ALSO BY BEN SHEPHARD

After Daybreak: The Liberation of Bergen-Belsen, 1945

A War of Nerves: Soldiers and Psychiatrists, 1914–1994

Kitty and the Prince: A Victorian Tragedy

The Long Road Home

The Long Road Home

THE AFTERMATH OF THE
SECOND WORLD WAR

Ben Shephard

ALFRED A. KNOPF · NEW YORK
2011

Copyright © 2010 by Ben Shephard
All rights reserved. Published in the United States by Alfred A. Knopf,
a division of Random House, Inc., New York, and in Canada by
Random House of Canada Limited, Toronto.
www.aaknopf.com

Knopf, Borzoi Books, and the colophon are
registered trademarks of Random House, Inc.

Originally published in Great Britain in slightly different form by The Bodley Head,
the Random House Group Ltd., London, in 2010.

Portions of this work previously appeared in *Journal of Contemporary History.*

Grateful acknowledgment is made to Edward Denny, Jr., and Lynda Garebedian
for permission to reprint excerpts from *The Wild Place* and *Undiscovered Country,*
both by Kathryn C. Hulme, as well as excerpts from the
unpublished letters of Kathryn C. Hulme.

Library of Congress Cataloging-in-Publication Data
Shephard, Ben, [date]
The long road home : the aftermath of the Second World War /
by Ben Shephard. — 1st American ed.
p.   cm.
"Originally published in Great Britain in slightly different form by
The Bodley Head, London, 2010"—T.p. verso.
"This is a Borzoi book published by Alfred A. Knopf"—T.p. verso.
Includes bibliographical references and index.
ISBN 978-1-4000-4068-1
1. World War, 1939–1945—Refugees.   2. World War, 1939–1945—
Forced repatriation.   3. Repatriation—Europe—History—20th century.
4. Repatriation—Asia—History—20th century.   I. Title.
D808.S44 2011
940.53086'914—dc22   2010023894

Jacket art: clockwise, upper left) Crowd of refugees, Germany, 1945. David E.
Scherman/Time & Life Pictures/Getty Images; German soup kitchen, 1944–45.
The Granger Collection, N.Y.; East German refugees, 1945 © dpa/Corbis; East Prussian
refugees, 1945. The Granger Collection, N.Y.; Jewish survivors of the Buchenwald
Nazi concentration camp stand on refugee ship *Mataroa* July 15, 1945, Haifa port,
during the British Mandate of Palestine. Zoltan Kluger/GPO via Getty Images
Jacket design by Jason Booher

Manufactured in the United States of America
First American Edition

For Sue

Contents

Germany and Austria in 1946

NORTH SEA

DENMARK

POLAND

Hamburg

Bergen-Belsen ▲

BRITISH ZONE

SOVIET ZONE

NETHERLANDS

Berlin

Cologne

Arolsen ▲

G E R M A N Y

Wildflecken ▲

Frankfurt

Aschaffenburg ▲

FRENCH

UNITED STATES ZONE

CZECHOSLOVAKIA

FRANCE

Stuttgart

ZONE

Munich

Landsberg ▲

SOVIET ZONE

Vienna

U.S. ZONE

SWITZERLAND

FRENCH ZONE   A U S T R I A

BRITISH ZONE

Berlin inset:
FRENCH
BRITISH
SOVIET ZONE
U.S. ZONE

Munich inset:
Schwabhausen
Dachau
Kaufering
St Ottilien
Landsberg
Ammersee
MUNICH
Feldafing
Starnberger See
Kempten

0   1   2 miles
0   1   2   3 km

.... Boundaries of occupation zones
▲ Major camps for displaced persons

0   50   100 miles
0   100   200 km

Author's Note

To avoid drowning the reader in a sea of acronyms, the names of official bodies have been kept to a minimum. But there remains an irreducible core.

RELIEF

Although the term "United Nations" was first used during the Second World War in the Atlantic Charter issued at the Anglo-American conference in Newfoundland in August 1941, the United Nations Organization (United Nations or UN for short) did not come into existence until October 1945. Before then, however, several international organizations were created in advance of the UN, the main ones being the Food and Agriculture Organization (FAO) and the United Nations Relief and Rehabilitation Administration (UNRRA), established in November 1943. UNRRA worked in both Europe and the Far East, but this book is concerned only with its European operations.

REFUGEES

UNRRA inherited some of the powers of an American body, the Office of Foreign Relief and Rehabilitation (OFFRO), created in November 1942, but remained bureaucratically divorced from the issue of refugees, which remained the province of the Intergovernmental Committee on Refugees (IGCR), created in July 1938, and also, in the United States, of the War Refugee Board, founded in January 1944. In 1947, when UNRRA was finally abolished, a new body, the International Refugee Organization (IRO), created the previous year under the auspices of the UN, inherited both UNRRA's and the IGCR's responsibilities. At the same time, a separate agency for children, The United Nations International Children's Emergency Fund (UNICEF), was established. When the IRO's mandate expired, yet another agency, the United Nations High Commissioner for Refugees (UNHCR), was created in 1950. It is still in existence.

THE MILITARY

During the the Second World War, the Allied armies created separate branches to administer occupied territory—a function known as military government or civil affairs. When Allied armies invaded Italy in 1943, they created a joint body, Allied Military Government of Occupied Territories (AMGOT, later shortened to AMG). At the end of 1943, when planning for the invasion of France began, General Dwight D. Eisenhower's staff was known as Supreme Headquarters, Allied Expeditionary Force (SHAEF). Based first in London, then in Versailles, and finally in Frankfurt, SHAEF was responsible for the initial government of Germany until it was abolished on July 14, 1945. Germany was then divided into zones by the four occupying powers, under the overall control of a four-power Allied Control Council, which met in Berlin. Each zone was, however, administered separately—with different terms, such as the Control Commission for Germany (British Zone).

PALESTINE

During most of the period covered by this book, Palestine was administered by the British under a League of Nations mandate. However, the Jewish Agency for Palestine acted as a "state within a state" and was responsible for a defense force, the Haganah, and, through the Mossad Le'aliyah Bet, for illegal immigration. *Aliyah,* or ascent, refers to immigration to the Holy Land; *Yishuv,* to the Jewish population of Palestine.

The Long Road Home

INTRODUCTION

"An Enormous Deal of Kindness"

"When this war is over," a young British officer wrote to his girl-friend in August 1942, "there will have to be an enormous deal of kindness to atone for all the senseless hate and suffering of these years."

Frank Thompson never lived to see the brave new world he dreamed of. A poet, Communist, and romantic, he was shot in Bulgaria in 1944 while working for the Special Operations Executive. But his girlfriend, a young civil servant named Iris Murdoch, shared his hopes. "Oh Frank, I wonder what the future holds for us all—shall we ever make of the dreamy idealistic stuff of our lives any hard and real thing?" she wrote back.[1]

While the young lovers were dreaming, more practical people tried to create something hard and real to bind up the wounds of the war. Many of them were haunted by memories of the previous war, when the suffering on the battlefield had been followed by yet more terrible loss of life among civilians, and were determined that this time they would get the peace right. For their own reasons, it suited British and American (and Russian) politicians to heed those cries and to create, before the United Nations itself came into existence in late 1945, a new international institution, the United Nations Relief and Rehabilitation Administration (UNRRA), intended to make sure that the armistice would not once again be followed by plagues and epidemics. In 1944, Iris Murdoch (and thousands of other idealists) joined UNRRA.

The Long Road Home tells the story of what then happened. It asks how far the war's aftermath in 1945 corresponded to the one which the Allies had planned for. There is a modern parallel here: postmortems of the débâcle which followed the conquest of Iraq in 2003 have routinely compared the Americans' failure to prepare for the aftermath in Baghdad with the years of planning which preceded the invasion of Germany in 1945. It has often been said that in the 1940s the Allies did not make this mistake; that then they *did* plan. Yet in many ways the long lead-up time in the 1940s was counterproductive, and much of the planning was based on past experience which turned out not to be relevant or which put into place, well before the end of the war, men and mechanisms unsuited to the task.

One aspect was particularly important. The new institutions designed to help Europe recover after the war were established in 1942 and 1943, when Allied planners were not fully aware of what was happening to Europe's Jews but were effectively monitoring the Germans' use of more than 10 million "slave laborers" in their economy. Consequently, the planners' model was based not on genocide but on the displacement of populations. "Displaced persons," the shorthand term they used for Adolf Hitler's victims, became the defining mental construct for the rest of the decade.

The concept of "the Holocaust" did not exist in Allied countries in the 1940s. As the American historian Peter Novick put it, "'The Holocaust,' as we speak of it today, was largely a retrospective construction, something that would not have been recognizable to most people at the time." Indeed, "to speak of 'the Holocaust' as a distinct entity," is, argued Novick, "to introduce an anachronism that stands in the way of understanding contemporary responses." Those responses were primarily influenced by the model of displacement. Consequently, the victims were "displaced persons"—whether inmates of Bergen-Belsen concentration camp in 1945 or Jewish patients at a hospital in Pittsburgh in the 1950s. "They were not 'Holocaust survivors,'" a social worker there recalled. "We had no sense of the Holocaust as we know it now, with a capital H."[2]

The concept of the "displaced person" determined the shape of the Allied humanitarian effort after the war, not just because the much-predicted public health catastrophe did not take place in 1945—thanks to extraordinary advances in medical science of which the politicians were largely unaware—but because, as it turned out, the war's most important legacy was a refugee crisis. When the dust had settled and all those who wished to had returned home, there remained in Germany, Austria, and Italy a residue of some 1 million people who were not inclined to go back to their own countries—

Jews, Poles, Ukrainians, Latvians, Lithuanians, Estonians, and Yugo-slavs. They had diverse and complicated wartime histories, for which modern terms such as "victims" and "perpetrators" do scant justice—some were by any definition collaborators of the Germans—but all, for complex political reasons, fell under the rubric "displaced persons." Meanwhile, several hundred thousand Germans died in the course of being expelled from Eastern Europe, but those that survived were not categorized as "displaced persons"; they were "refugees" and, as such, at the bottom of the pecking order.

For five years, between 1945 and 1950, as the Cold War between East and West began to escalate, the displaced persons crisis continued in Europe. While the DPs themselves sat in camps in Germany, a process of international lobbying and jockeying developed, in which each group used whatever weapon it had to hand—whether it be a claim on the Allied conscience, powerful friends in London or Washington, influence in the Vatican, the power of the Jewish vote in New York politics, contacts with American intelligence, or friends in the media. At the same time, the countries of Western Europe, the Americas, and Australasia began to see the displaced persons in a new light, as a pool of labor. But they tried to extract only those people who suited their labor needs and philosophy of immigration. The outcome of this process determined whether a DP ended up in Chile or Chicago, Manitoba or Melbourne.

This story has been largely ignored by historians, mainly because it sits uncomfortably among such historical behemoths as the Second World War, the Cold War, the Holocaust, and the Israeli-Palestinian question. In addition, the years in camps in Germany were for many of the refugees themselves a time of limbo, an interlude between stages in their lives—and therefore best forgotten.

But today, with the Cold War over and Soviet troops gone from Eastern Europe, we can see this period in a new light and appreciate the permanent mark it left on the modern world. The state of Israel, the transformation of U.S. immigration policy, the ending of the homogeneous Anglo-Saxon societies of Britain, Canada, and Australia, and the creation of a new framework of international law, under which individuals as well as nations have rights, are all legacies of this time. Beyond that, the postwar refugee crisis rehearsed many issues which still confront us today: How can mechanisms for international humanitarian aid be made to work? What levels of immigration can our societies absorb? Can the nationalisms of Eastern Europe live in peace with one another? How should an occupying power restore prosperity to a defeated enemy? At a more profound level, we can see Europe grappling with the psychological aftereffects of war and trying to reconcile the gulf between rhetoric and reality—on the one hand, the reality of the black market and prostitution on the streets of Hamburg and other German cities; on the other, the language of international brotherhood.[3]

One lesson of this period is clear. Wars shake the tectonic plates. They bring to the surface long-buried issues and grievances and pry loose forces which are normally kept nailed down. The Second World War was really several wars in one: not just the "good war" of Western memory—a military conflict prompted by Hitler's imperial ambitions—but also a bloody struggle between different nationalisms in Eastern Europe and a civil war that pitted partisan and resistance movements against collaborationist militias. By 1945, six years of titanic upheaval had let loose many of Europe's old demons—the place of the Jews; the future of Poland; the boundaries of the Russian Empire; Ukrainian nationalism; the viability of Yugoslavia as a state. For a brief while—and to the horror and mystification of British and American aid workers—these forces were in play; then the lowering of the Iron Curtain and the creation of the state of Israel controlled them again. But more recently, and particularly since the end of the Cold War, many of these forces have surfaced again. That is what gives this story its topicality today.[4]

It is not easy to write about the aftermath of the Second World War in a detached and objective way. Memories of the events themselves have been constructed ethnically—each ethnic group has recorded its own version. "Are we destined to remain forever entombed within these diametrically opposed versions of the Second World War?" a Polish historian has asked. "Each ethnic memory is so different from the other that at times it is difficult to believe that they portray the same events." Many of those who have published in this field have made no such attempt and have produced straightforwardly partisan or "pietist" accounts. The challenge is to reconcile the different versions of the war, to move beyond the competitive victimhood which has marked so much of the writing.[5]

How, though, should it be done? At a conference in New York in 2001, the historian Jan Tomasz Gross urged those who write about the 1940s to follow three simple rules: respect chronology, never use hindsight, and work from original documents. And certainly, if you apply Gross's rule to this period, many of its realities become startlingly different from our modern perceptions. For example, most of the Jewish displaced persons in camps in Germany in 1946 were not, strictly speaking, "Holocaust survivors," that is, survivors of the concentration and death camps; they were Jewish refugees who had fled to the Soviet Union from Poland in 1939 and were now hoping to make their way to Palestine. Yet, thanks to category creep, they are now routinely called "Holocaust survivors." Equally, we learn that, while thousands of Cossacks and Yugoslavs were forcibly repatriated to the regimes of Josef Stalin and Josip Broz Tito by the Allies in 1945—a so-called Final Secret which caused great outcry when it was revealed in the 1980s by the authors Nicholas Bethell and Nikolai Tolstoy—hundreds of thousands of Ukrainians and citizens of the Baltic republics were *not* handed back.

We forget now that the Allied occupation of Germany was a shambles and Germany itself a disaster area until the Currency Reform of 1948 and the coming of the Marshall Plan aid transformed the situation. And the issue which stirred the conscience of the British after the war was not the future of Jewish survivors but the plight of German refugees from the East. We may think of the United States as always being wary of involvement with international institutions, yet in the 1940s not only did a U.S. administration start the United Nations, the American taxpayer gave generously to international institutions and more American aid went to two Communist nations, Poland and Yugoslavia, than to any other states in Europe.

Another emerging theme of huge relevance today concerns international cooperation and the organization of charity—what in the 1940s was called "relief" and is today known as humanitarian aid.

From the early nineteenth century there emerged in Western society organizations concerned with addressing the wounds of war, especially those of civilians. Of these, the Red Cross, founded by the Swiss businessman Henri Dunant in 1863, is the most important but countless others, from Save the Children to Médecins Sans Frontières, have since played a major role. During the twentieth century, these organizations had some success in reducing the brutality of warfare—and many failures. All of them confronted the problem of somehow organizing the altruism of individuals into effective collective action.

Few subjects in twentieth-century history are more difficult for the historian. It raises what the writer Gitta Sereny has called the "goodie-goodie" problem. How, in our modern culture—where evil is sexy, goodness is dull, and organized goodness is dullest of all—can we find a way to make organized altruism interesting? The roots of this go back many years. The selling of Hitler was in the hands of Joseph Goebbels, Albert Speer, and Leni Riefenstahl, who created an iconography which still pervades popular mass culture; whereas the selling of the United Nations Relief and Rehabilitation Administration (and of the humanitarian ideal it stood for) was entrusted to the National Film Board of Canada, whose feeble efforts to create an imagery of international brotherhood and cooperation are long forgotten.[6]

Historians have faced a similar problem. Nowhere are the pitfalls of writing about international institutions that try to do good works better illustrated than in the official history of UNRRA which appeared in 1951. Even as its three mighty volumes were being composed, one of its authors predicted that it would be as "dull as ditchwater . . . so dull in its format that I doubt anybody will wade through it." She was right; it was, and nobody ever did. The book was condemned as "a damned awful history" by one of the main actors in its story, "a statistical record [with] absolutely not one word that matters over the operational capacity of UNRRA." Even for the expert, the UNRRA history, with its torrent of bureaucratic detail, self-referential tone, and sea of acronyms, is mind-numbing.[7]

But if the task is daunting, it is also necessary if history is to consist of anything more than "the mass killers of our time—crazed despots, the perverted henchmen, their army chiefs" and do justice to their opposites, "the healers who spent themselves in trying to prevent or reduce or redress the deliberate inhumanity of those with the power to hurt." I am not a religious person, nor have I worked in aid. My own interest in organized altruism was first aroused by writing about military psychiatrists—doctors who tried to alleviate the psychological effects of war—and then heightened by reading a book called *Humanity,* a "moral history" of the twentieth century written by the philosopher Jonathan Glover. What began as an attempt to explore the place of morality in public life soon lost its way in the dungeons and torture chambers of the SS, the NKVD, and Saddam Hussein. Hang on, I found myself crying, as the unending Cook's Tour of Horror took us from the building of the White Sea Canal to Auschwitz to Pol Pot's Cambodia, what about all the ordinary, decent people? Are we to believe that *all* of humanity is like this? Wasn't there some counter to the camps, the gulags, and the killing fields?[8]

This book's subject is, then, both important and neglected. But to do adequate justice to it, the modern reader does have to make certain mental adjustments and learn to look below the surface to what lies beneath. The first aspect of this involves the question of tone.

Take, for example, one of the best books about working with displaced persons. Margaret McNeill's *By the Rivers of Babylon,* published in 1950, is a lively, fictionalized account of a Quaker unit's work in Braunschweig in north Germany. The daughter of a Belfast Protestant businessman, McNeill dedicated her life to good works—from 1971 until her death in 1985, she was a peace worker in Northern Ireland—and unself-consciously expressed the attitudes of her class and time. There is more than a touch of Enid Blyton and the Famous Five in her account of how this group of Quakers came to Braunschweig and the adventures that befell them there.

McNeill conveys very well the Quakers' ignorance of the Europe they were dealing with. She reminds us, too, that her generation expressed its prejudices freely and did not hesitate to generalize; no one talked then of "racial stereotypes." For example, everyone loved but was exasperated by the Poles—generally regarded as sweet, feckless children, full of pride and honor, and quite without self-discipline. They would demand to be given all their rations at once—and then immediately eat them all, only to starve later. Margaret McNeill found the Poles "a paradoxical people":

> Their camps were nearly always in greater or less degree ramshackle and squalid, yet they showed a deeper, more artistic sensitivity than any other D.P.s. They were often overwhelmed with a forlorn misery, yet no D.P.s could laugh so gaily, or what was more, so laugh at themselves. They respected their Church and counted honour something to be defended to the death, yet they earned for

themselves a reputation for drunkenness, dishonesty and cruelty. They were often hopelessly lazy and unreliable as far as steady routine work went, but in a crisis they would, at the eleventh hour, rally and work with unparalleled speed and determination.

By contrast, Margaret found the Ukrainians hardworking but "peasants to the bone," with strange dark nationalistic politics: "We would have needed more than a knowledge of their language to understand their thoughts and feelings." The Braunschweig Quakers could more easily relate to displaced persons from the Baltic countries, who were much better educated, more middle class, more likely to speak English and to know how to represent themselves; though, of course, they had their obsessions, too. "Any conversation with Latvians or Estonians invariably turned to the lands that were lost to them; and they would recall with wistful pride the achievements of their shortage of independence. Faults and failures were forgotten, and the monotonous description would have been unreal to us, had we not detected in [their] voices the bitter cry of an outraged and homesick people."[9]

Yet, despite these prejudices, the Quaker team at Braunschweig worked tirelessly and enthusiastically for the displaced persons, each member of the team tending to identify with and champion the cause of a different group. *By the Rivers of Babylon* is one of those rare books that lives up to its blurb: it really is "informed throughout by a profound tenderness and compassion."

Margaret McNeill worked only briefly with Jewish displaced persons and left no observations on them. But Susan Pettiss, a young American welfare worker attached to UNRRA, was closely involved with Jewish survivors in Munich. "The Jews," she wrote to her aunt in October 1945, "have been terribly difficult to help."

They have been demanding, arrogant, have played upon their concentration camp experience to obtain ends. I saw rooms in our camp after they left—filthy dirty, furniture broken, such a mess as no other group left. They are divided into factions among themselves. One of our camps has to have six synagogues to keep the peace. They refuse to do any work, have had to be forced by gun to go out and cut wood to heat their own camps. American soldiers have developed bitter attitudes in many cases.[10]

The modern reflex would be to dismiss Pettiss as being anti-Semitic, yet her statement reminds us that Allied relief workers struggled to understand the psychological effects on Jewish survivors of the experiences they had been through. Over time, Pettiss's own views moderated and she would become a popular and highly effective manager of a section of UNRRA devoted to Jewish children.

This subject raises, however, issues not just of tone but of judgment. When discussing Allied immigration policy in the 1940s, it needs to be remembered that for most of the first half of the twentieth century, public debates about health in Britain and other countries were dominated by the language of eugenics, the first attempt to apply science to the understanding of individual conduct and development.[11] Between the wars, famous public figures—progressive intellectuals such as William Beveridge ("the father of the welfare state"), the economist John Maynard Keynes, and the popular writer H. G. Wells, as well as the leaders of the medical profession in Britain—belonged to the eugenics movement, which advocated birth control, largely as a way of controlling the fertility of the working classes, and voluntary sterilization of the mentally ill. Although the eugenists themselves moved away from this position by the late 1930s, embarrassed by the Nazis' campaign of compulsory sterilization and in the face of opposition from leading scientists, elements in public opinion and politicians raised in the Edwardian era continued to use the language of eugenics, routinely speaking about "the British race" and good "breeding stock." Similarly, in the 1940s most British people thought foreigners were funny; believed in national stereotypes; and talked about "Jews" or "blacks" in a way we would find offensive today. So did other nations. So far as immigration was concerned, British officialdom took it for granted that public opinion would accept as immigrants only people who would within a single generation be indistinguishable from the natives. They must therefore be white and northern European.

Much of the firsthand testimony in the pages that follow is, by modern standards, racist and xenophobic. We have traveled a long way in sixty years.

Questions of both tone and judgment arise particularly when writing about the Jews who survived the death camps—the *She'erith Hapletah,* or "Surviving Remnant." The survivors' first chronicler, the American Jewish lawyer and aid worker Leo Schwarz, cast his story in an epic mold, using dramatic Thucydidean reconstructions of historic events, conversations, and speeches, to produce a romanticized effect which reads very oddly today.[12] Two decades later, the Israeli historian Yehuda Bauer combined pioneering scholarship with deep sympathy and understanding; having known many of the survivors' leaders, he was able to depict them as flesh-and-blood human beings, a tradition maintained by Bauer's pupil Zeev Mankowitz.[13] More recently, however, some younger scholars in Germany and the United States have felt required to approach this subject in tones of reverence and awe and to cast the leaders as in a heroic mold.[14] I have tried to follow Bauer and Mankowitz. Similarly, I have steered a course between the two extremes of scholarship about the Jewish displaced persons—between those who see them as masters of their fate and those who portray them as "little more than clay in the hands of Zionist envoys."[15]

This tale should ideally be told from many vantage points, from above as well as from below. But the sources available are imbalanced: nearly everything comes from above—from Allied workers or from the leadership of the displaced persons—and only occasionally does one come across the voice of ordinary refugees—such as the Polish DP who told UNRRA workers at Hohenfels camp in October 1945, "You don't know our feelings; you don't know how to get in touch with us," and then tried to explain what six years as a slave laborer had done to his mind.[16]

In recent years, however, some major new sources have appeared: memoirs, literature, and oral histories. In researching this book, I unearthed—in a suitcase in north London—an important cache of new material, a collection of autobiographical essays written by DPs in 1946.

No doubt my own preferences and prejudices will be apparent to the reader. I am the product of a standard middle-class English education, but I grew up in Cape Town, South Africa, in the 1950s. My father's closest friends and associates there were a tall, solemn Prussian aristocrat and art historian whose brother had been executed by Hitler; a volatile Belgian painter who had spent time in the Congo; and a wonderful sculptor whose family was of Lithuanian Jewish background. Writing this book, I have come to understand more about all of them.

ONE

Feeding the War Machine

FOREIGN LABOR IN GERMANY, 1940–1945

"The Gestapo raid on our hospital came quite suddenly." One morning in the spring of 1940 the Germans arrived without warning at a hospital in Cracow and removed all the staff. The doctors were taken as they were, the nurses given five minutes to get ready. "Some of us were so taken aback that we did not even replace thermometers and syringes and were holding them as the doors of the trucks slammed," Anna, an art student working as a nurse, later recalled. The patients were simply abandoned.

The staff were driven to a nearby station. As they waited there, they observed little tragedies unfold: a boy who ran after his father was stopped by SS bayonets; a young man who had tried to escape was left with blood pouring from his face. Then they boarded the train.

Two nights later it stopped in the glass-halled station at Hamm, in Westphalia. An air raid was in progress. "It was very dark; only searchlights were crossing each other, in geometrical figures in the sky." They were taken down to a shelter. When they emerged, they saw their guards eating sandwiches and drinking beer. They themselves had not been fed for days.

At dawn they were marched off to the labor exchange seven miles away. On the autobahn they passed a long line of ragged, dirty human beings dragging their swollen feet, guarded only by well-groomed SS motorcyclists at either end, and met a column of French prisoners of war in tatty uniforms. As they approached the town, they noticed that every window was bedecked with red swastika flags and posters announcing a visit by Benito Mussolini. "In the labor exchange many future employers were waiting for us," Anna wrote later. "They began to look at us from every side; especially men were looked round. They fingered us like green pears in a basket, or cattle in a fair. We student-girls did not have many purchasers, therefore we were the last in the hall." The girls wanted to stay together, but they were all separated, given to masters in different parts of the country. Anna became a farmhand. She was a city girl and found the work hard.

The only chance to meet other Poles came on Sunday, at church. But fairly soon the Germans cracked down on that, too. When some of the Poles complained, they were flogged or sent to concentration camps. The others were told that they could not attend church or go back to Poland. "Abased, we returned to our plough and cattle, which were much more kind and friendly than their owners."[1]

That Polish girl, wrenched from her hospital and dumped in a foreign field, was not alone. Early in the Second World War, the German war machine had become dependent on foreign labor.

The Third Reich suffered from a chronic shortage of manpower and of agricultural manpower in particular. In the later 1930s, as economic recovery and rearmament gathered pace, it was estimated that there was a shortage of more than a million workers in the Greater German Reich, even with voluntary foreign labor. Germany's farms were especially undermanned; indeed, many of them were kept going by farmers' wives. When war came in September 1939, the authorities tried to protect agriculture, but the recruitment of some 800,000 men of prime working age was enough to produce a panic. The Ministry of Food and Agriculture, worried that the reduced workforce on the land would not be able to feed the urban population, as had happened in the First World War, insisted that foreign workers be drafted in. The 300,000 prisoners of war sent to the Reich from the rapid conquest of Poland were immediately put to work, but a massive shortfall remained. Plans were then drawn up to supply up to a million workers from the "General Government," the rump state of Poland. By the early months of 1940, ten trains a day, each filled with a thousand workers, were arriving in Germany.[2]

The employment of Poles unleashed violent ideological tensions within the Nazi hierarchy. On the one hand it was felt that the conscription of German women workers during the First World War had created dangerous social tensions and political unrest; it was also a cornerstone of Nazi social policy that a woman's place was in the home, not on the factory floor. Furthermore, the regime was determined that the war be waged without inflicting severe privations on the German public, as had happened in 1917 and 1918. From all those points of view, the use of Polish labor made good sense.

But what about the Nazi racial doctrine? As the historian Ulrich Herbert has written, "to bring millions of foreign workers, particularly Poles, to work in the Reich conflicted strongly with the ethnic principles of National Socialism, according to which the mass employment of aliens inside the Reich would be a threat to the purity of the blood of the German people." It would be doubly inconsistent, at a time when the SS under Himmler was drawing up plans to cleanse Eastern Europe of Jews and Poles, to bring thousands of Poles into Germany.[3]

The solution was to impose on the Poles a "system of penal apartheid." They were forced to live apart from Germans in separate barracks, to wear an identity tag with the letter *P,* and to accept inferior wages. Complete social apartheid was enforced by savage penalties and any sexual contact between Poles and Germans was punishable by death. This was no idle threat: from early 1940, Polish workers and POWs began to be executed for "sexual offenses"; in June 1941, a Polish civilian worker, of previously good character, was hanged for "having put his hand up the skirt of a German girl on agricultural labour service." There were some complaints from the local Germans, mainly because these executions were summary and carried out publicly, but the intention was to act as a warning to German women as much as to Polish men.[4]

Nonetheless, the German authorities in Poland expressed surprise when only some 200,000 Poles volunteered to work in Germany. Not having the troops needed to round up hundreds of thousands of Poles by force, the Germans introduced conscription of all inhabitants of the General Government between the ages of fourteen and twenty-five. The outside world was largely unaware of what was happening in Poland, because this action took place under cover of the German invasion of the West in May 1940.

The western blitzkrieg released a further huge reservoir of labor which seemed to solve Germany's manpower problems forever. By October 1940, 1,200,000 French and British prisoners of war had been deployed as workers in Germany, again mainly in agriculture. Contrary to popular mythology, most British prisoners of war did not engage in amateur theatricals, frustrated homosexual encounters, or harebrained schemes for escape; they worked on the land or, later, in factories.

At the same time, the Germans launched an enormous recruitment drive in the countries of Western Europe which attracted thousands of other workers. They then drew up special regulations governing the treatment, payment, and accommodation of each group, with a complex hierarchy of privileges: German workers at the top of the tree, followed by *Gastarbeitnehmer* from Axis countries such as Italy, then *Westarbeiter* from northern and Western Europe, POWs, and, at the bottom, Poles. The German population was supposed to act differently toward each of these four groups: "towards Poles as the 'master race,' towards POWs with reserve, towards Italians with friendliness and towards Belgians with neutrality." But in practice a different pecking order frequently operated at the workplace and farmyard level. The Italians were often regarded as lazy, arrogant, and overpaid for the poor work they did, and their criticism of German food such as potatoes, sauerkraut, sausage, and black bread was badly received. Poles, on the other hand, generally fitted in quite well in the countryside, and most of the civilians from the West, particularly the Belgians and French, were regarded as good workers. They were relatively highly paid, and their living conditions were not much worse than those of the average German worker.[5]

The war strategy that drove the Germans' use of foreign labor was consciously designed to avoid the mistakes of the past. The Nazi leadership were haunted by memories of the First World War when, as they saw it, the German army had not been defeated on the battlefield: rather, the British naval blockade had reduced the German civilian population to starvation and sapped its will to continue the war. The home front had then infected frontline soldiers with its defeatism and weakness and Germany had been "stabbed in the back." It was therefore vital to make sure that this time around Germany's population did not suffer food shortages.[6]

When 3 million German soldiers invaded the Soviet Union on June 22, 1941, Hitler and his generals expected the campaign to take a few weeks, at most a few months, and, even as the invasion of Russia was beginning, the planners in Berlin were shifting their focus to the next strategic goal, a campaign against Britain and the United States.

The expectation was that the German men called up to the colors would soon return to their factories and farms.

For about two months events in the East went according to plan. The Red Army put up little resistance and, in a series of massive encirclement battles, hundreds of thousands of Soviet soldiers were trapped in pockets and taken prisoner. At the end of July 1941, in an atmosphere of some euphoria, the Nazi leadership began to develop ambitious plans for the conquered lands. But then the pace of the advance slowed and signs of stiffening Russian resistance started to appear. While the Wehrmacht continued to move deeper into the vast Soviet hinterland—taking the Ukrainian capital, Kiev, and clearing the Baltic states of Soviet troops by the end of September— expectations in Berlin began to shift. Well before the successful Russian counterattack in front of Moscow in December 1941, it had become clear that a long campaign lay ahead.

This had obvious implications for Germany's already stretched reserves of manpower. Not only would German soldiers not be returning home in the near future, but huge numbers of new recruits would be needed, and they could come only from the industrial workforce at home. That, in turn, meant that if armaments production were to be maintained, more foreign labor would be needed. But once again, this proposal produced tensions within the system. On the one hand, Nazi propaganda depicted Russian prisoners of war as "animals," so it was unthinkable to bring them to work in Germany and allow them near German women. For that reason— and on the pretext that the Soviet Union had not signed the Geneva Conventions—no real effort was initially made to feed the 3.3 million Russians captured in the 1941 campaign and more than half of them froze to death, died of starvation or exhaustion, or were murdered. Ultimately, of the 5.7 million Russian prisoners taken in the war, some 3.5 million would lose their lives. But on the other hand, if more labor was to be found, what alternative was there to using Russians? In 1942, the policy was reversed and prisoners of war began to be fed and put to work. At the same time, the new "Plenipotentiary for Employment," the brutal gauleiter of Saxonia, Fritz Sauckel, began a drive to recruit civilian workers from the conquered lands to the east. "There are 250 million people now available to the German labour market," Hitler had told him.[7]

In Ukraine, the Germans had been welcomed as liberators, with the traditional gifts of bread and salt. Initially there was considerable interest in going to work in Germany, fueled by reports of the much higher standard of living there. Propaganda encouraging Ukrainian workers appeared in newspapers, posters were put up at workplaces, and a film titled *Come to Sunny Germany,* in which young Ukrainians sang and danced their way to a bucolic German farm, was shown in cinemas. At first the response was considerable. Driven by curiosity, the expectation of a good salary, the promise of a swift return, and a feeling that they had nothing to lose, volunteers came forward. In mid-January a brass band played as 1,500 young Kievans boarded a train for Germany decorated with flowers and banners. Two more trains followed in February. "We had a certain hope that in Germany we would earn something, and that we could get ourselves some decent clothes," one volunteer later recalled, "for we saw that all the Germans wore quality clothes made from good fabrics and well sewn."[8]

"The Russians have arrived," a Frenchwoman working in Germany wrote in May 1942. "They are Ukrainian girls, so young they are still virtually children. . . . Most of them are quite beautiful. They all wear their traditional scarf or a white kerchief round their heads, and they have a shy timid air like a flock of little sparrows. . . . They are so pretty, so innocent, so naïve with their cheap jewellery and their shabby little dresses."[9]

But within a few months the flood of volunteers had dried up; Ukrainians no longer came forward. Word had gotten back quickly about the abuse, poor housing, bad food, and general humiliation which awaited them. In practice, the Ukrainian workers were allotted a place below that of the Poles, confined to camps behind barbed wire "to prevent them spreading Communist propaganda," and obliged to wear a badge with the label "Ost." And so Sauckel was forced to use compulsion. The Ukrainian authorities were threatened with death if they could not provide a certain quota of recruits. Village elders often applied their own arbitrary criteria, protecting their own family members while packing off those disliked by the authorities, Communist Party members and activists, refugees, Poles, the physically vulnerable, and those thought to be poor workers. "A boss merely had to point at somebody and he was sent to Germany," one man recalled.[10]

Many years later, people remembered how their lives had changed. "I was ploughing the fields [when] the police appeared and said we were going to be taken to Germany," Anatolij Ljutikov told an interviewer. A seventeen-year-old farm boy from southern Ukraine, he became a welder in a munitions factory near Bremen. Nikolai Sjoma was fifteen when "a Policeman came to tell me I had to be at the collection point the next morning at 4 a.m. to be taken to Germany. . . . [He] went on to say that if I escaped, they would set my house on fire and hang my mother." A few months later, Nikolai was a laborer in an underground factory near Hildesheim. "In the summer of '42 they chased me to Germany," Klavdiia Ochkasova, a young girl living in a village near Kiev, would later recall. "At the distribution point, they gave us numbers and the masters already waited for their German slaves. They began to choose their free workers—like cattle on the market. I came to a good master. He was an antifascist. He treated me very well and didn't start anything with the other girls." However, Klavdiia wrote a letter back home urging young Ukrainians not to come to Germany as they would be beaten, humiliated, and made fun of there. It was intercepted, and she was sent to prison and later to a concentration camp.[11]

When appeals for volunteers and pressure on the Ukrainian authorities failed to produce the required numbers, the Germans simply resorted to rounding up people in public places. Purely in terms of numbers, they achieved impressive results. Between January 1942 and the end of June 1943, Sauckel's men delivered 2.8 million foreign workers to the German labor force; that is, every week, for seventy-eight weeks, some 34,000 workers were added to the industrial manpower.[12]

Nor was foreign labor only to be found in armaments factories and on farms. In 1942, Hitler finally allowed the Reich Labor Office to conscript German domestic workers into war work and employers to replace them with young women from the East. The justification for this ideological lapse was that earlier in the year, happening to see some Ukrainian girls, the Führer had been surprised by their fair hair and "Aryan" looks. He concluded that they had traces of Germanic blood, being descendants of the Goths who had at one stage passed through the area and, as such, would be acceptable as housemaids in German homes. In March 1944, there were some 100,000 foreign maids employed in German households, nearly half of them from the

Soviet Union. German children would later recall the arrival of a "Mary Poppins of the steppes" with "padded jacket, wooden clogs or boots and hair in bunches. She did not speak German, had never seen an indoor toilet or bath and the first instinct of the children's mother was usually to scrub the nanny clean and impose German hygiene on her." However, the Security Service reported that German house-wives preferred foreign maids because they were "willing, industri-ous, and eager to learn," whereas German domestic helpers were often "cheeky, lazy and licentious" and permitted themselves "every liberty, confident that they were indispensable." Furthermore, East-ern girls could be paid very low wages, would not expect holidays, and could be "assigned to any type of task, no matter how dirty or heavy."[13]

In the spring of 1942, the foreign labor program became the victim of its own success. Sauckel's ruthlessness in finding workers from all over Europe was outstripping the capacity of German industry to absorb them: both housing and food were completely inadequate. Employers were reluctant to spend much money on housing what they saw as a temporary and makeshift workforce, and construction materials were hard to come by in wartime. Even to provide the three basic barracks types specified by the Armaments Ministry—built to house eighteen civilian workers, thirty-six Russians, and twelve women workers, respectively—proved beyond the ability of many companies. Visiting the Ruhr in December 1942, even unsentimental bureaucrats were shocked by the living quarters and spoke of "a picture of desolation and immiseration" which would "never be extinguished."[14]

The real problem, however, was food. The arrival of all these extra mouths had put an even greater strain on Germany's already stretched reserves of foodstuffs. When the idea of using Eastern labor was first discussed, Hermann Göring had spoken airily about giving them cats and horse meat to eat. In the event, they were given what the 400,000 Russian POWs by now at work in Germany received—a bare subsis-tence diet, made up of 16.5 kilograms of turnips, 2.6 kilograms of bread (made from red rye, sugar beet waste, and straw), 3 kilograms of potatoes, 250 grams of horse or other scrap meat, 130 grams each of fat and yeast, 70 grams of sugar, and 2.5 liters of skimmed milk per week. Although high in carbohydrates and providing some 2,500 cal-ories a day, this diet was too low in fat and protein to sustain a man doing hard physical work, a fact that was rapidly becoming clear to German employers. Physical force and the threat of the concentration camp could achieve only so much; the real reason for the workers' low productivity was the inadequate diet. One armaments firm complained that it had "almost daily reports of Ukrainians who are willing to work collapsing at their machines." Stressing that its concern was only with productivity, it requested more food, "only for the purpose of getting the greatest possible performance out of Ukrainian workers who are undoubtedly diligent and usable." The *Ostarbeiter* themselves responded by trying to escape—in the second quarter of 1942, some 42,174 foreign workers were reported to have absconded, of whom the Gestapo claimed to have recovered 34,457. Tens of thousands more who were no longer able to work had to be shipped back eastward; many died on the journey—there were reports of corpses flung beside the railway lines. Sauckel himself demanded to know what was the point of bringing hundreds of thousands of workers to Germany, only for their productive potential to be wasted by the utterly inadequate diet being allocated to them by the Ministry of Food and Agriculture.[15]

What made the food crisis so serious was that it also hit the stomachs of the Germans. In April 1942, the Food Ministry was forced to announce cuts to the food rations of the German population, a drastic step given the regime's sensitivity to public morale and determination not to repeat the events of 1917–1918. Fears about the impact of the ration on the public mood were soon realized; the Security Service reported that it was "devastating" and like "virtually no other event during the war" and had produced "extreme disquiet amongst German civilians." Gauleiters found unhappiness in the ranks of the Nazi Party faithful.[16]

The 1942 food crisis was one of the rare occasions when the Nazi leadership acted in a coordinated and purposeful manner. Hitler's response was to replace the minister of Food and Agriculture, the influential Nazi ideologue Walther Darré, with his more dynamic assistant, Herbert Backe. A man accustomed to bold, strategic thinking, Backe had been the architect of the 1941 Hunger Plan, under which some 30 million Slavs would have been starved to death, a move which only the Wehrmacht's failure to capture Moscow and Leningrad had averted. Now he took decisive action. Supported by Heinrich Himmler and Göring, Backe decided that the distribution of food would be transformed. Germany would no longer send food to its armies in the field; instead, the Wehrmacht would live off the land. At the same time, the conquered territories—especially France, Ukraine, and the General Government of Poland—would send their grain to Germany. Moreover, certain groups—Jews, Ukrainians, and Poles—would no longer be fed at all. For Poles, the ration would be cut off in March 1943, but for 1.2 million Jews it was to cease almost immediately. Only 300,000 Jews classified as workers would receive any official food allocation, and all Jews in Poland not needed for work were to be killed by the end of the year.

The food crisis of 1942 did not initiate the "Final Solution of the Jewish Question," but it probably helped accelerate it. Since the conquest of Poland in 1939, the question of what to do about Europe's Jews had been preoccupying the Nazi leadership. In 1940, there was brief talk of sending them to the island of Madagascar in the Indian Ocean, clearly impractical so long as the British navy remained in existence. After that came vague plans to concentrate them in the General Government, the rump of Poland. By early 1941, with the invasion of the Soviet Union beginning to take shape, the scheme had changed. Now it was expected that, following victory over the Red Army, the Jews would be deported into the interior of the Soviet Union and worked and starved to death there over a period of years. Later that year the invading German armies were accompanied by *Einsatzgruppen,* SS troops supported by German policemen and local volunteers, which murdered "Judeo-Bolsheviks" among the Soviet population. The scope of this killing was quickly expanded, to take in first women and children and then whole Jewish communities. Huge numbers of people were killed in this way—at Babi Yar outside Kiev, some 33,771 Jews were executed. Nonetheless, the final step toward industrialized genocide had not yet been taken. Hitler himself seems to have hesitated.

However, in the last months of 1941, two factors changed his mind. First, it became apparent that there would be no quick victory in the East—and therefore no quick solution to the Jewish Question, unless a new strategy was devised. Second, the entry of the United States into the war removed any prospect of using the Jews as "hostages," an idea which Hitler had seriously considered over several years. Now, on the contrary, there was a world war, and therefore the

Jews who had instigated it, as Hitler believed, could be punished. According to Goebbels's diary, Hitler told the gauleiters on December 12, 1941, that "the world war is here so the annihilation of Jewry must be the necessary consequence."

At the same time, initiatives were being taken at a lower and local level which would transform the ghastly process of murder. Himmler's eager lieutenants were beginning to apply to the annihilation of the Jews the technology of poisoning by gas, first used against mental patients in the T-4 euthanasia project; special new camps were being built alongside the railways in Poland. After months of pressure from Nazi officials, Germany's Jews were now deported to the East. In January 1942, at a conference in the Berlin suburb of Wannsee, the Nazi bureaucracy accepted that the Jews would have to be destroyed before the war ended and that it would happen in Poland rather than the Soviet Union.

Over the next few months, the Jews of Poland were briskly exterminated at Belzec, Sobibor, and Treblinka, with German staff supervising Ukrainian volunteers, who shepherded them into the newly installed gas chambers. The killing soon extended to the whole of Poland. By the early summer of 1942, a comprehensive plan for the annihilation of Jews from all over Europe had been devised and was starting to be implemented. Auschwitz began to function as an extermination camp in the middle of 1942, and very soon Jews from occupied Western Europe—France, Belgium, Holland, and Luxembourg, as well as from Slovakia, Poland, and Ukraine, were being murdered there.

As of October 19, 1942, the food ration for both Germans and foreigners working in Germany was substantially increased.

From early 1942, Nazi Germany was confronted with the combined economic might of the United States, the Soviet Union, and the British Empire. It could hope to compete only by harnessing all the resources at its command—in particular of labor. The situation worsened after the defeat at Stalingrad in late 1942, as manpower began to hemorrhage steadily away; by the beginning of 1943, the Germans were losing 150,000 men a month on the eastern front, only half of whom would be replaced by men taken from the factories and farms of the Reich.[17]

Yet, despite this manpower crisis and in the face of the Allied bombing offensive, German industrial production continued to grow, reaching its peak in 1944. In part this was due to more efficient management, for which Hitler's armaments minister, Albert Speer, received too much credit in the past and now receives too little. But it was also due to the ruthlessness with which labor of all kinds was being exploited.

To fill the vacuum left on the shop floor, the Germans managed, despite the military reverse at Stalingrad, to lay their hands on millions more foreign workers from both Western and Eastern Europe. German economic planners argued that it made more sense to bring French workers to the Reich, where levels of output were much higher, than to leave them in factories in France.

French workers in Germany were now made up of roughly three groups—some 250,000 people who had originally volunteered to work in the Reich, a similar number of former prisoners of war set to work by their captors, and, after mid-1943, young men called up under a scheme known as Service du Travail Obligatoire (STO). French society put pressure on some young men to do their duty and go to Germany, their departure being seen as a price worth paying to protect their communities and families from reprisals. The novelist Alain Robbe-Grillet, for example, was persuaded by the head of his agricultural college to go to Germany and spent nine months assembling Panther tanks in a factory in Nuremberg; his foreman was a Turk. But although French workers enjoyed much better conditions than the Poles or Russians, the STO was also widely unpopular and proved a powerful recruiting tool of the Resistance. The wealthy and well connected were to some extent able to evade it, and the *grandes écoles* protected some of their pupils by enrolling them in the protected profession of mining. Two groups in society proved most vulnerable—the lumpenproletariat and those seen by the police as socially marginal, and those who were regarded as inessential to the war economy, such as shopkeepers, bank clerks, and postmen.[18]

Between November 1942 and December 1943, more than 700,000 Frenchmen, Belgians, and Dutch were recruited. However, this success came at a high political price. Sauckel's labor demands made the French, Belgian, and Dutch governments increasingly unpopular and drove young men to join the growing resistance groups. The Allied invasion of France in June 1944 effectively brought to an end the tide of recruits from the West.

While in Western Europe the Germans obtained labor by putting pressure on local governments, in Eastern Europe they simply kidnapped it. Although the conditions deteriorated after the defeat at Stalingrad, with the German armies in retreat and partisan activity increasing, "during a retreat able-bodied inhabitants of the sectors being evacuated were taken forcibly by the German troops into the rear areas." Children, too, now began to be systematically deported. Those crude methods were highly successful. Of the 2.8 million Soviet citizens working in Germany in the autumn of 1944, nearly half had been deported to the Reich *after* the defeat at Stalingrad. However, the most important and dramatic change in the use of foreign labor came from another quarter altogether.

In July 1943, the Allied landings on Sicily produced a coup in Rome. Mussolini was deposed, and the new Italian government, under Marshal Pietro Badoglio, in effect changed sides. The Germans responded quickly, occupying Italy north of Rome and disarming some fifty-six Italian divisions in northern Italy, France, and the Balkans. Those troops were then sent to Germany, and some 600,000 Italians were put to work in factories, farms, and, most important, mines.[19]

In that period, the tension between the pragmatists and the ideologues in Germany intensified. On the one hand, those elements in the regime aware of the wider political situation—such as Goebbels's Propaganda Ministry, Alfred Rosenberg's Eastern Ministry, and the army—tried to shape policy toward foreign workers in a more humane direction. With the political rationale of the war now that of a German-led European crusade against Bolshevism, it made sense to offer concessions to Ostarbeiter and to create some feeling of solidarity with the Germans. Their pressure did produce some talk of concessions, such as less-offensive badges, improvements in living conditions, and the erosion of the differentials between Western and Eastern workers. But on the other hand, the party and the security apparatus remained implacably opposed to any attempts to offer dignity and decency to the Eastern workers and constantly alert to any suggestion of the weakening of vigilance.

This tension between "victory" and "security" could also be found in the workplace. The food crisis in 1942 had shown that it was pointless to expect foreign laborers to work productively if they were being starved to death but, beyond that, how were employers to treat their foreign labor force, especially when so many skilled German workers were now being drafted into the army? Could they be trained or trusted to operate machinery on their own? In some parts of the German armaments industry, a change of attitude on the part of management did take place. Initially, the arrival of Eastern workers had obliged them to provide "social education" in order to create a manageable labor force: "We had to compel the Russian men to wash, use handkerchiefs, make proper use of toilets, etc.," a German employer complained. "Not only the men, the women as well—even more so, since the Russian women assigned to us had not learnt the most fundamental principles of female hygiene. We had to organize easy-to-follow courses for the Russian women, teaching them how a modern civilized woman behaves, because they were totally unfamiliar with even the simplest hygienic products."[20]

However, in 1943 a drastic reduction in the German workforce compelled some employers to train Eastern women for much more skilled work, give them more scope to use their initiative, and even trust them with expensive machinery. In some armaments companies, this new system proved highly successful. One firm proudly noted that "the Eastern worker is far more useful to the crew boss than before and can now work at his machine virtually independently." It was also found that the improved skill levels among Eastern workers as a result of better training acted to reduce tensions between German and Soviet employees. According to Ulrich Herbert, "once most firms made performance their first priority they began to see Eastern workers as ideal employees." The management at the great optical concern Carl Zeiss Jena, for example, found Eastern women to be "conscientious, rarely absent," and, unlike German workers, unable to "go away on vacation"—factors which greatly facilitated continuity of production at the plant. Correctly supervised, they were now performing many tasks. "For that reason, we want more Eastern female workers!"[21]

However, similar efforts to enhance output by providing better training and food in the mining industry were less successful. Here the workplace culture was male and traditionally brutal; below ground, physical violence toward the Soviet prisoners of war and Italian military internees, sent to supplement the dwindling numbers of German miners, flourished. If anything, the hostility toward the "Italian traitors" was even greater than toward the "hated Russians."

"Up to now we've had to treat these individuals gently because we'd have been guilty of a diplomatic insult. Now there's going to be a different tune," one German foreman was quoted as saying. A report in late 1943 found that the foreign miners were repeatedly flogged, given inadequate clothing and blankets, and harshly treated by doctors. Management was doing little to intervene. Not surprisingly, the Russians and Italians were dying like flies.[22]

Given the diversity of situations, it is not easy to generalize about the conditions under which foreign workers lived, though life was usually better on a farm than on a factory floor. After inspecting a number of camps for Eastern workers in the summer of 1943, a German Foreign Ministry official reported that they lived mostly on turnip soup, were preyed on by Western workers, and were at high risk of developing tuberculosis. Yet other reports speak of the general level of health being surprisingly good.

Women workers were exploited as workers and abused as women. There was, however, an important distinction between how the two main groups—Frenchwomen who had volunteered to work in Germany in the earlier years of the war and Eastern women caught up in Sauckel's drive—were perceived. Contemporary French accounts paint a lurid picture of the moral conditions these women endured.

> Morality. Here the degeneration of this mass of millions of workers is truly appalling. It has its roots in this barrack-room life of a promiscuous crowd of men, women, youngsters, young girls of all races . . . a mass which is completely cut off from its natural links; home town or village, neighbourhood, parish etc. . . . which are so important for morality. Depression, human indignity, boredom, tiredness, malnutrition all encourage the coarsest of satisfactions.[23]

French Catholic sources, such as this report of August 1943, deplored the failure of French women volunteers to resist this world. They were depicted as the "dregs," "young girls and women who came to try their fortunes" or who wanted to share in the Germans' spoils. The result, all too often, was that they were "practically condemned to concubinage or prostitution." Yet the same report added that "the behavior of the French women in Germany profoundly humiliates most French prisoners and workers."

These women may have been unfairly demonized, as the historian

Pieter Lagrou has argued. These reports were probably exaggerated to serve the needs of the Catholic Church, written by priggish young men unused to the earthiness of working-class life and colored by "clerical misogyny" and by the ideology of Marshal Philippe Pétain's Vichy government, "according to which women were not supposed to work outside the home, let alone to travel abroad unaccompanied." But the wealth of detail they contain suggests a world of degradation and brutality far beyond the easy promiscuity that Émile Zola described in his novels.

So far as the second group was concerned, there was less disagreement. More than half of the Polish and Soviet civilian workers were women, and they were below twenty years of age on average. "The typical slave worker in Germany in 1943," according to Ulrich Herbert, "was an eighteen-year-old schoolgirl from Kiev."* A German Foreign Office official who inspected several of the camps that year, on his own initiative, wrote:

> Despite their generally poor health, [the Eastern women workers] must often perform heavy or very heavy physical labour. In order to improve their lot a little, they fornicate with the German camp commanders and other superiors. For that reason, the situation in these camps is often indescribable. . . . To stress the fact that the "profession" of pimp is "thriving" in the camps and that women have a pleasant "source of extra income" with their German superiors and the German and foreign workers so they can buy bread and other food items on the "black market" is merely to lift a corner of the curtain behind which outrageous scenes are a daily occurrence.[24]

Fourteen months after noting the arrival of "Russian girls" at an artificial silk factory in Krefeld, a French political prisoner wrote, in July 1943:

---

* In the summer of 1944 about a quarter of the workforce in Germany was foreign— 7.8 million people. Of that number, 5.7 million were civilian workers and just under 2 million were prisoners of war. Some 2.8 million of them came from the Soviet Union, 1.7 million from Poland, and 1.3 million from France. At that time there were workers from almost twenty European countries employed in Germany.

The change in a year is startling. It's not that they are physically abused, as their work is quite bearable. But the promiscuity in which the wretched girls are forced to live, the shameful existence reserved for them here, has degraded them utterly and killed their spirit. Where have they gone, those pretty girls with their fresh, innocent faces framed by their traditional headscarves and head-bands? Most of them have abandoned their national headdress, and with it all the human dignity they had brought with them from their homelands. Now they all curl their hair and wear heavy make-up, shout and yell all the time and sleep with the lowest of the low from among the Belgian and Dutch workers. Many of them have been infected with disease, and twenty-five are pregnant. Those who make it back to Ukraine will have a handsome souvenir of "western civilization" to take with them.[25]

At first women who became pregnant were sent home. But when it became obvious that this policy was being used as a way to escape from Germany, it was changed and by 1943, a large number of "nursing homes for foreigners' children" had been set up by German companies. They were closely supervised by the racial authorities of the SS and a sharp distinction drawn between children with "good blood," that is, with German fathers, and the rest. Children of "good racial stock" born to foreign women were to be brought up as Germans in special homes, whereas those of "inferior racial stock" would be housed in other special homes and, in effect, allowed to die through neglect and malnutrition.

By 1943, another element was coming to dominate the lives of foreign workers in Germany. Although the British policy of "area bombing" had targeted the industrial regions of Germany since 1942, it took them (and the Americans) some time to muster the airplanes necessary for effective full-scale operations. But in mid-1943, Hamburg was devastated by a firestorm, and tens of thousand of tons of high explosives and incendiaries were being dropped nightly on the industrial heartland of Germany, the Ruhr, where most of the foreign workers were now concentrated. By and large, the foreigners were not allowed into the huge air-raid shelters to which the German population could retreat, and their rudimentary housing was very vulnerable to bombing. A single attack on Essen on March 5, 1943, left almost 10,000 workers homeless.[26]

Consequently, for the foreigners, this really was "terror bombing." Their response was to flee. Increasingly, French workers entitled to home leave did not return from it, while Eastern workers fled to safer parts of Germany and tried to find other jobs, with some success. By June 1944, Albert Speer was complaining to Hitler that 500,000 foreigners a year were absconding.

The bombing offensive drove the Germans to their final initiative. Much of the industrial production was moved underground, and much greater use was made of concentration camp labor. There had, of course, always been a policy of extracting labor from the concentration and death camps; this was the principle upon which "selections" at Auschwitz operated. (Goebbels wrote privately that he expected 60 percent to be killed at once, 40 percent to be worked to death.) But the SS labor system had always been both inefficient and detached from the general German economy. However, in late 1942, after taking over the construction agency Todt Organization, Albert Speer established a new scheme whereby labor gangs from concentration camps were made available to private business, housed in special external camps outside towns. In early 1944 came a further change. It was decided that, in the light of the acute shortage of labor and the fact that most of the Jews within the conquered territories had been exterminated, Jewish prisoners should be put to work within the Reich. Some worked for the SS; others were sent to work for private businesses.

Now concentration camp labor was also sent to work in the vast underground factories in which the German secret "V" weapons were to be constructed. At the end of the year, it was estimated that the total number of prisoners (Jewish and non-Jewish) from concentration camps was about 600,000, of which some 480,000 were reportedly fit for work. Of that number, about 140,000 were working on underground projects, 130,000 engaged in the Todt Organization's building projects, and another 230,000 employed by private companies such as Daimler-Benz, Messerschmitt, and Heinkel.

This switch in priority from extermination to the extraction of labor power undoubtedly saved the lives of many Jews, but the intention was simply to kill people more slowly. The conditions, particularly in the underground schemes, were appalling, and the diet consisted simply of turnip soup and a little bread and meat. "Towards the end of 1944," wrote Ulrich Herbert, "the life expectancy of prisoners was limited to an average of a few months. Here a man was worth no more than the amount of physical strength he could muster for the duration of a few weeks. For the hundreds of thousands of people in these camps, work was synonymous with extermination."[27]

By this stage of the war, foreigners were beginning to arrive in Germany voluntarily—people who had not been conscripted or snatched from the streets but were fleeing the Russians.

Following the failure of the huge German offensive against the Kursk salient in July 1943, the Red Army counterattacked and began to reclaim Soviet territory. The Dnieper River was reached by September 1943, and Kiev, the capital of Ukraine, was occupied on November 6. In January 1944, Dr. Olexa Woropay and his wife decided to take the road to the West. An agronomist whose career had not prospered before the war because of his "social origin," he had weathered the German occupation and now felt it politic to retreat with the German forces. Traveling in a horse-drawn cart, they had several narrow escapes before reaching Berlin. They were at first placed in a camp for foreigners but with help from the Ukrainian Relief Committee were able to find work as farm laborers in Bavaria.[28]

Later in the year, the Red Army launched Operation Bagration, a massive offensive across the entire front. In July and August 1944, as Allied armies were clearing France, the Russians reoccupied first the Baltic states and then western Ukraine. In Estonia a girl called Helena was among those who chose not to stay to welcome them:

> It was a summer day in September 1944 when we took leave of our home and native country. The work, responsibilities and joys of years had to be left behind. My mother called, "Shut the piano and throw the key through the window." From a rose tree beside the gate I took three buds and put them in my poetry book, which I have taken as the only souvenir.

They drove fast, and soon their white house had vanished behind the fir trees. At Tallinn harbor, chaos reigned, with thousands of people, horses, and crates of freight on the quayside and Russian aircraft dropping bombs. But they got onto a ship, and that evening, as Helena stood with her mother and brother watching the distant silhouette of the Estonian coast receding, she was reminded of the poet who had written, "When a man loses his native land, he loses all he has."

The ship was attacked from the air but eventually managed to reach "the golden towers of Danzig." There Helena found work in a rural kindergarten, "the dirtiest and most unpleasant work," until, drawing on a prewar acquaintance, she wrote to a Silesian baroness and was invited to the "splendid halls of her castle." She even managed to persuade the Arbeitsamt in Breslau to let her family work on the baroness's estate and in the evenings, after the family had gone to bed, was able to spend an hour practicing on the castle's piano. But in January 1945, the approach of the Red Army forced them to flee once more and to keep moving till Helena ended up as a kitchen maid in a military hospital in Saxony.[29]

On New Year's Day 1945, Hitler gave one of his last radio addresses to the German people. On that occasion, he supplemented his usual snarls of defiance with a mocking reference to the Allies' plans for the future of Europe. The German leader poured scorn on "the theoretical appointments of ever new commissions for the treatment of European questions after the war, the foundation of societies for the regulation of food supplies after the German collapse." The Allies, he said, "always acted as though they had already won the war, as though they could now already consider at their leisure all the measures necessary for those to rule Europe who have themselves set a sorry example of how not to rule people."[30]

In fact, such preparations for the aftermath of the war had been going on since practically the first shot had been fired.

TWO

Food and Freedom

PREPARING FOR THE AFTERMATH OF WAR, 1940–1943

British fortunes were at a low ebb in August 1940. The Germans, after occupying most of Western Europe, from Norway in the north to France in the south, had just embarked on the first stage of their planned invasion of Britain, an aerial attack. On August 20, with the outcome of the Battle of Britain still in the balance, it was time for the prime minister to rally the nation again.

Addressing the House of Commons that day, Winston Churchill sought to bolster British courage and to survey the "dark, wide field" of the war. He expressed his belief that "our science is definitely ahead of theirs" and his faith in Britain's command of the sea and ability to mobilize resources and preparedness to fend off invaders. He praised the role played by British airmen: "never in the field of human conflict was so much owed by so many to so few." Then the prime minister reaffirmed his government's determination to maintain and enforce a strict economic blockade not only of Germany but of Italy, France, and all other countries that had fallen into German hands; but he balanced that commitment to blockade with a passage on "Food and Freedom going into Europe together":

> We can and we will arrange in advance for the speedy entry of food into any part of the enslaved area, when that part has been wholly cleared of German forces, and has genuinely regained its freedom. We shall do our best to encourage the building up of reserves of food all over the world, so that there will always be held up before the eyes of the people of Europe, including—I say it deliberately—the German and Austrian peoples, the certainty that the shattering of the Nazi power will bring to them all immediate food, freedom, and peace.[1]

Churchill had made an extraordinary pledge. The British, struggling to stay in the war, were barely able to feed themselves, let alone victual half of Europe. Why, then, had he spoken as he had? The prime minister was attempting to reconcile Britain's determination to apply the policy of blockade—which, after the fall of France, was one of the few weapons left in its armory—with the need to placate powerful critics of "economic warfare." European governments in exile in London feared that the blockade would make their populations suffer and send them into the arms of the Germans, while humanitarian groups in the United States, led by ex-President Herbert Hoover, were calling for it to be partially lifted to allow relief supplies through to the occupied countries of Western Europe. And so, to justify the blockade before international opinion, the British were forced to raise the question of postwar relief to Europe.

Henceforward, economic warfare and the planning of postwar relief would be bureaucratically yoked together in Whitehall. On the one hand, the blockade was persisted with—and the fact that the Germans now controlled much more of Europe than they had in 1914–1918 and therefore found it easier to avoid its effects only made the British the more determined to enforce it. In the case of Greece, however, the government did eventually relent, after some 200,000 Greeks had died in the winter of 1941–1942 and a vociferous campaign involving many prominent churchmen, intellectuals, and doctors had brought British public opinion to bear. Otherwise, no exceptions were allowed. Overall, the blockade had some effect on the German economy but much less than belligerent optimists in the Ministry of Economic Warfare believed.[2]

But at the same time, a token effort was made to honor the commitment to "relief." Churchill's speech was given wide publicity, and a committee was created within Whitehall to organize the surpluses necessary for "food and freedom going into Europe together." It was chaired by the director general of the Ministry of Economic Warfare, Sir Frederick Leith-Ross, who was still nominally the government's chief economic adviser but had been sidelined by the return to the Treasury of John Maynard Keynes. "Leithers" was only fifty-five but seemed older, having started his public career back in 1910, and had become something of a figure of fun. His minister, the egomaniacal Hugh Dalton, found him "rather dull" but "not bad at certain jobs."[3]

The atmosphere within the "committee on surpluses" must have been surreal, but no more so than in many such bodies in Whitehall in 1941. Its main problem was that most of the world's surplus food was in the United States or in the Western Hemisphere, and most of the money and the shipping required to get it to Europe already committed to keeping the British afloat; Leith-Ross later recalled that "progress at first was slow." But following a conference in London in September 1941, a grander-sounding Inter-Allied Committee on Post-War Requirements was created and the European governments in exile in London were put to work compiling estimates of the food, raw materials, and other necessities they would need in the first six months after liberation. It was still uphill work. "Up to the present precisely nothing has been done to give effect to the Prime Minister's declaration," Leith-Ross wailed on October 29, 1941, "and at the present rate of progress, it seems to me that jolly little is likely to be done before the war ends."[4]

In fact, however, postwar planning was about to be transformed, thanks to the new direction the war itself was taking.

The entry into the war of first the Soviet Union and then the United States (after the attack on Pearl Harbor on December 7, 1941) transformed the politics of relief. From now on the complex interaction between Moscow and Washington would determine how relief was dispensed.

The Soviet government took a keen interest in relief. Already getting aid from Britain and Lend-Lease from the United States, the Russians had no problem with accepting relief, which they regarded as "a reward for fighting"—provided it was given without strings. But they, too, had memories of the past and, in particular, of the way the Volga famine of 1921 had forced the fledgling Bolshevik regime to accept aid from abroad. After months of negotiation, an American team led by Herbert Hoover had been admitted to the Soviet Union, where it had done steadfast work and saved millions of lives, but the ideological gap between Hoover and his Russian hosts had never been bridged, leaving a legacy of ill will on both sides. In London in 1942, Leith-Ross found the Soviet ambassador, Ivan Maisky, "full of the most ridiculous suspicions"—that "the Relief Organization might be intended to be supra-governmental" and might "distribute food in Russia as Hoover did last time, without any reference to the local authorities." Maisky also wanted to be "assured that it was not intended to send back White Russians into Soviet territory against the will of the Soviet government." On the other hand, Western politicians realized that the issue of relief could, if handled with a proper regard for Soviet sensitivities, be used as a diplomatic icebreaker. Hugh Dalton, the British minister of economic warfare, saw "much advantage in getting down to details with the Russians, partly because it will give them confidence in our good faith, and partly because it will keep us mindful of their state of mind."[5]

In January 1942, the Soviet government took the initiative. It proposed replacing Leith-Ross's British-run Inter-Allied Committee with an international organization with wide powers and an international staff from which the Americans and the British dominions would be excluded. Though clearly unrealistic, this scheme could not simply be rejected; some counterproposal had to be supplied, especially as it had by now also emerged that the Dutch and Norwegian governments in exile, ignoring Churchill's pledge, had quietly sent missions to South America to begin buying supplies for postwar use. They could be persuaded to desist only if they were convinced that their needs were being taken care of by "collective preparation for a common effort"; it had become "necessary to devise machinery for the prevention of an uncoordinated and unprofitable scramble."[6]

At the same time, with both the Soviet Union and the United States now in the war, the question of how to organize and pay for postwar relief in Europe assumed greater urgency, especially once it had been separated from the complex Anglo-American financial negotiations over how to pay for the war and create new financial institutions for the coming peace. The role of the Americans would be critical. Not only was most of the world's surplus food in the United States and Canada, but only the Americans were rich enough to pay the bill.[7]

American thinking came from several places, one starting point being the work of the American Relief Administration after the First World War. Informed American opinion was aware that, although the ARA had probably saved Europe from starvation by delivering some 7 million tons of relief aid to war-torn countries in 1919, it had never won the United States any great harvest of goodwill and gratitude—mainly because the ARA's highly competent administrator, Herbert Hoover, had insisted on running his own show, ridden roughshod over European sensibilities, used food as a weapon "to stem the tide of Bolshevism," and unloaded on Europe American agricultural surpluses accumulated while he had been the "food tsar" in wartime Washington. Nor had relief been given unconditionally: the United States' insistence that it be paid for had helped usher in the recriminatory climate of debt and repayment which had poisoned international relations between the wars. "Even if all the supplies came from the United States," an expert review concluded in 1943, "we ought not to play 'Lady Bountiful,' and expect the world to thank us for being so rich. It would be much better sense to take part in an international body, which will decide where and how supplies should go." The U.S. president was of the same opinion, but for different reasons. He took an instrumental view of relief, as part of his plans for the postwar world.[8]

Winston Churchill and Franklin Delano Roosevelt met for the second time on the British battleship *Prince of Wales* in Argentia Bay, Newfoundland, in August 1941. The two leaders conferred for several days, held an outdoor religious service at which they sang the hymn "Eternal Father, Strong to Save," and issued a communiqué which became known as the Atlantic Charter, a statement of British war aims (the United States was not yet in the war), in which the phrase "United Nations" was used for the first time. Roosevelt struck one British diplomat as "a headstrong man who means to monopolise the limelight at the peace but whose political ideas are still those of twenty years ago"; the President's draft for the joint declaration to be issued with Churchill he dismissed as "a terribly woolly document full of all the old clichés of the League of Nations period."[9]

That was only half the story. To be sure, Roosevelt's rhetoric had something of an internationalist tang—he had, after all, made some eight hundred speeches in favor of the League of Nations as the Democratic candidate for vice president in 1920—and he wanted to make another attempt to create a new international framework. But he was determined to avoid repeating both the mistakes of Woodrow Wilson after the First World War—when the president's arrogant refusal to compromise had led to the rejection of the League by Congress—and the mistakes of the League itself, which had become an irrelevant talking shop. Any successor to the League, Roosevelt recognized, would work only if it enjoyed the support of the Great Powers and, in particular, of the United States and the Soviet Union. That was Roosevelt's aim, but in advancing toward it he exercised the same tactical caution and political skill as he did in getting America into the war.[10]

The idea of an international body to administer relief thus fitted into Roosevelt's larger purpose of persuading the Russians to join a new international security organization dominated by the so-called Four Policemen—the United States, the Soviet Union, Britain, and China—with which he intended to replace the discredited prewar security system based on the League of Nations. At the same time, mindful of the failures of Woodrow Wilson in 1920, Roosevelt was careful to carry with him the leaders of Congress and American public opinion, a task made easier by a swing toward a more internationalist stance once the United States was at war. By 1942, some members of the American administration were offering "lofty visions of democratic cooperation and equality" after the war. Vice President Henry Wallace, for example, called for a "people's peace" in which the New Deal would be applied to the world at large. The following year, the book *One World,* containing an extended "sermon on internationalism" by the defeated presidential candidate Wendell Willkie, became a sensational best seller. The president was more cautious, however. "Roosevelt's world blueprint," a newspaper reported, was primarily concerned "not with aspirations toward a better world . . . but with the cold realistic techniques, or instruments, needed to make those aspirations work. This means he is concentrating on power." Because relief offered an opportunity to create the instruments of international cooperation, to slip the bridle onto the Soviets, Roosevelt gave it priority. Ignoring existing institutions on which the Soviet Union was not represented, in December 1942 he appointed the governor of New York State, Herbert Lehman, as the U.S. relief supremo. Lehman's task was to set up an international relief organization, plan its postwar mission, build up stocks of food, and organize shipping with which to carry it out.[11]

While politicians were establishing mechanisms for postwar relief, a parallel process was at work in which intellectuals, "experts," European émigrés, and relief workers sought to define and influence their role. Many of the prominent voices in this conversation were on the political left, pacifists and internationalists who were opposed to war in general and had no role in the current war effort. Yet this process was important because it helped to define, in advance, how the postwar landscape would be understood and categorized; in particular, it produced the central defining construct of postwar aid, that of the displaced person. It is not clear who coined the phrase, which was not in use in 1939 when the British think tank Chatham House produced a magisterial survey of the world refugee problem; but it may have originated in Leith-Ross's committee. By 1942, the concept of the displaced person had become part of the intellectual discourse of the Allied war, as was clearly seen when the left-wing think tank the Fabian Society staged a conference on the Relief and Reconstruction of Europe in Oxford on December 12, 1942.[12]

The timing was crucial. Following the British victory in the Western Desert at El Alamein and the Allied landings in North Africa, with the German Sixth Army newly cut off at Stalingrad, the prospect of victory was in sight. Roosevelt was clearly going to set up some sort of international relief body, so it was time for the pressure groups to make their voices heard.

The big guns of the intellectual Left set the scene. The publisher Leonard Woolf—bravely carrying on public work only a year after the suicide of his wife, Virginia—warned that Europe faced its greatest crisis since the Thirty Years' War. Then it had taken a century to recover fully; now it was clear that Hitler would bequeath to the continent an apocalypse of unprecedented dimensions. When the war ended, there would need to be an immediate relief effort, followed by longer-term reconstruction: projects so vast that they could not be left to private economic interests. Only large-scale intergovernmental action could meet this challenge. This theme was developed by the biologist and broadcaster Julian Huxley. The war, he declared, was just the symptom of a wider historical revolution. Capitalist laissez-faire and national political systems had broken down; what was needed in their place was more planning, more government control, and a higher degree of international organization, both economic and political. Finally, Harold Laski, a professor of politics at the London School of Economics, called on the Allied governments to show magnanimity in victory and not to punish innocent civilians in enemy countries. Echoing Leonard Woolf, he insisted that any machinery of relief must be capable of dealing not just with "immediate salvage" but also with long-term reconstruction. The United Nations—and above all the United States and Britain—must think of the machinery they had built "not as one thinks of a kind of International Red Cross, which moves in to do ambulance work after a flood or an earthquake, but as a system of institutions vitally related to the kind of world we want to build when peace comes."

The prophecies of the intellectuals were given substance by a second group of speakers, doctors, and aid workers who had witnessed the catastrophic aftereffects of the Great War. They were well aware that the 9 million–odd men killed on the battlefield between 1914 and 1918 were dwarfed by the numbers of civilians who had died after it, as Europe's population, weakened by wartime starvation and the British blockade, succumbed to disease. Relief workers were haunted by memories of the influenza epidemic of 1918–1919, which had killed 40 million people worldwide, many of them in Europe; the typhus which had accounted for another 3 million; the famine which had carried off 5 million people in Ukraine in 1921. They were determined that this time aid would not be used as a political weapon—as it had been in 1919–1921, when the maintenance of the Allied blockade had exacerbated starvation in Vienna and Berlin and the delay in admitting foreign relief to Soviet Russia had cost many lives. They wanted no more of the squabbling among the agencies that had impeded relief work in Serbia, for example. Their great fear was that history would repeat itself, that the appalling battlefield casualties of the Second World War, the dreadful loss of life in German concentration camps and slave labor factories, would once again be just a prelude to the true catastrophe to come in the aftermath of the war.[13]

The need for proper planning and coordination was underlined by the terrible reports now coming out of Hitler's Europe. The experts warned the Oxford conference that the war would leave a shortage of food at least as severe as in Germany in 1919, large-scale famine "to rival that of the Volga region in 1921–1922," with 330 million people needing about 700 calories a day to be kept alive. But the food problem was dwarfed by that of population displacement. The Germans had taken countless millions from their homes and, one speaker warned, "as soon as the war is over most of the people of continental Europe will wish to move." If not tackled firmly and dynamically, this problem might well bring to Europe a disaster greater than the war itself: "the magnitude of the task is such as to cause the heart to sink." The medical implications of starvation and displacement were also spelled out—malnutrition and typhus, a possible malaria pandemic, a vast tuberculous population, and rampant venereal disease.

Millions of people would carry the effects of years of underfeeding, and there would inevitably be "an enormous amount of mental breakdown from the lesser neuroses to frank insanity."[14]

The most surprising aspect of the 1942 Fabian conference, to the modern reader, is that only one of the speakers referred to what was then happening to Europe's Jews, and it was not Leonard Woolf or Harold Laski. In the course of a twenty-six-page discussion of "The Re-establishment of Displaced Persons," Kenneth Brookes devoted one half-page paragraph to the Jews. He quoted estimates that "throughout Europe 2,000,000 Jews had been put to death and that in some areas as much as 99 per cent of the Jewish population ha[d] succumbed." From Norway to France, he continued, "Jews have been deported to Poland, where they have been herded into ghettoes in which many spend but little time before being put to death." He then gave estimates of the numbers deported to the East. "The identification, repatriation or resettlement of these unhappy peoples" would, he concluded, be "one of the most difficult tasks to be faced as soon as the war is over"; but a solution had to be found. Not only was the Nazis' policy toward the Jews referred to only in passing, there was no suggestion that the Jewish problem was somehow separable from the wider question of displaced peoples.[15]

This overlap between the Germans' deportation of forced labor and their policy toward the Jews also misled British intelligence as to what was happening in Eastern Europe. Reports of the deportations of Jews from Western Europe in 1942 were initially interpreted by some in Whitehall within much more widespread intelligence of the mass deportation of foreign workers to Germany. As a result, it took interventions from outside to convince the British government of what was happening. In the second half of 1942, information from new sources reached London and Washington. A German industrialist revealed some of the Nazis' plans to a Swiss associate, and an underground courier from Poland reached London with a detailed dossier of what was happening in Poland. This new information caused the British and U.S. governments to issue a statement in December 1942 which declared that the Germans were "carrying into effect Hitler's often-repeated intention to exterminate the Jewish people in Europe." Both governments condemned this "bestial policy of cold-blooded extermination" and vowed to bring those responsible to justice. After the British foreign secretary had read the statement to the House of Commons, members stood in silence for a minute.[16]

Thus, by the end of 1942, it was generally recognized that the war's aftermath would pose a terrible challenge—and that a huge effort would have to be made if the catastrophe of 1918–1924 were not to be repeated. It was clear that it would take the cooperation of all the Allies. But as they began to occupy enemy territory, a new player emerged—the Allied armies themselves.

THREE

"The Origin of the Perpetual Muddle"

EXPERIENCE WITH RELIEF, 1943–1945

In the second week of February 1943, an armored Cadillac made its way into the rugged hills of northern Tunisia. It was bringing the supreme commander of the Allied armies in North Africa, General Dwight D. Eisenhower, from his base in Algiers to the front line five hundred miles away. In heavy rain, Eisenhower alighted and then spent two hours consulting with his generals. He found the overall disposition of forces to be satisfactory and was particularly impressed by Major General Lloyd R. Fredendall, in charge of U.S. II Corps, who appeared to have "a thorough knowledge of the battlefield." "He seems keen and fit," Eisenhower added in a cable to Washington, "and I am placing a lot of confidence in him." After further conferences with his commanders, Eisenhower and his retinue returned to his headquarters at Algiers, pausing to visit several Roman sites on the way.

The following day, a large force of German tanks attacked the U.S. positions, causing panic and confusion in the inexperienced troops. Entire units were obliterated. General Fredendall proved unable to handle the situation and began drinking heavily. He was soon sent home. But Eisenhower—who bore an equal, if not greater, responsibility for the overextended state of the Allied line, who had allowed political complications in Algiers to distract him from military matters, could not be sacrificed. He was the American commander, the protégé of the great General George C. Marshall, and had only recently been promoted to full general.

Fortunately, however, the Germans were unable to exploit their breakthrough. The ground lost was slowly regained, and in May 1943, the Allies were able to capture Tunis.[1]

Armies, it has been said, "never learn from other armies; they only learn from their own mistakes." As the tide of war began to turn in early 1943, the U.S. Army was still learning how to fight a modern war and, in the rush to expand a peacetime force of 200,000 into a mass army of 7 million men, was making many mistakes. But as well as battlefield tactics, it was having to learn other lessons: how to govern occupied territory and how to handle civilian relief.[2]

Their country's history made Americans uncomfortable as colonialists and uncertain how to play the role of the occupier. Early in the war, members of Roosevelt's Cabinet had mocked the Pentagon for establishing a School of Military Government and had demanded that there should be civilian control of any territories occupied by the military. But experience in North Africa soon showed this to be impractical. Civilians simply could not operate in the war zone without having military rank and access to army transport and military clearances, while all efforts to establish a single U.S. civilian government agency in charge of occupied territory ended in failure. The "real lesson" of North Africa, for General Brehon B. Somervell, the Pentagon's powerful logistics chief, was that "You cannot separate the handling of civil affairs from military operations in areas in which military operations are under way, and an attempt to do so in a hostile country would be disastrous." So the military got control of the "military phase," and soldiers were assigned new roles. Experience also taught them to take "relief" into account.[3]

Operation Torch, the invasion of Morocco and Algeria in November 1942, was the first Anglo-American campaign of the war; amid all the logistic and political complications, little thought had been given to the planning of humanitarian aid for civilians. That omission led to "the landing in North Africa, without permission, without previous intimation of arrival, and without any sort of coordination, of a number of parties dispatched by voluntary societies, mostly American, for work in the relief of civilians," as the British official historian put it; the presence of the voluntary agencies irritated the military. In Algiers, Eisenhower's political adviser, Robert Murphy, had to deal with a "continuous parade of Very Important Persons—or those who thought they were" because "almost every organization in the United States wanted to participate in this first major American campaign in World War II, and had drafted plans accordingly." Many of these American civilian relief workers were Jewish. Murphy, a Boston Irish Catholic who had served in Nazi Germany and Vichy

France, was not known for his philo-Semitism; neither was the U.S. Army.[4]

The lesson was quite clear: in future, these people must be kept out. The full implications of this policy would only become apparent in Germany in 1945.

From the invasion of Sicily in July 1943 to the end of the war, British and U.S. armies began to take control of Italy. It was not an easy task, with much of the country still under German occupation and a weak Italian government unwilling to take full responsibility. Nonetheless, the record of the Allied military government in Italy was as much a saga of incompetence, mismanagement, and missed opportunities as the Allied military campaign in Italy itself. Poor planning, a "fantastically elaborate and top-heavy machine" combining the worst excesses of the Pentagon and the British War Office, bureaucratic infighting, and weak leadership all played a part. Required to involve themselves in politics, economic management, and social policy, the soldiers brought inflation, starvation, and prostitution to Italy and restored the Sicilian Mafia and the Neapolitan Camorra to power. The devastating economic and social consequences of quartering U.S. troops on a poor country were first revealed. Some 60 percent of the canned food, wheat, sugar, cigarettes, uniforms, and underwear unloaded in Naples in 1944 disappeared onto the black market. "Those were the days when a truckload of goods smuggled across the Military Police roadblocks could make a man rich overnight, while the bulk of the city population subsisted on a little black bread and dried pea soup."[5]

However, the campaign in Italy did provide the military with a useful training ground in modern public health techniques. Confronted by starvation in Sicily, a typhus epidemic in Naples, and a refugee problem all over the peninsula, Allied commanders soon learned that in modern warfare they needed to manage civilians by feeding, fumigating, and sheltering them (unless, like the Germans, you simply terrorized them), and they found that recent advances in medical research had given them potent new weapons.

The Allies had invaded Sicily without making any provision for feeding the local population, having assumed that the granary of the Roman Empire could feed itself and taken on trust Italian official figures. They soon discovered that the arrangements for distributing food had broken down, farmers were not bringing produce for sale, a black market had developed, and there was starvation in certain areas. "The humble bean (fagioli) for generations scorned by everybody but the lowest classes" had "risen to a delicacy which can only be afforded by the rich at 150 lire per kilo as compared with a lire or less in normal times." A riot in Palermo further concentrated their minds. Rationing was attempted in Sicily, but conditions were not right; efforts to take action against hoarders failed. Allied officers spent four days of every week fruitlessly looking for illegal grain. A suggestion from Washington that military officials in Sicily "use calico cloth and jingles to attract the farmer's wife" into surrendering hoarded grain met with derision. "You would be simply astonished at the things you can buy in Italy. Pure silk stockings—you can buy as many as you want." A short-term crisis was averted by getting wheat from the French in North Africa and the Middle East. In the longer term, as the Allied armies moved to the Italian mainland, it was accepted that 50 percent of the population south of Rome would have to be fed with imported grain, diverting manpower and transport away from the military campaign itself. Civilians working for the Allied forces had extra rations, it being realized that "keeping the population quiet resolved itself, in practice, into providing adequate rations for urban heavy workers." Yet emergency food imports were only a crude solution to the problem and brought their own harvest—since most of the 416,000 tons of food imported into Italy had found its way onto the black market, those familiar with conditions on the ground argued that it made more sense to try to get the local commercial agriculture going again.[6]

The military's next lesson came in Naples, where typhus broke out in late 1943. Allied bombing of a prison allowed inmates already infected with the disease to escape and find refuge in overcrowded air-raid shelters. The retreating Germans then blew up the city's aqueduct and drained most of its reservoirs, so that Naples was without water for two weeks. Soon after Allied troops entered the city in late September 1943, typhus cases began to be reported, but it took the Allied military government two months to get a grip on the situation—or rather to call in the experts. Fortunately, this happened to be an area where remarkable progress had recently been made. Although doctors had long known that typhus develops when large numbers of soldiers or refugees are brought together in overcrowded and unsanitary conditions, it was not until 1909 that a French scientist established that the disease is vectored by the body louse. This finding enabled the vast armies of the world wars to contain the disease by regular delousing, using chemical disinfectants and mobile steam baths, but those traditional sanitary methods required considerable investment in equipment and the willingness of subjects to strip. They were therefore not ideal for handling civilian populations.

The fight against typhus was transformed by the Americans. In 1942, President Roosevelt established the U.S. Typhus Commission, specifically to find more effective ways of combating the disease in areas where U.S. forces would be fighting. By then there had been one further important advance, the development of an effective vaccine against typhus by the bacteriologist H. R. Cox, but better delousing techniques were still needed. Early in 1943, Dr. Fred L. Soper and a team from the Rockefeller Institute in New York began experimenting on Egyptian villagers, comparing an antilouse powder (MYL) developed by the U.S. Army with a newly marketed commercial insecticide, dichlorodiphenyltrichloroethane (DDT).

Fred Soper was an optimist and visionary, a man of great intellectual integrity and "fearless tenacity in dealing with superiors and government officials," who had helped to conceive and carry out effective campaigns against yellow fever and malaria in Brazil in the 1920s. Now, failing to convince the army of the importance of his work, he and his team moved to Algiers to collaborate with French doctors at the Pasteur Institute, who gave them access to nearly a thousand inmates in the Maison Carrée prison. In July 1943, comparative testing of insecticides showed that both MYL and DDT gave excellent results, but although MYL killed lice faster, DDT's effects lasted much longer. The typhus team then carried out further tests in Arab villages in Algeria. Warned by their French colleagues that in order to respect the modesty of the Arab women, they "would need to find a way to apply louse powder to the inner seams of clothing without undressing the wearer," the researchers simply pumped the powder with a hand duster up sleeves and skirts, down neck openings and waistbands. The powder was then evenly dispersed within the airspace between body and clothing. By the autumn, Soper had drafted a document setting out standard procedures which by the end of 1943 had been incorporated into the U.S. Army's military manuals.[7]

Fred Soper and the Rockefeller team arrived in Naples in early December. Ignoring the turf war still going on among the military government, the army, and the U.S. Typhus Commission, they established themselves in the city and on December 15 had seven hundred passengers on a train leaving Naples compulsorily dusted by hastily recruited and trained Italian teams, using the supplies of MYL immediately to hand. Soon afterward DDT began arriving. It was the start of an intensive program. In January 1944, some 1.3 million people were deloused, and in three weeks the typhus epidemic was completely mastered, with almost no deaths.

The New York Times hailed "the miracle performed in Naples" as a triumph of modern medicine. "Typhus, more dreaded than bullets in any Army, is now simply unknown among our soldiers and sailors," the paper stated. "DDT seems almost too good to be true." Soper himself later conceded that "the toxicology of DDT was relatively unknown, but we did not hesitate to pump it under the clothing of [millions of] people and to assign workers to the pumps in rooms which were unavoidably foggy from the DDT dust in the air."[8]

Here again, the lesson was quickly grasped: the men in charge of the military government must understand public health and have the authority to act, early preventive measures must be taken, and outside expertise must be used. However, the full significance of those developments—the extent to which medical research had tamed many of the bogeys encountered in 1918–1924, such as typhus—was not widely understood at the time. The British diplomat most closely involved with refugee policy, Sir George Rendel, later admitted, "We did not realize what miracles would be achieved by the new drugs and prophylactics which had been discovered since 1920."[9]

But there was a third plague in Italy: refugees. As the Allied armies headed north of Naples, the Germans adopted a scorched-earth policy that drove hundreds of thousands of civilians out of their homes and toward Allied lines. By 1944, Allied commanders were devoting substantial resources to the problem, using empty military transport to send refugees to the rear, where the Italian authorities were required to find lodging and care for them in Italian communities until large camps could be built. Later, it was realized that as the movement of refugees—first away from their homes and then back again—would always be to some extent uncontrollable, it was better to set up camps closer to their original residences and thus avoid clogging the roads used by the army.

The Italian campaign taught the Allied military how to handle civilians and devise simple drills for the purpose. To avoid disease, refugees must be sprayed with insecticide; to minimize conflict and make repatriation easy, they must be separated by nationality; to keep them alive, ration packs providing the basic vitamins must be distributed. But experience in Italy also brought out the limitations of the military's approach. Once they had gained control of the "military period," soldiers started trying to redefine their own role. They were unhappy with the more sophisticated aspects of looking after refugees. The army, they said, "could not get into the relief business" and did not "do welfare." They needed a civilian partner.[10]

Left to itself, the U.S. Army would have preferred to work with the American Red Cross, an organization with which it had long ties and felt at ease (and on which its officers relied for female company).[11] But it was not that simple. By now the seeds germinated by Churchill's speech in August 1940, the Leith-Ross committees, pressure from humanitarian groups to prevent a repetition of the disasters of the period after 1918, the Soviet interest in relief, and Roosevelt's wish to involve the Russians in any new organization were all coming together in Washington. In December 1942, the president had created a new branch of the State Department organization to look after refugees and brought in Governor Herbert Lehman to run it. But this was intended to be the predecessor of something greater.

In the first half of 1943—while the grim drama at Stalingrad reached its climax, a quarter of a million German and Italian troops went into Allied prisoner-of-war cages in Tunisia, and Allied airplanes hammered the German homeland—four bureaucrats spent five months negotiating a single piece of paper in a house near Dupont Circle in Washington, D.C. They were the "four wise men" nominated by Roosevelt to produce a draft agreement for an international agency to provide relief after the war. The Great Powers were firmly in control. Chairing the meetings was the dapper Anglophile U.S. deputy secretary of state, Dean Acheson, the son of an Episcopalian bishop, and round the table were the British, Soviet, and Chinese ambassadors: the tall, solemn, foxhunting British aristocrat and former foreign secretary Lord Halifax; the genial old Bolshevik Maxim Litvinov, who as foreign secretary had negotiated the entry of the Hoover mission to Russia; and Wei Tao-ming, an experienced Chinese diplomat.[12]

Why did it take so long to reach agreement? One reason was that the subject of relief evidently bored these great men. "Our group was a congenial one," Acheson later recalled, "often escaping from the confines of an uninspiring agenda to speculate about the world which was to be"; another, that the suspicions of the Russians were not easily overcome. Acheson was more fortunate than later Western negotiators: at this stage in the war the Soviets' desire for relief assistance made them readier to compromise than they would afterward prove. Though Litvinov was adamant that "nothing could be done within any country without that country's consent and through its agencies," he was prepared to give some ground elsewhere. Decisions in the new international body did not have to be unanimous, and the organization's director general was to be allowed some leeway. Finally, by June 1943, a draft was ready to be submitted to the members of the United Nations.[13]

There then followed a three-month interlude. In a rare misjudgment, Roosevelt proposed that U.S. participation in the new organization be secured through executive agreement (requiring no formal congressional approval) rather than via a treaty (subject to Senate approval by a two-thirds majority) and so aroused the suspicions of the powerful and, until recently, isolationist Senator Arthur H. Vandenberg that Congress was being taken for granted. It took time, concessions, persuasion, and "some judicious eating of crow" by Acheson to bring him round. With congressional feathers finally smoothed, however, the process could resume. On November 9, 1943, the president signed the revised agreement establishing the United Nations Relief and Rehabilitation Administration (UNRRA). "The sufferings of the little men and women who have been ground under the Axis heel can be relieved only if we utilize the production of *all* the world," he told the nation.

> In UNRRA we have devised a mechanism, based on the processes of true democracy, which can go far toward accomplishment of such an objective in the days and months of desperate emergency which will follow the overthrow of the Axis.

As in most of the difficult and complex things in life, nations will learn to work together only by actually working together. Why not? The nations have common objectives. It is, therefore, with a lift of hope that we look on the signing of this agreement by all the United Nations as a means of joining them together still more firmly.[14]

The following day delegates from forty-four nations gathered for the first meeting of the UNRRA Council in Atlantic City, New Jersey. Acheson had spent his childhood holidays in the resort, but it had gone down-market since then. "A bleak and barren situation, singularly devoid of charm or human interest," a British diplomat described it while conceding that the "keen and stimulating" air made it "easy to work long hours and do with little sleep." The delegates—who included the Czech foreign minister, Jan Masaryk, Jean Monnet of France, and the young Soviet diplomat Andrei Gromyko, who had just replaced Litvinov—spent most of their time discussing how UNRRA was to be paid for. Under the formula eventually agreed, contributing nations would donate 1 percent of their national income to the organization, giving UNRRA an overall budget of some $2 billion, of which the United States would provide $1.35 billion, nearly two-thirds of the total, and the United Kingdom £80 million, with the rest coming mainly from Canada and Latin America.[15]

There was also much debate about the "second R" in UNRRA. Would the agency provide "rehabilitation" as well as "relief"? Some delegates made Harold Laski's point that relief on its own (a "glorified soup kitchen") was pointless unless the means of getting the European economy going again were also provided.[16] That was the obvious lesson of the aftermath of the First World War. But at that stage it was not practical politics to ask the U.S. Congress to fund the recovery of European industries that might compete with American business. The British and U.S. governments regarded "rehabilitation" as an innocuous substitute for the more politically contentious "reconstruction" and wanted it kept within a fixed time limit, "coterminous with relief."[17]

There was less debate about another of UNRRA's functions. It was agreed that the organization would feed, give medical aid to, and repatriate the millions of foreign displaced persons in Germany. This term was now firmly established in the official lexicon, thanks to two comprehensive recent surveys. Leith-Ross's committee had finally produced a report on the scale of wartime displacement, and in the autumn of 1943 the book *The Displacement of Population in Europe,* written for the International Labour Office by the Russian-born demographer Eugene Kulischer, offered the public the first authoritative survey of the extent of wartime migration, both voluntary and involuntary. From now on the displaced person was one of the defining ideas in all postwar planning and propaganda, "one of the keywords of the decade," as Evelyn Waugh later wrote.[18]

At the same time, however, UNRRA's remit was clarified: Churchill's commitment to bring "food and freedom" to German civilians was quietly abandoned. At Atlantic City it became apparent that any attempt to use UNRRA to help German civilians would be bitterly opposed by the smaller nations of Western Europe, already annoyed that they were being excluded from UNRRA's inner councils. UNRRA was barred from assisting Germans to return to Germany from outside its frontiers, and any help given to Germany would have to paid for in full. Henceforward, as *The Economist* noted, "the scale of relief is to be divorced from need," and the principle which had so bedeviled relief after the First World War—"that capacity to pay and obligation to pay bear no relation to each other"—had been reintroduced. Here, once again, the humanitarian concern of the organization was being constrained.[19]

For all that, it was a great moment in history when both houses of Congress approved UNRRA's budget request by overwhelming margins—marking the dawn of a new age of international cooperation. In the First World War, the United States had acted alone to relieve the problems of starvation and misery in postwar Europe; between the wars it had not belonged to the League of Nations. Now it committed itself to a cooperative policy.

UNRRA immediately became a vessel into which wartime idealism flowed—not simply as an instrument for repairing the horrors of war but as the first of the UN agencies taking international action to tackle the problems of the world. The UNRRA draft agreement was hailed by the London *Observer* as "one of the most important and pregnant events of the war": "The enterprise there set on foot—we are measuring our words—[is] as bold, big and exciting a venture as any in the history of social organization." Harder-nosed commentators wondered how UNRRA would function when the food and supplies it was supposed to distribute were already largely allocated to the British and the shipping it would need was mostly committed to the military needs of the war.[20]

Much therefore rested on the shoulders of UNRRA's first director-general, Herbert Lehman. Sixty-five at the time of his appointment, Lehman came from an affluent and liberal-minded German Jewish Reform dynasty in New York City and had spent his early years working in the family business, the famous investment banking house Lehman Brothers. His association with the president went back to their first meeting in the Department of the Navy in 1917, and he had succeeded FDR as governor of New York State, going on to serve four terms in the post between 1932 and 1942, presiding over an impressive "little New Deal" which combined public welfare projects with relative financial orthodoxy. "A very nice, comfortable man, like a brown bear, swinging his little legs from his chair, honest, brave, slow and a personality," Lehman was not a colorful political campaigner like the president and the mercurial mayor of New York City, Fiorello H. La Guardia, but his solid, honest, and respectable persona complemented those of his more charismatic colleagues. He also had a long record in public service and relief work, having helped to found the American Jewish Joint Distribution Committee in 1914 and lobbied on behalf of Jewish refugees in the 1930s. The president in appointing him was heard to remark, "I want to see some of those Goddamned Fascists begging for subsistence from a Jew." Seen as "a man of known moderation, integrity, and competence," Lehman was acceptable to the British and Russians and to the U.S. military, whereas Hoover and La Guardia were not.[21]

Lehman had already been preparing for a year. In addition to drawing on the Leith-Ross committee's estimates, he had appointed twenty-four panels of experts (including many of those present at the Oxford conference) to assess the future needs of Europe's population. Now he established a large office near Dupont Circle in Washington, a European Regional Office in London, and purchasing missions around the world. He also began to recruit staff.

As an international relief agency, UNRRA aroused contradictory responses in the United States. Even after Pearl Harbor, one strand of American opinion remained wary of international institutions. "At no time during World War II," stressed the historian John M. Blum, "did the majority of the American people or of their representatives contemplate a postwar settlement in which the United States would not circumscribe its commitments, economic, political, and military, to other nations. On the contrary, at all times the majority of Americans seemed resolved that there would be no unconditional postwar giveaways—of American wealth, of American sovereignty, of American weapons. There was no chance that Uncle Sam would play Uncle Sucker." Congress voted for the UNRRA agreement, but only after inserting clauses requiring the organization to spend a substantial part of its budget on American agricultural products such as raw wool and cotton.

Against that, recent history had strengthened some Americans' faith in international cooperation. The Great Depression and Roosevelt's ambitious New Deal program had given them a belief in using large institutions to cure major social problems; the war had made them look again at the United States' role in the world. Many people who thought this way were currently out of a job, because by the end of 1943 Congress had abolished most of the New Deal agencies, such as the Civilian Conservation Corps and the Works Progress Administration.[22]

The office which UNRRA now established near Dupont Circle had "much of the atmosphere of a Communist headquarters," according to one right-wing American. Many of the people milling around in the halls and sitting at desks had, he thought, "that starry-eyed look which is usually associated with people who have visions of radically changing the world"; though he did concede that "many conscientious, well-meaning people" with backgrounds in welfare and the New Deal agencies entered UNRRA "who sincerely wanted to help humanity in any way they could." A journalist spoke to two such idealists in early 1944. For one Unitarian minister from Boston, UNRRA was "the first earnest step toward one world and I want to be in it," while a bank vice president from Baltimore was "eager to go across to 'alleviate the suffering of humanity.'"[23]

In wartime Britain, most relief workers were already busy with evacuee children and other problems, so UNRRA tended to attract long-term internationalists and veterans of foreign relief work. Will Arnold-Forster, who became UNRRA's chief instructor, was a longstanding advocate of the League of Nations and labor internationalist, while his friend, the journalist and activist Francesca Wilson, who joined UNRRA as principal welfare officer, had been involved in relief work with the Quakers since 1916. Having seen all the muddles and infighting among the agencies after the First World War, she had high hopes for UNRRA. In a memoir published in 1944, Wilson recalled how between the wars the idea that it was "better to plan beforehand than muddle through anyhow" had gained ground. For her, the fact that there was now an "official super-State body in charge of relief, the UNRRA" was "an advance of incalculable importance on last time when no prior survey of needs was made and nation was allowed to compete with nation for food and necessities." Furthermore, it opened the way to the first experiment in worldwide economic cooperation.[24]

By the end of 1944, UNRRA had in its Washington office a director-general and seven deputy directors general, a treasurer, a general counsel, a diplomatic adviser, a financial adviser, and directors of Divisions of Health, Welfare, Displaced Persons, and Public Information. In London there were three more deputy directors general, a general counsel, an executive secretary, a financial adviser, and directors of health, welfare, displaced persons, and public information. There were in addition relief missions to Albania, the Balkans, Ethiopia, Greece, Italy, and Yugoslavia (all based in Cairo) and offices in Switzerland and at Allied military headquarters for the Mediterranean at Caserta, near Naples. Outside Europe there were offices in Australia and China and a supply mission in Brazil.[25]

In terms of accomplishments, UNRRA had taken over from the British the responsibility for the refugee camps in Egypt, Palestine, and Syria which had been established to care for the many thousands of Greeks driven from their homes by Germans and Italians, Poles allowed to leave the Soviet Union by way of Turkey and Iran in 1942, and Yugoslav partisans, who had begun arriving via Italy early in 1944. In addition, its panels of technical experts had submitted reports on Europe's likely needs in terms of health, food, textiles, agriculture, and industrial rehabilitation, and UNRRA's Council had held a second meeting in Quebec.

But a sense of frustration and disappointment had also begun to surround the organization. As early as July 1944, *The Economist* was reporting a "general impression that UNRRA is in some way missing its opportunities and turning out not to be a vigorous experiment in the new internationalism, but another pale Genevan ghost." It had become obvious that UNRRA had not properly defined its own role, was not having much success in getting hold of supplies or transport, and had failed to overcome the distrust of the military and the voluntary societies, mainly because its staff were generally not respected.[26]

By the time UNRRA was created in November 1943, powerful wartime empires had developed. "Everyone in Washington was fighting for power," Herbert Lehman's biographer later wrote. "The Board of Economic Warfare was fighting for power. The Combined Boards— that is, the Raw Materials Board, the Production and Resources Board, the Food Board, and the Shipping Adjustment Board, all Anglo-American or Anglo-Canadian-American—were fighting for power. The Army, Navy and Air Force did not need power, for they had it, but they fought to keep power." The military's attitude was that "a lion's share was not enough: 'when in doubt take everything.'" Things were no easier in London, where the Ministries of Food, Shipping, and Economic Warfare divided the cake among them.[27]

These organizations couldn't see the point of UNRRA. Relief workers might dream of international collaboration; Roosevelt might favor it as a way of corralling the Russians; but that didn't make Whitehall or the Pentagon like the idea. The Washington warlords went through the motions but in practice did nothing to help UNRRA. The British, fearing that "UNRRA, when set up, with 'forceful' Americans in charge and a quantity of 'greedy and destitute' small European allies clamouring for supplies, [might] put us in the UK in a frightful hole," insisted on preserving the powers over the distribution of food of the existing Anglo-American Combined Boards and did their best to prevent UNRRA getting its hands on any supplies at all. Churchill, after the flourishes of 1940, was interested in relief only in the context of Anglo-Soviet relations, though he did, apparently, sing "UNRRA, runnrrah!" in his bath to a Gilbert and Sullivan tune.[28]

It didn't help that the quality of UNRRA's top management was poor. Anyone with talent or energy was already taking part in the war, so Lehman found it difficult to find suitably qualified staff; for all their fine words, neither London nor Washington made outstanding people available to him. The two distinguished British public servants seconded to UNRRA, Frederick Leith-Ross and Arthur Salter, were long past their prime.

But Lehman himself was also part of the problem. Though a decent and honorable man, liked and respected by all, the governor lacked the charisma, drive, and executive gifts needed to establish a new organization quickly. He was "an indifferent organizer," his planning was "worse than useless," and he had neither "guts nor common sense," according to British diplomats. Dean Acheson was equally dismissive: "the simplest executive task was beyond him." Lehman, Vice President Henry Wallace wrote in his diary, was "not a very good fighter" and did not "know the way things are done in Washington." His biographer concedes that the governor's approach "was that of a businessman, not a politician, evangelist or public personality. He had no distinction as a speech-maker, writer or diplomatist. He was even more a businessman in essential character than Hoover had been in the First World War."[29]

The British were particularly critical. "Governor Lehman has never shown any understanding of what is required and UNRRA has not therefore been put 'on the map,'" the Foreign Office concluded in September 1944. What was needed was an experienced publicist to "invent the slogans and organize the broadcast and press releases that would explain to the American public what UNRRA is, what it has to do, and what its relation [is] to the other postwar organizations." The British pleaded with Lehman to hire more PR men, only to be told that he "didn't believe in public relations." Then they begged him to hire Mary Craig McGeachy, an ebullient Canadian who had "done a wonderful job in 'putting over' our unpalatable blockade policy in the USA" and "could do an equally good job in 'putting over' UNRRA in the same way." She was indeed hired but inexplicably given a welfare job. The one outcome of British pressure was an agreement to spend some of Canada's substantial contribution to UNRRA on making promotional films.[30]

But an element outside anyone's control produced UNRRA's first crisis—the war in Europe dragged on far longer than expected. By the second half of 1944, as the Allied military offensives in Holland and Italy began to falter, it had become clear that UNRRA's budget of £450 million was not even half of what it actually needed. The initial estimates had been too low, and political constraints had further pushed up costs: the requirement that 90 percent of a country's contribution be spent inside that country (insisted on by the U.S. Congress) meant, for example, that UNRRA had to spend 67 percent of its overall budget in the United States, where commodity and supply prices were much higher than elsewhere.

Lehman was presented with a choice: to live with the funds allocated and risk doing inadequate work or to get UNRRA's mission done regardless of cost and assume that the U.S. taxpayer would pick up the overspend. It was no contest. As a banker, Lehman stood for financial prudence; by temperament, he loathed emotional blackmailers like La Guardia. Nor was it feasible, in an election year, to go back to Congress for more money. He insisted on financial rectitude. UNRRA must live within its budget, he made clear in the autumn of 1944.[31]

As a result, UNRRA took on a diminished role in Western Europe. It had originally been assumed that when the Allies invaded Europe, UNRRA would assume responsibility for relief in the liberated countries once the first "military phase" was over. But as the full cost of this became clear, UNRRA's policy evolved; it was decided that "those countries which could afford to pay for relief supplies should be required to do so." This meant that since France, Belgium, Luxembourg, Norway, and the Netherlands all technically had the national resources to pay for goods and supplies on the world market, they would not get free handouts from UNRRA. Those countries, having (as *The Times* of London put it) "first been led to believe that they could expect everything from UNRRA and subsequently [come] to the conclusion that they could expect nothing," saw little advantage in UNRRA's presence. "These tendencies to go elsewhere than to UNRRA for one's relief shopping were," according to the British official historian, "strongly reinforced by the general confusion and administrative ineptitude that reigned within UNRRA during the earlier days, and by the political desire of the governments concerned to demonstrate their zeal in caring for their own people. It was for these various reasons that the countries in which military operations took place decided, with few exceptions, to do without the aid of UNRRA." No doubt long-standing European suspicions that UNRRA was a Great Power stitch-up contributed to this decision.[32]

And so the end of 1944 saw a strange situation. The newly liberated countries of Western Europe were in desperate need of food, clothing, shelter, fuel, and medical supplies; yet the international organization specifically created to address those needs—supposedly "a crusade to bring food to the hungry, shelter to the homeless, clothing to those who are in rags"—was nowhere to be seen. In which case, what was UNRRA for? "The general opinion among the British public is that UNRRA is dead," a British diplomat reported. "His Majesty's Government is continually being asked in the House of Commons what has happened to the corpse."[33]

Nowhere were UNRRA's shortcomings more apparent than in its European Regional Office in London, housed in an assortment of buildings near the BBC and run by two European directors with equal and rather overlapping powers, Leith-Ross and Nikolai I. Feonov, a Soviet economist. Leith-Ross had difficulties with the Russians but put most of the blame on the Allied military command: "We were pressed to recruit staff and have them ready and when we arranged this they were kept kicking their heels, with much discontent and loss of morale," he later wrote. The resulting atmosphere of "inactivity and gossip and intrigue for better jobs" soon disillusioned Iris Murdoch, the young woman who had joined UNRRA in a flush of idealism after the death of her friend Frank Thompson. UNRRA, she wrote, was "rather too full of inept British civil servants (me for instance), uncoordinated foreigners with Special Ideas and an imperfect command of English." The result was "pretty fair chaos. V[ery] many noble-hearted good-intentioned—drown in the general flood of mediocrity and muddle." The general inertia also brought out international tensions. UNRRA, Murdoch wrote, was run "not by bowler hats from Ealing and Dagenham who behave approximately like gentlemen but by the citizens of Milwaukee and Cincinnati and New Haven, Conn., let loose in their myriads to deal a death blow to tottering Europe. They do not sit on office stools but lounge, with cellulose belts and nylon braces, behind enormous desks and chew gum and call their fellow citizens by their Christian names."[34]

UNRRA's Cairo office was another source of ridicule. Visiting the Egyptian capital in September 1944, a journalist found an assortment of picturesque characters sitting around there waiting to be sent to work in the Balkans: a florid British major who, when asked if he had done any relief work, had replied, "Good God, madam, I relieved Mafeking"; Lord Norbury, who had evacuated Salonika in the 1920s and now hoped to become chief of the Yugoslav mission—"with his red horsehair flywhisk and the monocle in his eye . . . the perfect popular idea of a British peer"; and Leo Gerstenzang, a millionaire friend of Governor Lehman and the inventor of the QTStick, "a small piece of cotton wool on the end of orange sticks used for cleaning out babies' nostrils and anuses." Also on the large staff were the erstwhile mayor of Louisville, Kentucky, and the former governor of Nebraska. The intense heat, prevailing idleness, and widely varying salary scales encouraged Anglo-American "jealousy and misunderstanding" to flourish.[35]

At the end of 1944, the British tried to do something about UNRRA. There was talk of sending in a Cabinet minister and of getting rid of Lehman, but it was soon recognized that it was an American show and Lehman was Roosevelt's appointee. Besides, whatever UNRRA's faults, it was costing the British less than any alternative would. "Our contribution to the expenses of UNRRA was likely to be only about 20 per cent while our contribution to any other organization might well be 50 per cent," a minister pointed out. In the end, Whitehall decided that UNRRA had to be made to work and began looking for someone to lick it into shape.[36]

The relationship which UNRRA most needed to resolve was that with the military. Although the Italian campaign had taught Allied generals that dealing with the problems of civilians was part of modern warfare, it did not alter their view that the best partner in this task was the American and British Red Cross. When France was invaded in June 1944, General Eisenhower asked those organizations to provide "welfare" in the wake of his armies. UNRRA played only a very minor part.

However, the campaign in France in 1944 further brought home to the military the problem of displaced persons—some 60,000 Russians, Poles, Czechs, and Yugoslavs had to be fed, housed, provided with sanitation and medical care, and moved out of the combat areas. When the Displaced Persons Branch at SHAEF began to prepare for the next phase of the war, it "soon realized that with the defeat of Nazi Germany the Allied armies would be faced with a staggeringly large and internationally complex problem of repatriating millions of Europeans." But how large exactly? Estimates of the number of refugees in Europe at this time ranged from 9 million to 30 million. Malcolm Proudfoot, in peacetime an urban geographer from Chicago, was one of the SHAEF staffers who tried to answer the question. Supplementing Leith-Ross and Kulischer's estimates with more recent reports, he and his colleagues concluded that there were in fact

11,469,000 people displaced in Europe and 7,738,000 displaced in Germany, of whom the largest groups were 2.3 million Frenchmen and -women, 1,840,000 Russians, 1,403,000 Poles, 500,000 Belgians, 402,000 Dutch, 350,000 Czechs, 328,000 Yugoslavs, 195,000 Italians, and 100,000 from the Baltic states.[37]

According to these figures, at least eight million people would have to be repatriated. SHAEF drew up elaborate plans for how this was to be done. Two lengthy documents set out the procedure, pamphlets were issued, military government staff trained, registration cards printed. The primary responsibility would fall to the military itself, but clearly it would need outside help. There was enormous opposition to involving UNRRA: both the British and the American military were collectively contemptuous of its personnel and felt that to involve them in military operations would create a security hazard. This hostility created what Proudfoot called "vexatious delays." Finally, however, in December 1944, Lehman and Eisenhower signed an agreement under which UNRRA would provide teams to look after DPs in Germany. In the detailed discussions that followed, the military first asked UNRRA to provide 200 teams and in February 1945 requested 450. UNRRA officials, desperate to please, agreed; in modern managementspeak, they "overpromised." And that, many people in UNRRA later believed, "was the origin of the perpetual muddle that never got sorted out."[38]

FOUR

"Half the Nationalities of Europe on the March"

GERMANY, 1945

On April 9, 1945, a Polish soldier escaped from a labor camp in Thuringia. A few days later, as he walked into a small village, he saw American tanks. "Dumbfounded with happiness I repeated only 'At last!' " he recalled a year later.

> This was the border behind which stayed years of slavery, endless hours of suffering and infinite hope. Faith materialized now, and was marching on the German road. She came exactly as we saw her in our dreams. Allied soldiers brought her in their steel tanks.
>
> A tank stopped. Young laughing American soldiers leaned forward. They were simple and spontaneous. We talked such natural simple chatter about nothing.
>
> They rolled through the village, and on the road the inhabitants poured out to greet the entering victors, with white handkerchiefs. Were they the same Germans who only a few days ago looked at our marching column with the arrogance of the masters?
>
> For a very long time we were standing on the road, greeting every machine which brought us freedom and the right to live—and freedom was continually passing by us. Suddenly a strange terror seized me, that perhaps this freedom will not remain with us, that it will always pass us by and we will stay alone on this German road.[1]

In the neighboring city of Erfurt, a group of displaced persons was asleep when General George S. Patton's troops arrived. After the brief battle was over, Russian, Italian, French, Polish, Belgian, and Ukrainian DPs rushed out, to find their saviors "standing at the shelter entrance, chewing gum and showering cigarettes on all." Most of the DPs then commandeered bicycles or cars and headed west to get away from the battlefront, but Bogdan Moszkowski, an eighteen-year-old Pole, stayed to watch with fascination as the American soldiers calmly went about fighting, eating their rations, and having fun with abandoned cars and motorbikes.

Soon, however, the Americans directed the DPs to a storehouse in Erfurt station, where they were issued with clothing. Bogdan received a complete new outfit and went to a local hotel to clean himself up. His account of the liberation—written in the third person—continues:

> The next issue is food and alcohol. The [DPs] eat so much that Bogdan thinks he will burst. [The] Germans went to earth before the Americans came, and stayed there for a week, all the rest of the town proceeded to get riotously drunk. They smoke—no more the butt ends of cigarettes found in the gutter, but brand new ones. In the stores many clothes remain. No one takes more than one set, but every one of them takes as much food as he can carry. They want to be surrounded with food—they do not want to part with it—they want to see it all the time.

Bogdan's group was then directed to a nearby barracks: "So many languages are heard there, that it is like the Tower of Babel." The biggest hall in the barracks was made into a ballroom and every night the DPs danced to a band formed of men from Buchenwald camp, who were now at Erfurt. "Bogdan did not like to talk to them, because they are always talking of their sufferings, Bogdan thinks he went through enough without going over it again and again."[2]

Allied troops had penetrated into Germany, taking the ancient town of Aachen toward the end of 1944. Then winter intervened and the Germans counterattacked in the Ardennes. It was not until late the following February that the offensive resumed and three weeks later that the Rhine was crossed. When Allied journalists began to see Germany for themselves, they noticed first the prosperity of the countryside. "The first thing that struck you," Alan Moorehead wrote, "was the cattle, so numerous, so well fed. Chickens and pigs and horses were running everywhere. The farms were rich, wonderfully well equipped and managed. The farming people and their foreign workers were well dressed, and they looked strong and healthy." Every house seemed to have a larder well stocked with preserved vegetables and fruits, sides of bacon, and dairy butter. The villages and towns, too, seemed to have a "solid bourgeois comfort," seemingly untouched by the war. However, as they ventured deeper into Germany, other impressions followed: the total devastation of many of the cities, the air of defeat—and then the slave laborers.[3]

The scale of this phenomenon astonished the liberators. "Thousands, tens of thousands, finally millions of slaves were coming out of the farms and the factories and the mines and pouring onto the highways," an American intelligence officer wrote. Alan Moorehead saw

> little groups of Frenchmen, then Dutch, then Belgians and Czechs and Poles and Italians, and finally, in overwhelming majority, the Russians in their bright green uniforms, with "SU"—Soviet Union—painted in white on their backs. Half the nationalities of Europe were on the march, all moving blindly westward along the roads, feeling their way by some common instinct towards the British and American lines in the hope of finding food and shelter and transportation there.

The laborers' clothes testified to their recent past:

> They wore the striped prison garb of the concentration camps, or the faded uniforms of their defeated army, or the scummiest rags. All along the highways lay little bundles of incredibly filthy and smelly tatters discarded by the slaves who found something better.[4]

This "tidal wave of nomad peoples" uncovered by the Allies' speedy advance into Germany overwhelmed the military machine. By the end of March, the number of liberated displaced persons totaled 350,000; by April 7, it had reached 600,000; by April 16, it was 1,072,000, and by May 14 (a week after the end of the war), 2,002,000.[5]

The numbers of prisoners of war and DPs on the roads forced SHAEF to halt its advance through Germany and left the Allied military government struggling to cope. "The displaced persons situation in large cities such as Frankfurt and Heidelberg has been in a state of near-chaos for the past week," Marguerite Higgens wrote in the *New York Herald Tribune* on April 7. "Military government officials themselves admit that facilities for caring for the freed Russians, Polish, French and other slave laborers are so inadequate as to produce very grave and often tragic results." In Frankfurt, twenty-one military government officers tried to care for 40,000 DPs, without a single Russian or French liaison officer being present to help them. In Hanover, the DPs turned the vaults of the town hall into what a British officer called "a scene out of Hogarth or Hieronymus Bosch." "Hundreds of Russians had smashed vat after vat of wine and spirits so that the floor was six inches deep in mixed alcohol. Kneeling down to drink this powerful draft, the Russians soon began to collapse into it, and many drowned before the military police closed the entrance and evacuated those inside." Driving through the streets of Hanover, a military government officer dispersed crowds of drunken looters by firing his revolver in the air. "This is the sort of thing that goes on all day," he told a journalist. "Looting, fighting, rape, murder—what a town!" It took more than a week to restore order.[6]

Nor was the unrest confined to the towns. Bands of displaced persons roamed the countryside, helping themselves to food and clothing and terrorizing the locals. "The Germans were terrified of the Russians," Moorehead noted. "Again and again women ran out to us to cry: 'Can't you leave a guard with us? The Russians have taken everything. The next lot will smash up the place if they find nothing.'" There were reports of rape, murder, and looting.

Saul Padover, an American intelligence officer, felt that the DPs were unfairly stigmatized and military government officers were too quick to side with the Germans against the famished slaves. *Everyone* was looting Germany; indeed, Padover thought, the foreign workers' response was surprisingly mild considering all that they had endured. But the general view of the Allied military was that Russian and Polish DPs were responsible for most of the crime and should be sent home as quickly as possible.

DPs from Western nations presented a different problem. They were eager to return home and, once they had sobered up, began to engage in "self-repatriation," as the military called it—a few commandeered trains, but most simply marched along the roads, often in "a joyous atmosphere of holidaymaking." The planners at SHAEF had anticipated this human tide and—fearful that it would obstruct the battlefield, spread infection and disease into the Western countries, and exacerbate feeding problems in Holland, Belgium, and France—had drawn up a system for establishing barrier zones at water obstacles such as the Rhine and the Elbe, where the refugees would be held until the campaign was over.

The plan was that the DPs would be rounded up by the military and transported to assembly centers or camps, where they would be fed, fumigated, and kept in order by special UNRRA teams. In December 1944—after, it will be recalled, "vexatious delays" caused by the High Command's reluctance to work with the new international organization—SHAEF had asked UNRRA to provide 200 such teams and then, on February 1, 1945, had requested a further 250. This was almost certainly an impossible task. At all events, thanks to further delays caused by the German offensive in the Ardennes, UNRRA's recruiting problems, and difficulties with transport and supply, only fifteen "spearhead" UNRRA teams (consisting of seven people each instead of the intended thirteen) were in the field by the end of the war. Three months would pass before UNRRA became a significant player in the displaced persons game. The military would have to man the assembly centers itself, with some help from the voluntary agencies. And so 20,000 soldiers—the equivalent of an entire division—had to be withdrawn from combat units and assigned to this task.[7]

On March 15, 1945, Lieutenant Marcus J. Smith, a young U.S. Army doctor, learned that he was to be transferred to a small "DP combat team." The next day he was sent to a DP camp, where a makeshift classroom had been created. A colonel strode in, pointed to a map tacked to the blackboard, and announced, "This is Germany! In Germany there are ten million displaced persons—DPs. *You* will take care of them." A soldier in the audience whispered that that meant that each person in the room would have to look after half a million DPs.

Smith was given a crash course distilling the lessons of the army's experiences with displaced persons in Italy into simple principles and procedures. His first task, he learned, was crowd control. Displaced persons and refugees must not be allowed to block the highways and obstruct the progress of the Allied armies. The plan was for the DPs in a newly liberated area to be ordered to remain where they were, until military police routed them to collecting points and temporary camps and then to larger "assembly centers" where they would be housed until they were repatriated.[8]

Smith learned that assembly centers should be created in "clusters of buildings located at outskirts of cities or towns, close to highways, and must be large enough to accommodate at least 2000 men, women and children." Small rooms should not be overcrowded, to minimize the risk of epidemics; similarly, close attention must be paid to sanitation and water supply. Food was vital: every DP was to receive a minimum of 2,000 calories a day. To maintain the camps, the team would also need to requisition medications, clothes, bedding, dishes, and other items—all of which had to come from German sources only; the U.S. Army would not provide any supplies. If necessary, the team must improvise.

In addition, Smith was told, the team had to provide "community services"—"opportunities for counseling, education, recreation, and religious activities," all things which had been denied to the DPs by their former masters. Red Cross workers should be permitted to work with the DPs; they would be particularly welcome because of their lines of communication to most European countries, which would enable DPs to contact their families. They were to involve the DPs to a "maximal extent" in community activities. To raise their fallen spirits and keep them out of mischief, they must be kept busy. The ultimate goal of their efforts, they were told, was speedy repatriation.

His brief induction left the young doctor reeling. Why was the army only now turning its attention to civilian problems? What could a small unit of soldiers hope to achieve? His doubts grew when he joined DP Team 115, a unit of four officers and six enlisted men commanded by an infantry lieutenant of three years' service who had worked with juvenile delinquents before the war. No one, Smith reported, had "any special knowledge of or desire to work with refugees or displaced persons, no unusual insight into European traditions or history, and no experience in organizing or caring for large numbers of people; none of us has been in the executive or administrative section of the Army." What they did all have in common, however, was "the traditional antipathy of the infantryman, the foot soldier, to unnecessary discipline—'chicken shit'": the army was using DP teams as a dumping ground for discontented soldiers. Their equipment was a jeep, two sickly captured German trucks, a shovel, four lanterns, two stretchers, and office supplies including an ancient olive drab typewriter. Smith's only medical supplies were a personal bottle of aspirin and a tube of penicillin eye ointment. "With these," his diary noted, "we drive bravely eastward, [to] provide and sustain the health and happiness of our share of ten million displaced persons."

But when their first assignment came, Team 115 proved surprisingly effective. Schwabach, near Nuremberg, had three labor camps— 1,200 Russians in a run-down, flimsy barracks; 400 French DPs and a few Italians in a single-story, low-ceilinged wooden barracks heated by potbellied stoves; and an identical building containing a dozen Frenchwomen. The American team leader decided to keep these camps going but to clean them out. While Lieutenant Smith worked on getting the water supply restored, water for drinking, cooking, and washing—five gallons per person per day—was provided by U.S. Army trucks and new latrines were constructed using DDT in kerosene to keep them clean. When medical supplies were stolen, Smith and a colleague helped themselves to replacements from a U.S. Army depot nearby; a visiting army colonel provided the DDT that Smith had frantically been trying to get hold of. The young doctor was even able to renew his civilian skills by delivering a baby. He addressed his patients in GI patois: "Dub Jay, Buddy. Wo ist der schmerz? Sprechen tout de suite."

There were no problems getting supplies from the Germans. When the local burgomaster warned them that some items on their long list would be hard to get, he was firmly told by the twenty-one-year-old lieutenant that "American policy concerning displaced persons is simple: all materials and services for their care will be provided by the German people, who brought them here. Only after they had accepted responsibility could the rest of the world treat them with respect." "We do not foresee any major difficulties," Smith wrote. "We know that the Germans have read the new 'articles of government,' which start with the ancient words, 'We come as conquerors.'" Sure enough, the Germans produced everything within twenty-four hours.

The small American unit had quite quickly made a real difference to the DPs' lives. But Smith realized that the more intangible part of the work—"providing recreational facilities" for them—was more complex. He became aware of national rivalries and psychological disorders simmering among the camp inmates. Smith and his team did what they could. "We have not been in the business long enough to think about kindergartens, occupational therapy, and vocational training," he wrote.

The thousands of assembly centers hastily improvised by combat troops and then handed over to the military government (and in a few cases to UNRRA units) were mostly in old military barracks. Beds and a few bits of furniture were found, and the DPs divided the rooms into units with blankets hung from above. Kitchens run by the DPs provided basic meals, supplemented by army rations and Red Cross parcels.

The physical health of the displaced foreigners liberated in Germany and Austria in the early summer of 1945 was "exceptionally good," according to Malcolm Proudfoot. Less than 1 percent required medical care, and only a fraction of those needed hospitalization. By immediately dusting each DP with DDT powder, the danger of epidemic typhus was eliminated; other medical problems were avoided by proper sanitary measures. The doctors' main task turned out to be dealing with the effects of looted or bartered poisonous liquor, which was estimated to have killed two thousand people in the two months after the Germans' surrender.

Their mental health, however, was more problematic: Allied soldiers were surprised by the behavior of many DPs. It had been assumed that, after their years in Germany, the liberated slave laborers would be "tractable, grateful, and powerless." Instead, they often suffered from what became known as a "Liberation Complex":

> This involved revenge, hunger and exultation, which three qualities combined to make displaced persons, when newly liberated, a problem as to behavior and conduct, as well as for care, feeding, disinfection, registration and repatriation.[9]

One of the first people to try to understand the DPs' state of mind was Marta Korwin, a Polish social worker attached to a British military government team. When she entered Bocholt in early April 1945, the fields around were still covered with gliders used in the Allied crossing of the Rhine and the town itself was on fire. It was decided to turn the only unbombed building, a five-story block in the Siemens and Halske factory, into an assembly center for displaced persons. According to Korwin, it "represented a sad sight: all nationalities mixed up, dirt, confusion, looting on a universal scale, most people dead drunk, and food inadequate."[10]

Once food, water, and sanitation had been arranged, Korwin assessed the DPs. There were deportees from Western Europe, Poles of all ages deported after the Warsaw rising, young Russians brought to work in Germany, and Italian prisoners of war. Each group wanted to assert its national identity. "Everyone wanted to have national emblems on their chests and flags as big as possible everywhere." Finding a cache of Nazi swastikas in a cupboard, the relief workers cut them up to form Polish and Russian flags. Then they grouped the nationalities together and appointed leaders, "not an easy task because so few people were sober." It was decided that Italians, Poles, Russians, and all Easterners, namely those who were likely to stay the longest, should occupy the factory building. The French, Dutch, and Belgians cheerfully accepted straw on the factory floor.

Korwin felt that they all shared a certain state of mind. During their captivity in Germany they had been

> counterbalancing the reality that was always extremely hard, and often sordid and horrible, by calling up daydreams of their past life, until they were almost certain that, the moment they were liberated, they would find themselves in the same happy, beautiful world they knew before the war. All their past difficulties would be forgotten, freedom would take them back to a world where nothing had ever gone wrong . . . a paradise in which all people were good, all wives loving, all mothers-in-law charming, all husbands faithful and all homes beautiful. There was no unemployment, poverty and unhappiness.

But when liberation came, the DPs found themselves, "instead of at once returning to paradise, being herded into camps in which, in many cases . . . they found themselves in worse conditions than before their liberation." Confronted by postliberation reality and "the ruin which had overtaken the world during the war years, seeing their hopes for a better future destroyed, and with time to reflect on it," most of them escaped into drink or sex. "Can anyone be surprised at the license found in the camps?" Korwin asked. She concluded that

"Fear of the future and revenge unrealized were the underlying factors responsible for the unbalanced behaviour which we met with in contacts with the DPs."

For many of those people, destroying machinery was a way of expressing revenge. "Russians especially, took special pleasure in ruining things and breaking them. . . . On the first morning I went through part of the factory filled with most expensive machinery, and I was shocked when I saw a number of Russians smashing with meticulous precision one machine after another."

The DPs' fragile state of mind meant they had to be handled very carefully if their cooperation was required, for example, in keeping the center clean. "It took so much more time to convince people that things should be done in a particular way, but once it was done we were working with friendly and helpful human beings and not a flock of sheep."[11]

On April 7, the 4th Armored Division of the U.S. Third Army captured the small town of Ordruf, just west of Weimar. On a nearby hill, in a cluster of filthy sheds, American soldiers found piles of naked bodies neatly stacked "like cordwood." Outside were pyres of half-burned corpses. On April 12, Generals Dwight D. Eisenhower, Omar Bradley, and George Patton visited the scene. Patton was sick. Soon other names hit the headlines. At Nordhausen near Göttingen, the Americans found 3,000 rotting, unburied bodies and 2,000 slave laborers on the brink of death after working in an underground V-2 rocket factory. In a dark wood near Weimar where Goethe had once wandered, American tanks were greeted by the survivors of Buchenwald.

On April 12, British units racing across the North German Plain were greeted by two German colonels carrying a white flag, who offered a truce in the area around a nearby concentration camp where typhus had broken out; its name was Bergen-Belsen. Three days later, the British entered the place and found huts full of dead and dying prisoners and mounds of unburied corpses. "The things I saw completely defy description," a British officer wrote. "There are no words in the English language which can give a true impression of the ghastly horror of this camp." Nor did that conclude the litany of horrors. At the end of April, the Americans reached Dachau, near Munich, and found forty open freight cars stuffed with corpses; in early May, they reached Mauthausen, the notorious quarry camp near Vienna.

The uncovering of the German camps made an overwhelming impression on Allied public opinion. Although the Red Army had entered Auschwitz in January 1945, Moscow had given that event no publicity. Now the ghastly scenes at Dachau and Buchenwald revealed the worst.[12]

The military was taken completely by surprise. "In 1945, little was known in the Army about concentration camps or even about the Nazi policy of exterminating the Jews and some other ethnic groups," one of the first officers to enter Belsen later wrote. "We were thus totally unprepared for the horrors that we saw in Germany." Brian Urquhart had been aware of Nazi anti-Semitism and had befriended German Jewish refugees at Oxford, yet "the 'final solution,' the actual extermination of millions of people, was simply unimaginable" to him. This testimony will puzzle the modern reader. How could the Allied governments, which had roundly condemned the Germans' policies in December 1942, allow their armies to be unprepared for the concentration and death camps in 1945?[13]

What the Allied military knew can be gleaned from the Handbooks on Axis Concentration Camps which were produced by the Displaced Persons Branch of SHAEF. The first edition, distributed to field units in August 1944, was an ill-edited collage of information, offering a brief account of the development of German concentration camps, based entirely on the prewar model of the camp as a place to lock up political dissenters; much unimportant detail about the hierarchy and regalia of the SS; and some ill-informed recent intelligence—for example, the statement that Hitler had personally ordered that a brothel be provided in Dachau. Attached to this, however, was an appendix listing camps all over Europe, in which Auschwitz, Belzec, Chelmno, Majdanek, Sobibor, Theresienstadt, and Treblinka were each defined as an "extermination camp for Jews"— but no further comments were made and no overall narrative provided. This, to the modern reader, clearly refers to the "Final Solution," but it is highly unlikely that it would, on its own, have been read in that way by Allied officers in 1944.[14]

Later that year, after the liberation of the first German camps, SHAEF produced an updated edition of the handbook which was much better informed and omitted most of the trivia. Now SHAEF made two main points—that the Germans were evacuating their camps as the Allies advanced toward them; and that inmates were "being transferred from one camp to another according to their working capabilities and the needs of the various enterprises run by the [SS]," which were then listed in some detail (and accurately) in the appendices. Here, the partial recognition of the "Final Solution" contained in the previous handbook had now been replaced by a perception of concentration camp inmates as a labor reserve, which accurately reflected what was happening at that time. By early 1945, Auschwitz was being evacuated and the distinction between the program to exterminate Jews and the general process of exploiting non–Jewish camp and slave labor had largely broken down. It is therefore hardly surprising that when Allied intelligence was at last able to get more accurate reports, SHAEF did not understand or at any rate did not emphasize such differences. This helps to explain why field units did not draw much of a distinction between Jews and non-Jews, especially as the liberated camp population was not exclusively Jewish: at Belsen they made up about 55 percent of the surviving inmates; at Buchenwald, much less.[15]

When the British went into Bergen-Belsen, they were ill equipped to deal with the medical emergency that greeted them there. A response had to be improvised, with tragic consequences. Unaware of the effects of starvation on the human system, army officers rushed up water lorries and food canteens containing army rations. When this rich food was given to the survivors, about 2,000 of them perished as a result. It also proved difficult to establish a clear chain of command at Belsen, and many of the strategies the British tried did not work. But the arrival of an American typhus specialist who had worked with DDT in Naples helped to transform the situation. The epidemic of typhus was soon brought under control, and by the end of April, when most of the corpses had been buried, the death rate finally began to fall. Nonetheless, some 14,000 people died at Bergen-Belsen *after* the British got there.

The Americans were able to apply most of the lessons of Belsen when they liberated Dachau concentration camp later in the month: within a few weeks, infectious diseases had been brought under control there and the sick nursed back to health. Then, however, other complications emerged. The liberated prisoners were not grateful but apathetic or paranoid. Inmate physicians refused to work, former prisoners failed to carry out tasks assigned to them. American soldiers grew exasperated by the incessant barrage of complaints and demands, the frequent requests for special privileges, and the ethnic hostilities that emerged among the prisoners. Few Americans spoke German or Yiddish, and there were no Jewish liaison officers, while the American Jewish charities had not been allowed into Germany. Relations between the army and Jewish survivors soon became strained.[16]

All this time, the military's main priority was to get displaced persons home—starting with those from the countries of Western Europe. The mass repatriation of the French slave workers began in March—a lorryload of French prisoners was filmed leaving Belsen in late April playing "The Marseillaise" on a trumpet and accordion. SHAEF was initially adamant that no military aircraft would be available for the repatriation of civilians, but the immensity of the numbers quickly made it change its mind, particularly as military aircraft carrying supplies into Germany were empty when they returned. Subsequently, more than 161,000 French repatriates were flown into military air bases close to Paris. Henri Cartier-Bresson's film Le Retour catches this moment in images of hope and rebirth: Frenchmen, clad in a motley assortment of clothing and clutching every kind of suitcase but with happy, smiling faces; tearful reunions on railway platforms; and, in the film's climax, fleets of Dakota aircraft, crowding the screen like flurrying ravens, bring home France's sons and daughters. By the middle of September more than 1.5 million Frenchmen had been repatriated; at the height of the odyssey reception centers were handling 55,000 people a day. One at Mulhouse claimed to process each DP in two and half hours. The arrivals were "cheerfully welcomed"; divided into groups depending on which region of France they came from; fingerprinted, photographed, and registered; screened by the Sécurité Militaire; given a complete medical examination, including X-rays, urine analysis, and immunization, as well as a dental checkup; barbered, reclothed, and fed; informed about their families, friends, and homes; and given 1,000 francs. Their morale was lifted by "paintings of French home life" inside and beds of colorful flowers outside, and music was continually broadcast through a loudspeaker.

Yet behind the logistical triumph and Cartier-Bresson's uplifting images lay political complications. At least four different categories of Frenchmen and -women were being returned to their motherland:

prisoners of war, migrant workers who had gone to work in Germany voluntarily, young men conscripted to work under the STO scheme, and political deportees. Charles de Gaulle's provisional French government, keen to use repatriation to overturn France's national sense of shame and to bind the nation together again, spent a fifth of its annual budget on the reception of these returnees and tried to present the different groups among them as a homogeneous mass, all enveloped in the flag of the resistance. It proposed that Bastille Day 1945 be dedicated to the dead and the Resistance, celebrating "the equality of all prisoners, deportees, and resisters." Local authorities were urged to exalt "the sense of union that exists between those who fell in the fighting and those who came back."[17]

This unity, however, did not last long. Quarrels soon broke out among the different categories of deportees; a competition developed over both the benefits to which they were entitled and, more important, the honor in which they stood. Returning STO workers in Touraine were incensed to receive double rations for only six weeks, whereas POWs and political deportees received them for six months. In terms of honor, a clear hierarchy emerged, with those with resistance credentials insisting on their moral superiority to those who had worked in Germany. Prisoners of war, who had enjoyed cult status under the Vichy regime, were now forgotten.[18]

By contrast to the French, the Belgians quietly welcomed back their returning workers. The government did not plan very far ahead, improvised, and left the initiative to local and voluntary associations, particularly the Catholic charities. The prime motive of the politician in charge, former prime minister Paul van Zeeland, was to win capital and work his own way back to respectability. The whole process was quickly and successfully accomplished. The Dutch had started planning for this moment very early in 1943 and appointed a senior minister in the government in exile, G. F. Ferwerda, to run it. But their long-laid plans were stymied by the course that the war took in Holland. Whereas Belgium was liberated by September 1944, much of Holland was not reclaimed from the Germans until right at the end of the war and had to undergo starvation and continued occupation, while the government in exile remained stuck in London. The ministers in London had all the detailed information, but the military in Holland took decisions more or less on its own initiative. The result was chaos and endless recriminations. In addition, the domestic population, having seen 16,000 people die of starvation, was not in the mood to be very generous to the returnees.[19]

What happened to the DPs once they got home was not the concern of the Combined Displaced Persons Executive at SHAEF. Purely in terms of logistics, its achievement was extraordinary. "By the end of September," Proudfoot wrote with some pride, "298,132 Belgians had been repatriated . . . by the end of July, 305,000 Dutch nationals." However, there was something of a hiccup when there turned out to be 700,000 Italians in Germany and Austria, almost twice as many as SHAEF had foreseen and more than 10 percent of all DPs. It took until September 1945 to organize their return home.[20]

Although SHAEF itself ceased to exist on July 14, its combined displaced persons executive was allowed to continue because the DP issue had still not been resolved. However, UNRRA was also finally playing its intended role. By July, it had 2,656 people in 332 teams deployed throughout the western zones. The plan was that UNRRA would more than double its personnel, set up a headquarters in Germany, and then take over entirely the care and supervision of the DPs from the military authorities.[21]

The scale of the task facing the Allies in Germany had by now become clear. The country was in a far worse state than had been foreseen; in particular, its transport network, on which economic recovery depended, was in ruins. It took weeks to restore power and sanitation in the big cities, somewhat longer to reestablish law and order and find people without a Nazi past to fill the higher posts in local government. Then, gradually, the schools began to reopen.[22]

The physical shape of the occupation was finalized at the end of June 1945, when the Allied armies withdrew within the zonal boundaries agreed at Yalta. Germany's political future was addressed by the victorious Allies when their leaders met at Potsdam in August. The country would now be run by an Allied Control Council, made up of the military commanders of the four zones, who would together develop policy under the direction of their governments. That much was agreed. But beneath the surface there was tension between two contradictory aims. On the one hand, the conference accepted the principle that Germany should be administered as a single economic unit. The Americans, who during the war had toyed with breaking up or deindustrializing Germany, now wanted to keep the country together and get it running again. The problem was "how to render

Germany harmless as a potential aggressor, and at the same time enable her to play her part in the necessary rehabilitation of Europe," as U.S. Secretary of War Henry L. Stimson put it. On the other hand, the Soviets' main interest was in extracting reparations from Germany—not just from their own zone, which they were already busily stripping, but from the western zones as well.[23]

Whatever happened in Germany, it was vital to send all the DPs home. "Until the Displaced Persons are removed from Germany they endanger the country and eat its diminishing food supplies," a reporter noted. "But their removal will also add a factor of confusion and collapse—for Germany has depended for years upon these unwilling foreigners to keep its fields and factories going." And the Western DPs represented only 40 percent of the problem. There remained the other 60 percent from Eastern Europe: Russians, Poles, Balts, Czechs, Yugoslavs, Greeks, Hungarians, and Romanians.[24]

For months it had been clear that this might not be a straighfor-ward exercise. "The most surprising thing is how many people don't want to go home," a Quaker relief worker in Germany wrote on May 31, 1945. "Very few people I have met from Eastern Europe want to go and live under the Russians."[25]

FIVE

The Psychological Moment

REPATRIATING THE REFUGEES, 1945

Soon after the Allies landed in Normandy in June 1944, they began to capture Russians in German uniforms. On June 14, when more than 1,600 of them had been taken, a British intelligence officer interrogated a group of twenty. He found that they came from various backgrounds—they included a doctor, a shoemaker, a student, a clerk, a schoolboy, two mechanics, and six peasants—and from all over the Soviet Union—"a mixture of Ukrainians, Central Russians, White Russians, Siberians and Mongols." All had been badly mistreated by the Germans, undergoing months of starvation and beatings, and their decision to "support" the German war effort had been taken only to ensure their own survival: those who had refused the German "offer" to serve in the Wehrmacht had immediately been shot. At the same time, the prisoners did not expect the Kremlin to understand their dilemma and were clear-eyed about the fate awaiting them in the Soviet Union. Stalin himself had declared, "We have no prisoners, only traitors—the last bullet should always be for yourself."

These men were in no doubt as to what would happen should the Allies win the war—"they would be handed over to their government which would deal with them mercilessly." One soldier reminded the interrogator of the fate of the 32,000 Russian prisoners of war exchanged against Finns after the 1939 Finnish campaign: they were shot by a machine-gun company which in turn was liquidated by the NKVD, the Soviet secret police. What, then, would induce others of these troops to surrender to the Allies? One soldier replied:

You don't seem to realise the desperate position our men are in; we know that the road back to our own people is irretrievably lost;

we dislike and distrust the Germans. Give our men just a hope of existence and work in your colonies and they are yours.[1]

The German invasion of the Soviet Union in June 1941 had produced millions of prisoners of war. More than half of them were almost immediately starved to death, thanks to a combination of racial ideology, cruelty, negligence, and logistical incompetence. It was not a matter of simple genocide: the war in the East did not end as quickly as expected, Hitler himself prohibited the transportation of Soviet POWs to the Reich on racial grounds, and the numbers of prisoners taken turned out to be far greater than expected. At all events, by February 1942, of the 3.9 million originally captured, only 1.1 million Soviet POWs were still alive and of those, only 400,000 were able to work.[2]

The Germans' treatment of Soviet prisoners was a great crime—and a serious political mistake. The sight of columns of marching, starving Soviet prisoners being dragooned and the emaciated corpses which littered the roads did nothing to endear them to the native population in Ukraine and Belorussia. But it was the loss of millions of potential laborers that was the most counterproductive aspect of the whole business from the Germans' point of view. The Nazi leadership awoke too late to the prisoners' potential value to the German economy.

At the same time, however, the German army almost from the start made use of Russians as indigenous helpers, *Hilfswillige*—those willing to help—or "Hiwis." As with slave labor, there was a contradiction between German ideology and practical requirements, but with the need for military manpower increasingly prevailing over that of racial orthodoxy after the defeat at Stalingrad, in 1943 the Germans began putting Soviet prisoners of war into fighting units. They were initially deployed on the eastern front, but in October 1943, after growing numbers of these *Osttruppen* had defected to the partisans—and thus confirmed Hitler's view that they were militarily useless—they were transferred to the West, away from Soviet partisans and propaganda, and used to fight local resistance groups in France, the Netherlands, Italy, and the Balkans.[3]

By the summer of 1944, British officialdom had begun to worry about this issue. On July 17, 1944, the War Cabinet decided that Russian prisoners would have to be returned to the Soviet Union if this was what the Soviet government wanted. The decisive factor was the need to ensure Soviet cooperation in handing back British and American prisoners of war—at that stage, some 50,000 British and U.S. prisoners from camps liberated by the Red Army were believed to be in Russian hands. But, beyond that, the Foreign Office needed good relations with Moscow on a number of issues and could not afford to incur ill will on a matter where no British interests were at stake. "In due course, all those with whom the Soviet authorities desire to deal must be handed over to them, and we are not concerned with the fact that they may be shot or otherwise more harshly dealt with than they might be under English law," wrote the Foreign Office lawyer Patrick Dean. However, the man who would bear responsibility for returning the Russians, the secretary for war, Sir James Grigg, insisted on a Cabinet ruling. "If we hand the Russian prisoners back to their death it would be the military authorities which will do this on my instructions and I am entitled to have behind me on this very unpleasant business the considered view of the Government."[4]

Accordingly, on September 4, 1944, the War Cabinet finally agreed to accede to the Soviet request for the return of its citizens, and at the Moscow Foreign Secretaries Conference a month later Anthony Eden verbally agreed to the repatriation of Soviet citizens "whether they were willing to return or not." This understanding was formalized in 1945 at the Yalta Conference, where, after a very brief discussion of the issue between Stalin and Churchill, a hastily cobbled together accord on the exchange of prisoners was signed. The vaguely worded document left the details to commanders in the field and made no explicit mention of the use of force, though, in the context of previous conversations with the Russians, it was implied.[5]

Early returns of Soviet prisoners had already raised some concern: there were reports of prisoners being taken behind sheds in Odessa and shot. But the full extent of the dangers involved only became apparent after the end of the war, in Austria.

In the spring of 1945, the Austrian province of Carinthia was like a trawler's net in the last stages of being hauled in, as the catch collects in the final loop. As the war ended, the British and Soviet armies and the forces of the Yugoslav Communist leader Marshal Tito all converged on a small plain, trapping German regular troops, Yugoslav anti-Communist Croats and Slovenes, and an assortment of pro-German Russian Cossacks, White Russians, and Ukrainians, many with women and children. All of these groups wanted to surrender to the Western Allies, and British troops in the area were heavily stretched coping with this task.[6]

Then came two fresh developments. First it seemed likely that a further half-million German soldiers fleeing Yugoslavia would arrive in the already overcrowded region. Second, the governments in London and Washington became worried that Tito's victorious Yugoslavs, having driven the Germans out, would advance into Italy and annex the province of Venezia Giulia. To stop this threat, the Allied commander in the Mediterranean, Field Marshal Harold Alexander, was ordered to get ready to take military action against Tito.

His staff reacted immediately to this situation. On May 16, 1945, Alexander told London that, with a million prisoners of war already on his hands, he could only take on Tito if he could first "clear the decks." Some German prisoners were transferred to the Allied military authorities in Germany, and preparations were made to hand over most of the Yugoslavs and Russians to their Communist enemies. It was recognized that force or deception would have to be used.

In the case of the Yugoslavs, it was mainly deception. They were "given no warning of their fate," a British officer wrote at the time, and "allowed to believe that their destination was Italy until the very last moment of their hand over." In this way, some 27,000 men were handed over to the Yugoslav Communists.[7] The operation involved "a good number of white lies and an equal number of pangs of conscience," Colonel Robert Caradoc Rose-Price of the Welsh Guards admitted. "The platoon were only able to continue in this harrowing task by constantly reminding themselves that former events had clearly proved that, had the boot been on the other leg, the kicks would have been no less savage." Another officer who complained that "the whole business is most unsavoury, and British troops have the utmost distaste in carrying out the orders" was summoned to headquarters and admonished. The future foreign secretary Anthony Crosland later described the event as "the most nauseating and cold-blooded act of war I have ever taken part in."[8]

The real problem, however, was the 40,000 "Cossacks"—Russians who had collaborated with the Germans. On May 21, 1945, at a meeting at the headquarters of V Corps, the British commanders present took decisions about their fate on the basis of the crude political guidelines available to them. The Yalta Agreement stipulated that all Soviet citizens liberated by the Allies should be handed over to the Russians, but it did not define what a Soviet citizen was. Some further clarification had been issued in March 1945, laying down that a Soviet citizen was someone living within the boundaries of the Soviet Union "as constituted before the outbreak of the present war," that is to say, on September 1, 1939. Poles and nationals of the Baltic states were thus explicitly excluded.

On this basis, it was decided that the 1st Ukrainian Division, many of whose members came from areas of western Ukraine, which on September 1, 1939, had still been part of Poland, was not liable to be handed over. And a unit of some 4,000 White Russians who had been living in Yugoslavia since the Bolshevik Revolution was saved by Colonel Walton Ling, a prominent British Red Cross official who had served with White forces in the civil war and now put in a word for them. The remaining four units, including an entire corps of Cossacks, should, it was decided, be handed over to the Russians. These rulings were made in the broadest-brush manner; the idea of carrying out individual screenings never entered anyone's head and would have been dismissed as totally impractical if it had.

The British commanders recognized that they would probably have to use force to implement this act of repatriation and were careful to get authorization to use it. But to carry out the orders, they also had to override the objections of several officers. The general whose unit would be responsible for what was likely to be the trickiest part, the moving of the Cossacks and a group from the Caucasus, including thousands of women and children, had a number of "heated exchanges" with his superiors and was told that it was "a matter of higher policy."[9]

The Caucasians responded to a modest display of force: only a few blows to a ringleader's head with a pickax handle were required. But the Cossacks proved much tougher. When their officers guessed their fate or were told it, a number committed suicide and others begged to be shot. The Cossack men held an outdoor service to stiffen their resolve, and on June 1, 1945, there were terrible scenes as the British tried to extract them:

As soon as the platoon approached to commence loading people formed themselves into a solid mass, kneeling and crouching with their arms locked round each other's bodies. As individuals on the outskirts of the group were pulled away, the remainder compressed themselves into a still tighter body, and as panic gripped them started clambering over each other in frantic efforts to get away from the soldiers. The result was a pyramid of hysterical, screaming human beings, under which a number of people were trapped.[10]

At another camp passive resistance was encountered; again it was necessary to take forceful measures.

One Cossack was hit across the head with the butt of a rifle. It was not until a platoon had advanced with fixed bayonets and administered some further blows that any movement started. The movement was continued only by the further persuasion of the bayonets and the firing of automatic weapons into the gaps between the groups of Cossacks. One party attempted to escape across the railway line. A burst of automatic fire was aimed to deflect them; most of them turned back, but several turned towards the firer and two were killed.[11]

In all, about 70,000 people were forcibly returned to the Soviets and Yugoslavs before the forced repatriations from Austria were stopped.

By the middle of June 1945, the crisis with Tito had subsided and British commanders had received strong protests from representatives of the Red Cross about the fate of the Slovenes and the Cossack women and children. On June 13, General Richard McCreery, the Eighth Army commander, met a Red Cross official and "explained at length the military situation, which had necessitated the clearance of certain areas without delay." He then gave assurances that there would be no more forcible repatriation and "no repatriation at all without proper screening by qualified Military Government officers." A few months later a Foreign Office official acknowledged that the handing over of the Yugoslavs had been "a ghastly mistake . . . It was not until some time later that we learned that the unfortunate Croats and Slovenes who had been expelled from Carinthia had been extensively slaughtered by Tito's troops after crossing the Yugoslav border."[12]

When historians rediscovered these events in the 1970s, they focused on the most dramatic and distressing event: the repatriation of the Cossacks to Stalin and the Croats and Slovenes to Tito. But what mattered much more at the time was the mass repatriation of Soviet citizens—and in particular of Ukrainians—from Germany.[13]

There were good reasons for sending the Russians back as soon as possible. At that time there were some 6 million Russians outside their homeland, who posed a danger to public order in Germany and were expensive to feed, being entitled (under Yalta) to the same rations as Allied soldiers. And the sooner its own citizens were returned, the more likely was Moscow to return the 50,000 Allied prisoners of war the Soviets had liberated.

As soon as the Allied and Russian forces met, they began making arrangements for exchanging prisoners at the local level. More formal procedures were agreed in Leipzig on May 22, 1945, at which reception and delivery points for exchanges were settled on. Once the plan was signed, the Allies lost no time in getting rid of the Russians. Over the next five days more than 100,000 Soviet DPs and prisoners of war were transferred, and by July 1945, only forty-two days after the Leipzig meetings, 1.5 million Soviet nationals had been moved and the operation was nearly three-quarters done. But although the Soviet authorities had made detailed plans and had built an additional hundred camps along the Ukrainian and Belorussian fronts, each capable of housing 100,000 people, to act as assembly/reception centers, they could not cope with these numbers: on July 4, the transfers had to be stopped. Ten days later they resumed, and by the end of September they were completed—by which time 2,946,000 Soviet nationals had been repatriated from the Soviet area of Germany, Austria, and Poland; 2,034,000 from the SHAEF area of Germany, Austria, and Czechoslovakia; 111,000 from France; 93,000 from Norway; and a further 34,000 from other Western European countries, making a grand total of 5,218,000.[14]

Soviet DPs were usually taken first to filtration centers in eastern Germany and Poland for preliminary screening. The atmosphere there was hostile. "They received us like enemies. They said, why didn't you kill yourself and so on," one DP later recalled. Another remembered a week of NKVD questioning as his story was checked. A survivor of Buchenwald and Belsen was held while the authorities questioned twenty witnesses to find out if he had lied or worked for the Germans voluntarily. The Soviet attitude was determined largely by gender: women were by and large regarded as innocent victims, whereas men encountered real suspicion.[15]

Once the initial vetting was over, the Soviet DPs were sent home. Transport shortages meant that only the sick and very young went by train—often spending weeks in crowded boxcars or waiting on station platforms with only a little black bread to keep them going. On June 6, Stalin ordered that physically healthy repatriates should be made to walk. Many survivors died on the march, although some were able to hitchhike home.

When repatriates got back to the USSR, they were filtered again, at the local level. By and large, the women were allowed to go home—though they would face subtle discrimination for the rest of their lives. Returning men were at first remobilized into the Red Army but in August 1945 Stalin set out a new policy under which liberated prisoners of war and DPs who had not completed their full term of military service were conscripted into People's Commissariat of Defense battalions and put to work in the coal-mining, black ore, and timber-producing industries in Siberia. They had to stay there for some time. They were more fortunate, however, than those found to have served in the German army, who were sent to work in NKVD special battalions. By March 1, 1946, 4.2 million people had been repatriated, of whom 58 percent went back to their hometowns (which in the case of "punished peoples," such as the Volga Germans, were not where they had been before the war), 19 percent had to join the Red Army, 14.5 percent had to work in the People's Commissariat, and 2 percent were still in transit camps or on their way through the system. That left 6.5 percent who had been handed over to the NKVD.[16]

Former *Ostarbeiter* were never fully reintegrated into Soviet society. For decades, the authorities remained suspicious of those who had been in contact with the outside world. But beyond that, participation in the Great Patriotic War now became the country's defining experience—replacing the Bolshevik Revolution. It was a narrative from which the foreign workers would always be excluded.

Even as the Allies hustled the Russians onto the trains, a new political problem was emerging: many displaced persons from Eastern Europe did not want to go home. It was thought there might be as many as a quarter of a million of these people in the three western zones of Germany and Austria. Not only did they not claim Soviet citizenship, they feared the consequences of returning to their home areas, which were now occupied and claimed by the Soviet Union. There were Estonians, Latvians, and Lithuanians; Poles, Ukrainians, and Belorussians who had been Polish citizens but whose home areas (after the movement of the border to the west) were now in the Soviet Union; Ruthenians from the Soviet-annexed portion of eastern Czechoslovakia; and, in addition perhaps 35,000 Ukrainians, Kalmuks, and other Soviet nationals who did not wish to be repatriated for undetermined personal reasons.[17]

What was to be done with them? The military was now getting clearer guidance from its political masters, and one important point left vague at Yalta had been clarified: Allied commanders should quietly ignore the Soviet line that all people originating from areas within its new (1945) borders were Soviet citizens and thus subject to forcible transportation under the Yalta accords. Western governments refused forcibly to repatriate people who had not been Soviet citizens before the Second World War. Although this had been left unresolved at Leipzig, Allied commanders were now instructed to apply their interpretation, not that of the Russians. "For your own information and guidance (but *not* for communication to Russians)," British commanders were told in July 1945, "Latvians, Estonians, and Lithuanians and Poles whose homes are east of the 1939 demarcation of the Curzon Line will not be repatriated to the Soviet Union unless they affirmatively claim Soviet citizenship."[18]

But what about the Ukrainians? They seemed prepared to resist repatriation. Putting them on trains might involve Allied soldiers in a rerun of the hideous scenes in Austria. "They are extremely law-abiding, hard-working people but are violently opposed to returning to Russia—their general attitude is that most of them will commit suicide if forced to do so," the British general Sir Brian Horrocks wrote on August 30. Were they to be returned, he asked? Couldn't the Russians be induced to "leave in this country all who do not wish to return?" The response from above was clear and immediate. Horrocks was told that British policy was "very defined and unlikely to be changed": Russian subjects had to go back to Russia. Nothing could be done. Similarly, Americans were told that "Ukrainian nationality will not be recognized. Persons claiming it will be dealt with according to their status as Soviet citizens, citizens of other countries, or stateless persons."[19]

"We knew very little about the Ukrainians," Margaret McNeill, the Quaker relief worker in Germany, wrote. After visiting camps housing Ukrainian refugees, a colleague of hers commented, "The more I see of them, the more confused I get." He thought the people decent and hardworking but found their leaders very difficult men: "They're all violently nationalistic." The Ukrainians explained to the Quakers that they were a nationality without a state, but since few of them spoke good English, they found it difficult to explain their complex history. One Ukrainian refugee whom McNeill befriended "knew and pronounced excellently a prodigious number of English words, yet somehow after one of his long statements" she "had the utmost difficulty in making out what he really meant." But eventually she became familiar with the rudiments of the past which defined the identity of the Ukrainians in the camps. It came down to four elements: there were two Ukraines; Moscow was hated more than Berlin; their political tradition was nationalistic, conspiratorial, and antidemocratic; and they had been both victims and transgressors during the war.[20]

People claiming "Ukrainian" identity in Germany in 1945 fell into two very different categories. Those from eastern Ukraine, east of the Dnieper River, had been subjects of the Russian Empire and of its successor, the Soviet Union, for more than a century and a half, and had mostly practiced the Russian Orthodox religion. Their capital city, Kiev, was very much in the Russian orbit. Against that, people coming from western Ukraine had been Catholics and subjects of the Austro-Hungarian Empire and then (between 1919 and 1939) citizens of Poland. These divergent pasts had produced profound differences in outlook between the two groups, but a sense of common identity had nonetheless survived thanks to the success of intellectuals in creating a Ukrainian literature and history, the discrimination and sense of being second-class citizens which Ukrainians on both sides of the Dnieper shared, and the fact that the dream of reestablishing a Ukrainian state had briefly seemed about to come to pass. Between 1917 and 1920, in the chaotic conditions then prevailing in Eastern Europe, three different Ukrainian governments had come into existence; more recently and less happily, the two Ukraines had been reunited between 1939 and 1941, when the Soviet Union had occupied Polish Ukraine under the Molotov–Ribbentrop pact.

Their history had left Ukrainian nationalists with traditional friends and enemies. The Poles and Russians were their great adversaries, whereas the Germans had been their allies. Margaret McNeill noted that in the camps the Ukrainians did not "hurl themselves into a passionate fury at the mere mention of Germans, as the Poles did. They treated the subject of their years in Germany with a kind of contemptuous resignation. What produced an instant excitement was any mention of the USSR." The charge sheet against Moscow soon became familiar to McNeill—the conduct of the civil war; the collectivization of agriculture in Ukraine; the famines of 1922 and 1933; the purges of the late 1930s; and the activities of the NKVD in the early years of the war. By contrast, the fact that the Germans had starved millions of Ukrainians to death and made millions more labor in Germany was seldom mentioned.[21]

Few Western soldiers or aid workers had any conception of what had gone on in Ukraine during the war. Their simple dichotomy between good and evil, victims and transgressors, had no meaning there. Caught between Hitler and Stalin, the country had been split three ways: most of its young men were conscripted into the Red Army, others helped the Germans to round up and massacre the Jewish population, and a third, substantial group become nationalist guerrillas who fought against both the Russians and the Germans. Whatever small capacity for moderation and Western liberalism Ukraine had possessed before the war had perished in the firestorm that had killed one in six of its population.[22]

Allied statesmen in 1945 did not question Stalin's right to reabsorb Ukraine into his domains. It was difficult enough to keep him out of Poland. It was thought that the Ukrainian question had been resolved, insofar as most ethnolinguistic Ukrainian territory had been brought together as part of the Soviet Union; and the Western Allies were not (at this stage) interested in establishing a separate Ukrainian state. The Foreign Office accepted the Soviet view, which the British diplomat Thomas Brimelow expressed (in an ironic parody of Moscow's jargon) as "Publicly the troubles of the Ukrainians, now reunited at last in their own state, are at an end. Any manifestations of discontent will in future be the work not of Ukrainian patriots, but of fascist bands, black reactionaries and enemies of the people. Thanks to the brotherly protection of the Great Russian people, this centuries-old problem has now found a complete and just solution."

Most Ukrainians longed to return to their homeland. This was especially true of the laborers, "the naïve, poor, peasant East Ukrainians" who had been forcibly deported to Germany. After being liberated by American forces "I returned to my Homeland, without which life was unthinkable," wrote Mykolai Burlak, a twenty-year-old who had spent three years in a German labor camp. Another young woman returned to Ukraine because she "could not imagine life far way from my mother, my family and my village."[23]

In the Ukrainian railway junction town of Zhmerinka, two hundred miles east of Odessa, a trainload of returning Ukrainian girls caught the eye of Primo Levi, a Jewish survivor then halfway through his journey from Auschwitz back to his native Turin. "Under the weight of their shame, they were being repatriated, without joy and without hope," he wrote later.

> Victorious Russia had no forgiveness for them. They returned home in roofless cattle trucks, which were divided horizontally by boards so as to exploit the space better: sixty, eighty women to a truck. They had no luggage, only the worn-out discoloured clothes they were wearing. If their young bodies were still solid and healthy, their closed and bitter faces, their evasive eyes displayed a disturbing animal-like humiliation and resignation: not a voice emerged from those coils of limbs, which sluggishly untangled themselves when the train stopped at the station. No one was waiting for them, no one seemed aware of them. Their inertia, their fugitive shyness, their painful lack of [modesty], was that of humiliated and tame beasts. We alone watched their passage, with compassion and sadness, a new testimony to, and a new aspect of, the pestilence which had prostrated Europe.[24]

For those Ukrainians unwilling to return, however, the events in Austria in May 1945 had come as a terrible warning. The political refugees who had fled western Ukraine ahead of the Red Army were especially alarmed. Even before the end of hostilities in Europe, they had begun to organize themselves by forming self-help committees in the camps, which communicated with one another and put out tentative feelers to the outside world. In some cases in the American Zone they also managed to have all-Ukrainian camps established.

But it took vigilance to survive. On June 14, 1945, while working as a farm laborer, the Ukrainian refugee Olexa Woropay heard that in the nearby DP camp at Augsburg "they were hunting down our people and forcibly sending them to Soviet camps." The following day came news of a fight in the camp between eastern and western Ukrainians. "A group who did not want to go back defended themselves against the 'Ostarbeiter' [workers from eastern Ukraine] who were Soviet sympathizers. Knives were brandished and the dead and wounded lay on all sides." On June 25, Woropay and his wife moved to the Augsburg camp themselves, following a rumor that the next day American troops were coming in trucks to their area to take all Ukrainians and Russians to a Soviet camp. In Augsburg he found a number of western Ukrainians but was alarmed to see ten buses going by, "packed with our people, guarded by Russian soldiers." The next day a Russian officer visited the camp and said that all Soviet citizens should be concentrated in a Soviet camp, but Woropay also got hold of a copy of *Stars and Stripes* in which an American colonel was quoted as saying that while DPs who did not want to return were causing the U.S. Army a great deal of trouble, there had never been any American policy to force them to return. Then, on August 7, everyone in the camp was extremely disturbed by rumors that the Americans had consented to deliver all the Soviet citizens over to the Soviet Commission in Augsburg. "The camp is stricken with panic," Woropay wrote. "I hear the women are preparing to go and see Miss Carpenter of UNRRA to beg for her protection."[25]

Soon after that, the Ukrainians' fears were fully realized when American soldiers were sent to Kempten camp in southern Bavaria to collect a group of Ukrainians. They entered the church where the DPs had sought refuge and "began to drag the people out forcibly. They dragged the women by their hair and twisted the men's arms up their backs, beating them with the butts of their rifles. One soldier took the cross from the priest and hit him with the butt of his rifle. Pandemonium broke loose. The people in a panic threw themselves from the second floor, for the church was in the second storey of the building, and they fell to their death or were crippled for life. In the church there were also suicide attempts." Soon afterward, another group of Ukrainian DPs requested that they be granted an extension of two weeks, in order to enable them to receive the Holy Sacrament in preparation for mass suicide.[26]

Such disturbances by Ukrainians opened the eyes of American soldiers. Forced repatriation, they now realized, was a nasty and unpleasant business. Soon American commanders learned not to give the troops prior knowledge that they were to be used in this way and took elaborate precautions to prevent suicides. The Americans found it not only shocking but incomprehensible when Soviet refugees targeted for extradition bit each other's jugular veins rather than submit to repatriation.[27]

The Ukrainians used other tactics to resist. The more experienced kept away from the camps or roamed from camp to camp, drawing rations and picking up news without registering on official lists. For Soviet Ukrainians the most common defense against repatriation was to fabricate or falsify identity documents. "Overnight they became citizens of Poland, claiming pre-1939 residence in that country. These false papers were produced on a massive scale by Catholic priests, political groups and enterprising individuals who most often used cut potatoes or war eggs for affixing authorization stamps." The Ukrainians also sent plaintive appeals to the press and to Allied political leaders. "Your Excellency Mr Eisenhower, Army General," one such document begged, "hand out to the military authorities in Germany an order, to make a stop with the brutality of the carried out return by force and give to each of the Ukrainians the possibility to speak for himself whether he will return to his home or not."[28]

Although the Ukrainians seemed powerless, they had weapons of their own, most notably support from the diaspora abroad. By July 1945, Ukrainian relief committees had been organized in Canada, the United States, and France and were monitoring events. On the ground, sympathetic Ukrainian-born officers serving in the Allied forces did what they could to help, the most important of them being Lieutenant Bohdan Panchuk of the Canadian air force. Raised in a remote rural enclave in the Canadian West, steeped in an idealized version of Ukrainian history, Panchuk was a tireless and selfless organizer, who had been active in Ukrainian-Canadian cultural activities before the war and created a welfare organization for Ukrainians in London. Now based in Hamburg, he was able to intervene on the Ukrainians' behalf. On one occasion, a Canadian military government official alerted him to the fact that 365 Ukrainians were about to be shipped off to the Soviet Union. "What could I do except send a telegram to Winnipeg and the same to Philadelphia?" Panchuk later wrote. "And they, in turn, sent telegrams of protest to Ottawa and Washington. Sometimes these helped to block such shipments, sometimes not. We did what we could. Still hundreds and thousands were sent back against their will."[29]

In fact, Panchuk and his London-based Central Ukrainian Relief Bureau proved to be effective lobbyists, constantly bombarding carefully chosen politicians in London, Ottawa, and Washington with detailed descriptions of the "shanghaing" of Ukrainians from Germany. At the same time, the Vatican and Catholic right-wing anti-Communist opinion in the United States was being mobilized. By September 1945, Ukrainian relief committees in Western Europe and the United States were actively pressuring their governments to resettle the refugees while religious leaders helped to convince the Vatican to intervene on the Ukrainians' behalf.[30]

This pressure had some effect. On September 4, General Eisenhower ordered a ban on the use of force, at least until Washington had time to reconsider its position. Another attempt to move 600 Ukrainians from Mannheim to Stuttgart on September 6 produced a riot which led to protests in the United States and questions by Congresswoman Clare Boothe Luce, the wife of the proprietor of *Time* magazine.[31]

But the situation in Europe remained confused. Both UNRRA and the military clamped down on Ukrainian organizations opposed to repatriation and tried to deny rations to Ukrainians unwilling to go home. By the end of the year, with all Western prisoners of war now returned from the Soviet Union, relations with Moscow beginning to sour, and Western public opinion more effectively mobilized, the Western Allies became increasingly reluctant to use force to repatriate Soviet nationals. In December 1945, repatriation became a purely voluntary affair in the American Zone—followed, by the summer of 1946, in the French and British areas of Germany. Consequently, the number of people returning to the Soviet Union fell dramatically.[32]

All that time, the Polish DPs had been waiting their turn for transport to go home. The departure of most of the Russians left the Poles as the largest surviving DP group—there were said to be a million of them, though that figure probably included many who would have described themselves as Ukrainians. The British were particularly determined to get rid of the Poles, whom they had come to see as troublesome nuisances. In August 1945, the British military government warned that a growing problem of law and order among Polish DPs was bringing British rule into disrepute. The British were divided about how best to respond to this. In Germany, Field Marshal Bernard Law Montgomery proposed shooting on sight to stop "looting, rape and murder by DPs" and warned that the German police might be rearmed; in London, the politicians urged greater caution. When forty-eight Poles were put on trial for acts of violence against Germans and four were sentenced to death in August 1945, there was an outcry in Warsaw that the British were "soft on the Germans and hard on the Polish DPs"; eventually, under pressure from London, the sentences were commuted. "The sooner we get back Polish displaced persons from the British Zone, the better for the Control Commission and for me," the British ambassador to Warsaw wailed.[33]

For that to happen, however, formidable logistical and political obstacles had to be overcome. During the summer, the Soviets insisted that all the railway rolling stock should be devoted to their citizens, and in September and October, when most of the 2 million Russians in Western Europe had been repatriated, they still refused to consider shipping Poles while a few of their own citizens remained in the West. For a while the Allies were able to send Poles back through Austria and Czechoslovakia, until that route, too, was stopped by the Red Army. In September, with the winter looming, it emerged that the Russians had never had any objection to Poles being returned in *Allied* transport. This news sent Major General Gerald Templer, the director of military government in the British Zone, into a fury of activity, drawing up detailed plans to use railways, roads, and the Baltic Sea route and getting the Polish authorities to establish reception centers.

Further frustrations followed. Seven successive plans foundered because of the inability of the Poles to accept more than 3,000 to 4,000 people a day and then only for the present at Szczecin; the unwillingness of the Soviet authorities to grant autobahn facilities or to cooperate over rolling stock; and the inability of the Polish government to accept DPs at Baltic ports. But the British persisted and got agreement for a circuitous route from Hamburg to Szczecin through a transit camp at Dessau. The evacuation of 3,000 a day was anticipated, alongside a sea evacuation to Gdynia. Nevertheless, of the 495,000 Poles remaining in the British Zone, it was estimated that 300,000 would still be there at the end of the year.[34]

On October 13, when news finally came through that the first British convoy of lorries carrying 1,000 Poles had crossed the Russian frontier toward Szczecin, General Templer announced his intention of getting drunk in celebration. But a British officer wondered how long this movement, which was supposed to grow in intensity in the next month, would continue and whether British personnel could keep order. They had been instructed not to interfere in any way if the returning Polish émigrées were raped by Russian soldiers—"they make a habit of this, stopping convoys and extracting the women that take their fancy for immediate treatment on the roadside"—but to defend their lorries, their supplies, and their petrol by force of arms, if necessary, the Russians being in the habit of trying to steal everything that came within their reach.[35]

These suspicions were justified. Two weeks later a train of repatriates arriving in the Polish town of Dziedzice was looted by Russian soldiers and the DPs beaten up and robbed. A Polish railwayman who tried to intervene was hit on the head, and when his colleagues made to help him the Russians opened fire with automatic weapons. "The Soviet soldiers occupied the whole railway station and then began to march around in the streets of Dziedzice, shooting wildly around them and beating up anyone they met. They screamed at us, 'We will murder all you fucking Poles!' "[36]

The behavior of these Russian troops was symptomatic of a wider problem. For with the Poles as with the Ukrainians, logistics alone were not enough. There also had to be a will to return home.

For many well-informed, educated Poles, that will had been sapped by distrust of the Soviet Union. They knew that Moscow had divided their country with Berlin under the Molotov–Ribbentrop pact of 1939; killed 10,000 Polish officers in the Katyn Forest (and then indignantly denied it); stood by as the 1944 Warsaw uprising was suppressed by the Germans; and installed a puppet regime, generally known as the Lublin government, in Poland. In addition, the Russians had appropriated a considerable area of Poland as it had existed in 1939. Some of the "political" Polish DPs would also have known that early in March 1945 the NKVD had invited sixteen leading figures in the Polish underground to a meeting, after giving assurances of their personal safety, and then had them arrested, flown to Moscow, and interrogated in the Lubyanka. After a three-day show trial in June 1945 the men were found guilty of anti-Soviet activity. Stalin's intention to crush all opposition in Poland was clear.[37]

Most of the Polish displaced persons, however, were not intellectuals or educated professionals but slave laborers. Their state of mind was more complicated. When a British relief worker began helping Polish DPs at Wolterdingen, near Hamburg, in the spring of 1945, she was amazed by how quickly they returned physically to an appearance of normal health and hugely impressed by the general enthusiasm.

> There were still hopes of a happy settlement to the problem of forming a government in Poland, which might be followed by the speedy repatriation of the people, and their pride and joy in their country, now at last permitted full vent, was genuine. . . . The good weather, the hope of news of the return home and of relatives from whom they were separated, helped to build up the hopes of the people.

Led by a priest newly released from Dachau, these Poles enthusiastically converted wooden garage sheds into a church, began to learn a trade, and enrolled in classes to make up for lost time. Relief worker Audrey Duchesne-Cripps noticed that the former concentration camp inmates who usually provided the leadership "tended to look down on the forced labourers who were more concerned to marry their girls and get on with everyday life in the camp. The slaves didn't intend to stay in Germany for ever, but they wanted a rest and perhaps a chance to exact revenge on the Germans before returning to face life back home."

But the long delay had a disastrous effect on the Poles' morale. "While other nationals were starting their lives anew in their own countries, five months of uncertainty and losing of hope must elapse before repatriation opened in Wolterdingen in October 1945," reported Duchesne-Cripps. During that period there was a marked decline in relations between the Poles and the British—the DPs acquired a reputation for lawlessness, while the British soon became pretty rough in their treatment of the Poles. To be slighted by their allies was "perhaps the bitterest blow of all," Duchesne-Cripps believed.[38]

Attitudes also began to change when news from home arrived. The setting up of the Polish Provisional Government of National Unity by the Soviets in late June 1945 and its immediate recognition by Britain and the United States was "a great blow," Duchesne-Cripps found, but "hope continued in our people's minds" until July 5, when the broadcasts of the Polish government in London came to an end. The announcement of Poland's new "western territories"—in land taken from Germany—created no enthusiasm, whereas the loss of the city of Lvov to the Soviet Union was keenly felt.

Then there was the question of Polish liaison officers. Until the end of June 1945, while Britain and the United States still recognized the Polish government in exile in London, 150 of its repatriation officers operated in the Polish DP camps in Germany. Once the new Provisional Government of National Unity in Warsaw had been recognized, however, it, too, sent a repatriation mission to Germany. With some naiveté, the DP staff at SHAEF allowed the London-appointed officers to remain "to assist with the welfare programme for Poles in the assembly centres." As Malcolm Proudfoot later admitted, this step "served, in part at least, to defeat the plan to repatriate the Poles." "The London Poles continued to counsel their countrymen against returning to Communist-dominated Poland."[39]

Despite all these factors, the occupying forces succeeded in repatriating 268,267 Poles before the arrival of winter made it difficult to continue. But at least twice that number remained. The delay had proved very costly. Had it been possible to return the Poles in the summer of 1945, they would nearly all have gone home. Now, living in relative comfort in camps in Germany, they might see things differently.

"If you ask me, we've missed the psychological moment as far as the Poles are concerned," one of the Quakers working at Braunschweig declared. "People who suffered during the war years as they suffered should all have been sent back in a triumphant body, prisoners of war and DPs all together and welcomed in Poland with bands playing and flags flying. If they'd done that I don't believe a single Pole would have stayed away."[40]

SIX

The Surviving Remnant

JEWISH DPs, 1945

On the morning of April 27, 1945, a flight of Thunderbolt fighters of the U.S. Air Force was patrolling the skies over southern Germany. Spotting two trains at a station near the small village of Schwabhausen, the pilots swooped to attack them.

One train was carrying soldiers and ammunition and armed with antiaircraft guns; the other contained a thousand sick prisoners from Kaufering labor camp, crowded into boxcars, on their way to Dachau, as part of a plan to keep them away from the advancing U.S. Army. Allied control of the skies had made movement difficult and the train had traveled only some twelve kilometers since setting out the previous morning.

When the American planes attacked, the SS guards fled. As bombs began to fall, the prisoners, too, escaped from the train and sought shelter in nearby woods. Eventually, when the planes had flown off, the guards attempted to round up the captives and got most of the sick back onto the train, which then continued on its way. But about 200 Jews remained in the forest. All night long they walked to and fro among the trees, arguing and discussing the situation they found themselves in. On the one hand, they had finally rid themselves of their "inseparable companions" for many years, the SS. At the same time, however, the U.S. Army had not yet arrived and no one knew when it might come. There were different opinions about what to do; some argued that they should be presenting themselves to the nearest German authority. A lawyer, Dr. Samuel Gringauz, was concerned that "in the last five, awful years we were legal, under the aegis of the law. Now, however, a number of days before the end, of all times, we've become illegal."

The next morning it was finally decided to send a delegation to the nearby German village to seek help for the wounded. It was to be led by Dr. Zalman Grinberg. Like many of his fellow passengers on the train, he was a Jew from Kovno in Lithuania.[1]

In spending half the night arguing over what to do and attaching great importance to their legal situation, this group was acting true to national stereotype. Lithuanian Jews, "Litvaks," had a reputation for seriousness, intellectual rigor, and rationality—by contrast with "Galitzianers," the Jews of neighboring Poland, Belorussia, Ukraine, and Galicia, who were seen as emotional, irrational, and uneducated. The Litvaks' approach to Judaism was marked by highly intellectual study of the Talmud, and the great center of Jewish learning, the former capital of the Lithuanian Commonwealth, Vilna (modern-day Vilnius), was known as the "Jerusalem of the North" thanks to its countless yeshivas and Great Synagogue. But when Vilna had passed to Poland in the post-1919 division of Eastern Europe, much of the vitality of Jewish life had migrated to the small garrison town of Kovno (modern-day Kaunas), which became the capital of the newly independent state of Lithuania. On the eve of the war there were approximately 35,000 Jews in Kovno, about 40 percent of the city's population.[2]

The Jews of Lithuania remained quite unassimilated when compared to those in Germany or even Poland; most saw themselves as Jewish, rather than as Lithuanian. In the 1930s, Kovno's small Jewish community supported three Yiddish daily newspapers and numerous other periodicals; both a Yiddish and a Hebrew theater; Jewish sports and youth clubs, banks and professional organizations. A Polish visitor was surprised to see the Jews of Kovno living their lives entirely within their own culture and language. "Walking the . . . streets," he later wrote, "you had the impression that it was a completely Jewish city. Perhaps it really was—in every respect—the most Jewish city in the world."[3] Relations between Jews and Lithuanians had traditionally been quite good. In the nineteenth century, both peoples had shared a sense of being oppressed by their Russian rulers, and it seemed in the early years of Lithuanian independence as though the country would serve as a model of toleration for other Eastern European countries. But after 1926, Lithuania, like most countries in Eastern Europe, swung to the right and became more nationalistic while the rising

Lithuanian middle class saw the Jews as competitors. The resulting "quietly" anti-Semitic policies caused many Jews to immigrate to South Africa, to South America, and above all to Palestine. Among those who stayed in Lithuania, there was strong support for the Zionist movement.[4]

Lithuania's brief period of independence came to an end in the summer of 1940, when the Soviet Union took over the Baltic states. In general the Jewish population accepted a Soviet Lithuania as the lesser of two evils and so became identified with the Bolsheviks in the eyes of many Lithuanians. The resulting anti-Semitism exploded violently when the Germans attacked the Soviet Union in June 1941: in the vacuum left by the sudden departure of the Russians, Lithuanian Nazi sympathizers initiated pogroms and beat Jews to death in public. The Germans, on arriving in Kovno, created a ghetto in the suburb of Vilijampole in which all the city's Jews were confined.

The Germans sealed off the Kovno ghetto and took a series of "actions" to reduce its population further. In early October 1941, they liquidated an area known as the "small ghetto," in the process locking the staff and patients into the hospital for contagious diseases and setting the building on fire. Three weeks later, they made the entire surviving Jewish population assemble in the main square and, in a rough and ready selection, winnowed out about a third of them, mainly children and the elderly, who were marched away to the Ninth Fort, a grim tsarist citadel on the outskirts of Kovno, made to undress and lie in ditches, and then shot at close range. This left some 18,000 surviving Jews.

There then followed what turned out to be a period of comparative stability. For almost two years, until the end of 1943, things were relatively quiet, with starvation and cold the main enemies. The Jewish council in the ghetto, led by a distinguished physician, Dr. Elkhanan Elkes, had from the beginning realized that the residents' only hope of survival lay in making themselves indispensable to the Germans and doing everything they could to provide them with a labor force for their war effort, even sometimes anticipating the occupiers' needs. This policy worked—it allowed some Jews to survive the war—but was not universally popular because it rested on an inequality of suffering—with some Jews in effect conscripted to carry out backbreaking work for the Germans and unable to supplement their diet by trading food, while others, well connected and middle class, were able to escape the worst of the work and engage in food trading.[5]

Dr. Grinberg owed his own survival to a mixture of good fortune and vigilance. He was fortunate to be among the small minority of professional people (including eleven doctors) to whom the Jewish council gave exemption certificates but unlucky in that his first child arrived on July 20, 1941, ten days after the ghetto was created. The boy was saved from death only by being farmed out to a Lithuanian wet nurse. When conditions in the ghetto stabilized somewhat, however, Jewish women began to reclaim their children from Gentiles, and Dr. Grinberg's distraught wife begged him to retrieve her son, too. With some difficulty this was achieved, and for a year or so the family lived together in cramped intimacy in a small wooden house. When the situation in the ghetto worsened again, they had to take the difficult decision to return the boy, now almost two years old, to his Lithuanian nurse. He was smuggled out in a wardrobe.[6]

In July 1944, as the Russian army neared Kovno, the Germans razed the ghetto and transferred the remaining 6,000-odd Jews to Germany. This time the sexes were separated. Dr. Grinberg's wife wept and reproached him for not taking her advice and committing suicide rather than be evacuated to this new camp. He begged her to wait and hope. The women were sent to Stutthoff concentration camp, the men to Kaufering. There they were put to work constructing an underground concrete bunker intended to house a Messerschmitt aircraft factory. The conditions were so poor that, in protest, Dr. Elkes refused to take nourishment for a week; in October 1944, he died. But some of the Kovno group were able to find managerial roles, and Dr. Grinberg eventually became an assistant to the camp physician. Paradoxically, an outbreak of typhus saved some of the inmates, by causing the Germans to put Grinberg in charge of quarantining the camp and giving the prisoners themselves a monthlong respite from the murderous work while being fed. Most of the physical labor was done by Hungarian Jews, who had not learned the skills of survival in the ghetto and died quickly.[7]

During the winter of 1944–1945 Dr. Grinberg was approached by a Jewish writer from Kovno, Michael Burstein. With the end of the war approaching, Burstein believed it was time to prepare for the moment of liberation by introducing in the camp "a kind of underground association whose function it will be to establish the nuclei for the rebuilding of European Jewry after its moral, cultural and national decimation." Burstein wanted him to make sure that "the handful of teachers, writers and academicians remaining alive in the camp get lighter work, as well as additional soup, to the extent that is possible." Grinberg later recalled how Burstein in his lectures

> spoke of the good tidings and encouragement, which fell on his audience like a life-giving dew. Like the primitive Christians in their catacombs, the inmates heard the sounds of the prophecy of salvation, which sounded so remote and mythical to them. . . . The lectures were now being conducted each day in each and every hut and the numbers of lecturers kept growing. . . . The People of the Book remained faithful to their spiritual heritage.

In fact, Burstein himself did not survive, but his influence did.[8]

The ghetto experience and the period of preparation for liberation enabled the group of Lithuanian Jews to seize their opportunity when their train was shot up near Schwabhausen. Drawing on his professional authority, Dr. Grinberg used the imminent arrival of the U.S. Army to extract some cooperation from the German population nearby. Then, learning from a sympathetic German doctor of a nearby military hospital in the Benedictine monastery of St. Ottilien, he telephoned the Germans, claiming to be the representative of the International Red Cross and demanding that they send ambulances to pick up the Jews wounded in the attack on the train. To his astonishment, his request was eventually carried out. Grinberg then installed himself at St. Ottilien and was making bold plans to transform the monastery into a Jewish hospital, when the Germans began to resist. Fortunately, American troops arrived just as the German head doctor was about to produce his pistol, whereupon he "gave [Grinberg] a military salute and said, subserviently, 'Doctor, sir, I am at your command.'" It was a precious moment for the doctor from Kovno. With the cooperation of an American captain, Grinberg was placed in charge of a special hospital for Jewish survivors.

A month later, on May 27, 1945, Grinberg organized a concert at St. Ottilien to mark the anniversary of the liberation. Survivors from all over Bavaria were present; the orchestra from the Kovno ghetto traveled over from Bad Tölz to play Mahler and Mendelssohn. In his speech, Dr. Grinberg recalled his own odyssey from Kovno to Dachau and the extraordinary events of the last month. "We have met here today to celebrate our liberation," he told the audience, "but it is a day of mourning as well. We are free, but we do not understand our freedom, probably because we are still in the shadow of the dead." This was followed by prayers, four minutes of silence, and then a concert. The program ended with the singing of the Zionist anthem "Hatikvah," the Song of Hope.

No political decisions were taken that day. But the gathering helped to produce a sense of shared identity among the survivors and of the need to take control of their future. Four days later, Dr. Grinberg wrote on the survivors' behalf to the World Jewish Congress expressing their "painful sense of abandonment."

> Four weeks have now passed since our liberation and no representative of the Jewish world . . . has come, in the wake of the greatest tragedy of all time, to be with us and to lighten our burden. We have been forced to take care of ourselves with our own meager resources.
>
> This is a grave disappointment to us. We are presently preoccupied with two important questions. We all want to know who among our kin died and survived. So we turn to you to obtain lists of Jewish survivors in Russia and in the occupied zones of Germany. We want to know over whom we must say *Kaddish*. The second question is what will become of us? Where will we be taken? Where will our miserable lives lead us?[9]

When the war in Europe ended, about 200,000 Jews emerged alive from the Nazi concentration camps, the remnant of possibly up to 500,000 Jews who were still alive in the camps toward the end of 1944. Between 50,000 and 75,000 survivors were on the territory of the future western occupation zones. Within a week, more than 20,000 of them had died. Many of the remainder were described as "physical and mental wrecks."[10]

In the following weeks, many of the Jews who were in better physical shape had gone back to Eastern Europe in search of their families: of the 200,000 survivors, well over 70,000 are thought to have returned more or less immediately to Hungary and Romania; tens of thousands of others returned to Czechoslovakia and Western

Europe or went back to their former homes in Poland and the Baltic states to look for relatives. A further 10,000 Jews were sent to Sweden for medical treatment. On June 20, 1945, it was estimated that only some 19,000 to 29,000 Jewish displaced persons remained in the American Zone of Germany and fewer than 10,000 in the British.[11]

It is difficult today to see these Jewish survivors as their rescuers saw them in 1945. Francesca Wilson, the experienced British aid worker and activist, at first found it impossible to look at camp inmates without revulsion. Despite having seen many victims of famine, she had never before seen victims of cruelty.

> They were wearing the convicts' striped blue and white pyjamas, and had the shaven heads and the number tattooed on the left arm which were the marks of Auschwitz. Some were walking skeletons, most had hollow cheeks, and large, black, expressionless eyes, which stared and stared and saw nothing. They had the furtive look and gestures of hunted animals.

Many of the liberators initially recoiled from the "smell of the monkey house" and the "strange simian throng" that greeted them in the camps. Arriving at Belsen for the first time, a Jewish rabbi turned with relief from the half-naked "animals" to "two young girls from good families in Prague" who were "still normal and human." Some Allied soldiers went further and regarded the survivors not as victims but as alien, even criminal, people. "I have never seen so many criminal-looking faces bundled together as I did at Belsen," a British officer wrote. General George S. Patton made no secret of his loathing of the Jews, most of whom came from Eastern Europe; they were, he wrote in his diary, "lower than animals." Patton did not think that their present way of life had any connection with what had happened to them in the camps but was, rather, the result of their being an inferior race.[12]

In those circumstances, it was hardly surprising that Allied soldiers often showed little awareness of what survivors had been through or of their resulting state of mind. An American working for UNRRA could not understand why a group of Jews from Belsen protested against having their clothing taken away from them or refused to have a steam bath. He was equally mystified by their "fanatical attachment to relatives and friends" and their reluctance to give information, especially their names. Francesca Wilson thought that what these "neurotic and unhappy" people needed was "a good motherly Jewish woman who could speak Yiddish, feel the call of the race when she saw the martyred remnants of her people, know how to appeal to them and cajole them into living again."[13]

In one sense, when Dr. Grinberg spoke of abandonment, he was correct: the main Jewish charities were nowhere to be seen. The U.S. Army's opposition to having "sectarian" organizations involved in relief, and its particular dislike of Jewish ones, meant that it was not until August 1945 that the well-funded and long-established American Jewish Joint Distribution Committee (usually known as "the Joint"), was allowed to function in the camps. Moreover, as Joint officials privately admitted, its own "failure to recruit and have available sufficient personnel for work in Germany" caused further delays.[14]

Furthermore, given that the military's main preoccupation in mid-1945 was with repatriation—getting displaced persons back to their home countries—its tactic with the small number of Jews remaining was to divide them by nationality, with, for example, no distinction being made between German Jews and ordinary Germans. At the same time they did allow some big Jewish camps to be created—at Belsen and at Feldafing on the Starnberger See near Munich, in a complex which had once been a holiday camp for the Hitler Youth.

In fact, this "abandonment" would be short-lived. Help was about to arrive for the Jewish displaced persons, and from many quarters.

Abraham Klausner came to the Dachau displaced persons camp in the third week of May 1945. A young Reform rabbi serving with the U.S. Army, he was given no particular assignment. Watching the doctors and nurses, he kept thinking, "What can I do?" Eventually, he forced himself to go and talk to survivors. They started asking him about relatives in the United States. One man asked Klausner if he knew his brother, a rabbi in the U.S. Army, and, recognizing something familiar in the man's voice, he replied, "Yes, I do." Later he was able to bring the inmate and his rabbi brother together. This first encounter with survivors seems to have given Klausner "the feeling that even though I had no resources, there was something I could do" and a growing sense of confidence and energy in doing it.[15]

Klausner quickly grasped that "the immediate need of the liberated was to regain their identity." They wanted more than anything to rediscover their own names, regain contact with their relatives, find out who had survived, and become once again part of a social fabric. Yet not only had the army failed to understand this human need, it did its best to thwart it because only military personnel could send letters. There was no mail service for the survivors.

After only a few days at Dachau, Klausner's unit was ordered out of the camp, to go off for a period of rest and recreation. The rabbi left with his unit but lingered as the trucks were unloaded at the rest center, and "when the sixth truck came past me, for reasons I can't explain, I just jumped onto the tail end of the truck, got myself in, and went back to Dachau." His decision to go AWOL, Klausner told an interviewer forty years later, was "part of the mystery of life."

> I felt that's where I belonged. I had started to do some work there, beginning to identify the people, making lists of those who had survived. I also began to hear of other people being located in different areas of Germany. I just felt it was going to be my work to find and identify them and make their identity known to the world.

It proved surprisingly easy, in the chaotic conditions then prevailing, for Klausner to operate independently. From time to time the military authorities caught up with him, and he was repeatedly admonished by superior officers and chaplains. But he was not arrested or court-martialed and, with the help of sympathetic officers, managed to move around Bavaria pursuing his own agenda. By June 1945, he had produced his first list of survivors' names, which he persuaded a German printer to print by providing him with tins of coffee and tea and some paper obtained through the military.[16]

Rabbi Klausner's tours of the camps soon brought him into contact with Dr. Grinberg and his associates from Kovno, who were trying to establish an organization among the survivors. He was able to get them petrol, supplies, and office space in the Deutsches Museum in Munich. "Zionists are organizing in every camp and a central secretariat for all the camps is now being set up in Munich," a Zionist from Lithuania wrote to the Zionist Executive in Jerusalem on June 9, 1945.

By then other allies were also arriving. Since late May, men from the Jewish Brigade serving with the British army in Italy had been traveling through Germany and Austria, ostensibly looking for relatives but in fact making contact with survivors on behalf of the Zionists in Palestine. These soldiers with a Star of David insignia on their shoulders were excitedly greeted by the survivors. In late June, the emissaries from Palestine, together with Rabbi Klausner, witnessed the first congress of Jewish survivors to be held in Germany, at St. Ottilien. The rabbi of the Jewish Brigade described the scene:

> Slogans of redemption, land, settlement and immigration cried out from the walls. Dark, wasted eyes are cast upward and hungrily take in what is written. There is a podium bedecked with pictures of Herzl, the Zionist fathers and the movement flag. On the chairs sit sunken skeletons with dry, thin hands, wearing tattered caps. Many are still in their prisoner garb. On the faces of all the immobility of death . . . an expression of apathy. They represented the millions of Zionists who had been asphyxiated, hung and burnt in Europe. The delegates bore a strong resemblance to their dead constituents.

The following day, a public proclamation was issued from the Munich beer cellar where Hitler had staged his putsch in 1922, calling for the immediate establishment of a Jewish state in Palestine, to be recognized by the United Nations.[17]

To maintain the political momentum, it was planned to have a further congress two months later, to which Jewish leaders from all over Germany would be invited—because in the British Zone, too, the Jewish survivors were organizing.

When Bergen-Belsen was liberated, it contained a diverse mixture of people, of whom just over half were Jewish, spread over two sites. Contemporary films show British soldiers chatting and flirting with well-fed, well-dressed, alert-looking young men and women while, in the background, "human skeletons" crawl about and corpses lie unburied. The fundamental distinction, however, was between the main concentration camp, in which some 40,000 people were crammed into stinking, typhus-ridden huts, and what the British called Camp 2, a few blocks of the German Tank Training School about a mile away, to which the very last batch of prisoners to arrive at Belsen had been sent. The British gradually evacuated all survivors to Camp 2, and on May 21, 1945, when the last hut in the "Horror Camp" was burned down, the whole population had been moved into the spacious and well-equipped Tank Training School, which had become the largest improvised hospital in Europe. It was this place, a huge German military garrison with well-built, four-story buildings grouped around some thirty parade squares, with broad avenues, leafy gardens, stables, a bakery, a ballroom, and a theater—more like a garden city suburb than a garrison—which became Belsen DP camp.

Only a few days after the liberation, prisoners' committees began to appear at Belsen, on which prisoners of all nationalities sat. But, with the departure of the Western Europeans in May, Polish Jews were left as the dominant group. A survivor of Camp 1 later recalled her disbelief when she learned that a Jewish Committee had been formed because she "simply could not imagine that there were any healthy Jews anywhere in Belsen." This group was in comparatively good health because most of them had arrived only a week before the liberation, in a shipment from the Dora concentration camp, and had been installed in the Tank Training School. They had therefore not been exposed to typhus.

According to the Israeli historian Hagit Lavsky, these young men, from Polish and Lithuanian shtetls, "belonged to Zionist youth movements and were preparing for a life of pioneering in Palestine."

> The spirited group had quite a significant impact on the mood in the camp. First of all they were quite numerous. Second, they were physically and mentally strong, which is probably why they survived in the first place. If anyone could organise the survivors, broken and exhausted by their ordeal, they could. Moreover, these young people had something to offer. They had a real goal. They were full of hope and their strong Zionist belief and enthusiasm transmitted itself to others. Their personal fate became inextricably linked to the fate of their own people, leading to a spontaneous decision not to return to Eastern Europe. Even before the survivors had recovered sufficiently to decide what to do next—to search for relatives, to try to build something out of the ruins, to think about the future—these young Zionists served as a compass and a guide.[18]

Here, as in Bavaria, it was the Zionists who provided the early leadership, the sense of purpose, for the dazed and bewildered survivors, as they struggled to come to terms with their new lives.

The dominant figure within this group was a Jew from Bedzin in Poland named Josef Rosensaft, whom everyone called Yossel. "Here was a man of small stature, but when he spoke you saw a giant," a survivor wrote later. "You thought you could look through him, but after a while, you had to stop. Something told you not to go any further." It was a miracle that Rosensaft was still alive. Born on January 15, 1911, he had worked before the war in the family scrap metal business and as a labor organizer. In July 1943, he escaped from the train taking him and his wife and stepson to Auschwitz by jumping into the Vistula River. He survived the guards' machine-gun fire but, after a period on the run, was recaptured and sent to Birkenau. Transferred, after two months of stone carrying, to the labor camp at Lagisza, he escaped once more in March 1943. But again his liberty was short-lived; by the end of April he was back in Auschwitz, where he survived months of torture without revealing who had helped him escape. When Auschwitz was evacuated, Rosensaft was taken to several labor camps and finally to Dora-Mittelbau, from which he was transferred to Belsen in early April 1945.

Only an extraordinary person could have come through this experience. "This small, militant, oversensitive man" became the dominant force on the Central Committee of Liberated Jews of the British Zone, which was formed on June 24, 1945. He was ably supported by other prominent Jews, including Dr. Hadassah Bimko, a dentist and passionate Zionist, who was invited to join the Central Committee and who married Rosensaft in 1946.

Much of the Central Committee's energy went into cultural and welfare work. In July 1945, the first Yiddish newspaper in the British Zone of Germany, *Unzer Sztyme,* appeared, and in September a theater company known as the Kazet Theater put on performances. An American observer was struck by the "stark realism and sheer drama" of its productions:

> Scenes with flames reaching out onto the stage depicting Jews being led to the crematoria, or showing Germans crushing the skull of a child, are commonplace . . . this is not acting but factual reproduction of what they have endured.

He also noticed that "at the finale there never is applause, just significant and painful silence that hangs over the theatre."

> It is not uncommon to see an audience of over 3000 persons burst
> into tears and hysterical sobbing throughout the production. In
> seeing their former miseries acted out, their lives projected onto a
> stage, so to speak, the displaced persons have come to regard their
> theatre as something a great deal more than "entertainment." The
> theatre symbolizes their will to live. It represents a culture that
> survived a systematic attempted extermination.[19]

In reclaiming their experience for themselves, members of the
Central Committee were helped by the belated arrival in the camps of
Jewish aid agencies. Until July 1945, the only Jewish people working
at Belsen were the army chaplains and a British welfare worker, Jane
Leverson, a member of the Red Cross team, who came from a grand
Hampstead Jewish family. Meanwhile, as we have seen, the Joint was
kept out because of the military's suspicion of "sectarian" organiza-
tions and its feeling that there were enough fingers in the pie already.
When pressure at the highest political level finally led to this policy
being rescinded and a Joint team arrived, more or less empty-handed,
Rosensaft's response was "OK, if you can't give us things, give us Yiddish typewriters so we can criticise the Joint to the Jews of the World."[20]

That confident tone reflected Rosensaft's successes in the political
arena, mainly in fighting the British. In the course of 1945, the Central Committee was engaged in more or less permanent war with the
military authorities. Rosensaft, an American aid worker noted, "has
had total disregard for military law and has incurred the wrath of the
military frequently who consider the Jewish Committee and their
activities illegal." Rosensaft did not endear himself to the British by
regarding it as a "matter of principle to address them in Yiddish, the
language of the people he represented."[21]

The fundamental question was whether the British would recognize Jewish survivors as Jews, rather than as Hungarian or Polish or
German nationals, and let them stay in the Tank Training School,
building it into a self-administered Jewish community. The British
plan was, initially, to ship all those who had recovered out of Belsen
and into other camps, turning the place into a purely medical facility;
but after vociferous protests that had to be abandoned. The British

also wanted to change the camp's name, from Belsen to Hohne, but the Central Committee valued the symbolism and successfully resisted that change, too.

The British view was that Rosensaft and the Central Committee were self-appointed troublemakers. It was noted that Hungarian and Romanian Jews, who tended to be Orthodox, were openly hostile to the younger and more secular Zionists on the Central Committee and that much of its equipment in the camp had been "organized" from the surrounding countryside. A British Red Cross nurse noted with distaste how "more and more as the months went by [the Jews] broke away from the other inmates and behind their strong Jewish leader they were compelled to follow his schemes and ideas. Jews who openly said they did not want to go to Palestine were ostracised and British interference was of little avail."[22]

Josef Rosensaft was one of the ninety-four delegates, representing some 40,000 Jews from forty-six centers in Germany and Austria, to attend the Conference of Representatives of the Surviving Jews in Germany, which convened at St. Ottilien on July 25, 1945, with the main objective of bringing the Jewish leaders together in a single organization. But Rosensaft refused to join the new body. An American who knew him thought "it was in character that Rosensaft, who treasured his power and independence, would not agree to have 'his' organization 'subordinated to' and 'diluted in' a larger body. Nor would he 'take orders from Munich,' where the projected central body would have its headquarters." There seems also to have been hostility between Rosensaft's emotional, populist Polish Jewish style of leadership and the more rational, intellectual approach of the Litvaks in the American Zone.[23]

Perhaps, also, Rosensaft was influenced by a new factor which had recently emerged: the growing interest of the U.S. government in the Jewish survivors.

In the spring of 1945, reports reached Washington that Jews who had survived the war were being kept in camps behind barbed wire and given less to eat than German prisoners of war. American Jewish leaders sprang into action. Their readiness to respond precipitately owed something to guilt; "strong feelings of missed opportunities and deeds undone," wrote the historian Zeev Mankowitz, "may have been a goad to quick action even without a significant accumulation of eye-witness reports." In addition, Zionists put strong pressure on the Truman administration to do something about the situation. Meyer Weisgal, the Washington representative of the Zionist leader Chaim Weizmann, persuaded Treasury Secretary Henry Morgenthau to take the matter up with the president. Harry Truman proved unresponsive, but Morgenthau persevered and eventually got the acting secretary of state, Joseph C. Grew, to send a representative to Europe to investigate conditions. Grew then appointed Earl G. Harrison, a law professor at the University of Pennsylvania, to lead this investigation and persuaded President Truman to authorize the mission.[24]

Earl G. Harrison, then forty-six years old, was a "spare-framed, square-jawed, red-haired" lawyer, a Roosevelt Republican, with long experience of refugee issues, having served during the war as commissioner of immigration and naturalization and then as the American representative on the body attempting to find homes for Jews fleeing from Europe, the Intergovernmental Committee on Refugees. Known as a "shrewd and level-headed observer" and "an almost indefatigable worker," Harrison was a Methodist, with a long record of community service, but was also involved with Jewish and African-American groups. Most important, he knew how shabbily Allied governments had behaved toward Jewish refugees in the past.[25]

Before leaving the United States, Harrison met with Meyer Weisgal, who persuaded him to widen the scope of his mission, looking beyond the immediate problem of rehabilitation to the wider question of the future of the 1.25 million Jews now left in Europe. As Weisgal saw it, the solution would have to be long term and political. The Jews of Europe, he said, had three options: to complete their demise, to obtain equality, or to emigrate. Only the third was a realistic option—and the only possible destination was Palestine. This encounter would decisively influence Harrison's approach.

Between July 7 and 25, 1945, Harrison toured the Jewish DP camps in Germany and Austria, accompanied by several experts, notably Dr. Joseph Schwartz, the European head of the American Jewish Joint Distribution Committee. In order to cover more ground, the group divided into two teams, with Schwartz writing independent reports which Harrison integrated into his final document. Harrison began by meeting Jewish leaders in Frankfurt and Munich, who emphasized two issues: the short-term need for Jews to be concentrated in separate camps and the longer-term question of free and immediate immigration to Palestine. He also met the head of the Press Office for the American military government in Munich, Joseph Dunner, who came up with what would prove to be Harrison's most telling statement: "as matters now stand, we appear to be treating the Jews as the Nazis treated them except that we do not exterminate them."[26]

Harrison's original itinerary was drawn up by the military and was intended to keep him away from the "worst places." But his colleague Schwartz made sure that he met the American who was closest to the DPs, Rabbi Klausner, and the rabbi in turn made sure that Harrison saw everything. "I took him to the partially bombed buildings into which we had crowded hundreds of refugees in flight from their lands with nowhere to be housed," Klausner wrote later. "I took him to the overcrowded camps." Several historians have argued that the young rabbi "decisively influenced" Harrison's perception of the physical and psychological suffering of the Jews, even to the point of providing him with much of the language he later used. In fact, Klausner was just one of many Jews who influenced Harrison. Indeed, the Gentile lawyer was not impressed by Klausner, whom he found "young, aggressive, irritating." The rabbi, he wrote in his journal, "gives credit to the army for good health job but deplores everything else."[27]

What made the greatest impression on Harrison was his visit to Belsen. "He looked at us and chain-smoked as the tears streamed down his face," a witness there recalled. "Finally, he whispered weakly: 'But how did you survive, and where do you take your strength from now?'" That evening, Harrison wrote in his diary: "Seldom have I been so depressed. . . . Only seven hours spent there but it seemed like a life-time." Harrison had been told not to bother going to Belsen because the original camp had been burned down and most of the Jews moved away, but he found some 14,000 displaced people, "including 7200 Jews still confined here. Oh yes, the building #1 with its fiendish gas-chambers and crematoria had been destroyed but the rest is bad enough. One loft, about 80 by 20, housing 85 people."[28]

Harrison's feelings rather got the better of him. Belsen had never had any gas chambers, though there certainly were crematoria. The Jewish DPs were now living in what Major Abraham S. Hyman considered "one of the best equipped DP camps in Germany," with a modern, well-appointed hospital. Of course, things were not perfect—the hospital was run by German doctors and nurses, and the British officer in charge at this time "had a colonial attitude towards the DPs" and treated them "as if they were idiots"—but the DPs, far from being "confined" at Belsen, knew the site's symbolic value and had resisted British attempts to move them from it.[29]

Earl Harrison produced a preliminary report in early August 1945, and the final version reached President Truman on August 24. In it Harrison concluded that the U.S. Army's treatment of Jewish DPs was unsatisfactory.

> Many Jewish displaced persons and other possibly unrepatriables are living under guard behind barbed-wire fences, in camps of several descriptions (built by the Germans for slave laborers and Jews), including some of the most notorious of the concentration camps, amidst crowded, frequently unsanitary and generally grim conditions, in complete idleness, with no opportunity, except surreptitiously, to communicate with the outside world, waiting, hoping, for some word of encouragement and action in their behalf.

In his report, Harrison accepted the argument that the Jews were a nation: "the first and plainest need of these people," he wrote, "is a recognition of their actual status and by this I mean their status as Jews." For the first time in history, an American official document acknowledged the Zionist case. How could Jews still be treated as nationals of countries whose peoples had been party to their extermination? He therefore recommended separate camps for Jews in Germany at once and asked that, where possible, UNRRA should take over the responsibility for running them from the army. Turning to longer-term solutions, he called for speedy immigration of 100,000 Jews to Palestine but expected the United States to make only minor amendments to its immigration policy. Harrison did not examine whether Palestine was capable of absorbing that number of Jewish survivors.[30]

Was Harrison's report fair? Most historians agree with Yehuda Bauer that the professor dealt in a "vastly exaggerated way" with the U.S. Army's treatment of Jews: "He grasped the essential point that the US Army was hostile to the Jews but failed to understand (or at any rate, to explain) that much of the squalor which he saw derived from the demoralization and hopelessness of the survivors themselves." He also got several things wrong—Jewish DPs were in fact free to come and go as they pleased and continued to wear concentration camp uniforms in the belief that it would get them preferential treatment. Harrison's colleague Joseph Schwartz was equally critical of the army but acknowledged that in view of its preoccupation with repatriation, "it was quite natural that little thought could be given to the non-repatriables."[31]

Fair or not, the report had an immediate impact. On August 25, Truman asked his adviser Judge Samuel Rosenman to read the report. "He said he had read it the previous night, and it made him sick. He said the situation at many of the camps, especially with respect to the Jews, was practically as bad now as it was under the Nazis." "The Harrison Report," Truman wrote in his memoirs, "was a moving document. The misery it depicted could not be allowed to continue, and I sent a message to Eisenhower, asking him to do what he could about conditions in the camps."[32]

In fact, Truman did much more than that. He ordered Eisenhower to take immediate steps to improve the conditions of the Jewish DPs, mainly at the expense of the German population, and took the unusual step of publishing his letter rebuking Eisenhower in the American press. Although the U.S. Army in Germany was incensed by the Harrison Report, which it considered biased and unfair, and although Eisenhower insisted on publishing a detailed rebuttal of many of its points, the general had throughout his career shown great sensitivity to the wishes of his political masters. He now saw that something had to be done. In the autumn of 1945, Eisenhower paid quick visits to five Jewish DP camps, appointed an adviser for Jewish Affairs, and set into motion a policy of putting Jews into their own camps—acknowledging, in effect, that they were a separate nation.[33]

Truman also tried to prod the British into action: he wrote to the British prime minister, Clement Attlee, supporting Earl Harrison's recommendation that 100,000 Jews be immediately admitted to Palestine. When a month passed without a response, he went public at a press conference on September 29, 1945. Truman's position was complex. He was an emotional man who had grown up on the Bible and had Jewish friends stretching back to his days as a young man in Kansas City, yet he was also capable of the casual anti-Semitic remarks common among American Gentiles of his generation. That being said, the plight of the Jewish DPs, as documented by Earl Harrison, had touched him deeply; once the issue had registered with him, it remained a continuing concern. A decent man, he wanted to see those people humanely treated.

However, there was also an element of straightforward political calculation in his attitude. Once when Truman was asked to explain his pro-Jewish policy, he replied, "I have to answer to hundreds of thousands who are anxious for the success of Zionism; I do not have hundreds of thousands of Arabs in my constituents." The 1940s had seen the rise in the United States of what is now called the "Jewish lobby"; from 1943 onward, the Zionists had organized the vast majority of American Jews behind support for a Jewish homeland in Palestine. Both the Republican and Democratic parties had included a plank endorsing this view in their platforms in the 1944 elections. The Jewish electorate had overwhelmingly supported Franklin Roosevelt, but the new president could be less sure of its support, which, in certain key states like New York and Pennsylvania, was very important. They were also substantial donors to the Democratic Party. Although Truman was in some ways "a resentful prisoner" of the Jewish lobby, as the historian Michael J. Cohen puts it, he recognized the need to appeal to Jewish voters. The timing of his press conference was largely determined by a forthcoming mayoral campaign in New York City.[34]

At the same time, Truman realized that he had to proceed with caution on the issue, given the hostility of much American opinion to further Jewish immigration to the United States. As Lord Halifax, the British ambassador to Washington, put it, the average U.S. citizen "does not want [the Jews] in the United States and salves his conscience by advocating their admission by Palestine." Nor did Truman want the United States itself to become involved on the ground in Palestine or American soldiers to be committed there. As far as he was concerned, this was a British problem.[35]

· · ·

It was one the British had chosen to take on. On November 2, 1917, the British foreign secretary, Arthur Balfour, sent to Lord Rothschild, one of the leaders of Britain's Jewish community, a "declaration of sympathy with Jewish Zionist aspirations" which had been approved by the British Cabinet:

> His Majesty's Government view with favour the establishment in Palestine of a national home for the Jewish people, and will use their best endeavours to facilitate the achievement of this object, it being clearly understood that nothing shall be done which may prejudice the civil and religious rights of existing non-Jewish communities in Palestine, or the rights and political status enjoyed by Jews in any other country.[36]

Many elements came together to produce the Balfour Declaration. The two decades since the Viennese journalist Theodor Herzl had launched the modern Zionist movement with his book *Der Judenstaat* (1896) had seen a sustained campaign of lobbying by the Zionists on behalf of the creation of a Jewish state. In Britain, the dominating figure was the son of a timber merchant in the Pripet marshes, Chaim Weizmann, who had gained an international reputation as a chemist before going to teach at Manchester University in 1906 and become a British citizen four years later. Weizmann's eloquence and charm found a ready audience in a generation of statesmen whose romantic alignment with the Jewish cause had been shaped by their early reading of Benjamin Disraeli's *Tancred* and George Eliot's *Daniel Deronda* or by youthful familiarity with the Bible. "When Dr Weizmann was talking of Palestine," David Lloyd George later recalled, "he kept bringing up place-names which were more familiar to me than those on the Western Front."[37]

The tactical concerns of the war gave a practical point to this issue. The Ottoman Empire, which had ruled Palestine for the last four hundred years, was now clearly on its last legs. In 1916, the British and French had agreed to divide the Turkish possessions in the Middle East between them, but there remained worries that the French might get involved in Palestine. Also, with Britain's ally Russia weakened after the Revolution of February 1917, it was felt that a gesture to world Jewry would give a boost to the Allied cause—the Zionists had promised as much to Lloyd George.

Nobody paused to ask the Arabs, who then made up nine-tenths of Palestine's population, what they thought about this idea, but several British Cabinet ministers did raise practical objections. What exactly was a national home? they wanted to know. Surely it was not being suggested that all the world's 12 million Jews could be fitted into this small and unproductive stretch of land? What was to happen to the Arabs? To deal with these objections, the original draft of the declaration, provided by the Zionists themselves, was altered. References to unrestricted Jewish immigration and self-rule were removed, and a clause safeguarding the rights of the majority Arab population in Palestine was inserted.

Thus the British created for themselves an insoluble conundrum. How could the establishment of a Jewish national home be reconciled with the maintenance of the place of the Arabs? From the moment General Edmund Allenby walked on foot through the gates of Jerusalem on December 11, 1917, the difficulty of squaring this circle was apparent to British administrators on the spot.

The Zionists did not immediately seize the opportunity given to them. Throughout the 1920s the levels of immigration to Palestine were lower than expected—the population rose from about 60,000 at the end of the war to about 180,000 in 1932. But the following year, Hitler came to power in Germany and the Jewish exodus began—with almost every country in the world tightening its immigration laws, Palestine was one of the few places the Jews could go to. In eight years the Jewish population more than doubled, until it reached 463,535 in 1940. Inevitably, this brought tensions with the Arab population to a head. Was Palestine to remain a traditional Muslim society or develop into a modern industrialized country?

The British tried to placate both sides and protect their own imperial interests. Several investigating committees were established and schemes propounded in an attempt to reconcile the two sides. An armed uprising by the Arabs led to the establishment in 1937 of yet another commission, which recommended that the only solution was to partition the country. Both Jews and Arabs rejected that solution.[38]

In May 1939, the British changed tack. With a war against Germany now looking likely, the Chamberlain government decided that Britain's strategic interests made the friendship of the Arabs more important than the feelings of the Jews—who had no option but to support the Allied cause. That meant buying Arab goodwill, damping down pro-Axis sympathy in the Middle East, and guaranteeing access to oil and land. The White Paper that appeared that month restricted Jewish land purchases in, and immigration to, Palestine. Churchill condemned this policy in 1939, but on becoming prime minister he did not reverse it, despite many pleas by those anxious to save the Jews from being exterminated later in the war. The Labour opposition, too, denounced the restriction on Jewish immigration to Palestine, and at its party conference in May 1945, Hugh Dalton, the party's expert on foreign affairs, asserted that "it is morally wrong and politically indefensible to impose obstacles on the entry into Palestine now of any Jews who desire to go there." The party reaffirmed its support for Zionism on no fewer than eleven occasions.[39]

When, however, the Labour Party was unexpectedly swept into power in the 1945 General Election, it was not Dalton but Ernest Bevin, the veteran trade union leader, the illegitimate son of a Somerset housemaid, who became foreign secretary. On Palestine, Bevin accepted the advice of his officials and did not reverse the 1939 White Paper. As Bevin's biographer Alan Bullock said, "British officials had no difficulty in convincing themselves that there was no necessary connection between the plight of the Jews in the DP camps and Palestine. If it were not for the pressure exercised by Zionist agents, they maintained, the Jewish refugees would prefer to remain in Europe or to go to other countries, preferably the USA." It was this position which the British now attempted to defend.[40]

The British were passionately opposed to the Harrison Report, in terms of both its effect in Germany and its effect in Palestine. Their opposition combined political objections with profound philosophical disagreement. "We do not of course admit that Jews constitute a separate nationality and are all against any attempt to label people as definitely and irrevocably 'non-repatriable' at this stage," Sir George Rendel of the Foreign Office wrote. "It would indeed be disastrous for the Jews themselves if they were accorded special treatment on this basis in comparison with the people of the country where they live."[41]

But the British were in a quandary. On every other question, it was vital to have U.S. cooperation: Britain's very economic survival depended on Congressional approval of a loan. Therefore a way would have to be found to make concessions to the Americans.

But if the Jewish DPs could not go to Palestine, where could they go? Even as the British wrestled with this question, the situation was being transformed with the arrival of thousands more Jews in the camps in Germany.

SEVEN

"Feed the Brutes?"

GERMAN REFUGEES, 1945

On August 23, 1945, two British journalists went to the Stettiner station in Berlin to meet a train loaded with German refugees fleeing from the East. The journey from Danzig had taken seven days. Inside a cattle truck they saw, on one side, four dead bodies lying on a stretcher and, on the other, four dying women. All over the station, on platforms and in the booking hall, people were dying. One woman, "emaciated, with dark rings under her eyes and sores breaking out all over her face, could only mutter self-condemnation because she was unable to feed her two whimpering babies." They watched her "desperately trying to force milk from her milkless breasts—a pitiful effort that only left her crying at her failure."[1]

Those people were just part of a tide of human misery reaching the German capital every day. Up to 25,000 a day were arriving by foot and being turned away by the authorities. Nearly all were women, children, and old men. Young Polish men could be seen boarding the trains and robbing the refugees; a young German girl, "her hair bedraggled, her clothes and stockings torn," was seen being led away from the station by Poles.

It was clear to Norman Clark of the *News Chronicle* that the expulsion of Germans from the East was producing "a tragedy of the greatest magnitude." There were now thought to be millions of homeless nomads in the areas around Berlin, and a further 5 million Germans expelled from Czechoslovakia would soon be on their way. What was being done about it? The refugees were receiving only the barest medical attention. The Allied authorities claimed that this was a German problem and refused to provide any relief themselves; nor were they helping the Germans. The local German Social Welfare Committee, with a staff of 33 and 220 helpers, had no telephones or cars at its disposal. As result, not much was being achieved. "Here in Berlin," wrote Clark, "we are living under the shadow, not just of hunger and of want, but of death, and epidemics on a scale that the world has not seen in recorded history."

Charles Bray struck a different note in the *Daily Herald*. "Today I have seen thousands of German civilians . . . reduced to the depths of misery and suffering that the Nazis inflicted on others," he began. "I didn't like it. It gave me no satisfaction, although for years I have hoped that the Germans would reap from the seeds they had sown." But the "miserable remnants of humanity" he had seen in the Stettiner station were past helping themselves; someone else would have to help them.

> This is the aftermath of war, raising problems more difficult to solve than almost any that existed during it. But if we are to prove to the German race that our methods, our civilization, our creed were right and theirs wrong, and if we are to keep faith with those who died, were maimed and suffered intolerable hardship, then these problems have got to be solved and have got to be solved quickly.[2]

In the stations of Berlin, Robert Capa and Margaret Bourke-White pointed their cameras at German refugees grouped like an opera chorus round ruined neoclassical pillars, dramatically lit by daylight streaming through the bomb-wrecked roofs. For the first time since the war, the Germans were shown as human beings and suffering victims. The journalistic language of death and dehumanization, of cattle trucks and innocent victimhood, coined earlier in the year when the concentration camps were opened, was now being applied to the Germans. But the reports and images also had a serious message. "These wandering millions," Reuters' correspondent wrote, "have upset all attempts to get Germany's food problem on to any workable basis. Without goal or control, they are rapidly spreading disease, particularly dysentery, typhoid and typhus."[3]

When it reached the attention of British newspaper readers in August 1945, the German refugee crisis was more than a year old. Its origins lay further back. During the war, the governments in exile of Poland and Czechoslovakia had made it clear that when victory came they would expel the German populations from their countries, citing as a precedent the transfer of populations between Greece and Turkey in 1923, which they said—wrongly—had taken place without violence. This policy of expulsion was consistently endorsed by the Allied governments, with both Churchill and Stalin giving robust support to it. The Russian leader advised the Polish Communists to "create such conditions for the Germans as they want to escape themselves," while Churchill informed Stalin at Yalta that there was unlikely to be much of a problem in absorbing the refugees into their mother country, as some 8 million or 9 million Germans had been killed in the war. "Expulsion is the method which, so far as we have been able to see, will be the most satisfactory and lasting," Churchill told the House of Commons on December 15, 1944. "A clean sweep will be made. I am not alarmed at the prospect of the disentanglement of the population, nor am I alarmed by these large transferences, which are more possible than they were before through modern conditions."[4]

That view was not shared in all quarters. Although academic experts had by 1939 come to accept the principle of "population transfers" as a solution to the "problem of minorities" which had plagued politics and diplomacy in Eastern Europe for the past twenty years, they doubted whether the sorts of wholesale transfers proposed by the Poles and Czechs could be painlessly achieved. The British Foreign Office was particularly skeptical.

Events rapidly made such reservations irrelevant. As the Red Army advanced into the eastern parts of Hitler's Reich and the Balkans at the end of 1944, a mass flight of Germans to the West began. By April 1945, some 3.5 million refugees had fled, made up of inhabitants of the eastern parts of Germany, such as West and East Prussia, Silesia, and Posen; wartime evacuees who had escaped from the bombing of the industrial West; recent settlers from annexed territories, such as Ukraine; as well as ethnic Germans—*Volksdeutsche*—from across Eastern Europe. These refugees had their own particular pathos—horse-drawn, four-wheeled wooden peasant carts trudging across a bleak wintry landscape under a lowering sky; little boys being fed at soup kitchens; old men and women dressed in timeless peasant garb with blank, expressionless faces.

When the war ended in May 1945, another flood of humanity was let loose. The Czechs and the Poles immediately set about expelling the Germans remaining in their countries. In Czechoslovakia, previous talk of allowing some "good" Germans to stay was swept aside by a wave of anti-German Czech nationalism that demanded revenge and retaliation for the activities of the Sudeten Germans, the insults of Munich, the loss of Czech sovereignty, and the massacre at Lidice. Indeed, the Czech government deliberately raised the temperature of anti-German feeling in the country. As a result, the surrender of the Wehrmacht was followed by an orgy of violence in which armed Czech fighters beat up, shot, humiliated, and tortured Germans. Villages were burned to the ground, Germans hanged in trees and set alight, beaten to death, and tortured. Czech paramilitaries, army units, and local vigilantes drove hundreds of thousands of Germans from their homes and across the border. The violence of the Czech response took even the Russians by surprise. Indeed, except for their habit of raping women, the Germans found Russian soldiers to be much more humane and responsible than the native Czechs.[5]

Why did the Czechs turn on their German minority with such savagery? Clearly, recent events provided part of the explanation, but there were also old scores to settle, stretching back many generations to the Battle of White Mountain in 1620, when troops of the Holy Roman Empire had wiped out the native Bohemian nobility. The Czechs were getting their revenge for being second-class citizens in their own country, subordinated to German culture and religion, dominated by German nobles, intellectuals, and professionals. It was soon obvious that nearly all of the 3 million Germans in Czechoslovakia would be forced to leave their homes and that there was nothing the Great Powers could do to stop the process.

The Poles' wish to expel their German population was easier to understand: the systematic destruction of Warsaw, the killing of millions of Polish citizens, the desecration of Polish culture—no country in Europe had suffered more from German occupation. What now happened was, as a German historian has said, "set in motion long before. It was the result of our own German madness." But in Poland as in Czechoslovakia, the expulsion of the Germans was seen as "a social as well as a national act. German exploiters, the German middle class, German landowners would be expelled and replaced by Poles. The Polish peasantry would no longer suffer at the hands of the German upper class." This view was shared across Polish life, by democratic politicians as much as by Communists. But Poland had other motives besides. In compensation for the land it was surrendering to the Soviet Union to the east, it had received German territory on the west, in Silesia and Prussia, as far as the Oder River. These lands had long been disputed, but in 1945 the majority of the inhabitants were German. For Poland to assert its claim to them, they would have to be expelled.[6]

Toward the end of June 1945, word went round the villages and farms of Pomerania that "the Germans must get out." Anna Kientopf, a farmer's wife, was given half an hour to pack and be ready to leave, shouted at by Polish and Russian policemen. She stuck her youngest children and a few possessions in a handcart and set out. As she looked back at the farm where she had been born and the cemetery where her parents were buried, she wondered who would milk the cows that evening. She joined a long column of refugees heading westward toward the new boundary, the Oder River.[7]

The refugees were old men, women, and children. At regular intervals they met Polish and Russian soldiers, who searched them and removed their possessions; if anyone tried to defend his goods, he was shot. One middle-aged widow from Sorau in Brandenburg, traveling with her only remaining relative, a baby grandchild, was later asked why she did not hide her jewelry in the seams of her skirt or in her hair. She replied that she had been "six times searched in my vagina for jewellery" while the gold crowns of the teeth of her friend, the wife of a district judge, had been knocked out of her mouth.

The refugees had to feed themselves, and though some had ensured they were well provided—with jars of meat, fat sausage, loaves of bread, potatoes, and milk—many others had almost nothing to eat and had to scavenge for food along the way, eating unripe fruit or potatoes from the fields. Nights were spent sleeping outside by the carts or in a hayloft or abandoned building. Anna Kientopf described the terrible sight and smell of dead bodies, human and animal, covered in flies, that lay in the countryside along the roads, and how "the breath of the plague" came out of the forest. Huge swarms of flies rose from the corpses and attacked them, creating festering sores. The heat was terrible, and they all suffered from thirst. They were drinking foul water from the wells of bombed-out houses and abandoned farms, which made them sick. Typhus and dysentery spread through the "endless columns of misery" and people began to die. The children began to get ill with dysentery.

Things grew worse as they neared the Oder. They had to pass through a line of Polish soldiers, who led people and their carts away from the column to a farm, presumably to be robbed. Young girls were taken screaming into the fields, and anyone trying to stop the soldiers was struck with rifle butts or riding whips. One man who tried to protect his daughter was shot by Polish soldiers. There were Russians standing by, "looking on cynically." "In our desperation we begged them for help. They shrugged their shoulders and indicated to us, that the Poles were the masters."

Anna and her family passed through the devastated town of Küstrin, and at last, in the late afternoon of July 6, reached the bridge over the Oder. The following day they crossed over. On the one side, they were fleeced by Polish soldiers; on the other, Russian soldiers turned their sacks and carts upside down and relieved them of the few possessions they still had. The journey through the Russian Zone proved as dangerous and painful as before, but Anna managed to reach Berlin with her two children, who by then were dangerously ill.[8]

The expulsion of the Germans was a humanitarian disaster. Nobody knows how many people died; estimates range from 200,000 to 2.3 million. But most of the deaths seem to have occurred between late 1944 and the end of the war, in areas where the German army was retreating in the face of Soviet and Yugoslav forces. They went largely unreported. Most of the refugees from Czechoslovakia, Hungary, and Romania entered Germany via Bavaria, but for the 5 million–odd people expelled from former German territories east of the Oder and from Poland, Berlin was the first port of call. Consequently, the Western Allies became aware of the sheer scale of the German refugee problem only when they took control of their sectors of Berlin in early July 1945.[9]

The German capital was in no condition to face this new challenge. Three months after Soviet troops had fought their way to the Reichstag, the city was ruined, paralyzed, and unfed. Transport connections with the countryside around, from which Berlin drew its food, had scarcely been reestablished, the bulk of the water was running to waste, only a fifth of the sewerage system was thought to be still functioning, no coal was available for domestic supplies, and gas and electricity were strictly rationed. Very few people had enough fuel for cooking. The British found a dysentery epidemic already in progress in their sector caused by "disorganized sanitary services, lack of personnel to advise on precautions, and flies breeding in the hot weather."[10]

Perhaps because of the prevailing view that this problem was not a British army responsibility, the British came to Berlin almost unprepared to deal with the German refugees who were pouring into the city at the rate of about 17,000 per day. They had neither the manpower nor the procedures in place, and—astonishingly—supplies of DDT did not arrive until a month later. Administratively, too, the British found themselves caught between two stools—powerless to prevent the Russians from letting refugees crowd into the British sector of Berlin, yet anxious that these new arrivals should not add to the overcrowding and strain in the bombed cities of western Germany by moving to the British Zone. They tried therefore to hold them in Berlin, in improvised transit camps and in what accommodation could be found in the city's rubble, while feeding them from soup kitchens.

The camps themselves were run by overstretched German relief organizations. Conditions "were not good," as two British doctors conceded. "Sick-bays were provided, and they were largely occupied by moribund cases which hospitals would not accept. One curious sign was the unemotional way in which a mother with perhaps four children would state that she had heard nothing of her husband for months or even years. Many seemed to have lost all normal human emotions." Lacerated feet in undernourished people proved particularly difficult to treat. The main concern, however, was with the diseases the refugees brought with them. In the crowded camps, it was comparatively easy to contain the threat of typhus by spraying with DDT powder (once supplies had arrived), but a typhoid epidemic broke out in August and raged for the next three months. With seven to eight hundred cases occurring each week, "shotgun" methods had to be adopted: compulsory immunization was introduced, the ration card system making it easy to check those who had been treated. Nonetheless, between July 1945 and January 1946, there were some 12,740 cases of typhoid in the British Zone, of which 1,600 were fatal.

The warnings of military doctors and relief workers that a political solution to the refugee problem in Berlin would have to be found went largely unheeded. District commanders in the British sector, as well as British personnel in other capacities, such as relief workers and those involved in the civilian side of occupation, were soon warning that unless a political as well as a practical solution were found to the growing refugee crisis, and the expulsion of German populations that was causing it, the Allies would soon be presiding over a humanitarian crisis of unknown proportions in Central Europe.

Despite the alarm on the ground in Berlin, senior British officials in the city and in the British Zone were slow to act. It was only because of press reports filed from Berlin which the Foreign Office wanted investigated and substantiated that their attention was finally brought to the developments unfolding beneath their very noses. The Foreign Office's man in Berlin expressed surprise "that such accounts were appearing in the British press, since these conditions were certainly not visible to the casual observer in Berlin."[11]

In the autumn of 1945, elements in the British press and the relief organizations began to mount a campaign. The situation in Germany was unsupportable, *Picture Post* wrote on September 8. There were still more than 2 million displaced persons in the country, and, in addition, 13 million homeless Germans, many removed from the Sudetenland and new Polish territory, were wandering about in a desperate condition. There was a danger of serious rioting in the winter, and administrators on the spot believed that some 5 million to 10 million Germans would die. "German misery this winter will be on a scale unknown in Europe since the Middle Ages."[12]

Over and over, critics railed at the administrative shambles in Germany. It was all very well to say that the United Nations had ruled that German refugees were no concern of UNRRA and that they were the responsibility of the German authorities. But if the infrastructure of Germany had collapsed totally, where was relief to come from? "If you dismantle the political apparatus of a nation, it is hopeless to expect it at the same time to perform a task so immense," wrote *Picture Post*. Henry Buckley of Reuters saw "a complete lack of any German or inter-allied organisation to deal with this problem. So far as provincial authorities exist, they order the burgomasters of small towns and villages to take in refugees equal in numbers to the normal inhabitants. But if a town or village gets short of food it usually sends the refugees on their way." Welfare officials he had spoken to saw "only one solution—that of a central organisation. Such a body, when set up, would prepare, in close collaboration with the Allies, some kind of plan to settle these wanderers, at least provisionally, according to the food resources, labour needs and similar factors obtaining in different parts of Germany."[13]

The press campaign reactivated a long-standing public debate about how to treat the defeated Germans. Noël Coward's famous song "Don't Let's Be Beastly to the Germans" was written in the spring of 1943, as a satire, Coward later said, on a small group of "excessive humanitarians" who, in his opinion, were "taking a rather too tolerant view of our enemies." He had in mind such figures as the philosopher Bertrand Russell, the writer J. B. Priestley, and the publisher Victor Gollancz, all of whom publicly opposed the notion of collective German guilt as advanced by the influential former diplomat Sir Robert Vansittart.[14]

In the autumn of 1945, their voices were heard again, with Gollancz in the lead. The son of a north London jeweler, Gollancz combined commercial acumen with strong (if inconsistent) moral convictions. Through his Left Book Club, his industry, and his genius for marketing, he had built up a unique position as an advocate for good causes. According to his biographer, Gollancz had a particular passion for the moral underdog and "enjoyed the sheer drama and excitement of being seen to take up an unpopular cause." He had already "become a self-ordained minister of moral values in the postwar world" by his attacks on what he called "the new morality." Provoked by a *Daily Express* article which seemed to gloat over German suffering, Gollancz argued in a letter to the *News Chronicle* that only "an act of genuine repentance" could save Europe from "utter destruction" and from "the evil [that] has already gone deep." Now Gollancz and his associates on the National Peace Council decided to mount a campaign to rouse British public opinion.[15]

They focused on a symbolic gesture—a voluntary (but officially sponsored) cut in British rations to "save" Europe—but also demanded that the government do more to stop the expulsions and allow the British to send parcels and to make voluntary reductions to their diet. The public response was formidable. The two appeals helped to draw attention to the plight of Europe in general and of German refugees in particular. A consensus was building: the presence of so many pestilent and starving refugees in the Soviet Zone, who at any moment might break out westward, was a matter of immediate concern that required resolute action for reasons of national self-interest, not sentimentality toward the Germans.

But if the stories coming out of Germany aroused the conscience of one strand of British opinion, they excited the fears of another. Should Germans be fed? Both sides in the debate, do-gooders and Hun bashers, agreed that they should—but for very different reasons. On October 5, 1945, the *Daily Mirror* carried an editorial, headed "Feed the Brutes?":

> The problem . . . must be faced and solved. In saying this we suggest no sympathy for the German people, or for the victims of those mass evacuations which have caused this nightmare of suffering, disease, and death; those pitiful ambling Belsens which move along the highways of Eastern Germany. . . . It is not any feeling of compassion which prompts us to emphasise the necessity of dealing with the situation. It is the practical matter which makes action imperative. . . . The longer Europe is allowed to sink into the bog, the longer it will take to raise up—the longer the occupation will have to go on.

At the opposite end of the spectrum, the right-wing, anti–German *Sunday Chronicle* acknowledged that "for the sake of Europe and ourselves, for the safety of our occupying troops . . . Germany must be prevented from becoming a plague spot and a danger to the world."[16]

One element in the British press coverage was fear of a pandemic if nothing was done. In Parliament, one Tory MP professed "not to care two rows of pins for what happened to the German people" but expressed concern that any epidemic of disease might "start in the East and spread like wildfire to the West, to Berlin further westward," and affect British troops. The English Channel had stopped the Luftwaffe, but it could not stop disease; an epidemic "knew no frontiers" and "needed no passport."[17]

The contradictions of British attitudes at this time are preserved in *A Defeated People,* a film which the director Humphrey Jennings shot in the British Zone in the autumn of 1945. Jennings's camera records with compassion the sufferings of the German people—bedraggled columns of prisoners of war, civilians living in rubble, ragged children playing in the dirt, notices put up by those desperately seeking relatives, crowded boxcars pulling out of Hamburg station. But his commentary has a harsher tone, blaming the Germans for their own fate and gloating over the fall of the "master race." Then it explains, with no great relish, that "we can't afford to wash our hands of the Germans." The military government—"that is, your husbands and sons"—have to "talk the Germans into putting their house in order. . . . Why? We have an interest in Germany that is purely selfish. We cannot live next to a disease-ridden neighbour. . . . Diseases of the mind, new brands of fascism, come springing up."[18]

By the autumn of 1945, some organization for dealing with the flood of incomers had been improvised. At the Potsdam Conference it was agreed that steps should be taken to make the exodus from the East more orderly and humane: there would be a hiatus while more of the DPs were sent home from Germany; then the expulsions would resume under controlled conditions. This was largely ignored by the Poles. Meanwhile, the Allied Control Council devised plans for distributing the refugees more evenly between the zones of occupation. The military government tried to get the newcomers dispersed away from the overcrowded cities into country areas, which had already absorbed large numbers of wartime evacuees from bombed cities. A central German organization for dealing with the problem was not established—the Allied military government remained in control—but at the local level German officials were required to organize accommodation for the newcomers in private houses. The German Red Cross and German Protestant and Catholic welfare groups established soup kitchens, provided first-aid centers in railway stations, and arranged hospital space for the refugees. Some attempt was also made to trace missing persons. Although the care of "expellees" remained outside UNRRA's remit, increasing numbers of non-German voluntary relief agencies were now sent to work with it. It was a measure of how far the Germans—or at any rate their women, children, and elderly—had now become "victims" in their own right that the traditional religious and humanitarian impulses of the voluntary societies could now come into play on their behalf. Among the British charities, only the Girl Guides and the Boy Scouts refused, saying they "did not feel like working to help [the Germans] when innocent nationalities they had treated like dirt were in need." The Guides eventually relented; but the Scouts remained steadfast in their opposition.[19]

The German expellees made their way to small villages and country towns, which soon became overcrowded. While the summer weather lasted, they could sleep out of doors or in improvised shelters, and in the autumn some of the buildings hitherto used to house DPs became available. But many of the refugees were still not properly housed when winter came, and the German food rations shrank to a near-starvation level of 1,550 calories a day. The attitude of the native Germans also began to change. Having initially felt a sense of duty to be welcoming to their fellow Germans, and previously having had slave workers and evacuees from the bombed cities quartered among them, they became increasingly aware that the expellees were different culturally—Eastern peasants, many of them—and not likely to move on. When the authorities began supporting refugees' demands for equal rights, they were no longer welcome at all.

The refugees were a problem for all the occupying powers. The Russians tried to shunt them through their zone and into the West but still had to absorb many thousands. At one stage tens of thousands of expellees were living in barns and shacks in the countryside of Mecklenburg and Pomerania, looking for work. The authorities also worried about their state of mind. There were said to be 28,000 "deeply depressed" refugees living in Leipzig in July 1946, unable to adjust to their new circumstances, dreaming of returning to their birthplace, and quite indifferent to the politics of their new surroundings. The American Zone was better able to absorb the influx, and the authorities there soon accepted that any idea of sending refugees on was unrealistic.[20]

But it was in the British Zone that the arrival of the refugees provided the greatest problems.

The Germans had deliberately used hunger as a weapon of war. The Hunger Plan they had produced at the time of the invasion of Russia in 1941 was frighteningly straightforward, laying down that Germany's army and domestic population would maintain more or less peacetime levels of diet while no attempt would be made to feed Soviet POWs or civilians. Although both these policies were moderated later in the war, the Germans had undoubtedly caused the deaths of many millions through starvation, most notably in Kiev and Leningrad.

The British, for their part, had maintained the blockade, which had also caused many deaths from starvation. Callousness, or "blockade-mindedness," persisted in official circles in the first half of 1945. The feeling was that it was now the Germans' turn to starve—and even to die. Sir Frederick Leith-Ross thought it "inevitable" that 10 percent of them would starve to death; Sir James Grigg expected 2 million people to die of hunger in the spring. "Conditions are going to be extremely difficult in Germany this winter and there will be much cold and hunger," General Lucius D. Clay wrote in June 1945. He thought "some cold and hunger" would be necessary "to make the German people realize the consequence of a war which they caused" but insisted that "this type of suffering should not extend to the point where it results in starvation and sickness." The Foreign Office mandarin Sir Orme Sargent thought the German population, outside the heavily bombed major cities, had had their lifestyle "cushioned" by the displaced persons. The implication was that it was time they *did* suffer.[21]

One obvious element in such calculations was the abrupt disappearance of Germany's rural workforce, the displaced persons. With Polish agricultural workers returning home or sitting in camps being fed by the Allies, who was going to bring in the harvest? Fortunately, the intelligent and decisive director of military government, Major General Gerald Templer, saw at once that if Germany's population were to get through the winter, steps must be taken to bring in the harvest, and the only people who could replace the departed or unwilling DPs on the land were the German prisoners of war now languishing in cages all over the country. Operation Barleycorn required German commanders to provide a daily quota of soldiers to be ferried in British lorries to farms in their home areas. By September the British had gotten nearly 800,000 prisoners of war released under the scheme and believed this had settled the labor shortage at harvesttime. But for all Templer's efforts, the harvest itself was disappointing, about 10 to 15 percent below expectations.[22]

In the autumn of 1945, the British managed to get their hands on some 542,000 tons of wheat left over from SHAEF supplies. But what would feed the British Zone when those reserves were exhausted? Soon gloomy forecasts were once again doing the rounds. Within

Germany a hierarchy of entitlement to what food there was had begun to develop. At the top of the tree were the occupying powers; whoever was starving in Germany in Year Zero, it wasn't the military High Command, which, it was noted, continued to enjoy "stupendous meals." American generals routinely ate two beefsteaks at a single meal. Meanwhile, horses kept for the amusement of British officers were receiving twenty pounds of oats a day, but the moment an underfed German horse collapsed in the streets of Lübeck, it would be butchered on the spot and eaten. The actors in Berlin's theaters were inclined to nod off during the evening performance, having spent their days cycling into the countryside to swap clothing for liver sausage and other rarities, and the theater doctor risked imprisonment to procure vitamin injections for them. The actors also had enforced typhus vaccinations and went on each night shaking with fever.[23]

People resorted to all sorts of stratagems to survive. Josef Rosensaft, the leader of the Central Committee of Liberated Jews in Bergen-Belsen, was in the habit of visiting the camp hospital to cheer the patients up. One day in the autumn of 1945, he noticed three heavyset men lying by themselves in a secluded corner of a ward. Intrigued by their bulk, he went over and greeted them in Yiddish but received only grunts in response. He then asked the doctors who they were and was told that they were Germans with Jewish parents or grandparents who had converted to Judaism in order to become eligible for DP rations. They were now recovering from the circumcision ritual. The rabbi at Belsen had promised each of them an orange. "Tell the rabbi," one said to Rosensaft, "he won't get us to do this again."[24]

For the Attlee government the problems of German civilians were an irritating distraction from more pressing matters. Britain was very nearly bankrupt, having exhausted its foreign reserves and drawn up enormous debts to finance the war, only then for the Lend-Lease arrangements to be abruptly terminated by the Truman administration a week after the end of the war in the Far East, in August 1945. From now on all purchases from the United States would have to be paid for in dollars. Caught unprepared, the British hastily sent John Maynard Keynes to Washington to negotiate a loan to keep them going. But the negotiations proved unexpectedly tough and dragged on. From mid-September to mid-December 1945, the leading members of the British Cabinet spent their evenings poring over the shoals of telegrams sent from Washington. Finally, on December 6, 1945, after "a long process of climbdown and capitulation" on the British side, an agreement was reached. Hugh Dalton, the chancellor of the Exchequer, was in the bath when the telegram announcing the end of negotiations came through. As his official read the details aloud, "Dalton waved, tossed and splashed a large sponge, to express his mixed emotions."[25]

Keynes had originally hoped that it might be possible to persuade the United States to make a free gift of £1.5 billion or, failing that, an interest-free loan of a similar sum. But the Americans took a tough line, conscious that public opinion was against any loan at all to Britain. While offering the British $3.75 billion, plus $650 million granted in final settlement of Lend-Lease, they insisted on an interest rate of 1.6 percent and imposed tough conditions. The British had to sign up for the Americans' vision of postwar economic arrangements by endorsing the Bretton Woods Agreement and, more controversially, to agree to restore convertibility between sterling and the dollar within a year. As many on the British side feared, this later proved to be a time bomb.[26]

Against this background, the British could not afford to occupy Germany at all. But since national prestige demanded that they do so, they tried by every possible means to cut their costs. (As we have seen, fears about the cost of occupation lay behind their wish to see UNRRA play a greater role.) Even so, it would cost them £80 million a year.[27]

No one in the Labour Cabinet shared Victor Gollancz's indulgent attitude toward the former enemy. Attlee, an infantry officer in the First World War, held the traditional anti-German views of the British upper middle class; Bevin had once said of the Germans, "I try to be fair to them but I 'ates them, really"; Dalton had favored "treating Germany much more harshly than in 1919" during the war. They had little interest in what happened in Germany after the war. Attlee visited the British Zone only once, Bevin made a few fleeting stopovers in the country, and even the junior minister responsible for British administration, the former railwayman John Hynd, preferred to stay in London most of the time. This meant that, in practical terms, the British military, not the politicians, was in charge in Germany. Nor could Attlee ignore the strength of British public opinion, especially as anti-German feelings were restoked by the protracted "Belsen trial," which went on through the autumn of 1945. And so the Cabinet publicly dismissed any talk of making the British tighten their belts so that Germans could eat. There was no possibility of making John eat less so that Hans could feed himself, Sir Stafford Cripps told the newsreels. Attlee brusquely dismissed a delegation led by Gollancz and the economist William Beveridge.[28]

What changed their mind was pressure from people on the ground, especially the military. The generals had been discovering a few realities for themselves. Although, in theory, the British had gotten their hands on the great prize by insisting on having as their zone of occupation the industrial area of the Ruhr and northern Germany, the reality in 1945 was rather different—as a contemporary joke acknowledged: the division of Germany, it was said, had given the Americans the landscape, the French the wine, and the British the ruins. The area the British now occupied had never fed itself. Historically, it had relied for most of its food on the breadbasket of Germany, the rich agricultural areas of East Prussia, which had been divided between Poland and the Soviet Union. It could be fed only with food imported from abroad—either from Britain herself or shipped from one of the grain-surplus countries of the world, imported at British expense.

But to let Germany starve might produce another Hitler—or the reverse: communism. In November 1945, the deputy military governor, Sir Brian Robertson, warned of the gravity of the food situation in the Ruhr:

> The ration card is not being met. Instead of 1,550 calories, the Germans are receiving lesser amounts from about 1,200 calories upwards. In some cases they are still able to supplement the ration from their stocks and gardens, but this reserve is dwindling fast now. The people are already losing weight noticeably and getting the yellow look that is a sure indication of pronounced undernourishment.

It was quite fruitless, he added, to conduct campaigns for the reactivation of political life, trade unions, youth movements, and so forth while the food situation was so bad: "The Germans simply will not take interest in these matters at this time." The military governor,

Field Marshal Montgomery, went further, warning the Cabinet that any suspension of imports into Germany would be catastrophic. It would mean "famine conditions to an extent which no civilised people should inflict upon their beaten enemies." He requested a further 800,000 tons of wheat by March 1, 1946, to tide Germany over the winter.[29]

In London, the Cabinet resisted, fearful of the drain on dollars involved and doubtful whether conditions in the British Zone were really as black as current information painted them. But it found that, far from exaggerating the case, Montgomery had actually understated it. "Very serious consequences would follow" unless a million and a half tons of wheat (or flour equivalent) were shipped to Germany over the next eight months.

Where and how was the food to be found? On December 3, 1945, Attlee and his ministers wrestled with this issue. They had already planned to spend valuable dollars on some 375,000 tons, but there was no guarantee that it would all get to Germany unless more shipping could be made available. And that still left the extra million-plus tons to be found; it could come only from the United States. Somehow the foreign secretary must persuade the Americans to provide it—but not until the American loan to Britain had been finalized.[30]

The Americans did provide food, but not enough of it. To keep Germany fed, the British were forced to take desperate measures. In July 1946, the government introduced bread rationing in the United Kingdom, a step which had not been taken during either of the world wars. With current stocks standing at less than eight weeks "in the pipeline," the government had no alternative, John Strachey, the new minister of food, told the House of Commons. Turning to the outlook for Germany, Strachey acknowledged that the dropping of the ration to a thousand calories was having a damaging effect on the population's health but made no promises to restore it to its earlier level. On the contrary, he emphasized the steps which would be necessary simply to maintain it at a thousand calories—the United States would have to ship some 120,000 tons of wheat to the British Zone every month, and Strachey was not sure it would be able to. But there was nothing more the British could do.

We have done our utmost to maintain it. Doing that utmost, has contributed to the necessity of rationing our own bread, and we now feel it necessary to say to our American friends in time, in advance, that we can do no more.[31]

He did not address the question of whether the British Zone, swollen by refugees and denied access to its former food sources in eastern Germany, was an economically viable entity.

EIGHT

Dollars or Death

By September 1945, the agenda was changing in occupied Germany. It was now being realized at the political level that not all the displaced persons would be going home before winter came—and some of them would not be going home at all. Some sort of improved camp system would therefore have to be created out of the improvised assembly centers in which the DPs were congregated—with heating, insulation, sanitation, and winter clothing: a task which the military was neither suited to nor keen to perform, as the Harrison Report had made clear. Therefore, faute de mieux, it would have to be done by the Cinderella organization with the unwieldy name: the United Nations Relief and Rehabilitation Administration.

In the early months of 1945, just as the war was ending, the British had tried to make UNRRA work: they had drafted in a boy genius to knock the organization into shape. Robert Jackson was a junior officer in the Australian navy whose fortunes had been transformed by the war: in four years he had gone from being tennis partner of the admiral on Malta to economic overlord of the eastern Mediterranean. The son of a Melbourne businessman, Jackson had excelled academically but been forced by his father's early death to enter the navy, where his ability was quickly recognized by the British commander of the Australian naval squadron. In 1938, he came to the attention of the Admiralty in London by writing a long report arguing that, contrary to the then-accepted doctrine, the island of Malta *could* be defended in a forthcoming war. When it was decided to put this to the test in 1941, Jackson became responsible for organizing supplies and supervising the loading of convoys in England and Alexandria, Egypt. The "aura of heroic accomplishment and unrivalled experience" which soon came to surround him led to his appointment in

November 1941, while not yet thirty, to run the Middle East Supply Center, an organization set up to mobilize the economy of the eastern Mediterranean for the needs of the Allied war effort. Taking advantage of the wartime power vacuum, Jackson became in effect the economic tsar of a vast region. Capable of intense work over long periods, he also proved to have the diplomatic and administrative skills needed to work closely with the military authorities and to coordinate teams of experts of different nationalities and from different disciplines.[1]

By the end of 1944, Jackson's talents were widely recognized; the question was how best to use them. The resident minister in the Mediterranean, Harold Macmillan, wanted to "detach" him from Cairo and make him his economic adviser; in London the Treasury was "holding him in reserve for big things in a few years," the War Office wanted to retain him in "a job where his present experience and contacts are being used," and the Foreign Office "believed Jackson would be used to greatest advantage in a 'field' job which could be found later—e.g. he might be put in charge of displaced persons for Germany and satellites." Instead he was sent to UNRRA.[2]

Jackson began by cleansing the "Augean stables" in UNRRA's Cairo office, which had long been paralyzed by vicious Anglo-American rivalries; among the first to go was the head of UNRRA's Albanian mission, who had commandeered a white stallion on which he planned to enter Tirana. Then Jackson turned his attention to operations in northern Europe. There he found UNRRA to be "still completely unprepared to carry out the task for which it had been created. No policy for any major aspect of its work had been developed," he wrote in a secret report to the British government. The organization was chaotic and the majority of the staff demoralized. So, he asked, was UNRRA worth saving, or should it simply be terminated?[3]

In the end it was decided to try to save it. As the first of the new international bodies, it had symbolic importance, and there was no time to create a new relief organization and get it functioning properly before the winter set in. But if UNRRA were to be saved, it would have to be reorganized. The first priority, Jackson believed, was to clear up "the mess in Europe (taking a chance that the headquarters in Washington would hold together for a little while) and then give attention to the Far East."[4] At the beginning of May 1945, he flew to New York and, over dinner with Herbert Lehman and his wife, Edith, at the Mayflower Hotel, offered his solution—that he take over the London office as Lehman's personal representative and turn it into the center of the European operation. Lehman was initially reluctant. The intention had been to use Jackson to stiffen UNRRA's central management in Washington, not in London; besides, it would mean Lehman delegating his authority to a young man, half his age, whom he scarcely knew. But he and Jackson got on, and, boldly, Lehman agreed to the scheme.[5]

Jackson's impact was immediate. His "effect on UNRRA" had been "electric," Lord Halifax reported from Washington on May 5, 1945; he had "amazingly woken up UNRRA" within a very short time. Jackson identified nine key positions which had to be filled— including a long-term successor to himself in the London office and men of proven administrative talent to run UNRRA's displaced persons work in Europe. He fired several members of UNRRA's London office, brought it together in one location, and used his contacts within government to put official pressure on the War Office to make outstanding military administrators available to UNRRA.[6]

But this all took months. In the meantime, Jackson's work at the higher levels had no immediate impact on the ground.

Throughout the summer of 1945, UNRRA struggled to meet its commitments, trying to honor the foolish promise made to the military to put into the field 450 welfare teams to handle displaced persons. Its task was hampered by the London office's failure, after the agreement with the military had been reached in November 1944, to establish an effective field organization in France and Germany; by the poor quality of many of the staff hired early on; and by the military itself. The result, one UNRRA welfare worker thought, was a "complete lack of administrative planning coupled with incessant rushing."[7]

Without a logistic infrastructure of its own, UNRRA was dependent on the military for transport, food, and supplies and frequently found itself in the role of the "kicked-around stepchild." "The trouble is that the military authorities, while paying lip service to UNRRA's noble aims and work, are not really prepared, except in exceptional circumstances, to cooperate more than they feel is absolutely necessary," a journalist noted. The UNRRA team which Lorna Hay of *Picture Post* accompanied into Germany in August 1945 "was gradually but insidiously made to feel that it was nobody's baby, that nobody quite expected it, and that it was rather a bore that it should have arrived at all, and should have to be given billets." Consequently, it was no wonder that when an UNRRA team began to work in the field, "it sometimes feels discouraged, inferiority complexes develop, national differences which simply did not exist when they were all full of hope and energy begin to peep out, and threats of resignation are offered."[8]

There were a few UNRRA liaison officers attached to the military commands, but in practice they could achieve very little. UNRRA's man at SHAEF, an ineffectual Canadian who had once been a major in the Judge Advocate's office, never commanded any status in the military hierarchy and did not even have an office or telephone of his own; so it was hardly surprising that he did not know where any of the UNRRA teams were and was not consulted or even informed when UNRRA officers were in effect relieved of their job. A vicious circle soon developed. UNRRA units in the field performed poorly, in large part because of lack of support from the military, yet it was UNRRA which received the blame; as a result, its standing with the military sank and the morale of its staff declined further.[9]

In February 1945, UNRRA had established in Granville and Jullouville, two seaside towns in Normandy, a continental base from which to assemble, train, and send into the field the 450 displaced persons teams which the military had asked it to provide. The idea was that recruits from Britain, the United States, and Europe would be brought together there and then dispatched to Germany.

The American volunteers had already undergone an eight-week course in College Park, Maryland, which some found enlightening and informative but others felt was too theoretical and vague— "lectures about displaced persons given by people who had never seen one." The British (and most of the continentals) had taken a similar course at Reading, where Will Arnold-Forster had done his best to instill the spirit of international cooperation into them; again, some were inspired while others talked of "idealistic chatter."[10]

The makeup of the continentals (who provided the bulk of the staff taken on in 1945) remains somewhat unclear—the Americans, as we have seen, were often New Deal professionals; the British, mostly army officers and welfare veterans. The UNRRA history claims that some European countries used jobs with the organization "to better the condition of some of their citizens" and the French to reward those with experience in their Resistance. In the French case, it adds, "the Administration was injured by the employment of a large proportion of unsuitable individuals." UNRRA instructors found the French "a strange mixture," including "outstanding persons who considered UNRRA a mission," a group of fifty young doctors mobilized by the government who were "sulky about their work that faced them," inexperienced girls in their twenties, and women in their fifties without obvious qualifications. The Belgians, Dutch, Danes, and Norwegians, however, were thought to be "quite good."[11]

Whatever their nationality, the recruits' idealism was soon put to the test. The center in France had been established at a time when it was "literally impossible to secure qualified labour in any category and, as a result eighty people with few qualifications" were sent to staff it. Two retired British officers presided over what everyone, regardless of nationality, agreed to be "the most inefficiently operated undertaking they had ever seen anywhere at any time," "with muddles and inefficiency from top to bottom." In Granville itself, a grand hotel fallen on hard times served as UNRRA's headquarters, while five miles to the south, in Jullouville, a "bleak and rather squalid" portable wooden barracks, occupied by the U.S. Army and then stripped by the French, housed the training center. The American women could not get used to the absence of toilet seats.[12]

The food, however, was good. But that in itself caused problems. At one point the kitchens had to be closed to stop the French chefs pilfering provisions. Moreover, the free availability of food also undermined the table manners of UNRRA's continental staff. "At the immense mess tables," an American later recalled, "the Europeans were like starvelings, gobbling up the U.S. Army white bread, jams and butter not tasted in five years, tearing into their meat like wolves, cornering platters and refusing to pass them on the pretext of not understanding the applicant's language—a mass national hunger that had to be appeased before any such lofty concept as international humanitarianism could be entertained. . . . If the torch I carried wobbled a bit in the first days," she added, "it was only from astonishment."[13]

Supplies had to be transported a distance of some eighty miles, from military dumps at the ports of Cherbourg and Carentan, which, as no one had thought to enforce discipline or security, provided more rich pickings for the local black market. "In a country bereft of economy and devastated by war, as France was in 1945, unguarded supplies and lack of security control in any department provided a fertile field for racketeers, one they accepted with alacrity." When a group of American students took over the driving, they found, on their first trip to collect rations, that "gangs were waiting on the way to receive the goods; cases were thrown from one truck to be picked up by the next; trucks were abandoned by their drivers." On one occasion, some two hundred lorries were sent over from England to Le Havre and more than a hundred French drivers went over to get them. Fewer than half ever appeared at Granville.[14]

The trucks were provided by the British as part of their UNRRA contribution and had all done many years' service in the Western Desert and other battlefields. They were parked in fields at Granville, and the local French were free to cannibalize them at will. By mid-summer 1945, 1,100 vehicles of all types were "spread-eagled over two large fields, without a semblance of control or protection." There were no records, fewer than a hundred of them were in running condition, and a Canadian sent over to sort out the mess found that "there was not a single screwdriver, tool or spare part on the base." In July and August 1945, the U.S. Army Criminal Investigation Department (CID) had four investigators at Granville looking into huge black-market operations on the part of the base staff personnel. It was reported that at that time at least 127 trucks were missing and probably more, together with huge supplies of food and clothing.[15]

But the real problems were delay and the incompetence with which the UNRRA management at Granville selected teams and sent them off to work in Germany. For six weeks, forty fully trained teams waited at the mobilization center because seventy tons of their equipment was sitting on the dockside in Britain and UNRRA's man at SHAEF could not get it moved. Consequently, "to many British and American UNRRA officers the names Granville and Jullouville are synonymous with frustration," Francesca Wilson wrote a year later. "They remember them for their empty days, with nothing to do but scan notice-boards to see if they had been 'teamed up' and for the impotent envy they felt for those who had." To find some way of occupying UNRRA teams, volunteers who had already undergone training in Britain and the United States were made to go through it all over again. Recruits were "at a loss to understand why another such period had to be undergone at the base; they wanted to get on with the job and saw no logical reason for delay." In June 1945, Herbert Lehman admitted to Congressman Everett Dirksen that there were 1,500 UNRRA personnel at Granville who were "drawing pay, subsistence and rations and who were doing nothing." When Dirksen asked why, he replied, "We are not getting cooperation from the military." Dirksen was amazed that an organization could "camp 1500 people in a little town in France and not know in advance."[16]

It was nearly two months before May Bingham, an eager young Canadian, was assigned; countless others were similarly treated. Granville was not a good place to linger, having become a "cesspool of blackmarketing, thieving and even immorality." Arriving there, May was "impressed by the obvious overcrowding, queuing for meals, bad food, filthy billets and undrinkable water." "Why on earth did you come here?" a young British UNRRA staffer asked her. "You should have side-tracked the base and gone direct to Germany. You'll be here for weeks." He was quite happy to stay himself. "The swimming is good, weather wonderful, one can have fun; it's a cheap holiday, if you haven't a conscience of course. There's little not obtainable for a packet of Luckies." May was horrified. Not surprisingly, "many of UNRRA's potentially best field personnel were reported as having resigned before they had even been deployed," and a journalist visiting Granville found herself approached by irate UNRRA personnel who asked her to "expose" the organization and told extraordinary stories about the rackets going on with UNRRA supplies. Lorna Hay was "astonished to see how even people with quite senior posts in the UNRRA administration approached me, knowing perfectly well I was a journalist, and told me long tales of dishonesty and inefficiency."[17]

Some people, though, enjoyed their interlude in Normandy. Francesca Wilson noticed that "there was an overweight of Indian and Colonial army men."

> Sitting in the lounge or bar of the Hotel Normandie, one heard many nostalgic stories about the regiment, the North-West Frontier and Poona, and one wondered how they would get on with the Russian and Polish "natives" in Germany. . . . A few, whose morale

had been corroded by the austerities of war-time London after a life in the tropics, found too much for them the sudden jump to a country where you could get calvados (the potent Normandy spirit), at seven o'clock in the morning, in the local café. In time they got their bowler hats—it was their own rueful expression. They disappeared noiselessly.

Others seemed to have joined UNRRA looking for adventure. A Polish welfare worker noticed "old spinsters who were never before looked upon as women—now with the hunger for women they were booked for weeks and were in a state of sexual dizziness, wanting to make up in the shortest time for 20 or 30 years of unfulfilled desire."[18]

The chaos at Granville was eventually sorted out by Anne Laughlin, a tough lady from Topeka, Kansas, who took over there on August 6, 1945. Her position was difficult because many ex–army officers resented serving under an American woman, but she proved "a loyal and inspiring leader [who] had the gift of attracting honest people who were devoted to her" and eventually managed to eliminate drunkenness and misconduct and establish discipline and order. According to the UNRRA history, "Her courage and shrewd administering . . . coupled with an iron constitution contributed so largely to the ultimate successes . . . she achieved."[19]

The shambles at Granville was just one of the problems that confronted Robert Jackson from his office in London. To turn UNRRA into an efficient relief organization, he needed to install competent management, create an effective field organization in Europe, and win the cooperation of the Allied military, without which nothing was possible. The medical services were a particular problem.

Health care was meant to be central to UNRRA's role. Its manifestos had boldly promised "an emergency international health service for displaced persons," providing medical teams in every assembly center and specialist medical care at the regional levels. Every displaced person would be medically examined and given a medical clearance certificate before being repatriated; appropriate food and medicines would be available to the young, the elderly, the sick, and pregnant women; welfare officers would provide comfort and entertainment; while mobile mass radiography units would monitor the levels of tuberculosis so as to alert the health authorities in the DPs' home countries. Venereal disease, it was hoped, would be treated with penicillin made available by the military.[20]

It hadn't turned out quite like that; because of its recruiting problems, UNRRA was particularly short of medical staff, and, although field teams were supposed to consist of thirteen people, including a doctor and a nurse, in practice they often became "spearhead teams" of seven people, without trained medical personnel. In June 1945, UNRRA had put only 205 such teams into the field instead of the promised 450, each with a doctor and nurse. Its medical chief blamed this on "the failure of subscribing governments to provide the necessary supplies, shipping and manpower" and of the military to overcome problems of transport and supply. The unwillingness of governments to ensure that medical expertise was made available forced UNRRA to cast its recruiting net very wide. The best hope seemed to lie in neutral countries such as Ireland, Sweden, and Switzerland.[21]

The lack of an administrative structure meant that UNRRA in London was unable to monitor the movements of its teams; they simply vanished into Germany. "Nary a body have I seen in the way of UNRRA nursing staff," an Australian matron noted eighteen days after arriving in Germany and after sending many an SOS both to London and to local headquarters. UNRRA's shortcomings made the military reluctant to collaborate with it and keen to continue its old associations. "The Army will not make up its mind to let the dear old Red Cross out at its appointed time," a Red Cross worker at Belsen noted at the end of August. "UNRRA ('You never really rehabilitate anyone' as it is called) is failing lamentably," she added. "High pay and people with no ideals" were to blame, she thought. On the other hand, the politicians were putting on pressure in favor of UNRRA, and the military was worried that there might be further epidemics—which it was not keen to deal with. If, as Jackson hoped, UNRRA (and not the British Red Cross) were to be given charge of the refugee crisis in British-occupied Germany, he urgently needed an expert in epidemic control. It was at that moment that Sir Raphael Cilento walked into his office.[22]

Sir Raphael seemed just what was needed—a distinguished Australian public health official, knighted in 1935 for his work on tropical hygiene but currently out of a job. Appointed to run UNRRA's campaign against malaria in the Balkans, working out of Egypt, he had started from Australia, only to find, by the time he had arrived in Cairo, that UNRRA's office there had been abolished by Robert Jackson. So after a brief attempt to muscle in on UNRRA's medical work in Greece, Cilento had wangled his way onto a London plane and come to see the new power in UNRRA, Commander Jackson. He was promptly offered the post of chief medical officer in Germany. Next, Jackson got General Templer, the head of the British military government in Germany, reluctantly to allow UNRRA to take over from the army certain medical duties, including the running of the hospital at Belsen. But Templer specified that UNRRA must establish itself in Germany within a fortnight; otherwise the British Red Cross would be given the job.

For the next ten days Cilento went mad with frustration as a bureaucratic catch-22 developed. UNRRA in London would not release to him the supplies and transport he needed until the appropriate military orders were received, while the military claimed to have sent the forms. Eventually, Cilento decided to "ditch channels" and take direct action. He rustled up staff and stole two cars intended for UNRRA's Austrian mission and a nurse bound for Poland. All went well until the last moment:

> As I stood in an office I had "borrowed" (and had twice been requested to vacate), looking over last minute details, the telephone rang and a female voice demanded shrilly why I had not filled in the "new transportation form" that had arrived from Washington and had been "issued in orders" that day. I said I had not seen it and that I intended to ignore it. Such sacrilege struck my questioner dumb for a moment—but only for a moment. She concluded by announcing that she was "issuing orders to have us stopped en route." We laughed and left.

Very early the next morning, as Cilento was waiting to board a landing craft at Tilbury, a dispatch rider came up to him and handed him a telegram. Suddenly feeling sick, he opened it. It was a cable from UNRRA, Washington, offering him a job as chief of staff, Ethiopia.

Once in Germany, Cilento's buccaneering approach continued. When the army was slow to provide him with premises, he occupied the small Westphalian village of Spenge and set up his HQ in a *Schloss* there. He then set about consolidating UNRRA's position, using health and welfare as the twin pillars of his strategy. By the time the zones in Germany were finally agreed (and the military government became the Control Commission for Germany) on August 15, 1945, UNRRA was well placed to play a major part on the postwar stage. Unfortunately, Cilento and General Templer took an instant dislike to each other, but Cilento got on well with his boss, Field Marshal Montgomery. At the end of August, Montgomery had Cilento raised to the rank of major general and offered him the job of chief of UNRRA operations in the British Zone of Occupation. Sir Raphael hesitated for a while—his sights were set on the newly launched World Health Organization—before accepting.[23]

By then UNRRA had more than two hundred teams in the field in Germany. But even as the organization finally began to play a bigger role, its very future was cast into doubt. Money and displaced persons dominated the third meeting of the UNRRA Council, held in London between August 7 and 24, 1945. Chastened but defensive, Herbert Lehman announced that the organization needed a fresh tranche of funding, his case dramatized a few days later when the first atomic bomb was dropped on Hiroshima, bringing the Pacific war abruptly to an end. This meant that UNRRA's long-planned program of relief in China and the Far East would have to swing into action much sooner than expected. To meet the new situation, the U.S. State Department proposed, and the British reluctantly accepted, that a further levy of 1 percent of national income, generating about $1.8 billion, would be needed. (Many of UNRRA's member countries had yet to come up with their first payment.)

Before the meeting, however, the Soviet Union and its allies launched a two-pronged offensive. On the issue of displaced persons, the Yugoslavs submitted a resolution which questioned UNRRA's authority both to "assist displaced persons in ex–enemy areas without the agreement of the country of which the displaced persons were nationals" and to "assist displaced persons who did not wish to be repatriated." To do so, Soviet Foreign Minister Vyacheslav Molotov argued separately, was counter to past UNRRA resolutions: "As an organization of the United Nations governments, UNRRA should not put itself in opposition to the United Nations governments." At the same time, in the second initiative, the Russians submitted a request for $700 million in relief payments from UNRRA on behalf of the republics of Ukraine and Belorussia.

These moves alarmed U.S. diplomats; they threatened the areas of UNRRA's work that were popular with Congress and the American public, while expanding yet further the liability of the U.S. taxpayer. The Yugoslav proposal, if accepted, "would mean that UNRRA could not assist German and Polish Jews who do not wish to return to their home countries." Equally, the Russians might block the expansion of UNRRA's program in Italy to something like $500 million, which was near to the hearts of many Americans but arguably well outside UNRRA's remit. Within the State Department it was accepted that there was no way that Congress would ever cough up $700 million for the Russians. But what about a lesser sum? James F. Byrnes, the secretary of state, felt that the Russians had already had "vast assistance" from the United States and dismissed as "ideological" their argument that "they are entitled to relief because of the greatness of their sufferings and contribution to victory." He thought it perfectly possible for the Russians to get loan credits from the United States without going through UNRRA. W. Averell Harriman, the ambassador in Moscow, agreed. Increasingly disillusioned with working with the Soviets, Harriman argued that there was no real food shortage in the USSR, especially as the Red Army was milking the territories it had occupied in Eastern Europe. But other American diplomats argued that Russia's need for relief was great and her moral case for receiving it as good as that of China, Czechoslovakia, Poland, and Greece (all of which were getting UNRRA aid) and very much greater than Italy's.[24]

These issues aggravated relations between the victorious Allies of East and West. The discussion about displaced persons who were unwilling to return home was particularly acrimonious. The Soviet Union, backed by Yugoslavia, Poland, and Czechoslovakia, was intransigent, while the United States, Britain, and Canada argued that "UNRRA should not be used as a political instrument to coerce refugees to return to their native lands against their will." In the end, deft work by the Canadian diplomat Lester Pearson produced an uneasy compromise. Resolution 71 permitted UNRRA to give help to refugees without the prior consent of their national governments but, at the same time, laid down that every effort should be made to encourage repatriation. The situation would be reviewed in six months.[25]

But it was the Soviet request for UNRRA aid that provided the real drama. The principal American delegate, Under Secretary of State William Clayton, could not oppose all UNRRA assistance to the Russians, particularly as the Canadians were in favor; that would have been to risk the future of UNRRA and a serious diplomatic defeat. But he found the Russians to be very tough bargainers, insisting on their full request for $700 million right until the last session. Privately they made it clear that the contrast between the American attitude to Italy and Austria—two former enemies—and its former Soviet ally was intolerable and threatened to bring this point before the UNRRA Council, thus exposing Allied disunity. According to the State Department, Clayton "became convinced that the Soviet Union would break up UNRRA, by forcing some form of Council action on its proposal, and by vigorously opposing the Italian action which was essential to Congressional approval of the additional contribution to UNRRA, unless some trade was made." And so a trade-off was made. The Americans managed to find $250 million for the Soviet republics out of the funds of UNRRA— "including the additional one percent contribution—without reducing other programs and giving Italy and China the amounts we had proposed."[26]

In another Great Power stitch-up, the Soviet Union allowed UNRRA to continue its work with DPs in return for substantial UNRRA programs to Poland, Yugoslavia, Belorussia, and Ukraine. The Americans felt they had done a reasonable job in the circumstances. "We did protect all of the UNRRA principles, saved UNRRA, and at the same time achieved an understanding with Russia whereby her continued pressure for additional aid from UNRRA should be entirely eliminated and her request very substantially cut down," Dean Acheson wrote to Harriman. But this experience left a bitter taste in Will Clayton's mouth. From now on, he was no friend of UNRRA.[27]

At the same time, Resolution 71, the vaguely worded agreement on DP operations reached in London, did not provide a clear direction on how the policy was to be applied in the field in Europe. It left much leeway for individual interpretation, and that in turn would lead to a considerable degree of confrontation throughout the DP operations in Europe.[28]

· · ·

On Saturday, September 1, 1945, Lieutenant General Sir Frederick Morgan received a letter from the War Office offering him a senior post with UNRRA. The following Monday, he saw Ernest Bevin, the foreign secretary, who was "brief and to the point," telling Morgan that he wished him to take charge of UNRRA's displaced persons operation in Germany and Western Europe. The general accepted at once—it seemed to him a job that had to be done. But could he count on the minister's support? he asked. He was assured that not only Bevin but the entire British government would support him. The foreign secretary explained his concerns. "Basically, of course, he was looking at things from the domestic British viewpoint," Morgan recorded in his diary.

> His chief fear was of an outbreak of epidemic amongst Displaced Persons in Europe which might rapidly reach the United Kingdom, get amongst the working people and so interfere disastrously with our industrial production. We parted on terms of some cordiality.

For the next few days, Morgan was briefed on his job by the acting head of UNRRA's London office, Commander Robert Jackson. The young Australian struck him as "tired and overwrought to the point almost of hysteria," having "over-worked almost to breaking point"; but, Morgan wrote, "he has achieved miracles in UNRRA." Morgan's recruitment was the climax of months of work (and Whitehall pressure) by Jackson to bring experienced military administrators to UNRRA. After several disappointments, he had secured General Humfrey Gale, Eisenhower's head of logistics, to run the London office. Now Morgan was his latest catch.[29]

"Freddie" Morgan was certainly a prize for UNRRA. Known as "the man who planned D-Day," he had done the preliminary planning for Operation Overlord before Montgomery took over (and heavily revised the plan) and had then served very harmoniously on Eisenhower's staff at SHAEF, where he was widely respected. "He considered Eisenhower as a god," Montgomery wrote of Morgan. "Since I had discarded many of his plans, he placed me at the other end of the celestial ladder." Morgan was "a tall cheerful soldier with a fresh complexion and blue eyes" who concealed a sharp mind behind a good deal of charm and a droll sense of humor.[30]

Morgan flung himself into his new task. After several days of meetings in London, he flew to Germany with Jackson and Gale to assess the situation on the ground, giving "joint performances" to UNRRA staff. His easy relations with his old American colleagues at SHAEF were at once apparent—he was repeatedly plied with drinks and beefsteaks and had no difficulty in cadging cars and airplanes from the military to supplement UNRRA's primitive logistics. Among the British military, too, he moved with ease. He was, though, unimpressed by some of the UNRRA staff and noticed that Cilento thought that "the Army is trying to do UNRRA down." It was clear that there had been "considerable feeling as between the British authorities and UNRRA. Certain of the exchanges between General Templer and Sir Raphael Cilento were pretty brisk."

There were also a couple of brief meetings with displaced persons themselves. Morgan found the Baltic DPs at a camp in Wiesbaden "the most charming people" but, after a couple of hours in their company, could "see very clearly the sickening, demoralising effect on the individual and on the family group of the complete absence of any coherent, positive policy up above." Elsewhere, he saw the looming problem of converting the flimsy huts that many DPs were currently living in for the coming winter.

Back in London for the last fortnight of September, Morgan struggled to clarify his task while mobilizing UNRRA's cumbersome machinery toward it. It was clear from Jackson that two immediate hurdles lay ahead: securing further funding for UNRRA from the U.S. Congress and reaching agreement with the Allied military in Germany on UNRRA's role; he was warned of the "difficulties and prospects" on account of Montgomery's role. And beyond that? The British government was not very helpful, not having the time to engage with the problem. It clearly had the "wind-up," a "vague fear of epidemic, unrest and so on," which it associated more with displaced persons than with expelled Germans.[31]

Morgan tried to sort the position out for himself. There were still around a million DPs in Germany and Austria, but he believed that more than half of them were comparatively easily repatriable and were being repatriated as fast as transportation and administration allowed.

Almost everything depends on the solution of the Polish problem. If the Poles agree to go home, and there is every likelihood that the vast majority of them will, the whole thing is comparatively simple.

There would, of course, still remain a "hard core" of the stateless and those who for obvious reasons, political and criminal and so forth, could not be repatriated, an estimated quarter of a million people. They would have to be "rounded up" in convenient locations for maintenance and administration until an organization had been created to take them over from UNRRA.

Morgan was quite clear that the whole UNRRA machine was "too vast and cumbersome for the task." Somebody, somewhere had gotten the thing out of all proportion. He confidently looked forward to gaining "tremendous kudos" by advocating enormous cuts in staff which would save the British government millions of pounds a year. While in London he also tried to prepare himself for the task. He wanted to address the "moral atmosphere" of the DP camps by giving the DPs something useful to do:

> [What] we must try to do is to bring out that which is inherent in our DPs rather than to superimpose anything on them from outside . . . there is little we can do for them materially, beyond the bare essentials of existence. We must therefore exploit the spiritual field.

To that end, he had a series of meetings with cultural figures such as the art historian Sir Kenneth Clark and a representative of the British Council. Nothing concrete emerged, but on September 29, as he flew to Germany to take up his job, Morgan struck an almost ecstatic note:

> I have the sensation that I have got something terrific by the tail. What exactly it is I still have no idea but I wouldn't be in the least surprised if once again the initiative didn't rest with me personally. Sticking out everywhere there is abundant evidence of immense goodwill, of realisation of an impending crisis and of desire for a sign of some kind. I wonder if my arrival may not be that sign. I feel it is up to me to try to make it so.[32]

By early November 1945, Robert Jackson felt that he had gotten UNRRA's London office, from which its European operations were run, sufficiently back on its feet to hand it over to General Sir Humfrey Gale. So Jackson went to Washington, to the job he had been hired to do as Herbert Lehman's deputy. But a fortnight later, he sent a confidential letter to the British government, warning that UNRRA faced its second major crisis: it was about to run out of money, and its Washington office was in chaos.

Under the formula agreed at Atlantic City in November 1943, UNRRA received 1 percent of the gross national product of its contributing members, which meant that the British, for example, had made a first payment of £80 million in January 1944 and a further £75 million in October 1945. But the United States was the main paymaster, providing 72 percent of the funds, and although Congress had authorized the first 1 percent payment, totalling $1.35 billion, back in March 1944 and the first installment of $800 million had been made in June 1944, in the autumn of 1945 UNRRA had yet to receive the second installment of the *first* tranche, the remaining $550 million. However, in the summer and autumn of 1945, UNRRA's expenditure had escalated rapidly as it began to operate in Italy, Greece, Poland, and Belorussia; and the unexpectedly sudden ending of the Pacific war had also brought its promised relief program in China into play and further strained its finances. The only way to keep UNRRA going was, therefore, immediately to get authorization for the *second* tranche of U.S. money. Thus it was that in November 1945 Congress was simultaneously holding two sets of hearings—one on the *second* installment of the *first* American tranche of $1.35 billion and another on the *first* installment of the *second* American tranche of $1.35 billion. With luck the first payment would be available to UNRRA by early December, which could be too late for the administration to make the best use of funds. Already, badly needed supplies were having to be frozen. This was, by any reckoning, bad politics and poor management.[33]

Jackson was angry that Lehman's staff had failed to monitor the situation—"the really desperate state of UNRRA's finances was not disclosed as early as it should have been"—and had not mobilized American public opinion; but the blame for the situation really lay with the governor himself. At least seven members of staff should be sacked immediately, argued Jackson, but, "mindful of his own political future," Lehman was not prepared to move any of them. "Over the next four weeks," Jackson concluded, "we have to win not one but two political battles. We intend to attack, however, using every possible argument and political manoeuvre—we have little to lose and everything to gain. Basically, it is matter of dollars or death for many people in Europe."[34]

The growing opposition on Capitol Hill was apparent in a debate on October 31. Uncle Sam was paying 72 cents of every UNRRA dollar, a thousand times what the Soviet Union was contributing, yet had only one vote on the UNRRA Council. Representative Frederick C. Smith, a Republican from Ohio, compared in great detail the salaries paid and results achieved after the two wars and concluded that UNRRA should be abolished forthwith. It had never been intended as a relief organization but to lay the foundation stone for an international governmental body. There were plenty of people capable of managing a real program of relief, he said, "who would be glad to take the job and do it gratis, as was done in World War I. And the right man could get all the volunteers he needs to help him in this work, as was done in the other war." UNRRA had been foisted on the United States and was now "an international racket of the first water," said others, "a great bottomless barrel for the diversion of relief and rehabilitation supplies for the sustenance of armies or political groups in Europe." It was accused of waste, overmanning, and corruption and of being the tool of Communist governments in Eastern Europe.

Few speakers defended the organization, but several admitted there was now no alternative. Illinois Republican Rolla C. McMillen stated:

> I hold no brief for UNRRA. It has made inexcusable mistakes. There is however, no other available organization now to carry on the necessary relief and rehabilitation for the cold months to come among these people. We must use this organization as best we can to rescue them from misery and death this winter.

Massachusetts Republican Richard B. Wigglesworth also supported the appropriation only because it was impossible to substitute any other agency which could contribute to the situation that winter. It was too late to make a change. Daniel J. Flood of Pennsylvania warned:

Hunger, destitution, sickness and disease will breed unrest and the specter of communism. Hungry people are fertile fields for the philosophies of the anti-Christ and for those who would make God of the omnipotent state.

The powerful Republican Everett Dirksen acknowledged that Robert Jackson's arrival had made a difference:

> He is a fine gentleman and a pretty good businessman . . . under his guidance and by his efforts there has been a measurable improvement in the administrative techniques of UNRRA, but we still have a long way to go.[35]

One of the few members of Congress to give UNRRA unequivocal support was Helen Gahagan Douglas, a liberal Democrat from California. Having recently returned from a tour of the DP camps, she believed there were "reasons other than altruism why we must ensure UNRRA's success."

> We won the war at great cost, but we can throw away the victory if we do not see that an orderly world emerges from the destruction. If we abandon these recently liberated peoples before their normal economies are functioning again, we deliver them in a sense to the leaders of violence and revolution.

Many members of Congress remained unconvinced that the internationalist approach was the right one. The bad publicity UNRRA had been getting had not helped matters. Critics such as Herbert Hoover were becoming vocal again, and UNRRA's supposed friends kept silent.[36]

Jackson and Lehman set to work on Capitol Hill. Lehman took the Democrats, Jackson, the Republicans. Their most potent weapon was General Eisenhower, newly returned from Europe. Now a five-star general with a chestful of medals, Eisenhower testified before Congress, speaking warmly of UNRRA's work in Europe and, more important, making it quite clear that the army had no wish to do UNRRA's job—an idea which had recently been touted by Hoover. In addition, the pope and the Catholic hierarchy in the United States declared their support. Reluctantly, in mid-December 1945, Congress voted UNRRA the two tranches of funding it needed to survive—in effect a year's reprieve. It was noticeable, however, that the organization received only token support from the Truman administration.

Meanwhile, in Germany, UNRRA had been formalizing its relationship with the military. After long negotiations, in which the friendships General Morgan had built up over many years served him well, agreements were reached. UNRRA would take over the running of the DP camps but would remain dependent on the military for law and order, security and transport. Right to the end, the British military governor, Field Marshal Montgomery, had opposed this move, considering UNRRA to be "quite unable" to do the job. But when Ernest Bevin spelled it out to him—"Britain has not got the dollars," he told Monty—he was persuaded to accept.[37]

On November 27, 1945, in a short ceremony at his headquarters (yet another *Schloss* in another picturesque Westphalian village), Montgomery signed the British agreement. Morgan noticed with glee how much his old enemy had aged and how keen he was to broach the gin bottle at 11 A.M. According to Cilento, Montgomery harangued them first.

> "You know this refugee business is becoming a nonsense, and will soon be very difficult, indeed very difficult. I am particularly worried by all the sentimentality that seems to be invading it—an overseas element, I think, I think," he added, cocking an eye a little mischievously at Morgan.
>
> "Understand me," he continued, "you have asked for it and you've got it. I agree that it is really a civilian matter—but it must not lag, it must not lag! In handing over to this civilian organization of yours, I want to say, very definitely, that every refugee must be out of Germany by April the first—and there is no joke in that date."[38]

Similar agreements regularizing UNRRA's relations with the military in the American and French zones were signed in early 1946.

But even as UNRRA's financial future was being assured and its relations with the military formalized, its director of displaced persons operations was having a crisis of faith. General Morgan's doubts had begun on his first trip to Germany, when he had been greeted by his many friends serving at U.S. Forces HQ, which had now taken over from SHAEF the great IG Farben building in Frankfurt. "What in God's name do you think you're at mixing yourself up in a god-damned racket of this sort?" one of them asked. The American told Morgan how, under the New Deal, "a vast business of unproduction known as the Works Progress Administration" had been set up, whose business was "the engagement of more and more individuals in less and less productive work. For people who for years had been engaged upon activities of which the most substantial could be described as nebulous, UNRRA came as dollars from heaven."[39]

Morgan's faith was further sapped by the sheer difficulty in getting anything done in UNRRA. For all Jackson's efforts to streamline the London office, it remained vast and inefficient, with rival bureaucracies competing to tie one another up in red tape. "We have got the whole thing wrong somewhere," Morgan wrote. "The whole machine seems much too vast and cumbersome for the task it is to perform." He found the internal culture of UNRRA quite alien: endless discussions, people taking initiatives on their own or making headlines in the papers; yet no discipline, hierarchy, or confidentiality. "None of the juniors seem to have any sort of regard for the seniors," he complained in his diary, "and in the absence of any sort of code of discipline, the simplest and most straightforward thing is quite absurdly difficult owing to the failure of organisation and failure to assume command."[40]

Morgan tried to impose his own methods. "I managed this morning to restrict my meeting to one hour of the clock. I can see I must do this by force until I get the personnel trained in military habits of brevity," he wrote on October 4, 1945. But he had only partial success. Two weeks later, "at intervals during the day, crises continued to arise of various descriptions." Petrol supply had failed in the French Zone, and there was a real threat that all of UNRRA's vehicles would grind to a halt: "One can only hope that something will turn up. I can't for the moment think what on earth this will be." In early November, he was horrified to find that "practically no supplies are on their way to us, owing to some absurd technical argument." A few days later, "for some reason that I shall never be able to fathom, today was regarded as a holiday by my headquarters." (It was Veterans Day in the United States.) "It is unthinkable to me that one should even contemplate taking five minutes off the job that we have in hand that simply must be done by next mid-summer. The attitude of these people in relation to hours of work, holidays and so forth just goes to show the rottenness of outlook of most of them."[41]

Then there were the scandals. UNRRA's chief in the American Zone brought him "a simply shocking tale of woe. I never heard anything like it even in the worst days of the British Army after the last war—not only dishonesty to an unbelievable degree, but also stories of the most sordid kind of vice which seems to be rampant among our employees."[42]

And there were the women. Morgan was not a womanizer, but he liked women and liked having them on his staff. They usually liked him—he was tall, handsome, and charming. But he preferred women of a certain kind, who fitted into the molds he was used to: British army officer's wife, Red Cross worker, and so on. Thus he found Marjorie Bradford, a Canadian nurse who handled the voluntary agencies, "a most capable girl [who] clearly has the whole of her business completely taped"; the glamorous Gitta Sereny was "a remarkable girl, originally a Hungarian of the upper class and now a Yank . . . one of the type of which UNRRA or anything like it should be exclusively composed"; and he always found time to listen to the lamentations of Hansi Pollak, a doe-eyed, warmhearted Czech/South African Jewess who struggled to organize welfare in Germany. Finally, Morgan was totally enraptured by two soignée young French girls who ran the Baltic DP camp at Junkers, near Kassel:

> Both had perfect poise. Miss Tabard could be glacially polite in the manner of the most sophisticated grand dame, and she could be the gum-chewing officer on active service speaking pure, or at least unexpurgated, GI English as the occasion demanded. No military inspecting officer, with one unfortunate exception at the end of their stay, ever failed to succumb to their charm and their technique in handling visitors.

On the other hand, "welfare queens"—domineering American career women—turned him right off. And UNRRA was full of them— middle-aged American women with loud voices and accents like sandpaper who had trained in social work under the New Deal and thought they knew everything and held forth about everything. So, although Anne Laughlin from Kansas had done a "magnificent job" and "nearly killed herself" in transforming UNRRA's training center, Morgan declined to have her to stay in his house in Germany, fearing a "flood of voluminous American" and "the usual garbled diatribe about everything in general and most things in particular."[43]

But his real bête noire was Mary Gibbons, who had worked on large-scale public welfare in New York City and was now in charge of relief services in UNRRA's London office. "There is no doubt she is a highly intelligent woman and knows her stuff," he wrote. "But it is always pathetic to me to see a woman trying somehow to ape the man. Attempts to emulate the high-powered executive just don't work somehow and the woman instead of, as she would wish, appearing masterful, is just plain ridiculous." Morgan's diaries intermittently develop a critique of UNRRA's whole welfare program, arguing that the American women who mainly ran it were diverting resources away from mundane, useful work into more high-profile, emotionally satisfying areas.[44]

As a result of all these frustrations, Morgan found it very difficult to conceal his own feelings toward the organization he was working for. "You trainee people must have heard some frightful things of what goes on in UNRRA," he told a newly arrived group of UNRRA recruits on October 28. "Most of them are true."[45]

The most satisfying part of Morgan's job was the field trips. Amid all his other concerns, he tried to visit as many DP camps as possible, cruising down the autobahn in a large Packard acquired from the U.S. Army.

When it came to the different DP groups, Morgan's sympathies were clear. Like most British soldiers and relief workers in Germany, he felt a strong—almost racial—affinity with the "Balts," the Lithuanians, Latvians, and Estonians. Of course, he knew whose side they had been on in the war, but he couldn't go to a Baltic DP camp or eat one of those "exquisite" Estonian meals without feeling an instinctive sympathy for them. They were educated, well-dressed people, often middle class, many speaking perfect English, with their families intact. The men were handsome, their womenfolk blond and beautiful; their camps were clean, well-organized places run by the inmates' elected representatives, with every available inch of space put to good use growing flowers and vegetables; the children were properly taught; the women produced beautiful textiles; and, to cap it all, their choirs sang brilliantly. The Balts, Morgan wrote, were "simply charming people."[46]

But he despised the Poles. Most of the Poles in German DP camps in 1945 were peasants and industrial workers who had been taken as slave laborers to Germany and had there been degraded and brutalized. Their camps were not renowned for their industry, internal democracy, sobriety, chastity, or cleanliness. "I went into a camp the other day full of Poles," Morgan told a group of UNRRA trainees in October 1945, "and honest to goodness that place smelt rather what I imagine a zoological garden would smell like after the animals had been dead for a fortnight." "One saw how almost hopeless the Pole is," he wrote after visiting another camp. "These people were just sitting about and had been sitting about for months without doing anything at all, and they all made trivial complaints with regard to the food, which I thought was ample and very good. . . . It is clear to me that the situation with regard to clothing, shoes, and blankets is already serious, and, if these people do not, in fact, go back to Poland this winter it is already critical." But by December 1945, it was pretty clear that most of the Poles, increasingly worried by the way things were going in their country, would not be going back immediately and would have to be fed along with everyone else.[47]

It is to Morgan's great credit that the DP camps were kept going throughout the winter. After months of sustained effort, he was able to record, on March 2, 1946, that "the whole supply situation has been sorted out for the rest of the year, and therefore for what looks like the rest of UNRRA. For the first time I got the feeling that some higher authority has really grasped our problem and put the procurement and supply business on a practical footing." He was particularly pleased that he now had his own proper reserve of medical supplies, could order basic supplies himself, and had "a budget of a million marks for local purchase in Berlin."[48]

By then, however, other problems were beginning to overwhelm the general.

On January 2, 1946, Morgan gave a press conference at the Park Hotel in Frankfurt, intending to take the opportunity of the New Year to talk about UNRRA's achievements in Germany and its hopes and fears for the future—and overcome some of the bad publicity the organization had recently been getting. At the end of his official briefing, he was asked about the large numbers of Jewish refugees from Poland who were beginning to arrive in Berlin. Exactly what Morgan said in response will probably never be known because, he said, "the reporters picked out only the more sensational bits." But according to the London *Evening Standard,* he did insist that his personal impression of the Berlin situation was that those Jews were well dressed and well fed and had "pockets bulging with money." He said that UNRRA's representatives had been unable to find a single concrete example of a pogrom inside Poland and then, according to one report, added that "the Jews seem to have organized a plan enabling them to become a world force—a weak force numerically, but one which will have a generating power for getting what they want." There was, Morgan said, evidence of an organization behind Jewish migration, and the idea was to have a Jewish exodus out of Europe. He added that the governments in Britain, the United States, Australia, and other places should try to absorb those people.[49]

Some of what Morgan said was true; some of it was not. The extent to which there was an anti-Jewish pogrom going on in Poland and the question of an underground Jewish refugee network will be examined in a later chapter. But his naiveté—his failure to understand that any suggestion of a Jewish "conspiracy" was, to say the least, unfortunate—revealed his political inexperience. The statement caused an immediate uproar in the Jewish world, especially in the United States. "I thought Hitler was dead," the entertainer Eddie Cantor declared in an advertisement in *The New York Times.* "His allegation is sheer Nazism," said the World Jewish Congress, "even in its wording, which might well have come from a speech by Hitler and his gang." "STUPID" was the headline in the London *Star;* "childish nonsense at best" and "at worst too close an echo of Hitler's ravings," wrote *The Manchester Guardian.*[50]

Was Morgan just expressing the traditional anti-Semitism of the British officer class? To some extent, yes. But to be fair, the General had made some effort to understand the Jewish problem when he was appointed to UNRRA. In London, he had sought advice from "the reigning Rothschild," Anthony, whom he found disappointingly "confused" and "very woolly with regard to Zionism," and in Germany he listened to a wider range of Jewish voices and struggled to understand the politics. "How one is going to deal with the conflicting claims of American and British Jewry, I don't know for the moment," he wrote after meeting a prominent British Jew. "It seems that there is yet a third gang to be considered, the Palestine Jews or Zionist Movement. Though most Jews seem interested in this when it pays them, there is I gather no sort of world Jewish organisation, where Judaism differs from Roman Catholicism, the other great religious block with whom I know I am bound to have all kinds of difficulty."[51]

Morgan liked several of the Jews he met. He found Edward Warburg "good, intelligent, and admirably broad-minded" and described Shalom Adler-Rudel, an Austrian working for the Jewish Agency, as "an interesting and most intelligent little man . . . the more I see [of him] the more I like him." Adler-Rudel gave Morgan "quite a new slant on the Jewish problem in Germany," by talking of "the astonishingly corporate spirit that has grown up in the Jewish DP camps, due, primarily, to a common sharing of horror and depression combined with the astonishing fact that practically all these Jews are individuals, each one being the survivor of some slaughtered family or group. The result of this is that the Jewish committees and camps feel that they stand *in loco parentis* to the few children that have survived." He also explained that the widespread Western assumption that "the Jews in Russia exercise influence on the Russian government" was wrong.[52]

But there were limits to Morgan's sympathies. A curious exchange of letters in December 1945 was caused by the visit of a sanitary engineer to the Jewish DP camp at Landsberg near Munich, where he found that "sanitary conditions" remained uncorrected because, he wrote, "the Jewish DPs were in no condition to pitch in and do the work involved." UNRRA's housing director, Joseph Berkman, Jewish himself, then remarked that "Jewish DPs lacked the morale or discipline needed to do the work and initiate self-government" because of their experiences under the Germans. "Engineers cannot accomplish anything for these people. What they need is psychiatrists." At that point, General Morgan became involved. "The last thing we want near here is psychiatrists," he wrote. "What these people need is to be treated like normal human beings and to be told firmly to get on and work. The sooner they are treated normally the sooner they will become normal." However, Morgan then added, revealingly, "Many of them have certainly suffered but in my view their sufferings cannot be compared to those of American and British nationals now returning from Japanese captivity. So far as I am aware no one is making all this fuss about them." Morgan came increasingly to feel that he was being pressured by the Jewish leaders and to complain about "the Jewish hysteria that is going round. They have an excellent case but in my view they are hard at work spoiling it by protesting too much."[53]

Whatever progress Morgan had made in understanding Jewish DPs, however, was completely stopped by the furor which his press conference provoked. The UNRRA hierarchy in Washington was infuriated that he should rock the boat at the very time that UNRRA's funding still had to go through Congress. Robert Jackson, besieged by telephone calls from Zionist leaders demanding that Morgan be fired, was particularly incensed, having specifically told Morgan when he had appointed him never to say anything publicly about the Jews. "He disobeyed orders. If he'd bloody well done that in the Army, he could have been court martialed on the spot and shot," Jackson later wrote.[54]

Morgan was indeed fired. But by refusing to accept the order, and by exploiting divisions within the UNRRA hierarchy and the weakness of Governor Lehman, he eventually had the order withdrawn. But it took a month of stubborn resistance and counterattacking and a visit to Washington—no simple matter in midwinter of 1946—before he was finally safe. What ultimately saved him was the view, expressed even by Jewish organizations, that it would have been inappropriate for him to be seen to be dismissed as a result of Jewish pressure.[55]

So much for UNRRA's higher management in Germany. But what was happening on the ground?

NINE

"You Pick It Up Fast"

WILDFLECKEN DP CAMP, GERMANY, 1945

Somewhere in northern Bavaria, on a foggy evening in July 1945, Kay Hulme got lost. She was one of a team of thirteen, drawn from five nationalities, which had just traveled for twelve days from UNRRA's Training Center at Granville on the French coast. Now they were looking for a camp near Bad Neustadt which housed 2,000 Polish refugees.

The French team director and a Dutchman went off to ask the way. They returned soon afterward. The camp was nearby, but, being sited in a former SS training center called Wildflecken, it was masked from the road by a forest of pines. And they had been misinformed; there weren't 2,000 Poles in the camp, there were 20,000.

The next day, a U.S. Army major briefed them. Wildflecken camp, he told them, was bigger, indeed, than Plattsburgh, New York, or Laramie, Wyoming—bigger than many cities. It took nine tons of bread a day to feed its population, though the flour kept being diverted into an illicit vodka still, which had just sent five blinded Poles to hospital. And forty-five babies were due in the month of September alone. His words were punctuated by pistol shots in the distance. The Poles, he explained, were still clearing out their *capos,* comrades who had collaborated with the Germans in the concentration camps. "You sure got to hand it to these Poles," said the major. "They never forget."

Kay Hulme was an American in her forties who had done a bit of everything, including a wartime spell as a shipyard riveter, with a passionate attachment to France and a wish to help the newly formed United Nations. By that afternoon, she was in charge of issuing passes to displaced persons, assisted by a countess from Warsaw, "with the cornflower-blue eyes of the Slav and the lean, *racé* face of the Polish nobility, but with all native hauteur beaten out of it so that every emotion showed instantly." The countess spoke flawless, Warsaw-society French, but Kay soon learned that her face did most of the interpreting. On their first day, they saw a famous tenor all of whose teeth had been pulled out by the Gestapo; a young girl made pregnant by a GI who had returned to the United States the previous week; a mother who wanted to go off and trade a silver cup for the raw liver needed to keep her anemic child alive; a "solemn and stately little Polish Boy Scout," who had managed to find his mother, brother, and sister and now asked permission to go in search of his father; an elderly woman camp survivor whose daughter was about to go into labor in Augsburg; and a gently deranged professor of botany who had lost all his family and wanted simply to roam the Bavarian woods in search of rare flowers.

The major had warned them that they would soon be over-whelmed by more DPs. "They're going to throw them at you fast. Army's got the cockeyed idea that every Pole in Germany will fit in up here." But he also told them not to worry. "You pick it up fast, this DP business. Boy, do you pick it up *fast!*"[1]

A few days later, a curt radio message informed the UNRRA team that 4,000 more Poles were on their way to them. Hastily improvising transport, they drove sixty kilometers to the nearest functioning train station (the RAF had disabled the railway viaduct near Wildflecken). There Kay saw for herself what happened to human beings crowded into cattle cars and what five days of unchanged diapers did to a baby's bottom. The nursing women and their babies had to be separated from their husbands, and the anguish this caused made Kay feel like a monster. "I was just another foreigner in uniform sending their wives and babies in different directions."

Kay and her colleagues were on their feet for the best part of two days, ferrying the refugees back to Wildflecken and ministering to their needs. Twice Kay had to commandeer ambulances from the military, once for a Polish woman about to give birth, the second time for a French driver whose lorry had crashed. Kay's emotional involvement with the Poles was so intense that she was astonished when a party of black U.S. Army drivers, who had already made two runs that day, insisted on halting, leaving several hundred Poles to pass the night beside the railhead. Kay marched up to where they were bivouacked round a fire and confronted the commanding officer:

> he refused flatly, said his men were "tahred" and needed rest. I pointed to 400 DPs huddled round baggage along the tracks (we had taken off earlier as many women and kids as we could) and asked him how he could refuse to get them into shelter that night, with rain imminent, etc. He refused with circuitous reasoning which suddenly exploded in my head, though the explosion came out in cold words to this effect: "The first time in my life I have been ashamed of the American Army and I'm so god-damned ashamed I could sink into the ground as I stand here."

Looking at the sleeping bodies, Kay remarked that it was like a Renaissance painting of the Last Judgment, "like Tintoretto's *Descent into Hell* in the Sistine Chapel★ . . . masses of forms contorted in firelight," "except that Christ was absent." Immediately, Marie-Louise Habets, the Belgian nurse with whom she was working, rebuked her. She must never say that again; Christ was never absent.[2]

A fortnight later the transports of DPs back to Poland began. With the broken viaduct by now repaired, a small engine pulling forty cattle cars chuffed into Wildflecken's own railhead, down the valley from the camp. Fifteen hundred people had been found, ready and willing to return to their motherland in appropriate style.

> The Poles had the cars decorated bravely with green branches torn from the surrounding pine trees, from the German apple orchards and plum groves. These plumes of green on all four corners of the cattle cars and festooned over the single entrance midway in each car give a very strange effect of festival. You'd think a vast train picnic were in the making. Flags accentuate this impression—the bold two-stripe red and white flag of Poland. . . . Some had got pieces of chalk and had inscribed on the sides of the cattle cars bold slogans in Polish about their never-dying race and the names and villages in Poland to which they hoped they were going.[3]

★ The Sistine's *Descent into Hell* was in fact painted by Michelangelo.

The final act was the loading of the special car which carried four days' food for fifteen hundred.

> It is a wondrous sight that draws the crowds—great sacks of bread, cartwheels of cheese, crates of tinned meat and always the tinned milk for babies and nursing mothers en route. The trucks back up tight against the train's doors as the rations are unloaded but the interstice is wide enough for hungry eyes to count and name each item and when the ten-pound tins of jam come down you hear a weird approving sound flutter through the crowd of onlookers. It's a word they've learned from Americans. It sounds like mummelid (marmalade) "Mummelid, *mummelid, MUMMELID!*"
>
> The engine has hooked on and is making stench and steam and now in each car the Poles are grouped around the open door as from a family portrait—youngsters sitting with legs hanging out, old folks on benches behind these and the men and young women standing brave and fine in their best clothes (which are often recognizable garments stolen from our clothing warehouses!) and as the wheels start turning and the cars slide slowly past, they all begin singing the Polish national hymn—and we outside stand still until the 40 cars go by, each one a burst of song, a flutter of women's handkerchiefs . . . huzzas, salutes, and smiles.[4]

The U.S. Army had always seen Wildflecken as a place of arrivals and departures. In the summer of 1945, when the military was rationalizing the different national groups, the camp there had been chosen as a DP center because it was large and close to a railhead the SS had built to handle two hundred railcars at once. The army intended Wildflecken to be a transit camp, a jumping-off point where Poles could be deloused and fed before being loaded into boxcars and sent home. Between August 12 and 31, it sent 8,562 repatriates home to Poland in five transports and received from other camps by boxcar and truck transports 7,340 DPs. The UNRRA team's task, as the army saw it, was not to service a community, but to keep the Poles alive and healthy while persuading them to go home.

Kay's boss, Georges Masset, was a French businessman who had traveled widely before the war and spent the war years in the Resistance. He was not simply "as full of emotions as a Paris taxicab driver and not ashamed of a single one" but tough, experienced, and determined. UNRRA reports speak of him as "eminently qualified," someone "who understands the things which must be done. His team works in complete harmony and agreement."[5]

Masset's UNRRA team began to evolve some sort of system of representation, based on the camp's topography—made up of some sixty-five blockhouses, each containing on average two hundred inhabitants. The sixty-five men chosen in this way became a sort of preliminary legislative body which called itself the Council of the Committee. Then, on August 26, 1945, full-scale elections were held in which every inhabitant of the camp who was of age had the right to vote, producing a Municipal Council of sixty-one, which on September 1, chose a seven-man Municipal Commission and a president of the camp, Zygmunt Rusinek, a well-known economist and former member of the Polish Parliament.

The reality behind this democratic facade was, however, evident at the banquet the new president gave to celebrate his sweeping victory. "The eyes of the invited UNRRA team popped when they saw that, even as the platform of the new party was toasted with 'impassioned speeches which promised suppression of Black Market, of schnapps stills, of cattle-rustling and hen-house marauding,' platters of prime roast beef and delicately baked chicken circulated up and down the 30-foot banquet table over the tops of brandy bottles spaced at 10-inch intervals."

There followed a period of difficult negotiations between Masset and Rusinek, "a delicate small man with a sensitive face and a mind like a steel trap." The president wanted UNRRA to provide everything for his people, while Masset needed a thousand young men to cut wood for the coming winter and hundreds of technicians to look after the camp's light, water, and sewage disposal systems. The weekly meetings saw intensive horse trading:

> [The president] would promise a garbage-disposal squad if we would make a special issue of clothing to the Concentration Camp group, numbering 350 of his faithful constituents. He would promise the wood-cutters if we would double their cigarette ration.[6]

Before this frail relationship could develop properly, however, there was a brutal interruption. On September 12, Wildflecken was inspected by two U.S. Army generals. "This was not an inspection of a DP center with accent on the conditions and needs of 15,000 DPs," Kay wrote.

> It was primarily a Sanitation Inspection such as might be expected in an Army barracks, where every small scrap of garbage (carefully concealed by our Poles in the corners of their basements where they never expected a General would go) resulted in penalties and future restrictions for one and all concerned. The physical and moral condition of our 15,000 Polish DPs was completely ignored.[7]

The generals ordered that there be guards in front of every block-house to enforce proper use of sanitation; the imprisonment of any DP dropping paper in the streets, hanging washing between trees, or concealing rubbish in basement corners; the arrest of any Pole not found working; the suppression of the Polish Committee as an organization functioning on "Soviet lines"; the repatriation of 1,500 Poles every fortnight; and the immediate VD examination of every woman in the camp. Kay drafted an impassioned letter to UNRRA's local headquarters. "We see our entire work of 'helping others to help themselves' pulled down, demoralized, even suppressed—if these orders were put into effect," she wrote. "Our camp will become a concentration camp worse than any the Germans devised. We see the ideal of UNRRA smashed under an Army boot." But the military "occupation" went ahead, and the local U.S. general's program was imposed. "In another month we will have snow and freezing weather and we will have no food reserve," Kay wrote on September 17. "But the camp will be clean as a barracks. We are in the midst of a military comedy but it could become a tragedy."[8]

Then, nearly two months later, on November 5, 1945, everything changed. Under the new policy the army handed over to UNRRA complete responsibility for the internal administration of DP camps. "We began, not where we had left off before the Army-control interlude, but where we had begun in the beginning, because so many projects had been suppressed or destroyed utterly. The Army's talent for relief work, we concluded, could hardly be called topflight."[9]

Once more in charge, the UNRRA people could concentrate on the important things. In November mass immunization began, with 15,000 Poles inoculated against typhus, typhoid, and diphtheria—it took a Belgian nurse and a doctor four hours to administer the 45,000 jabs this involved. Nearly 5,000 women were examined for VD— with exactly six glove fingers which had been sent in response to the requisition for two thousand from the military supply dump. Meanwhile, medical scrounging of heroic proportions was also going on. "Our nurses were on the hunt for thermometers, bed-pans, baby scales, breast pumps and syringes, purchasing these when they found them with anything the Germans would accept, generally silk stockings, cigarettes or coffee." One of the nurses returned from a trip to Würzburg on a gasoline truck with 5 million units of penicillin.[10]

Kay soon became familiar with a gruesome new word: "winterization." Preparing the camp for the coming winter required the acquisition and installation of stoves in every room in the blockhouses, the cutting down and stocking of enough wood to burn for the winter months, and the stockpiling of enough food to get the DPs through to spring. It was estimated that to give everyone the amount of wood officially required, 32,000 cubic meters had to be cut before mid-October. By the second week in the month they had 152 trucks operating daily, a third driven by Polish DPs. Meanwhile, huge convoys of winter clothing had to be unpacked.

The camp's food had originally come from the Germans. "We receive exactly 53 tons a week of potatoes, 47 tons of flour, 8 tons of meat, 5 tons of dried beans, 4 tons of fats and 1½ tons of sugar and salt," Kay explained. But the supply was never very reliable, driving Georges Masset on one occasion to threaten to put the secretary of the Bavarian Food Office in jail if fresh vegetables were not furnished; that threat produced 1,800 kilos of beets, 6,000 kilos of carrots, and other fresh vegetables. There were also periodic "moonlight requisitions"—"simply walking into German houses and taking what we needed." But in the late autumn, food became increasingly difficult to procure from the local burgomasters, who took it from the German farmers, and "one very much needed to vary the frightful potato diet we are forced to give these poor Poles."[11]

While Kay and her colleagues were wrestling with this question, there suddenly arrived an enormous convoy of lorries bringing Red Cross food parcels intended for American prisoners of war: cubes of sugar, tins of Cheddar cheese, sardines, Nescafé, corned beef, tuna, Spam, dried milk, Crisco, a half-pound chocolate bar, and seven packs of American cigarettes. Each DP, they were told, would get one box per month, containing 14,000 calories. It turned out that there was an unlimited supply of these boxes. It was the U.S. Army's bright idea of how to solve the winter food crisis.

Kay was full of resentment: "There is in that box all the things I had hungered for in the shipyards, all the things Americans 'gave up' during three years or more." Her director, Masset, however, quickly realized that the 10,000 cartons of cigarettes being given to the Wildflecken DPs were worth about 10 million reichsmarks on the black market. The UNRRA team was fearful of the effect of this. But it wasn't the black-market potential of the cigarettes that had the immediate effect; it was the Spam. The Poles immediately got wind of what was in the boxes, and all efforts to unload the two boxcars of parcels quietly came to nothing. The Poles "were positive that the packages were going to be handed out whole"—rather than used piecemeal to supplement the food extracted from the Germans—so that they could enjoy a "single night of magnificent celebration."

> *"Pakiety . . . pakiety."* The whole camp resounded to the one-word chant that picked up volume and insistence each time an UNRRA car threaded the striking crowds.
>
> There would have been something comical in the demonstration if you had not thought of the years of privation that lay behind it, the years of longing for a taste of the good things of life. *"Pakiety,"* they called like thwarted children.

Kay decided that no "spam-maddened adults" could be trusted to unpack the boxes and instead recruited some ninety Polish Boy Scouts to do the job—she learned that their nimble-fingeredness was the result of having worked for the Germans. But using the Scouts produced a sit-down strike by the DP workers and a demonstration by two thousand Poles. Kay did her best to sympathize with their "sudden awful mania," but when a special delegation accused the Scouts of cheating, she lost her rag:

> I flared like a harpy and said slowly for the interpreter to follow with her Polish, "If you see scouts eating chocolate in the camp, it is a chocolate bar I gave to them at the end of a day's work that any

of you is too damned lazy to do" . . . and I think I shook my fist in their faces, blazing with fury.

The disturbance was deftly handled by Georges Masset, who patiently argued and harangued the Poles until they accepted what was being done. To Kay, however, "the DPs' prompt obedience to anger and threats seemed almost the worst discovery I had yet made about them."

The uproar over the Red Cross parcels subsided when the food began to be distributed as a supplement to the daily ration—the DPs got one tin of tuna each on the days when the meat provided by German butchers was particularly bony.[12]

By demolishing parts of the old German barracks, the UNRRA team was able to create essential workshops where the Poles could be employed during the winter. And as fast as new workshops were created so the Polish Committee, "by now developed into a Tammany-like octopus with tentacles touching every aspect of camp life," supplied UNRRA with new labor. By October 1945, about a quarter of the total population was working hard to complete the preparations.

With every room in every blockhouse now containing a red-hot stove, the risk of fire was tangible. The UNRRA drivers "found" a German fire engine in near-working order and handed it over to the Poles, who insisted that it be painted the right color and managed to obtain red paint on the black market. A ceremony to inaugurate the camp's new fire brigade was duly organized, and on the appointed day, the camp band, the UNRRA team, the Polish Committee, and the U.S. Army colonel in charge stood outside the UNRRA headquarters building.

The band struck up the Polish national anthem as the glorious scarlet fire-wagon curved down the hill towards where we waited. Maybe the Polish driver thought he was already on the way to a fire. He accelerated on the down-grade, failed to make the left turn soon enough into the flat cobbled-parking space and crashed into the downside of the enclosure knocking down three trunk-sized blocks of yellow granite. Our beautiful fire-wagon looked like a red lobster flung against a stone wall. Every part of it was broken to bits but the driver and the cheering firemen escaped without a scratch. Our Colonel, unaccustomed to Polish anti-climaxes, thrust his swagger-stick under his arm and walked off speechless while we comforted our dismayed firemen and told them to find another fire-wagon. Meanwhile, we told them they might as well organize themselves into snow-removal squads which we would be needing very soon.[13]

On November 11, 1945, the first snow fell at Wildflecken. Everyone in the UNRRA team temporarily forgot the DPs and talked only about skiing in the Rhön mountains, "the poor man's Alps," according to Baedeker. The Poles' response was to convert their bedsteads into sledges by sawing off the roundel tops of their iron beds and using these curved pieces as runners on what Kay called "their home-made inflexible flyers."[14]

Meanwhile, the blockhouses had been transformed. Kay described in detail the atmosphere created:

> We had some twenty-eight hundred rooms in the camp in which the Poles were settling in for the winter in Slavic style. They nailed windows to stay shut till spring, bound babies like papooses in endless unhealthy yards of woollen swaddling clothes, and swung over-burdened clotheslines in the crowded interiors to produce, as our medical people said sadly, the proper incubating steam for swift transmission of respiratory diseases.
>
> Block-visiting was a queer haunting business. You never knew when you stood in the dim central hallways running the length of a blockhouse, with your hand on a grimy doorknob, what the opening of that door was going to reveal. A card on the door gave the number of square feet and the names of the individual souls the room contained, but that was no preparation. The entire scale of the human condition could be in any single room, or just one happy or forlorn note of it. It might be a bachelors' room bleak and bare with forty iron beds spaced at intervals along the walls and an ugly German army wardrobe standing narrow and tall beside each bed. Or, it might be a room where two or three families from the same village in Poland had managed to get together to create with

ikons, oleographs and lace bedspreads a semblance of the homes they had left behind.

Most generally, it would be a room into which the billeting committee had thrust heterogeneous families according to their size, with the old-timers secure by the windows and the newcomers in the dim spaces along the windowless walls. These were the rooms that always caught at one's heart, for they were partitioned off into family cubicles with the narrow wardrobes and stacked luggage built together to make one dividing wall, and army blankets hung from ropes to close in the remaining footage authorized to each.

You stared at these khaki labyrinths, the last ramparts of privacy to which the DPs clung, preferring to shiver with one less blanket on their straw-filled sacks rather than to dress, comb their hair, feed the baby or make a new one with ten or twenty pairs of strangers' eyes watching every move. You knew then that no matter what had happened to these people in the merciless herdings of them from homeland to enemy land, there was this one thing that could never be taken from them—the sense of privacy, the essence of human dignity.

Rising from the blanket-hung cubicles was a fixed medley of sounds descriptive of the private life each contained—a moan of a concertina, the tap-tap of a jeweler's hammer, the wail of a baby, the whirr of a sewing machine. Over all hung a redolent cloud of atmospheres composed of differing elements in the different communal rooms, but always smelling the same, a synthesis of drying diapers, smoked fish, cabbage brews and wood smoke from wet pine. It was not an unpleasant smell once you got used to it. For us it became the identifying odor of homeless humanity.

Always when you were looking for some specific person in those labyrinthine rooms, you visited first in the open space around the community stove that burned night and day and at all hours was covered with the pots of each family's food, which was brought in pails from the central kitchens and improved indoors with bits of meat or vegetables procured in that day's bartering. This open space in the partitioned rooms gave the peculiar impression of an inside public square to which drifted the inmates of the surrounding blanket-town when they got lonely, cold or hungry. Here was gossip, cooking, boot- and diaper-drying and all the other business that man has always performed before a fire. Here also could always be found someone with the soul of a concierge who could lead you through the maze of woollen-walled corridors to the room within a room that you were seeking, telling you meanwhile of what went on behind that particular khaki curtain.[15]

There was no way that the members of the UNRRA team, eighteen people at most, could relate directly to some 15,000 Polish DPs. Inevitably, their contacts were with those who worked for them as drivers and interpreters and with the camp leadership. "All life you see reduces to supply lines," Kay wrote.

> One talks airily of rehabilitation! I read the circulars and scream with ironic mirth . . . just to keep these thousands fed and housed is a job of such titan dimensions, a word like rehabilitation flutters around like a piece of useless lace under the wheels of our supply trucks grinding back and forth from station to warehouses—with overcoats, canned meat, coal, kegs of powdered soap and powdered milk.[16]

Occasionally, there were glimpses below the surface, a wedding or funeral. But mostly Kay remained an outsider, excluded by both language and culture, at once mystified and entertained by the doings of the Poles. "Today ended with drama," she wrote on December 15, 1945. "Our entire Polish police force was arrested [for corruption] . . . and a new one installed, guard post by guard post, we picked up the Old Guard, took away the guns." Five times in the first eighteen months the UNRRA team had to change the camp's entire police force. "Three to four months seemed the cycle of its rise and fall."[17]

But of one thing Kay became firmly convinced: the displaced persons' way of life was not good for their state of mind. DPs, she wrote,

> gradually lose all connections with the world of reality—the world we were all born and raised in where you had to work for what you got—and if you wanted a bigger car or a mink instead of a lapin coat, you worked harder than the other fellow. With this simple workaday scheme the DP has lost all connection whatsoever. As a result he has created for himself a weird Alice-in-Wonderland

world, and that's exactly what a DP camp is. We break our backs and souls to get enough food into the center to give them their 2000 calories (3000 to the heavy manual workers); we write endless requisitions to secure clothes for them; and never do we do enough. The more you give, the more they ask.

She was increasingly worried about their future.

What is to become of these DPs is beyond any guessing. . . . WHO, I ask, would choose to return to a beaten Poland, where there are no jobs, no food, no clothing, not even roofs to cover the head (you've all seen doubtless those pictures of Warsaw) when the other half of the option is to stay in a place where you can live as the lily of the field.[18]

The lives of the UNRRA team members were also very strange. "I never before encountered a life that requires so much intestinal fortitude as this one," Kay wrote. "It takes a lusty enduring nature to withstand this life, but I have that kind of nature." There was very little social life—the nearest big town was Frankfurt, two hours' hard driving away, and a "horror of destruction and a Red Cross canteen (even with its home-made doughnuts) [was] no reward for the trip." The response of most of the men on the UNRRA team was to set themselves up with mistresses selected from the Polish DPs. Kay was horrified, but Masset told her that after their treatment by the Germans and Russians the girls were probably happy to be taken up by Allied civilians. All the same, members of the team began to disappear. In early November, two French drivers took off for Paris, for which, Kay wrote, "they had been pining visibly for weeks. The people who stick it—what's left on my team—are plain wonders."[19]

Kay Hulme was not obviously qualified to be an aid worker. Born in San Francisco in 1900, a Berkeley graduate who had studied journalism, she had worked as a freelance reporter in New York in the 1920s and published several books based on her travels in Europe and Mexico before the war. The defining experience in her life was not her brief marriage to a San Francisco doctor but her meeting in Paris in 1935 with the Greek-Armenian mystic George Gurdjieff and the friendships she formed with other women who were studying with him.

For many people, Gurdjieff was a rogue and a rascal, a Rasputin; that was the conclusion to which Kay's former companion, a San Francisco milliner named Alice Rohrer, had come. When he tried to "free her of her possessions," she abandoned his sect. For Kay, though, Gurdjieff remained the man who had taught her how to find her inner spiritual strength, to look beyond externals in people and situations and see what lay inside; to accept her own sexuality. His little phrases, which many found meaningless, gave her strength and conviction, brought meaning to her life.

> He called me Krokodile because I had seven skins, was sentimental, fearsome, and sometimes fearless, had potential to become a dragon if I "worked on" myself and got myself up out of the mud (of ordinariness) where I liked to bask. He taught me to look at myself as I really was, and am, and life was never the same for me after those years with him.[20]

When she arrived in France in 1945—hanging around for weeks at Jullouville—Kay was appalled by the mutual suspicion of the different nationalities there. She astonished the personnel people by volunteering to work on a French team, even though they had acquired a reputation for being difficult. Having been appointed as an assistant director and aware that her job would include the fostering of "team spirit," she had marked down the team's Belgian nurse, a frail-looking woman who seemed to be perpetually asleep, as a "weak element." But in the course of the "twelve days of rocking in trucks over the broken roads of Germany to our destination camp in northern Bavaria," she learned enough about the Belgian woman's background to "put me in my place forever as an infallible judge of people." Marie-Louise Habets had been in the Belgian underground, worked as a nurse in a British field hospital—rescuing wounded Allied soldiers left behind by the Germans after the Battle of the Bulge—and survived a bomb which fell on a Brussels cinema, killing six hundred people. Then she had been sent to Germany to bring back Belgian nationals from the concentration camps before being administratively transferred to UNRRA with many other members of her unit, without having much idea of its mission. Small wonder she was happy to sleep at Jullouville. The two women became friends and shared a room at Wildflecken. But a month later Kay understood why Marie-

Louise was happy just to move on to UNRRA: "I left my convent last August—a nun who failed," she told Kay. "I tried for seventeen years to be a nun and failed."

Every night, Kay heard more about her roommate's past. She had spent seven years as a nurse in the Belgian Congo. "Her stories of operating alone in the bush . . . her life in the Belgian Army during the German occupation of Belgium, hunted most of the time by the Gestapo . . . make my life read like the Elsie books," Kay wrote to her friends. "She is a born nurse, magnificent in her work. She and I are kindred spirits in the matter of work. We are always the ones who turn out at weird hours—who stay latest in the camp—who never dream of turning in until things are accomplished."[21]

For each community in the camps, the first peacetime Christmas was special.

No one had a more interesting Christmas than Kay Hulme at Wildflecken. First her French team director disappeared to Paris for the duration, leaving her in charge. Then it became apparent that, as the DPs intended to celebrate their first postwar Christmas with true Polish gusto—their stills had been working overtime for months—they would be unavailable for any work until well into the New Year. Falling in with their wishes, Kay and her staff lovingly sorted out the special Red Cross Christmas parcels, making sure that each Pole received every luxury, bar of chocolate, and cigarette owing to him or her—whereupon the Poles insisted that their parties could not begin without the presence of UNRRA personnel, which meant a punishing round of drinking and dancing.

On December 24, a telegram arrived announcing that a further one thousand Poles would be coming on Boxing Day. Kay's protests were fruitless; the phones were unmanned. At 3 A.M. on December 26, in the grip of a terrible hangover, Kay was woken up by a U.S. Army major and told that General Lucian K. Truscott had just launched Operation Tally Ho, a carefully planned crackdown on black marketing among DPs. A ring of tanks surrounded the camp, and soldiers went from barracks to barracks, confiscating from the Poles all the Christmas goodies UNRRA had so lovingly given them.

Beside herself with rage, Kay screamed every expletive she had learned in the shipyards. In the midst of the confusion, the new consignment of Polish refugees appeared.[22]

TEN

"Even if the Gates Are Locked"

JEWISH DPS, 1946

Major Irving Heymont of the U.S. Army arrived at Landsberg displaced persons camp near Munich on September 19, 1945. His mission was to clean the place up. General Eisenhower had approved his task because it was from Landsberg that many of the criticisms of the army in Earl Harrison's report on the treatment of Jewish DPs had derived. If necessary he was authorized to cut the food ration by a third to force the inmates to clean up the camp.

The former German army barracks, in the town where Hitler had written *Mein Kampf,* now contained some 6,000 men, women, and children, of whom about 5,000 were Jews, mainly from Dachau. Heymont found it "filthy beyond description. Sanitation is virtually unknown. Words fail me, when I try to think of an adequate description," he wrote to his wife. With a few exceptions the people of the camp seemed to him "demoralized beyond hope of rehabilitation." "They appear to be beaten both spiritually and physically, with no hopes or incentives for the future." Touring the camp, he found "the toilets beg description," the hallways littered with trash, and idle people everywhere. In the kosher kitchen "the utter filth had to be seen to be believed." Yet the little dining room where the camp committee and functionaries ate was "a welcome contrast":

> The tables and chairs were neat and clean, and the room was nicely decorated. Pictures of Herzl, Ben-Gurion, F. D. Roosevelt, Harry Truman, the flag of America, and the blue and white Star of David flag adorned the walls.

Despite the filth, Heymont was surprised to find that the general health of the camp residents was good and an efficient two-hundred-bed hospital was at work. The schools were impressive—garages converted into classrooms and vocational schools run by an agronomist from Lithuania—though "the young and best elements" were organized into kibbutzim. "It appears that a kibbutz is a closely knit, self-disciplined group with an intense desire to emigrate to Palestine," he explained to his wife. "Each kibbutz is very clannish and little interested in the camp life." Landsberg was well equipped—a team from the Joint was doing a "superb job" buying supplies from Switzerland.[1]

Most of the Jews in the camp were of Polish origin, but the self-appointed camp committee largely consisted of better-educated Lithuanian and Latvian Jews. These were, in fact, Dr. Grinberg's companions on the train that had been shot up by the Americans, such as Samuel Gringauz, the lawyer with whom Grinberg had argued in the forest. While Grinberg had remained at his hospital at St. Ottilien, they had moved to Landsberg. As Heymont wrote:

> All the prominent members of the camp committee are up to their necks in politics. They are all connected in some way with a Central Committee for Liberated Jews with headquarters in Munich. It appears that the Munich committee has a strong influence on all Jews in Germany. It is very complicated and confusing, and I'm not sure that I have it quite straight yet . . . these people are jockeying among themselves for power in the camp and among the remaining Jews in central and eastern Europe.

The members of the committee, he learned, did not live in the camp themselves but lodged in German houses in the town nearby. Sometime, soon, the major told his wife, "he hoped to run an election, under U.S. Army supervision, for a democratically elected committee that would really be representative of the people in the camp."[2]

Heymont quickly drew up an agenda for change. The camp should become all Jewish, to make it a more coherent community, and the residents must all eat together in a central mess to sort out the sanitation problem because "if eating in the rooms and the storage of food in the wall lockers could be eliminated, a good part of the sanitation problem would solve itself." Heymont conceded that making everyone eat their meals at the same time certainly did not foster any personal sense of independence or freedom, but he could not see any other solution to the problem. Something must also be done immediately to prepare the camp for winter, everyone should be put to work, surplus population would be accommodated outside the camp, and, not least, elections would be held.[3]

On September 28, Heymont gathered the population together and gave a speech setting out his program for the future. He expressed great sympathy for what the inmates had been through and promised to make their lives better immediately by removing all barbed wire and guards and abolishing the pass system which regulated their movement in and out of the camp. The army and UNRRA would remain in charge, but if their elected leaders showed themselves competent, they would be given powers to run the camp. There was, though, a need for self-discipline and good organization if the dangers of an epidemic were to be overcome. It was time to relearn the habits of work and industry and to cut their own wood for the winter. He acknowledged that they had grievances and said he would try to resolve them, but he could give them autonomy only if they showed they were "capable of handling it."[4]

When Heymont began to implement his program, however, things immediately went wrong. The DPs started looting and pillaging the houses of Germans who had been evacuated, and the major was forced to bring in extra troops and restore the pass system. Then he discovered that, after their experiences in the camps, many Jews now saw work as their greatest enemy. "In the innermost of our hearts," he was told, "a complex was created that causes us to have a negative attitude toward labor." It turned out also that those who worked got fewer supplies. And so former members of the SS had to be brought in to cut the winter wood. But Heymont did have some successes. The central mess was finally opened on November 10— "a big affair complete with dinner music furnished by the camp orchestra—a pleasant surprise to see tablecloths on the tables"—and, greatest moment of all, the election was held. One of his officers carefully made voting booths from scrap lumber and canvas containing ballot boxes complete with padlocks, which were hard to come by in Germany at the time. There was only one fistfight, and many people voted for the first time in their lives. "We are all very proud of our success in reproducing the mechanics of an American election," Heymont wrote to his wife.[5]

Much to his surprise, the small group of Lithuanian intellectuals triumphed in the poll; but Heymont was delighted by the effect which the democratic process had on them. The camp committee showed new energy and began to take an interest in the daily administration of the camp, noticing things that were wrong without having to have them pointed out. At the same time, however, Heymont himself began to understand the mentality of the leadership better. Reading their speeches, he sympathized with their wish not to return home. Jacob Oleiski, a youth organizer from Kovno, had declared:

> Today . . . we can only grope and clasp with our finger tips the shadows of our dearest, and painfully cry: I can never more see my home. The victorious nations that in the twentieth century removed the black plague from Europe must understand once and for all the specific Jewish problem. No, we are not Polish when we were born in Poland; we are not Lithuanian even though we once passed through Lithuania; and we are neither Roumanians though we have seen the first time in our life the sunshine in Roumania. We are Jews! . . . We demand that the gates of Palestine be opened for us in order to live there as free people, as a free and independent nation. So if you wish to spare the coming generations a fate such as ours and to put life into the scattered *atsamot hajwejshot*—"dried beans"—we see the situation in that way: THE BUILDING OF A JEWISH COMMONWEALTH IN PALESTINE.

"This is obviously the major preoccupation of the camp committee," Heymont wrote. "Everything else is secondary—even the American Army and our desires for clean and healthy DP camps." He recognized, too, that it would not be easy to get people to join in community activities. Many were "still numb or completely preoccupied with efforts to locate family survivors." Although their hopes for immediate immigration to Palestine had been crushed, they were reluctant to participate because of "unconscious fears of sinking roots into a DP camp."[6]

One event played a major part in Heymont's change of perspective. On the very day the election took place, David Ben-Gurion, the head of the Zionist organization in Palestine, paid a surprise visit to the camp. Heymont received no advance warning. The first he knew of it was when he noticed people carrying flowers and hastily improvised banners and signs streaming out to line the street from Munich.

Inside the camp decorations of all sorts had suddenly appeared. Heymont doubted whether a visit by President Truman himself would
have generated so much excitement. "To the people of the camp he is
God. It seems that he represents all of their hopes of getting to Palestine. He had just come from England where he had been negotiating
with the British Government to allow more Jews into Palestine."

Heymont was able to talk at length to the Zionist leader, whom he
found sympathetic to his problems. After listening to inmates'
accounts of their reluctance to leave the overcrowded Landsberg for
other camps, Ben-Gurion commented, "It is a long and hard struggle
to overcome their psychology." Ben-Gurion, Heymont concluded,
"seems to be a man with keen insight and a practical approach to
problems." When he left, he offered further words of sympathy and
added, "In Palestine we too have comparable problems. A voyage on
a boat does not transform people."[7]

During the war a power struggle had been going on within the Zionist movement, as much about methods and personalities as about aims.
Chaim Weizmann, the elder statesman of Zionism who had charmed
the Balfour Declaration out of the British government in 1917, still
believed that the British could deliver a Jewish state in Palestine and
continued to put his trust in the methods of personal diplomacy and
high-level networking which had served him so well in the past. By
contrast, his main rival, the leader of the Jewish Agency for Palestine,
David Ben-Gurion, felt the time had now come to move beyond
diplomacy. Born in Poland in 1886, Ben-Gurion had immigrated to
Palestine as part of the "second wave" in 1908 and, apart from spells
in the United States, had spent his whole life there, rising through the
labor movement. By 1938, as the coming man in Zionism, he was
involved with Weizmann in negotiations with the British, an experience which had opened his eyes to both the duplicity of British diplomats and the vanity and unreliability of Weizmann as a colleague. For
months in London, Ben-Gurion watched as the British strung Weizmann along, even as they worked to win back Arab support in advance
of the coming war; yet he also came to see that, deep down, the British wanted to get out of Palestine—to rid themselves of the mandate.
During the war, therefore, Ben-Gurion came to advocate, more or
less openly, a different strategy of "combative Zionism," a three-
pronged approach combining illegal immigration to Palestine, appeals

to American public opinion, and a calculated use of terror against the British. Looking further ahead, he could see that a war with the Palestinian Arabs and their Muslim neighbors might be inevitable. For that, too, he was preparing.[8]

The issue of violence had long preoccupied the Zionist movement. Weizmann, an old-fashioned democratic liberal, was completely opposed to any use of violence, which he believed destroyed the moral basis on which the case for a Jewish state rested; yet such scruples were increasingly being abandoned by the younger men, conditioned by the political violence of the 1930s. Ben-Gurion saw that there was a danger that the Zionist leadership might be outflanked altogether by the new, more militaristic strands that were emerging. The assassination of Lord Moyne, the British minister resident in the Middle East in Cairo, in November 1944 by members of the Stern Gang, an extremist breakaway from the Zionist Irgun, not only shattered hopes for any wartime rapprochement between the British and the Jews of Palestine, it announced, in dramatic terms, the arrival of new kinds of Zionists with new methods. It had become a domestic political necessity for Ben-Gurion to prevent public sympathy and support from ebbing away to the extremists.[9]

For all these reasons, Ben-Gurion had become convinced that Weizmann was not the man to guide Zionism down the difficult road to statehood—and that he himself was. Throughout the Second World War, a state of armed neutrality had existed between the two men. Weizmann privately accused Ben-Gurion of "acting like a Fuehrer" and "developing fascist tendencies and megalomania coupled with political hysteria"; Ben-Gurion, meanwhile, concentrated on building up his power base.

Ben-Gurion's response to the Jewish survivors in the displaced persons camps came at both the human and the political level. Although some critics have accused him of indifference to the Holocaust, the reality, as his biographer Shabtai Teveth has convincingly shown, was more complex. Long before the war, Ben-Gurion had been prophesying that the Nazis would visit a catastrophe on the Jewish people in Europe, a disaster from which his cause would benefit because it would gain sympathy for the Judaic cause. But when those prophecies became reality, he found it as difficult as anyone to confront the awful truth. Despite being kept well informed about events in Eastern

Europe, he failed to realize until late in 1944 that what was taking place there was not a large-scale pogrom of the sort familiar in Jewish history but a program of industrialized genocide. (For the two years prior to El Alamein he was more worried that Palestine itself would fall to the Germans.) When he finally heard what was happening, he was shocked and shattered—as his private correspondence makes clear—but did not choose to make any public expressions of grief or outrage. That was not his way. Neither did any of the other Zionist leaders. He also did not seriously engage with any of the various attempts to "rescue" Jews because he was by temperament averse to any undertaking that could not be won.[10]

At the same time, however, Ben-Gurion was a man of ruthless political vision pursuing a single goal, the creation of a Zionist state in Palestine: in his mind, the fate of the European Jews always remained secondary to that primary objective. As a result, one ingredient in his reaction to the destruction of European Jewry was a fear that, were all of them to be lost, the moral leverage they could give him would also disappear. By the end of 1944, therefore, he was interested primarily in whether there would be any survivors and what sort of future they might want: "For the ability to exploit the disaster and the price that could be extracted from it were wholly dependent on their attitude to Zionism."

Immersed in planning the Zionist campaign for the postwar period, Ben-Gurion gathered data about the Jews in Europe and the world, taking particular interest in the Zionist pioneer youth movements and in the demographic composition of the Jewish communities that remained. By March 1945, he had formulated a plan for the immigration of a million Jews to Palestine in the eighteen months following the end of the war and found rich backers in America prepared to fund it.[11]

Ben-Gurion's clarity of purpose gave him a decisive advantage. Events, too, played out in his favor. He did not expect much from the Labour government in Britain and was therefore not surprised when it defaulted on its extravagant promises made while in opposition. In August 1945, he got the Zionist conference to endorse his aggressive approach rather than the moderation of Weizmann. The day after the British government rejected the Harrison Report, on September 21, 1945, Ben-Gurion demanded an end to talks with the British, an intense press campaign in England and the United States, and activity to step up immigration to and security measures in Palestine. He then created a united front between the Jewish military organizations in Palestine—the Zionist underground Haganah, the dissident armed Irgun, and the FFI, or "Sternists"—with which to put greater pressure on the British. The first act of this new resistance movement was the blowing up of 153 bridges in Palestine on November 1, 1945.

Ben-Gurion had intended to return to Palestine to take personal command of this new campaign. He did not do so because his visit to the displaced persons camps in Germany in October 1945 caused him to change his strategy.

Ben-Gurion's ostensible purpose was to "study the situation and needs of the Jewish DPs," but "his real intention," his biographer writes, was "to see for himself to what extent the power of their adversity could be used in his battle to establish the Jewish state." He was "interested not only in the votes of the 165,000 survivors in the camps he was to visit, but also, and perhaps primarily, in becoming their representative."[12]

Ben-Gurion spent eleven days visiting the camps. In his speeches to Jewish survivors, he did not talk primarily about what they had been through in the war. Instead, in dry and matter-of-fact tones, he addressed their future prospects in Palestine. Far from being a sign of his "insensitivity," as some critics have charged, this was a measure of his political skill. At St. Ottilien, with Dr. Grinberg standing by his side, the Zionist leader declared:

> I can tell you that a vibrant Jewish Palestine exists and that even if its gates are locked the Yishuv will break them open with its strong hands. . . . Today we are the decisive power in Palestine. . . . We have our own shops, our own factories, our own land, our own culture, and our own rifles. . . . Hitler was not far from Palestine.
>
> There could have been terrible destruction there, but what happened in Poland could not happen in Palestine. They would not have slaughtered us in synagogues.
>
> Every boy and every girl would have shot every German soldier.

As Shabtai Teveth has pointed out, "The news of a place where Jews had strength, where they could defend themselves, was the solace Ben-Gurion offered the survivors. His special instinct told him that neither caresses nor compassion was expected of him, but the bearing of a torch that lit a vision of hope for all."[13]

Ben-Gurion warned his listeners that, although the European war was over, their own war was just beginning. They, the surviving remnant, had to function as a "political factor" in the struggle for a Jewish state. Everywhere he went he was received with enormous enthusiasm. He wrote in his diary that "70 percent of the survivors do in fact want to go to Palestine" and were ready to fight for that right, even at the cost of their lives. He concluded that

> In the struggle ahead we have on our side three major forces: the Yishuv [the Jews in Palestine] and its strength, America [and] the DP camps in Germany. The function of Zionism is not to help the remnant to survive in Europe, but rather to rescue them for the sake of the Jewish people and the Yishuv: the Jews of America and the DPs are allotted a special role in this rescue.[14]

"Many Jews from Poland are drifting into the camp," Major Heymont wrote from Landsberg on October 11.

> Most of them returned to Poland after being liberated from concentration camps only to meet persecution again. Their attempts to repossess pre-war property met with violent opposition from the present owners. And the local police . . . often take no action and even join in preventing former owners from reclaiming their property.[15]

We have seen how the liberation of the concentration camps in the spring of 1945 was followed by the movement of thousands of Jews back to Eastern Europe in search of relatives or to reclaim property. Those who returned to Poland rapidly discovered that most Poles did not want them back and that the chances of recovering their property were slim; it did not help that several Jews occupied prominent positions in the unpopular Communist-dominated regime. The Polish people, a British diplomat observed, "appeared anxious to finish what the Germans had left undone." According to official figures, 351 Jews were murdered in Poland between November 1944 and October 1945.[16]

Confronted by this bleak outlook, many Polish Jews concluded that they had no future in the country and began to leave. In the summer of 1945, a second wave of Jewish migration began, this time overwhelmingly westward—and mainly into Germany. In August 1945, there were some 80,000 Jews in Poland, of whom 13,000 had been in the Polish pro-Soviet armed forces that had participated in the liberation of the country; others had come from liberated camps in Germany and Poland itself or had emerged from hiding or from partisan detachments. However, there were also between 150,000 and 200,000 more Polish Jews who had fled to the Soviet Union during the war and who were now beginning to return to Poland. The Soviet government did nothing to stop their passage from the Soviet Union, while the Polish government made no attempt to slow this exodus; indeed, it encouraged it. In exchange for 1,000 zlotys, Warsaw issued Jews with passports valid for a single crossing of the Polish border. A variety of routes was used.[17]

Was this, then, a simple flight from persecution or something more? It was both. A network for getting Jews out of Eastern Europe and smuggling them into Palestine had existed before the war. In the second half of 1944, Jewish ghetto fighters and partisans had created a clandestine organization known as Brichah ("flight") intended to help Jews escape from areas liberated by the Red Army. At first they used a route through Romania, but in the spring of 1945 they made contact with the Jewish Brigade in Italy and opened a route to Italy that was operational—on a small scale—from June to August 1945. When the British transferred the Jewish Brigade to Belgium and took steps to close the Italian frontier, the stream was diverted to Germany. By the end of 1945, some 40,000 Jews had found their way into the American Zone.[18]

The organizational core of Brichah—the people who helped refugees over mountains at night and bribed frontier guards—was initially young, highly motivated volunteers, veterans of the Jewish youth movement from before the war. But from the summer of 1945 onward, those local workers were stiffened and directed by agents of the Mossad Le'aliyah Bet, the body responsible (under the Jewish Agency and the Haganah) for organizing the illegal immigration of Jews into Palestine.[19]

These developments in Eastern Europe were very much in David Ben-Gurion's mind when he had a series of meetings with the American commander in Germany, Dwight D. Eisenhower, and his formidable deputy, Walter Bedell Smith, in Frankfurt in late October 1945. Introduced as "the head of all the Jews in Palestine," Ben-Gurion was treated with some ceremony by the American commanders. They were happy to accede to his request that the Jewish displaced persons in the American Zone be given a measure of self-government and allowed to carry out agricultural and military training. They also agreed to fly in teachers and instructors from Palestine while turning down his proposal that all the Jews in western Germany be brought together in one huge conurbation. But the decisive moment came when Ben-Gurion mentioned to Smith the daily influx of Jews from the East, which the Polish government was encouraging, and gently sounded him out on the U.S. Army's view. He was told that the military would not turn them away, that the U.S. Army was "duty bound" to save those Jews.[20]

There are no American records of those meetings. We do not know whether the military sought political guidance from Washington. But it is likely that the generals, still smarting from Harrison's criticism and Truman's public rebuke, thought it wisest to accept the inevitable, rather than risk the flak which any use of force to keep the Jews out would have caused. But whatever the reason, Ben-Gurion saw at once that he had been given a powerful political weapon—the green light to bring as many Eastern European Jews as possible into the American Zone and thus to put pressure on the British. "The Americans know that they will not be able to remain in Munich forever," he wrote. "The one place [those Jews] will be able to go to is Palestine and that will generate American pressure, they'll push and [the Jewish displaced persons] will be allowed to go." He took immediate steps to seize the opportunity. He had "told our people who deal with these matters to bring the refugees in quickly," he informed a Jewish Agency Executive meeting in Jerusalem a month later. That, he added,

[W]ill be the major factor for the Americans to demand their removal to Palestine. . . . It is possible to bring there all the European Jews, from everywhere, without any difficulty. . . . If we manage to concentrate a quarter of a million Jews in the U.S. Zone, it would increase the American pressure [on the British] not because of the economic problem—that does not play any role with them—but because they see no future for these people anywhere but in Palestine.

By then he had also reached an agreement with Edward Warburg and Joe Schwartz of the American Jewish Joint Distribution Committee that they would bankroll a new phase of clandestine immigration to Palestine.[21]

Ben-Gurion returned to Europe and began a double life. Officially, he stayed in London as chairman of the Jewish Agency Executive; unofficially, he established in Paris a control center from which to manage the underground network now being put in place in Germany and Central Europe.[22]

On November 14, at Landsberg DP camp, Major Irving Heymont learned that "all the Jews in Poland are either on the way or preparing to come to the American zone" and that, in addition, "there are groups from Palestine over here who are actively organizing the movement of Jews from Eastern Europe to Palestine." Landsberg, he was convinced, had become "a stop on this modern underground railroad." He noted, too, that men of the Jewish Brigade came frequently to the camp. No doubt they were active in the movement.[23]

Other elements were also recruited. Rabbi Herbert Friedman, then a military chaplain with the U.S. Army in Bavaria, was telephoned one day by a mysterious woman with a seductive voice who asked him to come to a hotel in Paris. Many years later, he recalled standing in the corridor of the Royal Monceau hotel on Avenue Foch and being asked if he would work for "them." For whom? he asked. She said "Haganah, Aliya Bet, Bricha." Friedman, normally a rational person who took decisions after long reflection, found himself saying yes immediately. He was then taken into a room and presented to a "short fellow with white hair" who thanked him for his commitment and left at once. "Who was that?" he asked the woman. "David Ben-Gurion," he was told. Friedman's orders were to get himself transferred to Berlin and wait to be joined there by men from the Jewish Brigade, at that time in Belgium, who would provide all the drivers, gunners, and mechanics he needed. In the meantime, he was to steal enough trucks and petrol tickets to enable him to drive every night from Berlin to Szcecin for a year, carrying Jewish refugees on the return journey. Using cigarettes provided by the Joint to bribe frontier guards, he successfully accomplished this task.[24]

In this way, the Jewish displaced persons, having been for a while entirely on their own, had by the end of 1945 become the vitally important moral spearhead of a much larger campaign. Were the survivors manipulated by a clever Zionist leadership bent on creating a Jewish state? Yes, they were. But, Yehuda Bauer argues, that is not the point: "the people *wanted* to be manipulated, they wanted to escape from an untenable situation first in Eastern Europe and then in the DP countries, and Palestine seemed to them to be the only practical way out."[25]

It soon became clear that the leadership of the Jewish DPs, too, was playing its part in a bigger drama. In three ways they helped the Zionist cause—in the case of the Jewish children, by exploiting Belsen for Zionist propaganda, and by appealing to American Jewish audiences.

In July 1945, the British and Swiss governments announced a willingness to take a certain number of "unaccompanied" Jewish children—that is, orphans—from the camps. There then followed several months during which arrangements were made for the children to be looked after by Jewish charities in their new countries. By October 1945, things were ready to go.

At first everyone's concern was entirely for the immediate welfare and comfort of the children. Their wishes were not in doubt. The children themselves "do not hesitate to say how much they would like to leave the camps and how they hated to continue living there," a Jewish visitor reported. There was a "stampede" of applicants when the scheme was announced. The leadership of the Jewish DPs agreed to the plan. However, after a member of the Jewish Brigade appeared before the Central Committee in Munich and explained that, in the light of the widespread resistance to the British in Palestine, the transfer of the children to England would be felt to be "a moral victory for the British and a blow to the Yishuv," the decision was reversed. A public statement on October 14 declared that in view of what was happening in Palestine, the Central Committee no longer trusted the "helpfulness and hospitality" of the British. No Jewish child should be transferred anywhere except directly to its only possible home: Palestine. A week later, after the first group of children from Belsen had gone to England, the Jewish Committee in the British Zone took a similar decision.[26]

Although it was evident at the time that the committees in Munich and Belsen "did not feel very comfortable" with their decision to put politics before the needs of the children and would happily have reversed it had the Jewish Agency authorized them to, they stuck to their line under pressure from Ben-Gurion. Plans to send thousands of children to France and Italy had also to be scrapped. Instead, a children's home was established at Blankenese, on the beautiful estate of the Warburg family, the founders of the Joint, and one hundred Jewish children were sent there from Belsen.[27]

The Jewish DPs in Germany also served the Zionist cause by providing bad publicity for the British in the American press. "The best British propaganda for Zionism is the DP camp at Bergen-Belsen. They behave like Nazis there," Ben-Gurion told the Jewish Agency in November 1945. *The New York Times* called the DP camp "the notorious Belsen camp—that very camp where thousands of Hebrews died and where today the survivors are still compelled to live." The British tried feebly to counterattack. "We ought to correct the idea about Belsen . . . it is not the horror camp I understand," Halifax wrote from Washington. Bevin agreed: "send a reliable press man there." But all efforts to explain that "Belsen" now provided some of the best accommodation in Germany were ignored, and when a fact-finding visit to the camp was organized, only "Mr. Goldsmith of the Associated Press" turned up. His story, which was never published, found that conditions were adequate, though there was still a shortage of shoes and the diet was monotonous.[28]

Equally important were the personal visits of Jewish DP leaders to the United States. When Josef Rosensaft was invited to address the United Jewish Appeal in Atlantic City in December 1945, the British tried to stop him from going; then they tried to stop him from returning to Belsen. Both times they failed. Rosensaft's fiery speeches were a hit with American audiences. He managed both to rebuke American Jewry for its slow response to the murder of the Jews and to praise it for the help it had so far given. Now it must get the Jews out of Germany and alleviate their condition while they were there. The following February, Dr. Grinberg spoke to the American Jewish Congress in Cleveland, Ohio, and addressed a mass meeting in New York.[29]

By the autumn of 1945, a profound difference in approach toward Jewish DPs had emerged between the British and the Americans, both in Germany and in London and Washington. The Americans had recognized them as Jews and given them separate camps, and President Truman, in the wake of the Harrison Report, had called on the British to allow 100,000 Jews to go to Palestine.

The position of the British was more complex. Officially, they still maintained that there was no Jewish nation and that the Jews' future lay in Europe and in the countries from which they had come. To accept Earl Harrison's proposals, the Foreign Office argued, was to accept that "there is no sure future in Europe for persons of Jewish race." It was "surely a counsel of despair which it would be quite wrong to admit at a time when conditions throughout Europe are still chaotic and when [the] effect of [the] antisemitic policy sedulously fostered by the Nazis has not yet been undone: indeed it would go far by implication to admit that [the] Nazis were right in holding that there was no place for Jews in Europe." Much better if the Jews could be persuaded to return to their "native lands"; the Allies' task was, surely, "to create conditions in which they will themselves feel it natural and right to go home rather than to admit at this stage that such conditions are impossible to create." Ernest Bevin "felt passionately that there had been no point in fighting the Second World War if the Jews could not stay on in Europe where they had a vital role to play in the reconstruction of that continent."[30]

At the same time, however, the British military government had made some concessions in its zone. Jews were allowed their own areas in the camps, if not separate Jewish camps, and "the need to throw a sop to world opinion" led to faltering steps being taken to improve the rations paid to "persecutees," that is, German Jews living outside the DP camps, who had hitherto been treated as "Germans."

In Whitehall, there continued to be resentment at the position of the Jews. Of course they had suffered—but so had others. It was pointed out that approximately 80 million Russians had been killed or exterminated during the previous three decades. When Bevin remarked that "Jews, with all their sufferings, want to get too much to the head of the queue," he was expressing in his unguarded way a commonly held British view.[31]

However, it was accepted that something more substantial would have to be done. The British could not afford to be isolated. U.S. support was vital to the Attlee government's economic survival; the last few months of 1945 were dominated by the long and difficult negotiations for the American loan, which was finally sealed on Decem-

ber 6, 1945. Confronted by the need to do something to appease
American opinion and to respond to the Harrison Report and Truman's proposal that 100,000 Jews go to Palestine, the British also
wanted to lock the Americans into Palestine, to get them to shoulder
some of the burden and make them face up to reality. So in October
1945, Bevin proposed the establishment of an Anglo-American Committee of Inquiry to look at the feasibility of Harrison's suggestions.
The Americans were understandably dubious—surely this was just
the classic Whitehall delaying tactic?—and insisted that the committee's remit be widened to include Palestine. Furthermore, nothing
could be said until the mayoral contest in New York City was out of
the way. The Democratic candidate was opposed by a Republican
rival who was Jewish, and Palestine was an important issue. As a
result, the plan was not announced till November.

It took some time to put the Anglo-American Committee of
Inquiry together; it proved difficult to find suitable people in America
who were not already publicly committed on the issue. Eventually,
though, an American delegation was produced, led by a conservative
Texan Democrat, Judge Joe Hutcheson, and made up of an academic,
two diplomats, a journalist, and a lawyer. Most of this group were, in
fact, pro-Zionist. Their British colleagues, also led by a judge, and
containing two Labour and one Conservative politician, a civil servant, and an economist, were anti-Zionist.[32]

The British unwisely agreed that the committee's hearings should
begin in Washington and so subjected themselves to a fortnight's
mauling in January 1946, as American Zionist leaders and Jewish
intellectuals engaged in predictable anti-British and anticolonialist
posturing. After sitting through Albert Einstein's attack on British
imperalism, even the sympathetically minded British Labour MP
Richard Crossman began to echo the Foreign Office view that "the
average American supported immigration to Palestine simply because
he did not want more Jews in America." "By shouting for a Jewish
state, Americans satisfy many motives," Crossman wrote in his diary.
"They are attacking the Empire and British protectionism, they are
espousing a moral cause, for whose fulfilment they will take no
responsibility, and most important of all, they are diverting attention
from the fact that their own immigration laws are one of the causes of
the problem." At the same time, he found it useful to see how, for
most Americans, the Arab cause simply didn't count; they were seen

as the indigenous people, the equivalent of the North American Indians, who would have to be pushed aside if progress and modernity were to prevail.[33]

The committee's next destination, at the end of January 1946, was London. Here again, the hearings were mostly a waste of time, as public figures rehearsed well-established positions. "Any gentile who is compelled to study Zionism for weeks on end reaches the point where he feels inclined to bang on the table and walk out of the room," Crossman expostulated. "Who exactly were these people who claimed to be both Jews and Englishmen and disagreed violently on the issue of whether there was a Jewish nation or not." But there was one very significant development. At a formal lunch for the committee at the Dorchester, Ernest Bevin pledged himself to "do everything in his power" to implement the committee's report if it was unanimous.[34]

Finally, three months after it had been established, the committee went to Europe and began to talk to the displaced persons themselves, in the camps in Germany and Austria. Everywhere they went they were appalled by the overcrowded conditions in which Jewish DPs were living and met by demonstrations demanding the right to go to Palestine. It was impossible not to be affected by the human suffering. Bartley Crum, a pro-Zionist San Francisco lawyer whom Truman had placed on the committee despite the State Department's objections, was particularly moved. As he was leaving one of the camps, a young boy pulled at his coat. "Mr. America, Mr. America," he said, "when are you going to let us out of here?" Crum patted him on the shoulder and urged him to have patience. "Patience!" he exclaimed. "How can you talk to us of patience? After six years of this war, after all our parents have been burned in the gas-ovens, you talk to us of patience?"[35]

Bartley Crum repeatedly heard the name of a Jewish physician, spoken of as an extraordinary person, who had "become almost a legend among the Jewish survivors of the concentration camps." Dr. Zalman Grinberg's reputation had recently been further enhanced when he chaired the first Constituent Assembly of the Central Committee in the Rathaus in Munich in January 1946, attended by Ben-Gurion and many foreign observers and journalists. After greeting the audience in English, German, and Hebrew, Grinberg delivered a powerful speech in perfect German calling on the Western leaders to redeem their failure to prevent the destruction of the Jews by giving them a homeland and a state. He was followed by Ben-Gurion himself, who mocked General Morgan's talk of a "Jewish conspiracy" at his now-infamous press conference earlier in the month and urged the Jewish DPs not to lose faith in their future. The proceedings were captured on film by Rabbi Klausner, using cans of stock acquired in exchange for tins of coffee.[36]

Crum duly made the pilgrimage to St. Ottilien hospital and found Grinberg to be a "slight little man, looking much older than his thirty-four years, with clear dark eyes and a simplicity of manner." In excellent English, Dr. Grinberg told him how, in the camps, they had continually asked themselves, "Why didn't I go to the land of Israel [Palestine]? I could have avoided all this." They had imagined that if somehow they came through the horror, the whole world would rush to help them. Instead of which they found themselves stuck. The state of mind of the average Jewish man in the displaced persons camps, said Grinberg, was "based on three factors: a bitter, terrible yesterday, an impossible today, and an undetermined tomorrow." The committee had to understand the psychological factors. The Nazis had taken from the Jewish survivors the love of work. Now, said Grinberg, "we have to re-educate our people to love work. And this job of re-education can happen only in Palestine, where two factors exist absolutely indispensable for such re-education: one is the love and comfort of our people; the other is the strength of conviction, the discipline of work." According to Crum, a colleague on the committee, the British trade unionist Sir Frederick Leggett, was "more deeply moved than I had ever seen him."[37]

Crum found that among the Jewish DPs morale was "highest where doubts about the future were least. Throughout Germany, wherever we found DPs on farms preparing for *kibbutz* life in Israel, the men and women were remarkably buoyant." His overall conclusions echoed Dr. Grinberg's views. "Certain facts became unmistakable," Crum wrote later.

These Jewish DPs had been deprived of two great needs, and from a psychiatric point of view they would not be made normal until they were satisfied. First was the need of family, of intimates upon whom they could lavish hopes and from whom they could receive love. Second was the need for purpose in their lives.[38]

But how representative was Dr. Grinberg? Did the Jewish displaced persons really all want to go to Palestine? Did they in fact know their own minds? Doubts have been raised. "Thorough groundwork was done by the Zionists," wrote the Israeli historian Yosef Grodzinsky. "Potential witnesses—residents of the DP camps—were prepared, in order to fortify and confirm the Zionist claim that all DPs wanted to immigrate to Palestine." It is clear that Ben-Gurion's men, with some help from elements in the U.S. Army, "met with all the . . . leaders and succeeded to unite them on this issue everywhere. We prepared materials for the Commission, wrote a memorandum, and selected persons who would give testimony." In their propaganda among the Jews in the camps, "they were not above anything," an anti-Zionist DP later complained. "They told the Jews: Go wherever you wish, no one will coerce you, but to the outside world, declare that you only want to go to Palestine." The success of this strategy was apparent when UNRRA conducted a poll among 20,000 DPs about their preferred future. The results exceeded the Zionists' wildest dreams: 96.8 percent of the Jewish DPs declared that they wished to immigrate to Palestine.[39]

Meeting exactly the same slogans and placards at each camp, hearing the same lines from witnesses, the committee members realized that the DPs had been drilled but felt nonetheless that their wish to go to Palestine was genuine.

Josef Rosensaft, the leader of the Jewish DPs at Bergen-Belsen, was in America in December 1945 when an urgent appeal from Ben-Gurion to return to be a witness before the committee sent him hurrying back to Germany. On February 10, 1946, Rosensaft told Judge Hutcheson and three British members that if he could not go to Palestine, he would rather go back to Auschwitz. Other witnesses before the committee made similar statements. The headmistress of the Jewish school at Belsen stated that "although she had refrained from teaching and disseminating Zionist ideology in her school, Zionism had spontaneously been introduced in the educational context. Hebrew was the only common language and Palestine was the only hope shared by them all."[40]

These witnesses had such a powerful effect on Bartley Crum that he urged the committee to produce an interim report calling for the immediate cleaning out of the camps, but he was overruled; the committee continued its planned schedule, which took it to Cairo and

Jerusalem. The visit to the Egyptian capital confirmed the Americans in their dislike for British imperialism and distaste for the Arabs. On the other hand, nearly everyone was impressed at once by Jewish Palestine. "At the edge of Tel Aviv, I saw the first houses," Crum wrote later. "There was a marked improvement. I thought to myself: *Here before your eyes is proof that Palestinian Jewry is bringing civilization to the Middle East.*" For Richard Crossman it was the vision of *socialist* progress, the sight of socialism in practice on Jewish kibbutzim in Palestine, which provoked his conversion to Zionism.[41]

In Jerusalem, the committee heard from both Zionists and Arabs. Weizmann—looking, Crossman noted, "like a weary and more humane version of Lenin, very tired, very ill, too old, and too pro-British to control his extremists"—spoke for two hours "with a magnificent mixture of passion and scientific detachment" which made a profound impression on the committee and alarmed his fellow Zionists. Weizmann, Crossman observed,

> is the first witness who has frankly and openly admitted that the issue is not between right and wrong but between the greater and the lesser injustice. Injustice is unavoidable and we have to decide whether it is better to be unjust to the Arabs of Palestine or to the Jews.

The Western world, he made clear, must favor the Jews. Weizmann was followed by Ben-Gurion: "stockily built, with a halo of white hair, a determined jaw set as in stone, with piercing blue eyes under heavy white shaggy brows, he was an extremely forceful personality" to Bartley Crum. Other committee members, though, were less impressed. Questioned as to his position on violence, Ben-Gurion equivocated and even claimed to have no knowledge of the Haganah. "He seems to want to have it both ways," Crossman wrote, "to remain within the letter of the law as chairman of the [Jewish] Agency, and to tolerate terror as a method of bringing pressure on the Administration." The most impressive of the pro-Arab witnesses, the Anglo-Lebanese scholar Albert Hourani, warned the committee that any attempt to send more Jews into Palestine would inevitably provoke war.[42]

At the end of March 1946, the Anglo-American Committee retired to Lausanne in Switzerland to consider its report. The mem-

200 · THE LONG ROAD HOME

bers were agreed on one thing—that 100,000 Jews should immediately be admitted to Palestine—but disagreed on nearly everything else. In the end, mindful of Ernest Bevin's wish that they produce a united report, they sank their differences and came up with unanimous recommendations: in addition to the admission of 100,000 Jewish displaced persons, the restrictions on Jewish immigration and land ownership imposed by the 1939 British White Paper should be lifted. However, the committee rejected the idea of partitioning Palestine between Jews and Arabs and, while urging the Jewish Agency for Palestine to cooperate in suppressing terrorism and illegal immigration, did not make the disarmament of Jewish illegal forces a condition for the admission of the Jewish DPs.

Many historians now argue that the British should have accepted the committee's proposals, which were in hindsight much the best offer that ever came along. Had they done so, they might have divided the moderate Zionists from the more extreme ones. Nicholas Bethell, for example, argued that if Britain had accepted the report and offered to take a good number of Jewish refugees from Europe "the steam would have gone out of the maximalist demand for a Jewish state." Had London, in addition, offered to take 25,000 Jewish DPs in Britain itself, it would probably have shamed the Americans into taking a further 50,000, say, which would have taken off the immediate pressure. In that case, the state of Israel might never have come into existence.[43]

Why, then, did the British not seize this opportunity? In fact, Ernest Bevin, the foreign secretary, was in favor of accepting the report, though he had doubts about how the Arabs would respond; it was Clement Attlee, the prime minister, who insisted that it be rejected. His military and political advisers were all of the view that to admit 100,000 Jews into Palestine would immediately provoke an Arab revolt and bring about the destruction of British interests in the area. Furthermore, it would be seen as a surrender to Zionist pressure at a time when the British government was feeling particularly unsympathetic toward the Jewish leadership because it knew (from intercepted cables) that Ben-Gurion and his closest associates, while claiming to be uninvolved in terrorist violence in Palestine, were in fact masterminding and coordinating it.[44]

The British did not immediately make their position clear; instead, they waited to confer with the Americans, hoping that something might be salvaged. But on the day the report was published, April 30, 1946, President Truman jumped the gun. At the instigation of American Zionists, including Bartley Crum and the White House assistant David Niles, Truman signed a statement accepting the committee's recommendation that 100,000 Jewish refugees be admitted to Palestine, without giving any indication that the United States would help implement the rest of the report. That provoked Attlee into an immediate statement of the British position: that the 100,000 refugees could not be accepted into Palestine unless the illegal Jewish organizations in Palestine were first disbanded and disarmed.[45]

In hindsight, the 100,000-refugee scheme was from then on dead in the water. But that was not immediately apparent in Germany. At the end of April 1946, newspaper headlines brought to the DP camps the news that the committee had recommended that 100,000 certificates for emigration be made available. There would soon be a mass exodus of Jews from Germany and Austria. The thoughts of the DP leadership began turning to the question of how the migrants would be transported to Palestine. In July 1946, when it was still thought that the plan might go ahead, a delegation was sent from Munich to make the necessary arrangements. It included Dr. Zalman Grinberg.

Grinberg had been trying to translate the promises made to him on his visit to America into action on the ground by the U.S. Army—to provide accommodation and food for the Polish Jews now flooding into the American Zone. As part of this campaign he even met General Morgan, who found him "a capable man though a fanatical Jew." But Grinberg was getting discouraged; according to his American friend Leo Schwarz, "at times the nervous strain made him feel 'sick unto death.' The whole country seemed a seething mass of rancor, the whole world bereft of charity."[46]

Above all, Grinberg's own circumstances had recently been transformed. He had been reunited with his wife, whom he had not seen since they were separated in Kovno in 1944, and with his child, who had been looked after by a Lithuanian woman ever since being smuggled out of the ghetto in 1942. Their reunion had been witnessed by an American soldier, Robert Levine. He and Grinberg were discussing the difficulty of maintaining the provision of supplies to St. Ottilien because it was not recognized as a regular DP camp:

In the midst of the conversation he suddenly stopped, remaining absolutely still. He moved only his eyes toward the door and stared as it opened and a woman came in followed by a boy. She looked at Dr. Grinberg, her face tight and wrinkled like those of the starving prisoners of the concentration camps. She tried to smile, then to laugh, but the sound became a plaintive wail as the tears poured from her eyes and her head shook up and down uncontrollably. It clearly was an effort for her to keep from sinking to the floor. The boy stood right behind her and stared at Dr. Grinberg with his eyes wide and his mouth open. Dr. Grinberg, still not moving, began crying, and then moaning through his tears, "Oh, my God! Oh my God!" over and over. Suddenly he pushed himself forward, took the woman into his arms, pulled the boy into his arms with her, began kissing the woman's face all over and did the same with the boy, his hands and arms moving all over them, around them, touching them, caressing them, making certain they were real, that they really were there.

Levine hastily left and, as he shut the door, could hear the sounds of laughter.[47]

The wife and son were now in Palestine. When Grinberg went there in July 1946, he found that the boy was dying of leukemia. He stayed on, even after his son's death in September.

The leadership of the Jewish DPs in Germany passed to others.[48]

ELEVEN

"Skryning"

REPATRIATING DPs, 1946

Marianna Kisztelińska went to Germany in 1939, age seventeen, as a seasonal worker, but when war broke out she was not allowed to return to Poland and became in effect a forced laborer. She met a fellow Pole in 1944, and they had a child together whom the sympathetic farmer for whom she worked allowed her to keep. After the war she and the child's father were married, and in January 1946 they returned to Poland, where they eventually settled on a smallholding in the "recovered territories." By contrast, Wera Letun, another woman at the same Polish DP camp in northern Germany, did not want to go back to Poland after the war—she came from an area in the East which had been swallowed up by the Soviet Union in September 1939. But Mikolaj, her boyfriend, persuaded her to return. They headed for Lublin, where they had heard of a farmer who needed labor, but on the way Wera developed typhus and spent weeks in hospital. When she recovered, she decided not to stay in Poland, and she and Mikolaj made their way with some difficulty back to the British Zone of Germany, where they registered as displaced persons. A third Polish DP, William Lubiniecki, wanted to go back to Poland with his family immediately after the war, but there were no transports and they had to wait. In the camp, they heard rumors about the situation in Poland and were glad that they hadn't gone back after all.[1]

Such were the choices facing Polish displaced persons in the spring of 1946—not that they were allowed to make up their own minds. Although Poles made up the largest national group in the camps in Germany, Austria, and Italy, they had, in the eyes of the military and UNRRA, the weakest claim to staying. The United States and Britain had recognized the changes to Poland's boundaries—and the new government in Warsaw—but still refused to recognize the Soviet annexation of the Baltic states. Both the military and UNRRA were keen to resume the process of repatriation of Poles which had been suspended in late 1945. To them it made political and administrative sense.[2]

The continuing presence of Polish DPs in Western Europe could only sharpen the divisions within UNRRA. The Soviets and their allies, as the UNRRA history put it, "believed that there were two classes of displaced person: good and bad. The good should be helped; the bad should not. The test of whether an individual was good or bad was whether he wanted actively and quickly to return to his country of origin." The British and Americans, by contrast, believed that there were three classes: "good, who wanted to return to their areas of origin; good, who did not, for legitimate reasons, wish to return; and bad (collaborators, criminals, etc). They were prepared to help both the first two groups; that is, they were prepared to help some who did not wish to return home. To this, the Slav nations objected." In practice, the Western position was more nuanced than that, with many factors determining where the line between "good" and "bad" was drawn.[3]

The difficulty of reconciling such fundamentally different views within a single body became apparent at UNRRA's fourth Council meeting in Atlantic City in March 1946. After prolonged and acrimonious debate, it was agreed that UNRRA should continue to look after displaced persons in Germany, Austria, and Italy; but, at the same time, in an attempt to meet the wishes of the Slav nations, Resolution 92 was passed. This emphasized the importance of aiding and encouraging the repatriation of DPs by removing any handicaps and committed UNRRA to make available to the governments of origin figures about the numbers of DPs wishing to return home. UNNRA teams were to continue repatriation and "overhaul registration with a view to compiling occupational data which may be made available to the governments of origin on request"—in plain English, send the rest of the Poles back and sift through the Ukrainians.[4]

Some of UNRRA's European staff thought that the execution of this mandate would be a simple matter of logistics. "It is assumed that with the advent of warmer weather, a majority if not all Polish citizens now in Germany will desire to return to their homeland," a senior UNRRA official wrote in late March 1946. With negotiations with the Czech and Polish railway authorities successfully completed, he expected the process to start in early April and to continue until all the Poles in both zones had been repatriated. Assuming that each train consisted of 50 wagons with a capacity of 1,500 persons and allowing 100 kilograms of luggage per person, it would be possible to move 8,500 persons a day from the British Zone and 9,000 a day from the American Zone and to complete the repatriation of the 200,000-odd Poles in the American Zone during the early summer and of their 400,000 compatriots in the British Zone soon after.[5]

Others were not so sure. A Polish-American UNRRA worker who had managed to persuade many Poles to return the previous year warned that the forthcoming repatriation effort would fail unless it was accompanied by a propaganda offensive giving information on the questions which worried the Poles in the DP camps: what were the conditions of life in the new Poland like, what jobs were there, how was resettlement progressing in the territories Poland had acquired from Germany, what was the position of the Catholic Church, and so on. Unless these uncertainties were addressed, the Polish displaced persons would not return, even though it was clearly in their long-term interest to do so. Such a campaign was particularly necessary because liaison officers sent by the London Poles and by General Władysław Anders's II Polish Corps (based at this time in Italy) were touring the camps disseminating literature which urged the DPs not to return. Although the London Poles had by this time lost their official status as repatriation liaison officers, they were still allowed to come and go by the Allied military and wielded considerable influence.[6]

The Allied hierarchy's response to Resolution 92 was mixed. The military authorities in Germany took it seriously but did not enforce uniformity. Even as some American officers allowed London Poles to operate in the camps, the U.S. military government in Frankfurt decided that the Polish displaced persons needed to be persuaded to go home. If they weren't returning because their life in the DP camps was too comfortable, the obvious thing to do was to make it *uncom*fortable. And so the military embarked on a campaign to disrupt the DPs' lives. "The Army is preparing to say that they must return home or get out of the camps, and is already beginning to move DPs from one camp to another and thus to make them as uncomfortable as possible," an UNRRA official reported. Such "population shifts," according to UNRRA's monthly team report in April 1946, were "attempts to merely unsettle the DPs and so drive them home." All the Polish camps in the Wiesbaden area, for example, were closed and their population transferred to camps in the Munich area.[7]

However, these tactics soon produced a howl of protest from the Polish DPs themselves and from Polish groups in the diaspora. The large Polish-American community had begun to mobilize itself the previous autumn, using as its ambassador the formidable Senator Arthur H. Vandenberg of Michigan; and, thanks to his pressure, the State Department had enabled Poles in America to make postal contact with their compatriots in Europe. Consequently, the army's initiative in Germany was now immediately condemned by the Polish American Congress, an umbrella organization established in 1944 which claimed 6 million members. To force Polish DPs to return to a Communist-dominated Poland would be "a cruel injustice and a flagrant violation of our American tradition of justice and humanity," declared Charles Rozmarek, the silver-tongued Chicago lawyer who led the Congress. In Britain, the Catholic newspaper *The Tablet* complained that UNRRA personnel had been telling Poles that if they did not return home soon, the best land would be gone or they would have to work for the Germans.[8]

In fact, however, UNRRA in Germany was itself split on this issue—"double talk and vacillation," was one view. Sir Frederick Morgan—although not always well-disposed to Polish DPs—was strongly anti-Communist. His implementation of Resolution 92 was dilatory and halfhearted; privately he voiced worries that there might be "unpleasant incidents" during repatriation and screening. Only in May 1946 did he pass on to UNRRA staff in the field a resolution taken by the UNRRA Council in March; even then he made no attempt to put greater muscle behind repatriation: in the U.S. Zone, for example, there was only one ill-equipped repatriation and emigration officer. Personal hostilities further complicated matters. UNRRA's director in the British Zone, Sir Raphael Cilento, was as opposed to repatriating Poles as Morgan but proved such a treacherous and unreliable colleague that the general found him impossible to work with—Cilento, he came to believe, suffered "not only from a complication of inferiority complexes but also, quite possibly, from some sort of mental disease." As a result, both men's energies were diverted into a personal battle which was finally resolved only when Cilento was recalled to Washington in June 1946.[9]

The confusion at the top meant that there was no coherent policy within the organization and a wide variety of approaches prevailed. Some UNRRA staff agreed with the military that only a tough line would work—such as the team director who concluded that, as all Poles living in comfortable housing were reluctant to return home, whereas those living rough were keen to go, the only thing to do was to chuck them out of the comfortable camps and shatter their "delusions of perpetual UNRRA care." Others took a different view. Officials in the British Zone denied that there was an official policy of persuasion or a propaganda team carrying it out: "UNRRA tried to be as neutral as possible." The policy was "not to encourage people to either stay or return," a British woman working in the American Zone later recalled. "We had at that time to be absolutely non-committal."

Kay Hulme, the deputy director of the UNRRA team at Wildflecken camp in Bavaria, heard about Resolution 92 early in April 1946. Six trains of repatriated Poles per day would be leaving the American Zone and probably one a week from Wildflecken. She immediately volunteered to go on the first transport, so as to help persuade other Poles to follow. Hulme passionately believed that it was in "her" Poles' best interest to return to their homeland. Snowbound in a remote Bavarian valley for the long winter months, she had seen the corrosive effects of DP life on the personality. "The DPs will be ruined utterly if they live off Reilly another half year," she wrote. For the Polish men, life was dominated by "incessant plundering and pilfering," punctuated by occasional episodes of murder and rape, with reprisals from the local German population. At the end of March, a raid by U.S. Army intelligence had "removed 11 of our banditti, including our chief of police." The fact that the DPs received a guaranteed 2,300 calories a day while their German neighbors made do on 1,800 (or less) created obvious opportunities.

> Centered in a continent of hunger, Wildflecken rose up before German eyes like a magic mountain made of sugar and Spam, or margarine and jam, bearing forests of cigarettes (four packs per week per worker) and carpeted with vitaminized chocolate bars.

The Poles had devised "a sort of New Year sport that broke the monotony of sitting around waiting for something to happen." They would go into the local bars, get talking to a German, invite him back to the camp for some trading, load him up with cigarettes and chocolate, and then arrest him for illegal entry and possession of unauthorized goods—before handing him over to the military government for trial.

As a welfare worker, Kay Hulme saw all too clearly the effect of camp life on the women. A mass VD examination ordered by the military revealed that 16 percent of them had gonorrhea, including the girl who had played the Virgin Mary in the camp's "Holy Manger" Christmas show. Nor did the penicillin treatment which UNRRA offered have much deterrent effect, the miracles of antibiotics being by now taken for granted by the inmates. What mattered to them was that the VD program came with three days' hospital food; it became known as "paradise."

Infanticide was also rife. "We had a murder in the camp yesterday which made us all mad with rage," Kay wrote on February 2, 1946. "When the sanitation trucks went their rounds in the morning, they dumped a newborn naked baby out of one of the barrels. It was a beautiful little full-term baby, with thumb prints round the neck from strangling, and marks where a finger had been thrust down the throat to complete the suffocation." After long investigation, it emerged that the baby had been murdered by her mother, the young Polish girl made pregnant by an American GI whom Kay had met on her first day in the camp. Nothing was done to prosecute her.

Kay also had her own good reasons for wanting to get away. The winter had offered her some compensations, such as learning to ski, but against that there were many frustrations—the monotony of the diet, a growing sense that UNRRA's hierarchy was useless, and a steady daily bombardment of brain-numbing U.S. Army "poop sheets" she had to read and implement.[10]

Kay was well aware that it would be a struggle to persuade any of the DPs to return—a contemporary UNRRA report found that only 65 people out of Wildflecken's population of more than 11,000 had initially expressed a willingness to go home. Nonetheless, the presence of Kay and the chairman of the camp committee combined to swell the number to 89 and ultimately to 220.

The prospect of accompanying the Poles sent Kay into a tremendous state of excitement. "I pray with an inner fervor that is a veritable fury that nothing will go wrong," she wrote. "Whatever it will be, it is the consummation of my heart's desire . . . to take the last ride with my Poles, to cheer them along."[11]

On the day, everything went wrong. The train arrived late, composed of the wrong sort of boxcars, the medical department complained it had had no notice, a siren that was supposed to warn the Poles that they were about to be picked up never blew, food delivery was delayed, and there was not enough clothing for the travelers, who were given large, thick mitts to wear.

But these initial problems were soon forgotten. "Ten days in a boxcar riding across Central Europe in the spring spoils you for any other kind of travel, especially if you have a little hobo blood in your veins," Kay wrote later.

> You sit on the swept floor with your legs hanging out on whichever side the April sun is shining, rolling along quite slowly just four feet above fields of young grain and clover which you can smell as intimately as if you were there face down on the sap-sweet earth. You rock along and wait for the incurves to come so that you can lean out and wave to friends in the forward and following cars and maybe point with excitement at a loping hare or a birch grove hazy pink in early bud. And everyone watches the engine wheezing and huffing at the head of the clanking linked cars, manufacturing hot water for a shave or a wash-up, which the engineer will spigot off into your bucket for the price of a few cigarettes at the next stop.[12]

Kay was on a perpetual high. She adored everything about the trip: the eighty-five-year-old granny she befriended who was going home to find her two surviving sons in Cracow; riding in a car with "nineteen boisterous bachelors"; the singing that accompanied the clanking of the train; the high-spirited bartering at stops along the way; the endless toasts in plum brandy; the sense of freedom when they entered Czechoslovakia; and, most exciting of all, the moment when they crossed into Poland itself—marked by a crescendo of national songs. At the first station inside Poland—Zebrzydowice—they "poured from the cars and sang their national anthem under a full moon until you thought your heart would crack."[13]

All the worst fears seemed groundless. There was no sign of any Russian soldiers, just a "small gay station" featuring a flag-decked pavilion of the P.U. (Polish Committee of Repatriation), posters of fine bold design saying *Welcome to Poland—We will all work together* and a loudspeaker giving off dance music. In a mere five hours all the train's passengers had been "discharged"—registered, photographed, and given an ID card. The strangest thing for Kay was to see her Poles going off by train to their final destination, having all bought second-class tickets, and "waving to her in her terrible box-car from their superior coaches."[14]

Kay got back to Wildflecken five days later, on Easter Saturday 1946, "burned bright red, haggard and ten years older." She told her colleagues that Poland seemed "to have been almost normal, except for prices, and everything, even salt, rationed." However, her "hallelujah accounts of the total absence of any signs of Communism in their land" did not prompt many more Polish DPs to volunteer. The second Wildflecken train to Poland carried only 154 repatriates, accompanied by a Norwegian welfare worker, Johnny Gulbrandsen, and Kay's friend, the Belgian nurse Marie-Louise Habets.[15]

Having lived through the German occupation of Belgium, Marie-Louise knew what to look for. Riding through Czechoslovakia the day after May Day, she saw scarlet hammer-and-sickle banners strung across every town, and in Poland she picked up things Kay had missed: evidence of partisan activities; "workingmen" helping the Polish repatriation committee who were Russian agents in disguise; the high price of food in ordinary shops (not the show ones Kay had visited). As a nurse, she "quickly spotted the excessively dry skins which denoted lack of fats in the diet. With lard selling for four hundred zlotys the kilo (twenty dollars the pound) the prevalence of the dry skins was explained." Instead of embracing the Poles in tearful farewells (as Kay had done), Marie-Louise stayed on the train as the box-cars were cleaned—and watched as they were stripped of all food scraps by desperate Poles. She also made a careful photographic record of conditions in Poland which, it was hoped, could be used to encourage the Poles to return.[16]

Back at Wildflecken, her prints were developed and made into a poster display. Unfortunately, one of her photographs caused consternation in the camp. It showed a postbox on a pillar; the Poles noticed that the eagle of Poland had lost its crown. That brought the repatriation movement to a standstill.

In Poland, a struggle was going on. The Communist Party, which had enjoyed negligible support before the war, was gradually maneuvering itself into power. On the military front, the Communists were using their control of state security to liquidate the main Polish underground organization during the war, the Home Army. In late 1945, this provoked an uprising, a sustained campaign of armed resistance, with as many as 35,000 anti-Soviet activists operating in the marshes and forests. However, this process played into the Communists' hands because it enabled them to associate their political opponents with the partisans and to use the machinery of state to destroy them.[17]

Having accepted the Western insistence on "free, unfettered elections" and party government in Poland, Stalin had arranged that the Provisional Government of National Unity, established in June 1945, should include members of the Polish Peasant Party and the Social Democrats as well as the Communists. Under the Potsdam Agreement, early elections were supposed to be held, but the Communists deferred them, arguing that the country needed to recover first. Meanwhile, the security police worked ceaselessly to surround, isolate, blackmail, and even murder the democratic politicians. Their particular target was the Polish Peasant Party, whose leader, Stanisław Mikołajczyk, enjoyed enormous popularity in the country: on his return from London, tens of thousands of people welcomed him in the streets of Cracow and Warsaw. While the Communists maneuvered with skill, Mikołajczyk proved to be a poor political tactician.

By early December 1945, the democratic political parties were under direct attack. "The massacre is in full swing," Mikołajczyk's deputy, Stefan Korboński, wrote. "The country reminds one increasingly of a slaughter house." Three prominent members of the Polish Peasant Party had just been murdered, the latest victims in a long list.

One is struck by the openness of these murders. Local security officials well known to the entire population either kill the victim in the presence of his family, or lead him ostentatiously through the village or town, and then shoot him in the neighbourhood.

Some cases indicate that the security officials intend to let the population know that they are murderers. The purpose of this is easily guessed—to arouse fear of the security police, and to establish terror as a basis of the regime.

Later that month, Korboński's name was struck off a list of deputies submitted by his party.[18]

In March 1946, the Peasant Party came under pressure to join the Socialists and Communists in a common electoral bloc. When it resisted, its offices were raided by the security police and the authorities announced that its party cards had been found on the dead bodies of members of underground gangs captured by the police. When one of the underground organizations was put on trial, witnesses were used to tar the party. In June 1946, the Ministry of Public Security announced that the party had been banned in two districts because of its "cooperation" with the nationalist underground organizations. Meanwhile, there were occasional signs of the Soviet puppet masters who were pulling the strings; the army replaced the traditional four-cornered Polish cap with "a round one whose style is only one step removed from the Russian *shapka*"; and, calling one day at the Ministry of Public Security, Korboński caught a quick glimpse of a Russian officer whom he had previously seen while being interrogated. This, he later discovered, was the real ruler of Poland, NKVD General Ivan Serov.[19]

The concerns of the political elite would not necessarily be shared by ordinary Poles. A peasant or former slave laborer in a DP camp deliberating whether to return home was more likely to be affected by the physical state of the country, the economic situation, and the prospects of advancement. In early 1946, Poland was still in a terrible physical condition. The destruction of Warsaw had surpassed even that of Berlin, leaving visitors speechless; in August 1945, the minister of health warned that the country was in "a catastrophic state with respect to sanitation and health." There was "a high death rate, a high tuberculosis rate, [and] an epidemic of venereal disease." Food prices had spiraled out of control. "An average worker's monthly pay was sufficient to buy 3 kilograms of fat or oil, or 5 kilograms of pork or 5 kilograms of sugar, or 20 kilograms of flour." There were also widespread food shortages. In February 1946, it became plain that Poland was facing a very serious grain shortage that might lead to famine; a party official reported that in Gdańsk a rail workers' strike had "erupted against a background of utter hunger and a lack of apartments."[20]

The political situation and physical condition of the country combined to create a black national mood. The Polish state had failed twice: in 1939, when it had proved unable to protect its citizens; and again in 1944, when it had been powerless to keep out the Russians. On top of that, trust in the Western Allies had turned to exasperation and a sense of betrayal.

Yet, against all these things, the situation in 1946 still offered opportunities. The war had created a terrible vacuum within Polish society, decimating entire classes. Landowners and officers had vanished; much of the intelligentsia had been murdered by Hitler and Stalin or gone into exile. It has been estimated that 30 percent of all Poland's scientists and academics perished; 57 percent of its lawyers; 21 percent of judges and prosecutors; 39 percent of doctors; and almost 20 percent of teachers and artists. This loss meant the prospect of social advancement for the ambitious. A humble doctor could run a hospital, a coal miner join management. Those who played the game could advance quickly through the police. And the "recovered territories"—the industrially rich lands around Breslau which Poland acquired from Germany—had to be rebuilt and settled.[21]

There is a discrepancy between UNRRA's official figures for the numbers of Poles returned and the perception within the organization. The figures show a steady flow of repatriation, which in the first six months of 1946 added a further 179,487 persons to the 150,773 who had already returned to Poland. This was a respectable figure but way below what the UNRRA hierarchy was hoping to achieve and well short of the complete removal of the "Polish problem" some policy makers had been anticipating. Hence the perception within UNRRA that, after an encouraging start, the tide of repatriation had stopped altogether by the summer.[22]

Why did Poles choose not to return? In their search for explanations, UNRRA and the military rehashed many old favorites: fears of a looming war between the United States and the Soviet Union, rumors of which were spread by Anders's officers; general apprehension that Poland had become part of the Soviet Union; the role of priests in resisting repatriation; and adverse reports sent back by those who had been back and by Jews fleeing from Poland. The economic situation in Poland certainly didn't help: in April 1946, internal UNRRA reports warned that the Polish government was considering putting a temporary stoppage to repatriation because of the Warsaw food shortage.

By June 1946, however, the media was being blamed, especially the American soldiers' newspaper *Stars and Stripes,* which had carried stories with lurid headlines:

ARMED TERRORISTS BURN AND PILLAGE POLISH VILLAGES; GIRL VICTIMS STRIPPED TO UNDIES AS POLISH CLOTHING BANDITS STRIKE; POLAND CUTS BREAD TO 200 GRAMS DAILY

Also blamed was the failure of the Polish government to set out its position vis-à-vis repatriates clearly. UNRRA had been trying since February to get something out of Warsaw, but "the complete and persistent absence of any authentic official public statement regarding Poland and the government's plans for repatriates, emanating from the Polish Provisional Government" meant there was only a reprint of a speech made by the Polish prime minister, Edward Osóbka-Morawski, in 1945, in which halfhearted appeals to patriotism were combined with a tone of menace—"bad psychology," an UNRRA person correctly observed. The UNRRA postmortem agreed that "the most important thing would be a statement from the Polish government that they desired all Polish DPs to come home."[23]

One aspect of the Polish problem was resolved, however. The British government had for some time faced the question of what to do about the large number of Polish troops serving under British command who were unwilling to return to a Russian-dominated Poland. Some 30,000 soldiers had agreed to go back, but that still left 60,000 in Britain and 100,000 in Italy, where their presence under the command of General Władysław Anders, who had made no secret of his anti-Communist and anti-Soviet feelings, had been denounced by the Soviet bloc.[24]

On March 14, 1946, General Anders was summoned to London to meet Attlee and Bevin and was presented with a fait accompli. The next day, he was told, Bevin would make public an Anglo-Polish understanding which "laid down the way in which Polish soldiers repatriated to Poland would be treated." According to Anders, it "contained a list of reprisals and punishments which would be inflicted on certain categories of them," while also making "vague promises that they would be treated in the same way as all other soldiers of the resurrected Polish army." Anders was indignant at the secrecy in which this important decision had been arrived at and at the short notice he had been given. He had believed that no decision would be taken in regard to the Polish forces until after elections had been held in Poland. He learned, however, that the British view had always been that the troops should return to take part in the elections. Bevin "seemed to think that their votes would really count and that by returning they would help in the attainment of Polish freedom." Bevin and Attlee were "kindly" in their explanations and assured him that no one would be repatriated against his will and demobilization would not be hurried. Nonetheless, it was clear that their main anxiety was that as many Poles as possible should be returned home.

The prospect of this happening was further diminished when the Polish government made it plain that it would receive soldiers of Anders's army not as military units in the armed forces of Poland but purely as individuals. The British then sent every Polish soldier in Italy a personal letter from Ernest Bevin, hastily translated into poor Polish, urging him to return home. It had the opposite effect. Anders recalled that "simple Polish soldiers" tore up Bevin's declaration, "revolted by the suggestion that they should return to Poland on the basis of the agreement made by Britain with the Provisional Government of National Unity in Warsaw." The Poles still clung to the declaration made by Churchill in 1944 "that the problems of Poland and her frontiers would be decided at a peace conference at which Poland would be represented."[25]

When it became clear that its approach was not going to work, the British government changed tack. In early May 1946, Bevin announced that he was now aiming at the earliest possible demobilization of the II Polish Corps and its transfer to Great Britain. The total of 160,000 men (many with families) would be formed into a Polish Resettlement Corps, which would prepare them for entry into civilian life in Britain or overseas. Announcing the scheme in Parliament on May 22, Bevin rejected Churchill's suggestion of using the Poles as part of the garrison for holding Germany. "I think it would be a bad thing for British policy if we were to go in for a system of foreign legions to undertake our responsibilities." Privately he wrote that such an arrangement "would only increase the outcry against a 'Fascist' army and make the political settlement more difficult."[26]

The transformation of the II Polish Corps, with its long and glorious military record, into a "resettlement corps" was almost the last chapter in the long saga of Anglo-Polish misunderstandings during the Second World War. British political opinion accepted Bevin's plan as the best way out of the difficulty, albeit without much enthusiasm: the London Poles had by now become a diplomatic embarrassment, but they could not be abandoned altogether. At the same time, however, the government concluded that by letting in so many Poles, the majority of whom could be expected to stay in the United Kingdom, the country had done its bit for refugees. The Cabinet ruled out taking any more Jewish refugees from the DP camps.[27]

General Anders accepted that, for the British, demobilization and resettlement in civilian life were something that needed to be done. At the same time, he wrote, "no Polish soldier was unaware of the significance of this British decision to demobilize the Polish army. All hope of an immediate return to a free Poland was gone, and all those ideals for which Polish soldiers had shed their blood on foreign soil were proved vain dreams."[28]

Repatriation was only half the story; screening was the other. Resolution 92 had also called for the "registration" of all DPs and the compiling of information about their employment skills and past history. As with repatriation, many different impulses lay behind this move, one of which was a wish simply to reduce the numbers that UNRRA was caring for. In Italy, such a process of "screening" had weeded out some 10,000 people who were not eligible for DP status and the perks that went with it. Nonetheless, for UNRRA and the army to screen all the million-odd DPs in camps in Germany and Austria was quite an undertaking. Was screening going to be a fundamental exercise in monitoring the wartime records of DPs—in which case according to what criteria? Or was it to be a much less ambitious exercise in reducing the numbers and eliminating some of the most obviously unsuitable people? In practice, it was often neither.

A first attempt at registration, in May 1946, soon encountered problems and had to be abandoned. In June staff were told that screening was to resume later that month, but further difficulties soon emerged. There were wide variations. In one area of the U.S. Zone, screening was carried out so fast by soldiers who were soon due to leave Germany, often using as interpreters people of the same groups as those being screened, that it was almost worthless. In another, the process was more thorough but equally unsatisfactory. The officers made available by the army, selected primarily because they would be in the sector for at least sixty days, were "youthful, newly recruited men, to whom UNRRA problems concerning DPs, and the task of screening in particular, were at first unknown quantities." The local UNRRA district director, seeing how unprepared they were, had hastily organized a three-day screening school in which the officers were given a crash course.[29]

This was mission impossible. "The Army and UNRRA tried hard to teach these boys in 12 hours what other people had tried to learn and understand during six or more years of intensive study," as one report put it. "They heard about minorities and languages, dialects and national hatreds; they learned of German occupation methods and Russian government methods. They were told of tricks used by people posing as displaced persons and they were shown both genuine and false identity papers." Most of these young soldiers were between eighteen and twenty-three years old; a few were first-generation Americans who still spoke a foreign language; some had holidayed in Europe before the war. But most of them did not know, like, or understand Europe and were entirely incapable of understanding the complex issues involved in screening.

> Looking over the crowd we could see two or three interested faces, one or two ambitious ones, scribbling away trying to store away all this information they were being swamped with . . . and all the others yawning, tired of a mass of words they could not possibly understand and frightened to death of an assignment they knew they could not do justice to. Some of them gratefully heard that an UNRRA official, chosen for special experience and qualifications, would be with them on each Team. Others obviously did not like the idea of having a civilian at work with them to whom they were asked to listen and from whom they were requested to take advice.[30]

A few individuals were committed to the exercise. The UNRRA member on one screening team was Gitta Sereny, the young, articulate, forceful, attractive welfare officer who had lived and traveled extensively throughout Europe and spoke and understood some seven or eight languages. She completely dominated the army lieutenant in charge of the team, a former rodeo rider and combat-tank officer from Texas. Sereny insisted that they process the DPs very thoroughly and uncovered some collaborationists. But she made herself unpopular with the UNRRA hierarchy by boldly interpreting the eligibility guidelines according to her own conviction that "the basic set of principles should be that any man or woman who had, during the six years of the war at any given moment, for any amount of time borne arms under the Germans, belonged to the national government or a minority group set up by the Germans, entered German territory and worked in Germany or annexed territory on a voluntary basis, or been evacuated by the Germans from his home country should be disqualified for DP care." In one camp Sereny estimated that between 15 and 20 percent of the Poles would be found ineligible, mainly as collaborators or as members of the Wehrmacht. She also argued

> that 80% of the Latvians should be ineligible since there was definite evidence that Latvians who came to Germany in 1941, 1942 or 1943 came without [any] pressure whatsoever, unless the inducement of high wages or the glories of the Wehrmacht, SS or Luftwaffe are considered to be pressures. It was only during two months in the summer of 1944 that Latvians were actually conscripted either to work or to fight. After that, there was no need to conscript manpower, for large numbers came to Germany as political refugees fleeing from the advancing Russians.

Then Sereny went further, calling for the whole screening process to be halted. It had become "a joke . . . a mere farce," she wrote on July 21. She proposed that "two hundred university graduates and undergraduates" be recruited from the United States to do the screening. Finally, she rejected the argument that "nothing can be done by UNRRA because the Army is in charge and not UNRRA."[31]

When Sereny's request to appear before the forthcoming meeting of the UNRRA Council was brushed aside by her superiors, she made contact with a friend in the BBC and offered him an exclusive story "exposing" UNRRA's screening program. He promptly informed UNRRA's hierarchy. Sereny was dismissed. Her insubordination had provided her superiors with the opportunity to ignore the bigger point she was making.[32]

Behind the scenes a battle was going on between, on the one side, UNRRA, and, on the other, Allied military and diplomats who were increasingly intervening to protect certain groups of DPs from having their pasts investigated. The "Balts"—the displaced persons from Latvia, Lithuania, and Estonia—had from the start enjoyed a privileged status. Not only had they been protected against repatriation since March 1945, they were able to claim DP status. They soon showed themselves adept at exploiting the system and taking advantage of the occupiers' ignorance of what had gone on in Eastern Europe. "Our Latvian nurses, who previously had led me to believe that they had come voluntarily during the war to work in the German hospitals, changed their mind the other day; perhaps it was because they saw the DPs in Hospital receiving special clothing issues, or perhaps we had misunderstood them before," an Australian working for UNRRA noted in September 1945. "The Latvian nurses now signed a statement that they had been forced by the Germans when they occupied Latvia to work first in German Hospitals there, and then to move into Germany to work in Military Hospitals. Having established themselves as DPs they now receive the special issue of rations."[33]

The Estonians even began to agitate on behalf of their menfolk who had served in the German army and were now being held as prisoners of war in Germany. In this they were helped by the Latvian diplomat Charles Zarine, who retained considerable influence in London, and by the dominant man in the British Foreign Office's Northern Department, Thomas Brimelow, who had been the British consul in Riga in 1939 and had then served in the embassy in Moscow. That experience had left him with very strong anti-Russian convictions, and he was now prepared to bend the rules to help the Balts. "Try to keep the Balts as long as possible and as quietly as possible in the status of prisoners of war until a decision has been made about their ultimate disposal," he told the military authorities in Germany in October 1945, "and if they have to be disbanded before such a decision is reached, they should be treated not as German civilians, but as Baltic DPs." This policy was quietly adopted in the British

Zone. Brimelow also took the view that it was in practice impossible to decide whether Baltic men who had served in the German army had done so voluntarily or under compulsion and argued that they should therefore be given the benefit of the doubt. He encouraged the authorities to fend off any Soviet requests for the extradition of war criminals; as a result, the Foreign Office created a double standard by which non-Germans in the Waffen SS were treated far more leniently than their German counterparts.[34]

The secrecy which surrounded screening aroused unnecessary resentment and fear among the DPs. Nor was the need for it adequately explained to UNRRA's own staff. "We were slow to see that in fact the screening would be of vital importance to every DP," Rhoda Dawson, a British welfare officer with UNRRA, later recalled.

> We were forbidden to explain the reason for it. We knew it was to separate the sheep from the goats, to clear out the Germans, the Volksdeutsch, infiltrees and criminals whom we knew to be hiding in the camps; and to find, among the real pre-V-day refugees, those who had been proved collaborators or willing workers with the Germans, and those who had come in after a dead-line date some months after the end of the war, and were therefore held to be fraudulently enjoying the benefits of UNRRA.

Dawson accepted that the need for secrecy was imposed by the technique of screening.

> But it was cruel for the muddled, neurotic people, who immediately saw in it another threat of forced return to terror. We should have been given some tale to tell them . . . and in some ignorant or careless hands it was used as a punishment, whereas in fact, incidental mistakes apart, it became rather a good thing in the long run.

On the first day of screening in the Polish camp where Dawson worked, about fifty men, women, and adolescents over fourteen were sat down at separate tables. They then took an oath in Polish and filled in a questionnaire. It was supposed to be foolproof, but frequently the DPs couldn't understand it and had to be helped by the screening team. The claimants backed up their answers by the production of their papers.

> Those questioned were forbidden to reveal the nature of the questions to other DPs following them. But after a fortnight two men were seen to come into the room with the answers already written down. In another camp members of one group undertook to learn one question off by heart, after which a class was held secretly.[35]

There was evidently considerable scope for individuals to assert their own loyalties. According to one account, the members of UNRRA Team 539 deliberately sought to strip Ukrainian, Polish, and Russian inhabitants of refugee camps of their DP status. "Refugees were interrogated with hostile intent and in a biased manner. The UNRRA team's Jewish interpreters even went so far as maliciously to introduce their own questions into the interrogating process. Reportedly they also 'deliberately' gave false or misleading information to the presiding officer and otherwise prejudiced the proceedings against those being screened." As a result, apparently, 64 percent of the camp's inhabitants lost their status.[36]

Screening most affected Ukrainian DPs, particularly those from eastern Ukraine who had been Russian citizens in 1939 but were by now determined to avoid going back to the Soviet Union. UNRRA's new policy, if properly carried through, threatened them directly. "Very quickly they realized that the screening boards were designed to facilitate repatriation by locating those still liable to the use of force and inducing voluntary repatriation," a Ukrainian historian has written. "The presence of Soviet officials at many screening boards further frightened the refugees. The trauma surrounding these procedures caused the word 'skryning' to enter the Ukrainian refugee vocabulary."[37]

The Ukrainians devised various countermeasures—false papers, false identities, hunger strikes, appeals to higher authority. Refugees from western Ukraine helped the eastern Ukrainians by providing them with information to enable them to assume new identities—as Poles, Czechs, or Romanians—and then to maintain them in the face of detailed and hostile questioning as to their school attendance, employment history, and geographical knowledge. The Ukrainian poet Rodion Berezov claimed to have lived before the war in Vilnius, then part of Poland, and was elaborately coached in the street names, possible workplaces, bars, and so on of that city. UNRRA frequently relied on DPs as translators, and those people were often able to mislead Allied officials as to a person's place of origin. Another Ukrainian vouched for the "Ukrainian-Russian-Polish gibberish" a group of DPs were spouting: "I, not looking into the lieutenant's eyes, confirmed that each of them spoke Polish. . . . He took it calmly, not showing any reservations, but at the end of the day he asked me not to return as he himself spoke Polish rather well." There were also prewar emigrants from Poland, Ukraine, and Russia working for UNRRA or the military who took it upon themselves to help DPs with documents and other forms of help. In a report sent to Stalin himself, two NKVD agents described how, after entering a DP camp posing as Russian "displaced persons," they had been told by a Canadian soldier named Bashkenich that they would have to register under false names if they wanted him to help them. The camp translator, another Ukrainian, had suggested they say that they had lived in Poland before the war. The two NKVD officers had followed this advice and duly been registered as DPs.[38]

Screening had another consequence, however. It highlighted the split in the Ukrainian nationalist movement created by wartime events.

Shortly after midday on May 23, 1938, a violent explosion shook the streets of Rotterdam. Several buildings were damaged, and passersby found the remains of a well-dressed man splattered across the pavement. Witnesses told the police that shortly before his death, the victim had met a man in a bar who had presented him with a box of chocolates. After several weeks, the Dutch police learned that the dead man was Yevhen Konovalets, the leader of the Organization of Ukrainian Nationalists (OUN). The identity of his assassin took longer to reveal, however; only in the 1990s was it finally confirmed that the man Konovalets had met was Pavel Sudoplatov, an NKVD agent. In his memoirs, Sudoplatov revealed that in November 1937 he had been summoned to see Stalin and ordered to "behead the movement of Ukrainian fascism on the eve of the war"; the NKVD had then devised a plan, taking advantage of the Ukrainian's well-known fondness for chocolate.[39]

Konovalets, who had fought for Ukrainian independence in 1918 and gone into exile in 1922, had been the undisputed leader of the Ukrainian nationalist movement since 1926. But his death, followed soon afterward by the Nazi-Soviet pact, brought about division. In 1940, the Ukrainian nationalists split into two factions, the more moderate, conservative elements supporting Andriy Melnyk, an army officer and engineer with close ties to the Catholic Church, while the younger and more extreme nationalists followed Stepan Bandera, who had led a gang carrying out terrorist attacks in Polish-ruled western Ukraine in the 1930s. Both factions were funded by the Germans, but whereas Melnyk's links were with the Abwehr, Bandera was closer to the army.

The German invasion of the Soviet Union gave the Ukrainian nationalists their chance. Battalions of soldiers drawn primarily from the Bandera faction accompanied the German army into Ukraine and took part in the killing of Jews and Communists which followed. However, in June 1941—in what became known as the *akt*—the Banderites proclaimed an independent Ukrainian state in Lvov. This provoked a sharp response from the Nazi leadership, which had decided against giving Ukraine independence. In the ensuing clampdown, Stepan Bandera himself was arrested and sent to Sachsenhausen concentration camp.

The removal of this charismatic leader left the field open to the Melnyk group, which now pursued a policy of cautious collaboration with the Germans, who allowed it considerable scope for activity. Gradually, however, as the harshness of German rule became clear and a million young Ukrainians were dragged off to work in Germany, this association made it increasingly unpopular.

For both nationalist groups, Stalingrad was a turning point. The more conservative elements associated with Melnyk responded to the call for non-German volunteers to join new Waffen SS units, intended to produce new manpower for their depleted forces in the East. The conservative Ukrainians remembered how in 1919 their country had been divided between the Poles and the Russians while they looked helplessly on; they believed that this time, by having a well-trained military force, they would be able to stand up to the Russians. Young Ukrainian men who wished to avoid labor in Germany were happy to volunteer. In July 1943, in an atmosphere of nationalistic fervor, recruits were blessed by the leadership of the Uniate Church and a vast crowd gathered in Lvov as the detachments of the new 14th Galician Waffen SS Division paraded past the opera house.[40]

Most of these expectations were unfulfilled. Without being properly trained, the Galician Division was flung into the German line during the great Soviet offensive of July 1944 and almost completely destroyed. It was then withdrawn, rapidly brought back up to strength (with men from Ukrainian police units), and sent to suppress anti-German uprisings in Slovakia and Yugoslavia. By the end of the war, the unit had changed its name to the 1st Ukrainian Division and acquired a Ukrainian commander, General Pavlo Shandruk. As we have seen, this force was saved from repatriation to the Soviet Union by the British in May 1945, following appeals by General Anders and Pope Pius XII, based on the fact that its soldiers were, in theory anyway, Polish citizens.[41]

The OUN–Bandera faction drew a different lesson from Stalingrad: it decided to go it alone. In March 1943, it created the Ukrainian Insurgent Army, (UPA), which aimed to fight the Germans, keep out the Soviets, and cleanse all Poles from Ukraine. The movement gained wide popular support; in particular, some 12,000 Ukrainian policemen who had taken part in the killing of Ukraine's Jews were recruited. The Poles, of course, were the softest target. In the course of 1943, the UPA killed between 40,000 and 60,000 Poles, in many cases applying techniques of ethnic cleansing learned from the Germans. However, the Poles began to retaliate; by the summer of 1944, as the Russians were starting to reoccupy western Ukraine, an all-out civil war between Ukrainian and Polish partisans was raging.[42]

Thus, as the historian Timothy Snyder has shown, wartime circumstances had created a situation in which "the most powerful representatives of Ukrainian political aspirations was the extreme branch of a terrorist organization, organized as an armed conspiracy, and directed in the main by young and inexperienced men." That armed conspiracy continued after the war. When the Red Army entered western Ukraine in 1944, the Ukrainian Insurgent Army numbered as many as 200,000, and nearly every peasant household had a shelter containing weapons, ammunition, and food. Despite reportedly killing some 110,000 "bandits" and arresting and deporting hundreds of thousands more, the Soviet authorities were not able finally to defeat the Ukrainian partisans until the early 1950s; at one stage Stalin had the Communist Party leader in Ukraine, Nikita Khrushchev, temporarily replaced.[43]

Against this background, the screening process had unintended effects. Because most of the DPs fearful of being repatriated were eastern Ukrainians, they became very dependent for help on the western Ukrainians, who were mostly followers of the ultranationalist group led by Stepan Bandera. The easterners, therefore, tried to prove citizenship of the western region, but they would be helped to escape repatriation only if they accepted the leadership of Bandera and his lieutenant Yaroslav Stetsko. The way that screening strengthened the hand of the Banderists was noticed at the time. Visiting DP camps in December 1946, the Canadian-Ukrainian activist Bohdan Panchuk found that "Things are not what they were when the war ended or when I was here before":

> For one reason or another there has been a noticeable deterioration in type and character. The camps are now full of "politicians" who are forever playing politics and games of God knows what instead of getting down to earth and realizing their true position, that they are displaced persons and not wanted by any country except the USSR. Instead of rolling up their sleeves and getting down to work, and learning something and making something of themselves, they find politics, black marketeering, and even banditry, looting, stealing, beating up those they don't like, etc. etc. etc. more "entertaining." This should never be spoken of or quoted publicly. We must defend the principle of the refugees and DPs . . . and victims of war, but, in actual fact, God forbid and protect us, if some of these parasitic bandits ever get into Canada.[44]

Panchuk's private worries in no way stopped the ceaseless flow of letters and telegrams to persons of power on behalf of his fellow Ukrainians. Similarly, the Catholic hierarchy in the United States continued to do what it could to help its fellow religionists in Germany. Secretary of State James Byrnes's attempt to close the DP camps in spring 1946 came to nothing when Roman Catholic leaders in the

United States put pressure on Truman. The president wrote to Byrnes on April 17, 1946, that the Catholic Church and the Poles "particularly are simply going to have spasms if we close out these camps without some sort of arrangement to take care of the people who can't go back." Byrnes's plan was shelved. [45]

At the same time, another form of protection for DPs was beginning to develop: that of the U.S. Army's Counter Intelligence Corps (CIC). Once the first wave of postwar Allied retribution had passed, the growing polarization in Europe gave new opportunities to those with skills or information to sell. "It was a visceral business of using any bastard as long as he was anti-Communist," an intelligence man later recalled, "and the eagerness to enlist collaborators meant that, sure, you didn't look at their credentials too closely." At the end of the war there was already in existence a "ratline" to safety leading via the Vatican to South America, run by the Croatian priest Father Krunoslav Draganović with the tacit approval of Pope Pius XII. At one time both Klaus Barbie, the notorious Gestapo chief in Lyons, and Franz Stangl, the former commandant of Treblinka, were enjoying the Vatican's hospitality. Despite his record, Barbie was taken up by the U.S. Army's Counter Intelligence Corps and quickly became a trusted operative until French clamoring for his head made it necessary to ship him hastily off to Bolivia.[46]

Similarly, the intelligence boss of the Organization of Ukrainian Nationalists, Mykola Lebed, who had played a prominent part in the "exhilarating days" of 1941—when thousands of Ukrainian Jews had been murdered in Kiev—escaped to Rome armed with files on anti-Soviet groups. At first rebuffed by the Americans as a "sadist and German collaborator," Lebed was put on CIC's payroll and taken to Germany, his expertise invaluable at a time when the military expected nuclear war to break out in six months, and was training an émigré army for use following an atomic attack on the USSR. When Lebed fell out with other exiled Ukrainians, he was spirited away to Washington.

At the same time, Allied intelligence was beginning to cultivate groups within the DP camps and was prepared to intervene on their behalf to shield them from screening. As early as 1945, Western agencies had begun contacting anti-Communist groups in Eastern Europe. In Poland and the Baltic republics, there was never substantial or sustained armed opposition to Soviet rule after the war—the British

attempt to train and finance operations in the Baltic states was moni-
tored almost from the start by the KGB—and though resistance
groups held out in remote areas for several years, the partisan movement never amounted to very much. In Ukraine, however, the
nationalists were a serious force. In 1946, they assassinated several
Soviet officials, blew up industrial plants, and mounted a revolt of
major proportions in the Donbas coal-mining region.[47]

The Ukrainian nationalists, already long-standing clients of both
German and British intelligence, acquired new patrons when the
American CIC took over the Nazis' intelligence chief, Reinhard
Gehlen, and his networks. The Ukrainians' resistance naturally
aroused interest in London and Washington. But nobody was under
any illusions. As early as 1945, London had taken a long look at Stepan Bandera's Organization of Ukrainian Nationalists and concluded
that it could "never be more than a 'nuisance' to the Soviets. But to
keep the Ukrainians going they had to talk the language of liberation." For their part, the Ukrainians were old hands at handling foreign intelligence networks, giving them exaggerated reports, and
playing one service off against the other. An American review of
"operations involving the use of Ukrainian nationalist organizations
for the purpose of collecting secret information on Eastern Europe
and the USSR" concluded that "duplication of effort" was inevitable
and "security hazards" very likely. While the Ukrainians were good
at pretending that "their past record is a clean one" and claimed an
"excellent intelligence service leading directly into the USSR," they
were "the most highly opportunistic groups in Europe, adroit political intriguers and past masters in the art of propaganda."[48]

What difference did any of this make to life in the displaced persons camps? Evidence of a direct trade-off is not forthcoming, but in
the spring of 1946, two Foreign Office mandarins, one of them
Thomas Brimelow, showed concern for the Ukrainians. They urged
the authorities in Germany to allow the Ukrainians to carry out
"welfare work" in their camps. "We are not suggesting that the
Ukrainians should be entitled to special privileges," Brimelow wrote.
"The only thought in our minds is that the denial to them of educational facilities in the Ukrainian language and the practice of treating
them as either Poles or Russians constitutes a definite hardship which
we should try to alleviate."[49]

Not surprisingly, Control Commission staff were at first baffled by this development. "We should all like to know what the Foreign Office mean by Ukrainian," they wrote. "We have always told people here that there really is no such nationality—a Ukrainian is a Pole, or a Soviet citizen, or stateless according to his origin. Now I see . . . that the FO think . . . that we ought to allow Ukrainians to organize their own non-political welfare work in the British zone." In May 1946, however, the Control Commission accepted the Foreign Office's recommendations and sent a letter to Allied HQ in Berlin stating that although Ukrainians were not to be officially recognized as a separate group, "[i]t is recognized that there is a need for welfare activities and facilities for teaching and entertainment in the Ukrainian language if the morale of the Ukrainian DPs is to be maintained. It has therefore been decided that there is no objection to the organization of welfare work for their benefit provided that all organizations are of a non-political character." However, since Ukrainians did not constitute a separate nationality, "it is not therefore possible to provide a precise definition of who are Ukrainians. It can only be said that they are those persons who speak the Ukrainian language and wished to be considered Ukrainians."

The people who benefited most from this change of policy, however, were the members of the Ukrainian Galician Division who had surrendered to the British in May 1945 and then been allowed to stay in Italy. As Italy regained its status as a sovereign nation—peace treaties were signed in 1947—its presence there became more difficult. In April and May 1947, the entire division was brought to Great Britain by the Attlee government.[50]

TWELVE

"Save Them First and Argue After"

LA GUARDIA AND UNRRA

On March 12, 1946, Herbert Lehman resigned as director-general of UNRRA, citing failing health. On the face of it, this was reason enough. "The governor" was nearly sixty-eight years old and had been involved in refugee relief for more than four years, three of them with UNRRA. In that time, he had flown hundreds of thousands of miles, suffered countless frustrations, broken his leg, and lost his son in the war. Only recently, he had lived through the drama of renewing UNRRA's financial mandate, faced increasing difficulties with the Russians, and had his long-needed holiday interrupted by General Morgan's dramatics. Now a fresh crisis loomed over food supplies. Lehman had had enough.

In fact, Lehman's health was not failing; he was well enough to run for the Senate in November of that year. There were other reasons for his departure. Increasingly, he felt that he could not rely on the new president as he had on the old, in confronting his critics in Congress, and he feared that Truman "would lack the comprehension and sympathy that Roosevelt had always displayed in dealing with UNRRA." His worries that the new administration was abandoning the international humanitarianism of the wartime period for a more narrowly national conception of relief were confirmed early in March 1946, when Truman asked UNRRA's archcritic, Herbert Hoover, to review the needs of Europe and Asia for food. The appointment was good politics for the president but more than Lehman's pride could stomach. Nor were his own political ambitions over.[1]

Who would his successor be? Under UNRRA's constitution, it had to be an American. There was talk of the former ambassador to London John Winant or of FDR's roving ambassador W. Averell Harriman. In the event, Truman asked Fiorello H. La Guardia to take on the job.

Already a major political figure, having served five terms in Congress and three as mayor of New York City, La Guardia was also well equipped for the job. For a start, he knew all about Europe. The son of an Italian father—a musician—and a Jewish mother, he had been raised on army posts in the American West before accompanying his family back to Trieste, then part of the Austro-Hungarian Empire. His first job, at the age of seventeen, had been for the American consular service in Europe, and by the time he returned to New York in 1906 he was fluent in Hungarian, German, Serbo-Croat, Yiddish, and Italian. Thereafter, La Guardia's career was a triumph of industry and idealism. After putting himself through law school by working as an interpreter on Ellis Island, he practiced law on New York's Lower East Side, while taking his first steps into politics. As an Italian American he gravitated toward the Republicans, rather than the Irish-dominated Tammany Hall Democratic machine, and made his name as a congressman in Washington before seeking election in his native city.[2]

La Guardia's executive talents were proven. He had brought honest government and a nonpolitical civil service to New York; transformed the city's roads, parks, airports, and public housing; developed ambitious new social programs and work creation schemes. But La Guardia was much more than a competent manager, he was a unique political personality. Compensating for his appearance—he was fat and only five feet, two inches tall—he was a powerful campaigner and natural showman who "read the Sunday comics over the radio to the 'kiddies' in his tenor-alto voice, and raced his own firemen to fires." He also "helped set an anti-Fascist and anti-Nazi tone as a national personality before the United States entered World War II."

If La Guardia was so well equipped, why had he not played a bigger part in the war—or been put in charge of UNRRA before? The answer was simple: he was not an easy man to work with. The mayor's personal style was "screaming, ranting, fist-shaking and more than a little irresponsible." As the historian Robert Caro has written, "Men who distrusted excess distrusted him. And he did not hesitate to play melting-pot politics, to wave the bloody flag, to appeal, in one of the seven languages in which he could harangue an audience, to the insecurities, resentments and prejudices of the ethnic groups in the immigrant district he had represented in Congress. His naked ambition for high office, his cockiness, truculence and violent temper . . . repelled them." Herbert Lehman had frequently lost patience with a man who "accused and vilified everyone who opposed or criticized him," but he respected his "indefatigable energy and shrewd judgment."[3]

The war years had been frustrating for La Guardia. Despite his best efforts, he was never given a job suited to his talents. The army refused to have him as civilian overlord in the Mediterranean theater; Roosevelt made a more orthodox Republican, Henry Stimson, his secretary of war; the UNRRA job went to Lehman. In fact, it suited FDR to keep the "little flower" in the United States, in the grand-sounding but impotent post of head of civil defense. In 1945, La Guardia's political career came to an abrupt end when Harry Truman, a loyal party man, declined to support a Republican mayor of New York, leaving him with little prospect of being reelected.[4]

Why, then, did Truman's administration now turn to La Guardia? The perception was that UNRRA was in a critical state, with possible scandals in the offing; that quick action had to be taken, especially on food; and that La Guardia could not refuse. He was seen as the man to sort out the food problem. But beyond that, his appointment was widely regarded as a decisive indication that the United States was determined to bring UNRRA to an end as quickly as possible. Washington's hostility to making further contributions to UNRRA, and its wish to terminate all its operations, was by now well known.[5]

Initially, La Guardia did not want the job. He was exhausted, and his health was poor. But eventually his sense of personal responsibility, his vanity, and the assurances of friends that only he could make UNRRA work wore him down. There remained, though, a contradiction in La Guardia's position. As UNRRA's man in Italy later put it, the mayor had been appointed "to take charge of the closeout" of the organization. "This was not a happy appointment. Fiorello was by his emotional nature best fitted for something that was growing, and that was improving and that was giving Fiorello the credit for it."[6]

La Guardia's own analysis of UNRRA's failings was largely emotional. Franklin Roosevelt's "magnificent conception," the "greatest relief operation in history" and the "future of international cooperation as an instrument of peace," had, he believed, been undermined and betrayed by the British Foreign and War offices and, to a lesser degree, by the United States State and War departments. Although UNRRA had accomplished great feats in rehabilitation among the displaced persons in Germany, it had been hamstrung by its dependence on the army for its supplies. Its prestige had gradually been whittled down, and Lehman was now bequeathing to him "a sorry stepchild."[7]

What, then, was to be done? Talking to his friend Ira Hirschmann on March 22, 1946, La Guardia was clear that his first job was to "get food to the people." Then they would have to find a "quick answer to the Displaced Persons' problem." Hirschmann broke in excitedly.

> "We need rescue squads, not committee meetings," [he] said. "We've got to move in and break every rule known to man, and that goes for the British Foreign Office and State Department too. We've got to improvise, slash red tape into ribbons—we've got to *save them first and argue after.*"

La Guardia agreed. He asked Hirschmann to get ready to go to Germany and prepare a study of the DP camps for him. The purpose of the mission, he said publicly, was "to enable us to kill the many, many rumors that are floating around and the gossip that is going on concerning these camps." There were continuing doubts in Washington as to Morgan's commitment to UNRRA, attitude to Jewish displaced persons, and effectiveness in enforcing Polish repatriation.[8]

La Guardia's envoy was an interesting, multifaceted man. Then forty years old, Ira Hirschmann was a business executive, broadcaster, and prominent figure in New York's cultural life. A graduate of Johns Hopkins University and the Peabody School of Music, he was a vice president of Bloomingdale's, ran a radio station, and, with his pianist wife, had created an organization to promote classical music, the New Friends of Music. A friend of Arturo Toscanini, Artur Schnabel, and Otto Klemperer, he was also an old associate of Mayor La Guardia and had been involved in helping Jewish refugees for many years.

Politically, Hirschmann was a supporter of the Bergson group, a radical right-wing Zionist organization which had effectively publicized the plight of the Jews of Europe by aggressive advertising and by mobilizing the support of sympathetic non-Jewish celebrities. In

1943, he had been sent as FDR's special envoy to Turkey and thereafter been much involved in the War Refugee Board's efforts to help Jews escape from Romania.[9]

Now La Guardia was giving him a new mission: to proceed "without fanfare, through the back door" to Germany and make "a complete inspection of the DP camps." He had, La Guardia said, been getting private information which did not jibe with the official reports coming across his desk. So he wanted to know exactly what was going on, to have "a full and complete report on Morgan and his work in the Displaced Persons camps." As Hirschmann was preparing to leave, the Anglo-American Committee of Inquiry reported, recommending that 100,000 Jewish displaced persons be admitted to Palestine. Much of the early part of his trip was, therefore, dominated by a scheme he hatched to mobilize UNRRA to move the 100,000 Jews to Palestine and use tents and equipment from deserted UNRRA camps in Egypt to feed them there. But by the time he reached London, in early June, he learned that the British were going to reject the report; his plan was irrelevant.

On June 12, 1946, Hirschmann landed at Frankfurt airport and was met by General Morgan's deputy. He was bundled into a large Packard and driven at high speed through the ruins of the city and, along a broad autobahn passing through fertile, rolling countryside to a small village in the heart of agricultural Hesse containing two castles called Arolsen. In one of them he found General Morgan. As he made himself at home in a large bedroom hung with portraits of the von Waldeck family, from whom the castle had been borrowed, Hirschmann found himself wondering why this "remote idyllic country place had been chosen as headquarters for an emergency activity dealing with nearly a million refugees." Arolsen was 150 miles away from U.S. Army headquarters in Frankfurt and at least 400 hundred miles from Munich, where the main clusters of DP camps were.

A sense of unreality began to take hold of me as I bathed and dressed; this was not a visit to UNRRA, Germany, to investigate human misery—I was a house-guest beginning a week end in the country. This sense of unreality grew on me as I descended a long, circular staircase into a baronial reception room where men and women amid brass and braid awaited me.

Among them was a tall, well-dressed British officer who turned out to be General Morgan. Hirschmann found him charming, disarming, and personable. The general, for his part, found Hirschmann "a good little chap, a New York German Jew obviously a great friend of the Mayor." "His mission seems to be to collect firsthand information for the Mayor."[10]

Visiting Washington in April 1946, Morgan had found La Guardia "quite an impressive affair":

> I took to the little man very much. A marked contrast to his predecessor. He is obviously a tremendous driving force but intensely amusing with it. He is obviously going to get something done or else. He told us frankly that he hated UNRRA and everything to do with it. But like the rest of us he has never found himself in such a spot in all his life. But having been asked by the president to take the job on, he had no alternative and having got it, he intends to do something with it or perish in the attempt.

Morgan and La Guardia had been able to clarify the lines of command. Morgan would in future report directly to the director-general or to his personal representative in Europe—who, just now, was Ira Hirschmann.[11]

The next day, Hirschmann began to plan his itinerary. Looking at a vast map of Germany that covered an entire wall, the sheer scale of the operation sank in on him. Between Denmark and Austria, UNRRA was running nearly three hundred camps with more than three-quarters of a million people. Each of these self-contained communities of between 500 and 6,000 people had to be operated by a small team of UNRRA workers, using supplies provided by the military. And the problem seemed to be getting bigger all the time. Were those displaced persons being returned to the East who wished to go? he asked. Were UNRRA's directives on screening out former war criminals and Nazi collaborators being followed?

Then Hirschmann had a moment of revelation. Why was the impression constantly given in America that displaced persons were principally Jews, "when by actual count the Poles outnumbered the Jews by more than four to one?" The statistics he was given were startling: of just under 800,000 DPs being cared for by UNRRA, there were 422,000 Poles, 187,000 Balts, 104,000 Jews, and 23,000 Yugoslavs. "Why was the presence of Poles and Balts soft-pedaled?" he asked. "The sense of unreality which struck me at my arrival grew steadily stronger." "What, then, was the real purpose of this high-powered, far-flung setup in this charming, medieval village in central Germany? Was it a façade? Was it there to conceal a Machiavellian game in which the DPs were only pawns on a political chessboard?" Recent press reports had suggested that the U.S. Army was considering arming disaffected Poles and Yugoslavs and forming them into guard and service companies to replace U.S. troops deployed elsewhere in Germany. UNRRA, Hirschmann decided, was feeding and sheltering "armies of mercenaries dominated by anti-Semitic anti-democratic elements." The Poles and Balts were being allowed to stay in Germany so as to form the basis for an anti-Communist army.[12]

This perception—in which an element of truth was compounded with much fantasy and exaggeration—accompanied Hirschmann around Germany and fueled a rising sense of anger. His mood, increasingly, was one of outrage. He was struck, for example, by the contrast between the Baltic DP camps and those of the Jews: "Well cared for by UNRRA, the Balts had set up a community life which lacked the nervous tension typical of a Jewish camp." In one camp a large, well-appointed recreation and concert hall had been set aside for them. Having collaborated with the Germans, the Balts now "posed as war victims and exploited the charity of UNRRA," whereas the Jewish camps he visited were all desperately overcrowded and squalid, flooded with Jews coming in from Poland at the rate of 2,000 a day. At Zeilsheim, he watched "an endless queue of refugees, packs and bundles on their backs, plodding up the path towards the camp . . . a group halted and, throwing their bundles on the ground, literally fell in their tracks from exhaustion." It turned out that they had arrived in the last few days from Cracow and Polish Silesia, more than seven hundred miles away." At the Funk Kaserne near Munich, Hirschmann found 1,800 men and women "herded together like cattle in an abattoir, for these 1800 there were three toilets . . . the stench of urine and human excrement was overpowering."[13]

Hirschmann was horrified to find that his own sense of urgency was not matched by the Americans on the ground. Eisenhower's directive that Jewish DPs should be given priority over Germans—now almost a year old—was being ignored. Ordinary GIs clearly preferred the neat, hardworking Germans to the Jewish survivors, while

American officials seemed interested mainly in their own comfort. Jack Whiting, the "dapper and carefree" UNRRA director for the U.S. Zone, lived in a luxurious home in Passing, a suburb of Munich; UNRRA's representative in Berlin had an "enormous residence in the swank suburb of Wannsee." All of Hirschmann's concerns coalesced when he returned to UNRRA's Munich office after a long and affecting day in the camps and was taken to a nightclub by Jack Whiting. After twenty minutes of watching the "shameful conduct between our soldiers and German fräuleins," Hirschmann made his apologies and left.[14]

It was not just a matter of fraternizing with fräuleins; Hirschmann was witnessing the first signs of a real shift in U.S. policy. Everywhere he was told that the main priority of the U.S. authorities was now to build up the German economy. When he reached Berlin, he found Robert Murphy, the political adviser to the American governor, more concerned with the problem of absorbing into the American Zone the 2.5 million Sudeten German expellees who were pouring out of Czechoslovakia than with that of Jewish refugees. The deputy military governor, General Lucius D. Clay, was hostile and not prepared to be questioned about the Eisenhower directive. When Hirschmann said that the army was going soft on the Germans, Clay replied that the criticisms he was receiving from the United States were quite different: "Senators in the Middle West insist that we're 'starving' and 'coercing' the German people. You must remember that we have 15,000,000 Germans in the United States. We must give attention to their point of view." Clay's parting words were "The American people are idealistic, not realistic."[15]

Three months later, in a major speech at Stuttgart, the U.S. secretary of state, James F. Byrnes, would formally put the seal on the new policy toward Germany and, in effect, bury the possibility of further cooperation with the Russians. "It is the view of the American government," Byrnes declared, "that the German people throughout Germany under proper safeguards should now be given the primary responsibility for the running of their own affairs." The Americans were starting to come to the view that only by giving Germans back control over their own affairs could the rehabilitation of Germany, which they now agreed was essential, be made to happen. There was a growing awareness that the Potsdam accord was incompatible with the objectives of Allied policy.[16]

. . .

Hirschmann's German trip concluded with a second encounter with General Morgan at Arolsen. This time, a musical evening was laid on at which Count Emeram von Lerchenfeld played the piano exquisitely, but Hirschmann was also treated by Morgan to a lecture on the strategic situation. "'To all intents and purposes we are at war with Russia now,' he said in a confidential half-whisper. 'You don't have to have shooting to have a war. This time the Germans will be on our side. And this time our plan will work.'" Morgan then "pulled out a pencil and began drawing lines on the tablecloth to indicate where the next military battles would be fought. It seemed that Poland would again be the battlefield." Hirschmann expressed some doubt as to whether the British people were ready for another war and went to bed.[17]

On his return to Washington, Hirschmann recommended that Morgan be fired, along with his deputies in the British and American Zones. But nothing happened until La Guardia himself came to Europe later in the summer of 1946, to inspect UNRRA's operations and attend the next meeting of the UNRRA Council at Geneva in August.

The mayor's "field visit" was an elaborate business, a mixture of campaign rally and triumphal progress. Accompanied by a considerable entourage, La Guardia flew to Cairo and then made his way to Germany via Athens, Rome, Belgrade, Vienna, and Paris. The high point was his stopover in Rome, where his motorcade was met by huge cheering crowds and he was presented with a replica of the statue of Romulus and Remus being suckled by a wolf. The mayor then addressed the Italian Constituent Assembly, kissed countless babies, and visited the Cinecittà film studios, now being used as a DP transit camp, where he flew into a huff when the pushing and shoving of the crowd prevented him from talking to inmates of the camp. A colleague recalled that La Guardia "spoke fluent but very bad Italian," was "the mortal foe of the subjunctive," and "got into trouble for confusing the Italian words for wolf and calf," but was still hugely popular. Most of the practical work was done behind the scenes by Robert Jackson.[18]

While in Rome, La Guardia confirmed that UNRRA's operation would be wound up at the end of the year. The news caused General Morgan "intense relief."

· · ·

Morgan's diary in the spring and summer of 1946 had been dominated by two themes: the prospect of war with the Soviet Union and his fury at the inability of UNRRA to control what was going on in the Jewish DP camps.

Historians still debate the origins of the Cold War. It is only with hindsight that events such as George F. Kennan's telegram from Moscow in February 1946 and Winston Churchill's "Iron Curtain" speech given at Fulton, Missouri, a month later can be fitted into a pattern. At the time, many took a different view. But General Morgan, like many in the military, was an early Cold Warrior. His hackles were raised when, on a visit to Washington in May 1946, he was subjected to a "vicious verbal assault" by the UNRRA representatives of the USSR, Poland, and Yugoslavia, charging him with deliberate obstruction of the flow of repatriation. Their "refusal to accept the truthful statement that the existing means of transport were fully adequate to convey the small numbers of those who wished to travel" convinced him that "there is no question whatever of international-mindedness on the part of the Eastern countries. They are simply out literally to liquidate the DP problem as early as may be and no holds barred. It is plainly the duty of UNRRA to protect the DPs from these people." On May 30, he worried that "London and Washington are getting into closer and closer contact with the Russians over all Baltic questions. This may be the beginning of the great betrayal that I feel is becoming more and more imminent." In June 1946, as we have seen, he had outlined to Hirschmann the shape of the next world war. In July, he spoke of the "full extent of the Russian peril."[19]

Morgan's irritation was only heightened by the efforts of the Russians to control his activities. At UNRRA's fourth Council meeting at Atlantic City in March 1946, they tried to set up a supervisory committee which would sit at his headquarters and oversee his work. When that scheme was defeated, they came up with a new idea and sent the chief liaison officer in Germany to keep an eye on him. Morgan was not taken in by the officer's smiling exterior: "it is evident that all these Russians want is to try and use UNRRA as a means of evading military restrictions." He barely managed to keep his temper while spending "two trying hours" with "Commissar" Mikhail A. Burinski, a Russian member of UNRRA's Washington staff.[20]

This new mood made Morgan increasingly reluctant to persuade Poles to go back to their country—and he began to soft-pedal attempts to get the Poles to return. But it also made him feel that in this hour of need his true place was back in the military, not with UNRRA, from which he felt increasingly detached. "I am now almost entirely in a state of not giving a damn," he wrote on July 15, 1946. "The issue as between the East and West becomes more clear cut every hour but it is not easy to fight a battle when the majority of one's immediate staff either cannot or will not see the problem in its true light and are intent on their own petty squabbles. . . . I am beginning to look forward more than anything to the end of this nonsense."

The second issue to preoccupy Morgan was that of Jewish displaced persons. His New Year's outburst had done nothing to stem the flow of Jewish refugees from Poland, which continued throughout the first half of 1946 and became a flood after what happened on July 4 in the Polish town of Kielce. Following allegations of the blood sacrifice of Christian children, a mob attacked a hostel for Jews, aided and abetted by local soldiers and policemen. Forty-three Jews were murdered, causing thousands more to hasten to get out of Poland. The Warsaw government made no attempt to persuade them to stay. While the British refused to admit these "infiltrees" to their zone or to grant them DP status and rations, the U.S. Army allowed them into the American Zone. Morgan's mood was further clouded by events in Palestine, where the Zionist campaign of terror had culminated in the bombing of the King David Hotel in Jerusalem. "It is distressing to have to admit it," he wrote on July 19, 1946, "but it seems as if these Jews for the time being at any rate have us defeated. There seems nothing whatever that any of us can do to prevent the carrying out of the Jewish plan of mass migration to Palestine." [21]

Morgan became obsessed by the way that UNRRA's Jewish employees in Germany seemed to be doing all they could to subvert British policy on Palestine, while turning a blind eye to black marketing and criminality among Jewish DPs. Some of his suspicions were justified—certain American Jews working for UNRRA were indeed involved with illegal Jewish emigration. Saul Sorrin, for example, UNRRA's director for the Munich region, helped the Brichah's efforts to infiltrate Eastern European Jews into the American Zone and on at least two occasions escorted transports of Palestine-bound DPs from Germany to France. Furthermore, Morgan was correct in believing that it went higher than that—to the director-general, Fiorello La Guardia, himself. We now know that when La Guardia visited Yugoslavia in August 1946, he urged Marshal Tito to assist the movement of Jewish refugees through his country to Palestine, warning him none too subtly that the continuation of UNRRA's aid to Yugoslavia was conditional on that country's aid to the Jewish movement. [22]

The tone of Morgan's diary now grew increasingly overwrought, encounters with Jewish leaders frequently provoking him to anti-Semitic outbursts. He found Rabbi Yitzhak Herzog, the chief rabbi of Palestine, "an excellent old man with a keen sense of proportion and a great sense of fun. He is of outstanding intelligence and, so, broad-minded," but his traveling companion, Rabbi Solomon P. Wohlgel-ernter, was "one of the most revolting Jews I have ever had the misfortune to meet."

> I took delight in telling him in front of the Chief Rabbi to take off the UNRRA uniform which he was wearing without authority. I happen to know that he has made use of it to obtain privileges in the way of travel to which he is not entitled. A really nasty piece of work.[23]

All in all, by the time Morgan watched La Guardia's plane touch down in Munich on August 1, 1946, he was close to the end of his tether. In his diary he referred to La Guardia, who wore a Stetson throughout his European tour, as "a figure of fun" surrounded by "a trickle of tenth-rate personalities."

Morgan was determined to talk to La Guardia alone, to voice his fears about the way UNRRA was being infiltrated. But no early opportunity arose, and he was forced to join the mayor's entourage as it visited camps, his fury mounting all the time. The Jewish camp at Feldafing provoked an anti-Semitic rant; he noted that the prominent American Zionist Rabbi Abba Hillel Silver was "of the traditional Shylock aspect," but he failed to get his private audience with La Guardia. The following day, the UNRRA party visited a Ukrainian camp at Augsburg, where Morgan was amused by the mayor's igno-rance of European political geography: "he had the bright idea that what we needed was a Ukrainian Liaison Officer, there being no such thing." At Haunstetten camp, Balts told the Mayor all the usual tales while he tried his normal technique of trying to persuade the people how groundless are their fears of what lay before them in their home countries. He was defeated hip and thigh by a magnificent woman in the camp office, a widow of an Estonian Army Major who was deported by the Russians some five years ago and from whom she has never heard since. The Mayor turned to her asking whether indeed she, an obviously sensible person, thought there was any truth in what he had been hearing from the Committee. She said with withering contempt that she not only thought it but knew it.

Finally, after the inevitable huge lunch at a U.S. Army officers' club, Morgan had his chance. He got the mayor alone in his car and gave him "the works on what was actually going on in Germany," and "how necessary it is to destroy this UNRRA racket without trace at the earliest opportunity."

I vainly tried to give the DG some account of what was going on both as a result of Zionist activities and the infiltration of Russian agents, all under UNRRA colours. He was not interested, so little interested that . . . he fell into a deep sleep.[24]

A few days later, Morgan was summoned to Geneva, where the fifth UNRRA Council meeting was being held. He spent a few hours observing the discussions in the Palais des Nations, where the League of Nations had met, but mostly sat about waiting to be called by La Guardia. On August 9, he gave a press conference, telling journalists off the record that UNRRA was "honeycombed" with Soviet agents. The following day, press reports citing an "Allied military source" claimed that UNRRA was serving as "an umbrella covering Russian secret agents and criminal elements engaged in wholesale dope peddling and smuggling." When the story was traced back to Morgan, La Guardia dismissed him. "General," he told him, "you are the right man in the wrong job." Morgan privately agreed.[25]

As his successor, La Guardia appointed Myer Cohen, an American welfare bureaucrat of the kind Morgan most despised—and a Jew. In fact, Cohen proved to be a low-key uncontroversial figure who was frequently off sick.[26]

·   ·   ·

Having finally cleared the decks, La Guardia and Hirschmann made another attempt to repatriate the Poles. This time they were careful to prepare the ground.

In some ways, conditions were more propitious. Ernest Bevin had dissolved Anders's army, Polish liaison officers had been banned from DP camps since August 1946, and Morgan's departure produced a purge of UNRRA in Germany which left the staff committed to repatriation. Furthermore, a UNRRA delegation visited Warsaw to plan a propaganda offensive with the Polish government and returned with "optimistic assessments." The Warsaw government was persuaded to adopt a less menacing, more welcoming tone. A leaflet, titled "What Every Returning Citizen Should Know," explained:

> Q. *Will I be welcomed having delayed my return for so long? Will there be any discrimination against me for this reason?*
> A. Poland welcomes all Poles who will work for the rebuilding of their country. The earlier you come the better prospect and job you will have and there will be no discrimination.

The leaflet stated that there were plenty of jobs and set out the steps for obtaining work and the training programs available. Turning to agriculture, it assured readers that holdings of seven to fifteen hectares would be private property:

> The tales you hear about collective farms are only rumors. It is in the interest of the Polish state to have private holdings which are sufficiently large to be self-supporting. Collective farms are not being introduced anywhere in the country and will not be introduced.

In addition, a film was produced to be shown to DPs. "Come back to Poland," the commentary of *The Road Home* urged:

> *In the north where the ruined house stands*
> *There will be freedom, justice, jobs for all.*
> *It's time to come back to the plow, to the pick,*
> *Time to rebuild the house, time to return.*

Last but not least, there was La Guardia's brainchild, the Sixty-Day Ration Plan, known officially as "Operation Carrot." Every repatriate who returned to Poland before the end of 1946 would be offered sixty days' rations of food.[27]

One night in September, while Wildflecken camp was sleeping, Kay Hulme and her team set out to implement Operation Carrot.

In the big general meeting-place of the camp canteen we set up a permanent preview of the sixty-day food ration, which amounted to some ninety-four pounds of food per person—flour, dried peas, rolled oats, salt, evaporated milk, canned fish and a small mountain of lard. [Kay's Polish driver] Ignatz worked with me on the visual display, giving it art touches like slashing the sack of flour and spilling a little on the table so everyone could see it was fine white flour and not the dingy tan mixture of German rye used in the camp's bakery, carving a floral design on the lard and stacking the tinned goods in perilous pyramids. And this was only the handout in miniature, the food for a single person. On another table longer and stronger we set out what a family of four would receive, 376 pounds of food, and the mound of lard in this display had enough mass to permit sculpture of the white eagle of Poland in its front surface.

This display certainly produced an effect:

All day long the Poles filed past the food displays. The awe-struck processionals continued for weeks and weeks until the sculptured lard had been whittled away by scooping fingers, until the spilled flour disappeared handful by handful, until the stacked tinned goods had no more buttresses to the rear as Ignatz had built them in to support the steep sheen of the front turrets.

It took time for its effect to be felt, but by October the home-bound movement was in full swing again.

Bigwigs from Army and from our own HQ swarmed the camp and made us proud of the speed of our repatriation machinery, which could process 800 Poles and load a string of boxcars every three or four days, with a numbered card in the hand of every repatriant entitling him to draw that wonder-working sixty-day food ration as soon as he arrived in Poland.

The crescendo of outgoing transports caught us up, swept us with braying brass bands and crashing of boxcars switching in and slamming out, back in the old familiar frenzy of continual movement with no time for thought or feeling.

Gradually we forgot the secret shame we had felt when we had first stood beside the free food displays and watched our DPs stare at the terrible fascination of the bait, thrashing, twisting and turning before they took the hook.[28]

Operation Carrot worked—but only in the short run. "U.S. Zone repatriation continues strong for third week," UNRRA's *Repatriation News* declared on October 21, 1946. But the numbers of DPs boarding trains for Poland soon fell again, and La Guardia's effort to put real pressure on the Poles and to sift through the nationalities in the camps, extracting Ukrainians, began to produce a reaction. Polish-American organizations protested yet again. And in the camps, the DPs fought back.[29]

In January 1947, the Polish Communists decided to stage an election. They had previously been adamant that no poll could take place in winter, but, having successfully stage-managed a plebiscite the previous July and continued to harass the political opposition, they were now confident that victory could be engineered. As polling day neared and reports of Communist coercion began to come in daily, tension rose in the DP camps in Germany. In the crowds at Wildflecken, Kay Hulme caught glimpses of Poles whom she had sent off with much ceremony a few months earlier, now come back to warn their fellows against returning to Poland. A fortnight before the election, the Wildflecken Poles decided to boycott a "nationality screening" that was going on all over the American Zone by order of the army and UNRRA, under the auspices of a group of Polish liaison officers accredited to Warsaw.

Our Poles simply sat down and refused to present themselves to the Polish officers for a one-minute interview and the showing of some such paper as a birth or baptismal certificate, proving Polish nationality. In vain we called mass meetings, explaining that this screening was our only way of knowing how many Poles (and Balts, Ukrainians, Yugoslavs and so on) our organization was caring for in the Zone. In vain we explained that there was no forced repatriation back of this simple nationality verification, that after a man proved by the showing of a single paper he was a Pole, he would not have to repatriate to Poland unless he wished.

However, there were divisions within the UNRRA team. Kay found that Georges Masset and other Europeans on the team "understood why Warsaw had become a symbol for Moscow in the minds of the Poles." But Kay herself, "with a stubbornness which I could not define," still thought that repatriation was better than stagnation. She "clung to [her] belief that Poland would vote free, and refused to read the writing on the wall."[30]

Meanwhile, UNRRA regional headquarters was adamant that the screening must go ahead. Kay summoned the seventy block leaders and read out their orders, warning them that severe sanctions, possibly even eviction from the camp, would be taken against any person, group, or organization that attempted to block the nationality screening. But three days later, when the Polish liaison officers came, there was no sign of the DPs in the mess hall. When Kay tried to find out what was happening, she was told by Masset that a demonstration was taking place and that he had called in the army. By now the liaison officers were surrounded by shoving Poles and fled to their car.

They got into it while its windows were being smashed. One of the officers got out to dislodge the ruffians who were rocking the car and I saw a hand snatch off his gold-braided hat and start tearing at the insignia on his greatcoat; then suddenly he disappeared before my eyes. I thought for one horrified moment that the Poles had him underfoot stamping on his face. [Masset] appeared with four jeeploads of armed constabulary, but from where he was at the far edge of the howling mass, he could not see the mission car or what was happening to it. It was being rocked violently by a five-deep cordon of strong-arms until it pitched into motion pointing downhill away from the street where the constabulary jeeps were stalled by a living wall. I saw the mauled Warsaw officer climbing or being dragged into the rocking car just as the mob closed in to give it the final shove that sent it careening down the icy hill toward the main gate.

Such was the "Wildflecken riot," quickly infamous within UNRRA.[31]

Soon afterward, however, Georges Masset allowed the man who had organized the demonstration, Krzysztof Krakowski, to become president of the camp committee. Kay was disgusted: "The expert little fascist clique that organized the ousting of the Liaison Officers was quietly elected to posts on the new Polish Committee," she wrote. She finally realized how much and for how long Masset had deceived her, going behind her back to deal directly with the Poles in the camp.

In response, Kay denounced Masset to her superiors in UNRRA. She had, she wrote on March 2, 1947, been "consistently tricked, bluffed and lied to" by her director since December 1945, when Masset had gone to Paris in an UNRRA truck and then lied about it. Furthermore, she said, Masset had given vast quantities of food from the Red Cross to the Polish Committee which had been uncovered during the famous Operation Tally Ho raid of December 26, 1945, while he was away in Paris; shielded fellow Frenchmen involved in the black-market work; and sent his wife on a trip to Paris in an UNRRA ambulance. But her real charge was that "by the grace of Mr. Masset, the cunning and capable enemy of all that we represent is riding into power."[32]

Kay later came to regret the use she had made of Masset's minor crimes. Her behavior showed how the strain of life in the enclosed world of the camp had finally affected her. She made no reference to this episode in the book she later wrote about her UNRRA experiences and invented a happy sequence in which Masset announced that he was being transferred to the French Zone. In fact, he was dismissed from UNRRA.

That was not quite the end of the repatriation effort. Soon after the Polish Communists had intimidated and falsified their way to victory in February 1947, UNRRA's principal repatriation officer, Ralph B. Price, visited Warsaw and held extensive meetings with Polish ministries. Naturally, said Price, "the question of Wildflecken" had arisen in discussions in Warsaw. Polish officials had not specifically criticized UNRRA, but "they felt we had maintained certain UNRRA Personnel in this camp who hold anti-repatriation attitudes." He had assured them that conditions in Wildflecken would be altered. The following month another spring offensive was launched, built around proclamations by U.S. military commanders, the Polish prime minister, and UNRRA's director-general and zone directors. Posters received from Warsaw, dealing with the three-year plan for the reconstruction of the Polish economy and general life in Poland, were distributed; still photographs of Polish life and reconstruction and tables of the specific labor needs of the new Poland were put up; pamphlets on the land grants and wages available in the "recovered territories" in Silesia were handed out. Polish Radio produced special items designed to interest DPs considering returning; newsreels showing reconstruction were made available to UNRRA; and *The Road Home* movie was reedited and shown again. Finally UNRRA's own newspapers were used to promote and record the repatriation.[33]

Once again, there was a brief movement of Poles. But by May 1947, repatriation was being given lower priority in UNRRA. It was now accepted that nearly all the remaining Polish DPs would not be going home. They would have to either stay in Germany or be found homes somewhere else in the world.

THIRTEEN

"We Grossly Underestimated the Destruction"

THE FOOD CRISIS IN EUROPE IN THE WINTER OF
1946–1947 AND WASHINGTON'S RESPONSE

Victor Gollancz spent the night of October 2, 1946, in a vast room at Schloss Nuremberg in the town of Lemgo, near Hanover. The building was the headquarters of General Evelyn Fanshawe, Sir Raphael Cilento's successor as UNRRA chief in the British Zone. It was, Gollancz reported, "grotesquely like a very-rich mid-Victorian English house."[1]

The British publisher and campaigner was on a fact-finding trip. For the past year, in numerous publications and letters to the press, he had sustained his campaign of pressure on the British government to do more to feed the Germans. Now Gollancz intended to stay longer than previous visitors and carry out a thorough survey of conditions. He was receiving wholehearted cooperation from the authorities in the British Zone and had spent the previous two days hobnobbing with generals in their "stolen châteaux." "The quiet luxury of the food at all these places is spiritually nauseating and physically delightful," Gollancz wrote to his wife. "One had forgotten such meals were possible."[2] He found that the attitude of the British to the Germans "varies from decent and even very heartwarming to disgusting . . . but even at its best [is] horribly the attitude of the superior conqueror to the inferior conquered." "I find myself loving Germans in general just because they're despised and rejected," he went on.

Four days later, after having begun his investigations, Gollancz wrote again from the Atlantic Hotel in Hamburg. "Much the worst thing I've seen is the condition of the expellees from Polish-occupied Germany, of which there are 1,300,000 in Schleswig-Holstein. It is beyond any possibility to describe their misery. . . . We visited a ship in Kiel harbour on which about a couple of hundred have been living for six months: it is the only time since I got here that I was quite unable to prevent myself from crying the whole time."[3]

It was hardly surprising that Gollancz should find the worst conditions among expellees from the East. Fourteen months after the appalling scenes at the Stettiner station in Berlin had brought this issue to the world's attention, the flood of refugees was still continuing. Allied attempts to slow down the expulsion of Germans from Poland and Czechoslovakia and to create the mechanisms for an "orderly and humane" transfer of populations at Potsdam had had some success. Nonetheless, 3 million Germans from east-central Europe entered western Germany between January and December 1946. While the Czech government tried to carry out the operation in an "orderly, humane and efficient way," the Poles did not bother, bundling refugees onto unheated trains in the depths of winter. But both states, and Poland in particular, sent to Germany their "useless mouths"—the elderly, women, children, the insane—while retaining fit workingmen in their own countries. The protests of the British authorities in Germany were overruled by the Foreign Office in London, which accepted Warsaw's argument that the "recovered territories" must be cleared of Germans before they could be colonized by Poles and the much-promised Polish elections take place.[4]

The influx of yet more refugees placed an intolerable burden on the British Zone. Only 17 percent of those who had entered the zone by June 15,1946, were adult males, and only 60 percent of those were fit for work. The arrival of 750,000 economically unproductive expellees aggravated the food, housing, and public health situation. In late 1948, there would be 243 people per square kilometer in the zone, compared to 167 in the American and 131 in the French; it was estimated that if you reckoned on one person per room, the British Zone was short of 6.5 million rooms. The situation was at its worst in Schleswig-Holstein, where 120,000 people were still living in camps.[5]

To feed the extra mouths, the British authorities made desperate efforts to raise food production and make the zone more self-supporting. They had some 650,000 acres of grassland plowed—to produce, it was hoped, a 10 percent increase in the grain harvest and a 75 percent increase in potatoes; they tried to persuade farmers to slaughter their livestock herds, so as to provide meat and reduce the demand on arable pasture and feedstuffs; forbade the growing of luxury crops;

cut the amount of grain allowed for brewing; encouraged the cultivation of vegetables in town gardens and allotments; and did what they could to compel farmers to bring their produce to market.

But this policy was only partially successful. The farmers of northern Germany, who were by long tradition animal husbandmen and not cereal growers, resisted attempts to change their ways; there wasn't the staff to enforce the changes. Food production was further handicapped by shortages of seed, fertilizers, and equipment. British policy fell between two stools, providing neither effective coercion nor effective incentives.[6]

It was clear that considerable imports would continue to be necessary for several years. The British would have to juggle the needs of the Germans against those of their own population—whose bread was rationed in 1946—and other regions of the world, such as India. For reasons which we shall presently explore, it proved difficult to guarantee a steady flow of foodstuffs from the United States. And so the German population lived "from shipment to shipment" and the official ration went up and down as conditions permitted. After the initial, dramatic fall in the daily calorie intake of the "normal consumer," from about 1,500 calories to only 1,100 in May 1946, it was raised to 1,500 in September 1946 and remained there for the next eight months, before falling again.[7]

Although these headline figures mattered politically, they bore little relationship to what people in the streets of Germany actually consumed. For a start, the official ration scale was rarely distributed all over the country, and the normal consumer usually got considerably less, under 1,000 calories a day. That would have been a recipe for death and starvation if continued over time; yet there was no mass starvation in postwar Germany and no famine-related epidemics. There were several explanations for this. First, only a minority of the population—perhaps 38 percent—were "normal consumers." The rest fell into special categories, such as nursing mothers, old people, and heavy workers—plus, of course, displaced persons and "persecutees"—who were entitled to extra rations. Second, as time went on more and more people managed to obtain certificates from their doctors entitling them to extra rations, until by 1948 the percentage of "normal consumers" had fallen to 22 percent. Third, about 15 percent of the population consisted of "self-supporters"—farmers and their families who lived off their own produce. Finally, most people were able to supplement their official ration by getting extra food at work, buying it on the black market, or having it sent from abroad. The former mayor of Cologne (and future West German chancellor), Konrad Adenauer, for example, received the extra rations allocated to persons persecuted by the Nazis but wrote repeatedly to friends in Switzerland asking them to send penicillin for his wife, "energy foods" for his teenage son, and Nescafé for himself; it gave him the "liveliness" needed for his political work. Over the next few years, he received cheese, honey, condensed milk, and the drug streptomycin from abroad. He also turned himself into a "self-supplier" by developing a vegetable garden and a chicken coop. Less fortunate Germans got by through "hamstering": they went into the countryside and bought directly from farmers, usually bartering items for food. It was estimated that a quarter of all agricultural produce was disposed of in this way. But the old, the poor, and the expellees from the East were the least able to compete in this marketplace. Most of the latter had arrived in western Germany minus all their possessions.[8]

Certain refugee groups were fortunate. Those who had been civil servants within greater Germany were now entitled to join the civil service or get a pension. A large percentage of bureaucrats in the new Germany were in fact refugees, and the fact that traditionally teachers were employees of the German state also aided the process. But that still left many people at the bottom of the heap. While Germans noticed that the newcomers often clung to the dream of returning to their former homes and resisted sending their children to local schools or marrying into local families, foreigners were more struck by their abject living conditions. In September 1946, practically all the children at a feeding center in Hamm, in Westphalia, were found to be infested with worms. Many refugee families were living in concrete air-raid shelters which had survived the bombing. Ella Jorden, a British Red Cross nurse, found the atmosphere inside them "foul beyond description" and the bunker population of refugees "a sullen army of helpless humans living in conditions that would be condemned by any livestock inspector of the Ministry of Agriculture." However, this was nothing compared to the conditions in the improvised refugee camps in the countryside around. One day Jorden "found a room in which fifty or sixty people were huddled together, with their meagre possessions around them."

The only space between them was cluttered up with vegetables and potatoes, which they were storing and their sole hope of food for the months ahead. The children were dirty and unkempt and the women had filthy abscesses on their legs; they were at the end of their tether, having travelled for days and nights on end without rest. A poor woman from the Baltic was prostrate with grief. . . . [H]er only child had died on the way to camp. Now, having fallen into a hole in the floor boards, she had lost the new baby she was expecting, so she was almost demented with misery. I was thankful to be able to get these people out of that awful room and settled into homes, and put them in touch with a German doctor who came from a nearby town to visit them.[9]

These living conditions inevitably affected public health. Victor Gollancz claimed that in Hamburg 100,000 people were suffering from hunger edema or equivalent, in Düsseldorf 13,000 people were being treated for the condition, and the incidence of tuberculosis in Hamburg under British occupation was five or even ten times greater than before the war; in Schleswig-Holstein, it was five times greater. These figures were at once challenged by British doctors, probably correctly; many of Gollancz's claims were certainly "wildly over-stated," being derived from German doctors, whom he made a point of talking to precisely because he was warned not to. This meant that much of the impact of Gollancz's work was dissipated in the subsequent row between German and British doctors.[10]

But Gollancz saw the bigger point. Although he dramatized the suffering of the expellees—and in his book *In Darkest Germany* published harrowing photographs of malnourished children—his real argument was that Germany, as a whole, was not recovering. It mattered more that miners in the Ruhr were not getting enough to eat and were therefore not digging enough coal to get the German economy going again than that women and children from the East were starving. Gollancz blamed this on two factors: the muddled and clumsy military government and the Potsdam Agreement.

British occupation policy in Germany had never been properly thought through. Instead it had grown out of early improvisations by the occupying military, onto which an elaborate system of bureaucracy and regulation had been grafted. The result was neither a centrally planned economy nor a free-market system—a "madhouse" in which "nobody ever knows what anybody else is doing." At the same time, Potsdam had envisaged a tight four-power regime in Germany, with the four zones cooperating to run the country according to a mutually agreed plan. The difficulty was that Britain, the United States, the Soviet Union, and France all had different expectations of Germany. Instead of attempting to resolve these at Potsdam, the Allied leaders had hastily assembled a "protocol" that was built on contradictions. Germany would remain united, yet would be divided into zones administered by the victorious Allies; it would pay reparations to her former enemies, yet also be economically self-sufficient. When the Allies began to implement these procedures within the four-power Allied Control Council in late 1945, the strains at once became obvious. Gollancz noticed that the "reparations monster" seemed to operate quite independently, like an out-of-control robot, and gave several examples of the "lunacy which results from the operation of these two factors." A blanket-making firm was allocated coal—but no power to run its machines; a pin and needle factory was allowed to restart—but not to use its stock of raw materials, without which it could do nothing; a firm which needed building materials was told it had to obtain them outside the city where it was based— and then refused a permit to take a lorry more than eighty kilometers; the only company in Düsseldorf able to operate a tram service was given a license, which was then taken away. Kiel harbor was to be destroyed, with the loss of 150,000 jobs.[11]

None of this was news to the British government.[12]

The British were the first occupying power to lose patience with the Potsdam protocol. They found themselves in an impossible position, faced with a zone of occupation which had to import 70 percent of its food and which cost them £80 million a year to run; expected simultaneously to get Germany's industries going again and to provide substantial reparations from them; and frightened that any Soviet political involvement in western Germany might allow Moscow to undermine the revival of German democracy. Concerned to restore the balance of power in Central Europe, they soon began to examine alternatives. A lengthy paper put before the British Cabinet in May 1946 acknowledged that the Potsdam framework had not been a success and asked whether it might be necessary to abandon working with the Russians and divide Germany. The British objective was to reduce the cost of occupation, keep the Russians out, prevent another war with Germany, yet restore the country to its natural place as the economic engine of Europe. Privately British officials were well aware that unless Germany's industrial workforce was properly fed, no recovery would take place. They also knew that they could not act alone; any initiative must come from the Americans.[13]

Among Washington, Frankfurt, and Berlin, American counsels were divided. Elements in the State Department favored confrontation with the Russians as early as February 1946, when George F. Kennan wrote his "long telegram" advocating a policy of containment. But soon afterward, when Winston Churchill, now leader of the opposition in Great Britain, delivered his "Iron Curtain" speech in Fulton, Missouri—at President Truman's invitation—in 1946, the president himself was forced publicly to disavow it because American public opinion still demanded a reduction of occupation forces in Europe. In Germany, General Lucius D. Clay, who became in effect the American proconsul, continued to champion a policy of cooperating with the Russians within the Potsdam framework, believing that he could control them.[14]

There was, however, a further complication. In addition to the Russian insistence that Potsdam and its reparation provisions be carried out, the French had their own agenda. Like the Russians, they wanted reparations to be paid, but they also wanted Germany's industrial heartland, the Ruhr, to be "internationalized" or, even better, given to France. It was to counter this French initiative that the Americans proposed that their zone be merged with those of the other Western occupying powers. The British responded immediately, desperate to find a way of sharing or reducing the costs of occupation. Accordingly, on July 30, 1946, the British and American zones of Germany were merged to create a new entity under the comic-opera name of "Bizonia."[15]

In hindsight, this fusion of the zones can be seen as a momentous step toward the future division of Germany and the creation of the Federal Republic of Germany. At the time, though, not only was the significance of the step not understood, it also failed to deliver the expected benefits. There seemed an obvious logic in combining Germany's industrial north and its agricultural south into a single economic unit; the hope was that significant economies of scale and savings could be made; in particular, that food shortages might be at an end. Bizonia, though, did not work out like that. Southern Germany proved unable to feed the north. Nor were the two bureaucracies of occupation easily synergized: there remained considerable differences in work methods, ideology, and approach to the Germans between the two Allies. Even the philosophies of their agricultural experts did not agree.[16]

The important consequences of Bizonia proved to be political. Although "fusion" did not bring the economic benefits the British had hoped for, it did mean that they lost political control over their zone. Not only were British plans, for example for the public ownership of German industry, now shelved; the whole question of Germany's future passed into the hands of the Americans.

As it turned out, the United States rose to the challenge: 1947 proved to be a momentous year in U.S. foreign policy. But that process took time and unfolded in a particularly American way. It is best understood if we return to the vital issue of food, this time from an American perspective.

On the face of it there should not have been a food problem at all after the war. More than enough was being produced in the Western Hemisphere—and in particular the United States—to feed the starving Europeans, and probably the starving Asians as well. The war years had seen a second agricultural revolution in the United States, as a severe labor shortage led to the systematic application of mechanization and fertilizers which transformed the productivity of the land. By 1946, American agriculture was producing a third more food and fiber than before the war, with much less labor.[17]

However, Americans now wanted to eat more meat, and it paid their farmers to feed their cereals to the livestock needed to produce that meat, rather than to human beings. For the first time in history, high meat consumption in one major country would distort agricultural output all over the world.

However, the roots of the problem went back further than that. The people who ran U.S. agriculture were mindful of the huge surpluses in the 1930s, when overproduction had destroyed farm prices; their main objective was to avoid any repetition of that nightmare. At the end of 1944, the U.S. War Food Administration (WFA) had decided from a few shreds of doubtful evidence that Europe was not going to starve when the war ended. Accordingly—and against the advice of Herbert Lehman—it took steps to avoid overproduction by reining in farm output, relaxing rationing controls so that American civilians could eat up existing food stocks, and stopping all stockpiling for relief. The object of this "bare-shelves" policy, said the historian Allen J. Matusow, was "to come as close as possible to see that the last GI potato, the last GI pat of butter and last GI slice of bread was eaten just as the last shot was fired." Its potentially disastrous effects on European relief were soon apparent, and by the spring of 1945 public figures such as Herbert Hoover were warning of the perils ahead. Yet it was almost a year before decisive action was taken, partly thanks to Lehman's ineffectiveness in Washington and partly due to the different priorities of the Truman administration and its secretary of agriculture, Clinton P. Anderson, who was determined to put the interests of American consumers before those of relief.

Which is where meat comes in. If there is a villain in this story, it is the sheer hoggery of the American military, which insisted on annually requisitioning 430 pounds of meat per soldier, thus taking up a fair amount of the available livestock and diverting grain production away from human consumption. However, in wartime meat had been rationed for the domestic American consumer; with the coming of peace and Americans now eating considerably better than in the 1930s, there was huge pressure on Washington to remove the rationing, while the incentive to American farmers to sell their cereals for animal rather than human consumption remained strong. In November 1945, the Truman administration lifted all rationing of meat, oil, and fats.

Barely a month later, however, the cabinet received stark warnings about the international situation. A "grain crisis of unimaginable severity" was taking place in the world, it was told. Not only would the United States not be able to ship to Europe the meat, sugar, fats, and oil that were being asked for, it would, more importantly, have great difficulty in providing the 6 million tons of wheat without which Europeans would die.

It was at this point, in February 1946, that "bumptious, bell-bottomed Fiorello H. La Guardia" (as *Time* called him) took over at UNRRA. The mayor at once energetically attacked the food crisis, putting the issue on the national agenda in a way that Herbert Lehman had quite failed to do. He pleaded with farmers, called on coal miners and dockers to do their bit "in the name of suffering humanity" and urged Americans to eat less. Some responded: in June 1946, Eleanor Roosevelt told her radio listeners how the burghers of Princeton, New Jersey, were denying themselves bread four meals a week and fats for one day a week. But *Time* magazine doubted whether the American people as a whole were in the mood for sacrifices. "They kicked about beer shortages, grumbled slightly over the one roll per customer" in restaurants, and noted that grain farmers were still hoarding their wheat, hopeful of higher prices.[18]

Thus, by the summer of 1946, food had become a potent issue in the United States. On the one hand, La Guardia was trying—with some help from sympathetic figures in the State Department, such as Acheson—to arouse the nation's conscience, overcome logistical problems, and get more of America's surplus food to the starving peoples of Europe and Asia; for it was not just in Germany that there were shortages in 1946. On the other hand, America's farmers and meatpackers were withholding foodstuffs from the marketplace and creating shortages, to drive up prices and see off any possible return to wartime rationing and controls. The Republicans were positioning themselves to take advantage of this issue in the midterm elections at the end of the year. Meanwhile, the Truman administration failed to take the lead and tried, ineffectually, to reconcile the different positions.

Then La Guardia went further. Forgetting that he had been appointed to close down UNRRA and passionately identifying with his new role as the savior of the world's starving millions, he launched a new scheme.[19] At the UN meeting at Lake Success, New York, in September 1946, the mayor proposed the creation of a UN World Food Bank, to be run by a much-slimmed-down UNRRA, with an executive board of UN delegates, each representing one nation and elected by the General Assembly, to determine where the food should be allocated. With a budget of $400 million (as against UNRRA's $1.3 billion in 1946) and with no nation contributing more than 49 percent of the money, it seemed to him a sensible interim solution to the food problem. The Russians and their allies supported the proposal. But La Guardia very quickly discovered that the main opposition to it came from his own government. "We wish to give relief as the United States," announced Secretary of State Byrnes, "not as a member of an international organization in which a committee composed of other governments determines the allotment of the relief given by us."[20]

The mood in the United States was changing. "Internationalism was fading from a phase to a phrase," as Ira Hirschmann later put it. La Guardia's emotional appeals were losing their power. The very interests largely to blame for the shortages—farmers and agribusinesses—were fighting back, shamelessly wrapping themselves in the flag. Grain traders in Chicago rebutted the mayor's attacks as "scurrilous," while the National Association of Commodity Exchanges and Allied Trades warned that his food plan would "put the whole American system in danger." Officialdom, they claimed, was seeking to "subject the country's food distribution to a worldwide totalitarian [control]."[21]

The Republicans exploited this mood ruthlessly in the elections of November 1946. "Voters were tired of effort, sacrifices, meatless days, rising taxes, and government restrictions; the mood of 1920 had come back," the historian Allan Nevins recalled. "Before the voters floated a vision of chops, butter, and low-priced canned foods, not to mention abundant new cars, refrigerators, and radios that would be theirs if the Republicans won. Once the call had been, 'Vote yourself a farm!' Now it was 'Vote yourself a steak!'" The Republicans took control of both Houses of Congress.[22]

These developments signed UNRRA's death warrant. The Truman administration had long been losing patience with the organization, largely because of what was happening in Eastern Europe.

It was with a sense of dread that Francesca Wilson went to Yugoslavia in the summer of 1946. She had loved the place and its people ever since working there thirty years before, but she knew full well what terrible things had gone on during the war. So, indeed, it proved. One day Wilson was exhilarated by an unexpected feeling of hope and purposeful reconstruction; the next, sucked into despair as she toured villages gutted and ruined by the fighting. She heard countless tales of the partisans' exploits during the war; watched two UNRRA experts trying to persuade Dalmatian peasants to treat their American tractor with more consideration; talked to anti-Fascist women; and watched a plastic-surgery unit funded by UNRRA patiently repairing the human damage of war. Her published account sensitively explored the tensions and fissures which would drive Yugoslavia apart four decades later. But its primary message was different: she wanted to sing the praises of UNRRA.[23]

UNRRA's success in Yugoslavia was all the more remarkable because its work there had begun so inauspiciously. Although the country was completely in ruins in 1945, Marshal Tito's Communist government was deeply suspicious of all outsiders and would accept UNRRA's aid only on very tight conditions. Months of haggling went by before the UNRRA mission was even allowed to enter. Yet, paradoxically, that delay was helpful. It gave the Yugoslavs time to assess clearly their own needs and to create an infrastructure; it gave UNRRA time to weed out "black marketeers and angels of mercy" from its team as it sat around in southern Italy. In the end, UNRRA sent only about 150 people to Yugoslavia, nearly all of them specialists, headed by a formidable Russian engineer, Mikhail Sergeichic.[24]

As a result, UNRRA's task in Yugoslavia was straightforward and clear: it was a supply, not a service, organization, dealing with a single client, without the military to provide a complicating interface. The Yugoslavs told UNRRA what they wanted and UNRRA got it for them, with remarkable success, because many of the wartime logistical blockages had by now been cleared and UNRRA's machine functioned well. "Yugoslavia has really been the relief worker's paradise," a jolly Lancashire schoolteacher told Wilson in Zagreb. "How often have I helped in the finding out and reporting on the needs of the country where I was doing relief but with little hope of getting anything but short-term supplies—food and clothing and perhaps horses and cows, but never tractors or bulldozers or diving suits for salvaging ships or twine for making fishing-nets." This time, however, he had been able to buy two-thousand-gallon petrol cisterns in France and (fending off French car thieves) have them floated to Marseilles and shipped to Split, where, converted into water cisterns, they saved Dalmatian villagers from dying of thirst in late 1945.

The statistics were extraordinary. UNRRA provided Yugoslavia with 10,000 trucks, 14,000 pack horses, 10,000 mules, 237 locomotives, 8,555 railway cars, more than 4,000 tractors, 4,000 tons of caustic soda to put the glass industry back into production, $7 million worth of mining equipment, 44 sawmills, and 433 woodworking machines. And the achievements were solid—the country was saved from starvation, its bridges and railways were made to function again, and its agriculture and industry were kick-started. Whereas Tito had initially been reluctant to allow foreign experts in, by late 1946 he was anxious not to lose them.[25]

It did not seem remarkable to the people Francesca Wilson talked to that UNRRA should be spending so much money in Yugoslavia—ultimately $415 million—of which 72 percent was provided by American taxpayers. But U.S. politicians saw things differently. Not only was Tito's government arresting and executing its political opponents, collectivizing the land, and outdoing Moscow in its anticapitalist rhetoric, it was distributing UNRRA supplies itself and, it was thought, using them for political purposes. And to cap it all off, Belgrade was engaging in saber rattling. On August 6, 1946, the Yugoslavs shot down a U.S. Army transport plane which overflew their airspace and then manhandled its crew, which included a member of UNRRA's staff. When they were put in jail, reported Secretary Byrnes in his memoirs, "They looked out of the window and saw an American-made locomotive over at the railway depot with the letters UNRRA printed on it. They knew that 70 percent of the cost of that locomotive was furnished by the US taxpayer and the thought contributed little to the comfort of their internment."[26] Thus, ironically, in Yugoslavia UNRRA fulfilled its original purpose by carrying out one of the most successful postwar recovery programs in history; yet it also helped to bring to an end the United States' brief engagement with internationally funded aid.

It was a similar story in Poland. UNRRA played a decisive part in helping the country to function again but in so doing brought American criticism on itself. Nobody, of course, disputed the Poles' claim to relief. "Poland, after being twice a battlefield and having suffered for six years every attempt to obliterate it as a nation, is one of the most devastated countries in history," an UNRRA publication declared. After suppressing the 1944 uprising, the Germans had tried to demolish Warsaw completely. "You can hardly get an idea of what it must have been like from just miles and miles of bricks and skeletons of buildings," an American visitor wrote to his wife. The city's population, according to UNRRA, was "ill-clothed, ill-housed and ill-fed"; "no country in Europe [was] more ravaged by disease than Poland." And any prospects of recovery were overshadowed by the physical destruction and depletion of the population. "With its transportation system shattered, its agriculture and industry paralyzed through lack of livestock and agricultural machinery, raw materials and industrial equipment, and its population depleted from 30,000,000 to some 20,000,000, Poland's national economy has suffered almost complete breakdown."[27]

At the same time, the political situation in Poland complicated UNRRA's role. The organization was not allowed into the country until London and Washington had recognized the Soviet-dominated government in June 1945, and Brigadier Charles "Bud" Drury, a young Canadian with a brilliant war record who ran the UNRRA program for most of its duration, had to steer a neutral course among the factions of Polish politics. "Tactful, suave, yet energetic," Drury privately doubted whether Poland would become a Communist state because of the individualistic qualities of its people and the influence of religion yet established good relations with the Communists and earned their trust.[28]

Like the Yugoslavs, the Poles wanted supplies, not aid workers. They got them. Poland was the largest single beneficiary of UNRRA's program, receiving more than $480 million worth of aid between 1945 and 1947. Foodstuffs accounted for more than 40 percent of the relief—in June 1946, Bud Drury estimated that UNRRA supplied 1,100 of the 1,500 daily calories for the Polish urban population and 70 percent of the bread and grain they consumed. But UNRRA also sent large amounts of clothing, textiles, medical and sanitation equipment, as well as agricultural and industrial goods—more than 50 percent of all the trucks in Poland, $11 million worth of seed, $5 million worth of nitrate and phosphate, 151,000 horses, 17,000 cattle, 2,685 boxcars, 871 gondolas, and 105 locomotives. This munificence had an obvious effect. Initially suspicious of UNRRA, Polish officials soon became profoundly grateful for the organization's presence. The influential Communist technocrat Hilary Minc acknowledged that UNRRA's aid played a vital role in bringing about Poland's recovery from the Second World War, a view echoed and reinforced by economic historians since.[29]

But the message reaching Washington was different. Diplomatic and press reports constantly referred to pilferage, waste, black marketing, and discrimination. The last charge was the most important— that "the Polish government distributed UNRRA supplies on a political rather than a humanitarian basis." Arthur Bliss Lane, the American ambassador to Warsaw, acknowledged that Drury did a creditable job but claimed that "as the agreement with the Polish Government gave UNRRA no control over the distribution of goods imported by UNRRA, Drury could not prevent supplies being used for political purposes." For example, said Lane, the government made sure that UNRRA supplies did not reach "reactionary" organizations such as the Roman Catholic Church.[30]

How do international agencies control the distribution of supplies they bring into a country? That issue remains topical today. In the Poland of 1946, it is doubtful whether UNRRA could ever have prevented distribution from being entirely in the hands of the government. The ration card system in place before UNRRA entered the country favored some groups over others, so that workers in key industries and government employees did better than those in the rural areas, the elderly, and employees of private industries. Polish authorities insisted that food and other scarce commodities be shared on the basis of the amount and nature of the work performed. They also insisted that the rationing system be used as a wage subsidy, apportioned according to the wages the individual earned. Critics, however, argued that the Polish government used the UNRRA supplies to subsidize itself.

Some of UNRRA's personnel were certainly naive and blind to the political realities. But the UNRRA mission did have its triumphs—managing, for example, to persuade the Polish authorities to give a daily milk allotment to all children under twelve years old in Warsaw and to provide supplementary rations for pregnant women and nursing mothers.[31]

American press coverage, however, tended to focus on a few details, most notably the appearance of UNRRA goods on the free market. Under the headline "Poland Abuses UNRRA," *Life* magazine revealed that "At Warsaw's Hotel Polonia, if you are willing to pay the price, you can drink vodka cocktails made with UNRRA grapefruit juice intended for Poland's undernourished children," quite unaware that most Poles regarded fruit juices as a luxury novelty and preferred to sell them for bread and other necessities—at that time "a quart of juice bought ten pounds of bread, four pounds more than even a package of American cigarettes." It was also standard practice, approved by UNRRA, for the Polish government to sell some of the supplies it received on the open market and to use the money generated for other purposes.[32]

But on Capitol Hill the message was plain. These and other incidents—when, for example, Belorussia accepted American tractors from UNRRA while exporting locally made models to the world—convinced U.S. legislators that UNRRA was a mechanism by which the United States was generously funding the economic recovery of Communist, anti-American regimes. This was the last straw as far as Washington was concerned. "To both Congress and the Administration, internationally administered relief had been a failure," Dean Acheson wrote later. "The staff obtainable had been weak and the leadership weaker. UNRRA supplies turned up all too frequently in black markets, but, far more serious, the bulk of them went to the wrong places and were used for the wrong purposes." UNRRA was already doomed when the midterm "beefsteak" elections at the end of 1946 returned a strongly Republican, neoisolationist Congress. To clear away another source of trouble on Capitol Hill, the Truman administration made it clear that UNRRA would be wound up at the end of 1946. President Truman decided that in future U.S. relief should be concentrated in areas where the United States had special responsibilities and interests.[33]

But if UNRRA was gone, what would take its place? There were still a million displaced persons in Germany, unwilling to return to their original countries, who would somehow have to be repatriated or resettled. Who would do that job? Was it necessary to create yet another new organization, or could the existing mechanisms of international cooperation do the job? And had the recovery of Western Europe which UNRRA was supposed to bring about been accomplished? These were questions confronting American policy makers in 1947.

There were precedents for dealing with the problem of refugees. The League of Nations had created the Nansen passport to enable the 1.5 million Russians left stateless after the civil war to be resettled in other countries. In 1938, in response to the flood of Jews fleeing from Nazi Germany, another body had been created, the Intergovernmental Committee on Refugees, designed to act as a link between the League of Nations and the United States. Initially something of a farce—"one full-time director and a few stuffed shirts, whose function is really little more than that of the patrons of a charity matinee," according to a British minister—the Intergovernmental Committee had earned itself a good reputation by the end of the Second World War. Many people considered it the obvious body to take over from UNRRA. But the British regarded the committee as too pro-Jewish and the Russians had never been part of it, so it was decided early in 1946 to create yet another organization, under the auspices of the newly established United Nations.[34]

The negotiations to create this new UN "specialty agency" for refugees eventually started in January 1946 and went on until December of that year. Those twelve months of argument, procedural wrangling, rhetoric, and misunderstanding were a measure of the discord which the issue produced. Although the delegates were ostensibly working out practical measures to deal with a particular emergency, all the talks, a British diplomat recalled, "took place against a background of profound ideological disagreement, so that we were from the first pulling in different directions. The Dutch and some of the neutrals helped in trying to work for a fair and humane settlement. The new Communist Yugoslavs were the closest allies of the Russians in trying to prevent any settlement other than forcible repatriation."[35]

The Russians consistently spoke in favor of establishing a new international organization to register, feed, and repatriate refugees and displaced persons and would have joined the organization if its mandate had been confined to these tasks alone. But they "opposed with increasing vigor the idea of using the international organization to assist in the resettlement of refugees who for political reasons refused to be repatriated"—"quislings and fascists"—and were adamant that they would not help to pay for such an organization. "How could you expect us to contribute towards the support and resettlement of those who are politically opposed to us and wish to work for other countries?" a Russian delegate asked privately.[36]

At first, the British and Americans wanted to cooperate with the Russians, so they made concessions. Critics would later argue that this eagerness to keep the Russians involved weakened the framework of the refugee organization, only to see the Russians walk away. By the later months of 1946, after the main Russian negotiator, Andrei Vyshinsky, had repudiated everything his subordinates had previously accepted, there was no alternative but to go forward in trying to reach a refugee settlement without the Soviets.[37]

The Western nations were not the saintly humanitarians they pretended to be; they had their own agendas. The British, as always, were looking to save money; the Americans, to help friends and those with clout on Capitol Hill—especially the Balts and the Jews. Consequently, the "eligibility criteria"—or definition of those who qualified for help—for the new organization, however generally phrased, were designed to favor certain groups. An American negotiator later conceded that "some of the categories were very broadly drawn," so that they "might be used to cover the Baltic peoples in Germany whose position was a source of embarrassment to all the Great Powers and who did not fit easily into the other categories." In the case of Jewish DPs, the Americans made sure that both the definition of a displaced person and the timing of the cutoff for eligibility allowed for "infiltrees"—Jewish refugees who had made their way into Germany from Poland after the end of the war—to be eligible for help. The Russians objected, pointing out quite fairly that a precedent would be created by including what were, in effect, postwar refugees among those for whom international responsibility was acknowledged. In the case of the Ukrainians, the Western countries agreed to exclude those actively plotting the downfall of the governments of their countries of origin, but not those simply hostile.

Throughout these negotiations, the U.S. delegation received very little support from the State Department. When one delegate, Eleanor Roosevelt, finally managed to have lunch with Secretary Byrnes, she asked him four times for instructions on how to proceed yet received no answer. So Mrs. Roosevelt and her colleague George L. Warren had to trust their own instincts and, at times, act boldly. When the British delegate, Philip Noel-Baker, tried to redefine the role of the new body, they contacted London and had him summarily removed by the prime minister, Clement Attlee. At another stage, they lopped $100 million off the new organization's budget overnight, cutting it from $250 million to $150 million, because they doubted that Congress would pay more. Afterward they discovered why they had so little support. "In another committee in the UN Assembly, Dean Acheson and Mr. Byrnes were desperately fighting against Mayor La Guardia's efforts to extend UNRRA," George L. Warren later recalled. "The reason that they were so opposed to it was that the Soviet Government had so exploited UNRRA that they just couldn't take any more of it. So the U.S. position in the General Assembly was terribly ambivalent. Here Acheson and Byrnes were fighting against any more UNRRA, while Mrs. Roosevelt and I were fighting in another committee for a hundred and fifty million dollar budget for IRO."[38]

It soon became clear that the new body, now called the International Refugee Organization, was a dead duck unless the United States agreed to meet its 46 percent share of its budget. In selling it to Congress, the Truman administration initially relied on two arguments: first, that the IRO's budget was one-ninth of that of UNRRA and its role was confined to repatriating and resettling displaced persons. Second, that in funding the IRO, the United States was paying for refugees to be sent elsewhere. Congressmen opposed to having refugees enter the United States were, Warren later recalled, "interested in creating IRO, in an effort to divert the pressure on the United States—to get refugees off to other countries."[39]

American public opinion was split. Sectarian pressure groups appealed to the humanitarian duty of the United States to ratify the organization's constitution and take a "fair share" of the refugees. Against that, a small but vociferous minority, spearheaded by veterans' organizations such as the American Legion and Veterans of Foreign Wars, appealed to traditional isolationist sentiment. The issue of ratification finally reached the Senate on March 1, 1947.[40]

By then, however, a major watershed in the Cold War had been reached. Over the weekend of February 22–23, 1947, the British ambassador in Washington had informed the Truman administration that his exhausted and near-bankrupt government could no longer give financial and military aid to Turkey and to Greece (where a civil war was in progress). Washington went into crisis mode, as the Americans scrambled to assume the role the British had decided to abdicate. At a White House meeting, Dean Acheson had sought congressional support by painting a bloodcurdling picture of the situation:

> Soviet pressure on the Straits, on Iran, and on northern Greece had brought the Balkans to the point where a highly possible Soviet breakthrough might open three continents to Soviet penetration. Like apples in a barrel infected by one rotten one, the corruption of Greece would infect Iran and all to the east. It would carry infection to Africa through Asia Minor and Egypt, and to Europe through Italy and France, already threatened by the strongest

domestic Communist parties in Western Europe. The Soviet Union was playing one of the greatest gambles in history at minimal cost.[41]

The United States now began to adopt the policy of "containment" of the Soviet Union advocated by George F. Kennan a year earlier. In an address to both houses of Congress, the president set out what became known as the "Truman Doctrine." In this new climate, the legislation authorizing the IRO's budget passed through the Senate.

This switch in U.S. policy, simultaneously becoming more detached from international institutions yet more involved in foreign policy, was given a decisive nudge by an act of God. In Europe, the winter of 1946–1947 was the coldest for a hundred years. In Britain, economic activity ground to a standstill; visitors to the Foreign Office found Ernest Bevin in a vast unheated room wrapped in a blanket. There were similar stories in Italy and France. But the winter's impact was most cruelly felt by Germany's already weakened population. A blanket of snow and ice descended for four months; the main rivers were icebound; the railways ceased to move; and arrests for stealing coal from trains rose dramatically. The miners in the Ruhr had to spend much time helping their families survive. Hamburg was without light or heat from seven in the morning till ten at night. Many of the Eastern refugees visited by Victor Gollancz the previous autumn died of starvation. "We face a situation here . . . in which the nation is slowly dying," wrote a Quaker team based in Hanover. "We can do nothing." "There is nothing we can do," echoed another team from Solingen. "In this ever growing ocean of distress, the Quaker relief drop seems quite ridiculously insignificant."[42]

American diplomats visiting Europe were astonished by what they found. They had assumed that a combination of UNRRA's relief effort and the restoration of normal economic relations would soon get Europe moving again and failed to understand how far the prospects for European recovery depended on having Germany functioning once again as the engine of the European economy. Now not only had the recovery faltered, there were real fears that Communist parties might be voted into office in France and Italy. For one man in particular, this was a Damascene moment.[43]

Will Clayton was an unusual figure in the Truman administration: a self-made cotton millionaire from Mississippi, by now in his midsixties; a passionate believer in capitalism, free trade, and monetary stability; a practical man of business, not an academic economist. As we have seen, Clayton had been more than happy to kill UNRRA off, after his experiences at the third UNRRA Council meeting in London in August 1945. But visiting Europe in early 1947, Clayton was horrified to find that capitalism was not working there. "It is now obvious that we grossly underestimated the destruction to the European economy by the war," Clayton's memorandum of May 27, 1947, to the new secretary of state, General George C. Marshall, began. The Americans, he said, had understood the physical destruction in the continent but had not grasped the extent to which the war had severed the social connections on which all economic activity is based. Instead of recovering, Europe was now steadily deteriorating. There were constant political crises, millions of people were starving in the cities, yet peasants were not bringing food to market because they had lost confidence in their currency. Large areas of the continent had reverted to a subsistence economy.

Most of the Western European countries now had to draw on their limited supplies of gold and dollars to pay for the importing of coal and food. It was vital to restore the continent to self-sufficiency as quickly as possible. Then Clayton gave a stark warning: "Without further prompt and substantial aid from the United States, economic, social and political disintegration will overwhelm Europe."

> Aside from the awful implications which this will have for the future peace and security of the world, the immediate effects on our domestic economy would be disastrous: markets for our surplus production gone, unemployment, depression, a heavily unbalanced budget on the background of a mountainous war debt.
>
> *These things must not happen.*

Clayton argued that the United States had ample resources to provide the necessary help if it was competently organized:

> It will be necessary for the President and the Secretary of State to make a strong spiritual appeal to the American people to sacrifice a little themselves, to draw in their own belts just a little in order to

save Europe from starvation and chaos (*not* from the Russians) and, at the same time to preserve for ourselves and our children the glorious heritage of a free America.

Europe would need a grant of about $6 billion or $7 billion worth of goods a year for three years, Clayton reckoned, made up of coal, food, cotton, tobacco, and shipping services from the United States. Food shipments should be stepped up beyond the 15 million tons the United States was already exporting to Europe. "We are wasting and over-consuming food in the United States to such an extent that a reasonable measure of conservation would make at least another million tons available for export with no harm whatsoever to the health and efficiency of the American people."

But Clayton concluded on a very different note. Recent experience, he wrote, suggested that other nations such as Canada, Brazil, and Argentina would no doubt help with their surplus food and raw materials, but, he emphasized, "we must avoid getting into another UNRRA. *The United States must run this show.*"[44]

Clayton's proposal quickly grew into the European Recovery Program, which George. C. Marshall unveiled in a speech at Harvard in May 1947. The scheme had many purposes: to restore Germany to its traditional role as the economic powerhouse of Europe in a way that was politically acceptable in Europe and the United States; to prevent the spread of communism in Western Europe; and to prevent America's overseas market from drying up.

Harry Truman insisted that the plan bear Marshall's name. "Anything that is sent up to the Senate and House with my name on it will quiver a couple of times and die," he claimed. The Republicans were determined to cut taxes and expenditures. Since the war, the United States had already spent $3 billion on foreign relief and loaned Britain a further $3.25 billion—to little purpose, it now seemed. The additional $6 billion or $7 billion which Will Clayton calculated the Europeans would need amounted to just over half the entire federal budget for 1948. It would be quite a job to sell that to Congress.[45]

Marshall and his team took a calculated gamble that the Russians would not accept the invitation to join the plan—had they done so, it would never have garnered the necessary support. In the event, Stalin was unable to accept two American conditions: that the Soviet Union should itself help to finance the rebuilding of Western and Central

Europe and that it provide a full accounting of how American money was being spent. As a result, although seventeen nations eventually took part in the Plan, Soviet pressure ensured that Czechoslovakia, Poland, Romania, and the other satellite countries of Eastern Europe did not. Stalin's refusal to take part in the plan virtually guaranteed its approval by Congress, though the risk of confrontation caused strong resistance by both conservative Republicans and liberal Democrats.

General Marshall tried to avoid the anti-Communist rhetoric that had underpinned the Truman Doctrine, selling the plan on the dire economic situation in Europe and the need to rebuild a region vital to U.S. security. He convinced the foreign policy elite, but the plan probably would not have gotten through Congress had Truman not played the Communist card, presenting it as the only way to stop Soviet domination in Europe. He was helped by the recent Communist coup in Czechoslovakia.[46]

The adoption of the Marshall Plan is rightly regarded as a turning point in postwar history. In Germany, however, its importance was more psychological and political than economic: it provided evidence that the United States was not going to abandon the Germans to their fate. What really brought about the recovery of Germany was the American decision finally to divide the country between the Western and Soviet zones; introduce a new currency, the deutsche mark; and put the Germans back in charge of their own economy. Yet by restoring sovereignty to the Germans, the Americans made it more urgent that the problem of the displaced persons be solved.[47]

FOURTEEN

"Dwell, Eat, Breed, Wait"

LIFE IN DP CAMPS, 1947–1950

In August 1946, Marta Korwin, the UNRRA welfare worker who was running an arts college for displaced persons in Kassel, set her students the challenge of writing an essay on their personal experiences. A month later, she translated and collated some of their writings. They have survived among her papers and today provide a rare glimpse of what the DPs felt at that time. Though the students struggled to express themselves, their individual voices nonetheless come through clearly. Over and over the same complaints can be heard—of betrayal and regret, mixed with apprehension and disbelief.

An anti-Communist Yugoslav expressed anger about being subjected to "strong and relentless propaganda" to return to Yugoslavia. The British had promised him uniforms and underclothing yet provided little more than rations and cigarettes. Then he had found that it was possible to buy anything from British soldiers on the black market. In British camps, he wrote, "We were slaves and in fact had not true freedom. But I was grieved still more that we were not treated as men." He felt frustrated that he could not correspond with his relatives at home and that his destiny seemed to be "decided at the conferences by the Great Powers." He also defended the behavior of his fellow DPs:

Whose fault is it that, in a large camp, the lower instincts grow and morale falls? This results from unemployment and boredom, which demand some distraction. Among us there are a considerable number of intellectuals who find ways to occupy themselves, if not in employment then by perfecting their minds; but the greater number of primitive people break boredom in a primitive way. This is most often by drinking, which is immediately followed by exaggerated enjoyment of sex.

Other writers had similar frustrations. Why was it that whenever the DPs began to develop any sort of worthwhile communal life in camp they were immediately moved on by UNRRA? Anna, a Polish art student, remembered the heady days after liberation in her first DP camp, when she and the other Poles had gotten together to establish schools and a theater "and to bring civilisation on to those who missed it during those long years":

> We worked furiously day and night and got the theatre to look, if not quite like a theatre, anyhow possible to give a daily entertainment [in]. Unfortunately our theatre never was used because, unexpectedly, an order came that we must leave this camp in a few hours and move to another one. In the new camp we set to work again on the schools, theatre, club reading rooms. Enthusiasm was not so high, especially in the young people. "Is it any use to work, if we may be kicked out again at a few hours' notice?" they used to say. Indeed when we got things going at great cost and privation and achieved some results, we were transferred from it, and later from another one as well. So we stopped working. The same with the gardens, the same with sports places. It looked as if someone would wait until we got things working and growing, to move us elsewhere. We often wonder, if those who give us those orders really do understand what harm they do us, or is it done with a purpose?

Many of the writers felt huge bitterness toward the British, often because they had once nursed dreams of solidarity. To one former officer in the Polish Home Army,

> England was a vision for which we were all longing, waiting, trusting she will come, our Polish army with her, and the Germans will go and then—then the law of force and violence will cease to exist—and Freedom and Justice will reign.

Now he felt very different:

I risked my life. For what? For those promises that England gave us? How stupid I was! They had the unlimited capital of our trust and enthusiasm, if they had only treated us like human beings.

A young man who had been kidnapped at sixteen and sent to work as a barman in Münster compared working for the Germans with working for the British:

Is there really much difference between "now" and "before"? I was a number. I am a number. I was called "Polish Dog." [Now] I am called "Wretched Pole." Food—the same. Despised by the Master Race Germans—rejected by the Master Race English. I hated the Germans before—I hate the English now.

A Polish DP who had worked in two synthetic oil factories in Germany recalled:

When we were drunk, our greatest pleasure was to picture the day when we in turn would see our "Allies" as DPs in Siberia, and "they" who treat us like dirt in camps themselves, and we pictured to ourselves how "they" would feel when they could get the same treatment of humiliation as the military and so many UNRRA officers do not spare to give us.

For the soldier in the Home Army:

Under the Germans whatever we endured, we remained Poles. Today we are described by two letters only, DP. The destiny of the people reduced to two letters is decided by one stroke of the pencil at a bureaucratic desk.

Only an Estonian girl managed a note of cheerfulness. She had escaped fairly lightly, having fled her country when the Russians approached, and had recently been reunited with her family. "Today, on the first Sunday in September," she concluded, "when I am sitting in my room, writing and thinking about the past, my heart is filled with great thankfulness to God, for saving our family, and letting those people who belong together, find one another."[1]

We do not know what happened to any of these DPs. We can only conjecture as to how they coped with their frustration and the uncertainty that lay ahead as they waited for a political outcome to their situation.

There were still more than a million displaced persons in Germany, Italy, and Austria in the latter half of 1947, the vast majority of them in the British and American zones of Germany. More than 60 percent of those people lived in camps, but about 400,000 had chosen to live outside them, mainly in German cities. The number of DP camps in the American Zone—134 in December 1945 and 400 by December 1946—had reached 416 in June 1947; in the British Zone, it had climbed over the same period from 78 to a peak of 443 in December 1946 but had now declined to 272. There were 45 in the French Zone, 21 in Austria, and 8 in Italy—bringing the total to 762 camps.[2]

In October 1948, *The New Yorker* writer Janet Flanner counted "three hundred limbos" in the U.S. Zone, camps run by UNRRA's successor, the International Refugee Organization, with a population of 598,000; 150,000 of the DPs had "merged with the Germans." She found that the camps tended to be monotonously alike, nearly all former Wehrmacht garrisons, typically "a quarter-mile square of harsh, four-story green stucco buildings that show signs of Allied bombardment and Allied repairs." According to IRO rules, each building had to house a minimum of three hundred DPs, "in rows of communal bedrooms, all furnished out of salvaged materials and all smelling of smeared cleanliness, hall-room cooking, and cramped decencies." "Like a well-functioning imitation of a town," she wrote,

> each DP camp has its mayor, police chief, rival political leaders, teachers, and garbage collectors, and one socially superior barracks, where the bourgeois remnants maintain the familiar notion of a select neighborhood, and where they cling together among fewer odors and try to keep up their French. Each camp is a microcosm of capitalistic society outside: DP shoemakers, tailors and carpenters ply their trades, participating in financial transactions for which the medium of exchange is now the Deutsche Mark but for which American baby foods, cigarettes, and canned goods, black-marketed by our occupying Army, provided the currency at the beginning.

German soldiers and refugees crowd the platforms of a Berlin train station, October 1945.

Displaced persons in the waiting hall of Frankfurt train station, September 8, 1945.

DPs being fed at an assembly center in the former German political prison at Ansalt, March 19, 1945.

Russians at Mosbach DP camp in southwest Germany stage a pageant to thank the men of the U.S. Seventh Army for their liberation, April 15, 1945. A drawing of Josef Stalin decorates the right of the podium.

Returning concentration camp survivors being given bread by UNRRA volunteers at Weimar station, Germany, before boarding a train, July 2, 1945.

Mayor Fiorello H. La Guardia (second from right) and Governor Herbert Lehman (left) attending Columbus Day ceremonies, New York, October 1, 1941.

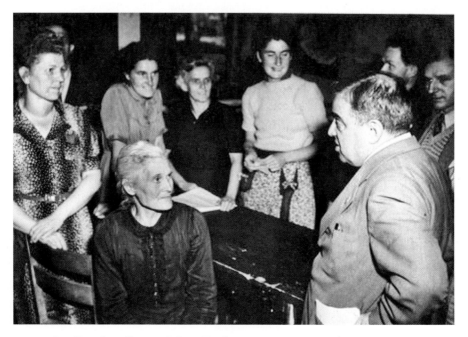

La Guardia talks to a DP at Funk Kaserne, near Munich, August 1946.

Lieutenant General Sir Frederick Morgan,
December 1944.

Marie-Louise Habets (left)
and Kay Hulme at
Wildflecken DP camp.

Major Irving Heymont converses with David Ben-Gurion during his visit to the Landsberg
DP camp, October 1945. A U.S. Army chaplain, Rabbi Abraham Klausner, is on the left.

A time of waiting: DPs at Weilheim camp.

An "interzone" football match is played at Belsen DP camp.

Jewish survivors of Buchenwald, some still in their camp clothing, stand on deck of the refugee ship Mataroa *at Haifa port, July 15, 1945.*

"Baltic cygnets": DPs from the Baltic States waiting for their medical inspection at a Ministry of Labour hostel in Havant, Hampshire, September 1947.

New York City, December 1950: Mrs. Zinaida Supe of Latvia, the 200,000th person brought to the United States under the Displaced Persons Act of 1948, and her children are welcomed by the executive director of War Relief Services, National Catholic Welfare Conference. The family, sponsored by the Catholic Daughters of America, was later flown to Colorado Springs, Colorado, where they planned to live.

The DPs, she added, "dwell, eat, breed, wait, and ponder their futures. Living a simulacrum of life that has no connection with the world outside except through the world's callousness and charity."[3]

In the early days after the liberation, when assembly centers were established by the military, it was usual for a nationality leader to be nominated by the army commander. This would normally be "an aggressive individual who was appointed (not elected) who seemed to have the ability to enforce discipline among the Displaced Persons of his nationality." The military's approach was based largely on the practical realization that there was no way a small army team could run a camp of 2,000 to 4,000 people without their cooperation. With UNRRA, however, it became more a matter of policy. "Camp self-government in the fullest sense was one of the goals of UNRRA camp administration," its official history declares, "indeed . . . the goal towards which all activities were pointed." When UNRRA took over the camps, a system of self-government based on democratic elections began to emerge, though along no uniform pattern. Some camps— between 10 and 15 percent—retained the old model of an appointed strongman.[4]

What determined these variations? Many DPs came from countries which had enjoyed only partial democracy between the wars or had no democratic tradition at all, countries used to politics organized around kinship networks or systems of patronage. Nor would their contacts with Soviet Russia and Nazi Germany during the war have fostered democratic ways.

In addition, according to an UNRRA report, a clear hierarchy emerged, with the Balts and the Jews at the top and the Poles and "mixed camps" at the bottom. The Baltic camps contained a high proportion of professional people, such as bank managers, engineers, and civil servants, had developed complete democratic institutions at an early date, and in general had "a complete constitution." Latvians, for example, used a basic constitution throughout the British and American zones prescribed by a central Latvian committee—under which the camp every six months elected by secret ballot an assembly of some fifteen to twenty members, which in turn elected a committee of five or six and a chairman who became the camp commander. The committee members became "ministers," whose portfolios matched those of the members of the UNRRA team: Welfare,

Employment, Administration, and so on. The only caveat was that the UNRRA team director had the right to strike from the lists the names of any candidate objectionable to him. The Jewish camps had developed equally democratic institutions but "without a highly developed constitution." By contrast, in Polish and mixed nationality camps, the democratic procedures were less exact and terms of office less clearly defined.[5]

UNRRA officials were clear that the greater the degree of democracy, the greater self-government was allowed. Whereas Baltic and some Jewish camps which had been long established were capable of operation with very little supervision, in other cases the camp commander or camp committee frequently was under the complete control of the UNRRA director and "merely carried out orders and disseminated orders to the people and submitted to the Assembly Centre Director complaints or requests from the population." But this was something of a constitutional fiction. In reality, the UNRRA teams had no way of imposing democratic practices. The Ukrainian camps, in particular, became nurseries of nationalism.[6]

By allowing the camps to be self-governed, the Western authorities made it relatively easy for political groups to assume control, either by enforcing party discipline or by intimidating opponents. The two factions of the Organization of Ukrainian Nationalists (OUN) saw control of the DP camps as part of a wider struggle to keep Ukrainian nationalism going, while fighting a guerrilla war in parts of Soviet Ukraine, which, in turn, they saw as the prelude to a wider conflict between Russia and the West. The OUN faction, owing allegiance to Stepan Bandera, was the more determined and ruthless and soon became the dominant force in the camps, with all the other political groups united in weak opposition to it. "Through its network of conspirators its members were able to take over most of the important positions and functions within the camps—first the internal camp police force, then the food supplies, and finally, the internal camp administration."[7]

Intimidation and violence buttressed the nationalists' authority. Suspected Soviet spies and political enemies were murdered, and terror was used to extract money from the camp populations: "The so-called liberals—persons who did not show sufficient zeal for patriotic lore, symbolic action, and pseudo-military drill—were especially under fire." It is unclear how widespread such practices were. The

Ukrainian exile masses were generally "socially apathetic," but "the charged atmosphere in the camps, the arrival from Ukraine of the guerilla fighters, and the enforced idleness of the men contributed to a shallow politicization of Ukrainian émigrés, who had leisure time for public meetings and constituted an audience responsive to nationally charged rhetoric." The overall impression is of most of the population falling into line. For example, the nationalists' traditional view of the place of women prevailed.[8]

However, divisions evidently remained. Refugees from Galicia, or Polish Ukraine, who had arrived in 1945 with their families, tended to be of a much higher educational level and to provide the leadership. Their tactics exacerbated the tensions between Polish and Soviet Ukrainians. According to the historian Yury Boshyk, "Members of the OUN, who were strongly anti-socialist and anti-Soviet, were suspicious of Soviet Ukrainians, believing them to be insufficiently nationalistic and tainted by communism. Soviet Ukrainians sometimes claimed they were misunderstood and discriminated against." One of their leaflets declared:

> Ukrainians! Enough is enough! The Galicians (Western Ukrainians) have seized power in all our camps. They pretend to be our older brothers, they talk of caring for us and teaching us. . . . We extricated ourselves from Stalin and Hitler and we will not let anyone rule over us. In all camps—Polish, Baltic and Russian, people live in safety and peace. Only in Ukrainian camps our "older brothers" have created a system of terror and suffocation. We too want to live under the guardianship of the democratic order. We have had enough of dictatorship. We demand the removal of the Galicians from the Ukrainian camps.[9]

Modern Ukrainian writers often paint a surprisingly positive picture of DP life. The camps, they argue, provided "a sheltering environment" in which "many people were suddenly given an extended holiday from some of life's most pressing problems." More than that, they offered a "temporary, artificial, insulated and protective social sub-system" within which Ukrainians could sit out hard times in postwar Germany, improve their industrial skills, and, for almost the first time in two centuries, freely express themselves as Ukrainians. According to this version, Ukrainians were able to develop a network of institutions and associations which included, beyond the official camp administration, churches, schools, and a host of voluntary groups; younger professionals could hone their skills; rural youths could learn "urban and urbane" behavior; and children had access not only to the family but to a well-organized larger community. Beyond that,

> Interaction became more egalitarian, as both the conditions of camp life and various external influences, including perhaps some of the ideas of western democracy, combined to reduce, slowly but irreversibly, the traditional distances and inequalities between male and female, old and young, villager and urbanite. Little remained of the stylized symmetry of relations between *pan* (Lord) and *khlop* (peasant) once prevalent in Ukraine's Western regions, even though the imagery itself proved quite tenacious.[10]

This upbeat picture of camp life is not borne out by the Ukrainian DP who recorded his day for researchers from Harvard University in 1949. He lived in a camp in the middle of the countryside, two kilometers from the nearest village and made up of nineteen old wooden barracks: those used by Germans during the war had been divided into small rooms, while those which had housed foreign workers contained dormitories.

> Let's take for example the room in which I live. This is a large room (one quarter of the barrack). There are 11 double decker beds in one room and on every bed there is an old cotton mattress and 3 thin blankets. They give us no bed sheets, and we have to sleep directly on the mattress. There are 22 people in our room. All are foreign DPs—Ukrainians from Poland, Ukrainians from Russia, Poles. The representatives of every nationality gather in one of the corners and tell each other stories, or about their experiences.
> Speaking of myself, I get up no earlier than 10 o'clock. There is no sense in getting up earlier—it's cold in the barracks and there is absolutely no comfort. After getting up I calmly proceed to do my morning toilet. When I am washed and shaved it's already time for lunch. What [do] we have for lunch? The first course some soup from pea powder or pearl-barley; the second—four potatoes boiled without being peeled, some sauerkraut on a little piece of blood

sausage. After my lunch I lie down on my bed for half an hour. After that I get up and go to the other barrack where the other families are living, to listen to the radio. There I stay until supper, that is, until 6 o'clock. For supper, we have 200 grams of bread with pork fat or butter, a small piece of cheese or sausage, and black coffee.

After having eaten I play chess or cards, and when I get a newspaper or a book no matter in which language it is: Russian, Polish or even German, I read until 9 or 10 o'clock in the evening. After that I go once more to listen to the Voice of America program and at 11 or 11.30 go to bed.

And so goes my daily life. There is no place to go. Four kilometers from us is a little town, Scheinfeld, where a movie may be seen. But I can afford it seldom for lack of money. Nine marks of so-called *Taschengeld* should be spared very accurately for purchases of tobacco and stamps. There is no possibility of earning some money. The life is dull and aimless.[11]

Such idleness was not universal. Many DPs worked, were involved in the black market, or were engaged in educating themselves or one another.

The more fortunate people could work in the camp itself, as part of the administration, employed by UNRRA or IRO. Alongside the small group of UNRRA workers known as Class I employees (men and women from various Allied countries who were well paid in their own country's currency), most of the actual work was done by Class II employees, who earned far less and were usually paid in German marks but, like Class I employees, wore military uniform and had residence privileges. Below these were ordinary office staff and chauffeurs known as "team workers" who received some salary, as well as special privileges such as food and housing. Finally, at the lowest level, came those who worked in storerooms or workshops. Some received little pay, but all were granted a larger food ration, plus a monthly handout (the "amenity supply"), which included soap and razor blades as well as chocolate and one packet of American cigarettes. Their ability to control the distribution of more sought-after jobs and better food rations gave enormous power to the camp committees and their tendency to reward their friends and supporters was a long-standing source of resentment among ordinary DPs. "As a rule social divisions in the DP community seemed to be reinforced by the few limited opportunities for employment available," a Lithuanian account argues. "Only those who had the support of the camp committee could expect to get decent work." This was often coupled with attempts to reassert the prewar social structure. A Lithuanian poet who tried to get a new coat from the clothes store in his camp was denied access to "the room where they kept quality clothes for special people" and told that "only venerable nationals were allowed there."[12]

Many DPs, especially the women, were expected to do manual jobs such as cleaning and working in kitchens and laundries. "I was sent to work in a laundry which was dreadful, with the cold water and so on, though at weekends I was allowed to sweep," Lizina, then sixteen years old, remembers. "I lived in part of the nurses' room, two or three in a room. We had food and a clean bed and were paid a little, a few deutschmarks a month." Her life improved after a friend helped her get an office job in the administration. Every young, educated Balt DP with secretarial or language skills was anxious to find a job in camp office administration.

From the start, some male DPs also did manual work. In August 1945, Marvin Klemmé, a forester from Washington State working for UNRRA, was loaned to the British army to get woodcutting started. At that time most military officials believed that "all DPs were lazy trouble-makers and couldn't be made to work." Klemmé set out to prove them wrong. By explaining to the camp leaders that if they didn't get some wood in they would freeze in the coming winter, he got plenty of volunteers; there turned out to be many skilled forest workers among the DPs.

Klemmé had more trouble getting the British military government to cooperate, but it was finally agreed that all DPs who were employed full-time could be placed on a German wage-scale basis. Yet German money was of little value to the DPs. When Klemmé tried to sort this out, he ran into endless trouble with British army officers: "I never saw a more unreasonable or impractical group of people in my entire life. They were constantly thinking up excuses why you couldn't do a thing but could seldom think of anything to help you get something done." And to get anything off the ground involved dealing with numerous departments, each with its own red tape. Klemmé wanted the forest workers all brought together in one barracks so that they could be fed and cared for as a unit, to get extra rations and cigarettes, and to have extra clothing. Whatever he tried to do, he ran into a stone wall. Only after General Morgan put his weight behind the scheme and the various military obstructionists were read the riot act was Klemmé able to get his way.[13]

However, a transport shortage created new obstacles. True to form, the British army refused to release any of its almost new American Lend-Lease trucks to haul wood, and Klemmé found it was difficult to get British drivers to put in a full day—to do more would mess up their tea break. British military incompetence "resulted in considerable suffering during the winter in certain DP camps in the British Zone. Probably the worst affected were some of the hospitals and children's homes . . . where lack of proper heating caused many to suffer exposure and frost bite and caused deaths from pneumonia." Klemmé believed that "comparatively few British officers want to take action on anything until an emergency stares them in the face."

Many of his best workers, Polish peasants, went home during the late autumn of 1945 and the spring of 1946, leaving a heavier percentage of DPs from the cities, who were of little use as forest workers. Klemmé thought that a dozen or so good foresters with experience in handling men would have been worth at least a hundred welfare officers that first winter. By contrast, the fuel situation was much better in the DP camps in the American Zone because the U.S. Army had had the foresight to bring in a number of trained foresters and start its program back in the summer.

But Klemmé was justifiably proud that during the winter of 1945–1946 something like 8,000 DPs were employed full-time in cutting wood within the British Zone alone. He believed this "proved conclusively that when these displaced persons were properly organized, properly supervised and were given some incentive to work, they would produce just about as well as anyone." As it became accepted that the "hard core" was not going to go home, official policy became more encouraging of any scheme which kept the DPs occupied. Klemmé was appointed zone employment and training officer.

There remained one major stumbling block, however. UNRRA and the military government insisted that workers had to be able to return home to their camp each evening: a DP who left the camp became a "deserter" and forfeited his DP status.

This meant that someone living in a remote rural area (such as Wildflecken) had no opportunity to work. This foolish ruling, before it was finally rescinded, deprived the German economy of millions of man-hours for almost two years after the war.

As Allied policy began to change and German economic recovery became a priority, greater efforts were made to tap into this reservoir of labor. Some DP camps were located very favorably for employment with German firms. In the Ruhr, many DPs went to work in the mines, between Hamburg and Bremen there were peat-cutting operations, and large numbers were employed in Hamburg repairing docks and doing various kinds of cleanup work. Probably the biggest employer of DPs was the Volkswagen works in Braunschweig, which used Ukrainians and Balts on its assembly lines.

In 1947, British military authorities decided that everyone living in their zone of Germany over the age of fourteen, male and female, Germans and DPs, must register for work. The registering of DPs was opposed by many in UNRRA because it would mean that the DPs would again be working for the Germans, but once the program got under way, no one seemed to object. The real opposition came from the German labor unions, which wanted the DPs to go home.[14]

The feeding of working DPs was another bureaucratic issue. After months of wrangling, military government officials set up four different ration scales. Extraheavy rations were for miners; heavy rations were for forest workers, mechanics, and suchlike; intermediate were for office workers, teachers, and the white-collar class; while the fourth ration scale was for nonworkers. There were further difficulties with getting them proper clothing and soap.

By the spring of 1947 about two-thirds of all employable men and one-third of all employable women in the British Zone were at work. The men not working were generally located in DP camps that were isolated in rural areas where work was seasonal. It was not always easy to find work for the women, although there was plenty for them to do in the country. The greatest percentage of the DPs employed, by nationality, were the Ukrainians; it seemed that nearly every one of them wanted to work. Then came the Balts, with almost as good a record; then the Yugoslavs and Poles.

Jewish DPs refused to work. According to Klemmé, "the British apparently were afraid to force them to work and the German 'Arbeitsamt' was glad to leave them alone. Up until the time that I left Germany, no one had even bothered to register them." In 1947, however, UNRRA and some of the Jewish welfare agencies came up with ambitious plans for setting up "cottage industries" inside their camps. The British were skeptical of the scheme. A British major voiced a common opinion when he said, "I reckon the blighters would be turning out uniforms for the Palestinian army if we didn't watch them."

Once DPs began to be offered some prospect of a future outside Germany, however, it became very difficult to interest them in work there. They now thought only of moving to a new land.[15]

Walking down a street in Landsberg, near Munich, one morning in 1947, the American writer Marie Syrkin heard a voice whisper in Yiddish, "Chocolates, cigarettes." Her interlocutor was a small, middle-aged man, "shabbily dressed and carrying the briefcase which was the hallmark of his occupation." He grew irritated when Syrkin replied that she had nothing to sell but wanted to understand the black market. "What's there to understand?" he demanded. "How are we going to live on calories? *You* could live on calories?" Besides, he added, who was to blame? "Who sells the stuff? Where do we get it? It's the high ups, the big people." Everyone was guilty, he insisted. Finally Syrkin asked if he could not manage without the black market. "Is opium necessary?" he replied. "What am I supposed to do with myself? I can't get work. I can't get out. This keeps me busy." It turned out that the man had lost his wife and child in Auschwitz. Before the war he had been a skilled leatherworker, but there was now no machinery for him to work with. He was most indignant when Marie Syrkin ended the conversation by thrusting a packet of cigarettes at him.[16]

Postwar Germany was run by the black market. As General Morgan himself said, "every man, woman and child in Western Europe was engaged to a greater or lesser degree in illegal trading of one kind or another. In fact, it [was] hardly possible to support existence without so doing." To meet almost every need, it was necessary to play the black market, and only a few people were too principled not to. A high-ranking Yugoslav who wore a handkerchief round his neck instead of a shirt fifteen months after liberation because he "could not buy honestly and would not buy dishonestly" was something of a rarity. "It was considered most dishonourable to abstain from the black market as long as members of one's family were starving," a German aristocrat later recalled. "Not to join because of some code of honour

or other was not a good thing. One has to be very careful about getting moral issues mixed up with something that was, at this time, a
most honourable business."[17]

The black market derived from the obvious scarcities of the time
but was exacerbated by the rigid economic policies pursued by the
Allies. In their determination not to replicate the devastating inflation that had swept Germany after the First World War, they stifled
all economic activity in Germany. As a contemporary report put it:

> The attempt to run the economies of the different occupation
> zones by detailed military orders only perpetuated the paralysis of
> the economy. Money ceased to a great extent to function either as
> a circulating medium or as a measure of economic calculations.
> Individual barter, compensation, trade, payment in kind and other
> atavistic forms of economic communication took its place.

In practice, the cigarette became the dominant unit of economic
exchange in Germany; there was almost nothing that could not be
bought for the right number of cigarettes.[18]

The different groups in occupied Germany approached the black
market from different angles. For Allied soldiers and occupation officials, it was a useful way of supplementing their official salary; for
Germans, a means of survival; for displaced persons, a way of supplementing the diet, an occupation, and (for some) a way of building up
capital. Of all these groups, the American soldiers started with the
greatest advantage, receiving a generous monthly cigarette allowance
which could easily be exchanged on the black market for items such
as cameras or jewelry that starving Germans were prepared to sell.
Most GIs sent their pay home.

The displaced persons were not quite so fortunate, but, as Kay
Hulme noticed at Wildflecken, their rations and Red Cross parcels
gave them a grubstake in the black—or, rather "gray"—market. Most
DPs at Landsberg engaged in "simple bartering for comfort items and
fresh food," Major Irving Heymont recorded, but there was also "a
small number of big black market operators." The standard DP scam
was the "dead souls" racket, whereby block leaders claimed rations for
inflated numbers of people in the camps and then used the surplus for
trading. Whether the proceeds thus generated were distributed round
the camp or converted by individuals into "portable wealth" such as

cameras, watches, diamonds, and hard currency was down to local circumstances.[19]

It is impossible to quantify the scale of the black market in general and in the DP camps in particular. Every group was involved. Sixty-seven Latvians and Lithuanians received prison sentences after a police raid on the Artillerie Kaserne camp in Lübeck in the week before Christmas 1947 uncovered 109 mature live pigs and a huge stash of other foodstuffs—enough edible meat, a German reporter claimed, to provide the standard weekly meat ration for 90,900 people or a year's meat allotment for 1,748 persons. And in a Polish camp a few days later, police found, in a huge network of underground tunnels, roughly 4,000 kilograms of high-quality leather and 415,000 gramophone needles, then the most highly prized item on the black market. The total value was said to be 2.5 million marks.[20]

Inevitably, though, it was the role of Jewish displaced persons in the black market which attracted the most attention. In the late 1940s, as the Germans recovered control of their affairs, they began to accuse Jewish DPs of dominating the black market, thus reviving "the ancient anti-Semitic stereotype of the Jewish profiteer and huckster." More recently, German historians have approached this subject with great caution, and the excellent museum at Bergen-Belsen does not refer at all to black-market activities in the displaced persons camp there.[21]

What does the evidence say? At Landsberg DP camp in late 1945, Major Heymont observed "a small number of big black market operators" using the opportunity to "accumulate portable wealth in order to be able to start again when they eventually reach a country of permanent residence." They fell into two types, he thought: "either former successful business men or individuals of previous criminal backgrounds or tendencies."

> The concentration camps tried the souls of men but did not necessarily purify them. . . . The enterprising man, especially if unscrupulous, can reap tremendous benefits if he has daring and nerve. Some are quick to take advantage of opportunities.

Many of the former businessmen, Heymont thought, were shrewd individuals who had been very successful in trade and industry before the war.

A free existence without participating in some form of commerce is meaningless for them. Unless their energies are channeled into constructive paths, they soon drift into the black market. They become big operators, because trade is all they know and they are desirous of accumulating capital for the future. The camps offer these individuals few opportunities as long as they refuse to become workers or artisans.

The Israeli historian Yehuda Bauer argued that the really big players in the black market were Germans but accepted that, with the arrival of a large number of Jewish refugees from the East, the black market "became a mass phenomenon in the camps." In 1947, a Joint report worried that "there are a people developing [in the Jewish DP camps] that resemble gangsters. They will stop at nothing and they threaten to kill."[22]

According to the Zionist elder statesman Nahum Goldmann, the Belsen DP camp was "the centre of one of the great black market rings in Europe; millions of cigarettes and other goods were channeled through it." Belsen was the hub from which the American Jewish Joint Distribution Committee sent goods all over Europe, both to DP camps and to German Jews living outside the camps. In the prevailing conditions, this presented Josef Rosensaft, the Belsen DPs' leader, with an obvious economic opportunity that he may have seized; as Rabbi Leslie Hardman recorded, Rosensaft "grew rich." At all events, in May 1946 a wish "to correct irregularities in the distribution system" led the Joint's director in the British Zone, David Wodlinger, to move the central warehouse from Belsen.[23]

The British kept Belsen under close observation. In February 1948, a German truck driver, caught on the autobahn near Hanover transporting 6 million cigarettes from Antwerp, claimed that his shipment was destined for Belsen and that he had earlier brought a truckload of 13 million cigarettes to the camp. At 1:30 A.M. on February 18, armed German police encircled the camp, accompanied by British soldiers to ensure their safety. Josef Rosensaft negotiated with the British in the early-morning hours about how the search was to be conducted, arguing that allowing German police or British soldiers to come into the camp was completely out of the question. In the end the British military authorities agreed that German police would not be involved. The search finally proceeded at 11:30 A.M.

with 150 British officers from every part of the zone. A Jewish policeman accompanied each search party.

According to a recent account, "the British conducted a very thorough search, examining every corner of the camp. The officers were
extremely considerate, and Rosensaft made a point of thanking them
for their thoughtfulness. Apart from a cow, twenty-five men's sweat-
ers, and a few cartons of cigarettes, the raid netted nothing. The British were surprised at how little black-market activity there was in
Belsen. An incident that had begun so disastrously with the deploy-
ment of armed German police ended peacefully with the agreement
of both parties." Yet the fact that nothing was found, after Rosensaft
had delayed the search by ten hours, can be interpreted in different
ways.[24]

Most modern authors claim that Jewish DPs were the victims of
racial stereotyping. Up to a point they were; they were also far less
likely to be involved in violent crime, which was an important element of black-market activity. But it is absurd to airbrush the past in
this way. As we have seen, almost everyone living in Germany at this
time participated in the black market to some degree. Moreover, in
the camps it provided the only outlet for people of Rosensaft's energy
and ability. Rosensaft was a survivor who had already taken on the
SS and the British. Yet, as Yehuda Bauer said, he was "by no means an
angel."[25]

One group among the DPs enjoyed a particular reputation for being
involved in crime: the Poles. In "Joining a Gang," one of the autobiographical sketches produced in Marta Korwin's class at the arts college in Kassel, the narrator describes how chance comments he made
while having his hair cut by the camp barber—who ran the biggest
distillery in the camp and whose schnapps was so good it was drunk
throughout the British Zone—led to his being invited to join a gang
operating from the camp. It was run by the assistant camp commandant, Bronek, who was famous for having robbed the safe in the
Reichsbank in the town of Bocholt during an air raid in March 1945.

The narrator then took an oath of silence on a revolver while
drinking schnapps and took part in plans to exchange the camp's store
of coffee for cows and sheep and to trade the cigarettes and chocolates
from Red Cross parcels. However, the gang came to a premature end
in February 1946 when Bronek the bank robber turned up for a meet-

ing completely drunk—which he had never done before. A raid had
gone disastrously wrong. While stealing two pounds of lard, he had
been discovered by a German farmer and had shot him dead. "There
is nothing else for me to do if I want to escape than to be repatriated
as soon as possible," Bronek moaned.

Aid workers in Germany generally thought that the people who made
the best of DP life were the Balts. Not only were they, as we have
seen, frequently better educated, but in many cases they had brought
their families and possessions with them. They were also on average
younger than other DPs. In the autumn of 1947, a quarter of the total
Lithuanian DP population of about 60,000 were children and only
3 percent were over sixty years old.

But there was also another factor particular to the Balts: national
pride. According to the Canadian historian Milda Danys, the Lithuanians "adopted a strategy that seemed naïve but was unexpectedly
fruitful: they refused to admit that their history had been snapped in
two, that their countries and cultures had ceased to exist. They denied
their impotence and lived and acted as though they still had power
over their lives. . . . One way to assert Lithuanian, Latvian or Estonian national pride was to participate as fully as possible within the
DP system, to become administrators of their own little worlds."
From this derived a fierce determination that their camps should be
cleaner and better run, their schools more efficient, and their culture
more vibrant than those of any other DP group.

To all the displaced persons, education was of fundamental importance—in keeping young people occupied, in handing on the national
culture, and in making up the lost wartime years. "In each DP camp,
the first order of business was to set up a hospital. The second order of
business was to open a school," one UNRRA veteran later recalled.
Ninety percent of the children between the ages of five and sixteen in
the American Zone were attending camp schools in April 1946. This
was in spite of formidable obstacles—bad physical conditions, inadequate buildings, and an enormous shortage of books and materials. At
first pupils often had to learn by rote. "The teacher would tell us, and
we would memorize what he said. We paid attention so we could
repeat it," a DP later remembered. Gradually, though, the facilities
improved.[26]

There were also political problems to overcome. The Poles, especially, had to weather harassment from UNRRA and the military, who were reluctant to let them get too comfortable in Germany and worried that too nationalistic a curriculum would upset the Russians. Of course, for most DPs, the very function of education was to inculcate national feeling: "We made all possible efforts to educate the children that they are Lithuanians," one educator-priest recalled. The Jewish DPs insisted that the medium of instruction in their camps be Hebrew.[27]

By 1946, the DP school system was expanding beyond the one-room schoolhouse state, and a variety of levels of higher education was being developed. The Jewish camps had especially thorough vocational training; the Lithuanians eventually opened a maritime academy at Flensburg, and the Estonians an agricultural college near Lübeck. In 1947, the occupation authorities made it possible for DPs to attend German universities (10 percent of places were kept open for them), and some of the better educated chose to do this; more than seven hundred Jews, for example, entered German universities in the American Zone. But there were also universities run by the DPs themselves. Probably the most successful was the "Baltic University" in the British Zone, but the most celebrated was the UNRRA University in Munich, which was the brainchild of several Eastern Europeans working for UNRRA and initially enjoyed the support of Jack Whiting, the organization's director in the American Zone. It has been argued that the UNRRA University represented an attempt to transcend national rivalries, cleanse the European university tradition of its complicity with both National Socialism and communism, and forge a new "transnational solidarity." In fact, the institution was strongly dominated by anti-Communist Russians and Ukrainians, and many of its staff were Ukrainian intellectuals already living in Germany. For that reason, it was felt to be too obviously anti-Soviet and in January 1947 the university was closed—according to an UNRRA handout, "as part of the Munich community's fuel conservation program."[28]

Besides education, there were other outlets for DPs' energy. For the Baltic women gardens held enormous significance, and not just as a source of vegetables to supplement the diet. Kay Hulme noticed how at Wildflecken, even in the "tide-like turbulence of a repatriat-

ing Polish camp" the DPs were "passionately garden-minded," growing mostly vegetables—cabbages, leeks, beets, and tomatoes. But in
the longer-term camps of the Balts

> the gardens had perennials like gooseberry, raspberry bushes, and
> two harvests of leaves had already been plucked from their flour-
> ishing tobacco plants and cured on strings stretched in the sun.
> Here there were landscaping effects and the crests of lost lands like
> Latvia, Lithuania and Estonia grew out of the earth in floral designs
> with marigolds, pansies and begonias spelling out the national
> colours.[29]

The Baltic DPs also put huge effort into organizing their social
and cultural life. Interviewed years later, young Latvian women recalled frequent dances, sports games, nature hikes, and camping trips;
being taught to darn and hem, to knit Latvian mittens with intricate
patterns, and embroider pillow covers with traditional designs. "We
had a lovely time. I was young and carefree then," reported one of the
women. Another, too, had enjoyed camp life but later realized how
much her parents had suffered. "We had our social life there in the
camps," she told an interviewer. "When you are young . . . it is just an
adventure. But when I think about my parents, they had to leave
everything behind, all their life, what they had saved. We only took a
few silver spoons to exchange later on in Germany for food. They lost
everything."[30]

The mass choral singing in which the Baltic peoples excelled was
a way of involving many people at once, but the Baltic DP camps
were also full of talented professional singers and artists. DPs particularly remember a staging of *The Barber of Seville* by members of the
Kaunas (Kovno) State Opera and a Latvian production of *Twelfth
Night,* which gave ten-year-old Agate Nesaule her introduction to
Shakespeare. "A simple trellis entwined with flowers on a platform at
the end of the dining hall was Illyria," she wrote later. "The Clowns
sang and played the *Kokle,* a traditional Latvian stringed instrument
similar to a zither; the air was full of music. The words did the rest, as
magical in Latvian as in English. I was entranced."[31]

Milda Danys believes that, having lost their self-respect, property,
careers, and power over their environment and being entirely dependent on others' charity for their survival, the Lithuanian DPs could

find meaning in their lives only in their national identity: "being a Lithuanian was a constant, and to this frail thread of identity Lithuanians clung." In fact, Danys claims, this period in the DP camps was for many Lithuanians critical to their future. Had those people been able to emigrate shortly after the war ended, they would never have taken with them to Canada, Australia, South America, England, and the United States the same sense of their national culture.[32]

In June 1945, a British military government officer recorded that Estonian DPs were nagging him for permission to produce a newspaper. Within months all the other groups had followed suit. As a result, in the Ukrainian language alone an estimated 327 newspapers and bulletins were published in 1945.[33]

To start a DP newspaper, one needed some capital, the capacity to operate in difficult conditions, staff prepared to work for minimal pay, and the ingenuity to get scarce materials on the black market—including, in the case of Ukrainians, Belorussians, Serbs, and Russians, Cyrillic typefaces. One also had to overcome the reluctance of local German businesses to enter into long-term contracts with foreigners. However, despite these initial hurdles, the publishing climate was good: "camp dwellers, thirsting for the written word in their own language, bought out even larger press runs." One Ukrainian newspaper was able to establish itself as an economically stable business in six months, despite having only one typewriter (an aged Underwood) in its office; it sold 10,000 copies weekly at 50 pfennigs, bringing in 5,000 reichsmarks.

The solidity of the readership was, however, offset by political complications. Freedom of the press and speech was in theory guaranteed, provided that nothing was said or done to undermine the activities of the Allied military government. Yet while some local commanders forbade the publication of newspapers, some UNRRA directors supported it enthusiastically. In general, newspaper publishers found it was better to get out of the camps, to avoid camp councils and commanders interfering in their affairs. Attempts to create an objective Ukrainian press agency, for example, soon fell foul of the nationalist factions, newspapers which accused the Banderites of waging a campaign of terror against their political opponents in the DP camps were urged to exercise self-censorship "so as not to discredit us in the eyes of the world and not provide ammunition to forces hostile to us." There was little substantial reporting on day-to-day life in the camps, as Ukrainian DPs seemed to "put more emphasis on ideology and politics than on material concerns."[34]

The Ukrainian DP camps also produced a substantial body of literature. The very size of their population—according to some estimates, over 200,000—created something new in Ukrainian cultural history, a large and concentrated audience for a wide range of genres and literary activities, whose material needs were taken care of by international charity and thus had ample time for the good literary life.[35] This climate proved more conducive to some art forms than others. The vitality of Ukrainian camp theater was remarkable: "theater flourished in every form from the most primitve farces to the most complex tragedies." Traveling companies mostly offered the traditional Ukrainan repertoire, but a professional company from Lvov put on modern European work and an experimental group staged modern satires.

Fiction proved more difficult. Under pressure to produce "great literature" which would at once advance the nationalist cause and draw the eyes of the literary world to Ukraine, the writers did their best, but literary genius does not call on demand. Two important novels have been described as marked by "dullness," "languid pace, and plodding problematics," while a long epic poem is "a monumental failure." As one might expect, the most "natural" and "organic" genre of camp literature turned out to be the memoir.[36]

The DP years did, however, produce some interesting writers, among them the Poles Tadeusz Borowski and Tadeusz Nowakowski and the Lithuanian poet and filmmaker Jonas Mekas. The son of Poles living in Ukraine, Borowski had spent time in Auschwitz as a *capo* and was in DP camps in Germany after the war before being repatriated to Poland in late 1946. Best known today for *This Way for the Gas, Ladies and Gentlemen,* a collection based on his time in Auschwitz, Borowksi also wrote stories about DP life—later filmed by the Polish director Andrzej Wajda as *Landscape After the Battle*—which seized on the absurdity and unreality of the DPs' condition, their faltering efforts to adjust to the new world after liberation, and to draw meaning again from the mundane realities of drink and sex. Borowski himself never did quite manage it. After returning to Poland, he enjoyed some success but struggled to find a place in the new Communist regime and committed suicide in 1951, at the age of twenty-eight.[37]

Borowski's harshly satirical picture of a Polish DP camp, dominated by outdated traditions and maintaining discredited social structures, is taken further in Nowakowski's novel *The Camp of All Saints.* Here the eponymous camp is situated near the German–Dutch border, in a gloomy, flat, unhealthy landscape. The novel's hero, Stefan, is an independent-minded schoolteacher, contemptuously dismissive of Polish traditions. He proudly recalls how, as a schoolboy, he laughed at "his own first encounter with Martyred Poland, a thousand lines of abysmal chauvinistic claptrap" which represented the "first stage of the initiation into the dark mysteries of national masochism." Yet Stefan is also a romantic, happy to engage in "the one pitiful diversion of the camp inmate, chewing over one's past": "Suddenly, in his cold, damp barracks room, Stefan felt a surge of warmth, of love for his native city. A feeling as intense as love for a human being."

The novel is full of loving descriptions of the minor occurrences of prewar Polish provincial life, the promenading after church on Sundays, the fierce rivalries between the prominent tradesmen, the youth associations and the men's clubs, the actress his father wasted his money on—the whole social canvas ripped up by the Germans in 1939.

Nowakowski's DP camp is run by a Polish army major in high boots and cavalry trousers and with all the mannerisms of his discredited class, assisted by a bossy female librarian. These two are constantly going off to Hamburg, claiming that it improves their morale to look at the ruins, but it soon emerges that they are using the trips to sell the camp's cigarette rations on the black market. When Stefan challenges their ascendancy, they counterattack by staging an evening of patriotic songs and national stories, which rallies the DPs behind them. Stefan goes off in disgust to live with a German girl he has fallen in love with. They marry but the relationship does not prosper as Stefan begins to realize that he cannot shake off his Polish identity.

> There's no getting away from it. I'm a man without a country, but I can't stop being a Pole. Can a man stop being a German, a Chinese or Zulu, or whatever, can he get out of his own skin? Wherever you go, your greedy, jealous, vindictive fatherland goes with you.

On September 1, 1948, the ninth anniversary of the German invasion of Poland, Stefan leaves his wife, Ursula, and returns to the camp, where he is forced to make a groveling apology to the major before he can once again claim DP rations.

Nowakowski himself got out of the DP camp within a year—to work as a journalist—and his picture of DP life is as bleak as Borowski's. The inmates in his book all suffer from a "barbed wire complex," and most are "mental cripples, slaves of habits, afflicted with prisoner's psychoses of all kinds."

> The intellectual and emotional climate of the DP camp was stifling. Day after day, one saw the same people, the same faces, heard the same clichés. Any trifle could provoke a quarrel, an "affront to honour." Animals, too, when shut up in cages, fight with one another out of sheer boredom.

Some of Nowakowski's most interesting passages, however, deal with the relationship between those who give aid and those who receive it, the liberators and the liberated. Although his own contact was with the British, in the novel the local military and UNRRA officials are all gullible, innocent, ignorant Americans, who cannot understand the one great truth about war:

> Suffering, Stefan thought, never unites people, it only separates them; only joy can bring them together. There is no fraternity in defeat, the only fraternity is in victory. Nor is there such a thing as a brotherhood of arms, or a common feeling based on sharing the same war experiences, the same camps or prisons. Contrary to all the clichés about how suffering and injustice ennoble their victims, experiences that originate in moral defeat do not bring people together.[38]

It would be a mistake, however, to regard Nowakowski's book as a realistic portrait of DP life. Written in the 1950s, it draws heavily on the author's later experiences working for the Voice of America in Munich and is pitched in the absurdist tone of much Polish literature. We get a better sense of the realities of camp life in the diaries of the Lithuanian poet Jonas Mekas.

Like most young intellectuals, Mekas was self-obsessed and given

to self-pity and valued his privacy. The "miseries of communal living" in overcrowded camps are recorded in misanthropic ranting:

> We can hear every sound behind [the wooden boards], their vapid
> conversations, jokes, every fart. And nights, when they bring home
> German and international prostitutes, we hear their fucking too,
> and we can see their insane faces, eyes bulging out from eating too
> much fat in the American army kitchens, where they work.

Yet DP life also offered Mekas, his brother Anastas, and their Lithuanian friends great opportunities—greater perhaps than they would
have had in their native land. Jonas was able to enroll in the University of Mainz, study philosophy, and had his plays put on in a drama
studio. He received a monthly stipend and a basic weekly ration:

> We picked up our weekly food ration on Friday and of course we
> ate it all in the same day. Now, the whole week to go and all
> we have left is this pile of boiled potatoes. . . .
> This morning, to avoid the breakfast problem, we stayed on
> our cots till noon. But our eyes have been open for hours, moving
> from object to object.

The young men sold their possessions for food: "We ate the radio, we
ate the typewriter, the clothes, the books. Now the room feels a little
bit emptier, more space. But the stomach feels as empty as before."[39]
Mekas read prodigiously—Thoreau, Stanislavsky, Rilke, and Dos-
toevsky are just a few of the writers he mentions—and greedily drank
in all the culture available to him. When he and his friends got a
room to themselves, they painted on the wall a long, incomprehensible sentence from the philosopher Heidegger. "The sentence has gone
already three times round the room and no end yet in sight," he notes.
But Mekas was racked by conflicts. Unlike most of his friends, he
came not from the bourgeoisie but from a humble country background and his cultural roots lay in the landscape of his childhood.
The more he was exposed to European modernism, the more Lithuanian he felt:

> Such longing suddenly takes over, overpowers me, that sometimes
> I think I won't be able to hold it. No, I hear the breaking of the ice

on the rivers. I hear the sound of sleds on the road, the hoofs of the horses. A branch moves on a fir tree, in the forest, snow falls down. I can hear it all, see it all again. I sit and I dream. Silently the snow falls again on the landscapes of my childhood. And only when somebody suddenly opens the door, the voice breaks the silence, I wake up, I startle—I wake up—and I see the table, the books, the walls.

In 1948, while in a DP camp in Germany, Mekas published *Idylls,* the volume on which his reputation as a poet still rests.[40]

An Estonian psychologist living among the DPs was initially surprised at how little mental illness there was. Eduard Bakis had expected wartime experiences, culminating in the loss of their homeland, to do more "harm." But by the summer of 1947, after two years in the camps, more serious symptoms had become conspicuous. Almost everyone was "showing at one time or another behaviour that had to be classified as neurotic. Crime became more serious, absenteeism from work more frequent, interest in camp affairs—elections—was vanishing. Participation in cultural entertainments dropped and even artists of international repute could no longer attract a full hall of listeners." The most obvious and widespread features seemed to be procrastination and apathy.[41]

What was causing those problems? A questionnaire revealed that most of the people wished to leave Europe because they feared a war with Russia and were afraid of what might happen to them if the Russians were to conquer Germany; but after years of living on 1,700 or 2,000 calories a day, they found it difficult to make the mental effort needed to plan overseas migration for the first time in their lives.

Other factors contributed. The DPs worried about friends and relatives left behind but had by now discovered that it was impossible to communicate with them—for those behind the Iron Curtain, it was dangerous to receive a letter from abroad. "It is as if the mind of my father were 'Off the air,'" one man wrote. About a third of those questioned reported having had telepathic experiences or prophetic ones.

Then again, the insecurity and meaninglessness of DP life—the absence of any clear direction—coupled with the tensions caused by overcrowded camps contributed to hypertension. Many people worried about their identity. Coming from a country which had only recently gained its independence, they did not have deep-rooted traditions and feared that they were "losing the habits and social code of normal life." This made all the more valuable the things which remained:

> family, such as had survived; native language and native schools for the children; the churches; national and European literature and culture; occupation, for such as were fortunate enough to be able to continue it. Among these factors the language was probably the most important, because of its continuous use by everyone. We can assume that the nationally organized DP camps contributed a great deal to the mental health of the inhabitants.

Often those who were supposed to provide leadership, such as ministers, psychiatrists, and psychologists, were themselves also affected. The DPs, Bakis believed, "lacked both guidance from a tradition and inspiration from the future, and each had to rely upon his own thinking to develop some kind of practical philosophy of living, if he was to survive."

Not surprisingly, many went astray. "The people have to follow *only* their own moral codes and moral experiences," a teacher wrote. "So much cannot be expected from the majority. As a consequence people 'lose their heads.' . . . Orders and laws are violated because there is nobody to watch the obedience of these laws; quarrels are common because there is nobody to make one ashamed of oneself." Anyone who adhered to the old prewar moral code would not survive long in a DP camp. Mothers had to get black-market food and medicine for their malnourished children; the elderly and infirm had to forge papers to become eligible for DP rations; wives whose husbands had been deported to Siberia eight years previously, and had almost certainly died there, had to manipulate the records to get their new marriages legalized; wartime orphans had been "educated by the world." The old traditions, beliefs, and hopes had collapsed and "a new morality—if one can call it a morality" had taken their place.

Many bourgeois Estonians talked of depression and nervousness. But the most important theme to emerge was the "extinction of personal gaiety," the loss of the ability to enjoy yourself. "In the past I was able to experience joy heartily," a middle-aged woman wrote, "but since June 1941 [the date of the first mass deportation in Estonia] no more. . . . Even if there is something to enjoy, painful recollections kill at once the little gaiety. It is as if I would sin if I should feel joy for a moment, and this is always so. I am sorry about that. My mouth is singing, but the heart worries, and I am entirely free from that." Many people turned to alcohol. But, as one DP observed, because there was so little food, "one was narcotized before he could enjoy the artificial ecstasy."

The psychological pressures of DP life were, however, most strongly felt by the Jewish DPs.

The first people to try to come to terms with the meaning of the Holocaust were its victims. Well before the liberation, while still in Kaufering labor camp near Dachau, a group of Jews from Kovno in Lithuania had begun to develop their own ideology, based on the biblical concept of the *She'erith Hapletah*—the "Surviving Remnant," which carries the promise of the future. This idea was carried further after the liberation, most clearly by the lawyer and scholar Samuel Gringauz—who, together with Dr. Zalman Grinberg, provided the early leadership for the survivors.

The task confronting the Surviving Remnant, Gringauz argued, was nothing less than to lead the Jewish people in a new direction, "empowered by its own martyrdom and the legacy left it by the dead." The destruction of the European Jews—the "great catastrophe" of Jewish history—had, said Gringauz, abolished the distinctions between Jews; from now on all Jewish survivors must accept that their fundamental identity was as Jews. Second, they had no future in Europe, though they should not renounce Western culture. Third, in the new American-Palestinian epoch of Jewish history, it was only in Palestine that Jews could be truly Jewish. "The task with which we are confronted is a double one: political struggle in and for Palestine, and the spiritual unification of the Jews of the rest of the world." Gringauz was asserting, on behalf of the survivors, a claim to lead or, at any rate, to steer the Jewish people.[42]

Central to his argument was a belief that only Zionism provided the way forward. This was acknowledged by nearly all those who worked with the survivors. "The events of 1939–1945 seemed to discredit completely those philosophies of Jewish life prevailing before the war which were not centered around Palestine," wrote the American historian Koppel S. Pinson, the Joint's education director in the American Zone. "The Zionists were the only ones that had a program that seemed to make sense after this catastrophe."

The Zionists' sense of purpose quickly found concrete expression. By October 1946, the Jews in occupied Germany were politically organized both within camps and at the zonal level and had created more than sixty schools with 10,000 pupils, about twenty libraries, historical commissions to gather eyewitness testimonies of German crimes against the Jews, four newspapers and one journal, and several dramatic and musical groups. With help from the American Jewish Joint Distribution Committee and volunteers from Palestine, young Jewish DPs were encouraged to join kibbutzim, which took them away from the unstructured lassitude of camp life, channeled their energy in a positive direction, trained them in skills they would need in Palestine, and offered them a group identity. By the beginning of 1947, there were 276 kibbutzim with 16,238 members.[43]

At the same time, the process of Jewish regeneration and revival expressed itself in a massive baby boom. The birthrate among the Jewish DPs was one of the highest in the world. A network of hospitals, crèches, and clinics sprang up to cope with this phenomenon.[44]

The psychological effect of all this activity was undoubtedly beneficial. "The creation of a community of fate imbued with a sense of purpose," Zeev Mankowitz has argued, "was a critical factor in deflecting, mitigating and transmuting the destructive effect of massive psychic trauma." Certainly the way in which camp survivors recovered astonished those who nursed them. The psychotic symptoms common at the time of liberation mostly disappeared once the survivors had been treated for typhus, fed, clothed, and partially resocialized. Other problems then emerged, such as "immorality" and delinquency. "The moral standing of many of these survivors from the concentration camps is very low; theft is of daily occurrence and sexual irregularity has reached appalling proportions," Dr. Henri Nerson of the French charity OSE wrote in August 1945. "Many young girls give themselves up to debauch without restraint." He then added, "There can be no question of reproaching these poor creatures, who have passed through a hell of suffering, sadistic persecution and systematic demoralisation . . . they are now seized by an irresistible desire for affection and forgetfulness, which they seek to satisfy with the means at their disposal."[45]

Boys, too, were affected. Children evacuated from Buchenwald were found to be "undisciplined, unstable, primitive, even bestial," though desperate for affection. Such findings prompted an American psychologist to ask magazine readers, "Will these children be an asset or a liability to the nation which receives them? Will they be welcome young blood to nations that have lost so much, or will they be juvenile delinquents now and future criminals?"[46]

By the end of 1945, however, order and morality had been restored. The structure of Jewish family life was reestablished; rabbis and camp authorities encouraged young couples to marry as a way of reasserting moral authority. Youth workers from Palestine were able to discipline the vagabonding boys. But doctors continued to express concern about the "disconcertingly inappropriate affect" evident in survivors' social behavior. Children did not laugh and play; were "emotional at the wrong moments" and "preternaturally calm"; came unmoved through tragedies yet flew into a rage over trifles. Psychiatrists wrote of loss of affect or "affective anesthesia," "emotional numbness or shallowness" and "distortion of the ego." Laymen said simply that the survivors were not normal, that they were neurotic or hysterical.[47]

One vital element must be remembered, however. Nowadays we routinely talk of "Holocaust survivors" as if they made up a single group. But Jewish DPs in 1946, far from being a monolithic unit, were composed of at least four different categories: survivors of the concentration and death camps; those who had spent the war in hiding; those who had been in Russia; and those who had fought with the partisans or had Aryan papers. There were, in addition, differences of nationality—Polish Jews had been persecuted since 1939, Hungarians since 1944.

These divergent wartime experiences had produced very different states of mind. Camp survivors were numb, apathetic, neurotic about food, often hysterical, and incapable of normal emotional responses. But the moment they came into contact with "the strong and almost authoritative leadership of ex-partisan fighters, ex-Jewish army men and others who have a positive program," the contrast was obvious. Jews who had been in hiding were "more self-sufficient, more social, and more rational" than those who had remained in the camps, Ralph Segalman, a psychologist with the Joint, noticed. Ex-partisans and anti-Nazi fighters had "a strong sense of discipline and also a strong group interest. . . . These are the people who look to the future among the DPs and try to plan for it." Jews who had come from Russia via Poland—the so-called infiltrees—were "the healthiest element among the Jews in Germany," according to Koppel S. Pinson. They had not completely lost all sense of organized community life. Jews from Russia were also less "resistive to work"; they did not have the attitude that "we have worked so much for the Germans; it is about time the Germans worked for us."[48]

Aid workers expected those "healthier elements" to assert themselves, to become the dominant group and lift the survivors out of their inertia. But that did not happen. Although the newcomers played an active part in cultural and political life, they did not challenge the established ideology; as Samuel Gringauz put it, "the experiences of concentration camp prisoners and partisans were decisive in creating the ideology of the Jewish DPs; even those Polish Jews who during the war took refuge in Siberia and later came across Poland to Germany have in the course of time accepted it."

The Jewish DPs' achievement in putting their lives together was remarkable. But it came at some cost, Koppel Pinson concluded after spending a year working with them. Pinson found the Jewish DP to be "preoccupied almost to the point of morbidity with his past," especially experiences under the Nazis. He was constantly engaging in "gruesome recapitulation of concentration camp incidents" and had a "heightened historical sense" that led to an "almost passionate devotion of the DPs to the collection of historical and material data on ghetto and kotzet life and death." He was self-absorbed—"the interest of the Jewish DP in Germany revolves almost entirely around himself"—yet restless; this derived partly from the situation in the camps and from the way, after the war, "driven by a mad fury the first thought of liberated Jews was to rush about seeking traces of their lost relatives."

The vast majority of Jews were ordinary people who had suffered more and were therefore more emotionally tense, but, given normal surroundings and community life once again, these exaggerated and intensified personality traits could easily be reduced to something approximating the healthy. The problem was that the DP camps did not provide "normal surroundings." "Contact with Nazism" had also "left certain traces of totalitarian influence even upon these very victims of Nazism." Jewish DPs, Pinson said, feel they must maintain a totalitarian conception of unity at all costs. In many ways they have become totalitarians. All cultural activity must have only one aim, to make propaganda for Palestine. The leaders do not trust open discussion of intellectual problems. They are cold and at times arrogantly indifferent to pleas for tolerance, intellectual freedom and the like. Their approach to such matters dangerously resembles that of their former masters— an emphasis on the state of crisis, a mistrust of the ordinary person's intelligence and a burning conviction in their own possession of truth.

Pinson felt that the paramilitary atmosphere in the Jewish camps— the "concern with marching, demonstrations, banners and uniforms, the widespread resort to agitation, propaganda and indoctrination and the persistence on the whole of a certain regulated intolerance"— also "betrayed, perhaps unconsciously the effects of living for many years under Totalitarian rule."

Pinson knew and admired Samuel Gringauz. But for all the latter's fine rhetoric about the historic role to be played by the Surviving Remnant, the reality Pinson found in Germany was rather different. The Jewish DP camps were supposedly self-governing but in practice entirely dependent for their survival on UNRRA or the Joint. Their cultural life, though heroic and commendable in the circumstances, was primitive—how could it not be when the cultural elite had been exterminated? Teachers had a difficult job:

> In one class you may have children from Hungary who know no Yiddish, children recovered from Polish gentile families who still have to be taught and convinced that they are Jews, children coming from Samarkand or Uzbekistan or some such place in the USSR and who speak nothing but Russian—all together with little Lithuanian or Carpatho-Russian Jewish children, who run about conversing in a juicy and fluent Yiddish.[49]

Nor was Pinson impressed by the theatrical work, which he thought offered yet another means to revisit the past. "In most cases the . . . performances are more in the nature of revues dealing with ghetto and kotzet life and enabling the spectators to relive their gruesome experiences all over again." He thought the Jewish DP press, with some exceptions, was marked by "narrowness and fanatical emotionalism."

As the Joint's educational chief, Pinson tried to get the DPs to widen the school curriculum beyond its narrow Jewish focus, but he met with strong resistance. Similarly, when an UNRRA welfare worker gave a lecture on social work in the United States, one Jewish youth leader remarked, "We do not need social work, we need nationalism." In response, UNRRA workers pointed out the dangers of a narrow nationalistic education and criticized the obsessive exploitation of the horrors of the past to help bind the kibbutzim together in the present. The welfare officer Lotte Lotheim regretted that

[t]hose who are called upon to "lead" hold on to their provoking experience of the past—with such great emotional need—that it is difficult for them to be objective. Intellectually they admit this and find the following excuse: "We must hold on to it—in order to keep alive among our people that our goal is Palestine."[50]

Relations between the DPs and those who tried to help them were never easy. Lucy Schildkret, a young American aid worker who spoke fluent Yiddish, found that "almost to a man, the survivors regarded all *goyim*—non-Jews—as unmitigated anti-Semites. They were convinced that they all would, sooner or later, even in the United States, do to the Jews what the Nazis had done." However, they were also contemptuous of American Jews, including the Joint workers, whom they despised as rich and self-satisfied: "They called us *amerikaner Khazeyrim* ('American pigs'), they resented being dependent on our handouts." Most of all, she believed, "they hated the functionaries from the Central Committee and the camp committees, believing them to be crooked and corrupt."[51]

When Schildkret first got to Germany, she found that camp survivors had a compulsion to talk: "Telling their story helped to expiate the guilt feelings that tormented them." She felt humbled in their presence. Gradually, though, she came to see that she was sentimentalizing the survivors as a class, "endowing them not only with courage and endurance, but with mythical properties." As she came to know more of them, "I saw that they were not all stamped from the same mold. Suffering, I learned, did not always ennoble. The experiences of suffering were more likely to bring to the fore the dominant elements in a person's character, the good or the bad, selfishness or ruthlessness." Similarly, some psychiatrists who worked with DPs came to feel that they might have achieved more if they had been tougher with them. "They recognised that their own feelings of guilt in relation to their persecuted fellows made them over anxious to placate them . . . the refugees, apart from those in the kibbutzim, got no moral guidance but were rather encouraged to continue their regressively dependent behaviour."[52]

FIFTEEN

"The Best Interests of the Child"

CHILD SEARCH IN GERMANY, 1945–1950

On April 18, 1945, a baby boy was found beside the road leading into Schwabach, near Nuremberg, in Bavaria, lying between a dead woman and a suitcase. In the suitcase were baby clothes and papers as well as identification documents for two women, one French, the other Yugoslav. Who was the baby, and who was his mother? No one knew. In the meantime, Frau Fanny Spiess, the German woman who had found the child, continued to care for him.

Seventeen months had passed when, in September 1946, the Child Search team in UNRRA's Munich office wrote to Eileen Davidson, the district Child Search officer on UNRRA Team 1048 at Regensburg, asking her to establish the identity of the baby. They were fairly certain that the dead woman was Mademoiselle Paulette Robin from Neuilly in France and the baby was her child. But inquiries in France revealed that Mlle Robin was in fact alive and had been repatriated after treatment for injuries. Interviewed by the mayor of Neuilly, Robin confirmed that she had been a munitions worker in Germany but denied any knowledge of a Yugoslav woman or a baby and swore that she herself had never had a child. UNRRA officers knew that it was common practice for the mothers of illegitimate babies to leave them behind when returning home.

The trail now returned to Germany. Dozens of letters and inquiries were sent to German, French, and Yugoslav offices (all of which had to be translated into the relevant language and the replies translated into English). It was discovered that both women named in the documents in the suitcase had been foreign workers in the Dynamit AG factory and had lived at the same camp. German ex-employees of the factory and foreign workers there were interviewed. Eventually, Smiljana Milojkovic and her daughter Dula, two Yugo-

slav ex–ammunition workers traced to a DP camp, told child searchers that they had known both women—the Yugoslav, whose name
was Marija Puskaric, and the Frenchwoman, Paulette Robin—and
that both had given birth to babies around the same time and had
been confined in the camp hospital together.

However, Margaret Heider, the German head nurse of the factory
camp, had a different version. She told interviewers that Marija Puskaric and her husband (who had been killed by partisans in Yugoslavia) had had a baby boy and immediately recognized the photograph
of the child shown to her. She claimed to have been a close friend of
Marija and to have packed the small suitcase containing baby clothes
herself but made no mention of a French mother. A German midwife,
Margareth Reder, also testified that she had been present at the birth
of a boy to Marija Puskaric at fifteen minutes past one on February 8,
1945; the boy had been named Stefan. Several witnesses described
Marija as twenty years old with blond hair and blue eyes and "strongly
built." But the dead woman found with the baby had dark hair and
was slim. "Perhaps," wrote one child searcher rather desperately, "the
hair of the dead woman was blood-stained and thus looked black."

It took several more months of determined work by numerous
individuals before the boy's story was finally told.

On April 17, 1945, the night before the baby was found, U.S.
troops were approaching the city of Nuremberg. The French, Italian,
and Croatian workers in the Dynamit AG factory in Fürth were
ordered to abandon the camp and go to Schwabach under armed SS
guard. Near a cemetery in the suburbs of the city they came under
artillery fire, and several were killed and wounded, including Paulette Robin. A witness, Anna Steituchar from Croatia, described how
she and her brother had survived but as they passed the cemetery had
heard a baby crying and seen the dead body of Marija, but the SS
guards would not allow anyone to stop or help. As the survivors fled
toward Schwabach, they were met by American troops. Paulette
Robin was taken to hospital. It remained a mystery why her letters
and papers were left in the Puskaric suitcase. Despite inconsistencies
in the descriptions, it was concluded that Marija Puskaric was the
mother of the baby.

On January 13, 1947, the Yugoslav liaison officer in Munich sent
his authorization to Eileen Davidson for Stefan Puskaric to be repatriated to Yugoslavia. Fanny Spiess, the German foster mother who

had been caring for Stefan for nearly two years, was reported to be "very anxious about the boy's future." She said "she will not give him up to anybody and she wants to keep him as her own child, despite the fact that she knows he is not a German child." But she was overruled. Stefan was returned to Yugoslavia, to be cared for in an orphanage. So far as UNRRA was concerned, his case was closed.[1]

Baby Stefan was just one of millions of children to suffer in the Second World War. Touring Europe in the summer of 1947, the Irish journalist Dorothy Macardle found everywhere children who were homeless, ill fed, in poor health, and very often without parents. There were 50,000 orphans in Czechoslovakia, 200,000 in Poland, and 280,000 in Yugoslavia. It was estimated that in all 2.5 million Polish children were in urgent need of care and 8 million children in Germany, 6.5 million in the Soviet Union, and 1.3 million in France remained homeless. Infant mortality rates were double the prewar rate in France and nearly four times as high in Vienna.[2]

However, the psychologists and child welfare experts Macardle talked to all agreed that far more important than the material conditions was the war's likely emotional legacy: as a Polish doctor put it, children "saw, with their own eyes, people being arrested, rounded up, beaten, murdered." What would be the effect, Macardle asked, of the exposure to violence, the "tensions and agitations of life under enemy occupation," the loss of education? "The calamity which has befallen Europe's children," Macardle concluded, was "immeasurable," and only a "tremendous and swift crusade of rescue" could save millions of them from "growing up ignorant, wretched and embittered, with sick, stunted bodies and minds."[3]

The response to this situation was, however, complicated by several factors.

There was, on the one side, the sense of outraged nationalism on the part of the victims in the countries the Germans had occupied. At the same time, however, children aroused equally powerful feelings in both aid workers and the general public. Idealized, romanticized, and made to bear a weight of expectation; symbols of innocence in a world of terrible evil; vessels of hope for the future, children carried the burden of adult projections. Thus Yugoslav refugees in camps in Italy in 1944 were, for the British aid worker Ann Dacie, "the most naturally disciplined, eager children possible to know." She marveled at how "children who had suffered from barbaric and needless cruelty" could still keep untouched within their little starving bodies "the spirit of their country which had endured and achieved so much against overwhelming odds." But the humanitarian response was also shaped by new intellectual and organizational currents: the growth of psychology (and, in particular, of Freudian psychoanalysis) in the first half of the twentieth century; the evolution of welfare bureaucracies; and the arrival of women in positions of executive power within large organizations.[4]

Between the wars, in advanced Western societies, the academic discipline of psychology was gradually applied to such areas of everyday life as education, advertising, the industrial workplace, and the handling of teenage delinquency. In particular, as the role of religion declined, psychology successfully colonized the domain of child rearing, particularly through the medium of popular journalism. As part of this process, the effects of war came also to be seen in psychological terms.

And so, for the first time in history, those who planned postwar relief in the 1940s factored in psychology; they had a vision of ameliorating the psychological aftermath of the conflict. "In a shift from earlier efforts, postwar humanitarian activists saw themselves as agents of individual psychological reconstruction and rehabilitation," the historian Tara Zahra has written. In June 1945, UNRRA proclaimed itself "concerned not only with relief—that is with the provision of material needs—but also with rehabilitation—that is with the amelioration of psychological suffering and dislocation. For men do not live by bread alone." In that spirit, it commissioned several reports from leading psychiatrists and psychologists on the "psychological problems of displaced persons" and "special needs of women and girls during rehabilitation and repatriation." Those reports echoed the dire predictions of postwar epidemics made by experts but added a new note of psychological warning:

> However great the physical devastation caused by German policy, the moral and psychological disturbance is probably greater. This policy has erected in young people a wall of cynicism and brutishness which will require years of both mass and individual psychotherapeutic or social treatment to put right.

The experts were, however, vague about the form such a program should take.[5]

It was the job of UNRRA to translate these aspirations into reality. Its Welfare Division had been established in Atlantic City in November 1943, but only after some struggle. The difficulty arose from a difference of opinion "over the meaning of the terms *relief* and *welfare,* how welfare services should be delivered, and by whom."

> To many people on both sides of the Atlantic, the two terms were synonymous. They meant material assistance such as food, shelter, clothing, fuel, medicines, and other necessities of life, made available for people unable to provide for themselves. Charities had dispensed relief for centuries, and the Hoover relief campaign after the First World War subscribed to this interpretation.[6]

However, this traditional approach had now been overtaken by the development of social work as a profession, especially in America in the 1930s.

The United States had gone into the Depression with a public assistance program still grounded in the Elizabethan poor law code, in which relief still carried the stigma of the workhouse. But by the end of the decade the New Deal programs of emergency relief and public assistance had turned the federal government into a giant social work organization and made a former social worker, Harry Hopkins, into Roosevelt's effective deputy. Hopkins's Social Security Act of 1935 created three huge new bureaucracies employing thousands of social workers. It also changed the profession. Whereas the social worker had traditionally been "an agent of middle-class or religious philanthropy, often in fact a volunteer or at least altruistic in spirit," the New Deal programs attracted a host of people who saw themselves as professionals, line workers in a bureaucracy who wanted better working conditions and job security. At the same time, a new ideology emerged. Social workers now felt close to their clients and their woes and believed that proper welfare services should be active, not passive—that they should stimulate self-help among the recipients. At Atlantic City in November 1943, this view was energetically promoted by advisers to the American delegation, who succeeded in persuading Herbert Lehman to establish a Welfare Division within UNRRA.[7]

Unfortunately, however, welfare soon became one of UNRRA's black holes, thanks to one of Lehman's disastrous appointments. Mary Craig McGeachy was a forceful, intelligent, and attractive Canadian who had worked for the League of Nations before the war and then made her name by brilliantly selling the British policy of economic blockade to the American public; she became the first woman ever to be accorded full diplomatic status by the British Foreign Office. However, she had no background in welfare work; British diplomats were thus astonished when Lehman put her in charge of welfare instead of giving her the public relations job for which she was obviously suited (and which UNRRA desperately needed). According to her biographer, to her mainly American staff in Washington she was ideologically suspect: she seemed to personify "the image of an English, *noblesse oblige* approach to the old-fashioned kind of relief which they were at pains to dispel."[8]

McGeachy began promisingly. In her writings and speeches she set out an inspiring vision of how UNRRA's welfare role would draw on three different strands—the spirit of cooperation engendered by the resistance movement in Nazi-occupied Europe, British experience of feeding and sheltering large groups of people dislocated by air raids, and American social welfare work in the Depression—to create a new model of international welfare. Fearful that Americans would impose their own social norms on European culture, she emphasized that UNRRA should "see to it that our plans bring out the values that exist in the Occupied Countries and lend support to the institutions and voluntary groups there rather than impose new ones." At the same time, she commissioned numerous expert reports into the social and psychological problems of the displaced persons of occupied Europe.[9]

Unfortunately, this bold vision was never realized. McGeachy proved a poor administrator and a weak leader. She failed to fight her corner in UNRRA's Washington office, did not win resources or respect from her colleagues, could not motivate her staff, and was unable to give UNRRA workers in the field a clear sense of their mission. Her protracted absences from Washington while conducting a relationship in London further weakened the Welfare Division. Yet McGeachy's skill in manipulating old men such as Lehman and Leith-

Ross repeatedly saved her from dismissal, and it was not until August 1946 that La Guardia managed to force her out.[10]

Given this vacuum at the top, welfare became UNRRA's problem child, mostly kept firmly subservient to the organization's other tasks such as repatriation and resettlement. It was constantly beset by tensions between its ambitious intentions and the realities on the ground.

UNRRA was one of the first major organizations to employ women in large numbers and in positions of responsibility. Of its 12,889 personnel in December 1946, 44 percent were women. There were sound reasons for this practice. Decades of experience led the British relief worker Francesca Wilson to conclude that "women are better than men for all the improvisations and make-do-and-mends that relief work entails."

> They give trouble sometimes through emotional instability and because power goes to their heads, but, on the whole, they are harder working and more successful in relief work than men. A man wants a real, clear-cut job; relief work is temporary, messy and clamorous; it seems unworthy of his best efforts. Moreover, the trained woman usually recruited to relief work is less susceptible to the temptations of life away from home, especially in a conquered county.[11]

The political and ideological fault lines in UNRRA's offices in London and Washington were replicated in its field operation in Germany. But there were also local factors. The environment in Germany was male-dominated and the scope for any welfare program severely limited. The resources were tiny, particularly in the British Zone, where such things as cinema projection screens and personal transport were hard to come by, when compared to the American Zone. One UNRRA welfare worker's only achievement, after four months in the British Zone, was to get herself a car with which to cover "her" area. Furthermore, the Welfare Division had, a British adviser acknowledged, to "operate within the reality that the military held the real power." Even on such matters as the welfare of children, nothing could be achieved without the cooperation of the military authorities, and UNRRA, by and large, was powerless to resist the military's wishes.[12]

There were further tensions between UNRRA and organizations such as the Quakers, with their own long-standing traditions of charitable work. "UNRRA respected theory; to them much of our method appeared deplorably unorthodox and often inadequate," Margaret McNeill wrote. The Quaker team at Braunschweig, in common with many relief workers, spent much of their time teaching young Polish or Ukrainian women brought to Germany as slave workers the simple skills of motherhood they would normally have learned from their mothers and aunts. The Quakers found the visits of young UNRRA nursing officers, seeking to impose fashionable Western child-rearing practices on Eastern European women, both comic and tiresome. One such person "roamed tirelessly round the camps seeking milk kitchens" and found none—"unless you could say that Mrs Pawloss in the Ukrainian Camp, placidly ladling milk into a large open can with a very dubious cup in one corner of the storeroom, was a milk kitchen." She then stopped to speak to a young Ukrainian woman sitting in the sun with a baby in her arms. When the baby started to cry and the mother clapped him to her breast, the UNRRA nursing officer looked at her watch disapprovingly; in line with then-current Western orthodoxy, she was a firm believer in set hours for feeding. Worried that they might be "reported to Zone," the Quakers hastily arranged a baby-welfare organization among the DP mothers and achieved "a compromise between the mothers in Polish and Ukrainian camps and the methods of Dr Truby King," though they knew the change would arouse suspicions among the DPs. On another occasion, an UNRRA doctor was outraged to find in a mothers and babies' home "all the children with two pullovers on each, all windows closed, and husbands smoking," not realizing that progress had been made by persuading the mothers to wash their babies every day and to put *only* two pullovers on them and that, having been forbidden by the Germans to marry, they now wanted to keep the fathers of their children close to hand—"the fear of being separated was so great that it could not be overcome from one day to another."[13]

Within UNRRA itself, the battle between grand theory and day-to-day reality was also played out. The politics of relief determined many careers. Francesca Wilson, for example, came from the do-gooder tradition, "one of the last survivors of that unique English type of middle-aged unmarried woman, with independent means and an inherent urge towards philanthropy." By 1945, she was a veteran of thirty-odd years of relief work, with a gift for picking up languages, skill in handling people, and wide experience of the policy issues in relief. Wilson was one of the first to join UNRRA, hoping, like many others, that it would make a better job of relief than the quarreling charities had after 1918.[14]

Yet Wilson soon found herself at odds with the UNRRA hierarchy in Germany, composed mainly of American women with social science degrees and no knowledge of European languages. "This plus ambition and the desire to win credit in their profession made so many of them seek administrative jobs, especially those at 'area level,'" Wilson wrote later. She conceded that professionally trained Americans were more methodical, "but this very method means, perhaps, that they are at their very best in stable conditions, and less able to deal with the chaotic and the unexpected than their European opposite numbers." Many of their schemes were excellent on paper, "but sometimes they seemed to hesitate about trying them out themselves in the rough-and-tumble of the field and to prefer supervising those who did."[15]

Wilson was particularly critical of the questionnaires that began to pour out from UNRRA's headquarters in Munich:

> What about our Personal Counselling Service? To how many people did we give personal counsel every day? How many handicapped had we discovered? Social science has neat labels and appropriate pigeon-holes for everyone: handicapped, under-privileged, maladjusted, deprived, introvert and extrovert. Does it sometimes forget the person in his label?

From her Quaker past, Francesca Wilson was "accustomed to relief work on a much smaller scale, and where she was able to do things her own way," as her friend Rhoda Dawson noted. "She had in fact a much more humane and experienced approach, but it was completely useless in the current situation" because there was not the time or the resources to function in this hands-on, personal way. In addition, her long career had left Francesca with clear preferences as to whom she felt able to help among the DPs. She liked the "gaiety and resilience" of Serbs and Russians and was attracted to blond Baltic women ("they are freedom-loving sturdy peoples") but was less responsive to the "unsmiling faces with haunted eyes" of Jewish concentration camp survivors. For its part, the mostly American UNRRA administration did not like Francesca Wilson, and when she became unwell, briskly sent her home.[16]

By contrast, aid workers with other qualities thrived; some people built entire careers out of their ability to get soldiers to cooperate. Susan Pettiss joined UNRRA to get away from her alcoholic and abusive husband in Mobile, Alabama, and was in one of the first teams sent to Munich in May 1945. There she quickly found a role. "Being one of just a handful of American women there also gave me a powerful weapon—my femininity," she wrote later.

> Those in command were all men, mostly Americans, and it was a new and exciting job to get their acquiescence to what I needed to get the job done. My Belgian director learned early to send me to the Army. . . . Because I had a Southern accent and blue eyes, we got lots more from the military than many teams.

In a memoir published years later, Pettiss wrote frankly about her work in Germany.

> The headiest part of this remarkable experience was finding myself in the center of a large number of American men. . . . I thrived on the male attention. It was cathartic and balm to a bruised ego and soul after a disastrous marriage. Yet I was also spared dealing with the complexities of deep relationships. . . . No relationship could be more than a light flirtation, which suited me fine.

Early on, a U.S. Army captain about to be sent home gave her a brand-new BMW car he had commandeered as "confiscated enemy material." As a result, "I was the absolute envy of everyone in UNRRA as there was no provision for transportation for teams. For the next two years I managed with a lot of smiling, fast talk, and some flirting, to get proper registrations and stickers to keep the car." Another admirer, a Canadian working for UNRRA's transport section, adorned his fleet of vehicles with her name.

Susan Pettiss arrived in Germany knowing very little about Eastern European history and speaking only English. Unaware of the hatreds and hostilities among the various nationality groups, she did not understand why the army immediately separated the nationalities.

"Imbued with the idealistic sense of the goal of 'one world,' I felt disillusioned when that unity didn't materialize right away," she later recalled. By the end of the first year she could speak French and German without an interpreter, but she never really communicated with the displaced persons themselves and preferred liaison jobs where she provided the interface among UNRRA, the voluntary agencies, and the military. At those, she was enormously successful and very popular and rose to an important position in the UNRRA hierarchy. "A lot has happened in those two years," she wrote when she left Germany in May 1947. "I have been more than fortunate. I am certainly a different Susan Pettiss."[17]

By then it had become accepted that the most effective welfare was done by people from within the same culture as the DPs they were helping, especially with Jewish DPs. A good example was Cecelia "Zippy" Orlin, a young South African woman who worked with Jewish children at Bergen-Belsen for twenty-seven months. She was recruited in the spring of 1946, at a time when the Joint was looking for volunteer workers with the right linguistic skills, and, although without previous experience of relief work, she spoke Yiddish, having lived in Lithuania for the first six years of her life. Her primary job was to care for the youngest children in the camp, including some orphans, but she also served with the camp hospital nursing staff, trying to make the children feel safe, help them to enjoy life again, and build up their sense of self-esteem. One of the many photographs she took is captioned, "By love, tears make way for joy, crying makes way for singing, repression gives way to expression"; another, "sturdy little toddlers romped and played in the flower-covered fields, and expressed the childish emotions so long suppressed." When Zippy left Germany, her performance was rated as "very good" by her boss at the Joint, who praised her "application of energy, interest, skills, initiative, resourcefulness," and especially "cooperativeness and ability to work with others," which he felt more than made up for her lack of training. His only criticism was that she "over-identified" with the children.[18]

The problems described so far in this chapter—the terrible impact of the war on children, the gulf between aspiration and reality, the frustrations of the UNRRA workers, and the tensions between UNRRA and the military—all came together around the issue of "stolen children." In the words of one aid worker, "The lost identity of individual children is *the* Social Problem of the day on the continent of Europe."[19]

It was a problem that took a while to emerge. In the summer of 1945, when UNRRA and the military were establishing assembly centers for displaced persons and trying to deal with the people's basic needs, they soon became familiar with the DPs' worries and anxieties. As an UNRRA report explained:

> These people went to the Welfare Officers with problems and sorrows of every imaginable type. One compelling and recurrent request came from parents who cried in utter despair, "Where is my child?" or "Help me find my children!"

The natural response, the Canadian welfare worker Jean Henshaw explained, was to try to help:

> For two years this heartrending cry of desperate parents has echoed through Europe. In April 1947, when the first official transport of unaccompanied children went by rail to Prague, Czechoslovakia, the station and streets were massed with parents and relatives pressing forward, with imploring hands upraised in urgent entreaty, beseeching UNRRA to find and return their children with the next—and the next—transports.[20]

From the moment they entered Germany, Allied soldiers found children separated from their families—"unaccompanied children," as they were called.★ These included child survivors of concentration camps and forced-labor brigades and "GI mascots," boys who had attached themselves to the U.S. Army and then been abandoned. UNRRA soon began to create children's centers where they could be brought together. The first, established in July 1945 at the monastery in Kloster Indersdorf in Bavaria, soon attracted children of all ages

---

★ An "unaccompanied child" was defined by UNRRA as one who was not with either parent or member of its family, had been born in, brought into, or infiltrated into Germany since October 1, 1938, and one of whose parents was known, or suspected to be, a national of one of the United Nations or of assimilated status of unknown parentage. This included children who had been adopted or were being cared for in a German family or institution.

and nationalities. Many were found by the military or by workers from UNRRA or the voluntary organizations; others found their own way there. Greta Fischer, the principal welfare officer at Indersdorf, described sleeping by the front door so that she would not miss the quiet knock of a child in the middle of the night. When a child arrived, he was examined and his possessions searched for papers, letters, and photographs that would help identify him. Many were too traumatized to give coherent explanations, some were too young, and others preferred to say nothing—they were just glad to be safe and given food. Soon several more camps for unaccompanied children were set up in the U.S. and British zones, where they could be cared for pending identification and repatriation.[21]

Then, however, another issue emerged. When UNRRA began to carry out surveys of the DPs living outside the camps, groups of children who were clearly not German were found in institutions and private homes in the region of Passau and Regensburg in north Bavaria. UNRRA workers reported that "when questioned about these children, the Germans were evasive, resistant and even hostile for they had come to regard these children 'as their own.'" As Jean Henshaw put it:

> Remembering the tragic, despairing parents, the officers commenced to feel that there was a link between their questions and these children. At once they felt the urgency of this work, to such a degree that, although there was no formal search program in progress, they spent their free time searching and registering children.

A similar survey in the Heidelberg area produced smaller numbers but confirmed the need for a "thorough combing of all welfare agencies and institutions in search of Allied children." Military requests to the German authorities for more information soon produced further children. By now the international scope of the problem and the need for special UNRRA teams to search for the "lost and missing children" had become clear.

Child welfare workers had at first thought that most of the children living in German households and institutions were the offspring of Eastern slave workers who had been separated from their families, which was the usual Nazi policy. They were wholly unprepared for the revelations they now uncovered as letters began to pour into SHAEF from Poland, Russia, Ukraine, the Baltics, and Yugoslavia, imploring them to find missing children.

The Lebensborn program had begun in the winter of 1941. Initially Lebensborn centers were set up for children born to selected Nazi men and women in order to swell the Aryan population—the future *Herrenvolk*. Later a scheme was created to kidnap blond, blue-eyed children from families mostly in German-occupied Poland, where, it was reported, there was a large number of children whose racial appearance made them suitable for "Germanization." Other intelligent, healthy-looking children of the "Nordic" type aged between two and twelve, found living in Yugoslavia, Czechoslovakia, Romania, the Netherlands, Belgium, and France, were targeted by teams of officials who snatched them from parks, school playgrounds, or their homes. Children vanished from the forced-labor camps while their mothers were working. In Poland entire orphanages were emptied and put onto trains and sent to Germany where they were assessed and put in institutions or fostered in a family which had pledged to bring them up as good Germans in return for maintenance payments. All were given new German names and instructed in the German language and German ways. Those who failed the tests were sent to hospitals for medical experiments and invariably died. None was ever sent home.

UNRRA's welfare workers were understandably horrified by these discoveries. For them, this, even more than the Holocaust, was the Nazis' greatest crime—their "most dastardly plan," Jean Henshaw called it. They were galvanized into action. In less than three months, searchers had successfully traced nearly 6,000 kidnapped children in regions of Bavaria and Silesia. In Austria an appeal to foster parents to give up stolen children revealed 800 mostly Polish children. After six months about 10,000 lost and kidnapped children were identified. But it was still only one-sixth of the total number for whom inquiries had been registered with UNRRA.

By the second half of 1945, the Child Search program had become a formal part of the Allied welfare effort. Colonel Charles L. Schottland, the head of SHAEF's D P Division, with the cooperation of a child welfare specialist, Dorothy de la Pole, organized a Central Tracing Bureau based at the UNRRA headquarters near

Frankfurt, staffed by a hundred workers who among them spoke twenty-seven languages, with the aim of locating and identifying all unaccompanied UN children found in Germany and repatriating them to their countries of birth. Meanwhile, Child Search teams were formed in the U.S. and British zones and given authorization to enter German homes and institutions with powers to interview families and staff and remove a child if it was a national of another country. They examined police records and captured enemy documents—although the Germans had done a thorough job of destroying such records. As one UNRRA worker noted, "amnesia seemed to be a prevalent malady in Germany."★

Child Search work was challenging and difficult, calling for great persistence, self-belief, and forcefulness, as well as perseverance in the face of German obstructiveness. But it was also intensely rewarding: "a mighty worthwhile job, for we feel we are saving children, we are doing our part in this marvellous work; Rehabilitation," a Dutchman working for UNRRA wrote. One of the great satisfactions was getting children to reveal their true nationalities. Most had been forbidden to speak their mother tongue (usually Polish, Yugoslav, Baltic, or Czech). In several convents the nuns "schooled" children in their replies to questions from UNRRA investigators. A Czech child worker found five children in a German village whom he believed to be Czechs or Slovaks. The families swore that the children, who apparently spoke only German, were their own. The searcher stayed in the village; within a few days the children were all chatting away in Czech.[22]

For those running the program, however, this was only the beginning. To carry out their ambitious aim, they wanted to compile information from all over Europe, send experts to Poland and other countries from which children had been abducted, and get access to the records of the German agencies involved in the Lebensborn program. In addition, the Child Search teams would need to be strengthened.

At the end of 1945, responsibility for the Child Search program

★ Child Search was defined as the process of looking for and locating children believed to be in occupied areas whose names and particulars were not known. Child Tracing was the process of locating children at the request of someone who could give particulars about them and of locating relatives of children found without their family.

passed from the military to UNRRA, just as General Sir Frederick Morgan began running its displaced persons operation in Germany. At first he was interested in the program and very supportive of UNRRA's efforts to get the Allied occupation authorities to put pressure on the Germans to produce their records. But by April 1946, he was having his doubts. On May 29, he wrote:

> I was at last able to square up to this complicated child care business, and on reading carefully the documentary evidence, I fully believe that we may be completely wasting our time. These dear girls who are in charge of this side of our business are in the main, middle-aged, frustrated virgins suffering from all kinds of repressions. As a result they completely lack all sense of proportion and resent all kinds of control or direction. I foresee all kinds of trouble over this, but the affair must be brought within bounds.[23]

How could Morgan so easily dismiss the whole program? Was he simply voicing male prejudice? The general certainly had a low opinion of Eileen Blackey, the child welfare officer at UNRRA headquarters and successor to Miss de la Pole. She was the sort of American professional social worker he could not abide; listening to her stating her case for "a joy ride to Poland" was a "waste of time." But the issues involved went beyond personalities and prejudices. We can see why if we look at a particular case.

In the spring of 1946, the UNRRA child welfare officer Gitta Sereny went to a Bavarian farmhouse and persuaded the farmer and his wife to give her a photograph of Johann and Marie, the blond six-year-old adopted children they so obviously adored; the photograph had been taken on the day the children had arrived in Germany. That image, which Sereny passed to her superiors in UNRRA, enabled a couple in Lvov, Poland, to recognize the twin children taken from them in 1942 and UNRRA officials to reclaim them on the true parents' behalf. By the time the decision was enforced, however, Sereny had been moved elsewhere, so she did not herself have to carry out the removal of Johann and Marie—though, after taking a child from another German couple, she always remembered the "inconsolable grief of the parents" and the "wild uncomprehending anger of the child himself."

That was not the end of the story, however. Two months later, when

Sereny arrived at a children's center in Bavaria, she found Johann and Marie still there. Their return to Poland had been delayed to allow them more time for psychological readjustment, but it had only made them worse. Johann was now violent—he attacked Sereny when he saw her, shouting "Du, du, du,"—and Marie had regressed to babyhood and was wetting her bed and drinking from a bottle. Soon afterward, they were returned to their natural parents.[24]

Sereny's account of this episode, published years later, may have colored or simplified some of the details; for example, she worked as part of a team and would probably not have visited the couple on her own. Nonetheless, this case clearly illustrates some of the dilemmas inherent in this kind of work. Was it in Johann's and Marie's best interests to remove them from the German couple who were so attached to them (although it should be emphasized that not *all* German families were devoted fosterers)? Supposing the children did in the end overcome the distress caused by being removed, would they have been better off in the long run in Poland? And what about those like Stefan, whom we met at the beginning of this chapter, who did not have natural parents left in their own country? Would they have been better off returning to an orphanage or staying in Germany?

Morgan's view was that quite apart from the interests of the child, the Child Search program took up huge resources, was not within UNRRA's remit, disturbed relations with the Germans, and raised huge "strategic issues"—that is to say, had to be seen within the wider context of East-West relations. This was pretty much the general opinion among the military by 1946. Child Search teams, Marvin Klemmé thought, "did some very good work at first but became a disgrace to both the organization and to humanity, later on in the game. As long as they were helping to reunite families it was all right, but in the end many of them spent more time in breaking up families."

> Children five or six years old were snatched out of their foster-mother's arms with both the child and the mother wailing its eyes out. Had the child been going home to rejoin its real mother, or even an aunt or grandmother, the act could possibly have been justified, but in most cases they were being sent to orphanages. Quite a number were shipped back to Poland under such conditions as that.

His view was that there should be no more "baby snatching" unless it could be proved that the child's blood relatives were living and actually wanted the child.[25]

But the UNRRA welfare workers continued to fight for their program. Eileen Davidson, the Australian social worker who ran the main Child Search team, later recalled that she had several times "longed to give up and run away from all this sordidness for ever, but, in my mind's eye, I have a mental picture of a group of distraught women from whom SS troops are wrenching their children . . . and now, I feel that we who were so long in coming to the rescue have a small, very, very small opportunity of undoing what was done." The child welfare workers did find some allies within the military system, most notably the war crimes investigators in the U.S. Department of War, then preparing the second round of trials due to follow Nuremberg. The prosecution of several of the Germans involved in the Lebensborn program in October 1947 was an important boost to the child searchers' morale, as well as providing them with valuable new information.[26]

Then, after General Morgan's dismissal, the prevailing wind within UNRRA changed. In August 1946, Eileen Blackey was at last able to visit Warsaw and confer with the Polish authorities. As she had foreseen, by meeting the Poles she was able to uncover a great deal of new information. In Lodz, they had found more than five thousand case records of children selected for Lebensborn; in Katowice, another five thousand. With their usual thoroughness, the Germans had photographed the children, and recorded their birth details, their new German names, and information about their new German foster families. Some files carried the formula "no special care required," the code for liquidation.[27]

Fired up by this new material, Eileen Blackey returned to Germany to continue the task. In November 1946, she was back in Poland to resolve another problem—making sure that the reception arrangements in Poland for returning children were adequate, especially for those without parents. Again she was completely satisfied. Like many on UNRRA's Warsaw team, Blackey was sincere in her identification with the Poles. What she encountered during her visits to Poland was serious-minded fellow professionals doing their best to rebuild their country after a devastating war.

But for all that, in Germany itself the results were disappointing.

By July 1946, some 6,000 to 7,000 children had been reported in the U.S. Zone, of whom about 2,000 had been found directly through Child Search efforts; the rest were part of large groups of DPs. Very few children had been found in German families; most had turned up in German institutions and orphanages. At a conference in October 1946, Child Search workers attributed the poor results partly to shortages of staff (there were only thirty-four full-time workers in the British Zone, few of them with the necessary languages, and forty-four-plus voluntary helpers in the U.S. Zone). But their real anger was vented at the military authorities, who, on the one hand, were refusing to allow children to be removed from German families until elaborate safeguards had been met; and, on the other, were very half-hearted in pushing the German authorities for records and information. In her final report before handing the problem on to her successor at IRO, Eileen Blackey expressed her belief that a great opportunity had been lost. Had the military authorities effectively enforced the search directives issued by the Allied Control Council in January and March 1946, she argued, it might have been possible to get an effective grip on the problem of missing children. But they had not, and by then—she was writing in June 1947—the Germans were regaining more and more control over the administration and could no longer be put under the same pressure. Similarly, the importance of centralizing all the information had not been grasped by the occupying powers. The Central Tracing Bureau had been closed down.

In addition, a further mystery had emerged, said Blackey. "The children who are being found by the Search Teams in the field do not tally with the children who are being asked for by their families." Most of the children located thus far were those who had been evacuated into Germany, been born in Germany, or been brought forcibly with their families and later become separated from them. The children who were stolen from their families in their home countries with the intention of taking them to Germany for "Germanization" were in the vast majority of cases still unaccounted for. "These children are living in German families as German children and can be found only through the discovery and perusal of documents and records which reveal what disposition was made of those children during the Nazi regime."[28]

Not all UNRRA workers shared Blackey's sense that a great opportunity had been lost through the shortsightedness of the military. Some came to feel they should examine their own records and consciences. "Vindictive factors have often coloured our motives," Ella Dunkel, child search officer, 460 UNRRA HQ, wrote in June 1947. She was very critical of the rhetoric which surrounded the program: "the terms 'stolen,' 'hidden,' and 'kidnapped' children are loosely used without regard to analysis." Another Child Search worker, Michael Sorenson, questioned many of the dominant assumptions. It was absurd, he said, to suggest that 100,000 French children had been abducted. Actually, "100,000 was a guess made by the French government for the number of children born to French mothers while working in Germany." Indeed, most of the children living with German families had been born to non-German mothers who had gone or been sent to work in Germany during the war. They were mostly illegitimate and not wanted by their mothers. "They have usually been with foster parents since they were very small babies and have grown up and been treated as actual children of their foster parents." There was generally no question of their being hidden, for the papers were available for inspection in the local welfare office. Indeed, Sorenson had found most German officials—except nuns— to be very cooperative. "The German in general does not like acting on his own in defiance of authority."[29]

Ella Dunkel even assailed the core belief of UNRRA's whole Child Search operation. "Another contentious statement," she wrote, "is that a child of complete or half foreign origin left in Germany will suffer a great psychological shock when in adolescence he begins to enquire into the past and finds that he is not of German origin." She continued:

> Has this been psychologically proved? It would seem that the shock sustained as a result of removing a child of tender years from good family care where he finds security, to the unknown, would be considerably greater. The reaction of the adopted child to his past in any case and in any country depends upon the wisdom with which the foster parents have presented it to him. Our feelings of nationality grow with us, we are not born with them.

Far from deploring the safeguards introduced by the military authorities, she commended them. "This serious decision involving the disposition of a human life should not be left, as it has been, to one or two individuals." A measure of protection had been secured by giving the military the right to review all child repatriation cases, but she demanded that in future decisions be made by a committee of six consisting of representatives of the military government, the IRO, and the International Red Cross, a legal officer, a social worker, and a psychologist.

In January 1948, Eileen Davidson, by then deputy chief of IRO's Child Search section, felt it necessary to reassert the true faith. The policy of returning every child to his country of birth represented "the best interest of the child" from a psychological, social, moral, and political perspective, she declared. Davidson's argument, as Tara Zahra has pointed out, "rested largely on her conviction that as German society had not yet been purged of Nazi racism and authoritarianism, the possibility of true assimilation and integration for east European children in post-war Germany was therefore slim. Even German-speaking children from Eastern Europe often faced discrimination as foreigners in Germany." Children removed from German institutions, meanwhile, showed telltale signs of authoritarian Nazi behavior, according to Davidson:

> These children are apparently subjected to rigid routines and discipline and ordinarily they are shy, extremely fearful, and do not know how to play, even amongst themselves. Their behaviour is that of very repressed children, and it is in marked contrast to the behaviour of children in this group who have been with us any length of time who ordinarily are extremely friendly to adults, very active and free in their play and activities.

Eileen Davidson also reaffirmed her faith in "nationalization"— that is, the process by which a child who had become "Germanized" was turned back into a Pole or Czechoslovak in a UNRRA children's home before being repatriated. She recalled that a group of Polish children who had been adopted by Germans were "gradually absorbed into the life of the centre, and began to speak Polish, and on their own request were enrolled into the Polish class. After a few weeks they were eagerly learning Polish songs and folk dances. . . . By the time they had made the decision to go back to Poland, they were identified with the Polish group and had thus severed their relationship with their German friends." She did not discuss cases such as

Sereny's Johann and Marie, where "nationalization" clearly went wrong, but warned that Allied children left in German foster homes would surely suffer permanent psychological damage, even if they were loved and well cared for. "Far from securing the best interests of the child, one had run the danger with the passage of years of contributing to the development of a warped and twisted personality, a misfit with roots neither here nor in his home country."[30]

With the onset of the Cold War in earnest, all prospect of harmonious cooperation on this issue vanished. Allied military authorities grew more determined not to return children to the East unless they could be shown to have close relatives.

According to the official IRO history, after 1948 some 2,000 children were repatriated to Eastern Europe, mainly Poland, after quasi-judicial hearings, but twice that number were dispersed throughout the United States, Israel, and Canada. Gitta Sereny has claimed that this policy of resettlement of children overseas was in fact in place in 1946 and was fiercely resisted by UNRRA personnel, but she admits that no records of such a protest survive.[31]

It is impossible to say which side in this debate was right. For a start, there are no agreed statistics. According to one source, more than 15,000 stolen children were recovered by the time the IRO took over in June 1947; according to another, 5,000 children were returned home. Yet the UNRRA official history lists only 12,843 children as having been given into care by the agency, 2,703 repatriated, 1,889 resettled, and 1,016 reunited with their families.

The process of tracing—in which UNRRA and the IRO were by no means the only or, indeed, the main actors—went on for decades after the war. Ultimately, according to the Poles, only about 40,000 out of a possible 200,000 returned to Poland, but that figure included children born to Polish "slave workers," so most of the children who had been kidnapped remained in Germany. However, the German scholar Isabel Heinemann has recently questioned these figures. Detailed study of the German records led her to conclude that in fact only 20,000 (not 200,000) Polish children were kidnapped and up to 50,000 from all over Europe.[32]

And what was in the best interests of the child? The few cases which have been followed up (usually by television producers) may not be typical. Most have not fitted easily into any category or proven the case either way. Certainly, Eileen Davidson's conviction that a Polish child, once "Germanized," could be hastily and happily re-Polonized is not borne out; but, on the other hand, some children managed to have two sets of parents. In addition, national identity was not quite as clear cut as it seemed to the UNRRA workers, many people in Eastern Europe having had an ill-defined and flexible sense of nationality. Nor was every country's policy the same. The French, with their long-standing anxiety about a declining population, claimed any child who might be thought "French," whereas the Belgians refused to take a child unless he or she was shown to have relatives able to keep it.[33]

In hindsight, it is curious how the agenda of war-damaged children disappeared in the 1950s. For a while organizations such as UNICEF continued to monitor progress, but it soon ceased to be an issue of general public concern, replaced by worries about youth culture, teenagers, pop music, and so on. It is thus very difficult to say whether the fears expressed in the 1940s, and given powerful voice in Dorothy Macardle's *Children of Europe,* were legitimate or exaggerated. Certainly, some of the doom mongering was culturally ill informed, based on then-prominent psychoanalytic models of child development which focused particularly on the mother-child relationship and ignored the still very powerful role of the extended family in Eastern Europe. One long-term study of the impact of war and civil war on Greek children taken away from their mothers found that they were not nearly as damaged as the researcher had expected; indeed, they had turned out to be fairly similar to ordinary Greeks of their generation, largely because of the love and support they had received within their extended families.[34]

SIXTEEN

"Good Human Stock"

RESETTLING DPs, 1947–1950

Kay Hulme left Wildflecken displaced persons camp on March 24, 1947. After all the recent dramas—the Polish riot, Kay's denunciation of her director, Georges Masset, and his subsequent dismissal—it was felt better that she move on. UNRRA in Germany was now being downsized and reorganized prior to handing over to its successor, the International Refugee Organization. Kay was promoted to director of a team of only four people based at Aschaffenburg, twenty-five miles southeast of Frankfurt, running seven camps containing 9,000 DPs of five nationalities—a job which had previously been done by thirty. Kay was able to take her friend Marie-Louise Habets and her welfare director from Wildflecken with her. "It is practically a matriarchy," she wrote. "I've always believed that I would end up as the head gorgon of a matriarchy. I've always believed that women could do things. The women associated with me are rather elated at the opportunity of 'showing the men.'"[1]

Kay was now working mainly with Ukrainians and Estonians, "a static, irrepatriable group, organized beautifully, with most key people in the same jobs for more than a year." She had inherited a going concern.

> I deal now, not with simple Poles, but with the wily Ukrainians who have brain power and many thoughts about the way they want things run in the camps . . . it is talk, talk—day and night, winning my way slowly on each point and somehow holding the control and making them respect me for it.

But Kay did not have the same passionate sense of engagement with her new charges that she had had with the Poles. After watching their Easter festivities, she wrote:

It is amazing to see how much emotion is pent up in these Ukrainian and Baltic people over which I rule. One cannot but feel that the majority came into Germany of their own free will . . . somehow they passed Army screenings and were declared eligible for UNRRA care, but sometimes as I sit with their leaders, attired like gentlemen of Wall Street, all in fine tailored suits and smart cravats, I feel as if I am in some high-ranking diplomatic group and am embarrassed to use the phrase "displaced persons" before them.[2]

One afternoon in April, a new chapter in Kay's work began when a dapper little man with a lisp and a limp suddenly appeared in her office, accompanied by the Polish priest from one of her camps and an official of one of the major voluntary agencies. He announced himself as Ludger Dionne, a member of the Canadian Parliament and prominent industrialist, who had come to Germany, with the approval of the Canadian government, to recruit a hundred girls of spotless moral character to work in his spinning mill in a small town in Quebec. As the girls had to be Roman Catholics, he had first sought the approval of the camp priest. The successful recruits would be flown to Canada at once and be housed in a convent near the factory. They would receive £3 7s. a week and have to pay only 2 guineas for their board. The girls would have to go on their own.

Amused and appalled, Kay rang up her area director. Amid much masculine laughter, she gathered that Dionne's visit had already aroused attention. A *Time* reporter was also pursuing the story, attracted by the "spotless morals" angle. UNRRA's position on the matter was not quite clear, but in the meantime the director suggested that Kay show Dionne round the camp since he had come so far.

> "From slave labor to slave labor!" I banged on the switchboard. "You don't have to be a crystal-gazer to know what's going to happen to those girls with twenty-five shillings a week spending money, most of which they'll probably send back to their families." "They won't be virgins long," sang out my director.[3]

Dionne's mission was allowed to proceed. By the time the girls reached Canada, they had become known as "the Flying Virgins." It also turned out that Dionne had already been using Polish displaced persons as strikebreakers and, after a storm of bad publicity, a debate in the Canadian Parliament, and a row with the Polish government, he did not return for further shipments. But Kay noted sadly that the Polish girls who had not been picked continued to wait for him to return. They were quite happy to exchange the DP camps for a sweatshop in Quebec.[4]

In his way, Ludger Dionne was a pioneer. By early 1947, governments and individuals around the world were following his example: starting to see the European displaced persons in a new and more positive light, not as "idle bloodsuckers" but as a valuable pool of employment. Many countries needed workers to do jobs such as mining or forestry that their own populations were no longer prepared to do. Yet each government also wanted to be selective, to cherry-pick among the DPs. This contradiction gave to each of these transactions its own particular character.

In many Allied nations, the displaced persons filled the void left by the return of prisoners of war. Nearly three years after the end of the war, over 1 million German and Austrian POWs were still being used for labor—"the new slavery," *The New York Times* called it. More than half were held in the Soviet Union, but many other countries had also hung on to their prisoners. The Americans had repatriated 2.5 million of the 8 million prisoners they had held soon after the end of the war and had loaned some 600,000 to 700,000 to the French (who had never taken many themselves) and another 30,000 to the Belgians. By the end of 1947, there were hardly any German prisoners left in the United States, but France still had some 383,000 and they were such good workers that the French wanted to hang on to as many as possible. The British, too, dragged their feet. By November 1946, only 31,200 of the 385,000 POWs held in Britain had been sent home. After criticism in press and Parliament, for a time the repatriation rate rose to 20,000 a month, but at the end of 1947 there were still almost 200,000 German POWs in Britain, most of them working on the land.[5]

By then, however, the British had begun to recruit displaced persons. There was nothing humanitarian about their initiative; rather, as Marvin Klemmé said, it was a "cold-blooded labor recruiting program" driven by hard economics. The Attlee government's only chance of staving off national bankruptcy—while maintaining the position of a Great Power, with substantial forces stationed overseas and a high percentage of the country's manpower in the armed forces—rested on an economic recovery spearheaded by a drive in export sales. This could take place only if key sectors of the economy, such as coal mining, agriculture, and cotton textiles, were running at full capacity. Yet these were precisely the areas suffering from acute shortages of labor, as foreign prisoners of war began to be repatriated and women and the elderly, drafted into the workforce during the war, returned to their homes. Matters were further complicated by the government's commitment to improve general working conditions, its ties to the trade union movement, and the abandonment of some wartime controls over the direction of labor. Moreover, ministers believed that they could, at the same time, offset the decline in Britain's imperial power and "keep the Dominions loyal" by encouraging British immigration to Australia and Canada. This only exacerbated the manpower shortages.[6]

Where, then, were the necessary workers to be found? The 200,000 Polish soldiers who had refused to be repatriated and were now in the semimilitary Polish Resettlement Corps provided one obvious source. However, the Polish scheme had run into practical difficulties (only 910 Poles turned out to have experience in coal mining) and aroused resistance from British trade unions, fearful of a return to prewar unemployment levels and hostile to "landlords" and "fascists," as the anti-Communist Poles were seen. In the agricultural sector, the government simply ignored the unions' protests and put the Poles to work on the land; by the autumn of 1946, they were gathering the potato harvest in Scotland. In the coal industry, the more powerful National Union of Mineworkers was bribed to accept foreigners by the introduction of a five-day workweek in May 1947.[7] But there still remained severe labor shortages; finding domestic staff to work in hospitals was especially difficult. Workers in other European countries were not interested. British attention now turned to the DP camps.

"Britain is not by tradition a country of immigration," a Whitehall official declared in 1952. Despite their long history of settlement from abroad, the British had ceased to welcome foreigners by the mid–twentieth century. Between 1815 and 1914, the population of the United Kingdom had quadrupled, and some 20 million people had been exported to America and the colonies without any large-scale immigration. Yet the arrival of small numbers of Chinese, Italians, and Eastern European Jews was enough to set off a wave of anti-immigrant feeling leading to the passage of the Aliens Act of 1905, restricting the entry of foreigners. Their right to work in Britain was further curtailed in 1920, with workers admitted only under permits granted to individual employers by the Ministry of Labour, which were issued very sparingly. Between the wars the main labor shortage was in domestic servants—which was why many Jewish refugees from Austria and Germany trying to enter Britain in the late 1930s were obliged to plead their suitability for such employment. It was hard work: British consular officials were not convinced that Jews made good butlers.[8]

At the same time, however, members of the policy elite had for some time been fretting that Britain's population was in decline and her national "stock" in need of regeneration. In the 1930s, there were fears among some progressive intellectuals that a shrinking population and falling birthrate would hinder economic development and require an injection of new blood into the country. There needed to be immigration—but of the right sort. "Immigrants on a large scale into a fully established society like ours could only be welcomed without reserve," the Royal Commission on Population declared in 1949, "if the immigrants were of good human stock and were not prevented by their religion or race from intermarrying with the local population and becoming merged with it." Similarly, *Population and the People,* a 1945 Fabian Society pamphlet, declared that "From the population point of view we need to encourage potential parents of healthy stock to settle in the British Isles, and to discourage those whom we already have from leaving." The left-wing think tank concluded that "men and women of European stock, between the ages of 20 and 30, are the immigrants best suited to assist population policy." They would have to be carefully selected to "ensure they are assimilable and can adapt to the British way-of-life" and "the utmost care should, of course, be taken to admit only those physically and mentally sound, and free from criminal records, who will introduce a sound stock into the country. The eugenics of immigration cannot be overstressed." That phrase, with its chilling echoes of Nazi ideology, had a specific meaning to older officials educated in the eugenic assumptions of Edwardian Britain—that preference be given to

"Anglo-Saxon stock" and "sturdy womenfolk." For those reasons, British officialdom was wary of migrant workers from the Caribbean and Jewish refugees from Eastern Europe, who were felt to pose a threat to social cohesion, while Irish migrants, though racially compatible, were thought to be poor workers.[9]

From those assumptions, certain conclusions followed. British officials and relief workers agreed that the Balts—middle class, well organized, industrious, anxious to please, racially compatible, and (in the case of the Latvians and Estonians), Protestant by religion—"would be the easiest to assimilate in Great Britain or her Dominions," as Francesca Wilson wrote in her 1946 Penguin Special *Aftermath*. She acknowledged that there were collaborators among them, as in every country of occupied Europe, but "they are freedom-loving, sturdy peoples, and the proportion of pro-Nazis amongst them is certainly not high." After visiting Germany, Ministry of Labour officials reported that among the Baltic DPs "an exceedingly good type of woman is available for hospital domestic work in this country." The general standard of education was good, many already spoke English quite well, and they were "of good appearance" and "scrupulously clean in their persons and habits" and had "a natural dignity in their bearing." Those selected to come to Britain would form "an exceptionally healthy and fit body."[10]

Nonetheless, officials had their worries. Would it be possible to return unsatisfactory workers? What would happen to the displaced persons once they had settled in? Wouldn't the more intelligent of them resent doing domestic work and try to better themselves elsewhere? Might some of the refugees of peasant stock fail standards of cleanliness? Might women workers marry and leave their work? For politicians the concerns were different: recruiting foreign workers was politically sensitive and would represent a substantial shift in immigration policy. However, in April 1946, continuing labor shortages finally forced the Cabinet to approve Baltic Cygnet, a scheme to recruit one thousand unmarried Baltic women DPs to serve as domestics in TB sanatoria and hospitals. It was felt that single women would be less controversial, less visible, and more easily housed. The "Baltic cygnets" would work under the same terms and conditions as British workers, and, after their initial stint, other employment of "national importance" would be found for them. In the process, their official status would be transformed from that of refugee into economic migrant: the term "displaced persons" was replaced by "European volunteer workers," or EVWs.[11]

The first ninety-six "cygnets" arrived at Tilbury Dock on October 19, 1946, to be greeted by newsmen eager to see these gentle young swans coming to help the sick in Britain. To the *Evening Standard* they were the "intelligentsia of the Baltic States"; to *The Manchester Guardian,* "student doctors or dentists . . . hairdressers and office clerks." But instead of looking like poor refugees, they were dressed in their smartest hats and coats: "ocelot, some musquash, sealskin and others just rabbit." A few were elderly, but "the great majority are young, strong-looking and healthy and just as much interested in their personal appearance as any other girls of their years." Soon afterward came glowing reports from hospital matrons that they were "first class workers," "keen and enthusiastic," and "liking their fresh life in their new homes so much that many want to stay here for good—and hopefully marry English men." By the end of November 1946, 1,150 cygnets had been accepted.[12]

The contradictions in the British approach—balancing long-term eugenic criteria with short-term economic needs—were soon apparent. Middle-class Balts found themselves doing menial work alongside working-class Englishwomen. Agnes, a Latvian "cygnet," later recalled that she "couldn't hold conversations" with many of her English colleagues in a Yorkshire hospital: "We had nothing in common. I mean I am not a snob but they really knew nothing."[13]

At first the cygnets sent back positive impressions of life and work in Britain to their families in the camps: their letters arrived at a time when life there was rapidly deteriorating, with cuts in rations and the introduction of a compulsory work order in January 1947. The Ministry of Labour's recruiting officer in Germany was hopeful—"The tide of opinion has set very strongly in our favour, and we are being hailed as Liberators," he wrote—and advocated expanding the scheme to take on more recruits "while the iron is hot." Once the less popular TB sanatoria quota had been filled, it was decided to recruit 5,000 women for domestic work in general hospitals. But soon the numbers began to falter. The original estimate of 20,000 employable Baltic women in the British Zone, "of whom as many as 10,000 may be unmarried and childless and thus suitable for domestic work in En-

gland," proved overoptimistic, so the Ministry of Labour was forced
to consider single women from Ukraine, regarded as distinctly second
best, "aging more quickly than the Balts," and being "suitable [only]
for the rougher types of hospital domestic work (kitchen maids, cleaners, laundry maids, etc.)." They were "essentially peasants" and would
not fit into English life as easily as the mainly middle-class Balts.
Despite the extension of the Baltic Cygnet scheme to take in other
nationalities, the 5,000 quota was never met. Ultimately, only 3,891
women were recruited for hospitals and institutions.[14]

However, in the initial euphoria a more ambitious British scheme
took shape. Westward Ho!, approved by the Cabinet in December
1946, aimed to bring in 100,000 people from the DP camps to work
in the British cotton, coal, and agriculture industries. By March 1947,
recruiting teams were scouring Germany. When the actual details of
the scheme were explained, however, the DPs "were by no means
stunned with joy at England's beneficence. The fact that families
would have to wait behind dashed to pieces the cherished dream of
mass emigration." Nonetheless, the younger DPs without families
"flocked enthusiastically to register as volunteers. A wave of optimistic urgency swept through the camps and the first chance to break out
of the bondage of dependence and uselessness was grasped with almost
hysterical hopefulness."[15]

Eva, a Latvian woman, came to England under Westward Ho! in
1947. "I will never forget that day because it was Princess Elizabeth's
birthday. That is 21 April," she later recalled. "We were coming by
boat lots of girls together." After a night in a hostel in London, they
were met by a welfare officer who asked them what part of England
they wanted to go to. The girls spoke little English and had no idea
where to go but liked the sound of one job.

> They needed four girls for this mental hospital and we were four
> and they said it's in the Midlands. So we thought "oh well, in the
> middle that would be good, that would be best, not far away from
> anything."

They were registered for a mental hospital near Warwick: "We were
talking among ourselves and 'I wonder what mental means' . . . we
didn't know what mental means." One girl looked the word up in her
dictionary and cried "Aagh." "And we said 'Oh God, we don't want

to go to a mental hospital.'" But after being reassured that they would not work with the patients, Eva and her three friends did go to the hospital and were quite happy together polishing floors and serving meals and making beds—upgraded to ward orderlies, "one up" from the rougher domestic work. "We thought we were in paradise," Eva recalled. The four of them each had a small room with a sink with hot and cold water and shared a bathroom and a separate little sitting room. They did not socialize with the English hospital staff. "The matron, the sisters, they all told us that we are not really the lower class people. I am sorry to say that, but we couldn't fit in so we kept to ourselves mostly."[16]

Others had different memories. Women sent to isolated hospitals were lonely and overworked; being a domestic in a men's hostel was fun, but everyone hated working for private employers. The most demanding job was working in the textile industry. The Baltic women were unused to the harsh, noisy environment of the mills and factories and lacked the speed and dexterity required to do the jobs. "The first day at the mill I wanted to kill myself," eighteen-year-old Lizina remembered.

> I'd never been in a mill before. All the noise and the dust and the people—Oh Lordy. After the first day, I got back to the room and I screamed and cried. My mother said "you wanted to come to England, so here we are and I don't want to hear another word."[17]

From some official pronouncements, you might have thought that Britain had imported a shipload of prize heifers. Ministers spoke of "the benefits that come from the assimilation of virile, active and industrious people into our stock," and MPs of both main parties described the new arrivals as "first class people" who would "be of great benefit to our stock" and who would "replace the vigorous young blood of our nation," which was immigrating to the Commonwealth. The British government put considerable energy into "shaping" public opinion to accept European volunteer workers; special documentary films were made, and items presenting the new arrivals in a favorable light inserted into BBC radio shows. Nonetheless, there was some public opposition, especially in the popular press. In July 1948, an article in the *Daily Mirror*, headlined "Let Them Be Displaced," suggested that Britain had recruited "most of the scum" from the camps rather than the cream that other nations had taken and that the EVWs were responsible for swelling the crime wave and engaging in black-market rackets. In 1949, the *New Statesman,* while appreciating the efforts of some EVWs, also ranted that the "illiterate, the mentally deficient, the sick, the aged, the politically suspect and the behaviourally disruptive" should be excluded from EVW schemes.[18]

Initially the British took only Balts and Ukrainians, but the net was eventually widened to include Poles, Yugoslavs, Hungarians, Bulgarians, Czechs, and Slovaks—and a few, carefully vetted *Volksdeutsche.* Between 1946 and 1951, a total of 81,000 DPs was admitted under the two British schemes, and most made a favorable adjustment, with only 4,000 insisting on returning to Germany and Austria, the majority of them being people who had left dependents in the camps. At the same time, several thousand DPs left the United Kingdom on completing the scheme when opportunities arose in other countries. Britain had gotten itself a bad name, mainly because of the very restrictive policy about bringing in dependents, determined partly by the great housing shortage in Britain—and because of attempts to maintain restrictions on where the DPs could work.[19]

The next major scheme involved Belgium, a country which had suffered heavy damage in the war and had a considerable manpower shortage. Under an agreement reached on June 11, 1947, the Belgian government agreed to admit 50,000 DPs to work as coal miners, promising equal working conditions, the right to social security benefits, and Belgian citizenship after a period of five years. Unlike the British, they laid down no restrictions on nationality.

The Belgian scheme caused a stir of interest among the DPs. Kay Hulme watched a "vivacious" Belgian colonel address the camps in Bavaria, playing a tape recording of Poles who had worked in the Belgian mines since before the war and explaining why V-bomb damage to housing in his country made it impossible to accept workers' wives straightaway. Then a mine doctor examined the recruits, and "the cream of the crop" lined up, "all husky young men with eyes alight for adventure, clutching their contracts as if they had the world by the tail." Kay watched their departure. As dawn broke over the camp parade ground, fifteen army trucks containing 180 men formed up for a blessing from Orthodox and Catholic priests:

From where we stood on the ground the whole thing was lifted against the dawn sky—the dark crosses, the brilliant magenta caps and the rows of young men standing bareheaded and motionless in the trucks, listening with gravest intensity to what was doubtless the last service they would hear in their native tongue for a long time. They bowed low and crossed themselves at the final prayer and then watched in utter silence while their priests climbed from the altar truck to pass down the lines of [army trucks] and sprinkled holy water on each flat green hood.

The departure of the trucks left Kay drained and emotional. "This affair lifted my heart," she wrote. "It was the opening of a door . . . the first full-scale legitimate emigration offer to the DPs. . . . I saw suddenly the fitting and proper end to my book."[20]

Alas, the Belgian scheme was not a success. Conditions in the mines were very severe, and the DPs were given the worst jobs. At the same time, many unsuitable men had applied—and the medical vetting had been cursory, whereas that of the British had been thorough—and many recruits quickly proved unequal to the physical demands of the work. Soon a chorus of complaints and demands to return to Germany could be heard, posing for the IRO the difficult question of whether to abandon those who had rejected the Belgian scheme or resettle them for a second time. Ultimately, some 15,000 displaced persons did stay in Belgium and in 1956 were well on the way to the eight or ten years' residence in the country that would qualify them for naturalization. The Belgians had evidently raised the time required to qualify.[21]

By 1947, there were signs of increasing impatience with the DP problem. Displaced persons were "a dead weight on the ailing economy of Europe," a committee of American experts reported. "They are a drag on European recovery." An essential step to economic revival must be the relocation and rehabilitation of the uprooted millions so that they would at least produce as much as they consumed. The report recommended that DPs be sent to the labor bottlenecks in the European economy, with due care being taken to look after their "human needs." The remaining "hard core" should then be redistributed around the world. This committee was clear that the real problem—that of feeding the German expellees and integrating them into German society—could be addressed only when the DPs had left Germany.[22]

This new sense of urgency infused the agency now responsible for the DPs. UNRRA's successor, the International Refugee Organization, conceived in prolonged discussion throughout 1946, was functioning in the DP camps by mid-1947. The decision of the Soviet Union and its allies not to join the IRO meant, according to the French diplomat René Ristelhueber, that the organization was "crippled at birth." "A humanitarian organization," Ristelhueber wrote in 1951, "the very purpose of which should have been enough to gain unanimity, took on a political character which was to become even more marked as a stream of refugees continued to arrive from eastern Europe." Certainly, with only eighteen out of the fifty-four members of the United Nations belonging to it, the IRO became in practice the instrument of the Western powers, especially the United States, which contributed more than half of its operating funds; and that, according to its official historian, the American academic Louise Holborn, was the secret of its success. "The IRO's amazing achievement," Holborn wrote in 1957, was "chiefly due to the extraordinary unity of purpose prevailing in its policy and administrative organs, partly because of the absence of the Soviet Union and its satellites and partly because of the objectivity of the IRO's General Council, whose policies were dictated by the needs of the refugees."[23]

The IRO was, then, an American show, a partial return to the Herbert Hoover model. The three successive executive secretaries who ran it were American, and so was the culture of the organization: at its headquarters in Geneva, one observer found "offices and corridors in democratic uniformity, simple wooden furniture, banks of telephones, cleanliness and austere comfort, along with an atmosphere of good humour and cordiality." Learning from UNRRA's mistakes, the IRO made a point of being independent of the military, in terms of both transport and resources, and negotiated directly with the zonal authorities in Germany and governments around the world. It even leased its own shipping fleet. Overall, it was a triumph of good management. "Working closely with sixty volunteer relief agencies from various countries," the historian Michael Marrus has written, "IRO spent $450 million, an enormous sum for the time, and did so while maintaining a high reputation for efficiency and integrity."[24]

For the staff on the ground in Germany this meant continual

economies. "Every mail," Kay Hulme wrote, "brought orders from the struggling new IRO as it endeavored to condense within its narrower financial frame the vast sprawling empire which UNRRA had created for the needs of the early days." Particularly irksome for Kay was the constant process of "closing out" camps: by bringing the DPs together in larger, more efficiently run camps, the bureaucrats could not only hand housing stock back to the Germans but also save money that could be channeled into the resettlement centers now being created. Although the IRO continued the repatriation program (and did manage to send 54,687 people back to Eastern Europe during its four years of life), its primary focus was now on the resettlement of displaced persons.[25]

Learning from the Belgian experience, the IRO persuaded the French to take DP workers with their families, and ultimately 30,000 refugees found a home in France itself, while a further 5,000 were taken by Morocco, Tunisia, and French Guiana. By that time, however, the DPs were reluctant to go into mining and agriculture, the two sectors in which the French needed labor. Equally, the Swedish offer to accept 10,000 single Baltic refugees was not attractive and was taken up by only 4,330 DPs. By far the most generous offer came from Turkey, which agreed to take all the 3,000-odd Muslim DPs (Albanians and Yugoslavs), regardless of their fitness for work, and offered them immediate Turkish citizenship.[26]

Among them the nations of Western Europe would eventually take some 170,000 refugees, a fifth of the whole. But by 1947, it was becoming clear that a permanent solution to the refugee problem would be found only "overseas"—in North and South America and the British Commonwealth.[27]

Canada would probably not have taken any refugees at all had public opinion had its way. An opinion poll in 1946 revealed widespread hostility to immigration, with only 37 percent of Canadians willing to consider northern European displaced persons and an overwhelming majority opposed to Eastern and southern European immigrants. "This vast country with a population of only twelve million was terrified of swamping the employment market," the historian Modris Eksteins has written. Memories of the Depression combined with hostility to foreigners. On the other hand, Canadian politicians knew that there was a price to pay for their prominence in international organizations such as the United Nations: if Canada wanted to command the world stage, it would have to take its share of the refugees. Added to that, the wartime economic boom had left real shortages of labor in the fields of domestic service, mining, forestry, and construction. As the IRO began pressuring Ottawa to play its part, the deputy minister of labour argued that, as Canada was duty bound to take some DPs, she might as well cream off the best of the "useful" ones before other nations took them. "We might get some good people from this refugee list, particularly those from the Baltic States," he wrote.[28]

In November 1946, Canada launched a scheme whereby displaced persons who already had relatives in Canada could join them—which was expected to bring some 30,000 people to the country. A year later, a "labor selection scheme" followed, under which the IRO was to provide Canada with DPs capable of working as miners, loggers, farmworkers, general laborers, and domestics. DPs going to Canada would have to sign a two-year contract for a specific occupation.

The Canadians wanted young, strong, willing workers who would be content to stay in the jobs they were sent to yet were also "of a type likely to make good citizens," as Prime Minister Mackenzie King told Parliament. From the start, Canadian officials had clear preferences. Vincent Massey, the high commissioner in London, reported from Germany in 1945 that if Canada had to take new settlers, the Balts—and especially the Latvians—might be the best of the lot. In one camp he had visited, "there were about 1,500 Balts of all ages and of both sexes, most of them from Latvia. I am deeply impressed by the quality of these people who appeared to be industrious, clean, resourceful and well-mannered. The camp itself was a model of self-help, and I could not help feeling that of all the Europeans I have seen these Balts would make the most admirable settlers." Another official called them "excellent citizen material." But Massey was unimpressed by the Poles: "one did not want too many of them about." A major in the Canadian Eighth Army Corps in Germany pointed out that if Canada let Poles in, "they will be unemployed or in jail, and in either case quite happy." He had little time for Lithuanians either—"as bad as the Poles"—but the Latvians and Estonians he appreciated. They were "honest, ingenious and good workers. They would make good immigrants."[29]

The other great British dominion also needed labor but had her own geopolitical agenda as well. Australia, like Canada, had enjoyed a wartime boom which continued into the peace and left holes in the labor market, even after its armed forces had been demobilized. By 1947, Australia's need for workers was becoming critical. But the country also wanted to boost its population for strategic reasons. The Second World War had dramatized its global isolation and left its politicians fearful of Japanese aggression and invasion from Asia at a time of waning British power in the Far East. "We must populate or we will perish," declared Arthur Calwell, Australia's first minister for immigration and architect of its mass migration scheme. "We must fill this country or we will lose it. We need to protect ourselves against the yellow peril from the north." Feeling that the current population of 7,391,000 (about one person per square mile) left a land as vast as Australia "underprotected," Calwell aimed to increase the population to 20 million by the end of the twentieth century, at an average rate of 2 percent per year.[30]

He expected the bulk of these new migrants to come from Australia's traditional source—in 1945, 90 percent of its population was of British origin. There was certainly no shortage of people wishing to flee postwar "austerity Britain" for sunnier climes: in late 1945, the announcement of an assisted passage scheme produced queues from Australia House right down Fleet Street past the Law Courts. But it took time to organize assisted passages, and there was, furthermore, a shortage of shipping. When Calwell came to London to sort out the problems in early 1947, he met officials from the IRO who pointed out that they had their own fleet of ships and could therefore send potential laborers to Australia within a matter of months. Calwell was interested at once but realized that, with other nations already competing for the best "immigrant types," he needed to act fast.

A deal was quickly struck. In return for a £10 contribution for each individual refugee's fare, the IRO agreed to provide the desperately needed shipping. Australia was able to insist that migrants be of a particular race and of a certain standard of health and physical development and be prepared to be placed in specified jobs for two years. However, the Australian (and later New Zealand) policy demanded that as a precondition of their resettlement DPs enter into an open-ended indenture without having any knowledge of the type of work they would be assigned. Other countries had selected DPs for specific companies to work on contract and could tell immigrants not only the type of work they were to undertake but the name of the company, its location, and the wage they would be paid. In contrast, the Australian scheme entailed no such contract.[31]

On July 21, 1947, Calwell signed an agreement for the dispatch of 12,000 DPs per year and immediately sent selection officers to Germany. One of them later recalled that Calwell told them to take "lots of warm clothes" and find "good, healthy young persons of the type from which we are sprung," suitable for farm labor, mining, domestic work in hospitals, and labor in the construction industry. They had to work fast. "We had six weeks from scratch to fill the first ship which involved getting cars, getting accommodation, setting up procedures and writing leaflets." The IRO insisted on a leaflet in German, the lingua franca of DPs, setting out the conditions under which they would be accepted for migration to Australia, what their obligations would be, and, in turn, what entitlements they would have when they arrived.

Selection was therefore a pretty rough-and-ready business. Working in teams of two or four, selection officers conducted approximately twenty interviews per day.

> You were given a card and an interpreter was provided by the agency. You went through the card and questioned the person on their age, their background, what they had done during the war years, why they were a displaced person and then, if it was a family group, you asked them questions about the family. Then you made up your mind and later you made a brief notation on the card as to your opinion of the family and marked it "accept" or "not accept." If the person said he was a doctor, pianist or a painter, I always warned him, "Look, you may not be able to be employed as a painter or a doctor or an artist in Australia. You've got to accept whatever the Australian government is prepared to offer you and you are under a two year contract. You've got to do what the Australian government tells you for the first two years."[32]

In the spring of 1948, immigration fever swept over the DP camps. At the peak of recruitment there were some fifty national missions seeking immigrants. Kay Hulme described a recruitment center with a central hall that "appeared at first sight as provocative as a corridor through Cook's, with neat signs angling out from the repainted doors, naming the mission within—CANADA, BELGIUM, UNITED KINGDOM, FRANCE, AUSTRALIA, SOUTH AMERICA."[33]

Suddenly everyone was writing to relatives around the world, discussing the merits of one country over another and different types of employment. Nobody wanted to be left behind to face the new war between the Soviet Union and the United States that they all anticipated. Everyone longed for a chance to settle down somewhere and find peace in their lives and some security for their families. It might mean sacrifices, humiliating work, and hard economic times, but anything would be preferable to staying where they were in the camps of occupied Germany. DPs anxiously scanned the camp notice boards listing all the options for escape.

The United States was many DPs' first choice, but the Americans took their time to agree and implement their policy on DP settlements. England was already taking DPs, but word was filtering back that it was not a good place to go: unfriendly, overcrowded, shabby, and rationed. South America and Australia were thought to be too far away and too exotic in climate and culture. Canada, on the other hand, was huge, empty, and safe.

Kostas Dubauskas, a seventeen-year-old Lithuanian in 1949, later recalled how his family had held a council of war to decide to where they should emigrate. "My father said, 'America is today, Canada is tomorrow, Australia is the day after, New Zealand—God knows when!'" All but one sister voted for Canada, the land of tomorrow. Their contract was for sugar-beet work, two spring-to-autumn seasons in Alberta. Another Latvian family chose Canada for want of an alternative. "America was the dream. But America dallied. Sweden or Britain would have been fine, but they didn't want us. And so it was Canada, *faute de mieux*. For the year ending March 31, 1949, Canada admitted 3,331 Latvians. We were four of those." "Our country was divided, and we thought it had no future," one German emigrant recalled. "We were afraid the Russians would move in. Canada seemed so big, so safe, so far away from our troubles."[34]

Each country had slightly different criteria for selection: Brazil wanted agricultural workers, without young children, of all nationalities and religious groups except Jews and people of Asiatic origin; Luxembourg asked for single workers with no dependents, Balts preferred; Holland had jobs for tailors, weavers, and spinning mill hands, again without dependents; Sweden wanted graduate nurses; and so on. But as we have seen, most countries were looking for young, sturdy people without dependents, and, after all their efforts to reunite their families after the war, very few DPs were single. Families were now being split up by demands for single emigrants. There were other difficulties: according to Kay Hulme, 10 percent of the women who applied to work as domestics in Canada under one scheme were "thrown out for illiteracy or tangled marital relations—such as having once been married and having lost track of the man."[35]

A system quickly evolved. IRO resettlement officers would make a preliminary selection of the displaced persons whom they thought fitted a particular country's needs and a "labor selector" would then visit the camps interviewing the candidates before further filleting out the numbers. If the selector and the candidate were satisfied, he and his family were sent to a "resettlement processing center" for final screening and selection. Medical tests were the next hurdle. Chest X-rays and blood and urine tests were no problem for a healthy person, but many of the DPs now applying for sturdy physical work had been weakened by the years in the camps. TB was rife, and so was venereal disease. If one of its members had TB, a whole family's chances of a future life would be spoiled. Not surprisingly, the process of medical testing soon became enveloped in corruption and pathos. "Bribery of officials and kind-hearted oversights of negative results were far too common," Kay noted, "this process involving all-powerful officials and woefully weak supplicants." It quickly became apparent that medical tests carried out by UNRRA and IRO doctors, often of the applicants' own nationality, were worthless. For that reason the British insisted, from the start, in doing their own testing. The immigrants were selected, said one critic, "like good beef cattle."[36]

Tests constituted another hurdle. Most countries demanded literacy but were suspicious of intellectuals—anyone with education or professional aspirations, men who would try to reestablish themselves in professions in a country that had no need for such skills. The DPs soon learned how to pitch themselves. Intellectuals with doctorates hastily reinvented themselves as sturdy proletarians. "If they wanted to go to Canada they had to say that they had already worked in the woods," Kostas Toliusis remembered, ". . . they shook hands with you. If you don't squeeze his hand, you weren't strong. We caught on to that trick fast. If a Canadian shakes your hand, then squeeze it so hard you crush it!"[37]

· · ·

The screening process lacked two significant elements. There was no psychological testing, and, more important, there was no meaningful investigation of the DPs' wartime records. Given the sheer numbers involved, the complexity of Eastern European wartime politics, the staff available, and the state of the records, that was probably inevitable. But in addition, the Cold War was beginning to upset old certainties; the British had declared that the time for prosecuting minor war criminals was over. Above all, the mood of the times was forward-, not backward-looking: everyone wanted to get the displaced persons out of Europe, get the postwar economy moving— and get on with life.[38]

The political issues which arose did not address today's sensitivities. The question of "national quotas" provides a good example. The Canadian team in Germany was instructed that great care should be taken "to ensure a reasonable division of nationalities"—that is, mostly Latvians, Lithuanians, and Estonians—but that it was also "advisable to include a number of Ukrainians as such action will be favourably received in some quarters here." (Prime Minister Mackenzie King had Ukrainians in his constituency.) According to the historian Milda Danys, Canadian officials sent to Germany were unaware that Baltic DPs had more education and were therefore far more likely to be professionals or clerical workers unsuited to work in mines, forests, and factories; it was more a question of what they did *not* want: Poles, Ukrainians, and Jews, with whom they were more familiar and whom they disliked.[39]

The Canadians began cautiously but soon became enthusiastic about the potential for displaced persons. Industries rushed to contract new labor. "Like a shopper at a Boxing Day sale," wrote Danys, Canada's "initial wariness had disappeared under the shock of finding so many bargains: now it was scrambling to buy, determined to carry off the prize items at rock-bottom prices."

In the process, there were disappointments on both sides. Mining work held few attractions, being regarded as dirty and dangerous, but hundreds who had applied for forestry work in Canada had to make do with a contract in the gold mines instead. Juozas Krucas recalled that, with a wife and child, he had no option but to take a mining contract, which did at least offer to bring over his family as soon as he had secured housing for them in Canada. "On the way, I thought, I'm going to Dante's Hell." For their part, Canadian employers' efforts to

find skilled craftsmen among the immigrants were not always successful: ornamental ironworkers, plasterers, and brickmakers brought
to Canada at some expense often turned out to be schoolteachers or
unskilled laborers. The Southern Saskatchewan Wool Growers Association's request for twenty-five experienced shepherds eventually
produced a single candidate who, within a few months, broke his
contract and fled to Toronto. No further shepherds were called for.[40]

The countries of Central and South America were seldom the first
choice of a displaced person. Few of those states were particularly
affluent or had any proper mechanisms for receiving new immigrants.
The new arrivals would be joining a complex ethnic mosaic, primarily Latin and South American Indian, in which people of Slavic, Baltic, and Jewish origin did not really belong and would be confronted
with "hard work in a tropical or semi-tropical climate, a low standard
of living, a patriarchal agrarian system which made it difficult to get
permanent titles to land, and an uncertain political future." It says
something for the desperation of the DPs that nearly 100,000 of them
ended up in the seventeen countries of this region, nearly 80,000 in
Venezuela, Brazil, and Argentina. On the other hand, because the
Latin American countries did not carry out preliminary selection in
Europe, many old and infirm people went to countries where they
had few contacts or prospects. Many of the DPs found a new home in
Argentina, where the Juan Perón government encouraged immigration. Argentina took about 33,000 IRO-sponsored immigrants, plus a
further 17,500 Poles who chose not to stay in Britain.

Brazil admitted about 29,000 DPs and encouraged them to live in
the countryside. That policy was largely unsuccessful, but several DPs
quickly established themselves in local industries, such as hatmaking
or metallurgy. A further 17,000 DPs, including some 6,000 Spanish
Republican refugees, went to Venezuela.[41]

Arthur Calwell himself masterminded the first boatload of DPs to
arrive in Australia. The handpicked group of 843 young male and
female DPs had to be between fifteen and thirty-five years old, have
successfully passed police, political, and health checks, preferably
speak English, and, according to a Latvian who was one of them,
only DPs without any scars on their bodies could be selected. The
immigrants on this inaugural voyage to Australia were known as the

"Beautiful Balts," not just because they were handsome and beautiful but because many had the same blue eyes and red or blond hair as the Australians. When the half-empty *General Stuart Heintzelman* berthed at Fremantle, Calwell was able to say, "It was not hard to sell immigration to the Australian people once the press had published their photographs." In a radio speech welcoming the first DPs he said, "If shipping can be provided we will bring 20,000 people to Australia of your type next year."

The first group of refugees made an excellent impression on everyone. The warm reception given to the shipment in Australia convinced Calwell that the Baltic image of the DPs should be preserved. From then on, he often referred to the displaced as "Balts" or "Baltic people" long after approval had been given for the inclusion of other nationalities. In fact, to maintain the high standards of selection and the narrow age criterion, it soon became necessary to include other groups—Slovenes and Ukrainians from September 1947, Yugoslavs and Czechs from January 1948, Poles (without children) from May 1948, followed in the same year by Hungarians and Belorussians, and even, eventually, by some *Volksdeutsche*. Nonetheless, for years most Australians referred to non-British, non-Mediterranean immigrants as "Balts"—a misuse of the term to which many of the immigrants, including some from the Baltic area, vehemently objected. Australians were assured not only that the newcomers would look like them but that they would soon renounce their culture and languages and become indistinguishable from them and perform the jobs Australians had rejected. Similarly, Australians were encouraged to think that the employment found for the displaced persons would help create a better standard of living in housing, public works, and consumer goods, which could only improve the lifestyle of the average Australian.

After the improvised beginning, Australia adopted a far more aggressive and successful strategy for luring DPs (the right kind, of course) to immigrate. Books, pamphlets, films, and posters were distributed around the camps extolling the wonders of Australia as a land of good wages, housing, food, fine weather, and so on. All that was required was that prospective immigrants meet age and health criteria and remain for two years in the type of employment selected for them. From 1949 to 1954, DP immigrants made up nearly 50 percent of the new arrivals to Western Australia.

SEVENTEEN

"We Lived to See It"

JEWISH DPs AND THE CREATION OF ISRAEL, 1947–1949

The Zirkus Krone was one of the shrines of National Socialism. As Munich's largest indoor arena, it provided the setting for many of Hitler's earliest rallies in the 1920s; it was there that he found his powers as a mass orator and made the transition from beer-hall ranter to full-blown demagogue.

Many of the 2,000 people who packed into the Zirkus Krone on the evening of January 29, 1947, to watch a boxing match were aware of the venue's past history. The audience—nearly all men, well wrapped up against the winter cold, screaming their fighters on, jumping with excitement—were Jewish displaced persons. So, too, were the fighters themselves: circling the ring warily, gloves flailing, pummeling against the ropes, hanging in a clinch. Some fighters wore the Star of David on their chests, and the event had begun with the singing of a Zionist anthem. This was the finals of the boxing championship of the *She'erith Hapletah,* the "Surviving Remnant," the Jewish DPs living in the American Zone of Germany.

Sport had become increasingly popular among the DPs over the last couple of years—by this time some 16,000 of them belonged to more than a hundred clubs. The tradition of Jewish sporting clubs went back to the early years of the century, when they had provided a means of self-protection, but in the DP camps sport kept young men occupied, gave them a sense of brotherhood, and reaffirmed their masculinity. The Zionist organizers saw sport as a way to "raise physical capabilities and, in a comprehensive way, to prepare our youth for the tasks that await them in the near future in the land of Israel." The boxing championship had a particular intensity:

The contenders, fighting superbly and bitterly—three of the seven won by knockouts—demonstrated the superiority of experience over youth. . . . Hirsh Dileski, captain and trainer of the Landsberg team, provided the sensation of the whole event. The solid Landsberg deputation in the stands broke into hysterical applause.

Each of the new champions was awarded a specially designed silver cup, and the runners up carried away beautifully engraved certificates. These were proudly exhibited at the victory banquets which . . . were held in the camps in the following weeks.

The boxing event was particularly enjoyed because it provided a break from the very charged buildup to fresh elections being held by the Jews in the American Zone.[1]

The position of the Jewish displaced persons in early 1947 was, on the face of it, much stronger than a year earlier. The enormous infusion of immigrants from the East, driven by the pogroms in Poland, had completely transformed the size of the community: in the American Zone, where nearly all the new arrivals congregated, the population rose from 60,000 in late 1945 to more than 160,000 a year later, and in April, when the U.S. Army declared that it could take no more refugees into its zone, there were more than sixty-one camps housing Jews.[2]

Because the Americans recognized Jewish "infiltrees" as displaced persons and the British did not, most of the Jews fleeing to Germany from Poland made their way to the American, not the British, Zone. Consequently, from the middle of 1946 the political center of gravity among Jewish DPs was to be found in southern Germany. In addition, in March 1947, the British attempted to reduce the Jewish population in their zone by allowing DPs from Belsen to immigrate legally to Palestine under the annual quota. The four hundred *aliyah* certificates a month were allocated solely to Belsen, but the Jewish leadership believed it was their duty to share them with other Jews in Germany and did.

The new influx had also changed the complexion of the Jewish population. Many of the newcomers had children, for example, or came from groups which had not survived in the concentration camps, such as intellectuals and old people. Some aid workers saw these changes in a positive light and were hopeful that a new dynamism might be given to the Jewish community in Germany. On the surface all seemed well. A description of Landsberg DP camp published in the United States at this time struck an almost idyllic note:

> The visitor enters the camp and walks through the cleanly swept streets. Men are moving about—many with a look of purpose, obviously about work. On a huge sports field set with goal posts, a group of boys is noisily playing soccer. In a little tree-shaded park, young women sit with infants in their arms.

The American sociologist Leo Srole then explained that "into this fabric of communal life" in the Jewish camps had been "woven variegated and vigorous motifs of cultural activity": kindergartens, a compulsory elementary school for children between six and sixteen, a technical high school, a university, library, camp newspapers (both printed and on walls), a radio station, three cafés, a cinema, a theater created in the old Wehrmacht parade hall, and a gymnasium. There were political parties and, most important of all, kibbutzim, "pioneer youth organizations composed largely of orphans and patterned after the agricultural settlements in Palestine."

> To facilitate the processes of re-education, the *kibbutzim* have adopted boy-scout methods. Marching, with their distinctive khaki shorts and white shirts, their Jewish and *kibbutz* flags, and their spirited singing, they are one of the most colorful of camp sights. And by their discipline, high morality, and morale, they act as a steadying influence on the adults.

Yet after this long catalogue of social enterprise and self-help, the article concluded that to "allow the present slow rot of the DP camps—against which their inmates are increasingly defenseless—to continue its course" would be "an accessory to a form of genocide."[3]

Srole was not alone. Every outside observer agreed that unless something was done soon the Jewish DPs would be lost souls. Abraham Klausner, the young American rabbi who had helped the survivors organize after liberation, found a "radical change" in the spirit of the people when he returned to Germany in early 1947. "There is no longer an air of excitement, a darting of the eyes, a flood of questions—there is a feeling of resignation," he wrote. Many of the leaders spoke to him of the demoralization of the people. The Palestinian kibbutz leader and politician Yitzhak Tabenkin found that "despair was rampant in the camps and many of the inmates had begun seeking out relatives in America, who would help them financially, and especially send them the permits necessary for entry into the United States." An American journalist, David Bernstein, noticed "a new and absolute dependence on charity." The Jewish communal organizations, "which were once so self-reliant and ruggedly independent," Bernstein wrote, "now quiver in fear of antagonizing the all-powerful functionaries of JDC [the Joint] and other relief agencies."[4]

The time between the autumn of 1945 and the summer of 1947 came to be seen by Samuel Gringauz as "the humanitarian period . . . marked by an enormous growth of self-help organizations and self-administration." "Looking back, it seems a kind of golden age," he wrote in 1948. The precondition of this, Gringauz believed, was the "profound understanding and human sympathy" shown by the U.S. Army toward Jewish DPs. So what had brought the golden age to an end? Gringauz blamed the new international climate. He argued that the speech by Secretary of State James F. Byrnes in Stuttgart in September 1946, calling for a new policy toward Germany, had ushered in a new era in which Germans were allowed to reassert themselves against the displaced persons in their midst. As a result, the U.S. Army became less favorably inclined toward Jewish DPs and there was a revival of anti-Semitism. Newly established Jewish cemeteries were desecrated, and when a newsreel of General Clay visiting a Munich synagogue was shown in cinemas, a line of commentary saying that 6 million Jews had been killed caused many members of the audience to shout, "They didn't kill enough of them," to deafening applause.[5]

But there were other reasons. The new migrants from the East brought with them a new approach to politics. The Zionist "united front," which had hitherto prevailed, was now replaced by a more factious approach, in which the divisions among Jews in Palestine were replicated in the camps in Germany. "Deprived of a productive existence, languishing in overcrowded huts or barracks, with no real prospect of emigrating from an increasingly anti-Semitic German environment, DPs took to abstract politics with gusto," wrote Yehuda Bauer. The second Congress of the Central Committee of Liberated Jews in the American Zone, held at the Bavarian ski resort of Bad Reichenall in February 1947, was a much more subdued affair than the first, at which Grinberg and Ben-Gurion had spoken in front of the world's press. Now, instead of great charismatic speakers, there was an argument between those who wanted to ally the movement in Germany with the Irgun in Palestine and those who wanted to stay loyal to Ben-Gurion. The Orthodox Jews, who now made up 40 percent of the camp population, also demanded more power.[6]

Despite the rise of anti–Semitism, among ordinary Jews there was an increasing tendency to try to join the German community outside or to emigrate. This worried the leadership. There was particular distress when Dr. Samuel Gringauz himself went to the United States in September 1947, having been offered one of the few visas available for Jewish displaced persons. Ever since the liberation, Gringauz had occupied a unique position among the DPs, both as a nonpolitical figurehead, providing guidance and shrewd counsel, and as an intellectual leader, shaping the identity of the Jewish survivors. But he felt increasingly marginalized in the new political climate and had also lost faith in the rehabilitation programs he had been running. Only emigration or the chance to go to Palestine, he now concluded, would allow the Jews really to begin life anew. His decision to leave must have been a difficult one.[7]

The fundamental problem, however, was that the Jewish DPs were now players in a wider drama, and, until that was resolved, they could only look on and wait.

The British refusal to allow the entry of 100,000 Jewish displaced persons into Palestine, as proposed by the Anglo-American Committee of Inquiry in April 1946, brought a swift response from the Jews there. On the night of June 16–17, 1946, ten of the road and rail bridges linking Palestine to neighboring countries were blown up; numerous similar incidents followed. The British countered by arresting most of the Jewish leadership in Operation Agatha at the end of the month. Although this caused the mainstream Zionist leaders to reconsider the use of terror, the Irgun faction, under the leadership of Menachem Begin, went ahead with a plan to attack the King David Hotel in Jerusalem, where the British command had its headquarters. On July 22, seven members of Irgun, dressed as Arabs, planted seven milk churns containing 250 kilos of explosives in the hotel's kitchens. In the blast that followed, ninety-one people died.[8]

For the next year the cycle of tit-for-tat violence continued in Pal-

estine, culminating in the kidnapping and murder of two British ser-
geants by the Irgun, in response to British brutality, and the inevitable
British response. The steady stream of casualties sapped British morale,
gradually posing the question of whether the mandate was worth
hanging on to. It also gave an unreal quality to continuing British
efforts to come up with a proposal that would satisfy the moderate
Zionists such as Weizmann and the Palestinian Arabs. Various schemes
which involved sharing the country between Jews and Arabs were
discussed. The moderate Zionists were prepared to compromise in
order to help the Jews of Europe at once. But it was difficult to get the
Arabs to accept anything.

Whether this process could ever have gone anywhere is debatable.
But it was abruptly torpedoed in October 1946 when President Truman made a statement on Yom Kippur which seemed to give support
to the creation of a viable Jewish state in Palestine controlling its own
immigration and economic policies and a sizable amount of territory.
The president had aligned himself in this way, with some reluctance,
on the insistence of his party officials in order to mobilize the Jewish
vote in the forthcoming congressional elections. His words, though
watered down by the State Department, were widely interpreted to
mean that he was advocating a separate Jewish state and the partition
of Palestine. The British now began to lose patience. If the Zionist
lobby in the United States could so easily put pressure on the president, what hope was there of the British getting the Jews in Palestine
to compromise?[9]

That belief was further strengthened when David Ben-Gurion
decisively defeated Weizmann and the moderates at the Zionist Congress held in Switzerland in December 1946. With his usual tactical
skill, Ben-Gurion steered a course between Weizmann and the increasingly popular terrorist groups in Palestine by forming a short-
term alliance with the American Zionist leader Rabbi Abba Hillel
Silver. Weizmann made a great speech but, amid dramatic and bitter
scenes, was defeated because of his blind trust in Britain. Ernest Bevin's response was to refer the whole Palestine question back to the
United Nations.

British attitudes toward the Palestine Mandate underwent a sea
change in early 1947. Although the military continued to argue that a
presence in Palestine was vital to the maintenance of British strategic

interests in the eastern Mediterranean, the Cabinet slowly came round to the view that a way had to be found to "scuttle"—to get out.[10]

The British expected nothing decisive to happen at the United Nations because concerted action on Palestine required the involvement of both the United States and Russia, and that was thought most unlikely. There was therefore consternation when, on May 14, 1947, the Soviet delegate, Andrei Gromyko, addressed the General Assembly in tones of honeyed friendship toward the Jews, even suggesting that, if necessary, Palestine would have to be partitioned to give them a country of their own. This swing, which came even as Stalin was persecuting and murdering prominent Jews within the Soviet Union, was intended to undermine the British position in the Middle East.[11]

Thanks in part to the new Soviet line, the UN special session on Palestine decided to send yet another committee to consider the options on the ground. The United Nations Special Committee on Palestine (UNSCOP), made up of members from eleven "minor" neutral states, set off for Palestine in June 1947. Quite by chance, its arrival in Palestine coincided with the Zionists' greatest propaganda coup.

Together with terrorism, illegal immigration remained part of the Zionists' strategy for putting pressure on the British. They sent some thirty ships packed with Jews from Europe into Palestinian waters between July 1945 and the end of 1946. Eighteen of them were intercepted by the Royal Navy, and some 18,000 passengers were detained first in Palestine and then in camps which the British opened on the island of Cyprus. Conditions there were reminiscent of the German camps, and doctors found that for many inmates this reopened old wounds. But the ships and Jews continued to come.[12]

The Mossad, the branch of the Jewish Agency responsible for immigration, bought the *President Warfield,* an elderly Baltimore ferry due for the scrapyard, in September 1946, intending to use her to run Jewish refugees to Palestine from camps in Italy. But difficulties in crossing the Atlantic meant that it was not until the following May that she arrived at La Spezia in Italy, by which time British pressure on the Italian government had closed that route to Palestine. Another scheme, to bring displaced persons out through the north German port of Bremen, also had to be abandoned. Instead, it was decided to run the operation through France, where the Mossad had its head-quarters and had spent several years cultivating French politicians. This switch meant, however, that the Mossad had to bring 4,500 people from the American Zone of Germany to France in next to no time. As a result, the passengers were a mixed bag of kibbutz members, children, and ordinary Jews, selected to represent the various political factions in the American Zone. Whereas earlier shipments had consisted almost entirely of pioneers, this time they made up only 60 percent. The passengers represented an accurate cross section of the Jewish DP population in the American Zone of Germany in spring 1947, including, for example, pregnant women. The mass exodus of 4,500 people in less than two weeks did much to improve the general atmosphere in the camps.[13]

Some of the DPs left by trains but most were driven by the Brichah from the American Zone in a convoy of 170 trucks, with the U.S. Army turning a blind eye. In the south of France, the documents necessary for their organized exit from France to Colombia (so it said on the certificates) were prepared during the immigrants' brief stay in the training camps, with street photographers brought in from Marseilles to take passport photographs.[14] Nothing would have been possible without the cooperation of French officials at all levels. In particular, members of the French Socialist Party, the cornerstone of French governments in those days, saw Zionism as a socialist national liberation movement and felt class solidarity with the organizers of illegal immigration. The small port of Sète was chosen as the embarkation point as it was situated in the constituency of Jules Moch, the French transport minister and an old friend of the Mossad. The clerks at the port, the customs, border control, and other authorities were all Socialist Party activists.[15]

This support enabled the *President Warfield*, now renamed *Exodus 1947*, to sail despite heavy British pressure on the French government to have it stopped. Apart from the death of a woman in childbirth, the voyage itself was uneventful. The ship was well supplied with medicine and food and the passengers very well drilled by the organizers. It took only seven days to reach Palestine, arriving off the port of Haifa on July 17, 1947. The atmosphere on board, according to Aviva Halamish, was one of " 'all Jews are comrades,' one for all and all for one, and this went hand in hand with clannish sectarianism, separatism and deep loyalty to the group and the party."[16]

Exodus was carrying far more passengers than any previous illegal immigrant ship. The leadership on board came mostly from the Palmach, the young, elite spearhead of the Haganah, which had long advocated a more aggressive use of the illegal immigration strategy. In line with their belief that "unarmed resistance must be exhibited, as firm and prolonged as possible," their final plan was to break through the British blockade, run the flat-bottomed ship aground on a sandbank near Tel Aviv, and set the passengers ashore with the help of the local population.

However, the British—increasingly infuriated by illegal Jewish immigration—had decided on tougher measures. When *Exodus* was still in territorial waters about seventeen miles off the Palestine coast, she was surrounded and rammed by eight British warships and boarded by a small force of soldiers who seized the wheelhouse. In the ensuing battle, the British used firearms; three members of the crew and two young Zionists were killed. Eventually the ship's commander, who had seen people killed on an earlier illegal immigration ship, overruled the captain, a Palmachite with dreams of glory, and ordered resistance to cease so that the wounded could receive attention. At four in the afternoon of Friday, July 18, 1947, *Exodus* arrived in Haifa, escorted by eight British warships. Her arrival, witnessed by members of the UNSCOP delegation and much of the world's press, provided the Zionists with their greatest propaganda coup. The image of the old ferryboat coming into harbor, one side shattered like matchwood, her decks lined with weary but determined passengers, went immediately round the world. The leadership in Palestine, which had made no effort to recruit the public to help the immigrants on the Tel Aviv beach—as called for in the original plan—now quickly switched to an alternative tactic, designed to get more publicity. The intention had been to use *Exodus*'s passengers as activists, demonstrating Jewish resistance; instead they arrived at Haifa as victims of British brutality. The name *Exodus* spread immediately round the world.[17]

The British did their best to compound their defeat. Determined to punish the Zionists, Bevin ordered that the ship's passengers be returned to their port of origin. Now carried in three British troopships, they were shipped back to France. There they were offered asylum by the French, but, apart from a few of the elderly and sickly, they declined the offer and heroically stayed on the ships for more than a month in sweltering conditions while their future was decided. Bevin finally had them sent back to Germany, where demonstrators from Bergen-Belsen, organized by Josef Rosensaft, greeted them on the gangplank at Hamburg. They were then shipped by train to two camps near Lübeck, where the British surrounded them with barbed wire, searchlights, and watchtowers.[18]

David Ben-Gurion had not initiated the voyage of the *Exodus*. Feeling that the strategy of illegal immigration had already served its purpose, he was preoccupied by the next phase in the struggle and was preparing for war with the Arabs. But when presented with a golden propaganda opportunity, he took advantage of it with his usual mix of deft manipulation, assertion of his own authority, overblown rhetoric, and shrewd tactical sense. Rhetorically he saluted the *Exodus* passengers: "in our generation, there has never been an epic of the Jewish war like this one." But when Weizmann tried to intervene to prevent their being sent back to Germany (or possibly to Denmark), he rebuffed him vehemently while at the same time making sure that the demonstrations in Hamburg were restrained and did not result in bloodshed.[19]

The scenes in Tel Aviv had a powerful effect on the UNSCOP commissioners—but so too did skillful Zionist lobbying (with Weizmann's eloquence prevailing yet again) and the refusal of the Arabs to engage seriously with this latest group of inspecting foreigners. After some debate, the UNSCOP commissioners also visited the DP camps in Europe and were duly much moved. "That night I was in hell," the Uruguayan Enrique Fabregat wrote after visiting a TB hospital for displaced persons in Vienna. The commissioners learned that "one hundred per cent" of the DPs at Belsen wanted to immigrate to Israel.[20]

Following in the footsteps of the Anglo-American Committee of Inquiry a year earlier, the UNSCOP group adjourned to Geneva to discuss its report. Eventually, the representatives of Sweden, Holland, Canada, Uruguay, Guatemala, Peru, and Czechoslovakia produced the majority report, which recommended the partition of Palestine between Jews and Arabs, with the Jews getting 62 percent of the country and Jerusalem and Bethlehem being divided. The British mandate would continue for another two years, during which 150,000 Jews would be allowed into the Jewish-designated areas. By contrast, the minority report, written by the Yugoslav, Iranian, and Indian representatives, proposed the establishment of a unitary state under Arab domination, with limited Jewish immigration.

The focus now switched to the United Nations itself. After weeks of lobbying and arm-twisting, the crucial vote on the resolution embodying the UNSCOP report took place on November 29, 1947. At first, to the Zionists' horror, the United States did not seem to be supporting their cause, as anti-Zionist State Department officials mounted a last-ditch resistance; but after yet another visit by Weizmann to the White House, the might of U.S. diplomacy was duly mobilized. The Zionists had mounted a brilliant lobbying operation. In the words of the Israeli historian Benny Morris, "the underlying argument was the two-thousand-year history of Jewish suffering and statelessness, culminating in the Holocaust, and the international community's responsibility to make amends."[21]

Yet there was concern about the twenty-member Latin American bloc, the largest in the United Nations. Although officially aligned with Washington, many of those countries reflected the anti-Jewish feelings of the Vatican and their local German and Arab populations. The votes of at least two Latin American ambassadors had to be bought, and the influence of the United Fruit Company in Central America also proved vital. The Zionists wheeled in the widow of the British pro-Zionist and military adventurer Orde Wingate to influence Emperor Haile Selassie of Ethiopia, while the Firestone Tire Company threatened to boycott Liberia if it abstained. But not even Albert Einstein could persuade India, with its large Muslim population, to change its mind. Surprisingly, in view of the support given to the *Exodus* passengers, France initially proved reluctant to commit itself publicly to the Zionist cause—the drama being heightened by the fall of the French government ten days before the final vote. But the threat of resignation of three members of the Cabinet—and hints that the American Marshall aid program might have to be revised—eventually brought France, as well as Belgium, Holland, and Luxembourg, into line. The British intended to abstain, but the dominions—Australia, New Zealand, Canada, and South Africa—all favored the resolution.[22]

The tactics of the Arabs have not been studied in the same detail. They seem not to have appreciated the tremendous impact of the Holocaust on the international community while also doing their share of diplomatic arm-twisting behind the scenes, but with less success. Publicly, the Arabs' main tactic was to blackmail—to threaten that any vote for partition would immediately be followed by war. "We will have to initiate total war. We will murder, wreck and ruin everything standing in our way, be it English, American or Jewish," one Arab commander declared. Not until the vote itself did the Arabs realize that the resolution would be carried by a two-thirds majority.[23]

Some delegates may also have been influenced by the atmosphere in New York at the time. According to the strongly pro-Arab British diplomat Harold Beeley, the "cumulative effect of [press coverage] on many Delegates must have been to convey the impression that an opponent of partition was an enemy of the American people. Final Meetings . . . in the Assembly Hall at Flushing . . . were packed with an almost exclusively Zionist audience. They applauded declarations of support for Zionism. They hissed Arab speakers. They created the atmosphere of a football match, with the Arabs as the away team."[24]

When the vote was finally taken, Resolution 181 [II] was passed with the necessary two-thirds majority—with 33 states voting yes, 13 no, and 10 abstaining. The Arabs were mystified. What right did the international community have to award their country to the Jews? As a Palestinian historian later put it, "they failed to see why they should be made to pay for the Holocaust."[25]

News of the vote in New York reached the DPs the following day. Leo Schwarz, who worked for the Joint in Germany, later described the reaction.

> Sunday [November 30, 1947] was a radiant day. The German radio had been silent, but in the early hours of the morning [the] BBC broadcast the first announcement of the news. From all sides the people streamed to Siebertstrasse and Moehlstrasse [in Munich]. The blue-and-white Zionist banner and the stars and stripes waved from flagpoles at the headquarters of the Central Committee. The streets resounded with congratulations. An ethereal joy imbued the very air. Happy faces were everywhere; people kissed and embraced. *Mazel tov.* On the corners where the people usually hunted for a pat of butter, an egg, an apple, there was a festive spirit.
>
> "Well, we lived to see it! This calls for a drink!"[26]

In fact, it took six months of fighting and diplomatic drama for the resolution to be realized. The British announced that they would be pulling out on May 15 and began to scale down their occupying force, while a civil war between Jews and Arabs began to smolder in Palestine. At 8 A.M. on May 14, 1947, the British lowered the Union Jack in Jerusalem. Eight hours later, in a ceremony held in the museum in Tel Aviv and broadcast across the country, David Ben-Gurion read the declaration of independence of the new state of Israel. At once fighting began to intensify.

Two days later the Americans recognized the new state. President Truman listened to the advice of his legal counsel, Clark Clifford, and ignored the warning of General Marshall that "if the President were to follow Mr Clifford's advice and if in the elections I were to vote, I would vote against the President." A State Department official later complained that "the President's political advisers, having failed to make the President the father of the new state, have determined at least to make him the midwife." That was unfair. In truth Truman *was* one of the fathers of Israel. He had consistently championed the cause of the Jewish DPs, from a mixture of human sympathy and political calculation, and had repeatedly shown himself willing to intervene on their behalf when prompted by his advisers or even by Chaim Weizmann. But occasionally, like all fathers, Truman complained privately. On July 21, 1947, for example, a phone call from Henry Morgenthau (whom he had never liked and had dismissed as Treasury secretary) prompted an angry entry in his diary:

> He'd no business whatever to call me. The Jews have no sense of proportion nor do they have any judgment on world affairs. . . . The Jews I find are very, very selfish. They care not how many Estonians, Latvians, Poles, Yugoslavs or Greeks get murdered or mistreated as long as the Jews get special treatment. Yet when they have power, physical, financial or political neither Hitler nor Stalin has anything on them for cruelty or mistreatment of the under dog.[27]

There was some tut-tutting about "country club anti-Semitism" when these comments were made public in 2003.

· · ·

As they looked forward to long-awaited independence, the Zionist leadership prepared for the war against the Arab states which it knew was inevitable. They recognized that there was no prospect of the new Israeli state matching the military manpower of its adversaries; at the end of 1947, the size of its regular armed forces was very small—a mere 4,500 men and women, with an additional 40,000 poorly trained reservists. Therefore, to stand any chance at all, the Jews would need to mobilize all the manpower available to them. What about the young men in the DP camps?

A secret Haganah delegation had been sent to Europe in early 1946, when its commander, Nahum Shadmi, had begun to sign up young men among the DPs for military training, initially as a way of giving them back dignity and respect. "Each of them," he said, "still has his private burden to bear . . . and no faith in anyone," so that "great patience is needed in order to turn this human dust into people of stature." In Italy the Haganah did in fact create a force of three battalions, 600 fighting men. Now, with war in Palestine in the offing, Shadmi submitted to the Jewish Agency leadership a more ambitious proposal to recruit an army of 20,000 men. Initially there was strong opposition from Zionist aid workers, who doubted whether it would be fair, in the darkening climate in Germany, to skim off the remaining young and fit people and leave a depleted DP population to fend for itself. But David Ben-Gurion, with his usual clearheadedness, saw the overwhelming logic behind this argument and supported the proposal: desperate times called for desperate measures.[28]

In March 1948, Shadmi told the Jewish DP leaders in Germany that it was their duty to comply. "Every young man and woman, aged 18–35, must join the Haganah whose role is to protect us from the Arabs, perhaps even from the British Army," he told them. "Everyone must be in the Haganah—there are no excuses. All those capable must mobilize and come to Eretz Yisrael and join the army." The Central Committee of Liberated Jews in the American Zone was enthusiastic, and the mobilization of DPs for Haganah was formally underwritten at its third Congress in late March 1948. At the same time, a War Fund for the purchase of weapons for the Haganah (to which everyone was expected to contribute) was created, and speakers warned that Jews who did not fulfill their duty and register would be declared deserters, "removed from the social and political life," and denied entry to all offices. "In the months that followed," an American Jewish chaplain later wrote, "the word 'Giyus' (Mobilization) dominated the air in all the DP camps in Germany, Austria and Italy." *Giyus* stations were set up in all the DP camps. "The social pressure to volunteer was so strong that men of military age were embarrassed to appear in the streets of the DP camps."[29]

In fact, voluntary enlistment proved a failure. It became clear that the DPs themselves were not keen to engage in further struggle; even members of Jewish sports clubs showed reluctance to play the role for which their training had supposedly prepared them. "Most Jewish refugees who had been through the hell of the ghetto, slavery and death camps under the Nazis, Soviet forced-labor camps, and other disasters, yearn for some quiet place," an anti-Zionist DP wrote. "Regardless of their views on current events in Palestine they feel physically drained and have no desire to go into the fire again. They rightfully ask—even the Zionists among them—why do we, having been so pained and tortured, need to go back into the fire?" The first mobilization operation failed. "The recruitment of the first thousand was not easy," Haganah's deputy commander in Germany admitted. "In fact the organization succeeded to draft only 700 persons."[30]

The failure of the DPs to rise to their "historic role" produced a strong reaction among the Jewish leaders. Some advocated force. At a meeting of American Jewish advisers in Germany, Abraham Klausner argued that the DPs "should be forced to go to Palestine . . . we are dealing with a sick people. They are not to be asked but told what to do." Klausner reported that "most of the people were idle; had lost their moral standards. Most of them were not concentration camp victims. Only 30 percent wanted to go to Palestine." There was no support for Klausner's advocacy of force but widespread agreement that demoralization and black-market activity were rampant. The Zionist leader Nahum Goldmann and the advisers to the U.S. Army William Haber and Abraham S. Hyman all agreed that the Jewish DPs had "served their historical purpose"—contributed decisively to the creation of the state of Israel—and need no longer necessarily go to Palestine.[31]

The Central Committee introduced compulsory enlistment backed up by strong sanctions, such as denial of Joint supplementary rations, dismissal from public posts, and ineligibility for immigration to Palestine. The last sanction was never put into effect. According to William Haber, the pressure was "crude, often reflecting techniques which the people had learned from their own oppressors"; but when an American general protested to Haber about heavy-handed recruitment methods, the latter assured him that the reports were "probably exaggerated." "Fortunately," he added, "General Harrold was not aware of all the methods being employed." In fact, it seems that the U.S. Army knew what was going on and unofficially approved because it would ultimately remove from Germany the families to whom the recruits belonged.[32]

By those means the numbers of DP "volunteers" rose dramatically, from 700 to 7,800. The camps gave stirring farewells to the volunteers when they left for Palestine.

How, then, did the reluctant soldiers fare? How important was their contribution to the Israeli victory in 1948? And how were they treated by their fellow Jews?

Israeli historians have picked over the evidence and come to contradictory conclusions. The DP soldiers, together with other (more willing) fighters recruited from the camps on Cyprus, made up about 22,000 "Holocaust survivors" who took part in the war—making up one-third of the Israeli army. They had a reputation among other members of the Israel Defense Forces (as the Haganah was now known) as "melancholy, cowardly soldiers, prisoners of their past . . . difficult, stubborn and cowardly men." According to the Israeli historian Tom Segev, they were generally excluded "from the legendary brotherhood of arms." They did not speak Hebrew and hardly knew the customs of the country they were now defending; it was therefore impossible to use them at staff level. Despite their inexperience and poor training, they could only be sent to the front. Consequently, an internal IDF report noted, many described themselves as "cannon fodder." In line with this picture, it was for many years believed that hundreds, maybe even thousands, of these "foreign draft" soldiers died without being able to fire a single shot.[33]

Recent research has shown, however, that of the 7,800 men drafted from the DP camps, in fact only about 100 were killed; and the foreign draft of 22,000, despite being a third of the army, suffered only a twentieth of the casualties. Presumably the foreign draft was used mainly as support troops, bringing up ammunition, transporting the wounded, and guarding prisoners.[34]

There are very few accounts by DPs themselves of their experience. Thus we simply do not know what they made of Nahum Shadmi's statement that, by volunteering to fight for Israel, they had regained their self-respect or of Segev's later comment that military service "gave the soldier who had survived the Holocaust a part in the victory compensating him at least for some of what he had endured in Europe."[35]

Even while the war was still in progress, DPs from Germany began going to Israel. In 1948, 118,993 immigrants arrived, of whom 86 percent had survived the Holocaust; in 1949, 141,608 arrived, 95,165 of whom were Holocaust survivors, constituting 67 percent of that year's immigrants. "The significance of these numbers," according to Hanna Yablonka, "lies in the fact that the Holocaust survivors made up some 70 per cent of the total immigrant population during the first two years of Israel's existence as a state." Unfortunately, Yablonka made no attempt to define what she meant by the term "Holocaust survivors"; as we have seen, by now most of the DP population in Germany was made up of Jewish refugees from Poland and the Soviet Union, not survivors of the German concentration camps.[36]

The need to help the newcomers to adjust was clearly grasped. In 1946, it will be recalled, Dr. Zalman Grinberg had gone to Palestine to organize reception arrangements for displaced persons coming from the German camps, but, in the event, he became the head of Beilinson Hospital near Tel Aviv and was not directly involved with newly arriving DPs. When they did come in large numbers in 1948, conditions were difficult and no coordinated plans for receiving the refugees were ever carried out. There was already a housing shortage, and Israeli families proved reluctant to take their immigrant relatives. Although the Jewish Agency and other public bodies built apartments for the immigrants—consisting of one room and a kitchen—many remained in squalid camps.[37]

What rescued the immigrants was the so-called Arab miracle. When hostilities broke out in Palestine, many of the Arabs fled, leaving their houses empty; in other instances, the Israeli army removed the inhabitants. Once they had gone, the Israeli Cabinet decided not to allow them to return. According to Tom Segev:

Entire cities and hundreds of villages left empty were repopulated in short order with new immigrants. In April 1949 they numbered

100,000, most of them Holocaust survivors. The moment was a dramatic one in the war for Israel, and a frightfully banal one, too, focused as it was on the struggle over houses and furniture. Free people—Arabs—had gone into exile and become destitute refugees; desperate refugees—Jews—took the exiles' places as a first step in their new lives as free people. One group had lost all they had, while the other found everything they needed—tables, chairs, closets, pots, pans, plates, sometimes clothes, family albums, books, radios, and pets.[38]

Although a passionate Zionist and close supporter of David Ben-Gurion, Josef Rosensaft decided to remain in Europe. When Rosensaft married Dr. Hadassah Bimko at Belsen DP camp in September 1946, the leader of the Jewish Agency sent the couple a warm and effusive letter of congratulations. "Destiny brought you together," he wrote. "It is a symbol that fate is not so terrible, but is a little bit, although seldom, decent, because it could not have made a better union."

Though Rosensaft was happy in the role of the prophet's disciple, his own autocratic manner of leadership brought him into conflict with "party politics"; he found himself out of sympathy with Palestinian Jews, who "came from a country where party politics were a matter of course." His wife was an admirer and supporter of Chaim Weizmann, whom she had met when she accompanied a group of children from Belsen to Palestine in the spring of 1946. At the end of that year she was deeply disappointed when Weizmann was removed as president of the World Zionist Organization. "I was disgusted by the infighting and political greed at the Zionist Congress," she wrote later. "As we watched the political parties maneuvering for position at the Congress we were convinced, to our dismay, that the party strife pushed the recent calamity into the background."[39]

When Josef Rosensaft visited the newly independent state of Israel in April 1949, he was received at the highest levels. His presence happened to coincide with the arrival of a transport of Jews from Belsen, and he was shocked by the living conditions in the transit camps they were sent to. A previous transport, forced to live in waterlogged huts, had even asked the Israeli authorities to send them back to Belsen. According to his wife, "this experience had such an impact on Yossel that he decided he could not live in Israel," even though she had already made detailed plans to work there as a dentist. On his return to Belsen, Rosensaft gave a powerful speech to the Jews in the camp, telling them that Israel was a wonderful but difficult country. He urged them to go there as long as they were prepared for the harsh conditions they would encounter there. He also warned them that they would be on their own. "Ben-Gurion will not meet you at the boat," he said, "and Eliezer Kaplan [Israel's first finance minister] will not present you with a check."

There may have been other factors behind his decision. Rosensaft was by now making his way in the European commercial world; after his years of heroic exertion, he was entitled to a quieter life. Nahum Goldmann remembered Rosensaft saying to him, half jokingly, half seriously, "Palestine has too many Jossels. I can't do business there." But that wasn't what he said in public. According to one source, Rosensaft told Israelis, "You danced the hora while we were being burned in the crematoriums."[40]

EIGHTEEN

America's Fair Share

THE UNITED STATES AND DPs, 1947–1950

From the beginning of the displaced persons saga, one thing was clear: given a choice, most DPs wanted to go to the United States. Not only were its streets believed to be paved with gold, it enjoyed in the late 1940s a much higher standard of living than any other country and was safe from communism and from the threat of another world war. In addition, many displaced persons already had relatives or countrymen in the United States whom they wished to join. Furthermore, as the main paymaster of UNRRA and of its successor, the International Refugee Organization, the United States was intimately involved with the whole business of resettlement, providing most of the money and the shipping.

Yet the United States took longer than almost any other nation fully to engage with the question of whether it should give DPs a refuge. When it did so, its response was defined by its ethnic makeup, its history of immigration policy, and the vagaries of its political system.

At that time the United States was by far the most ethnically diverse country in the world—a "nation of immigrants," a unique society in which refugees from all over Europe mingled with descendants of Native Americans, African slaves, and Asian and Hispanic immigrants to form a new nationality. Americans were proud of their diversity and had produced several metaphors to describe it. The most famous of them was coined in a play in 1908:

> Understand that America is God's crucible, the great Melting-Pot where all the races of Europe are melting and reforming! A fig for your feuds and vendettas! Germans and Frenchmen, Irishmen and

Englishmen, Jews and Russians—into the crucible with you all! God is making the American.[1]

All the national groups in the camps in Germany could already claim to have played some part in the epic of American history. The travails of Lithuanians in the Chicago stockyards were recorded in Upton Sinclair's famous novel *The Jungle;* Louis Adamic, one of the best-known American authors of the 1940s, was a Slovenian who had worked among Croatian fishermen in California; and, visiting the mining communities of Pennsylvania on a Sunday, travelers felt they were in Ukraine. But three groups in particular stood out: the Germans, the Jews, and the Poles.

For most of the nineteenth century, between a third and quarter of immigrants to America had come from Germany—craftsmen and peasants escaping rural overpopulation and (in some cases) religious persecution to settle in the Middle West, especially in Wisconsin and Minnesota. They were admired for their skill, diligence, thrift, and family strength; but the need to demonstrate their loyalty to their new country during the two world wars had taken away much of their separate identity: the enormous German-American press, for example, had largely disappeared. But, although by the 1940s German culture was largely hidden below the surface, German Americans remained a formidable group in terms of numbers and their place in national life—President Hoover, General Eisenhower, and the aviator Charles Lindbergh were all of German stock. At a political level their views had to be taken into account.[2]

By contrast, the Polish community was much more visible yet lacking in political clout. One of the biggest groups numerically, the Poles were mostly descended from peasants who had arrived between 1890 and 1914, looking for a better life, and become industrial laborers in Chicago, Pittsburgh, Buffalo, and other big cities. More than other groups, the Poles had tended to remain where they were, their comparative lack of social mobility born of distinctive social attitudes: they spent their money on houses for their families and on donations to the Catholic Church, rather than on education. "Most Polish parents," wrote the immigration historian Victor Greene, "were reluctant to see their children through high school, much less college. A basic education up to the age of confirmation was felt to be sufficient; the immigrant child was expected to go to work even before finishing grammar school." And, insofar as Poles did not advance in America, so they remained Polish. "The degree to which ethnic ritual and traditions were maintained in Polish-American homes may have been surprising to observers in the 1930s," wrote Greene, "but it was likely the result of the essentially static socioeconomic conditions of the group." Although Polish Americans produced very few political leaders, they were an important, well-organized constituency with strong views on events in their homeland and on Russia, which were usually ventilated through the hierarchy of the Catholic Church and the Polish associations. As we have seen, interventions by the Catholic hierarchy had played an important part in keeping the displaced persons camps going.[3]

The influence of America's Jewish community on national life was out of all proportion to its numerical size. Eagerly embracing the public education system, Jews had risen to prominence in politics, the media, and the professions; the best-known figures, such as Herbert Lehman, Treasury Secretary Henry Morgenthau, and Supreme Court Justice Louis Brandeis, coming mostly from the older German-Jewish emigration of the mid-nineteenth century. But by the 1940s, Jews from Eastern Europe had also reached the top in many areas of American life. After the destruction of the European Jews, the United States contained the largest Jewish community in the world— 4.5 million people, living mostly in the cities of New York, Chicago, Cincinnati, and Philadelphia. There were 2 million in New York City alone.[4]

The growing prominence of Jews in American life had, however, produced a backlash. In the 1920s, Ivy League universities felt it necessary to introduce a "Jewish quota," and Jewish organizations learned to present an American front. Jewish actors in Hollywood Anglicized their names. This fear of provoking American hostility partially explains the caution with which the leaders of American Jewry had responded to the Nazis' persecution of Germany's Jews. But by 1942, the dreadful events in Europe had brought most of America's Jews together, united in support of the demand for a Jewish homeland in Palestine.[5]

By the late 1940s, the "Jewish lobby" had arrived. "Jewish groups in the U.S. were well organized and had friends strategically located," wrote Leonard Dinnerstein. "Their defense organizations hired top lawyers, publicists, and community relations personnel to promote group interests and thwart potentially unfavorable legislation and executive actions. An indication of their success is that they never seemed to have any difficulty in reaching people at the highest levels of government." The role of David Niles, President Truman's special assistant for minority affairs, was particularly important; according to Truman's biographer, Niles "would keep key Zionists informed of what was going on in Washington and within the White House at almost every step." He helped orchestrate Truman's Yom Kippur message in October 1946, organized American lobbying on behalf of a Jewish state in Palestine in November 1947, and intervened on behalf of Jewish DPs. Thus, for example, when the secretaries of state and war advised Truman in July 1946 to close the West German border to further infiltration from East Europeans, "the Jewish lobby," wrote Dinnerstein, "orchestrated counter pressure . . . to prevent this action." Numerous congressmen were mobilized, and, "as a result of these contacts, Truman kept the West German border open and East Europeans continued to flock into the DP centers."[6]

For most of the twentieth century, immigration had been a deeply contested area of American political life. Indeed, in the 1940s attitudes to immigration were still determined largely by the debates of a generation before.

Immigration policy has always been important in the United States. "From the moment they managed their own affairs," the historian Aristide R. Zolberg has argued, "Americans were determined to select who might join them." Immigration policy, Zolberg has shown, "emerged from the outset as a major instrument of nation-building, equivalent in the fashioning of the United States to the amalgamation of divers regions in the making of the United Kingdom, France or Spain." At the same time, however, the United States presented a paradox: it was at once the most cosmopolitan country in the world and one of the most insular and provincial; the federal system of government, by, for example, assigning two senators to every state regardless of the size of population, enhanced rather than minimized local feelings and prejudices.[7]

One such feeling was a powerful hostility to new immigrants, who came in three waves in the nineteenth century: first, anti-Catholic feeling, driven by Irish immigration; then hostility to Chinese laborers; and finally opposition to all immigration, in response to the great wave of migration from Eastern and southern Europe which reached its climax in 1907, when more than a million new Americans arrived in one year. Even as Emma Lazarus's poem

> *Give me your tired, your poor,*
> *Your huddled masses yearning to breathe free,*
> *The wretched refuse of your teeming shore*

was being engraved on the Statue of Liberty, U.S. legislators were taking steps to exclude the huddled masses, trying to introduce controls on immigration into the United States. According to a prominent Republican, they were driven by two fears—first, "a very deeply held feeling of our people that the future immigration of racial stocks should be so limited as to coincide with the existing ratio of such stocks already within the country"; and second, a wish to keep out emigrants from Eastern and southern Europe, born of a strong fear "that an uncontrolled immigration from such countries would modify the proportion of the racial stocks already existing in our own population and would introduce into the United States many people who would with difficulty be assimilated into our own population and brought into conformity with our own institutions and traditions."[8]

The eventual outcome of this process was the two Immigration Acts of 1917 and 1924, which still governed American policy two decades later. They limited the number of immigrants and established a national quota system which controlled the numbers coming from each country. The system was designed to rein in immigration from southern and Eastern Europe and maintain the existing ethnic balance of the American population by favoring immigrants from the countries of northern and Western Europe. The total annual quota of 154,277 immigrants could not be carried over from one year to the next, and while the smaller quotas for Eastern and Central Europe were always filled, only about a quarter of those from northern and Western Europe were used. As a result, since the early 1930s the United States had admitted only an annual average of 54,095 immigrants, rather than the 154,277 theoretically entitled to visas each year.[9]

Between 1933 and 1940, about 127,000 Jewish refugees entered the United States, more than the number admitted to any other country. Most were refugees from Germany, but, as Zolberg has pointed out, "another 110,000 could have been admitted within the limits of the German quota alone in the years before it was filled." At the same time, the Jews widely understood to be at risk, those living in Poland, Hungary, and Romania, were nearly all denied entry because of the extremely small quotas for Central and Eastern Europe.[10]

It is a remarkable fact that the Second World War and the German concentration camps produced no discernible shift in Main Street American opinion. If anything, the feeling that the country needed more time to absorb its existing immigrants hardened. At the end of hostilities, Congress and the country were in an anti-immigrant mood and had no wish to lower the barriers. A Gallup Poll taken in December 1945 found that 32 percent of Americans wanted immigration to remain at the same level, but 37 percent wanted it reduced and only 5 percent wanted it higher. Patriotic groups such as the Daughters of the American Revolution, the American Legion, and Veterans of Foreign Wars wanted to ban immigration to the United States for a decade. Eleanor Roosevelt noted that every representative in Congress with whom she had talked "has told me that the general feeling is that they want to stop all immigration."[11]

It therefore took some political courage for President Truman to issue, in December 1945, a directive mandating preferential treatment for all DPs, especially orphans, within the existing U.S. immigration laws. This helped the DPs only slightly because the entire yearly quota for all the Eastern European nations, from which most of them came, amounted to only 13,000, while another 26,000 places were reserved for Germans. In August 1946, Truman announced that he was seeking congressional legislation to bring an unspecified number of DPs to the United States. Seventy-two percent of respondents to a poll disapproved of Truman's idea, and only 16 percent were in favor. Opposition came from nativist congressmen but also from Zionists who feared that bringing DPs to the United States would weaken the pressure to establish a Jewish homeland in Palestine.[12]

As we have seen, the war years in the United States had seen a successful lobbying campaign by Zionists, thanks to which both Republican and Democratic parties went into the 1944 elections committed to the creation of a Jewish state in Palestine. But American Jewry was not itself united. A small but powerful and important minority of American Jews, mainly wealthy German Americans, remained opposed to Zionism. When it became apparent in 1946 that the British would not allow 100,000 European Jews into Palestine, they began to campaign for them to come to the United States. Composed mainly of older Jewish immigrants, this group included such rich and influential figures as the Sulzbergers (the owners of *The New York Times*) and Lessing J. Rosenwald, whose family controlled the Sears, Roebuck retail company.

Peter Novick has described Arthur Hays Sulzberger, the publisher of *The New York Times*, as "a Jew of a sort now rare: a believer in the classical reform position that Jewishness means solely religious belief—not ethnic 'peoplehood.' His political loyalties were strictly American, his sensibility was liberal and universalist, and he was an opponent of the campaign for a Jewish state in Palestine. And he didn't want the *Times* to become—or seem to be—a spokesman for any parochial concern." As a result of this stance, it has recently been alleged, "he bent over backwards to deny the specificity of Jewish victimhood, refused to allow the *Times* to give prominent notice of the Holocaust and withheld support for rescue programs that focused on European Jewry."[13]

Lessing J. Rosenwald's position was more complex. After giving up the day-to-day running of Sears, Roebuck in 1939, he was for a time associated with the isolationist America First campaign led by Charles Lindbergh, until its obvious anti-Semitism caused him to withdraw. After the war, Rosenwald felt strongly that the United States had a duty to take as many of the Jewish displaced persons as possible, but he and his associates recognized that the only way to overcome public hostility was to launch a major campaign of public education and persuasion. Such an initiative, if it were to have any success, would have to be fronted by prominent non-Jewish Americans. Accordingly, Rosenwald persuaded the nation's best-known champion of DPs, his Philadelphia neighbor Earl G. Harrison, to become the campaign's chairman. He also brought prominent figures in business, labor, education, and the Christian churches into what became known as the Citizens Committee on Displaced Persons. In its publicity, the Citizens Committee emphasized the fact that 80 percent of the displaced persons were Christians, and in its private deliberations, it recognized that, in order for America to admit 100,000 Jews, it would probably be necessary to allow four times that number of DPs into the country. It acknowledged that this would inevitably mean letting in some Nazi collaborators but believed that "a calculated risk should be taken since it was unavoidable if a haven were to be found in this country for a significant number of displaced Jews." On the other hand, it did not intend to spread the net to include *Volksdeutsche* or any of the millions of Africans and Asians whom the war had displaced. As far as it was concerned, it was a question of getting Jewish, as well as Polish, Ukrainian, Baltic, and Yugoslav, DPs to America. This was emphasized in its publicity and propaganda.[14]

The Citizens Committee, as its name made clear, was pitched at Middle America. For that reason, it contained no representatives of the nations making up the vast majority of the DPs—Latvians, Lithuanians, Poles, Ukrainians, Estonians, and Yugoslavs. It wanted to avoid associating its campaign with "migrants and foreigners" and believed that Congress would bring in new legislation only if pressured to do so by a significant number of respected Protestants. The Citizens Committee, Peter Novick has pointed out, was "ostensibly nondenominational, but in fact largely funded and staffed by Jews"; two-thirds of its $1 million budget was underwritten by Lessing Rosenwald himself.[15]

The Citizens Committee was subsequently recognized as one of the most effective lobbying exercises in postwar America. Much of its energy went into influencing media coverage. According to Leonard Dinnerstein's exhaustive study, "almost all the editorials on the displaced persons problem appearing in the press of the nation were inspired, if not written by, the Committee." For example, shortly before the second anniversary of VE Day, on May 8, 1947, the committee circulated a draft editorial to newspapers across the country, explaining helpfully that "if your newspaper is the sole publication in your community this editorial may be reproduced without risk of conflicting publication":

Who are these people? They are the "displaced persons." More than 75 per cent of them are victims of one or another of European dictators, no matter under what cause or name the dictatorship flourished—communist or fascist. They are, these 80 per cent, of the Christian faith, a good many of them Polish or Baltic Catholics. Another portion of them, by far the smallest number, only one out of five, is of the Jewish faith.

The committee also provided speakers and films and gave support to prominent local people who might promote its cause. Over the next eighteen months, nearly six hundred radio stations used its materials, and millions of Americans saw the film *Passport to Nowhere,* made with professional actors and technicians and distributed by the Hollywood studio RKO.[16]

The Citizens Committee also tried to get Congress moving on the issue. In April 1947, William Stratton, a congressman from Illinois, was persuaded to introduce into the House of Representatives a bill which would have allowed 400,000 DPs into the United States over the next four years. But the public mood was still hostile. "We have enough foreigners already and I think we should get rid of them rather than bring in additional ones," a congressman from South Carolina declared. Mail to Congress ran seven to one against letting DPs in. Despite the Citizens Committee's work, most of the public continued to believe that nearly all DPs were Jews. A New York radio broadcaster told his listeners that the proposed legislation would admit 400,000 Jewish displaced persons to the United States; Church leaders shied away from assisting the campaign morally or financially because everyone thought this was a Jewish problem. With only weak endorsement from the administration, the bill made slow progress in the Republican-dominated Congress.

Then, gradually, the climate began to shift. Dinnerstein attributed the "miraculous" change in public opinion to several factors. Undoubtedly the Citizens Committee's work began to have some effect. A senator from Wisconsin complained that "he could not walk down the streets of his home town without someone like his banker, butcher or former Sunday School teacher stopping him and saying 'Senator, why aren't you a good Christian? Why are you against DPs?'" Then again, steps to educate the political leadership were beginning to bear fruit. Important congressmen were sent to Europe, and the minds of some were changed by the experience of going round the camps, especially when they also saw that most of the DPs were not Jews. Skillful lobbying had also converted the powerful veterans' organization the American Legion, whose leaders "did not want this country flooded with Jews," as one of them put it. However, once it had been convinced that "most of those Jews in the DP camps want to go to Palestine and not the USA," the Legion withdrew its opposition. [17]

But what undoubtedly made the greatest impact were events in Europe: the Communist coup in Czechoslovakia, the Berlin Airlift, the Marshall Plan. Nineteen forty-eight was the year Hollywood brought the Cold War to Main Street America. Although the wartime mood of Allied cooperation still lingered in one film released that year—the thriller *Berlin Express,* in which a sympathetically portrayed Russian helped American GIs foil a neo-Nazi plot—the new mood was apparent in Twentieth Century-Fox's *The Iron Curtain,* soon to be followed by Howard Hughes's *I Married a Communist* and other similar titles.

The Communist takeover in Eastern Europe mobilized, in particular, America's Catholic hierarchy, whose interest in DPs had hitherto been somewhat intermittent. In terms of providing relief in Germany, for example, the Catholics had lagged far behind the Jewish agencies. In 1945, the American Jewish Joint Distribution Committee spent $317,000 on relief for DPs in Germany and Austria, but by 1946 its expenditure had risen twelvefold, to $4 million, and in 1947 it reached $9 million, an enormous sum for that time. By contrast, Catholic War Relief had only five people working for the 400,000 Catholic DPs in the American zones in Germany and Austria in April 1946—a ratio of 1 worker per 20,000 DPs—whereas the Jewish agencies had a staff of 117 persons serving 117,000 DPs, a ratio of 1 worker for every 1,000 DPs.[18]

The disparity was even greater when it came to fund-raising in America. "The Jews are after 170 million dollars this year (100 million last year) and they will get it," a Catholic welfare official wrote in March 1947. "We in the Sunday collection last year got less than 2 million and anticipate 5 million for the current effort." He warned that if Catholics really did make up 75 percent of the DPs, his organization might have to resettle some 350,000 people: "Let's get down to brass tacks. Who would foot the enormous bill of transportation and support?"[19]

By 1948, the Catholic hierarchy in the United States was taking a definite interest in DPs, though the Protestant churches remained largely indifferent. However, as some of the leaders of the Citizens Committee acknowledged, there was a danger. The Christian organizations recruited to the campaign were more interested in those fleeing communism than in victims of the Nazis. The greater the emphasis on communism, the less provision there might be for Jewish displaced persons. These fears proved well founded. The legislation which ultimately emerged, the Displaced Persons Act of 1948, was blatantly designed (by senators from West Virginia and North Dakota) to exclude Jews and favor Balts. It stipulated, for example, that only people who had reached Germany before December 22, 1945, were eligible to come to the United States, thus automatically excluding the more than 100,000 Jews who were released from the Soviet Union in the spring of 1946 and who fled the Polish pogroms that summer. It also favored agricultural workers, people whose countries had been annexed by a foreign power—that is, citizens of the Baltic republics—and former residents of the Soviet Union. President Truman called the act "flagrantly discriminatory" but reluctantly signed it.[20]

There was a double irony here: a skillful public education campaign, funded and controlled by Jewish groups, had ultimately produced an act which not only discriminated against Jews but also undercut the advantages that had accrued to them under the provisions of the Truman directive of 1945. Not surprisingly, this provoked fierce argument within the American Jewish community. The strategy of "always getting up a non-Jewish front to press for Jewish causes" was fiercely attacked, especially by pro-Zionists. The Citizens Committee's campaign, they argued, had only made it easier for Nazi collaborators to get into the United States. The Zionist Abraham Duker attacked the "self-delusion" of those Jewish organizations which still refused to "see the indecency, the shame and the danger of rewarding the killers and their kin by admitting them to our hospitable shores." In response, the Citizens Committee accused the Zionists of not putting their full weight behind the campaign.[21]

To apply the 1948 act, President Truman established a Displaced Persons Commission and appointed Ugo Carusi, a Protestant; Edward M. O'Connor, a Catholic; and Harry N. Rosenfield, a Jew, to run it. They, in turn, staffed the organization with senior- and middle-level staff who had worked for UNRRA and the IRO and were strongly committed to the refugees. The Displaced Persons Commission, said Leonard Dinnerstein, "showed how a government bureau could change the intent of a law by the nature of its administration. Congress passed a complex and restrictive measure in 1948. The DPC, however, sought every loophole and stretched every ambiguity to help bring people to the United States under the terms of that Act." For their part, the U.S. government agencies did their best to restrict the flow of immigrants.[22]

There would inevitably have been difficulties in applying the 1948 act. Congress had, for example, stipulated that 40 percent of DPs admitted had to come from "annexed areas"—territory taken by the Soviet Union after the war—whereas even under the State Department's definition, only 19 percent did. Thirty percent had to be engaged in agricultural pursuits; but, by the most generous definition, only 20 percent of them were. So the definition had to be widened. But the main administrative stumbling block was the cutoff date of December 22, 1945. Thousands of people were unable to prove their eligibility because, even among those who had entered Germany by then, accurate records of DP residence often did not go back that far. In trying to resolve this situation, the indulgence of the Displaced Persons Commission and the IRO staff in Germany was matched by the complexities of the law and the prejudice and obstructionism of the immigration and visa authorities. As a result, it took nine months to process every applicant. One journalist thought it "a miracle that any displaced persons have arrived in America . . . in the face of all the obstacles that have been placed in their way . . . the entire complicated process is confusing, humiliating and brutal."[23]

The slowness in processing applications was not due to any vigilance in investigating DPs' wartime records. Once again, the army used undertrained soldiers to carry out screening, expecting them to master the complexities of European history in a day and a half's training. According to Dinnerstein, the records "show countless examples of completely arbitrary evaluations being made." In addition, the arrival of the Cold War in earnest meant a new interpretation of the past, with greater emphasis being placed on whether groups had been anti-Soviet rather than pro-German. After September 1950, the Displaced Persons Commission took its cue from the State Department in ruling that, although wartime military units such as the Latvian Legion had fought alongside the Germans, they were separate in purpose, ideology, and activities from the German SS and therefore "not considered to be a movement hostile to the Government of the United States under section 13 of the Displaced Persons Act."[24]

The new mood was also apparent in the way the DPs were received on arrival in America. While the major Jewish resettlement agency quietly tried to disperse the DPs it sponsored all over the country and allowed only those DPs with close relatives in New York to remain there, press coverage of the arriving DPs focused almost exclusively on the Balts. In 1950, the Displaced Persons Commission chose a frail Latvian woman bound for Colorado Springs to be honored as the 200,000th DP; newspapers pictured her with four healthy-looking children, born between 1939 and 1944. American Jews were astonished by the number of Latvians with children and loads of possessions. According to Abraham Duker, "one of the ways to identify the collaborationists was to see which ones had their children with them. Those who had been taken as slave laborers had been separated from their families."[25]

Favorable stories about a few such cases, lavishly illustrated and spread across the pages of periodicals, helped make the public more receptive to DPs—and to a broadened, and less discriminatory, Displaced Persons Act. "Forget that term 'displaced persons' quickly," a community leader in North Dakota declared. "When they come into their new country they're no longer displaced. They're in the right place. They're home. They're new neighbors!" The problems of adjustment which many of the newcomers faced were largely ignored, though it was soon apparent that many of the "agricultural workers" admitted under the Displaced Persons Act were nothing of the kind. Although 27 percent of those admitted were "agricultural workers," by December 1951 less than 3.4 percent remained in that occupation.[26]

The presidential election of 1948 was one of the great upsets in American political history. President Truman was widely expected to lose to his Republican opponent, Thomas E. Dewey. Dismissed by the *Los Angeles Times* as "the most complete fumbler and bumbler this nation has seen in high office for a long time," Truman was written off by the opinion polls; when *Newsweek* asked America's top fifty political journalists to assess his chances, not one expected him to be reelected. But, by tirelessly taking his case to the American people—and with the help of a cynical, lackluster campaign by Dewey—Truman pulled off one of the great political upsets in history. The image of Truman triumphantly holding up a newspaper front page, with its banner headline DEWEY DEFEATS TRUMAN, defined the moment.

Not only was Truman reelected, but an overwhelmingly Democratic Congress was returned and many prominent opponents of immigration were defeated; Herbert Lehman was among the new senators. During his campaign, Truman had reminded city audiences that the Republican Congress had discriminated against Catholics and Jews. It was therefore widely expected that a new Displaced Persons Act would soon be passed.

However, no one took account of Pat McCarran.[27]

The American political system gives power to chairmen of Senate committees, who often come from remote constituencies and have illiberal views. Senator Patrick A. McCarran of Nevada, who now became chairman of the all-important Senate Judiciary Committee, was, even by these standards, an authentic, twenty-two-carat monster. An isolationist Democrat who considered himself responsible for safeguarding the national interest, McCarran had opposed the New Deal, Lend-Lease, and aid to Britain and France. He considered the United Nations' presence in New York City to be "an open door for foreign spies and communists" and believed that "too many" DPs entering the country were "active subversives" who had "no other purpose but to undermine our American way of life." He wanted no more. Like many Irish-American Catholics, he was also very anti-Semitic.[28]

In early 1949, a new DP bill was brought forward which dropped the provisions for 40 percent from annexed territories and 30 percent agricultural workers, moved the cutoff date, and made specific provision for several groups: 18,000 members of the Polish army, 4,000 Jewish refugees from Shanghai, and 15,000 recent political refugees.

Although the bill passed the House of Representatives in June 1949, it made little headway in the Senate in the face of McCarran's delaying tactics. In September, he asked for a three-week leave of absence to investigate the situation in Europe—and then disappeared for eleven weeks, taking time to have an audience with the pope, hold talks with his friend General Francisco Franco in Madrid, and visit his mother's birthplace in County Cork. On his return, McCarran continued to stall. In February 1950, he began hearings into the workings of the existing DP legislation, using his position to accuse the Displaced Persons Commission of falling down on the job and letting Communists into the United States. "Instead of discharging its duties in Europe," McCarran charged, the DPC had "turned the operation over to former UNRRA employees, social workers, persons of that caliber, who are not concerned primarily with the best interests of the USA." He found enough disgruntled former staff members willing to endorse his argument that the Displaced Persons Commission, "in favoring quick processing and ignoring minor or unsubstantiated accusations, was following neither the letter nor the restrictionist spirit of the 1948 Act, which placed the burden of proof of eligibility on the DP."[29]

At the same time, McCarran and his associates inserted into the new bill amendments which transformed it by changing the definition of a displaced person again—from those people victimized by the Nazis to anyone forced to flee from his last residence because of persecution or fear of persecution between September 1, 1939, and January 1, 1949. In effect, this new definition added to the pool 12 million *Volksdeutsche* expelled from Eastern Europe and Czechoslovakia during and after the Second World War and thus diluted the number of places available to the DPs already registered. At one point Herbert Lehman claimed that the Judiciary Committee's real object was to "change the entire nature of the program from one of relief for displaced persons to one of relief for German expellees." The rejoinder came from Senator James Eastland of Mississippi: the *Volksdeutsche,* he said, were "the real displaced persons." "One of the greatest crimes in history," he claimed, "was uprooting people whose only offense was that through their veins flowed German blood. . . . They were turned out into the cold and snow, driven like cattle across eastern and central Europe into Germany, where many of them died on the march like flies. I say that is one of the greatest crimes in all human history."[30]

Once again, a complex trade-off had taken place among America's ethnic groups. A senator from a small state, with a population of 135,000, had used his position to hold the entire political process at bay. But the liberals in the Senate had learned some lessons from the debacle of 1948. Whereas they had then allowed the bill to be emasculated in committee, this time they made sure to block parliamentary maneuvers that might bury the legislation. Opponents of liberal legislation, on the other hand, took advantage of every stratagem available to delay a vote. Finally, in June 1950, the new Displaced Persons Act became law. Nine days after the president signed the bill, the Korean War began. If McCarran had succeeded in delaying the progress of the legislation a few more weeks, he might have achieved his goal of blocking the passage of the liberal measure.

Leonard Dinnerstein has argued that though McCarran lost the legislative battle, he nonetheless won the administrative fight. His visits to the Displaced Persons Commission's offices in Europe in the autumn of 1949 and his subcommittee hearings in Washington had unnerved the commissioners and their subordinates and destroyed the agency's morale. Many of its staff were frightened into resigning or intimidated into taking a tougher line with the DPs. Thanks to his pressure, "screening procedures tightened; processing of applicants slowed."

When the Displaced Persons Act finally expired in 1952, the United States had taken in 380,000 people under its provisions, about 40 percent of the displaced persons registered in Europe—far more than any other nation. Overall, some 45 percent of the new immigrants were Catholic, 20 percent were Jewish, and 34 percent were either Protestant or Greek Orthodox.[31]

In the end—in its own time, in its own way—the United States took its fair share.

NINETEEN

Legacies

HOW DPs MADE NEW LIVES

Between 1940 and 1951, more than a million people left their home-lands in Europe, spent years waiting in displaced persons camps for their future to be decided, and were then resettled overseas. What did the process mean for them as individuals? How were the contours of their lives shaped and altered by that experience? In the last years of the twentieth century, answers to some of these questions began to emerge as former displaced persons began to write memoirs of their lives—or, more usually, when their children did it for them. We can see in these narratives how great historical forces affect, and are refracted by, ordinary people.

Agate Nesaule was born in Latvia in 1938. Her father was a Lutheran minister; her mother, the daughter of a Latvian socialist exiled to Russia for his political activities. "A stylish woman," she would have liked to have gone to university but instead became a village teacher. Agate's later memories of her childhood in the Latvian countryside were "forever associated with sunlight." In the middle of 1944, the family fled to Germany, where they spent three months in a detention center before being released to work in an institution for the mentally defective near Berlin, the menfolk as laborers, the women as kitchen staff.

As the Red Army approached in early 1945, many of the Germans fled to the West, but Agate's mother refused to abandon her elderly and sickly mother. When the Russian soldiers came, they took every-one's watches and shot several of the men, including the kindly doctor who had managed to keep the inmates alive. Agate and her mother were put in a cellar with the other women and witnessed a young German girl, Hilde, being repeatedly raped by "Mongolian" soldiers before she drowned herself in an ornamental lake. But Agate's mother managed to persuade a Russian officer to intervene on their behalf, and eventually they were able to escape and make their way to Berlin. After waiting all day in a long line, and as rain began to fall, they were admitted to a receiving center run by the British. The raspberry jam and tea the British gave them would always remain "the most wonderful meal" of Agate's life.

In due course the Nesaules found themselves in a DP camp in western Germany. Both her parents kept very busy, and Agate attached herself to Mrs. Saulitis, a childless woman who had gotten a room to herself "after having been seen walking in the woods with a British soldier." When they moved to other camps, Agate began to seek out other women without children of their own. Her other great consolation was the camp school. Coming from an academically minded family, she was expected to do well, but education also offered her something very important:

> We were constantly told of the importance of learning. The most frequently quoted lines—"the riches of the heart do not rust"— were from a poem by Karlis Sklabe. This was interpreted to mean that one could lose all one's material possessions in looting and wars, one could lose one's family, friends, and country, but that knowledge was a precious, everlasting possession. I did not question this. Here at last was something positive and permanent. I knew that if I tried hard enough I could master almost everything and this gave me real satisfaction and a sense of control.

Agate took away many happy memories from the camps: the coat her mother had made out of a purple blanket; the patent-leather dancing shoes everyone wore at one stage; and, especially, a performance of *Twelfth Night*.[1]

In 1947, Agate's extended family, by now more or less re-formed in the camps, began to break up again. A girl cousin went to Canada as a domestic, a boy to the mines in England. Her own parents were divided as to whether they should go to Brazil—where her father could work as a pastor—or to the United States, where there was education for women. Her mother prevailed, but their departure was delayed by the fact that the United States would take only one dependent per worker, so that Agate's grandmother would have to be left behind. Finally, an uncle and aunt who had only one daughter took the old woman.

Agate's family reached the United States in 1950, when she was twelve years old, and settled in Indianapolis, where many Latvian DPs worked in the metalworks owned by the father of the novelist Kurt Vonnegut, Jr. The Nesaules were sponsored by a Lutheran pastor, who wanted to bring whites into a run-down inner-city neighborhood then being settled by black migrants from the South, but he made them pay steeply for their accommodation. They also discovered that the house next door was used as a brothel—the prostitutes were black, but the clients, who drunkenly urinated on their porch, were white. Agate's mother had to work as a dishwasher at La Rue's Supper Club in the evenings, and her father worked unpaid for the Latvian community. He remained entirely Latvian, whereas her mother quickly came to terms with American life and culture, while having few illusions about the society. Overall, the Latvian women did better: many of the men failed and turned to drink—Agate's Latvian brother-in-law drank himself to death. After two decades the family was able to move to a better neighborhood.[2]

Soon after her arrival, Agate caught tuberculosis and was in bed for a year, but was too ashamed of the living conditions at home ever to invite a school friend home. She and her grandmother also encountered abuse on the bus for speaking Latvian. Once again, though, education provided a lifeline. Soon after her arrival, Agate was taken by her officious but kindly Latvian mentor, Mrs. Čigāns, to the local public library. While Agate marveled at the sheer numbers of books, Mrs. Čigāns attempted to communicate with the librarian, crying "Whoosh, whoosh," waving her arms and cupping her hands over her mouth and blowing. The librarian went off and returned with a pile of volumes, topped by *Gone with the Wind*. In the camps, Agate had read the first volume in Latvian translation three times. Now she began laboriously going through the English text with an English-Latvian dictionary. By the end of her first summer, she could read English.

While still at college, and against her mother's advice, she married a handsome young American boy, who turned out to have many problems of his own. He refused to listen to Agate's wartime experiences; "Everybody had a lousy childhood," he would say. Only when she was divorced and had acquired a new partner did Agate feel confident enough to explore her own past and to realize how many of her problems derived from her wartime past—and how much she had handed on to her own son. "For more than forty years my own life was constricted by shame, anger and guilt. I was saved by the stories of others, by therapy, dreams and love," she wrote.[3]

In America Agate missed "the DP camps in Germany, where at least I was among people like myself, rather than among strangers from whom I was always different, as I now am in America."[4]

Joseph Berger's parents were Jewish refugees from Poland who fled to the Soviet Union in 1939. Rachel, his mother, escaped from Warsaw with two of her brothers, leaving the rest of her family behind and, while working in the industrial city of Lysva near the Ural Mountains, met Marcus, a peasant from southeastern Poland who had been drafted into the Red Army when the Soviets occupied that part of the country. He was now assigned to a work battalion with Rachel's younger brother, making boots and shoes. Marcus and Rachel were an odd couple: he a shy peasant farmer who fell asleep in the cinema but knew how to find food; she a nervy, intelligent, ambitious woman who worked as a hatmaker. But in that place and time, their relationship made sense; she was grateful for his strength and skills. They married in 1943.[5]

In 1945, after their son Joseph was born, they decided to return to Poland and find the rest of their families. On the train through Poland, Marcus overheard a Pole at a station shout, "Jesus Maria! So many of them survived. I thought Hitler had killed them all." They found two surviving relatives in Warsaw and Marcus worked as a shoemaker, but when they heard of the pogrom at Kielce in late 1946, they decided to flee to the American Zone of Germany. After selling every possession and scrap of spare clothing she possessed, Rachel bought passages on two trucks going to Germany via the Baltic port of Szczecin. After a difficult journey, they reached Berlin, where Rachel found an uncle still alive. They ended up in Schlachtensee DP camp, in the suburbs of the German capital.

Later Rachel recalled the "blocks of long, low wooden buildings arranged around a sandy field" which provided her temporary home. "We had four olive-green American army cots, four olive-green blankets, four olive-green sheets and four olive-green pillows. I began thinking of this room as my home." There were few middle-aged and elderly people and only a handful of children over five in the camp. Schlachtensee also housed Christian Poles, Latvians, and Estonians—and there was considerable tension. Yet she also remembered that all the DPs wanted to put the past behind them and get on with their lives and create new families and bring Jewish children into the world. In April 1947, Rachel's second child, another boy, was born.

Meanwhile, Marcus and Rachel's brother Yasha "began doing what most of their Jewish acquaintances were doing: dealing with German farmers and merchants who were trying to sell their goods to the Displaced Persons." They started by buying fruit and reselling it to the camp's inmates, then moved up to the more lucrative business of cigarettes and chocolates. They would drive the goods, which originally came from American GIs, to the Russian-occupied zone, tipping the guards to let them through the checkpoint, and then sell them to Germans in exchange for cash, meat, eggs, and chocolate. On one occasion, Marcus's truck was stopped by the Russians and its German driver questioned. Marcus immediately jumped out of the truck and fled. It cost him an entire truckload of cigarettes, but he was soon back in business.

Most of the time, Rachel felt "quite prosperous" as a refugee; indeed, like many DPs, she was able to hire a German babysitter for her children: "When a grandmotherly woman desperate for money came to your door and offered her services for a few marks, it was irresistible." The German woman, Elsa, was good-natured, affectionate, and very good with the children.

However, in 1948 the crisis in Berlin caused the authorities to evacuate DPs from the German capital, and Rachel and Marcus were flown to Landsberg camp near Munich. There, the question of where they should immigrate to began to loom. Rachel favored Israel. "I wanted to go to Israel," she wrote later. "It had just declared its independence. The refugees were buying refrigerators, stoves, sewing machines to take with them. I wanted my children to grow up in a Jewish country." But her husband disagreed. He had heard that in Israel the new immigrants slept in tents and there was not enough milk for the children and no jobs for people like him. Besides, people were afraid that there would be another war with the Arabs.

The problem about going to America was that they were not eligible under the 1948 Displaced Persons Act, having entered Germany after the cutoff date of December 1945; indeed, they had come from the Soviet Union. But a solution was found: "We got rid of our Soviet papers and were able easily to get false documents that said we were married in Germany." Rachel also managed to handle the detailed questions of American interrogators looking out for spies and Communist infiltrators, and although medical tests revealed that Joseph had had tuberculosis in the past, probably when he was weak with pneumonia in Russia, he was fine now, thanks to the new streptomycin drug. The family was approved and made their way to Bremerhaven, where they sat through a long quayside lecture on American table manners from an agency worker.

The USAT *General A. W. Greeley* left Germany on February 18 and arrived at Ellis Island on March 3, 1950. Rachel was sick for the first week of the voyage, but then she began to enjoy the chance to relax for the first time in years. As their ship neared the Statue of Liberty, the passengers all screamed and cried, and eventually Rachel—who "knew nothing about this solemn woman with a torch, and . . . had so many concerns about how we would earn our livelihood in a strange land and where we would live and whether we would be isolated and lonely"—also "felt in my soul that my family had finally reached its true refuge, and I cried the tears I had denied myself during so many painful moments of my life."

After an initial struggle, Rachel and Marcus did reasonably well in the United States, but Marcus—the daring black-market operator in Russian Berlin—was less at ease in the new country. He stayed with the General Textile Company for twenty-five years making ironing board covers, an unpleasant job that involved handling asbestos. Rachel worked sewing hats, had another child (a daughter this time), and finally, in 1987, graduated from Hunter College in New York City. In the classic immigrant manner, the next generation was able to improve itself. Their son Joseph Berger became a reporter on *The New York Times* and drew on his mother's journals to publish a fine memoir of his childhood "growing up American." He noted that his father, who had lost five sisters in the Holocaust, never lost his sense of being alone.

In 1981, when his paper sent Joseph to Israel to cover the first world gathering of Jewish Holocaust survivors, he took his parents along. He watched as elderly survivors still looking for relatives gave names in Yiddish, Polish, and Russian to young students, who punched the data into computers. But his father preferred to stick a note on a board. Joseph realized that he had never stopped searching for his relatives.[6]

Ella Schneider was born in Kiev, Ukraine, on June 23, 1936. Her father was a Volga German, a handsome but feckless carpenter and cabinetmaker, and the family spoke German among themselves but Russian to neighbors. They lived on borscht and bread in a small apartment in the better district of Kiev, without an indoor toilet, and bathed once every six weeks. Ella and her little sister shared a bed with their grandmother.

The night before her fifth birthday her father beat her up in a drunken rage and then forgot to listen to the radio. As a result, he did not hear about the German invasion of the Soviet Union. Early the following day, June 23, 1941, he was taken away by the secret police, the NKVD. "Where are you taking him? Tell me so I can bring him his razor," her mother demanded. "Where we're taking him, he won't need a thing" was the reply.

The next day her mother went to the bazaar, with other German-Russian women, to search for their fathers, husbands, and sons. She "turned over one bullet-ridden body after another, into the hundreds. All were cold and stiff—the men had been executed during the night." But she did not find her husband's body. Soon after, the women and children fled, first to stay with neighbors and then to their aunt's village, returning two months later only when they heard that the Germans were in Kiev. Most of their neighborhood was now in ruins, but the German authorities told them to move into their neighbors' more spacious apartment. German officers gave them food, and Ella's mother got a job working for the occupation authorities. She told her children that from now on they must say they were born in Poland, but Ella did not know where Poland was. Their Russian neighbors no longer spoke to them.

In the autumn of 1943, as the first snow fell and the Red Army approached, the German army evacuated Ella and her family to Berlin. They were taken from the station to a processing camp on the outskirts of the city, where they were given a thorough interrogation to make sure they were not Jewish. Soon afterward, the air raids began, and the family was then evacuated to the city of Regensburg, where Ella was sent to school. Once again, Allied air raids intervened. On February 12, 1944, Ella's *oma,* her grandmother, was killed. Her mother cursed the Americans: "They will someday have to answer to God for this." The end of the war found Ella, her mother, and her sister in a camp for *Flüchtlinge* (refugees) in a monastery in Passau in Bavaria.

In the middle of October 1945, Ella's mother went off for a few days on her own and returned with a new husband, Theodor Puder: she explained that, doubting whether her husband would ever return, she needed a man to take care of the family. Later, Ella learned that, had her mother not cut five years off her age, Theodor would not have married her.

The family group, now consisting of six people, lived for a while in homes run by a monastic order, but early in 1946 they were moved to Camp Hofstetten, a former German army training camp a few miles outside Straubing, where they would remain for the next six years, living in a small three-room apartment in a wooden block. Initially, Ella attended the school in the nearby village, but after a few months the hostility of "real Germans" to the refugee children led to her being withdrawn. After that, a school was organized inside the camp.

Ella never discovered exactly what had happened to her stepfather during the war, but she noticed that he avoided company and isolated himself within his family. He was certainly a sour and embittered man. "He hated everybody," Ella later remembered. "He blamed the Jews for starting the war. The Russians for killing his first wife. The Germans for losing the war. The Americans for getting into the war and bombing Germany. Most of all, the Communists who would continue to pursue him to the end of the world." Theodor beat his new family all the time; most of all he beat Ella's mother, but she never complained. Ella thought afterward that "men, those who came home from the war, were in control and letting out their frustrations on their families." Theodor cheered up somewhat when his new wife gave him a son.[7]

Ella helped her mother with domestic chores, went gleaning in the fields with her new grandmother, begged for bread and milk, stole fruit and vegetables in the fields, and gathered cigarette butts for her stepfather. Gradually, life began to improve. Her mother grew vegetables, kept chickens, and even fattened a pig—slaughtered with great ceremony in October 1948 and turned into ham, sausages, and other delicacies. Another great day came on April 2, 1950, when Ella was confirmed. The ceaseless Hail Marys all around her during the air raids had left her fascinated by Catholicism, but in the end she remained a Lutheran. The only difficulty was that the ceremony required her to wear a black dress, which she did not have. However, a miracle happened: at the last minute the pastor announced that clothes had come from America. " 'From America? The same people who almost killed us two years ago?' I asked."

In 1951, when Ella was fifteen, her schooling came to an end and she had to find a job. She quickly discovered that German employers did not hire anyone from Camp Hofstetten. Fortunately, however, her stepfather had applied for them all to go to America, having found out that the 1950 Displaced Persons Act specifically provided for the admission into the United States of "54,744 refugees and expellees of German origin."

A few months later, vetted by the U.S. Immigration Office in Munich, the family told the truth about coming from Kiev. After they had been examined and interviewed, a soldier took their file and stamped "DP" on it. Ella did not know what that meant. "Displaced person," she was told. When they reached Bremerhaven, prior to embarking for America, her mother suddenly disappeared for a day and returned looking pale and ill. Later, Ella learned that she had become pregnant and, because the Americans would not take a woman in her condition, had undergone an abortion.

The USNS *General Harry Taylor* entered New York Harbor on April 27, 1952. Only then did Ella's family discover that they would be going to Holly Springs, Mississippi. Nobody in the Puder family had the slightest idea where that was. The Tyrone Power movies Ella had seen in the camps, and the brief language course she had taken in Bavaria, had not prepared her for America. After a long train ride, they were met by their sponsors, the Deans—who had arranged their transportation from New York—and dumped in their new dwelling, a tumbledown shack. Two weeks later, they learned that they would be "indentured servants" for a year, expected to pay off the cost of their travel and maintenance by working as field hands in the cotton fields.[8]

The family got through it. They coped with the snakes that lived in their well, the red clay dirt in which nothing would grow, and the long-legged spiders. They chopped and picked cotton and tried to understand the social customs in their new home: racial separation, class distinction among whites, harsh and backward living conditions for many. Once Ella suffered sunstroke in the fields and was briefly taken up by Mrs. Dean and trained to be a housemaid in her air-conditioned house. Ella learned that American women showered and washed their hair, shaved under their arms, changed their sanitary towels frequently, used deodorant daily, and brushed their teeth twice a day—to contain "body odor." But Mrs. Dean soon lost interest in her and she returned to the shack. The smell of her family horrified her.

Before the year was up, neighbors intervened to make sure that Ella and her siblings went to school. Mrs. Dean responded by cutting short their stay on her farm and removing the fridge and cow she had given them. The Puder family's Christmas was saved only when a local Methodist group arrived with a turkey and all the trimmings. Theodor was grateful but completely mystified: he had never heard of the Methodists and wasn't sure if they were Christians.

Thereafter, Ella began to attend the local school and her life to diverge from her family's. She was now a teenager in 1950s America, a world of bobby-soxers, soda fountains and drugstores, drive-in cinemas and necking in cars; of "nice" girls who didn't "go all the way" and "easy" girls who did; in which the cares of the universe collapsed down to the question of which boy would take you to the prom. Ella was foreign and strange, always "the German girl" who did not speak English as the locals did, but she was attractive and willing, and, though she didn't break into the best social circles, she got to a religious college in Jackson, Mississippi, and found herself a good husband who rose to be a lieutenant colonel in the U.S. Army.

Her parents, though, did not prosper in America. Her stepfather never had a proper job or owned a house and made only one new friend, an émigré Latvian. Ella's mother never spoke more than a few words of English, stuck to her old recipes, and concentrated on raising her other children and watching television, of which she became a passionate devotee.[9]

The process by which DPs were resettled was not a lottery, but there was certainly a high element of chance in how their later lives panned out. By the mid-1950s, winners and losers were becoming apparent. Perhaps the most important distinction was between people who went to a country where there was already a community of their own nationals and those who did not.

In this respect, the 180,000 displaced persons who went to Australia were probably the least fortunate. Without much of an ethnic support network, they were often powerless to resist exploitative conditions; even to move around in Australia was difficult. Unskilled laborers were comparatively fortunate; at the end of the two-year contract period, they could stay in their existing jobs or take other similar ones and within a few years buy property. Similarly, craftsmen found themselves in demand, especially those who had received the thorough technical training normal in Eastern Europe. But professional people faced naked discrimination. Their arrival posed a threat to Australia's middle classes—Latvian men, for example, were five times as likely to have a university education as their Australian equivalents. So the professional associations did all they could to exclude them and, in the most notorious case, the Australian Medical Association made sure that medically qualified immigrants could not practice as doctors, except in Antarctica and Papua New Guinea. Immigrants also found that Australian culture was intensely individualistic—based, indeed, on a distrust of and contempt for collective activity and thus quite at odds with the community-oriented cultures they had brought from Eastern Europe. Yet for those prepared to work there were plenty of opportunities in Australia.[10]

Similarly, Slovenians who went to Argentina had to readjust their expectations quickly: "Reports of prosperous farms so fertile that the farmers could sleep during the afternoon turned out to be a fantasy. The farms were in the hands of big landowners who only offered poorly paid, unskilled jobs." Like many immigrants, the newcomers had to start life again at the bottom of the ladder, as carpenters, cleaners, and factory hands, but by hard work and helping one another, "fortified by the community spirit fostered in the camps," within seven or eight years they had a footing in their new country.[11]

In Britain, too, most of the DPs who arrived under the European Volunteer Workers scheme had no fellow nationals to give them a leg up. Many found themselves trapped for decades in the doomed industries, such as textiles, to which they had been sent. Hopes of upward mobility often came to nothing—particularly for women. A follow-up study of twenty-five Latvian women found that almost all had remained in largely working-class areas and seldom achieved more than an adequate standard of living. At the same time, these immigrants tended to stay within their own community and find husbands of their own nationality, so that British officialdom's fantasies of Baltic women providing sound breeding stock were not immediately realized.[12]

Where, however, the displaced persons joined long-established ethnic communities, they usually found it easier to rewrite the contract on which their resettlement was based—the extreme example being Jewish DPs sent to the southern states of the United States as farm laborers, who usually escaped to cities such as New York within a few months. Lithuanians who crossed the Atlantic to work in Canada's forests, gold mines, sugar-beet farms, and homes were often sponsored by "old Lithuanians" who had migrated in the 1920s. "They were good to us," a young woman who worked as a domestic in Winnipeg later recalled. "They invited us to come to the Club; they found us jobs and places to live. We were surprised at how beautifully they spoke Lithuanian." There was, however, one important source of misunderstanding and suspicion: many of the older generation were leftists, sympathetic to the Soviet Union—a social club in Winnipeg had a picture of Stalin on the wall—whereas the newcomers were passionately anti-Communist. But despite these disagreements, the Lithuanians stuck together and helped one another. As a result, many of the younger DPs did very well and, if they had the technical skills and expertise that were in demand, were able to buck the immigrant trend and leap upward—into the middle class—within the first decade. However, those involved in the arts seldom found any new outlet. Baltic displaced persons were shocked by the "unbearable narrowness" of Canadian rural culture—what one of them called the "strange values and even vulgarity of the land to which they had come." "The architecture was banal, literature and music was the preserve of a small elite and the metropolitan life of the mind was rarely felt."[13]

If the Lithuanians in Canada resolved their differences harmoniously, others found it more difficult. Polish immigrants to the Americas in the late 1940s tended to be better educated than their predecessors, and some DPs later recalled that the well-established Polish community in Pittsburgh "had everything ready for us—churches, organizations, newspapers and clubs." They were grateful for the welcome. But they were also appalled at what they perceived as a lack of respect for educated people. The new arrivals were ridiculed—called "princes," "barons," or "masters" as if they had been Polish aristocrats. "We simply did not have much in common with the old," Lidia M. told an interviewer. "What shocked us and is a continuing irritation was the equation of being Polish with the polka and eating kielbasy and pierogi . . . they had such limited notions of Polish culture. We did not blame them, but nevertheless, that's why Polish jokes exist—because these people present Polish culture from A to B and do not know the culture from B to Z." When, however, prominent new arrivals such as Stanisław Mikołajczyk and Stefan Korboński—who had been leaders of the anti-Communist parties in Poland—tried to take over the Polish leadership in the United States, they met with strong opposition from the established groups.[14]

The Canadian-Ukrainian activist Bohdan Panchuk had hoped that the arrival of Ukrainian DPs would revive the community in Canada but had also expressed private fears: "God forbid if we let some of these parasitic bandits into Canada," he had written. Some 35,000 Ukrainians were admitted, partly for political reasons and partly because the government wanted their strong anticommunism to counter Communist influences in Canada's existing Ukrainian community. The latter objective was achieved: within a few years the feuding and violence between Ukrainian DPs in the camps in Germany had been transferred to Canada, much to Panchuk's horror. Following an explosion in a Ukrainian Labor Temple in Toronto in 1949, the pro-Moscow group faded from sight. However, the Canadian government quickly decided that no purpose was served by actively supporting movements or organizations which aimed at breaking up the Soviet Union, and though it was happy to support Ukrainian cultural activities, it was careful not to allow anything more overt.[15]

The newcomers regarded themselves as true Ukrainians and insisted on creating their own separate institutions. Interviewed in the early 1980s, Panchuk recalled that, at a funeral he had recently attended in Quebec, "there was a great steel fence in the cemetery, eight feet high, dividing the cemetery of the old-time Ukrainians from that of their neighbours. There's no difference between the people but they're buried on different sides of the fence—an iron curtain between the dead. What have we learned when you see that sort of barrier?"[16]

· · ·

Jewish displaced persons, who went primarily to Israel and the United States, found that though they were given practical help, they were expected to put the past behind them and get on with life in the present. Some found it easier than others.

In the United States, Jewish DPs got much more support than other groups did. The main Jewish charity, the United Service for New Americans, was the second largest voluntary social service agency in the country (after the Red Cross), with a budget for 1947 of $9,153,500 and a staff of six hundred. But the Jewish agencies, once the full scale of the immigration to the United States became apparent, adopted a ruthlessly practical approach. They would not support anyone for longer than a year, and their workers' priority was to get the DPs "functioning and self-sufficient" as soon as possible. To achieve this, they were encouraged to take the first job that came along, and considerable pressure was exerted to that effect. The agencies also wanted to disperse the DPs around the country as much as possible, whereas the DPs naturally wanted to stay in New York City, where 2 million of the country's 5 million Jews lived. Again, this caused tension.[17]

Jewish social workers made a genuine effort to understand what the newcomers had been through, but they also wanted to get them moving again. In retrospect, it was clear that some mistakes were made. "We didn't really understand what the people were telling us. Their stories sounded too terrible," Ethel Landerman, who worked for a Jewish charity in Pittsburgh in the 1950s, later recalled. Although hospital staff were given classes in Yiddish, they found it hard to make proper contact with the survivors, and the Freudian psychotherapy they provided was not very effective. Beyond that, Landerman remembered, "some of the medical personnel had no patience with the survivors. They complained that the DPs were mourning too long, that they were not becoming American fast enough, that the war was over: 'enough already!' And the survivors felt their impatience. . . . They used to tell me."[18]

The consequences of the policy of speedy placement were apparent a few years later, when survivors began to develop physical and psychological problems which made it difficult for them to hang on to their jobs—or to bring up their children. Some of the cases might perhaps have been avoided had the survivors been given more time to settle themselves and adjust to the United States before being thrust onto the labor market. But in the circumstances of the time it simply was not possible to give all the 140,000 people the breathing time they wanted. For some of them, the shock therapy of being thrown into a job seems to have worked.[19]

Jewish DPs who went to Israel were, of course, a special case; they were going to a country largely populated and governed by their own people. Yet there, too, it was not all plain sailing. The flip side of the charge made by some historians—that the Zionist leadership "used" the Jewish DPs for its own purposes—is that in addition, when the survivors migrated to Israel, they were not given the respect and honor they deserved: that David Ben-Gurion, in Idith Zertal's vivid phrase, "forced silence upon the survivors"; he did not allow them "room for their pain and anguish."[20]

A fine historian, Zertal is here imposing the modern culture of psychotherapy on the past. Her own research has shown that Ben-Gurion was in fact much affected by the plight of the survivors he saw and wrote movingly and perceptively about them. In a letter to his party in Israel from Paris in August 1946, for example, he referred to the "terrible and cruel" experiences of "this crowd of people," who could not be brought back to the path of life by charity or guardians or inundation with gifts, nor by politeness or sermons. "Only friends who come to live among them, be with them, are like them, who will share of themselves in every way, in loyal love, in natural and simple friendship; which in their deeds and lives will set an example and role model—only these can be accepted by them and will anoint their spirit and selves."[21]

Ben-Gurion also had views about how the survivors should be treated in Palestine. "If they [the survivors] arrive and perceive us as the prosecuted and they the prosecutors," he told the youth of the farming movement in November 1947, "we will have to bear it, to get used to it, to understand their soul, to treat them with love, even if it arouses anger and revulsion within us. If we do not gird ourselves with love, we shall not be able to work with them." Zertal thinks that in this remarkable passage, never repeated, Ben-Gurion was revealing his own feelings of guilt. He then went on to try to explain to young people what the new arrivals had been through and warned that to turn them into citizens of the Jewish state would be no easy task.

"Who can demand something of a man whose wife was killed, whose children and parents were annihilated?"[22]

At one stage, the Zionist leadership intended to take practical steps to meet the special needs of survivors. As we have seen, Dr. Zalman Grinberg and other Jewish DP leaders in Germany visited Palestine in 1946 to supervise arrangements for receiving the 100,000 Jewish refugees then expected to go there under the Anglo-American Committee of Inquiry's plan. But that scheme never materialized, and thereafter the flow of events—the blowing up of the King David Hotel, *Exodus,* the war of independence, and so on—thrust such concerns to one side. "Unfortunately, I cannot—nowadays less than at any other time—deal with the integration of immigrants," Ben-Gurion wrote in February 1948 in response to an appeal that he get involved. Tom Segev has argued that in addition to the lack of funds for integration programs, "the yishuv also tended to scorn organized planning and to prefer improvisation." The politician who declared, "We just need to throw the immigrants here and there and they will be absorbed somewhere" was not a lone voice.[23]

None of the three main institutions in Israeli society—the army, the kibbutz movement, and the trade unions—had made serious plans for accommodating the 200,000-odd survivors who arrived in Israel in the first two years of its existence. Although survivors were valued as a way of persuading international opinion of the need for a Jewish state in Palestine and as soldiers, they were not expected to play an important role in the society being forged—there being "a general lack of faith in the human quality of the Holocaust survivors."[24]

Visiting Israel in 1950, the Scottish psychiatrist H. B. M. Murphy concluded that, at a practical level, "the pattern of service supplied to the immigrant is remarkably complete and could be studied with profit by other countries." However, because the psychological state of the refugee immigrants was "not normal," any resettlement scheme needed also to be accompanied by special measures to rehabilitate the refugees mentally as well as physically. Such rehabilitation was being carried out with remarkable success on children by the Youth Aliyah and associated bodies; Murphy was impressed by "the transformation of these orphans from the savage, half-animal, conditions in which they were found after the war to the balanced, sociable, hard-working condition in which one finds them in the *Kibbutzim.*" However, recovery of this sort was easier to effect in children than in adults and easier immediately after the traumatic experience ended than several years later. "In Israel little is being attempted on adults allegedly because they do not think it would succeed but probably for less conscious reasons."[25]

The situation was aggravated by Zionist propaganda, which had aroused exaggerated expectations in immigrants. The gap between the DPs' dreams and the reality they found in Israel led to "disappointment and bitterness"—a common theme in early letters back to Europe. Murphy also thought there should have been more direction of immigrant labor by the state, instead of leaving DPs to discover for themselves what work was available in the new country. Ben-Gurion obviously came to similar conclusions, because in 1949 he toyed with a plan for conscripting immigrants into military or paramilitary units to work on "development projects." The intention was to get rid of "the demoralizing material" among the newcomers and to instill "discipline" and the skills needed to function in the new state. But though the plan was discussed several times, it was never implemented. Perhaps Ben-Gurion recognized that such an approach would be counterproductive—it already being clear that most of the survivors were not prepared to make the psychological changes necessary to function in a kibbutz; indeed, "many immigrants rejected the collective idea in principle," finding the atmosphere there all too reminiscent of the camps.[26]

The popular belief in Israel today is that in the 1950s the survivors were simply abandoned and that there was a "conspiracy of silence"— a general agreement that the events of the past should be swept under the carpet. Another way of putting it would be that they were left to rebuild their lives in their own ways. They did so, on the whole, with some success, and numerous individuals with talent and ingenuity emerged, but they did not produce leaders and they did not make a collective mark on Israeli society. Mystified by the survivors' lack of "collective-public impact," when compared to "the great vitality" of the period immediately after the war, Hanna Yablonka concluded that it was wrong to assume that "Holocaust survivors" remained a separate public group: "Holocaust survivors, notwithstanding their mutual fate during the Second World War, came from different countries in Europe, countries with varied political and cultural traditions. Thus, any long-term organization as a single group with singular objectives was virtually impossible."[27]

. . .

For Dr. Zalman Grinberg, things did not work out well. Soon after his arrival in Palestine, he was appointed the head of Beilinson Hospital in Tel Aviv, the largest in the country, and played a part in the treatment of soldiers and civilians with injuries during the war of 1948. As a protégé of Ben-Gurion, he was spoken of as a future Cabinet minister, and visiting American celebrities such as Leonard Bernstein and Senator John F. Kennedy toured his hospital. This successful and fulfilled life suddenly unraveled in the mid-1950s, when Grinberg became mentally ill. Manic depression had dogged him all his life; the terrible events he had lived through in the 1940s—and in particular the death of his son Emanuel, on whose survival so much energy had been expended—caught up with him. Israel in the early 1950s, his family recalls, was "a cut and dry, do or die, place where mental illness was not tolerated, let alone treated." After going abroad several times during episodes of mania, Grinberg was eventually obliged to give up his job. He moved with his family to the United States and retrained as a psychiatrist, becoming one of the first doctors in America to use the new lithium drug therapy for depression.[28]

In America, Dr. Grinberg reestablished contact with Dr. Samuel Gringauz, his old colleague on the Central Committee of Liberated Jews, now the head of the restitution organization in America. "My father never wanted to apply for any restitution payments from the Germans," his son recalls, "but my mother, who had gone through some very difficult times in the early 1960s, when my parents were almost divorced and my father was hospitalized for about three years, had a more practical attitude and prevailed." Thanks to relatives, their children went to college.

Dr. Grinberg's second son, Yair, now a successful anesthetist in northern Connecticut, remembers his father as a gentle, defeated man. Once, going through old photographs, the boy found one taken in 1946, showing Mayor William O'Dwyer giving Dr. Grinberg a large symbolic key to the city of New York. Impressed and excited, he asked to see it. His father turned pensive for a moment but then his face lit up; " 'You know I always lose my keys,' he said with a laugh." One of the speeches Dr. Grinberg gave during his multicity tour of the United States that year was printed in a book of great speeches. "It was a speech in which he passionately recounted how for centuries Jews contributed to the culture, education and life of Europe, and that same Europe turned to build crematoria for us," his son recalls. "After that he spoke about how the remnant of the survivors had become stuck in the throat of international politics. It was a truly stirring speech, and when I first read it, I could not believe the fire in his heart, especially when contrasted with the person I [knew]."[29]

When Dr. Grinberg died in 1983, he was the assistant attending psychiatrist at a small hospital on Long Island. He received a five-paragraph obituary in *The New York Times*.

After deciding not to go to Israel, Josef Rosensaft remained at Bergen-Belsen, defending the rights of the Jewish DPs and helping to smuggle arms out of Germany to Israel, until the camp was closed in September 1950. After ensuring that the remaining DPs were satisfactorily housed in their new camp, he and his family moved to Montreux in Switzerland. There Rosensaft began a new career as a businessman. The sum of $3,000 which the American Jewish Joint Distribution Committee gave to each member of the Belsen Central Committee's executive board to enable them to take the first steps in their new life, plus introductions to Swiss bankers from friends in London, gave him a start in finance and real estate. According to his friend the Zionist elder statesman Nahum Goldmann, Rosensaft's business "began with jewels and he became in a few years a multimillionaire." His business methods, however, were "quite unconventional." Goldmann later recalled:

> he never kept books, never had a bookkeeper, never paid with checks, but only in cash, and used to go around with ten thousand dollars in cash in his pocket. He probably never broke the law, but he practiced in business what the former Secretary of State John Foster Dulles described politically as "brinkmanship" and had with it for the great part success. He had unusual luck and was a passionate gambler. When he came to a casino the croupiers began to shake; he broke the bank in Monte Carlo and Deauville many times.[30]

In 1958, the Rosensafts moved to New York, and four years later they became American citizens. Josef now began to engage in a new passion, acquiring works of art. Having entered the art market for purely financial reasons, he soon began to take an interest and became a true connoisseur. At one stage he owned some two hundred paintings by Renoir, Pissarro, and his particular favorite, Chagall.

Throughout the postwar period, Rosensaft continued to act as the leader of the Belsen survivors. He financed the publication of two books about the camp, established survivors' associations throughout the world, and every year organized a great meal on the day the British had liberated the camp. He also showed boundless generosity to other survivors from Belsen. Anyone who was in need or whose daughter was getting married had only to turn to him, and he at once sent him money.

In September 1975, Josef Rosensaft collapsed and died of a heart attack in the lobby of Claridge's Hotel in London, two days before Yom Kippur, the Day of Atonement, for which he had planned to return to New York. It turned out that his speculations had been going badly, and, because there were no proper records, his estate had to be sold cheaply. His picture collection, including the twenty Chagalls, mostly went for knockdown prices, and many people lost money. "For the countless Jews and non-Jews who knew him," Nahum Goldmann wrote, "he nevertheless remains unforgettable: his life was the stuff of a novel by Balzac."[31]

Those who worked with and for displaced persons often had similar difficulties readjusting. For example, Robert Jackson, the young Australian whose tireless labors had turned UNRRA round, seemed to have a great career ahead of him when he finally left the organization in August 1947, aged only thirty-seven. In fact, he was burned out. Before he could adequately recover, he was sent to perform a similar miracle at the United Nations. He soon fell foul of the secretary-general, Trygve Lie, was fired, and never again held a senior post.[32]

The American UNRRA worker Kay Hulme and her friend the Belgian nurse Marie-Louise Habets were able to make a gentler adjustment. Nineteen forty-nine was a bad year for Kay—both her mother and her guru G. I. Gurdjieff died, and Marie-Louise went off as an escort nurse on a ship taking DPs to Australia, briefly escaping the austerities of postwar Europe for colonial sunshine and optimism. Back in Germany, Kay "had a twinge of envy for the way [Marie-Louise] was ending her UN service—*with* the DPs in their dramatic moment of delivery to a new life in a new land." She also found the atmosphere within the IRO unappealing.

The humanitarianism that had characterized the early days of the UNRRA appeared to have come full circle; it was a cloak-and-dagger business now. I counted the days until my walking papers would deliver me. It was nip-and-tuck, I said to my roommates, whether I would get out with a shred of faith in my fellow beings left. In short I was fighting mad.[33]

But she soldiered on. She decided she would "finish her refugee job as honorably as the law allowed and then sail for the States with Marie-Louise and the doings and try again to be a writer." She had earned enough to pay for herself for a year and to guarantee sponsorship for Marie-Louise as an immigrant to the United States under the Belgian quota.

The two women sailed with the dogs they had acquired in Europe. Kay found herself, returning to America after six years, "as much of a DP as any of my refugees," hastily catching up with "the new paraphernalia of American life"—television sets, LPs, and best-selling books by authors she had never heard of. To her relief, the literary agency that had sold her last book twelve years earlier was still in business and liked her proposal for a book about her experiences with DPs, to be called *The Wild Place*. She and Marie-Louise drove to California and on the way discovered Arizona. For a year, Marie-Louise worked there as a nurse with Navajo patients while Kay wrote her book. As she finished it, she became a convert to the Catholic Church.

The Wild Place won the 1953 *Atlantic Monthly* Non-Fiction Award and received much critical praise, but only 8,200 copies were sold. When Kay was thinking of a subject for her next book, Marie-Louise suggested that she turn her life into a novel. In *The Nun's Story*, which appeared in 1956, Kay managed to convey Marie-Louise's struggle with her vocation—the conflict between her sense of duty as a nurse and her vow of obedience as a nun—in a way that was acceptable to both Catholics and non-Catholics. The book became a best seller and was filmed with Audrey Hepburn. Its success enabled Kay and Marie-Louise to retire to Hawaii, where Kay continued to write. She died in 1981; Marie-Louise followed a couple of years later.

In 1949, as the IRO's resettlement program was under way, some aid workers fondly imagined that the refugee problem was finally being resolved. Yet even as they sent the DPs on their way, new waves of refugees were being created, as nearly a million people were massacred in riots between Hindus and Muslims in India and Arabs fled from Palestine. By 1952, there were roughly 15 million unsettled refugees around the globe. Then came the Hungarian uprising and the war in Algeria, which together displaced another million or so people. And all that time, there remained in Germany a "hard core," a residue of some 200,000 people whom the IRO had not resettled.[34]

The persistence of the refugee problem led to discussions at the United Nations as to what should take the place of the IRO—debates in which many of the old arguments were rehearsed again. The Russians did not want any UN refugee body to have a "political" role; the Americans were determined not to incur a permanent obligation to pay for the world's refugees. What emerged was a compromise or, putting it more cynically, another illustration of the gulf between ambition and reality which seems endemic to international institutions. The United Nations High Commissioner for Refugees (UNHCR) was a tightly funded organization with a small staff, yet its remit was vast and its definition of refugees and the scope for further action infinite. As a result, wrote the historian Michael Marrus, "like Nansen's High Commission, it became an international mendicant, constantly faced with the UN delegates' and the governments' flagging interest."[35]

It was to overcome official indifference that in 1958 four young British politicians came up with the idea of World Refugee Year, intended to galvanize the international community into doing more to help refugees, not least by using voluntary agencies to overcome some of the bureaucratic obstacles which had arisen. To dramatize the issue, the campaigners devised stunts such as asking the public to "adopt a camp" and building replica camps in British cities where "synthetic refugees" endured at least some of the hardships of real ones. Yet the refugees themselves, as the historian Peter Gatrell has noted, "mostly had a walk-on part in World Refugee Year." A hundred countries took part, and the campaign raised some $90 million, of which $17 million went to UN refugee agencies and the rest to voluntary agencies. As far as the United Nations High Commissioner for Refugees was concerned, the purpose of World Refugee Year (1959–1960) was to "clear the camps"—finally to resettle the 130,000 DPs then still living in and out of camps in Europe.[36]

According to the public rhetoric, this was achieved: World Refugee Year eliminated the few remaining DPs by relaxing the entry requirements of countries such as Canada and Great Britain to give the chronically ill and those with minor criminal records a second chance. But when the British journalist Robert Kee visited DP camps in Germany in 1960, he found numerous individuals who were either still ineligible for emigration, were eligible but had been overlooked by the bureaucrats, or were simply so institutionalized and numbed by camp life that they had failed to take the opportunities offered. Kee criticized the UNHCR for complacency, bureaucracy, and a lack of courage. An aid worker told him that it wasn't really about emigration anymore. Most of the DPs had been in Germany for so long that it made sense to help them integrate. Individuals had the best chance of getting out if they could get sponsored or taken up by religious groups and charities. Drunkenness and asocial behavior were both common and inevitable among the DPs, which only made the resourcefulness and cheerfulness of some of them all the more admirable. "One visits the refugee world," Kee wrote, "expecting to sympathize, pity and help, and one goes away, not only shamed out of all patronage, but inspired by example for the whole business of living."[37]

The DPs still in camps were living in makeshift accommodations—an old Wehrmacht ammunition dump, a former Luftwaffe camp, a collection of back ends of old motor buses and bits of corrugated iron, a clay pit on the outskirts of Heilbronn. By contrast, Kee noticed outside every city huge new blocks of apartment houses being put up for German refugees. Since 1945, West Germany had directly absorbed some 7 million expellees from the East, plus a further 2.5 million Germans who had come from East Germany between 1949 and 1961, the year the Berlin Wall was built.[38] It was by then acknowledged that the vast reserve army of labor represented by the German expellees from the East had played a major part in the economic miracle, or *Wirtschaftswunder,* which by 1958 had made the West German economy once again the largest in Europe; in 1960 it was growing at an annual rate of 9 percent, compared to 2.6 percent in Britain. The *Vertriebene* were hardworking, saved their earnings, and were prepared to move in search of work—by the mid-1950s only about a third of them remained in the villages where they had originally been settled. As Kee put it, "the refugee flood had actually worked to West

Germany's advantage by providing her both with a tremendous labour force and a vast internal market."[39]

However, the process of integrating the expellees into West German society was still going on. The Konrad Adenauer government had tried hard to make them welcome, passing an Equalization of Burdens Law, which made Germany's businesses pay for the cost of rehousing them, and establishing in Bonn a Federal Ministry of Expellees, which chronicled their suffering in enormous detail. No German political party could afford to offend them by accepting Potsdam and recognizing the new frontier with Poland. And so the place of the expellees in German life meant that the country could not quickly put the war behind it. Only when Willy Brandt became chancellor could Germany accept the new boundaries to its east and so begin to make peace with Poland and Russia. When, in 1970, Brandt knelt at the monument to those killed in the Warsaw ghetto, Europe could start to move on.

During the 1960s, the way in which the history of the Second World War was perceived and discussed in Western societies—most notably, in the United States—changed profoundly. The concept of the Holocaust emerged.

For two decades after the war, the Nazi extermination of the Jews was not an important part of Western public culture. In the United States, as the historian Peter Novick has shown, non-Jews simply did not take this phenomenon on board; their attention was focused on current political questions—such as communism and civil rights—and on the aftermath of Hiroshima. Jewish leaders, for their part, chose not to emphasize the subject either. At the time of the Cold War, they had no wish to reinforce the equation in the public mind between Jews and Communists by drawing attention to the Germans' wartime behavior. Nor was the role of victim one to be sought after; in the upbeat, confident culture of the 1950s, it aroused contempt rather than sympathy. Finally, the survivors themselves were still a marginalized element within the American Jewish community. Much the same was true in Europe. "In the two decades following 1945," the historian Tony Judt has concluded, "Jews and non-Jews alike paid only occasional attention to Auschwitz and its implications."[40]

In the 1960s, a remarkable change took place. Although this was in part due to the passing of the anti-Communist hysteria, its main catalyst was the trial of Adolf Eichmann in Jerusalem in 1961, during which the Nazis' plans for the extermination of Europe's Jews were ventilated at some length. "This was the first time that what we now call the Holocaust was presented to the American public as an entity in its own right, distinct from Nazi barbarism in general," wrote Peter Novick. "In the United States, the word 'Holocaust' first became firmly attached to the murder of European Jewry as a result of the trial." A further consequence was that American Jews lost most of their inhibitions about discussing events in the 1940s.[41]

As far as the DP story is concerned, the foregrounding of "the Holocaust" had two important consequences. First, it led historians to look again at the wartime period, examining from the modern perspective the failure of the Western Allies to rescue the Jews from their fate. Second, it provoked a reexamination of the process by which displaced persons had been resettled in the 1940s. The public was now astonished to discover that some of the "quiet neighbors" living respectably alongside them were in fact "war criminals."

In the late 1970s, pressure from the U.S. Congress and newspapers such as *The New York Times* led to the creation of a Special Investigations Unit in the Justice Department to investigate and prosecute ex-Nazis in the United States. Allan A. Ryan, the lawyer put in charge, was horrified by what he found. "Nazi war criminals came here by the thousands, through the openly deliberated public policy of this country, formulated by Congress and administered by accountable officials," Ryan wrote in 1984. "And it is the more disturbing because the proof is abundant. . . . The overwhelming majority of Nazi criminals came through the front door, with all their papers in order. They came here not by conniving with lawless government officials but by the infinitely easier method of simply deceiving the honest ones."[42]

Such discoveries generated a worldwide initiative to find and prosecute war criminals. The legal difficulties were often enormous: in 1991, the introduction of a War Crimes Bill, intended to extend the jurisdiction of British courts so that they could try people alleged to have committed or abetted mass murder during the Second World War in other countries, and while they were not British citizens, provoked a constitutional battle between the two chambers of the British Parliament. Younger politicians tended to favor such initiatives, older ones to deplore them. Some countries, such as Norway and Sweden, refused from the start to take part in the process.[43]

Since the 1970s, some major war criminals have been tried and convicted. But the most famous example of such retrospective justice, the thirty-year prosecution of the former Cleveland car mechanic John Demjanjuk, is more complicated. Born in Ukraine, Demjanjuk went to the United States as a DP in 1952 after telling immigration officials that he had lived in Poland before the war. As we have seen, it was common for Ukrainians to invent such stories, but Demjanjuk stated that he had worked on a farm at Sobibor—at that time little more than a railway halt but later notorious as the site of a Jewish death camp. However, it was because he resembled a certain "Ivan the Terrible," a Ukrainian who had committed appalling atrocities as a guard at another death camp, Treblinka, that Demjanjuk was stripped of his U.S. citizenship in 1981, deported to Israel, tried, and sentenced to death in April 1988—only for it then to emerge during the appeal process that prosecution evidence provided by the Soviet government had been faked and that Ivan the Terrible was in all likelihood a certain Ivan Marchenko. By that stage it was clear that Demjanjuk had probably been at Sobibor as a guard or driver and had therefore been present when horrible crimes were committed, but in a minor capacity. He was small fry: in the 1940s, no one would have bothered with him. But the prominence of his case and—as Gitta Sereny has argued—the need to justify the Justice Department's expensive office meant that the legal process was restarted. Eventually, in 2009—by then eighty-nine years old and thirty-two years after his first arrest—Demjanjuk was deported to Germany and put on trial, charged with 28,060 counts of accessory to murder. The case had become symbolic of the willingness of the Americans and Germans still to prosecute Nazi war criminals. For the Ukrainian-American community, however, Demjanjuk had become a martyr, one of their own attacked by the traditional enemies, the Communists and the Jews.[44]

In one other way, the displaced persons era has repeatedly resurfaced: the question of whether compensation should be paid to those who were forced laborers in Germany has refused to go away.

One of the principal charges against defendants in the Nuremberg Trials such as Fritz Sauckel and Albert Speer was that they managed a "program of slave labor." Though the court never defined precisely what was meant by the term, it was the major count on which Sauckel and other defendants were tried and convicted. So one might have expected some at least of the laborers to be compensated.

However, the complex diplomatic and legal issues involved enabled the West German (and later German) government to play a very clever hand, paying reparations only when necessary to make particular foreign policy gains—to Israel, Western Europe (mainly France), Poland, and finally (after the reunification of Germany) to other parts of Eastern Europe. The fundamental point, however, is that until recently West German courts did not accept that forced labor was a "typical Nazi wrongdoing." Indeed, in a key ruling in 1960—rejecting the claim of a Pole who had been arrested during the war, sent to Germany for forced labor, and later worked at Dachau and Buchenwald—the Federal Constitutional Court argued that the thinking of the labor authorities had been "solely to recruit new workers to bolster the German economy, particularly the armaments industry." In line with this ruling, the German government has never admitted liability to individual claims. Instead it has made "voluntary" payments, not to individuals but to organizations—which have then distributed the moneys.[45]

In the 1950s, the Bonn government pleaded poverty: it argued that the much-needed recovery of the country could not take place if it were saddled with huge compensation claims (as the Weimar Republic had been with reparations). It also persuaded the Americans that priority should be given to the repayment of creditors, the main one being Washington. In the event, the rapid recovery of West Germany's economy enabled Bonn to pay off its foreign debt ahead of schedule. During the Cold War, claims from the countries of Eastern Europe were met with counterclaims on behalf of Germans expelled from the East, but those from Western European countries—with which Bonn was by now linked economically and militarily—were more difficult to ignore. Consequently, in the early 1960s the Bonn government "voluntarily" paid out some 876 million deutsche marks to eleven Western European countries, with France receiving almost 400 million.

In the 1970s, Willy Brandt's policy of *Ostpolitik*—of normalizing Germany's relations with its Western neighbors, especially Poland—required some resolution of the long-standing Polish claim for compensation. Under the agreement finally reached in 1975, the Germans, while continuing to deny the legality of Poland's claims, agreed to grant it a "soft" loan of 1 billion marks, and to provide a further 1.3 billion marks in settlement of pension claims. In return, Poland allowed some 125,000 ethnic Germans still in the country to immigrate to the Federal Republic.

The next payment became necessary in 1990. Following the fall of the Berlin Wall, the German people and Germany's politicians made it clear that they wished to form a united German state and were willing finally to accept the terms of the Potsdam Agreement as they affected their country. The question of compensation for enforced labor played an important part in the so-called four-plus-two negotiations (among the foreign ministers of the Soviet Union, the United States, Britain, and France, on the one side, and the two Germanys, on the other); once again, the Germans agreed to make payments, without conceding the legal principle. The Bonn government reached agreement with the states of the former Soviet Union and with Poland for a one-off payment of 1.5 billion marks, to be distributed to victims of the Nazis by foundations established in those countries. However, the historian Ulrich Herbert wrote, "during these negotiations, Bonn stuck to the view that forced labor was not a typical form of Nazi wrongdoing that entitled its victims to compensation. The Bonn government was determined not to give up the legal position it had always adhered to; it was concerned to avoid opening the door to further demands by forced laborers from other countries."[46]

In the 1990s, that position became less tenable. American law firms brought group actions in the U.S. courts against particular companies such as Daimler-Benz, posing a threat to their capacity to operate in the U.S. market, while German courts began to take a different line. The award, in November 1997, of 15,000 marks to an elderly Jewish woman who had worked in a munitions factory at Auschwitz aroused fears that it would "open the floodgates": with at least 100,000 "ex-slaves" still alive who had received no compensation, the total bill "might run to billions." The German response was two-pronged. On the one hand, giants such as Volkswagen—which had hitherto denied access to its archives and ruthlessly airbrushed its past—now hired prominent historians to investigate its record under the Third Reich. Critics who asserted that such businesses "either tried to hamstring historians or retained researchers who viewed corporate wartime transgressions as unavoidable" missed the point. Sophisticated German managements saw that by washing all their dirty linen in public—by revealing every shameful detail of their past with academic thoroughness—they could simply kill off journalistic interest in the story: it was cheaper to pay historians than to pay compensation.[47]

Then, in 1999, the government of Chancellor Gerhard Schröder suggested a way of finally settling the issue. He proposed that a fund be established, jointly funded by the German government and German industry, to pay compensation to victims; and that, in return, the German concerns be granted legal security against further action in the U.S. courts. His idea was quickly accepted in principle, but months of legal wrangling followed; the two sides disagreed over the size of a proposed compensation settlement; the companies initially offered $1.7 billion, against claims of more than $20 billion; then there were further challenges in the German Bundestag. During the process, it was estimated that two hundred elderly survivors were dying every day. But, finally, on August 12, 2000, a German law came into effect designating seven organizations to make payments to former slave and forced laborers. The ensuing process was not perfect. German industry was slow to come up with its half of the 5.1 billion euros needed to run the operation, despite getting tax write-offs and legal security against further claims. Many former slave workers' claims were denied because they did not have documentary proof that they had not gone to Germany voluntarily—such documents as existed had often been removed by the Soviet authorities in 1945. Inevitably, too, there were claims that much of the money stuck to the fingers of lawyers.[48]

When the fund was closed in June 2007, more than 4.37 billion euros had been paid to 1.7 million victims of the Hitler era around the world. The largest group of recipients was non-Jews in Poland and Ukraine. The sums individuals received were not large—up to 7,669 euros for "slave labor," up to 2,556 euros for forced labor in industry, and up to 1,022 euros for forced labor in agriculture. But for some individuals they made a difference. Thus, an elderly Ukrainian woman stood to receive an amount which was many times her monthly pension and would enable her to afford the expensive medication she needed.[49]

For all that, this chapter is now finally closed. "At least with these symbolic payments," said the German president, "the suffering of the victims has been publicly acknowledged after decades of being forgotten."[50]

If there was a single defining characteristic to the communities which the displaced persons created in exile, it was anticommunism. For four decades the refugees did all they could to keep alight the flame of opposition to Moscow. The Russians, for their part, periodically retaliated, as when the Ukrainian Nationalist leader Stepan Bandera was assassinated with a cyanide gun in Munich in 1959. But with the passing of time, as those who had fled Eastern Europe aged and their children grew up in Western societies, the task of keeping the flag flying grew more difficult. In 1960s Canada the son of Ukrainian DPs found his parents' obsession with their homeland embarrassing. "When our parents tried to pass on their mantle to us, most of us declined the offer," Lubomyr Luciuk wrote. "We were schooled to think that their nationalism was an evil, responsible for some of the greatest crimes of the century, that nationalism was a dirty word." Two decades later, a study of Lithuanian exiles found that "despite its effort to resist it, the Lithuanian Diaspora is being increasingly absorbed into American society." Yet while the relations between the superpowers gradually improved, the fundamental division in Europe remained. "The Cold War seems a permanent fixture," the historian Mark Wyman wrote in his study of displaced persons published in 1989.[51]

That very year, it all began to change. The collapse of the Soviet Empire in 1991 gave many displaced persons the chance finally to fulfill their dreams and to return to their homelands. There were many emotional reunions: personal ones with family and broader national ones, often centered round choral festivals, where choirs from Canada and the United States joined singers from the Baltic states in moving assertions of their common culture—in Riga in 1990, some 19,000 people from all over the world sang together in the festival chorus before marching to the Freedom Monument to lay flowers at its base. Groups and individuals from the diaspora quickly joined in the emerging politics in their former homelands—or, in some cases, made quick killings by buying up real estate at knock-down prices.

But as the euphoria subsided, practical problems appeared. Half a century of separation had created many barriers. Returning DPs often found it impossible to recover confiscated property and met with resentment from ordinary people who had lived through the rigors of Soviet rule. "You had a good life while we suffered" was a common refrain. "The locals are not very keen on having us move in," a Lithuanian woman admitted after her first visit to the country since 1944. Experience of Communist rule, not life abroad, provided the dominant narrative; and though the exiles' money and experience of democracy and capitalism were valued, they remained apart. Very few chose to return permanently. There were, though, several prominent exceptions, such as Valdas Adamkus, who was elected president of Lithuania in 1998 after a distinguished career as a civil servant in the United States.[52]

"When the immigrant tries to maintain his identity through embracing the 'old country,'" the archbishop of Toronto wrote after attending a reunion in Slovenia in 1995, "that identity becomes idealized. Returning to it the emigrant sees at first only what he or she wants to see; on the second or third visit he may see that for which he is not prepared; he may perceive that his ideal country either never existed or has ceased to exist."[53]

Notes

ABBREVIATIONS

AP S. Armstrong-Reid and E. Murray, *Armies of Peace: Canada and the UNRRA Years* (Toronto, 2008).

ASH L. Dinnerstein, *America and the Survivors of the Holocaust* (New York, 1982).

BC 2003 J.-D. Steinert and I. Weber-Newth (eds.), *Beyond Camps and Forced Labour: Current International Research on Survivors of Nazi Persecution. Proceedings of the International Conference, London, 29–31 January 2003* (Osnabrück, 2005).

BC 2006 J.-D. Steinert and I. Weber-Newth (eds.), *Beyond Camps and Forced Labour. Current International Research on Survivors of Nazi Persecution. Proceedings of the International Conference, London, 11–13 January 2006* (Osnabrück, 2008).

CAMGCOP F. S. V. Donnison, *Civil Affairs and Military Government: Central Organisation and Planning* (1966).

CAMGNWE F. S. V. Donnison, *Civil Affairs and Military Government: North West Europe, 1944–46* (1961).

DBPO M. E. Pelly et al. (eds.), *Documents on British Policy Overseas,* series I, volume 5. *Germany and Western Europe, 11 August–31 December 1945* (1990), series I, volume 6. *Eastern Europe, August 1945–April 1946* (1991).

FRUS *Foreign Relations of the United States, 1942–1950* (Washington, D.C., 1967–78).

HEAEG S. Thernstrom et al. (eds.), *Harvard Encyclopedia of American Ethnic Groups* (Cambridge, Mass., 1980).

HFW U. Herbert, *Hitler's Foreign Workers: Enforced Foreign Labour in Germany Under the Third Reich* (Cambridge, England, 1997).

HST/OT Harry S. Truman Library, oral testimony.

IWM Imperial War Museum.

KHL Letters and Papers of Kathryn C. Hulme, Beinecke Library, Yale University

LR M. Z. Rosensaft (ed.), *Life Reborn: Jewish Displaced Persons 1945–1951* (Washington, D.C., 2001).

NPA National Planning Association, Washington, D.C.

NYT *The New York Times.*

ODNB *Oxford Dictionary of National Biography.*

PCW Kathryn C. Hulme, Polish Camp Wildflecken Report, June 1947. UNA: S1021, Box 81, File 1.

TLS *Times Literary Supplement.*

TNA The National Archives, Kew, London.

UC Kathryn C. Hulme, *Undiscovered Country: The Search for Gurdjieff* (1966; Lexington, Ky., 1997).

UD Sir Frederick Morgan, "UNRRA Diary," Imperial War Museum.

UNA United Nations Archive, New York.

USHMM United States Holocaust Memorial Museum, Washington, D.C.

Woodbridge *UNRRA: The History of the United Nations Relief and Rehabilitation Administration*, 3 vols. (New York, 1950).

WP Kathryn C. Hulme, *The Wild Place* (Boston, 1953).

INTRODUCTION: "AN ENORMOUS DEAL OF KINDNESS"

1. Conradi, *Iris Murdoch*, pp. 205, 152–3.
2. Novick, *Holocaust*, p. 20; Burstin, *After the Holocaust*, p. 112.
3. D. Reynolds, "From World-War to Cold-War: The Wartime Alliance and Postwar Transitions, 1941–1947," *Historical Journal* 45 (2002), pp. 211–27.
4. Mazower, *Dark Continent*, p. 215.
5. Piotr Wrobel, quoted in Burds, "Ethnicity, Memory and Violence."
6. Sereny, *German Trauma*, p. 25.
7. Hansi Pollak to Sir Frederick Morgan, November 5, 1947, Morgan Papers, IWM; Sir Robert Jackson, oral history, Bodleian Library Ms. Eng. C, 4678; Woodbridge, *UNRRA*.
8. Oldfield, *Women Humanitarians*, p. xi; Shephard, *War of Nerves;* Glover, *Humanity.*
9. McNeill, *Rivers of Babylon*, pp. 37, 53–64, 49.
10. Pettiss and Taylor, *After the Shooting*, p. 126.
11. A. Oakley, "Eugenics, Social Medicine and the Career of Richard Titmuss in Britain 1935–1950," *British Journal of Sociology* 42 (1991), pp. 165–94; G. R. Searle, "Eugenics and Politics in Britain in the 1930s," *Annals of Science* 35 (1979), pp. 159–69.
12. Schwarz, *Redeemers.*
13. Bauer, *Flight and Rescue;* Bauer, *Out of the Ashes;* Bauer, "The DP Legacy."
14. Hitchcock, *Bitter Road*. Papers given to conferences on DPs at the Remarque Institute, New York, in 2001 and the Imperial War Museum, London, in 2003 and 2006.
15. Mankowitz, *Life Between Memory and Hope*, p. 9.
16. Letter to Mr. Fuller, Deputy Director, and Mrs. Brown, Welfare Officer, of Team 71, DP Camp Hohenfels, from a Polish Scout, October 12, 1945, UNA.

CHAPTER I: FEEDING THE WAR MACHINE

1. "VAD Nurse. Student of Painting in the Art Academy of Cracow Before the War," unpublished memoir, written 1946. Appendix to Korwin, "No Man's People," in Arnold-Forster Papers.
2. Tooze, *Wages of Destruction*, pp. 166–99.
3. U. Herbert, "Forced Labour."
4. Tooze, *Wages of Destruction*, p. 363; *HFW*, p. 132.
5. *HFW*, p. 105.

6. Hitler's *Mein Kampf* took this view. Modern historians such as Avner Offner have argued that the blockade was nothing like as effective as was thought at the time. However, as Hew Strachan has written, "The memory of the blockade is central to German thinking about the war and the future waging of war in Europe, however solid or not the analytical foundations on which that thought rested." E-mail to author, February 11, 2008. I thank Professor Strachan for clarifying this point.

7. Tooze, *Wages of Destruction*, pp. 515–22; Mazower, *Hitler's Empire*, pp. 159–66; Sereny, *Speer*, pp. 313–16; Dallin, *German Rule*, pp. 409–50.

8. Berkhoff, *Harvest*, pp. 25–74

9. Humbert, *Résistance*, pp. 132–3.

10. Berkhoff, *Harvest*, p. 261.

11. Nolte (ed.), *Häftlinge*, pp. 54–9.

12. Tooze, *Wages of Destruction*, p. 517.

13. I have borrowed the phrase "Mary Poppins of the steppes" from Nicholas Stargardt. Stargardt, *Witnesses of War*, p. 157; Berkhoff, *Harvest*, pp. 265–6; HFW, pp. 188–9, 439. There is disagreement over figures: 50,000 "eastern maids" (Berkhoff); 500,000 "forced nannies" (Stargardt); 100,000 "foreign maids" (Herbert).

14. Homze, *Foreign Labor in Nazi Germany*, pp. 264–71; HFW, pp. 313–25.

15. Tooze, *Wages of Destruction*, pp. 539–40.

16. Mazower, *Hitler's Empire*, pp. 274–90; Tooze, *Wages of Destruction*, pp. 538–51.

17. HFW, pp. 256–358.

18. Vinen, *Unfree French*, pp. 247–312; Robbe-Grillet, *Ghosts*, pp. 89–91, 103–8.

19. HFW, pp. 282–3.

20. Ibid., p. 303.

21. Ibid., pp. 304–8.

22. Ibid., pp. 239–47.

23. Lagrou, *Legacy*, pp. 144–5.

24. "Notes on the Situation of Eastern Workers in Germany," Embassy Secretary Starke, quoted in HFW, pp. 322–3. Ulrich Herbert gives no more information about Starke, nor does he explain why a German Foreign Ministry official should have concerned himself with this matter.

25. Humbert, *Résistance*, pp. 200–1.

26. HFW, pp. 317–23. Many historians have argued that had the RAF continued to attack the Ruhr in late 1943 instead of switching to Berlin, it might have won the war—or at any rate done Germany much more damage.

27. Tooze, *Wages of Destruction*, pp. 618–24; Mazower, *Hitler's Empire*, pp. 307–28.

28. Woropay, *Road to the West*, pp. 1–20.

29. "An Estonian Girl Speaks," in Marta Korwin, "No Man's People," in Arnold-Forster Papers.

30. Mazower, *Hitler's Empire*, p. 367.

CHAPTER 2: FOOD AND FREEDOM

1. Medlicott, *Economic Blockade*, vol. 1, pp. 551–7, 666; Pimlott (ed.), *War Diaries of Dalton*, p. 76; Gilbert, *Finest Hour*, p. 743; Olsen (ed.), *Harold Nicolson, Diaries and Letters*, p. 19.

2. Mazower, *Inside Hitler's Greece*, pp. 23–48; Black, *Cause for Our Times*, pp. 5–21. The

British felt that there was no way, when dealing with a regime like that of the Nazis, of making sure that food reached those it was intended for.

3. *CAMGCOP*, p. 137; Pimlott (ed.), *War Diaries of Dalton*, p. 229; Leith-Ross, "by no means an uncritical admirer" of Keynes, was "the frequent recipient of acerbic comments for his over-eagerness to commit Britain to expensive relief schemes which it could not afford." Skidelsky, *Keynes*, vol. 3, pp. 110, 142.
4. Leith-Ross, *Money Talks*, p. 289; TNA: T 188/253.
5. Patenaude, *Big Show;* Weissman, *Hoover and Famine Relief;* Pimlott (ed.), *War Diaries of Dalton*, pp. 525–6.
6. Acheson, *Present at the Creation*, pp. 65–7; *CAMGCOP*, pp. 138–9.
7. Leith-Ross, *Money Talks*, p. 289.
8. NPA, *Relief for Europe*, pp. 37–44; Patenaude, *Big Show*, pp. 28–48.
9. Harvey, *Wartime Diaries*, p. 31. Churchill and Roosevelt had met for the first time in London in 1918; Roberts, *Masters and Commanders*, p. 9.
10. Speaking to Eden in March 1943, Roosevelt "reiterated his belief that the Big Four should make 'all the real decisions,' since they 'would be the powers for many years to come that would have to police the world.' " Divine, *Second Chance*, p. 114.
11. Hoopes and Brinkley, *FDR*, pp. 1–74; Divine, *Second Chance*, pp. 98–135.
12. Huxley et al., *When Hostilities Cease.*
13. Asquith, *Famine;* Fry, *Quaker Adventure;* Marrus, *The Unwanted*, pp. 15–21; Vincent, *Politics of Hunger;* Baron and Gattrell (eds.), *Homelands;* Weissman, *Hoover;* Healy, *Vienna and the Fall of the Habsburg Empire.*
14. Chatham House, *Relief and Reconstruction in Europe;* Mackenzie, *Medical Relief in Europe;* Save the Children Fund, *Children in Bondage;* Bourne, *Starvation in Europe;* NPA, *Relief for Europe;* J. Marrack, "Food for Starving Europe," A. Bourne, "Postwar Medical Relief," K. G. Brookes, "The Re-establishment of Displaced Persons," in Huxley et al., *When Hostilities Cease*, pp. 99–124.
15. Brookes, "The Re-establishment of Displaced Persons," in Huxley et al., *When Hostilities Cease*, pp. 99–124.
16. Terry, "Conflicting Signals"; Breitman, *Official Secrets*, pp. 88–109; Wasserstein, *Britain and the Jews of Europe*, pp. 155–6.

CHAPTER 3: "THE ORIGIN OF THE PERPETUAL MUDDLE"

1. Atkinson, *Army at Dawn*, pp. 327–92.
2. Roberts, *Masters and Commanders*, p. 297.
3. Coles and Weinberg, *Civil Affairs*, pp. 3–62, 65; Ziemke, *U.S. Army*, pp. 3–23; Murphy, *Diplomat*, p. 185; Acheson, *Present at the Creation*, p. 42.
4. *CAMGCOP*, pp. 178–81; Murphy, *Diplomat*, pp. 160–61. Murphy also came under pressure from American Jewish groups to restore Algerian Jews to the favored status they had enjoyed prior to the Vichy government. He felt that to take such a step in wartime would provoke Algeria's Muslim majority.
5. V. Petrov, *Money and Conquest: Allied Occupation Currencies in World War II* (Baltimore, 1967), pp. 91–2, quoted in Ellwood, *Italy*, p. 64.
6. Coles and Weinberg, *Civil Affairs*, pp. 188–216.
7. Ibid., pp. 322–6; Weindling, *Epidemics and Genocide*, pp. 374–5.
8. Snowden, *Conquest of Malaria*, p. 199. The use of convicts and Arab women as trial subjects prefigured the way the contraceptive pill was later tried out on Puerto Rican

women. After the war, when DDT was heavily marketed in the United States, the "miracle in Naples" featured prominently in advertisements and helped to raise the hydrocarbon insecticide to the miraculous status it enjoyed until Rachel Carson's *Silent Spring* exposed its devastating effects on the food chain.

9. Harrison, *Medicine and Victory*, pp. 128–84; Weindling, *Epidemics and Genocide*, 322–33; Snowden, *Conquest of Malaria*, pp. 198–212; Rendel, *Sword and Olive*, p. 232; Coles and Weinberg, *Civil Affairs*, pp. 322–7, 232.

10. Coles and Weinberg, *Civil Affairs*, pp. 328–33.

11. Ibid., pp. 153–6.

12. Acheson, *Present at the Creation*, p. 79; Coles and Weinberg, *Civil Affairs*, pp. 153–4. British military planners assumed that relief would consist of 2,000 calories a day, the minimum needed to "prevent disease and unrest"—an ambitious goal, as it turned out; *CAMGCOP*, p. 146.

13. Acheson, *Present at the Creation*, p. 68.

14. Vandenberg (ed.), *Private Papers*, pp. 66–74; Fox, "Origins of UNRRA."

15. Fox, "Origins of UNRRA," p. 584; Rendel, *Sword and Olive*, p. 235; Divine, *Second Chance*, p. 157. Fox claimed that news of the signing of the UNRRA agreement, "broadcast by radio, press and pamphlets dropped from the air, gave immediate courage to peoples suffering under the controls of the Axis."

16. Leith-Ross, *Money Talks*, pp. 294–5. Knowledge of the experience of Austria after the First World War made Leith-Ross a consistent advocate of this view.

17. Woodbridge, vol. 1, pp. 30–2. "To us," Acheson wrote later, "the word had no definition; rather it was propitiation by ignorance of the unknown. UNRRA would have done its work and passed away before we were to know what rehabilitation really required from us." Only in 1949 would rehabilitation be politically feasible, in the form of what became known as Marshall Plan aid. Acheson, *Present at the Creation*, p. 69.

18. Kulischer, *Displacement of Population;* Evelyn Waugh, *Sword of Honour* (1965; 1999), p. 605.

19. "UNRRA Decides," *The Economist*, December 4, 1943; "Potiphar," *They Must Not Starve*, pp. 12–23.

20. NPA, *UNRRA. Gateway to Recovery*, pp. 15, 17–24, 57; Arnold-Forster, "UNRRA's prospects." The first UN agency was actually the Food and Agriculture Organization, which never attracted the same attention as UNRRA.

21. Nevins, *Lehman;* H. G. Nicholas (ed.), *Washington Despatches*, p. 123; Berlin, *Flourishing*, pp. 363, 375.

22. Blum, *V Was for Victory*, pp. 304–7; Borgwardt, *New Deal*, pp. 76–9; Brinkley, *End of Reform*, p. 141.

23. Klemmé, *Inside Story*, pp. ix–x, 8; *NYT*, May 21, 1944: "The great zeal and fine idealism possessed by these people turned to disappointment later on when they faced Europe's almost insoluble problems."

24. The son of a Conservative politician, Will Arnold-Forster trained as a painter, served in the navy in the First World War, and became a fervent advocate of the League of Nations Union in the 1920s. Although much respected within the League, he never managed to gain acceptance in mainstream academia and remained a marginal figure within the Labour Party's foreign policy establishment. "He still thinks and talks in the terms of long ago," Hugh Dalton complained in January 1941. Will's first wife, Katherine "Ka" Cox, had as a young woman attracted the attention of both Rupert

Brooke and Virginia Woolf, whose diaries and letters contain many spiteful references to Arnold-Forster. Arnold-Forster Papers; F. Wilson, *In the Margins of Chaos*, p. 269.

25. Woodbridge, vol. 3, pp. 3–18.

26. *The Economist,* July 15, 1944.

27. Nevins, *Lehman,* p. 226.

28. Ibid., pp. 224–9; Pimlott (ed.), *War Diaries of Hugh Dalton,* p. 613; House of Lords, December 15, 1944; Dallas, *Poisoned Peace,* p. 429.

29. Keeny, "Reminiscences," London School of Economics; Salter, *Memoirs,* p. 277; Rendel, *Sword and Olive,* p. 237; Acheson, *Present at the Creation,* p. 43; Blum, *Price of Vision,* p. 251; Nevins, *Lehman,* p. 238.

30. TNA: FO 371/41164.

31. Best, "British Foreign Office," pp. 87–100.

32. *The Times,* February 14, 1945; *CAMGCOP,* pp. 163–5.

33. Woodbridge, vol. 2, pp. 342–7; House of Lords, December 14, 1944. See *CAMGNWE* for problems in liberated Europe.

34. Leith-Ross, *Money Talks,* p. 305; Conradi, *Iris Murdoch,* pp. 206–7.

35. Calder-Marshall, *Watershed,* pp. 42–6 (Calder-Marshall thought the product's name was "Kutiestix."); Woodbridge, vol. 2, pp. 88–9; Macmillan, *War Diaries,* p. 541.

36. Richard Law, December 1994. TNA: FO 371/41144.

37. Proudfoot, *European Refugees,* pp. 107–19; id., "Anglo-American [DP] program . . . "

38. Proudfoot, "Anglo-American [DP] Program"; Hansi Pollak to General Morgan, November 5, 1947. Morgan Papers, IWM.

CHAPTER 4: "HALF THE NATIONALITIES OF EUROPE ON THE MARCH"

1. "A Soldier from the Home Army," Korwin Papers.

2. "A Man at Fourteen," Korwin Papers.

3. Moorehead, *Eclipse,* p. 195.

4. Padover, *Psychologist,* p. 273; Moorehead, *Eclipse,* pp. 212–13.

5. Proudfoot, *European Refugees,* p. 158. Over the same period, the Soviet forces liberated about the same number of displaced foreigners in Central Europe, eastern Germany, and Austria. Of these, the overwhelming majority (76 percent) were Russian. In Italy there was a total of 95,590 persons, Denmark had some 250,000, and Norway had 84,000 Soviet nationals and 57,000 other displaced persons.

6. Hitchcock, *Bitter Road,* pp. 255–6; Urquhart, *Life in Peace and War,* p. 79; Mosley, *Report from Germany,* pp. 66–83; TNA: WO 171/8004.

7. Padover, *Psychologist,* pp. 276–7; Ziemke, *U.S. Army,* pp. 200–207, 239; Jacobmeyer, *Zwangsarbeiter,* pp. 46–8; Shephard, *After Daybreak,* pp. 29–30.

8. M. J. Smith, *Dachau,* pp. 7–67. Smith learned the difference between refugees and displaced persons: "Refugees are civilians in their own country who want to return to their homes but, because of the chaotic conditions created by the war, need help to do so. Obviously homeless Germans are refugees, but not our responsibility unless they are concentration camp survivors. DPs are people outside the boundaries of their own countries who, because of the war, need help to survive and later to go home or to some other country. There are many categories of DPs, such as stateless persons, political prisoners, fugitives, enemy and ex-enemy nationals, and ex-prisoners of war. However, most of the DPs will be the people driven into Germany by the Nazis and used by them as laborers." Ibid., p. 8.

9. Coles and Weinberg, *Civil Affairs,* p. 858.

10. Korwin, "No Man's People," pp. 13–33, in Arnold-Forster Papers.

11. Ibid.

12. Ziemke, *U.S. Army,* pp. 234–8. See also Abzug, *Vicious Hearts;* Bridgman, *End of Holocaust;* Shephard, *After Daybreak.* There were, though, Alan Moorehead argued, special reasons. "A shudder of horror went round the world when the news of the concentration camps was published," he wrote, "but only, I think, because of the special interest and the special moment in the war." Moorehead believed that the timing was crucial. "We were engrossed with Germany and it is perhaps not too subtle to say that since Germany was manifestly beaten, people wanted to have a justification for their fight, a proof that they were engaged against evil." Contemporary reports tended to rely on a simple dichotomy between good and evil, perpetrator and victim. They did not emphasize the fact that most of the victims were Jewish, let alone see what was uncovered in 1945 as the last act of the Germans' "Final Solution" of the Jewish question. They did not explore the complex web of economic and ideological processes which lay behind the camps and dealt only in the most rudimentary way with the Nazi chain of command; neither did they disentangle the complex internal divisions within the camps.

13. Urquhart, *Life in Peace and War,* p. 81. Following the stern words in 1942, London and Washington did their best to bury public discussion of the Jewish issue—partly because of the scrutiny of their own actions it produced, partly because they did not want to be depicted by Nazi propaganda as fighting the war for the Jews, and partly because (in the British case) they were frightened that Hitler might call their bluff and ask them to take hundreds of thousands of Jews. They had had some success in this. At the same time, however, the terrible fact that most of Europe's Jews were dead by the end of 1943 inevitably took some of the urgency out of the issue, even as the concept of the displaced person became dominant both in general discourse and in military planning. In addition, UNRRA as an organization was accountable to sovereign states and the Jews did not constitute a nation. Attempts by Jewish representatives to change this situation met with little success. For example, representatives of the World Jewish Congress who called on Lehman's London deputy, Sir Frederick Leith-Ross, in June 1944, urging that "Jewish needs" be considered in UNRRA's planning of relief, were rebuffed, though they were told that a large part would be played by voluntary organizations.

14. SHAEF, Evaluation and Dissemination Section G-2 (Counter-Intelligence Sub-Division), "Basic Handbook. KLs. Axis Concentration Camps and Detention Centers Reported as Such in Europe." USHMM. My thanks to Martin Smith for lending me a copy of this document.

15. It states, for example, that Auschwitz inmates are being employed in some thirty different—and specifically named—enterprises. But the list of camps which provided the appendix to the previous edition has now been dropped, in favor of a reference (in the main text) to the fourteen main camps from which satellite labor camps were developed.

16. Shephard, *After Daybreak,* pp. 55–132; Shephard, "Medical Relief Effort at Belsen"; M. J. Smith, *Dachau,* pp. 79–148.

17. Proudfoot, *European Refugees,* pp. 204–6.

18. Gildea, *Marianne in Chains,* pp. 365–76; Lagrou, *Legacy,* pp. 106–28. When Alain Robbe-Grillet returned to France in the summer of 1944, after working in the tank

factory in Nuremberg, he noted that the director of the institute who had a year earlier urged his students "Go to Germany, young people, you will know a great country" had, in the meantime, become "a long-standing member of the resistance and therefore had no trouble keeping his job."

19. Lagrou, *Legacy,* pp. 91–105.
20. Proudfoot, *European Refugees,* pp. 204–6.
21. Botting, *Ruins of the Reich;* MacDonogh, *After the Reich,* pp. 227–355.
22. Ziemke, *U.S. Army,* pp. 297–319.
23. Ibid., pp. 344–6; Balfour and Mair, *Four-Power Control,* pp. 80–91.
24. Gordon Walker, *Lid Lifts,* pp. 76–7.
25. McClelland, *Embers of War,* p. 16.

CHAPTER 5: THE PSYCHOLOGICAL MOMENT

1. C. J. Murphy, "SOE and Repatriation."
2. Mazower, *Hitler's Empire,* pp. 159–66.
3. Dallin, *German Rule.*
4. Tolstoy, *Victims of Yalta,* p. 5; Cowgill et al., *Documentary Evidence,* p. 18.
5. Ibid.
6. Booker, *Looking-Glass Tragedy;* Bethell, *Last Secret;* Cowgill et al., *Report;* Tolstoy, *Victims of Yalta.*
7. 12,196 Croats, 5,840 Serbs, 8,263 Slovenes, and 400 Montenegrins were handed over.
8. Booker, *Looking-Glass Tragedy,* pp. 210, 218, 244.
9. Ibid., pp. 242–74.
10. Cowgill et al., *Report,* pp. 127–8.
11. The process was often fairly arbitrary. One British unit had just succeeded, with the use of a flamethrower, in persuading a group of intransigent Russians not to get themselves shot when an officer arrived with new orders from corps "containing a definition of a Soviet Citizen as (amongst other qualifications) someone who had been in the Soviet Union since 1930, [which we thought] might possibly apply to our political refugees. Since our [previous] order stated definitely that only Soviet Citizens were to be sent back to Russia, but at the same specifically classed our particular concentration as Soviet citizens, these two orders were completely at variance since the 50 Cossacks concerned had not been in the Soviet Union since 1920. There was at once a mad rush for the telephones, the transport was held, interrogators were rushed to the scene and then the answer came back that a reprieve was possible. Interrogations produced the answer expected, namely that the party of 50 were in the non-Soviet category and amidst, it must be admitted, a general rejoicing, they were returned to their cage. Their final fate is not known." Cowgill, *Documentary Evidence,* pp. 343–9.
12. John Selby-Bigge, quoted in Booker, *Looking-Glass Tragedy,* p. 271; *DBPO,* series I, vol. 6, p. 101.
13. In 1986, Count Nikolai Tolstoy alleged in *The Minister and the Massacres* that the handover in Austria had been masterminded by the adjutant of British V Corps, Brigadier Toby Low, who had conspired with Harold Macmillan (then political adviser to Field Marshal Alexander) to send to their deaths several White Russian generals whose fate was not covered by the Yalta Agreement. This charge provoked a massive counterattack by the British establishment. A meticulous three-man

inquiry, led by Brigadier Anthony Cowgill, reproduced all the main documents in the case and established that there was no substance to Tolstoy's charges; in 1989, Brigadier Low, by now Lord Aldington, was awarded record libel damages of £1.5 million against Tolstoy and a codefendant. This episode, according to the historian Robert Knight, "conforms closely with the dynamics of contemporary history: the opening of archives after thirty years leading to sensational 'discoveries,' media attention and bad history, followed after several more years by a methodical rebuttal (and fewer headlines)" (*TLS*, October 19, 1990). Three further comments are worth making. First, Tolstoy romanticized the "Cossacks," many of whom were guilty of atrocities. Second, Low was of a particular English psychological type, the public school hyperconformist; his eagerness to please his masters had brought him high military rank while still in his twenties. Had a more experienced and independent-minded officer been in his position, the response might have been more circumspect and more humane. Third, the Cowgill Report claimed to have been unable to find any archival record relating to the circumstances under which the Ukrainian Division was spared. It then offered a somewhat implausible account of how the surrendered division appeared to have walked more than three hundred miles, from Austria into Italy, with no logistical support or transport, in approximately eighteen days. As David Cesarani has remarked, "That an unsupplied, war-weary and hungry division of 10,000 men managed this without being molested on the way or creating something of a fuss as they passed through the densely populated and partisan-controlled north-east of Italy may be considered to be stretching credulity." Cesarani, *Justice Delayed*, p. 282.

14. Proudfoot, *European Refugees*, pp. 208–20; Dyczok, *Grand Alliance*, pp. 52–62. The Soviets repatriated some 32,000 U.S. POWs; plus 25,102 British; 294,699 French; and 794,113 other Allied nationals; including 33,150 Belgian; 32,530 Dutch; and 756 Danish citizens. "Most Americans freed by the Red Army passed undramatically from Soviet to U.S. control in Germany after VE Day. Only about 10 percent were repatriated via Odessa." Elliot, *Pawns of Yalta*, pp. 62, 76.

15. Nolte (ed.), *Häftlinge*, pp. 143–7.

16. *CAMGNWE*, pp. 350–1; Proudfoot, *European Refugees*, p. 210; TNA: FO 1030/300 CCG (BE), PW & DP Division; Jeffrey Burds, e-mail to author, October 10, 2005; Dyczok, *Grand Alliance*, pp. 46, 56–62; Nolte (ed.), *Häftlinge*, pp. 205–25; Applebaum, *Gulag*, pp. 395–8.

17. Proudfoot, *European Refugees*, p. 217.

18. TNA: WO 219/2427. The Curzon Line, named after Lord Curzon, the British foreign secretary, was a demarcation line drawn between the Second Polish Republic and Bolshevik Russia in 1919, which broadly speaking followed the border between the Prussian kingdom and the Russian Empire when Poland was divided in 1797 and 1914. Although ignored by both Russians and Poles in the 1920s, the Curzon Line was used as a diplomatic tool by Stalin during the Second World War. He argued that the Soviet Union was only asking for territory which the British government had already allocated to it, via Curzon, two decades earlier.

19. TNA: FO 1030/301; Dyczok, *Grand Alliance*, pp. 46–7. On May 27, SHAEF forces were given an order which immediately exempted Balts, Poles, and Ruthenians from being classified as Soviet citizens, and caused doubt concerning the status of many additional DPs whom the Soviet repatriation officers claimed were their nationals.

20. McNeill, *Rivers of Babylon*, pp. 53–64. On Ukraine: Berkhoff, *Harvest of Despair;*

Dallin, *German Rule;* Boshyk, *Ukraine During World War II;* Armstrong, *Ukrainian Nationalism.*

21. McNeill, *Rivers of Babylon,* p. 56.
22. Snyder, *Reconstruction,* pp. 154–78.
23. Dyczok, *Grand Alliance,* p. 47.
24. Levi, *The Truce,* pp. 292–3.
25. Woropay, *Road to the West,* pp. 28–32.
26. Ibid., p. 33.
27. Elliott, *Pawns of Yalta,* pp. 90–1.
28. Letter from Neubeuren camp, September 22, 1945. Similar appeals were sent to the head of the International Red Cross, President Truman, Herbert Lehman, and the British minister Philip Noel-Baker. All were intercepted before they could be delivered. UNA S-0425, Box 8, File 4, PAG 4/3.0.11.3.0.
29. Luciuk (ed.), *Heroes,* p. 70; Janco, "The Soviet Refugee."
30. Luciuk, *Searching for Place,* pp. 63–80.
31. This was not quite the end of American forced repatriation. In January 1946, the U.S. Army's attempts to load 399 Russians onto a train at Dachau bound for the Soviet Zone produced eleven suicides and a very ugly scene. At the end of February 1946 a carefully planned dawn operation to load the last sizeable remnant of the Russian Liberation Army, held at barracks in the Bavarian town of Plattling, onto waiting lorries met further resistance and attempts at suicide. Five more Russians died. *FRUS,* 1945, p. 1,106. There was a parallel attempt by Ukrainian POWs in Britain and the United States to resist being returned to the USSR. A group of Vlasovite soldiers who rioted at Fort Dix in New Jersey was eventually handed over to Soviet repatriation officers on the Nuremberg–Leipzig autobahn on August, 31 1945. The United States forcibly repatriated at least 4,000 Soviet citizens from U.S. soil. Elliott, *Pawns of Yalta,* pp. 102–26.
32. Dyczok, *Grand Alliance,* pp. 98–112.
33. There were probably some one million Poles in the SHAEF area of Germany, Austria, and Czechoslovakia and the same and more in the Soviet area. Proudfoot, *European Refugees,* pp. 220–3; *DBPO,* series I, vol. 5, p. 43, no. 9.
34. *DBPO,* series I, vol. 5, pp. 221–3, no. 48, Conference October 12–13, 1945.
35. *UD,* p. 43, October 13, 1945.
36. Jacobmeyer, *Zwangarbeiter,* pp. 69–70.
37. Davies, *Rising '44,* pp. 459–70; Kersten, *Establishment of Communist Rule,* pp. 134–60; Hilton, "Pawns"; Holian, "Political Prisoners"; Siedlecki, *Beyond Lost Dreams,* pp. 232–3.
38. Duchesne-Cripps, "Mental Outlook of Displaced Persons." The "unsettling influence of Warsaw radio" also made the management of Polish DP camps very difficult. "The radio station encourages Poles to return immediately to Poland, ignoring completely the fact that only Russians are accepted at the exchange points." "No movement of Poles from Germany will be possible for several months since priority must first be given to Russian DPs." Duchesne-Cripps, Library of Congress, pp. 62–70.
39. Proudfoot, *European Refugees,* p. 222.
40. McNeill, *Rivers of Babylon,* p. 40.

CHAPTER 6: THE SURVIVING REMNANT

1. Z. Grinberg, "Our Liberation from Dachau," trans. Israel Eiss, reprinted from *Kamah,* the yearbook of the Jewish National Fund, 5708 (1948); Z. I. Kaplan, "Marsch aus den Kauferinger Lagern," from *Fun letstn churbn* (Munich, 1947). Thanks to Dr. Zeev Mankowitz and Dr. Edith Raim.

2. Levin, *Litvaks,* pp. 10–13. "A LITVAK, in prosaic terms, is simply a Jew whose family happens to come from Lithuania; mythopoetically speaking, however, being a Litvak is a state of mind. The Litvak thinks of himself (especially vis-à-vis his traditional 'enemy,' the Polish Jew) as endowed by Providence with a true sense of values: he is committed to reason and realism instead of fantasy—he is intelligent, open-minded, ironic (in the style of Hamlet) but immovable on principle. The enduring purpose in Jewish life, he is sure, is expressed in the Litvak connection." Chaim Raphael, *Commentary,* May 1976.

3. Quoted in Reich (ed.), *Hidden History,* p. 28.

4. Mendelsohn, *Jews of East Central Europe,* pp. 213–39; Tory, *Surviving the Holocaust,* pp. xii–xxiv. After 1939, the Soviets returned Vilna (Vilnius) to Lithuania. "The annexation of Vilna and its region added some 100,000 Jews to the population, 75,000 of them in Vilna alone. There was also a considerable population of Polish Jews, fleeing both the Nazi and the Soviet zones, who needed assistance in the necessities of life and in obtaining papers to travel onward to other destinations." Reich (ed.), *Hidden History,* p. 28.

5. Reich (ed.), *Hidden History,* pp. 15–24.

6. Ibid.; Mishell, *Kaddish for Kovno;* Gringauz, "The Ghetto as an Experiment"; Elkes, *Values, Belief and Survival,* pp. 22–34.

7. Grinberg, "Our Liberation from Dachau"; Hilliard, *Surviving the Americans;* Schwarz, *Redeemers,* pp. 3–7; Klausner, *Letter,* pp. 65–6; Elkes, *Values, Belief and Survival;* Mishell, *Kaddish for Kovno,* pp. 279–335; Gordon, *Shadow of Death,* pp. 152–72.

8. Mankowitz, *Life Between Memory and Hope,* pp. 29–30.

9. Ibid., chap. 2.

10. *ASH,* p. 28; Königsweder and Wetzel, *Waiting for Hope,* pp. 15–21.

11. Bauer, "DP Legacy," in *LR;* Bauer, "Initial Organization"; Königsweder and Wetzel, *Waiting for Hope,* p. 10. USHMM, p. 217: "On the eve of the Holocaust there were 37,000 Jews in Kovno. At the end of the Holocaust an estimated 500 survived in forests, in hiding, or in bunkers, and some 2,500 survived the KZs in Germany. In liberated Lithuania only 8,000–9,000 Jews remained from the prewar population of 235,000. More than 95 percent of Lithuanian Jewry had been destroyed." Bridgman, *End of the Holocaust,* p. 76.

12. F. Wilson, *Aftermath,* pp. 40–1; Sington, *Belsen Uncovered,* quoted in Shephard, *After Daybreak,* p. 36; Levy, *Witness to Evil,* p. 13; Rickman Papers; Blumenson (ed.), *Patton Papers,* p. 751.

13. Klemmé, *Inside Story,* p. 86; F. Wilson, *Aftermath,* p. 116; Hilliard, *Surviving the Americans.*

14. Bauer, *American Jewry,* p. 452; Bauer, *Out of the Ashes,* pp. 41, 55; Milton and Bogin (eds.), p. 1269; Peck (ed.), *World Jewish Congress,* p. 30; speech by Edward Warburg, Atlantic City, September 1945; Rosensaft Papers, USHMM.

15. Klausner, *Letter,* pp. 10–11; "Rabbi Abraham Klausner," in Harris (ed.), *Long Way Home,* pp. 20–33; Mankowitz, *Life Between Memory and Hope,* pp. 39–40; König-

sweder and Wetzel, *Waiting for Hope,* pp. 19–20, 80; Bauer, *Flight,* pp. 57–62; Bauer, "Initial Organization."

16. Harris (ed.), *Long Way Home,* p. 24.
17. Grodzinsky, *Shadow,* pp. 42–54; Bauer, "Initial Organization."
18. Lavsky, *New Beginnings,* p. 66.
19. Rosensaft, *Yesterday,* p. 62; Sington, *Belsen Uncovered,* p. 191; Somers and Kok (eds.), *Jewish Displaced Persons,* pp. 76–8.
20. Shephard, *After Daybreak,* p. 160.
21. Ibid., pp. 155–8; M. Eigen, "Belsen Camp, 31 August 1945," in Milton and Bogin (eds.), *Archives of the Holocaust,* pp. 1312–20.
22. Beardwell, *Aftermath,* pp. 48, 51.
23. Hyman, *Undefeated,* p. 79; Bauer, *Flight,* pp. 72–3. Historians have faithfully repeated the zonal split: Leo Schwarz and Zeev Mankowitz, the chroniclers of Jews in the American Zone, barely mention Rosensaft, while Hagit Lavsky's book about Jews at Bergen-Belsen ignores Grinberg and his colleagues.
24. Mankowitz, *Life Between Memory and Hope,* p. 53; Dinnerstein, "American policy," in *LR,* pp. 104–5.
25. *ASH,* pp. 34–7; *DBPO,* series I, vol. 5, p. 1232.
26. Mankowitz, *Life Between Memory and Hope,* pp. 54–7.
27. Klausner, *Letter,* pp. 67–8; Earl Harrison, "Diary," USHMM.
28. Trepman, "On Being Reborn," p. 134. To comfort himself, Harrison thought of man's essential goodness, as revealed by the charitable workers he was involved with at home, "so different in their objectives from man's degradation of man." It "warmed my heart" to think of the "loyal devoted men and women who rally each year." Earl Harrison, "Diary," USHMM.
29. Hyman, *Undefeated,* p. 55; Rosensaft, *Yesterday,* p. 77.
30. *ASH,* pp. 291–305.
31. Bauer, "DP Legacy," in *LR,* p. 27; Bauer, *Flight,* pp. 77–8; Hyman, *Undefeated,* pp. 44–53.
32. Ferrell (ed.), *Truman,* p. 72; Truman, *Years of Trial,* p. 164, quoted in Kochavi, *Post-Holocaust Politics,* p. 305.
33. Kochavi, *Post-Holocaust Politics,* p. 91; Clay, *Decision,* p. 232; Blumenson (ed.), *Patton Papers,* p. 752.
34. Louis, *British Empire,* p. 422; M. Cohen, *Palestine,* pp. 109, 113; Bauer, "DP legacy," in *LR,* p. 27.
35. Kochavi, *Post-Holocaust Politics,* p. 100.
36. Sachar, *History of Israel,* p. 109.
37. Sanders, *High Walls,* p. 133, quoted in Johnson, *History of the Jews,* p. 428.
38. Sachar, *History of Israel,* pp. 163–248.
39. Crossman, *Palestine Mission,* pp. 60–3.
40. Bullock, *Bevin,* p. 16.
41. Rendel to Strang, August 24, 1945, *DBPO,* series 1, vol. 5, p. 183.

CHAPTER 7: "FEED THE BRUTES?"

1. Norman Clark, *News Chronicle,* August 24, 1945, quoted in de Zayas, *Nemesis at Potsdam,* pp. 109–11.
2. Quoted in Frank, " 'The New Morality.' "

3. Henry Buckley, Reuters, August 21, 1945, TNA: FO 371/46812.
4. Naimark, *Fires of Hatred*, pp. 108–10.
5. MacDonogh, *After the Reich*, pp. 125–61; Schieder (ed.), *Documents on the Expulsion*, vol. 4, pp. 345–579.
6. C. von Krockow, *Die Reise nach Pommern* (Munich, 1985), p. 215.
7. Schieder (ed.), *Documents on the Expulsion*, vol. 1, pp. 285–302.
8. Ibid., p. 300. The children did survive. In March 1946, they and Anna finally got to the British Zone, where she found her husband again. According to another witness, about seventy families had thrown themselves into the Oder; they were farmers who could not understand why they had lost their farms.
9. In the 1950s and 1960s, the *Vertreibungsverluste*—the question of how many Germans died during the expulsions—became an issue in West German politics and Cold War propaganda, while being officially taboo in Poland and Czechoslovakia. It was occasionally claimed that this episode represented the "German Holocaust"—a manifestly ridiculous claim. According to West German statistics, 1,618,400 Germans died during the expulsion from Poland and the total number of victims was 2,239,500. An overall figure of 2 million deaths has often been quoted by German historians, for example by Wolfgang Benz, but other scholars tend to be skeptical. Rüdiger Overmans has questioned these figures, arguing that only about 400,000 casualties have in fact been documented and offering an estimate of about 600,000 as the entire number of "victims of expulsion." However, issues of definition arise. Norman Naimark quotes a Polish study which found that "some two million Germans died in the process of Soviet occupation, Polish occupation, and forced deportation—most in the western territories—of violence, hunger and disease." Naimark adds, "disease was the biggest killer; many Germans died en route and after arrival in occupied Germany of a variety of maladies. Suicide, hunger, and exposure also took a serious toll. In other words, the lower numbers may well accurately reflect the numbers . . . murdered and killed in the course of the deportation; the higher numbers would include the number who died from other causes during the uprooting, detention, transport and resettling." The British historian Matthew Frank argued that "the 2 million figure is almost certainly too high. That number certainly did not die as direct result of the expulsions post-May 1945." Frank believes that "most deaths occurred between the end of 1944 and the end of the war (or into late May), in areas that roughly correspond with movement of the eastern front and Soviet (and Yugoslav) occupation" (e-mail to the author, July 27, 2007). The Czech historian Tomás Stanek estimates that between 25,000 and 40,000 Germans were killed during the expulsions from Czechoslovakia. In 1996, a Czech–German historical commission put the figure at 40,000. Naimark, *Fires of Hatred*, pp. 168–32; Ther, "Integration of Expellees."
10. Horsburgh and Raeburn, "Health Problem in Berlin," pp. 423–9.
11. Ibid., TNA:FO 371/46812.
12. The situation may have been better in some other parts of Germany. "In spite of the gross overcrowding ever more refugees are drifting into Lübeck," a British military government official reported in June 1945. "The German Red Cross is doing excellent work in the thirty refugee camps and bunkers of Lübeck. In these they have charge of some 14,000 of a total of 70,000 German refugees. They maintain a staff of twenty-five doctors, solely at work on these people. Yet another hospital has been opened in a school building, making the start of education appear more remote than

ever. I pass daily a clean and efficiently-run Red Cross home for the hundreds of parentless children found hereabouts. The German Red Cross is also helping in the welfare schemes for both concentration camp victims and German prisoners. A great deal of its usefulness is due to voluntary labour and one observes a staggering proportion of the women in the streets wearing nurse's uniform. On the whole the Germans are doing well in this type of self-help—it is something they understand already and calls for devotion rather than special gifts of improvisation." Dickens, *Lübeck Diary*, p. 150.

13. TNA: FO 371/46813. Eleanor Rathbone, August 25, 1945, PNB, quoting *News Chronicle* the previous day: "This proportion of Germany's population must die before winter if nothing is done. The Allied authorities are neither tackling the problem themselves nor helping the German Welfare Committees to do it. . . . If the Allies can't tackle the job themselves they should give every possible help to the accredited German bodies."

14. Reinisch, "Public Health," pp. 51–7.

15. Edwards, *Gollancz*, pp. 401–32.

16. Frank, "'New morality.'"

17. For three days in early November, a strange panic seized Fleet Street. Although experts knew that recently developed techniques of mass inoculation were preventing the spread of disease, fears were ventilated that any outbreak of disease in Germany might quickly spread westward and the health disasters of the early 1920s be repeated after all.

18. *A Defeated People*. Jennings privately shared this view. Jackson, *Humphrey Jennings*, pp. 308–10.

19. Frank, "British Voluntary Societies."

20. Naimark, *Russians in Germany*, p. 148.

21. Pimlott (ed.), *War Diaries of Dalton*, p. 846; "You and the Army must do all you can to mitigate it, but you won't be able to cure it" (Cloake, *Templer*, p. 149); Smith, *Clay Papers*, vol. 1, pp. 24, 41, quoted in Tooze, *Wages of Destruction*, p. 672; Jul. 26, 1945 *DBPO*, vol. 1, pp. 915–16, no. 421. Sargent warned against the military government making common cause with the Germans against the DPs; there was "no room for exaggerated sympathy." He hoped that the repatriation of the DPs would put an end to the problem.

22. *CAMGNWE*, p. 231; Annan, *Changing Enemies*, p. 149; Balfour and Mair, *Four-Power Control*, pp. 73–4; Farquharson, *Western Allies*, pp. 55–60. Not all the released POWs were farmworkers. Many Wehrmacht members had simply claimed to be farm laborers to get early release from POW camps. Operation Barleycorn was by no means a permanent solution to the problem, as rural migration had been in progress too long for that. Ziemke, *U.S. Army*, pp. 292–5, suggests that German POWs were being discharged anyway as there wasn't enough food to keep them in cages.

23. *UD*, passim; McClelland, *Embers of War*, p. 58; Dickens, *Lübeck Diary*, p. 260; Knef, *Gift Horse*, pp. 113–25.

24. *LR*, p. 79.

25. Jay, *Change and Fortune*, pp. 136–9; Pimlott (ed.), *War Diaries of Dalton*, p. 432.

26. Pimlott (ed.), *War Diaries of Dalton*, pp. 429–34; Skidelsky, *Keynes*, pp. 378–444.

27. Balfour and Mair, *Four-Power Control*, pp. 123–51.

28. Meehan, *Strange Enemy People*, p. 54; Pimlott (ed.), *War Diaries of Dalton*, pp. 546–7; *DBPO*, 1945, series I, vol. 5, pp. 273–6.

29. *DBPO,* series I, vol. 5, pp. 379–80; Farquharson, *Western Allies,* p. 93.
30. *DBPO,* 1945, vol. 6, pp. 417–20.
31. Thomas, *Strachey,* pp. 230–4; Jay, *Change and Fortune,* pp. 140–2; House of Commons debates. Part of the explanation was the international obligations the United Kingdom had discharged. Since November 1945, said Strachey, the British government had sent or diverted 60,000 tons of cereals (mainly wheat) to India; 60,000 tons through UNRRA to Italy, Poland, Greece, and Yugoslavia; 60,000 tons to Germany; 10,000 tons to South Africa; and 10,000 tons to Belgium. This tonnage had all been lent and would in due course be replaced by the Americans. But in addition, the government had sent to the British Zone in Germany 192,000 tons of wheat, 109,000 tons of flour, 105,000 tons of barley, and 132,400 tons of potatoes. Strachey himself privately believed it was not necessary to introduce bread rationing in Britain but was unable to prevail over his cautious civil servants. Bread rationing was highly unpopular and cost the Labour government much political capital. "Even if the bread ration was adequate, as most acknowledged it was, the very fact of peacetime rationing would remain a symbolic sore as long as it remained in force. This was especially so in the middle-class." Kynaston, *Austerity Britain,* p. 118.

CHAPTER 8: DOLLARS OR DEATH

1. Gibson, *Jacko,* pp. 1–62; Wilmington, *Middle East Supply Centre,* pp. 41–4.
2. *ODNB;* Jackson interviews, Bodleian Library; TNA: FO 371/41144.
3. Robert Jackson to Philip Noel-Baker, November 25, 1945, Jackson UNRRA papers, C256, no. 20, Lehman Suite, Columbia.
4. Ibid. It became clear later in the year that British support for UNRRA derived mainly from the fact that this organization, which was 72 percent funded by the Americans, provided a cheaper mechanism by which the British could discharge their aid commitments than any other.
5. Jackson, untitled document, Jackson UNRRA papers, C256, no. 20, Lehman Suite, Columbia. Jackson's arrival stopped all talk of sacking Lehman.
6. Best, "British Foreign Office," p. 167; FO 371/51336.
7. UNA: UNRRA, Office of the Historian Monographs, Box 78/7, May Bingham, "Mobilization and Training."
8. Lorna Hay, "Can UNRRA Relieve the Chaos in Europe?," *Picture Post,* September 15, 1945.
9. Arnold-Forster, "UNRRA's Work," Arnold-Forster Papers; *AP,* pp. 162–5.
10. Floore, *Bread of the Oppressed,* p. 27; UNA: UNRRA, Office of the Historian Monographs, Box 78, Roger Carter, "Training of Personnel for Displaced Persons Operations."
11. Woodbridge, vol. 1, pp. 251–2; Korwin, "No Man's People," p. 58, Arnold-Forster Papers; F. Wilson, *Aftermath,* pp. 26–9; "There were certain criteria on which Welfare officers were assigned Principal or Assistant. They all had five years' university training and wide experience. Two or three ladies only came with letters or recommendations from high persons instead of degrees and experience. The UK sent people with Social Science diplomas and experience, but also people without qualifications. This caused difficulties and discontent. The criteria for recruitment in France were beyond my powers to judge. Some people said it was a reward for resistance activities." The Personnel Department "had no psychological knowledge and

no field experience. They were supposed to make use of the evaluation of the training, but more often than not they assigned people to teams by holy inspiration." Korwin, "No Man's People," Arnold-Forster Papers.

12. Klemmé, *Inside Story,* pp. 28–32; Wilson, *Aftermath,* p. 10; Dawson, "Stagnant Pool," IWM.

13. *UC,* p. 157.

14. UNA: UNRRA, Office of the Historian Monographs, Box 78, Roger Carter, "Training of Personnel for Displaced Persons Operations"; Korwin, "No Man's People," Arnold-Forster Papers.

15. "One morning, at breakfast, it was difficult to recognize the dining table. Everything was there: fruit juices, butter, sugar. Word had come that there were American CIDs investigating. Many things changed overnight." Korwin, "No Man's People," Arnold-Forster Papers.

16. Wilson, *Aftermath,* p. 30; U.S. House of Representatives, *Congressional Record,* October 31, 1945.

17. Lorna Hay, "Can UNRRA Relieve the Chaos in Europe?," *Picture Post,* September 15, 1945; UNA: UNRRA. Office of the Historian Monographs, Box 78/7, May Bingham, "Mobilization and Training."

18. Best, "British Foreign Office"; Wilson, *Aftermath,* p. 28; Korwin, "No Man's People," Arnold-Forster Papers.

19. UNA: UNRRA, Office of the Historian Monographs, Box 78/7, May Bingham, "Mobilization and Training"; Korwin, "No Man's People," p. 67, Arnold-Forster Papers.

20. Coigny, "Displaced Persons."

21. Topping, "The Task of UNRRA."

22. Doherty, *Letters from Belsen,* pp. 63, 71, 120; Effie Barker, Barker Papers, IWM (D); Fisher, *Cilento,* pp. 176–93.

23. Cilento, "Escape," pp. 60–5, University of Queensland Library. Both Cilento and Montgomery were "vain and ambitious." Fisher, *Cilento.*

24. *FRUS* (1945), vol. 2, pp. 993–1,009; Woodbridge, vol. 1, pp. 41–3; *AP,* pp. 55–62.

25. *FRUS* (1945), vol. 2, p. 1,024.

26. Ibid., pp. 1,025–7.

27. Ibid., Acheson to Harriman, p. 1,027; Fossedal, *Finest Hour.*

28. *AP,* p. 59.

29. Morgan, *Peace and War,* p. 220; *UD,* pp. 1–2.

30. Bond, "Sir Frederick Morgan," *ODNB;* Morgan, *Peace and War.*

31. *UD,* pp. 12–15.

32. *UD,* September 19–28, 1945, pp. 20–8.

33. UNRRA's U.S. funding:

March 28, 1944: Congress authorized the first 1 percent	$1.35 billion
June 30, 1944: First appropriation	$800 million
December 14, 1945: Second appropriation	$550 million
December 18, 1945: Congress authorized second 1 percent	$1.35 billion
December 28, 1945: Appropriation of	$700 million
May 27, 1946: Appropriation of	$135 million
July 23, 1946: Appropriation of	$465 million

34. Robert Jackson to Philip Noel-Baker, November 25, 1945, C256 #20, Jackson Papers, Lehman Suite, Columbia.

35. According to *Time,* December 31, 1945, the "sparkplug of UNRRA's present spurt was the Royal Australian Navy's fast-talking, reddish-haired RGA Jackson."
36. Helen Gahagan Douglas is perhaps best remembered now for calling Richard Nixon "Tricky Dick" after he defeated her in 1950.
37. Rendel to Strang, *DBPO,* series 1, vol. 5, p. 207.
38. *UD,* p. 82; Cilento, "Escape," pp. 103–4, University of Queensland Library.
39. Morgan Papers, IWM.
40. *UD,* pp. 6, 31, 24.
41. Ibid., pp. 32, 48, 65, 67.
42. Ibid., p. 68.
43. Ibid., p. 78; Sereny, *German Trauma,* p. 45; UNA: PAG 4/4.2, Box 81, Office of the Historian Monographs, no. 20/2. Donald F. McGonigal, "Baltic Camp at Kassel."
44. *UD,* pp. 55, 80, 88.
45. UNA: UNRRA Archives, Office of the Historian Monographs, Box 78. No. 7.
46. *UD,* p. 345.
47. Ibid., pp. 39, 164; UNA: UNRRA Archives, Office of the Historian Monographs, Box 78, no. 7.
48. *UD,* p. 165.
49. Ibid., pp. 109–110.
50. Bauer, *Flight,* pp. 194–8; *ASH,* pp. 109–110; Kochavi, *Post-Holocaust Politics,* pp. 163–4.
51. *UD,* pp. 25, 32. Meeting Leslie Hore-Belisha in St James's Park in February 1943, Sir Alan Brooke noted that he was "looking more greasy and objectionable than ever." Danchev and Todman (eds.), *Alanbrooke War Diaries,* p. 385.
52. *UD,* pp. 62, 77, 88, 90. Shalom (Solomon) Adler-Rudel (1894–1975), originally from Czernowitz in Poland, had been the leader of the exiled German-Jewish community in London.
53. UNA, S 425, Box 8, File 6.
54. Jackson interview, Bodleian Library.
55. *UD,* pp. 110–44.

CHAPTER 9: "YOU PICK IT UP FAST"

1. *WP,* pp. 3–8.
2. Ibid., pp. 9–20.
3. KHL: letter, August 19, 1945.
4. KHL: letter, August 30, 1945.
5. Hitchcock, *Bitter Road,* pp. 272–7.
6. PCW, p. 9.
7. Ibid., pp. 10–11.
8. PCW, pp. 11–12. Letter, G. Masset, Director, UNRRA Team 302, Wildflecken, to J. H. Whiting, Acting District Director, UNRRA, September 13, 1945. UNA: S-0436 Box 8 File 5. PAG 4/3.0.11.3.2 (clearly written by Kay Hulme); Report of Investigation of Displaced Persons Center at Wildflecken (No. 91-252), September 5–6, 1945 (by H. E. McDonald). Technically the Polish Committee was now a municipal council. Kay continued the old usage.
9. PCW, p. 12.
10. KHL: letters, November 4 and December 15, 1945.

11. KHL: letter, October 1945; PCW, p. 3.
12. KHL: letters, October 9 and 12, 1945; *WP*, p. 62.
13. PCW, pp. 19–21.
14. *WP*, p. 85.
15. Ibid., pp. 90–2.
16. KHL: letter, December 15, 1945.
17. PCW, p. 5.
18. KHL: letters, November 4 and 22, 1945.
19. KHL: letter, November 13, 1945.
20. *UC*, pp. 241–4; Patterson, *Ladies of the Rope.*
21. *UC*, pp. 156–61, 170–2, 178–82; KHL: letter, October 27, 1945.
22. KHL: letter, December 31, 1945: *WP*, pp. 99–123. According to Ziemke, *U.S. Army*, p. 318, Tally Ho was a check-and-search operation conducted in July 1945.

CHAPTER 10: "EVEN IF THE GATES ARE LOCKED"

1. Peck (ed.), *Among the Survivors*, pp. 5, 10–12, 21.
2. Ibid., pp. 14–15.
3. Ibid., pp. 16, 22.
4. Ibid., pp. 15, 29.
5. Ibid., pp. 36, 31, 59–60, 82, 62.
6. Ibid., pp. 47–8. Olieski's speech had been made in August 1945.
7. Ibid., pp. 64–6.
8. Teveth, *Ben-Gurion*, pp. 695–831; Rose, *Weizmann*, pp. 356–400.
9. Shapira, *Land and Power*, pp. 277–352; M. Cohen, *Palestine*, pp. 68–70.
10. Teveth, *Ben-Gurion*, pp. 843–62; Teveth, *Ben-Gurion and the Holocaust;* Segev, *Seventh Million*, p. 97.
11. Zertal, *From Catastrophe to Power*, pp. 225–9; Cohen, *Palestine*, p. 68.
12. Teveth, *Ben-Gurion*, pp. 870–3.
13. Ibid., p. 872.
14. Ibid., p. 873.
15. Peck (ed.), *Among the Survivors*, pp. 49–50.
16. Bauer, *Flight and Rescue*, pp. 113–51; Kochavi, *Post-Holocaust Politics*, 162–3; Gross, *Fear*, pp. 31–80.
17. Bauer, "DP Legacy," p. 25. All figures are necessarily approximate. Bauer estimates that there were at that point approximately 120,000 survivors in Germany, Austria, Poland, and Lithuania and in Hungary some 180,000 survivors, made up of returnees from the camps and the Jewish Labor Battalion in the Hungarian army and survivors of the Budapest ghetto. Finally, there were some 200,000 Jews who had fled eastward into the Soviet Union when the Germans attacked.
18. Bauer, *Flight and Rescue;* Mankowitz, *Life Between Memory and Hope*, p. 17.
19. "Up until September 1945, the whole thing was run without the presence of a single person from the Palestine center." But in early October, the first Zionist emissary arrived, soon followed by others sent by Mossad. At first the locals remained in control, but as they gradually emigrated themselves the Palestinians took over, and by the late spring of 1946 they were "definitely . . . running the *Brichah*." Bauer, *Flight and Rescue*, p. 121.

20. Mankowitz, *Life Between Memory and Hope,* pp. 67–8; Bauer, "DP Legacy," p. 28.

21. Bauer, *Flight and Rescue,* pp. 95–6; Kochavi, *Post-Holocaust Politics,* pp. 92–7. Yehuda Bauer has argued that Bedell Smith was partly influenced by the fact (of which no one else was aware at the time) that he was part Jewish. The archivist at the Eisenhower Center, where Smith's papers are now housed, can find no evidence to support this theory. The U.S. commander in Austria, General Mark Clark, was, however, half Jewish.

22. Zertal, *From Catastrophe to Power,* pp. 74–8; Cohen, *Palestine,* p. 69.

23. Peck (ed.), *Among the Survivors,* p. 93.

24. Friedman, "Military Chaplain's Perspective," in *LR.*

25. Bauer, "DP Legacy," p. 31.

26. Grodzinsky, *In the Shadow,* pp. 80–99; Shephard, *After Daybreak,* pp. 162–5. One element in this was the rivalry between Zionists and the Jewish religious groups which had mounted the effort to bring Jewish children to England.

27. Dr. Grinberg himself declared, "either the children go to the place they need and have a right to go to—Palestine—or they stay in the camps." Ben-Gurion: "I object to the removal of Jewish children to England, even to Sweden—the best country in this respect. It is necessary that they be there—it's good for them, it's good for the Jews . . . it is a Jewish interest that in the American Zone there will be a large Jewish force. America will pressure Britain, de Gaulle will not." Grodzinsky, *In the Shadow,* pp. 97–8.

28. Segev, *Seventh Million,* p. 130; *DBPO,* series I, vol. 5, pp. 457–8, microfiche document no. 98iiia. Control Commission for Germany to Refugees Department, Foreign Office, enclosing confidential report by Mr. Goldsmith, December 24, 1945. The journalist found the Belsen DPs unaware that they were probably getting more to eat than the British. Dr. Hadassah Bimko suggested to him "that the DPs were actually entitled to a higher rations scale than British civilians because of the privations they had suffered." Both the Jewish and Polish representatives agreed that they were quite prepared to see some German people starve in order that they have more food than they were getting at present. By that time, considerable quantities of aid from the Joint were reaching Belsen. TNA: FO 1049/81.

29. Bauer, *Out of the Ashes,* pp. 99–100; Schwarz, *Redeemers,* pp. 99–100. Grinberg found American Jewry "over-organized" yet sharply divided.

30. TNA: FO 1049/81/77, quoted in Reilly, "British Policy," p. 110.

31. R. Ovendale, review of Kochavi, *Post-Holocaust Politics,* in *English Historical Review* 117 (2002), p. 1296; Bullock, *Bevin,* p. 181.

32. Nachmani, *Great Power Discord;* Louis, *British Empire,* pp. 397–419.

33. Crossman, *Palestine Mission,* pp. 46–7.

34. Ibid., pp. 63, 75.

35. Crum, *Behind the Silken Curtain,* p. 73.

36. Schwarz, *Redeemers,* pp. 81–8; Grossmann, *Jews, Germans, and Allies,* pp. 168–9; *These are the People,* film (Steven Spielberg Film Archive).

37. Crum, *Behind the Silken Curtain,* pp. 78–81.

38. Ibid., p. 83.

39. Grodzinsky, *In the Shadow,* p. 138; R. Ovendale, review of Kochavi, *Post-Holocaust Politics,* in *English Historical Review* 117 (2002), p. 1,296.

40. Lavsky, *New Beginnings,* p. 189–92.

41. Crum, *Behind the Silken Curtain,* p. 145.

42. Louis, *British Empire,* p. 412; Crossman, *Palestine Mission,* pp. 138–9; Crum, *Behind the Silken Curtain,* pp. 126–9.

43. Bethell, *Palestine Triangle,* p. 237; Bullock, *Bevin,* pp. 255–8; Louis, *British Empire,* pp. 418–19: Bauer, "DP Legacy."

44. Bullock, *Bevin,* pp. 292–4; Louis, *British Empire,* pp. 415–19.

45. Louis, *British Empire,* p. 418; Cohen, *Palestine,* pp. 113–15.

46. Schwarz, *Redeemers,* pp. 120–8; UD, p. 180. In a letter to General Templer of July 4, 1946, Morgan described Grinberg as "a tremendous personality . . . a militant visionary of the Maccabean type, capable of anything." Morgan papers, IWM.

47. Hilliard, *Surviving the Americans,* pp. 100–1.

48. Schwarz, *Redeemers,* pp. 122–5; Bauer, *Flight and Rescue,* p. 275; Yablonka, *Holocaust Survivors,* p. 270. The dedication to Grinberg's account of his survival reads, "A light in memory of the soul of my first-born son, Emanuel, born in the Kowno Ghetto on 25 Tammuz, 5701 (July 20, 1941); saved by one of the Righteous Among the Nations, Matas Jonushaukas; entered the land of our forefathers on 24 Nissan 5706 (April 25, 1946) and passed away and was buried in Zion on 24 Elul 5706 (September 20, 1946)."

CHAPTER 11: "SKRYNING"

1. Dölger, *"Polenlager Jägerlust,"* pp. 75–102.

2. Hilton, "Pawns," p. 90.

3. Woodbridge, vol. 1, pp. 486–7.

4. Ibid., pp. 490–1; *AP,* pp. 62–3.

5. UNA: Vincent Meyer, UNRRA Deputy Chief of Operations, Berlin, March 23, 1946, S 402, Box 1, File 1. Danylyszyn, "Prisoners of Peace," p. 74, gives a figure of almost 850,000 displaced Poles remaining in Germany, drawn from the *UNRRA Journal.* This may have included Jews and "Ukrainians." According to Proudfoot, *European Refugees,* pp. 238–9, there were 816,004 Poles in the western zones of Germany on September 30, 1945—253,981 in the American, 510,320 in the British, and 51,703 in the French zones.

6. UNA: "Historical Report—Repatriation Division," written by Ralph M. Price, May 1947, S-0524-0104. PAG 4/4.2:80 (hereafter "Price Report"); UNA: F. E. Morgan, Narrative Report, February 1946, S-0518-0800, PAG 4.1.1.3.5.6.2:133.

7. Hilton, "Pawns."

8. Lukas, *Bitter Legacy,* pp. 109–10; Jaroszyńska-Kirchmann, *Exile Mission,* p. 49.

9. Price Report, p. 2; Cilento, "Escape," p. 99. Having established UNRRA in the British Zone in the Wild West days of autumn 1945, Sir Raphael may have resented Morgan's patronizing army manner. He found Morgan "at first sight . . . a striking personality, tall, well built, with a deliberate charm of manner, a ready wit, and a most engaging chuckle" but "on closer acquaintance, he seemed to me to show a love of public and private recognition, an intolerance of differing viewpoints, and an almost cyclic sequence of euphoria and cacophoria [a generalized feeling of unhappiness] that indicated the intensity of the nervous strain of his wartime responsibilities." Cilento, while making loud noises in favor of repatriation, did his best to deny liaison officers sent by the Lublin Poles access to the records of the Polish Red Cross held in Germany. To that extent the sabotage charge is warranted. He also accused Morgan of a long delay in implementing Resolution 92 and of contradictory instruc-

tions thereafter: "the double talk, the vacillation, the insecurity of purpose and the fluctuations of policies in all the parties concerned, ultimately ruined the resolution of the refugees. . . . In effect . . . killed the repatriation programme."

10. KHL: letters, January 20, February 2, February 27, and March 29, 1946; *WP*, p. 125.

11. KHL: letter, April 7, 1946. "We of course did nothing to persuade people to go. . . . The policy so far was not to encourage people either to stay or to return. We had at that time to be absolutely non-committal. In fact, I heard the Director say that in the previous autumn, he had been criticised by superior officers for trying to encourage repatriation, as being incorrect." Dawson, "Stagnant Pool," IWM, pp. 155A, 157A.

12. *WP*, p. 136.

13. KHL: letters, April 23, and May 5, 1946.

14. Dawson, "Stagnant Pool," IWM, p. 146; KHL: letter, April 23, 1946.

15. Dawson, "Stagnant Pool," IWM, p. 146.

16. *UC*, pp. 196–7.

17. Kersten, *Establishment of Communist Rule*, pp. 163–231.

18. Korboński, *Warsaw in Chains*, p. 49.

19. Ibid., p. 67; Toranska, *Oni*.

20. Kersten, *Establishment of Communist Rule*, pp. 163–71; Lane, *Poland Betrayed*.

21. Kersten, *Establishment of Communist Rule*, p. 166.

22. Woodbridge, vol. 3, pp. 426–7. In all, 35,557 Poles returned in March, 58,314 in April, 36,319 in May, 22,964 in June, 35,564 in July, and 25,516 in August 1946.

23. UNA: S 402–0004 Subject Files of the Repatriation Section, Romuald Nowicki, Director, UNRRA Team 109, to J. H. Whiting, February 15, 1946; Paper, June 1, 1946; documents pertaining to implementation of UNRRA Resolution no. 92; Price Report.

24. Bullock, *Bevin*, p. 274.

25. Anders, *Army in Exile*, pp. 288–95.

26. Bullock, *Bevin*, p. 274.

27. Ibid.

28. Anders, *Army in Exile*, pp. 288–95; Sword et al., *Formation*, pp. 200–202.

29. UNA: Screening Operations in the U.S. Zone. Report by Jay B. Krane, Chief, Reports and Analysis Division, July 10, 1946 (hereafter "Krane Report"); Dyczok, *Grand Alliance*, pp. 138–47.

30. UNA: Gitta Sereny to J. H. Whiting, UNRRA Director, U.S. Zone, July 21, 1946.

31. Ibid.; Krane Report. The young officers were mystified by Sereny's attempts to explain the political forces at work in the camps—"stories like that sound like Hollywood to Hollywood-minded kids." They "regarded male DPs as lazy criminals"; the women were "either one thing or another depending on their looks." Sereny did succeed in uncovering evidence of a collaborationist organization or movement that had operated among the predominantly Belorussian (Ruthenian) population of eastern Poland during 1942–1944 in the period of the German occupation.

32. Sereny's UNRRA boss wrote: "Her background is that of a journalist rather than a welfare person." While recognizing her "considerable international feeling, education and experience," she also had a "record of volatility, volubility and self-expression that has been a source of disquiet in her several assignments. She is a belligerent champion of lost causes, or weak ones. . . . She is never far from a phone and apparently she knows many people." UNA: A. C. Dunn to C. J. Taylor, July 22, 1946. Sereny left UNRRA in October to undertake a lecture tour of schools and colleges in

America. Sereny, *German Trauma,* pp. 50–1.

33. Doherty, *Letters,* p. 98. A Canadian nurse working for UNRRA wrote to Mackenzie King, the Canadian prime minister, "Practically all the Baltics and some of the others, notably Eukrainains [*sic*] came of their own free will, aided and abetted Germany in her fight . . . worked in their factories for good wages . . . helped to manufacture guns . . . which helped to kill our own men and those of our allies. . . . These people merely bet on the wrong horse and regret that it did not win. They now stand around demanding, yes, and getting the handout. . . . No good screening has been done . . . almost always [they want to immigrate] to the U.S. or Canada. What I hope and pray for is that these Baltics especially be not allowed into our country. They are red hot Fascists . . . may they never step on fair Canadian soil." Luciuk, *Searching for Place,* p. 203.

34. Cesarani, *Justice Delayed,* pp. 45–65; Benton, *Baltic Countdown.*

35. Dawson, "Stagnant Pool," IWM, pp. 169–70.

36. Luciuk, *Searching for Place,* p. 203.

37. Dyczok, *Grand Alliance,* p. 139.

38. Janco, "The Soviet Refugee."

39. Jansen and de Jong, "Stalin's Hand"; Sudoplatov, *Special Tasks,* pp. 23–4.

40. Armstrong, *Ukrainian Nationalism;* Littman, *Pure Soldiers.*

41. Littman, *Pure Soldiers,* pp. 59–112; Snyder, *Reconstruction of Nations,* pp. 165–6.

42. Snyder, *Reconstruction of Nations,* pp. 154–78; Lotnik, *Nine Lives.*

43. Snyder, *Reconstruction of Nations,* p. 164; Bower, *Red Web;* Laar, *Forgotten War;* Burds, "Early Cold War"; Taubman, *Khrushchev,* pp. 193–7. Khrushchev was closely involved in the brutality and sanctioned the assassination of Catholic leaders who were not proving sufficiently helpful.

44. Luciuk, "Unintended Consequences."

45. Wyman, *DPs,* pp. 82–3.

46. Goni, *Real Odessa;* Simpson, *Blowback.*

47. Aldrich, *Hidden Hand,* pp. 142–4, 169–70.

48. Ibid., pp. 167–72.

49. Dyczok, *Grand Alliance,* pp. 127–32.

50. Ibid.; Cesarani, *Justice Delayed,* pp. 102–33; Luciuk, *Searching for Place;* Littman, *Pure Soldiers,* pp. 156–69.

CHAPTER 12: "SAVE THEM FIRST AND ARGUE AFTER"

1. Nevins, *Lehman,* p. 297; Lehman was defeated but later served as a senator from 1949 to 1957.

2. *Dictionary of American Biography,* suppl. 4 (New York, 1974); Kessner, *La Guardia.*

3. Caro, *Moses,* pp. 355, 699; Nevins, *Lehman,* pp. 218–19.

4. Coles and Weinberg, *Civil Affairs,* pp. 55–9; Sherwood, *Hopkins,* pp. 720–2; Caro, *Moses,* p. 699.

5. Hirschmann, *Embers,* p. 3; Jackson, UNRRA papers, C 256, no. 54, Lehman Suite, p. 40. The State Department was "completely barren of ideas" about displaced persons and "conscious only of the fact that DPs cost money and they can't get money." UD, April 29, 1946.

6. Hirschmann, *Embers,* p. 7; Keeny, "Reminiscences."

7. Hirschmann, *Embers,* pp. 6–7.
8. Ibid., pp. 7–10.
9. Hirschmann did an excellent job in publicizing his work, but historians are divided about its effectiveness. Henry Feingold considers him to have been "highly effective" and credits him with helping to save some 7,000 Jews who were extracted from Romania via Turkey and a further 48,000 whom the Romanian government was persuaded to protect. Yet for Yehuda Bauer, Hirschmann's rescue attempts, "though made with the best intentions and with great energy, failed completely." He may have had some slight influence over the Romanians, says Bauer, but "it was the Red Army bursting into the country that made the Rumanians rebel . . . and join the Allies, and it was the weakness of the German forces there that enabled this change-over to be effected without serious harm to the Jews." Bauer, *Jews for Sale,* pp. 184–5; Gutman (ed.), *Encyclopaedia of the Holocaust;* Feingold, *Politics of Rescue,* pp. 285–91. For further harsh judgements see Rapaport, *Shake Heaven* ("weak, vain, inglorious") and Wyman and Medoff, *Race against Death.*
10. Hirschmann, *Embers,* pp. 58–69; UD, June 12, 1946.
11. UD, April 30, 1946.
12. Hirschmann, *Embers,* pp. 63–73.
13. Ibid., pp. 74–94.
14. Ibid., pp. 94–5.
15. Ibid., pp. 106–11.
16. Byrnes, *Frankly Speaking,* pp. 187–92.
17. Hirschmann, *Embers,* pp. 124–8; UD, June 25, 1946. Von Lerchenfeld was a relative by marriage of Count von Stauffenberg.
18. After first intending to fire Jackson, La Guardia had found him indispensable and retained him. C. Tylor Wood, Travel Diary, George C. Marshall Foundation. La Guardia's visit to Europe, "was for some countries a considerable catastrophe, and for us in Italy . . . little more than a joke. He fired quite a number of his officials and demanded that the government fire others because in Austria and Czechoslovakia they used some of the imported grain to make the beer without which every workman's lunch is unthinkable in those countries—they like lager beer—and it never occurred to him that lager beer is to those people what table wine is to ordinary Italian families in Italy. But he came like a typhoon to the various countries and fired people, and threatened people, and scared many more that he didn't threaten directly." Keeny, "Reminiscences," LSE.
19. UD, May 2, May 20, and July 19, 1946; Morgan, *Peace and War,* p. 255.
20. UD, July 21, 1946. Burinski was "even for a Russian" a "bad type. The most palpable Moscow agent."
21. UD, June 10, July 15, and July 19, 1946.
22. USHMM, Saul Sorrin, Interview October 11, 1994 (and Picture no. 21010); Kochhavi, *Post-Holocaust Politics,* p. 214.
23. UD, June 10, 1946
24. UD, August 1 and August 2, 1946, Morgan Papers, IWM; Morgan, *Peace and War,* p. 255.
25. UD, August 8–15, 1946; Morgan Papers, IWM. Morgan ran the British atomic energy program from 1951 to 1956. He died in 1967.
26. Cohen later had a long career at the United Nations.

27. UNA: Box S 0402-0004, Subject Files of the Repatriation Section, File 3, Repatriation of Polish Displaced Persons; Nowakowski, *Camp of All Saints,* p. 21.
28. *WP,* pp. 151–60.
29. Hilton, "Pawns."
30. *WP,* pp. 153–60; UNA: S 1021, Box 81, File 3, "Incident Camp Wildflecken," Appendix to Price Report on Repatriation.
31. WP, p. 159–60; UNA: "Incident Camp Wildflecken."
32. KHL, letter, February 3, 1947; KHL: "Mr. Georges Masset as viewed by his deputy"—Kay Hulme to A. C. Dunn, Director UNRRA District 3, March 2, 1947. Afterward Kay discovered why the army had been reluctant to rush to their help when the situation got difficult: "we learned that Army had NEVER ordered that screening. That UNRRA had pranced ahead and ordered it and that all of this is the result of some obscure friction between Army and UNRRA."
33. UNA: S 1021, Box 81, File 3, "Plans for Spring Polish Repatriation Resulting from Conferences Held in Warsaw," March 1, 1947, Appendix 4 to Price Report on repatriation.

CHAPTER 13: "WE GROSSLY UNDERESTIMATED THE DESTRUCTION"

1. Dudley Edwards, *Gollancz,* pp. 434–5.
2. Gollancz was quite uninhibited by the fact that he himself had no experience of rationing and had continued to eat at London's exclusive Ivy restaurant throughout the war. On one occasion during his visit to Germany, while staying with a British army unit, he went down to breakfast early and ate his hosts' entire bacon ration for the day. Ibid., p. 438.
3. Ibid., pp. 434–7.
4. Frank, *Expelling Germans,* pp. 235–40.
5. Ibid., pp. 244–73; Wiskemann, *Germany's Eastern Neighbours,* pp. 144–51. On October 24, 1946, the Czech minister of the interior announced that the transfer of Germans was now complete. Of the 2.5 million Germans referred to at Potsdam, some 2,165,135 had been repatriated: 750,000 to the Russian Zone, the remainder to the American. However, 300,000 Germans had been retained "in essential industries," and some 820,000 Germans had been killed in the war, had fled in 1945, or were prisoners of war. The operation to remove the remaining Germans from Poland was known by the British as Operation Swallow. One relief worker wondered whether this was "an attempt to romanticise this trek of broken-hearted old people, patient mothers and numbed children . . . as the flight of swallows to a distant land" or whether it had "a more cynical significance—that an already reduced German land must swallow several millions of economically useless people." A British diplomat complained, "We are always being told what an essentially Christian people the Poles are. Could they not for once behave like Christians?" "Jews, some from as far afield as Russia, began arriving as 'Swallows' in ever increasing numbers from May 1946 and, following the Kielce pogrom of July 1946, the British authorities braced themselves for a deluge. Swallow transports were sometimes found to be 100 per cent Jewish and there were suspicions that Jewish organisations were providing 'forged papers on a vast scale.'" Polish local authorities also began loading the inmates of lunatic asylums, hospitals, orphanages, and old people's homes onto Swallow. Frank, *Expelling Germans,* p. 253.

6. Farquharson, *Western Allies,* pp. 44–60.

7. For calorie charts, see Steinert, "Food and the Food Crisis," p. 275; Kramer, *German Economy,* pp. 76–7.

8. Enssle, "Five Theses."

9. Jorden, *Operation Mercy,* pp. 73–9.

10. Gollancz, *Inside Darkest Germany,* pp. 23–7; Farquharson, "Emotional but Influential"; Reinisch, "Public Health."

11. Gollancz, *Inside Darkest Germany,* pp. 87–93.

12. Attlee wrote privately to Bevin, "Quite apart from the coal and food factors, the economic machine is running down. Reparation demands cause uncertainty and hopelessness as to the future. . . . I am myself apprehensive as to the future if we continue to be held to the Potsdam decisions . . . much longer." Meehan, *Strange Enemy People,* p. 199.

13. Deighton, *Impossible Peace,* pp. 54–80; Balfour and Mair, *Four-Power Control.*

14. Eisenberg, *Drawing the Line;* Yergin, *Shattered Peace.*

15. Murphy later argued that at the time no one appreciated the significance of Bizonia. Deighton's account suggests that the British did.

16. R. M. Raup, review of Farquharson, *Western Allies and Politics of Food,* in *Agricultural History* 62 (1988), pp. 110–11.

17. This section is largely derived from Matusow, *Politics of Food.*

18. *Time,* April 22, 1946; *NYT,* April–May 1946; Eleanor Roosevelt, "My Day," radio broadcast, June 3, 1946.

19. There were also personal factors. Part of La Guardia's reason for hastening the end of UNRRA was that he was seeking the Democratic nomination for senator from New York. When, however, Herbert Lehman won the nomination, La Guardia "changed his colours." Gibson, *Jacko,* p. 85.

20. Hirschmann, *Embers,* pp. 146–7. Sir John Boyd Orr, director-general of the UN FAO, proposed the establishment of a World Food Board, "which would operate to stabilize agricultural commodity prices in world markets, to create a world food reserve for use in case of shortages, and to dispose of surplus farm products on special terms to countries needing them." The U.S. Cabinet "accepted the principles of Sir John Orr, but not the method" on August 2, 1946. Wallace himself supported Orr's scheme, and Acheson "came out flat-footedly and wholeheartedly for the agreement" but Agriculture Secretary Anderson was "lukewarm" and Wallace concluded that State and Treasury would also be opposed "due to the influence of the grain trade." Blum (ed.), *Price of Vision,* p. 607.

21. *NYT,* September 7, and October 13, 1946.

22. Nevins, *Lehman,* p. 306. La Guardia resigned from UNRRA at the end of 1946 and died at his New York home nine months later. His successor as director general, former U.S. Army staff officer Major General Lowell W. Rooks, presided over UNRRA's obsequies.

23. Wilson, *Aftermath* (1947). UNRRA's staff in Yugoslavia included long-standing authorities on the region, such as the journalist Doreen Warriner, and others, such as the economist Michael Barratt Brown, who would later become stalwarts of the British Marxist Left.

24. Woodbridge, vol. 2, pp. 138–70; Barratt Brown, *Tito to Milosevic.*

25. Lampe, *Yugoslavia as History,* pp. 234–7; Pavlowitch, *Improbable Survivor,* pp. 187–92.

26. Byrnes, *Speaking Frankly,* pp. 145–6; Petrovich, "View from Yugoslavia."

27. Vachon, *Poland 1946* and "UNRRA at Work, no. 5," both quoted in Reinisch, "We Shall Build Anew," pp. 451, 464.

28. Lane, *I Saw Poland*, p. 176. The U.S. State Department regarded Drury as an "ardent, if naive propagandist for the Communist-dominated Warsaw government," led by his wife's "communist tendencies." Lukas, *Bitter Legacy*, p. 98; *AP*, pp. 87–92.

29. *AP*, p. 88; Lukas, *Bitter Legacy*, pp. 96–104; Woodbridge, vol. 2, pp. 200–30.

30. Lane, *I Saw Poland*, p. 176.

31. Woodbridge, II, p. 221.

32. *Life*, December 16, 1946; Lukas, *Bitter Legacy*, p. 102.

33. Acheson, *Present at the Creation*, p. 201.

34. Huntford, *Nansen*, pp. 634–8; Stoessinger, *Refugee*, pp. 18–23; Sjöberg, *Powers and the Persecuted*; Richard Law, quoted in London, *Whitehall and the Jews*, p. 249; Rendel, *Sword and Olive*, pp. 250–1.

35. Rendel, *Sword and Olive*, pp. 251–3.

36. Penrose, "Negotiating on Refugees."

37. Rendel, *Sword and Olive*, pp. 253–4. Vyshinsky was a bogeyman in the West after his role in the prewar show trials.

38. HST/OT, George L. Warren; Holborn, *IRO*, pp. 39–46.

39. HST/OT, George L. Warren.

40. Stoessinger, *Refugee*, pp. 92–5.

41. Acheson, *Present at the Creation*, p. 219; Patterson, *Grand Expectations*, pp. 127–8, McCullough, *Truman*, p. 542.

42. Rabbi Herbert Friedman in Mark Jonathan Harris's film *The Long Way Home*; Meehan, *Strange Enemy People*, pp. 239–42; Frank, "Working for the Germans"; Connor, *Refugees*.

43. Yergin, *Shattered Peace*, pp. 303–35.

44. *FRUS*, 1947, vol. 3, pp. 230–2. Clayton admitted, "we will have to lick the shipping lobby, fattening as it is off the U.S. Treasury."

45. McCullough, *Truman*, pp. 563–4.

46. Divine, review of Bonds, *Bipartisan Strategy*.

47. Hardach, "Marshall Plan in Germany."

CHAPTER 14: "DWELL, EAT, BREED, WAIT"

1. "A Yugoslav Speaks," "A Cutting from a School-teacher's Paper," "A Soldier of the Home Army," "VAD Nurse," "Adolescent in Nazi Hands," "A Man at Fourteen," "An Estonian Girl Speaks." Korwin, "No Man's People," part 2, Arnold-Forster Papers.

2. I have averaged three sets of figures. In June 1947, it was estimated that there were 558,851 DPs under UNRRA care or supervision in Germany, 28,059 in Austria, and 17,985 in Italy, making a total of 604,895. An American congressional committee, in late September 1947, found 643,763 in camps and 652,500 out of camps, a total of 1,296,263. A third report calculated that in November 1947 there were 637,800 in camps and 325,400 out of camps, a total of 963,200. Between September 1946 and June 1947, the number of Poles and Ukrainians fell from 302,725 to 235,258, a drop of 67,467. Woodbridge, vol. 2, pp. 498, 502; *ASH*, quoted in Grodzinsky, *In the Shadow*, p. 118.

3. Flanner, "Letter from Aschaffenburg."

4. UNA, "Camp Self-Government," UNRRA, Office of the Historian, UNA DP US 17, S1021, Box 81, File 1.

5. Ibid.; Woodbridge, vol. 2, pp. 522–5. Behind their united front, the leaders of the Latvians DPs were bitterly divided between groups representing different eras of the country's political history; the first wishing to purge Nazi collaborators and return to the democratic politics of the 1920s; the second consisting mainly of Nazi-era politicians. With the support of former Latvians soldiers in the German Army, the second group eventually prevailed. Purrs, "Latvian National Politics." in Gatrell and Baron (eds.), *Warlands*.

6. Ibid. Although academics seeking to categorize DP camps have invoked Irving Goffman's idea of the total institution, the social system the DP camp most resembled was the prisoner-of-war camp. In both, rival elites tended to emerge: one based on individuals' prewar status or military rank, the other on their capacity to adapt and thrive in the economic conditions of the camp. Nardini, "Survival Factors."

7. Y. Boshyk, "Repatriation and Resistance: Ukrainian Refugees and Displaced Persons in Occupied Germany and Austria, 1945–1948," in Bramwell (ed.), *Refugees*, p. 205.

8. Bohachevsky-Chomiak, "Women's Movement."

9. Y. Boshyk, "Repatriation and Resistance: Ukrainian Refugees and Displaced Persons in Occupied Germany and Austria, 1945–1948," in Bramwell (ed.), *Refugees*, p. 205.

10. H. Zielyk, "[Ukrainian] DP Camps as a Social System," in Isajiw et al. (eds.), *Refugee Experience*.

11. Harvard University Refugee Interview Project, Schedule B, Respondent 360, quoted in Dyczok, *Grand Alliance*, p. 188.

12. Danys, *DP*, p. 54; Balkelis, "Living in the Displaced Persons Camp."

13. Tools were scarce; instead of "indenting" officially for them, Klemmé's teams got axes off the Germans for a few cigarettes. The Germans, though, were reluctant to see their limited supplies of forest timber cut down to heat foreigners who could go home. Klemmé found that national rivalry produced more wood. The Balts, and especially the Latvians, were the best workers, while the Poles were "always doing things one would ordinarily expect of thirteen- or fourteen-year-olds." Klemmé, *Inside Story*, pp. 193–210.

14. Klemmé thought fourteen was a bit young, but the British insisted that their own boys started to work in the mines at fourteen and that the Germans and DPs were not entitled to a higher minimum wage.

15. Ibid.; Woodbridge, vol. 2, pp. 519–21.

16. Syrkin, quoted in Schwarz, *Redeemers*, pp. 226–8.

17. Morgan, report to Bevin, September 14, 1946, Morgan Papers, IWM; "A Yugoslav speaks" in Korwin, "No Man's People," p. 23, in Arnold-Forster Papers; Botting, *In the Ruins*, p. 289.

18. UN Report 1953, quoted in Balfour and Mair, *Four-Power Control*, pp. 110–11.

19. Peck (ed.) *Among the Survivors*, p. 63. At Belsen DP camp, people who had died or left but whose name remained on the camp roll were known as *malochim*, or angels. Bauer, *Out of the Ashes*, p. 99.

20. Eksteins, *Walking Since Daybreak*, pp. 128–9.

21. Königsweder and Wetzel, *Waiting for Hope*, pp. 200–1.

22. Peck (ed.), *Among the Survivors*, pp. 63–4; Bauer, *Out of the Ashes*, pp. 204–5.

23. Goldmann, *Mein Leben*, p. 335; Hardman and Goodman, *Survivors*, p. 106; Königsweder and Wetzel, *Waiting for Hope*, p. 175; Bauer, *Out of the Ashes*, p. 100. In July

1946, General Morgan began to take an interest in Belsen. He recorded that the Joint had been allowed to create a small fleet of trawlers, "ostensibly to fish for extra food for the starving Jews," but "little or no fish seems to have been brought ashore" and the trawlers were in fact being used as lighters, to ferry illicit goods ashore from cargo shipping in or off the port of Hamburg. This material was taken to a Joint depot near the Jewish children's home at Blankenese, which had been drawing large quantities of surplus rations. "Distribution to black markets is undertaken by the AJJDC fleet of lorries based on Belsen." Morgan found the CCG's intelligence chief, Brigadier John "Tubby" Lethbridge, "most interesting on the subject of underground trading that is going on organized by the American Jews"—he apparently believed that Joint officials were using "gold and jewels" distributed in small packets around Germany before the Nazi crash and now recovered, "in exchange for food for the Germans and for dope." This sounds like an anti-Semitic fantasy. UD, July 3, July 16, and July 19, 1946.

24. Königsweder and Wetzel, *Waiting for Hope*, p. 201.
25. *LR,* p. 28.
26. Danys, *DP,* pp. 55–64; Wyman, *DPs,* pp. 101–2.
27. Duchesne-Cripps, "Mental Outlook," Library of Congress.
28. Wyman, *DPs,* p. 122; Brodzki and Varon, "The Munich Years"; Holian, "Displacement"; *UNRRA Team News,* February 8, 1947. General Morgan was opposed to the "much advertised UNRRA University." "I cannot believe that [it] is going to produce anything other than a quantity of publicity," he wrote on March 25, 1946.
29. Nesaule, *Woman in Amber,* p. 112.
30. McDowell, *Hard Labour,* pp. 79–80.
31. Nesaule, *Woman in Amber,* p. 139.
32. Danys, *DP,* p. 64.
33. Dickens, *Lübeck Diary,* p. 69; R. Ilnytzkyj, "Ukrainian Camp Periodicals," in Isajiw et al. (eds), *Refugee Experience,* pp. 272–3.
34. Ilnytzkyj, "Ukrainian Camp Periodicals," pp. 279–86.
35. G. G. Grabowicz, "A Great Literature," and Revutsky, "Theatre in the Camps," both in Isajiw et al. (eds.), *Refugee Experience.*
36. Ibid., pp. 246–64.
37. Borowski's *This Way for the Gas* is available in English (with a biographical sketch by Jan Kott), but his DP stories have been translated only into French. Borowski's postwar life is sketched in Czesław Miłosz's *Captive Mind.*
38. Nowakowski, *The Camp of All Saints,* pp. 18, 290, 14, 162–3, 149.
39. Mekas, *I Had Nowhere to Go,* pp. 109, 129–31.
40. Ibid., p. 186.
41. Bakis, "DP Apathy."
42. Gringauz, "Jewish Destiny."
43. Pinson, "Jewish Life"; Mankowitz, *Life Between Memory and Hope,* p. 144. See also Patt, *Finding Home.*
44. Grossmann, *Jews, Germans, and Allies,* pp. 184–96.
45. Mankowitz, *Life Between Memory and Hope,* p. 285. OSE, *Report,* p. 52. Dr. Gisela Perl and Dr. Odette Rosenstock, who worked as physicians at Auschwitz and Belsen, made similar observations. Perl, *I Was a Doctor,* p. 182; Abadi, *Terre de Détresse,* p. 158; "Some Aspects of Jewish Social Work in Europe," *Jewish Social Service Quarterly,* 1946, p. 114.

46. Papanek, "They Are Not Expendable," pp. 312–19.

47. Grossmann, *Jews, Germans, and Allies,* pp. 150–1.

48. Segalman, "Psychology"; Pinson, "Jewish Life"; Milton and Bogin (eds), *American Jewish Joint Distribution Committee,* p. 1,329.

49. Pinson, "Jewish Life."

50. Mankowitz, *Life Between Memory and Hope,* p. 142.

51. Dawidowicz, *From That Place,* pp. 302–4.

52. H. B. M. Murphy, "Editor's Note," in H.B.M. Murphy, *Flight and Resettlement,* p. 64.

CHAPTER 15: "THE BEST INTERESTS OF THE CHILD"

1. UNA: UNRRA, Office of the Historian [Jean Henshaw], "Child Welfare in US Zone," S1021, Box 81, File 13, Exhibit 52, Stefan Puskaric.

2. Macardle, *Children of Europe,* pp. 58, 107, 154; Zahra, "Lost Children," p. 46.

3. Hrabar et al., *Fate of Polish Children,* p. 182; Macardle, *Children of Europe,* p. 301.

4. Dacie, *Yugoslav Refugees,* pp. 15–16.

5. Zahra, "Lost Children," p. 47; UNA S 518-0363, UNRRA Subject Files, PAG 4/1.13.5.6.0.129—UNRRA, "Psychological Problems of Displaced Persons."

6. Kinnear, *Woman of the World,* pp. 149–50.

7. Woodroofe, *Charity to Social Work,* pp. 151–77; Leiby, *History of Social Welfare,* pp. 241–4.

8. *AP,* pp. 104–15; Kinnear, *Woman of the World,* pp. 150–1.

9. Kinnear, *Woman of the World,* pp. 153–74.

10. General Morgan took her measure at once. "It was evident from her conversation that she had had little experience in the practical field," he wrote on September 24, 1945. "I gave her the idea to take away with her that from now on I am the head welfare officer in Frankfurt, though I shall be glad to have technical advice to assist me on some of the finer points. I think she got the idea." UD. In January 1946, General Gale ordered her to report to Washington but found Robert Jackson reluctant to sack her. Kinnear, *Woman of the World,* p. 172.

11. Zahra, "Lost Children"; F. Wilson, *Aftermath,* pp. 25–6. Thirty-seven percent were American, 34 percent were British.

12. British welfare administrator Geraldine Aves, quoted in Wilmot, *Singular Woman.*

13. McNeill, *Rivers of Babylon,* pp. 103–10; Korwin, "No Man's People," p. 41, in Arnold-Forster Papers.

14. F. Wilson, *Margins of Chaos,* passim.

15. F. Wilson, *Aftermath,* pp. 15, 31–3.

16. Dawson, "Stagnant Pool," IWM. Rhoda Dawson "heard that it was partly because she allowed her French second-in-command to take the secretary to his bed." She felt his was "a poor sort of excuse," particularly as the next director would "shout cheerfully through the door of her Chief Welfare Officer's bedroom where she and the American town Major were carrying on." "How indulgent Americans are to all the little 'irregularities' involving their own officers and how fierce if a Frenchman has a girl-friend," Francesca wrote to Rhoda. "What hypocrisy." Dawson Papers, IWM.

17. Pettiss and Taylor, *After the Shooting Stopped,* pp. 65–6, 54, 62, 210–17.

18. Pinson, "Jewish Life"; Somers and Kok (eds.), *Jewish Displaced Persons,* pp. 22–7.

19. Zahra, "Lost Children," p. 45.

20. Henshaw, "Child Welfare."
21. Ibid., Exhibit 29.
22. Henshaw, "Child Welfare"; Macardle, *Children of Europe*, p. 237. Colonel Schottland was in peacetime a distinguished social worker.
23. UD, March 4, March 12, April 2, May 29, 1946.
24. Sereny, *German Trauma*, pp. 33–52.
25. Klemmé, *Inside Story*, pp. 257–8. On July 16, 1946 C. J. Taylor, deputy zone director, commented on a document on UNRRA's responsibilities to unaccompanied children: "Nationality is not decided by UNRRA" and asked "how far the removal of [children of undetermined nationality] from German institutions to UNRRA children's homes [was] justified. . . . This would appear to be a military responsibility and not UNRRA's."
26. Eileen Davidson to Richard Winslow, January 22, 1948. Winslow Papers, quoted in Nicholas, *Cruel World*, p. 507.
27. Henshaw, "Child Welfare."
28. E. Blackey, "Closure Report on Unaccompanied Children in Germany," April 1947, UNA PAG-4/1.1.3.5.4.:21. Thanks to Gitta Sereny and Don Honeyman. On Austria: Brownlee, "Whose Children?," Hoover Institution.
29. Ella Dunkel, "Memorandum on Child Search, June 13, 1947"; Michael Sorenson, "Some Observations at the Conclusion of Six Months of Child Search and Investigation," August 1946. UNA, PAG 2/4.2:82/S-0524-0106. Thanks to Nick Stargardt.
30. E. Davidson, "Removal from German families of Allied Children: Reasons Why This Is in the Best Interests of the Child," February 21, 1948, quoted in Zahra, "Lost Children," p. 79.
31. Holborn, *IRO*, pp. 493–512; Marrus, *The Unwanted*, pp. 350–1; Sereny, *German Trauma*, pp. 49–52.
32. For differing numbers, Marrus, *The Unwanted*, pp. 350–1; Woodbridge, vol. 2, p. 531; Sereny, *German Trauma*, p. 52; Heinemann, *"Rasse,"* pp. 508–9, quoted in Zahra, *Kidnapped Souls*, p. 260.
33. Clay and Leapman, *Master Race*, followed up several individuals. Blackey, "Closure report," UNA.
34. Brosse, *War-Handicapped Children;* Dalianis and Mazower, "Children in Turmoil."

CHAPTER 16: "GOOD HUMAN STOCK"

1. KHL, March 30, 1947. The following day she discovered that her Belgian nurse was having a miscarriage and had to drive her to Frankfurt.
2. KHL, March 23 and April 17, 1947.
3. *WP,* pp. 173–8.
4. *Time,* May 19, 1947; Sangster, "Polish 'Dionnes.'"
5. Clark, *Role of Uprooted People.*
6. Paul, *Whitewashing Britain*, pp. 25–89. What follows draws on Cesarani, *Justice Delayed;* Kay and Miles, *Refugees;* Tannahill, *European Volunteer Workers.*
7. Orwell, *Smothered Under Journalism 1946,* p. 482.
8. Tannahill, *European Volunteer Workers;* Winder, *Bloody Foreigners;* Neal Ascherson, review of London, *Whitehall and the Jews,* in *New York Review of Books,* March 29, 2001.

9. Overy, *Morbid Age,* pp. 93–135; Cesarani, *Justice Delayed,* pp. 66–73.

10. F. Wilson, *Aftermath,* p. 152. TNA: LAB 8/90. "Draft Report on Recruitments of Balts for Hospitals," quoted in Kay and Miles, *Refugees,* p. 50.

11. Kay and Miles, *Refugees,* pp. 42–65; Tannahill, *European Volunteer Workers,* pp. 19–30.

12. *The Manchester Guardian,* October 21, 1946; *Evening Standard,* October 5, 1946; *The Star,* February 28, 1947, quoted in Kay and Miles, *Refugees,* pp. 51–2.

13. McDowell, *Hard Labour,* p. 102.

14. Kay and Miles, *Refugees,* pp. 52; Tannahill, *European Volunteer Workers,* pp. 133.

15. McNeill, *Rivers of Babylon,* pp. 200–3.

16. McDowell, *Hard Labour,* p. 103. Matrons and hospital staff found the Baltic EVWs to be willing workers. Several were given additional responsibilities, which their English and Irish codomestics resented: "There was some jealousy in the hospital. We were good workers and some of the English girls were jealous."

17. Ibid., p. 117.

18. Paul, *Whitewashing,* p. 84; Kay and Miles, *Refugees,* p. 116.

19. Some of the restrictions on dependents were eventually lifted.

20. *WP,* pp. 178–86.

21. The "Belgian miners' scheme" was originally developed by the IGCR. By the end of 1949, "nearly 32,000 refugees had gone to Belgium, 21,649 of the miners and their families having been moved by the IRO. By the same date 7,413 persons had returned to Germany." Holborn, *IRO,* pp. 377–82.

22. Clark, *Role of Uprooted People,* the report of a "special group working on the human aspects of European reconstruction." Its members included Earl G. Harrison, the demographer Eugene Kulischer, Joseph Schwartz of the Joint, and Ernest Penrose, the diplomat who had helped establish the IRO.

23. Ristelhueber quoted in *American Political Science Review* 51 (1957), p. 239; Holborn review of Stoessinger, *Refugee and World Community,* in *American Political Science Review,* 51 (1957), p. 529.

24. Marrus, *The Unwanted,* p. 343. The IRO's second executive director, William Hallam Tuck, a friend of Herbert Hoover and Congressman Jerry Voorhis (who had helped to get funding for the IRO), proved to be a poor administrator. He was quickly and silently removed. HST/OT, George L. Warren.

25. *WP,* pp. 196–8; Holborn, *IRO,* p. 355.

26. Only 2,358 refugees were actually resettled in Turkey. Stoessinger, *Refugee,* p. 121.

27. Holborn, *IRO,* pp. 433–42.

28. Eksteins, *Walking Since Daybreak,* p. 100; Danys, *DP,* pp. 67–85. See also *AP,* pp. 324–42.

29. Eksteins, *Walking Since Daybreak,* p. 105.

30. Peters, *Milk and Honey,* pp. 5–8.

31. Ibid., pp. 14–18; Kunz, *Displaced Persons.*

32. Peters, *Milk and Honey,* pp. 63–4.

33. *WP,* p. 207.

34. Danys, *DP,* pp. 169–70; Eksteins, *Walking Since Daybreak,* p. 91.

35. *WP,* pp. 199–202.

36. Holborn, *IRO,* pp. 365–440.

37. Danys, *DP,* p. 93.

38. Agate Nesaule tells the story of a twelve-year-old boy who sexually attacked girls.

"The vigorous screening process for emigration did not single him out, and he went to Canada, where he later murdered a ten-year-old girl." Nesaule, *Woman in Amber,* p. 133.

39. Danys, *DP,* pp. 89–90.
40. Ibid., p. 198–9.
41. Holleufer, "Seeking New Horizons"; Holborn, *IRO,* pp. 401–10; Goni, *Real Odessa.*

CHAPTER 17: "WE LIVED TO SEE IT"

1. Schwarz, *Redeemers,* pp. 206–7; Finder, "Muscular Judaism"; "Boxing Championship," Steven Spielberg Jewish Film Archive, www.spielbergfilmarchive.org.il.
2. Klausner report, March 20, 1947, in Klausner, *Letter to My Children,* pp. 130–7. Grodzinsky, *In the Shadow* (p. 147), gives a figure of 200 camps exclusively for Jews out of 732 camps in all in Germany, but his source (the appendix to Königsweder and Wetzel, *Waiting for Hope*) lists only 109 in the U.S. Zone.
3. Srole, "Why the DPs Can't Wait."
4. Klausner, *Letter,* pp. 130–7; Halamish, *Exodus Affair,* p. 276; Bernstein, "Europe's Jews."
5. Gringauz, "Our New German policy." The cemetery which Gringauz and Dr. Zalman Grinberg had established in the village of Schwabhausen for the Jews who died in April 1945 when the train taking them to Dachau was shot up by the Americans was among those vandalized.
6. Bauer, *Out of the Ashes,* pp. 196–201; Schwarz, *Redeemers,* pp. 212–18.
7. "A strange, inexplicable silence envelops his departure—no speeches, no thanks, no good wishes." Mankowitz, *Life Between Memory and Hope,* p. 191.
8. Rose, *"Senseless, Squalid War,"* is a good recent account. See also Bethell, *Palestine Triangle.*
9. Cohen, *Palestine,* pp. 162–70; Louis, *British Empire,* pp. 439–43.
10. At that time a debate was raging on the government's decision to pull out of India, the economic climate worsened sharply, and the country suffered one of the worst winters in its history.
11. Cohen, *Palestine,* p. 261. Louis, *British Empire,* p. 483, surveys historians' explanations for the Soviet move. Meir Zamir, "Britain's treachery, France's Revenge," *Haaretz,* February 7, 2008, argued that "France kept the Soviets abreast of British activity in the Middle East and North Africa" and that France and the Soviet Union made common cause to defeat British schemes for Arab federation in the region.
12. Stewart, *Royal Navy;* Friedman, "Road Back."
13. Halamish, *Exodus Affair,* pp. 15–51.
14. Ibid., p. 49.
15. French officials were still smarting from events the previous year, when the British had prevented them from reoccupying their former colonial possessions in the Levant, notably Syria. "You have insulted France and betrayed the West," de Gaulle had told the British ambassador. "Do they think we have forgotten Syria?" one bureaucrat asked in 1946. Zamir, "Britain's Treachery, France's Revenge."
16. Halamish, *Exodus Affair,* p. 72.
17. Ibid., pp. 66–102; Stewart, *Royal Navy,* pp. 112–28.
18. Somers and Kok, *Jewish Displaced Persons;* pp. 184–213. The barbed wire, intended to stop outsiders coming in and helping the *Exodus* DPs, was quite ineffective. Within a

few months, most of the passengers had been removed, smuggled out of the British Zone, and returned to Palestine. Klausner, *Letter to My Children,* pp. 142–5.

19. Zertal, *From Catastrophe to Power,* pp. 239–54.
20. Louis, *British Empire,* pp. 464–77; Cohen, *Palestine,* pp. 260–8.
21. Weizmann's intervention with Truman ensured that in the partition of Palestine the Negev Desert was saved for the Jews. Morris, *1948,* pp. 51–65.
22. Louis, *British Empire,* pp. 478–93; Cohen, *Palestine,* pp. 276–300; Sachar, *History of Israel,* pp. 283–95.
23. Fawzi al-Qawuqji, quoted in Morris, *1948,* p. 61.
24. TNA: 371/68528, quoted in Cohen, *Palestine,* pp. 298–9.
25. Walid Khalidi, *Before Their Diaspora* (Washington, D.C., 1991), pp. 305–6, quoted in Morris, *1948,* p. 163.
26. Schwarz, *Redeemers,* p. 266.
27. Louis, *British Empire,* pp. 526–8. Truman, Diary, July 21, 1946, HST Library.
28. Yablonka, *Survivors,* pp. 81–98; Grodzinsky, *In the Shadow,* pp. 166–87. According to Grodzinsky, there is little evidence that the Yishuv leadership was concerned with the legal issues posed by a draft on foreign soil.
29. Grodzinsky, *In the Shadow,* pp. 190–1; Hyman, *Undefeated,* pp. 365–6.
30. Finder, "Muscular Judaism"; Moshe Ajzenbud, quoted in Grodzinsky, *In the Shadow,* pp. 193–4.
31. Novick, *Holocaust,* pp. 80–1. Klausner had returned to Germany on an army assignment. Klausner's fear was that "if nothing was done, the Jews would sink into a moral morass and, with the reconstitution of an independent Germany, would be singled out for physical destruction." Bauer, *Out of the Ashes,* pp. 265–6.
32. Conversations with General Harrold, April 13 and 20, 1948; Novick, *Holocaust,* p. 299. Bauer's emphasis is different. "The process of recruitment," he wrote, "which at first seemed to be fairly straightforward, soon caused a great deal of trouble. Enthusiastic recruiters from among the DPs moved from persuasion to force, in their attempts to get the largest numbers of recruits possible. While the majority really were volunteers, others were persuaded by social pressure. . . . Ugly scenes occurred and camp committees refused to give such people the JDC supplementary rations to which they were entitled." Bauer claims that both the Joint and the Central Committee were powerless to prevent this: "The camp committees really were a law unto themselves, and did not care what the people in Munich were saying. Yet at the same time there were scenes of mass support for the drive, and even a few manipulators and black marketers were smitten with enthusiasm to go and fight. It was really the only way of escaping Germany; recruits had priority in illegal immigrant ships and those who could not be accommodated on the ships and had to wait for an opportunity, were prepared to join the Jewish forces in Palestine the moment this became possible." Bauer, *Out of the Ashes,* pp. 264–5.
33. Segev, *Seventh Million,* pp. 176–9.
34. Grodzinsky, *In the Shadow,* pp. 209–15. Segev stated that "one out of three of the war's casualties was a Holocaust survivor," *Seventh Million,* p. 177.
35. Segev, *Seventh Million,* p. 178.
36. Yablonka, *Holocaust Survivors,* pp. 18–42.
37. Ibid., pp. 270–1; Murphy, "Resettlement of Jewish Refugees."
38. Segev, *Seventh Million,* pp. 161–2. According to Ben-Gurion, "a total of some 110,000 people settled in abandoned accommodation." Yablonka, *Holocaust Survivors,* p. 18.

Historians still debate as to whether the Israelis practiced "ethnic cleansing"—had a plan to evict the Arabs—or their flight was spontaneous. For a recent discussion, see Morris, *1948.*

39. H. Rosensaft, *Yesterday*, pp. 106–10; J. Rosensaft, "Our Belsen," in *Belsen*, pp. 42–3.

40. H. Rosensaft, *Yesterday*, pp. 114–15, 120–1; Hardman and Goodman, *The Survivors*, p. 107; Goldmann, *Mein Leben*, p. 337; Ruth Aliav, quoted in Segev, *Seventh Million*, p. 181.

CHAPTER 18: AMERICA'S FAIR SHARE

1. Israel Zangwill, *The Melting-Pot.*

2. Polenberg, *One Nation Divisible*, pp. 32–45; Brown and Roucek (eds.), *One America*, pp. 104–20; *HEAEG*, pp. 405–25.

3. Greene, "Poles," in *HEAEG*, pp. 787–803. These were, of course, the attributes of this group of Polish immigrants to America, not of Poles in general.

4. Crossman, *Palestine Mission*, pp. 37, 39; Glazer, *American Judaism;* Feingold, *Zion in America;* Johnson, *History of the Jews.*

5. Goren, "Jews," in *HEAEG*, pp. 571–98.

6. McCullough, *Truman*, p. 596; *ASH*, pp. 36–8; Sachar, *Redemption of the Unwanted.*

7. Zolberg, *Nation by Design*, p. 1.

8. Henry L. Stimson, quoted in Bendersky, *"Jewish Threat,"* pp. 336–7. Stimson was secretary of state in 1924 and was Roosevelt's secretary of war at the time of his remarks.

9. Daniels, *Coming to America*, pp. 287–306; Graham, *Unguarded Gates*, offers a different interpretation.

10. Zolberg, *Nation by Design*, pp. 285–6.

11. *ASH*, p. 173; Genizi, *Fair Share*, pp. 66–7. Dinnerstein's remains the classic account, but Genizi provides useful extra detail.

12. *ASH*, p. 115.

13. Novick, "Looking Back in Anger," *The Washington Post*, May 1, 2005. Novick argues that Laurel Leff's criticism of Sulzberger in *Buried by the Times* is misconceived: "The great difficulty with blaming the behavior of the *Times* on Sulzberger's belief system is that so many others—Jews and gentiles, universalists and particularists, Zionists and anti-Zionists—believed more or less identically. Yehuda Bauer . . . writes that the wartime Palestinian press would 'go into ecstasies about some local party political affair, while the murder of the Jews of Europe is reported only in the inside pages.' "

14. *ASH*, pp. 116–36; Genizi, *Fair Share*, pp. 70–2.

15. Novick, *Holocaust*, pp. 81–2; *ASH*, pp. 117–36.

16. *ASH*, pp. 128–9.

17. Ibid., p. 159.

18. Burstin, *After the Holocaust*, p. 69; Königsweder and Wetzel, *Waiting for Hope*, p. 62.

19. Bruce Mohler, director of the Bureau of Immigration of the National Catholic Welfare Conference, Washington, D.C., March 3, 1947, quoted in Burstin, *After the Holocaust*, pp. 69–70.

20. *ASH*, pp. 163–77; Genizi, *Fair Share*, pp. 74–80.

21. *ASH*, pp. 177–8; Genizi, *Fair Share*, pp. 81–111.

22. *ASH*, p. 183; Genizi, *Fair Share*, pp. 114–127.

23. "Annexed areas," according to State Department directives, ultimately included, in

addition to the Baltic States, eastern Poland, Silesia, Bessarabia, and Moldavia, the former city of Danzig and what was once East Prussia.

24. *ASH*, pp. 183–98.

25. Cohen, *Case Closed,* pp. 30–49; *ASH*, p. 209.

26. *ASH*, p. 211–12.

27. Lehman's Republican opponent, John Foster Dulles, tried to portray him as "soft on communism" for having hired "Reds" at UNRRA. Nevins, *Lehman,* pp. 307–31.

28. Gunther, *Inside U.S.A.,* pp. 76–84; Ybarra, *Washington Gone Crazy,* pp. 459–84.

29. *ASH*, pp. 217–53.

30. Ibid., pp. 243–5.

31. Although Jews made up 20 to 25 percent of the DPs, they represented only 16 percent of those admitted to the United States under the 1948 and 1950 acts. However, when the disproportionate numbers of Jews admitted under the 1945 Truman directive are also considered, the figures are fairer.

CHAPTER 19: LEGACIES

1. Nesaule, *Woman in Amber,* p. 121.

2. Nesaule witnessed a formal debate at the Latvian Center in Indianapolis on "Who had the hardest time during the war, men or women?" The men spoke of exhaustion, wounds, and death and gave casualty figures, whereas the women, living in a culture in which even to mention the word "rape" was unacceptable in polite society, could only refer to "terrible things, more destructive in their own way," that had happened to their sex in war. The men won the debate. Ibid., pp. 182–3.

3. Ibid., pp. 272–80.

4. In his fine memoir, *Walking Since Daybreak,* the Latvian-born historian Modris Eksteins explains that, despite his academic triumphs in the Anglo-imperial culture of 1950s Canada, he identifies most strongly with the north German Protestant world he encountered as a young child in the DP camps. Eksteins's father, like Nesaule's, was a Latvian minister.

5. Rachel's eldest brother was strongly pro-Communist but was imprisoned by the Soviet authorities, perhaps for Zionism or for black-market activities.

6. Berger, *Displaced Persons.*

7. Hilton, *Displaced Person,* pp. 101–2.

8. The Puders were cosponsored by the Lutheran Church and the Deans.

9. Theodor, being German, was fond of beer yet had found himself in a dry state. The local sheriff was very understanding when he celebrated the birth of another child too vigorously.

10. Kunz, *Displaced Persons,* pp. 173–209; Murphy, "The Assimilation of Refugee Immigrants in Australia." The Australian Medical Association was at the time still technically known as the Australian branch of the British Medical Association.

11. Corsellis and Ferrar, *Slovenia 1945,* pp. 166–79.

12. McDowell, *Hard Labour,* p. 157.

13. Heberle and Hall, *New Americans;* Eksteins, *Walking Since Daybreak,* p. 88; Danys, *DP,* pp. 217–32.

14. Burstin, *After the Holocaust,* p. 134; Jaroszyńska-Kirchmann, *Exile Mission.* Polish intellectuals who made their way to Chicago, hoping to become valued professionals, discovered that neither American society nor the Polish community in the

United States valued and revered intellectuals as they traditionally had been in pre-war Poland. Unable to adapt, not happy to drive taxis or collect garbage, such intellectuals clung to their shrunken status and their internal world. Iwańska, *Polish Intelligentsia*.

15. Luciuk, *Searching for Place*, pp. 245–63.

16. Luciuk (ed.), *Heroes of Their Day*, p. 124.

17. B. Cohen, *Case Closed*. Some cities were more receptive than others. New York, unsurprisingly, was not particularly welcoming, whereas in Boston and San Francisco more imaginative resettlement schemes were based on a greater understanding of what the survivors had been through. In Denver, Colorado, where the Jewish community was quite small, social workers were convinced that the city was being used as a dumping ground for hard cases and constantly complained that unsuitable people, such as Orthodox rabbis and people for whose skills there was no demand (such as clothing workers), were being sent there. Social workers helping Jewish DPs to adjust produced numerous articles in journals.

18. Burstin, *After the Holocaust*, p. 112.

19. Cohen, *Case Closed*. The extensive literature on Holocaust survivors in the U.S. is surveyed in Niewyk and Nicosia, *The Columbia Guide to the Holocaust*, pp. 363–70.

20. Zertal, *From Catastrophe to Power*, p. 219.

21. Ibid.

22. Ibid., p. 220.

23. Segev, *Seventh Million*, p. 161.

24. Yablonka, *Survivors*, pp. 267–78.

25. H. B. M. Murphy, "The Resettlement of Jewish Refugees."

26. Segev, *Seventh Million*, p. 175.

27. Yablonka, *Survivors*, pp. 277–8.

28. E-mail, Yair Grinberg to author, February 23, 2009.

29. Ibid.

30. H. Rosensaft, *Yesterday*, pp. 127–48; Goldmann, *Mein Leben*, pp. 334–41 (author's translation). According to his son, Rosensaft gambled only on holiday in Europe. Menachem Rosensaft, telephone conversation with the author May 2010.

31. Ibid.

32. Gibson, *Jacko*. Jackson had a variety of jobs with the British government, including the Volta River dam scheme in Ghana, and produced an influential report on development in the 1960s but was something of a forgotten figure when he was brought in to handle the UN relief operation in Bangladesh in 1971, following devastating floods and a civil war. Although he was by then sixty years old and in poor health, his experience, skill, and imagination made this operation a model of "large-scale professionalism." Thereafter he was used to coordinate UN assistance programs, most notably in Kampuchea in 1981. Shawcross, *Quality of Mercy*.

33. *UC*, p. 235.

34. According to official IRO figures, there remained 140,011 foreign refugees in Germany as of December 31, 1951, but Vernant, *Refugee*, p. 147, gives a figure of 200,000. Kee, *Refugee World*, p. 7, speaks of "300,000 still unsettled refugees." By the 1980s, UNRRA was looked back on as "probably the broadest and most effective disaster-relief agency ever formed—at one time it employed almost 50,000 people, and, over its existence, it spent $4.25 billion on food supplies, medical supplies and programs,

industrial and agricultural reconstruction, and aid to refugees—in Greece, Yugoslavia, Albania, Czechoslovakia, Poland, Italy, Austria, Finland, Hungary, Ukraine, Ethiopia, China, the Philippines and Korea—8.5 million in all." Shawcross, *Quality of Mercy,* pp. 80–1.

35. Marrus, *The Unwanted,* pp. 354–8.
36. Gatrell, "World Refugee Year." The British government's response was niggardly. Many countries issued stamps, and World Refugee Year is now remembered largely by philatelists. The instigators also hoped to reawaken a spirit of idealism in a generation of young people made cynical by Suez, the atom bomb, and colonial policing scandals in Kenya and Cyprus. There are obvious parallels with modern events such as the 2005 "Make Poverty History" campaign.
37. Kee, *Refugee World.* Kee quoted a UNHCR estimate of some 35,000 DPs left in Germany and a Ukrainian estimate that there were about 14,000 Ukrainian refugees in Germany, of whom 6,000 were in need. One thousand of those were in camps. Many of those out of camps were working for farmers. Most of the refugees in Austria were "economic migrants" from Yugoslavia.
38. About a third (800,000) were expellees. Connor, *Refugees,* p. 143; Ther, "Integration," p. 300.
39. Judt, *Postwar,* pp. 354–9: Ther, "Integration"; Kossert, *Kalte Heimat;* Connor, *Refugees,* pp. 139–96; Kee, *Refugee World,* p. 26.
40. Novick, *Holocaust,* pp. 102–23; Judt, *Reappraisals,* p. 38.
41. Novick, *Holocaust,* p. 133. Novick goes on to argue, more controversially, that once the concept of the Holocaust had become present in American minds, it was then invoked, first, as a way of raising support for Israel and, second, as a way of reversing the secularization and declining Jewish commitment of the young. Novick, *Holocaust,* pp. 132–3. Other reasons why the Holocaust is now at the center of Western consciousness include the powerful memoir literature, from Anne Frank's *Diary* to Primo Levi's *Is This a Man?;* a psychiatric literature derived from the West German survivor compensation process, which strongly influenced modern approaches to trauma; meticulous historical scholarship, notably by Raul Hilberg; and, at a more popular level, Claude Lanzmann's 1985 film *Shoah* and the vulgar, meretricious, and hugely popular 1987 television miniseries *Holocaust.*
42. Ryan, *Quiet Neighbors,* p. 5.
43. Cesarani, *Justice Delayed,* p. 1.
44. Sereny, *German Trauma,* pp. 309–57. Sereny's 1974 book *Into That Darkness* dealt with Franz Stangl, the commandant of Sobibor and Treblinka.
45. U. Herbert, "No Compensation for Forced Labour," *Frankfurter Allgemeine Zeitung,* July 19, 1999.
46. Ibid.
47. Deutsche Bank commissioned Harold James; the insurance company Allianz, Gerald D. Feldman; Bertelsmann, accused in the Swiss press of publishing anti-Semitic books during the Nazi years, Saul Friedländer; Volkswagen, Hans Mommsen. See Eley, "Historical Accountability," *NYT,* September 8, 1999.
48. In an attempt to claim the moral high ground, the German government also established the Remembrance, Responsibility and Future foundation, whose sanctimonious pronouncements, couched in truth-and-reconciliation claptrap, leave a nasty taste.

49. Polish American Congress, "Forced Labor Compensation Programs: A Mid-term review and assessment"; Foundation Remembrance, Responsibility and Future, Final report to the U.S. government, press release, March 9, 2009; "Paying for the Past," *Central European Review,* January 8, 2001.

50. "Germany Ends War Chapter with 'Slave Fund' closure," Reuters, June 12, 2007.

51. James D. White, review of van Reenan, *Lithuanian Diaspora,* in *Slavonic and East European Review* 70 (1992), p. 189; Luciuk, *Searching for Place,* pp. 273–4; Wyman, *DPs,* p. 3.

52. Wyman, *DPs,* pp. 1–13; Lieven, *Baltic Revolution,* p. 276; Skultans, *Testimony of Lives.* Adamkus served as president of Lithuania from 1998 to 2003 and again from 2004 to 2009. The largest group to return was Croatians from Argentina, where economic conditions had not been good.

53. Wyman, *DPs,* p. 12.

Bibliography

UNPUBLISHED MATERIALS

WILL ARNOLD-FORSTER PAPERS (PRIVATE COLLECTION, LONDON)

Correspondence, 1943–1946

Marta Korwin, "No Man's People," part I. memoir written ca. 1950

Marta Korwin, "No Man's People," part II, essays by displaced persons, 1946:

"A Yugoslav Speaks"

"A Cutting from a School-teacher's Paper"

"A Soldier of the Home Army"

"Joining a Gang"

"VAD Nurse, Student of Painting in the Art Academy of Cracow Before the War"

"An Estonian Girl Speaks"

"So Many Were like Him"

"Adolescent in Nazi Hands," A

"Adolescent in Nazi Hands," B

"Bozenka"

"A Man at Fourteen"

BRITISH PSYCHOANALYTIC SOCIETY, LONDON

John Rickman Papers

COLUMBIA UNIVERSITY, LEHMAN SUITE

Sir Robert Jackson Papers

HOOVER INSTITUTION, STANFORD UNIVERSITY

Aleta Brownlee, "Whose Children?"

IMPERIAL WAR MUSEUM, LONDON

Effie Barker Papers

Lieutenant General Sir Frederick Morgan, "UNRRA Diary"

Lieutenant General Sir Frederick Morgan Papers

Rhoda Dawson, "The Stagnant Pool"

LIBRARY OF CONGRESS, WASHINGTON, D.C.

A. Duchesne-Cripps, "The Mental Outlook of the Displaced Persons as Seen Through Welfare Work in Displaced Persons Camps" (1955)

LONDON SCHOOL OF ECONOMICS

Fabian Society Papers
Spurgeon M. Keeny, "Reminiscences"

GEORGE C. MARSHALL FOUNDATION

C. Tylor Wood, Travel Diary, 1946

NEW YORK CITY ARCHIVE

Fiorello H. La Guardia Papers

HARRY S. TRUMAN LIBRARY

Anne Laughlin Papers

UNITED NATIONS ARCHIVES, NEW YORK

UNRRA Archives

UNITED STATES HOLOCAUST MEMORIAL MUSEUM

Earl C. Harrison, Journal, 1946
Rosensaft Papers

UNIVERSITY OF CAPE TOWN LIBRARY

Hansi P. Pollak Papers

UNIVERSITY OF QUEENSLAND LIBRARY, AUSTRALIA

Sir Raphael Cilento, "Escape from U.N. Reality," unpublished MS, n.d., ca. 1953

BEINECKE RARE BOOK AND MANUSCRIPT LIBRARY, YALE UNIVERSITY

Kathryn C. Hulme Papers

INTERVIEWS

BODLEIAN LIBRARY, OXFORD

Sir Robert Jackson, MS Eng. C 4676, C 4678.

HARRY S. TRUMAN LIBRARY

Charles P. Kindleberger
C. Tylor Wood
George L. Warren

PUBLISHED SOURCES

Unless otherwise indicated, London is the place of publication.

Abadi, O. *Terre de détresse* (Paris, 1995).

Abzug, R. H. *Inside the Vicious Heart: Americans and the Liberation of Nazi Concentration Camps* (New York, 1985).

Acheson, D. *Present at the Creation: My Years at the State Department* (New York, 1969).

Ahonen P., et al. *People on the Move: European Population Movements in Europe in the Second World War and Its Aftermath* (Oxford, England, 2008).

Alberich, T. and R. W. Zweig (eds.). *Escape Through Austria: Jewish Refugees and the Austrian Route to Palestine* (2002).

Aldrich, R. J. *The Hidden Hand: Britain, America and Cold War Secret Intelligence* (Woodstock, N.Y., 2002).

Anders, W. *An Army in Exile* (1949).

Annan, N. *Changing Enemies: The Defeat and Regeneration of Germany* (1996).

Applebaum, A. *Gulag. A History of the Soviet Camps* (2003).

Arendt, H. *Eichmann and the Holocaust* (2005).

Armonas, B. *Leave Your Tears in Moscow* (Philadelphia, 1961).

Armstrong, J. *Ukrainian Nationalism* (New York, 1963).

Armstrong-Reid, S., and D. Murray. *Armies of Peace: Canada and the UNRRA Years* (Toronto, 2008).

Arnold-Forster, W. "UNRRA's Prospects," *Political Quarterly* 15 (1944), pp. 57–65.

———. "UNRRA's Work for Displaced Persons in Germany," *International Affairs*, 1946, pp. 1–13.

Asquith, M. *Famine: Quaker Work to Russia, 1921–1923* (Oxford, England, 1943).

Atkinson, R. *An Army at Dawn: The War in North Africa* (2004).

Bakis, E. "DP Apathy," in H. B. M. Murphy (ed.), *Flight and Resettlement* (1956).

Balfour, M., and J. Mair. *Four-Power Control in Germany and Austria, 1945–1946* (Oxford, 1956).

Balkelis, T. "Living in the Displaced Persons Camp: Lithuanian War Refugees in the West, 1944–54," in Gatrell and Baron (eds.), *Warlands*.

Baron, N. "Remaking Soviet Society: the Filtration of Returnees from Nazi Germany, 1944–49," in Gatrell and Baron (eds.), *Warlands*.

Baron, N., and P. Gatrell (eds.). *Homelands: War, Population and Statehood in Eastern Europe and Russia, 1918–1924* (2004).

Brown, M. Barratt. *From Tito to Milosevic: Yugoslavia, the Lost Country* (2005).

Bauer, Y. *American Jewry and the Holocaust: The American Joint Distribution Committee, 1939–1945* (Detroit, 1981).

———. "The DP Legacy," in M. Z. Rosensaft (ed.), *Life Reborn* (2001).

———. *Flight and Rescue: Brichah, The Organized Escape of the Jewish Survivors of Eastern Europe, 1944–1948* (New York, 1970).

———. "The Initial Organization of the Holocaust Survivors in Bavaria," *Yad Vashem Studies* 8 (1970), pp. 127–158.

———. *Jews for Sale? Nazi-Jewish Negotiations, 1933–1945* (New Haven, Conn., 1994).

———. *Out of the Ashes: The Impact of American Jews on Post-Holocaust European Jewry* (Oxford, England, 1989).

Beardwell, M. *Aftermath* (Ilfracombe, Devon, England, 1953).

Bendersky, J. *The "Jewish Threat": Anti-Semitic Politics of the U.S. Army* (New York, 2000).

Benton, P. *Baltic Countdown* (1984).

Berger, J. *Displaced Persons: Growing Up American After the Holocaust* (New York, 2001).

Berkhoff, K. C. *Harvest of Despair: Life and Death in Ukraine Under Nazi Rule* (Cambridge, Mass., 2004).

Berlin, I. *Flourishing: Letters, 1928–1946* (2005).

Bernstein, D. "Europe's Jews," *Commentary,* August 1947.

Beschloss, M. *The Conquerors: Roosevelt, Truman and the Destruction of Hitler's Germany, 1941–1945* (New York, 2002).

Bessel, R. *Germany 1945: From War to Peace* (2009).

Best, S. R. M. "The British Foreign Office, The United Nations Relief and Rehabilitation Administration (UNRRA) and the Displaced Persons Problem in British-Occupied Europe, 1944–1947" (PhD thesis, London School of Economics, 1991).

Bethell, N. *The Last Secret: Forcible Repatriation to Russia, 1944–7* (1977).

———. *The Palestine Triangle: The Struggle between the British, the Jews and the Arabs, 1925–48* (1980).

Biber, J. *Risen from the Ashes* (Asheville, N.C., 2005).

Black, M. *A Cause for Our Times: OXFAM—The First 50 Years* (Oxford, England, 1992).

Blum, J. M. (ed.). *The Price of Vision: The Diary of Henry A. Wallace, 1942–1946* (Boston, 1973).

———. *V Was for Victory: Politics and American Culture During World War II* (New York, 1976).

Blumenson, M. (ed.). *The Patton Papers, 1940–1945* (Boston, 1974).

Bohachevsky-Chomiak, M. "The Women's Movement in the DP Camps," in W. W. Isajiw et al. (eds.), *The Refugee Experience* (1994).

Bonds, J. B. *Bipartisan Strategy: Selling the Marshall Plan* (Westport, Conn., 2002).

Booker, C. *A Looking-Glass Tragedy: The Controversy over Repatriations from Austria in 1945* (1997).

Borgwardt, E. *A New Deal for the World: America's Vision for Human Rights* (Cambridge, Mass., 2005).

Boshyk, Y. (ed.). *Ukraine During World War II: History and Its Aftermath* (Edmonton, 1986).

Botting, D. *In the Ruins of the Reich* (1985; 2005).

Bourne, G. H. *Starvation in Europe* (1943).

Bower, T. *The Red Web: MI6 and the KGB Master Coup* (1989; 1993).

Bramwell, A. C. (ed.). *Refugees in the Age of Total War* (1988).

Breitman, R. *Official Secrets: What the Nazis Planned. What the British and Americans Knew* (2000).

Brenner, M. *After the Holocaust: Rebuilding Jewish Lives in Postwar Germany* (Princeton, N.J., 1997).

Bridgman, J. *The End of the Holocaust: The Liberation of the Camps* (1990).

Brinkley, A. *The End of Reform: New Deal Liberalism in Recession and War* (New York, 1995).

Brodzki, B., and J. Varon. "The Munich Years. The Jewish Students in Post-war Germany," in J.-O. Steinert and I. Weber-Newth (eds.), *Beyond Camps* (2006).

Brosse, T. *War-Handicapped Children* (Paris, 1950).

Brown, F. J., and J. S. Roucek (eds.). *One America: The History, Contributions, and Present Problems of our Racial and National Minorities* (3d ed., New York, 1952).

Bullock, A. *Ernest Bevin: Foreign Secretary* (1983; Oxford, 1985).

Burds, J. "The Early Cold War in Soviet West Ukraine, 1944–1948," no. 1505 in *Carl Beck Papers in Russian and East European Studies* (Pittsburgh, 2001).

———. "Ethnicity, Memory and Violence: Reflections on Special Problems in Soviet and East European Archives," in F. X. Blouin and W. G. Rosenberg (eds.), *Archives, Documentation, and the Institutions of Social Memory: Essays from the Sawyer Seminar* (Ann Arbor, Mich., 2006).

Burstin, B. S. *After the Holocaust: The Migration of Polish Jews and Christians to Pittsburgh* (Pittsburgh, 1989).

Byrnes, J. F. *Speaking Frankly* (1947).

Calder-Marshall, A. *The Watershed* (1947).

Caro, R. A. *The Power Broker: Robert Moses and the Fall of New York* (New York, 1974).

Casey, S. *Cautious Crusade: Franklin D. Roosevelt, American Public Opinion, and the War Against Nazi Germany* (Oxford, 2001).

Cesarani, D. *Justice Delayed: How Britain Became a Refuge for Nazi War Criminals* (1992).

Chatham House. *Relief and Reconstruction in Europe: The First Steps. Report by a Chatham House Group* (1942).

Cirtautas, K. C. *The Refugee: A Psychological Study* (Boston, 1957).

Clark, J. P. *The Role of Uprooted People in European Recovery* (Washington, D.C., 1948).

Clay, C., and M. Leapman. *Master Race: The Lebensborn Experiment in Nazi Germany* (1995).

Clay, L. D. *Decision in Germany* (1950).

Cloake, J. *Templer of Malaya* (1995).

Cohen, B. *Case Closed: Holocaust Survivors in Postwar America* (New Brunswick, N.J., 2007).

Cohen, M. *Palestine and the Great Powers, 1945–1948* (Princeton, N.J., 1982).

Coigny, R. L. "Displaced Persons: The Medical Problems," *Lancet 1,* (1945), pp. 477–8.

Coles, H. L., and A. K. Weinberg. *Civil Affairs: Soldiers Become Governors* (Washington, D.C., 1964).

Connor, I. *Refugees and Expellees in Post-war Germany* (Manchester, England, 2007).

Conradi, P. J. *Iris Murdoch: A Life* (2002).

Corsellis, J., and M. Ferrar. *Slovenia 1945: Memories of Death and Survival After World War II* (2005).

Cowgill, A., et al. *The Repatriations from Austria in 1945: Cowgill Inquiry: The Documentary Evidence* (1990).

———. *The Repatriations from Austria: The Report of an Inquiry* (1990).

Crossman, R. *Palestine Mission: A Personal Record* (1947).

Crum, B. C. *Behind the Silken Curtain: A Personal Account of Anglo-American Diplomacy in Palestine and the Middle East* (1947).

Dacie, A. *Yugoslav Refugees in Italy: The Story of a Transit Camp* (1945).

Dalianas, M., and M. Mazower. "Children in Turmoil During the Civil War: Today's Adults," in M. Mazower (ed.), *After the War Was Over* (Princeton, 2000).

Dallas, G. *Poisoned Peace: 1945—The War That Never Ended* (2005).

Dallin, A. *German Rule in Russia* (2nd ed., 1980).

Danchev, A., and D. Todman (eds.). *Field Marshal Lord Alanbrooke: War Diaries, 1939–45* (2001).

Daniels, R. *Coming to America: A History of Immigration and Ethnicity in American Life* (New York, 1991).

Danylyszyn, J. "Prisoners of Peace: British Policy Towards Displaced Persons and Political Refugees Within Occupied Germany, 1945–51" (PhD thesis, London School of Economics, 2001).

Danys, M. *DP: Lithuanian Immigration to Canada After the Second World War* (Toronto, 1986).

Davies, N. *Rising '44: The Battle for Warsaw* (2004).

Davies, N., and R. Moorhouse. *Microcosm: Portrait of a Central European City* (2003).

Dawidowicz, L. S. *From That Place and Time: A Memoir, 1938–1947* (New York, 1989).

Deane, J. R. *The Strange Alliance: The Story of American Efforts at Wartime Co-operation with Russia* (1947).

Deighton, A. *The Impossible Peace: Britain, the Division of Germany and the Origins of the Cold War* (Oxford, 1990).

Dennett, R., and J. E. Johnson (eds.). *Negotiating with the Russians* (Boston, Mass., 1951).

Dickens, A. *Lübeck Diary* (1946).

Dinnerstein, L. *America and the Survivors of the Holocaust* (New York, 1982).

Divine, R. A. Review of J. B. Bonds, *Bipartisan Strategy: Selling the Marshall Plan,* in *Political Science Quarterly* 118 (2004), pp. 686–7.

———. *Second Chance: The Triumph of Internationalism in America During World War II* (New York, 1967).

Djilas, M. *Conversations with Stalin* (1963).

———. *Wartime. With Tito and the Partisans* (1977; 1980).

Doherty, M. D. *Letters from Belsen, 1945* (St. Leonards, New South Wales, 2000).

Dölger, K. *"Polenlager Jägerslust": Polnische "Displaced Persons" in Schleswig-Holstein* (Neumünster, Germany, 2000).

Donnison, F. S. V. *Civil Affairs and Military Government. Central Organisation and Planning* (1966).

———. *Civil Affairs and Military Government. North West Europe, 1944–46* (1961).

Dyczok, M. *The Grand Alliance and Ukrainian Refugees* (Basingstoke, England, 2000).

Edwards, R. D. *Victor Gollancz: A Biography* (1987).

Eisenberg, C. *Drawing the Line: The American Decision to Divide Germany, 1944–1949* (Cambridge, England, 1998).

Eitinger, L. *Concentration Camp Survivors in Norway and Israel* (Oslo, 1964).

Eksteins, M. *Walking Since Daybreak: A Story of Eastern Europe, World War II and the Heart of the Twentieth Century* (2000).

Elkes, J. *Values, Belief and Survival: Dr Elkhanan Elkes and the Kovno Ghetto* (1997).

Elliott, M. R. *Pawns of Yalta: Soviet Refugees and America's Role in Their Repatriation* (Urbana, Ill., 1982).

Ellwood, D. W. *Italy, 1943–1945* (Leicester, 1985).

Farquharson, J. E. "'Emotional but Influential': Victor Gollancz, Richard Stokes and the British Zone of Germany, 1945–9," *Journal of Contemporary History* 22 (1987), pp. 501–19.

———. *The Western Allies and the Politics of Food. Agrarian Management in Postwar Germany* (Leamington Spa, England, 1985).

Feingold, H. *The Politics of Rescue: The Roosevelt Administration and the Holocaust, 1938–1945* (New York, 1970).

———. *Zion in America* (New York, 1974).

Ferrell, R. H. (ed.). *Truman in the White House: The Diary of Eben A. Ayers* (Columbia, Mo., 1991).

Finder, G. "Muscular Judaism after the Shoah: Sports and Jewish DPs," in J.-D. Steinert and I. Weber-Newth (eds.), *Beyond Camps and Forced Labour* (2008).

Fisher, F. G. *Raphael Cilento: A Biography* (St. Lucia, Queensland, 1994).

Flanner, J. "Letter from Aschaffenburg," *The New Yorker,* October 30, 1948.

Floore, F. B. *The Bread of the Oppressed: An American Woman's Experience in War-Disrupted Countries* (Hicksville, N.Y., 1975).

Folly, M. *Churchill, Whitehall and the Soviet Union, 1940–1945* (Basingstoke, England, 2000).

Foreign Relations of the United States, 1942–1951 (Washington, D.C., 1967–78).

Fossedal, G. A. *Our Finest Hour: Will Clayton, the Marshall Plan and the Triumph of Democracy* (Stanford, Calif., 2003).

Fox, G. "The Origins of UNRRA," *Political Science Quarterly* 65 (1950), pp. 561–84.

Frank, M. *Expelling the Germans: British Opinion and Post-1945 Population Transfer in Context* (Oxford, England, 2007).

———. "'The new morality'—Victor Gollancz, 'Save Europe Now' and the German Refugees in 1945–46," *Twentieth-Century British History* 17 (2006), pp. 230–56.

———. "Working for the Germans: British Voluntary Societies and the German Refugee Crisis, 1945–50," *Historical Research* 72 (2009), pp. 157–75.

Friedman, H. A. "A Military Chaplain's Perspective," in M. Z. Rosensaft (ed.), *Life Reborn* (2001).

Friedman, P. "The Road Back for DPs: Healing the Psychological Scars of Nazism," *Commentary,* December 1948.

Fry, R. *A Quaker Adventure* (1926; 1943).

Gatrell, P. *A Whole Empire Walking: Refugees in Russia During World War I* (Bloomington, Ind., 1999).

———. "World Refugee Year, 1959–60: A Chapter in Refugee History," paper dated January 14, 2008, on the Internet.

———. "World Wars and Population Displacement in Europe in the Twentieth Century," *Contemporary European History* 16 (2007), pp. 415–26.

Gatrell, P., and N. Baron, eds. *Warlands: Population Resettlement and State Reconstruction in the Soviet-East European Borderlands, 1945–50* (Basingstoke, England, 2009).

Gay, R. *Safe Among the Germans: Liberated Jews After World War II* (New Haven, Conn., 2002).

Genizi, H. *America's Fair Share: The Admission and Resettlement of Displaced Persons, 1945–1952* (Detroit, 1993).

Gibson, J. *Jacko. Where Are You Now? A Life of Robert Jackson* (2006).

Gilbert, M. *Finest Hour: Winston S. Churchill, 1939–1941* (1983).

———. *The Holocaust* (1986).

Gildea, R. *Marianne in Chains: In Search of the German Occupation of France, 1940–45* (2003).

Gill, A. *The Journey Back from Hell: Conversations with Concentration Camp Survivors* (1989).

Gimbel, J. *The Origins of the Marshall Plan* (Stanford, Calif., 1976).

Glazer, N. *American Judaism* (Chicago, 1974).

Glendon, M. A. *A World Made New: Eleanor Roosevelt and the Universal Declaration of Human Rights* (New York, 2001).

Glover, J. *Humanity: A Moral History of the Twentieth Century* (1999).

Goldmann, N. *Mein Leben als deutscher Jude* (Munich, 1980).

Gollancz, V. *Inside Darkest Germany* (1947).

Goni, U. *The Real Odessa* (2nd ed., 2003).

Gordon, H. *The Shadow of Death: The Holocaust in Lithuania* (Lexington, Ky., 1992).

Goren, A. A. "Jews," in S. Thernstrom et al. (eds.), *Harvard Encyclopedia of American Ethnic Groups* (Cambridge, Mass., 1980).

Graham, L. *Unguarded Gates: A History of America's Immigration Crisis* (Lanham, Md., 2004).

Greene, V. "Poles," in S. Thernstrom et al. (eds.), *Harvard Encyclopedia of American Ethnic Groups* (Cambridge, Mass., 1980).

Grinberg, Z. "Our Liberation from Dachau," a private translation by Israel Eiss from *Kamah,* the Yearbook for the Jewish National Fund (Jerusalem, 1948).

Gringauz, S. "The Ghetto as an Experiment of Jewish Social Organization: Three Years of the Kovno Ghetto," *Jewish Social Studies* 11 (1949), pp. 3–20.

———. "Our New German Policy and the DP's," *Commentary,* June 1948.

———. "Jewish Destiny as the DP's See It," *Commentary,* December 1947.

Grobman, A. (ed.). *In Defense of the Survivors. The Letters and Documents of Oscar A. Mintzer, AJDC Legal Advisor, Germany, 1945–46* (Berkeley, Calif., 1999).

———. *Rekindling the Flame: American Jewish Chaplains and the Survivors of European Jewry, 1944–1948* (Detroit, 1993).

Grodzinsky, Y. *In the Shadow of the Holocaust: The Struggle Between Jews and Zionists in the Aftermath of World War II* (Monroe, Maine, 2004).

Gross, J. T. *Fear: Anti-Semitism in Poland after Auschwitz—an Essay in Historical Interpretation* (Princeton, 2006).

———. *Neighbors: The Destruction of the Jewish Community in Jedwabne, Poland* (Princeton, 2001).

Grossmann, A. *Jews, Germans, and Allies: Close Encounters in Occupied Germany* (Princeton, 2007).

Gunther, J. *Inside U.S.A.* (New York, 1947).

Gutman, I. (ed.). *Encyclopedia of the Holocaust* (New York, 1990).

Hagen, M. von. "Does Ukraine Have a History?," *Slavic Review* 54 (1995), pp. 658–73.

Halamish, A. *The Exodus Affair: Holocaust Survivors and the Struggle for Palestine* (Syracuse, N.Y., 1998).

Hammond, T. T. (ed.). *Witnesses to the Origins of the Cold War* (Seattle, 1986).

Hardach, G. "The Marshall Plan in Germany, 1948–1952," *Journal of European Economic History* 16 (1987), pp. 433–85.

Hardman, L. H., and C. Goodman. *The Survivors: The Story of the Belsen Remnant* (1958).

Harris, M. J. *The Long Way Home* (Los Angeles, 1997).

Harrison, M. *Medicine and Victory* (Oxford, 2005).

Harvey, O. *Wartime Diaries* (1970).

Healy, M. *Vienna and the Fall of the Habsburg Empire: Total War and Everyday Life in World War I* (Cambridge, England 2004).

Heberle, R., and D. S. Hall. *New Americans: A Study of Displaced Persons in Louisiana and Mississippi* (Baton Rouge, La., 1951).

Heinemann, I. *"Rasse, Siedlung, deutsches Blut": Das Rasse- und Siedlungshauptamt der SS und die rassenpolitische Neuordnung Europas* (Göttingen, 2003).

Helton, A. C. *The Price of Indifference: Refugees and Humanitarian Action in the New Century* (Oxford, 2002).

Herbert, U. "Forced Labour," in I. C. B. Dear and M. R. D. Foot (eds.), *The Oxford Companion to World War II* (Oxford, 1995).

———. *Hitler's Foreign Workers: Enforced Foreign Labor in Germany Under the Third Reich* (Cambridge, England, 1997).

————. "No Compensation for Forced Labor: Legal and Historical Dimensions," *Frankfurter Allgemeine Zeitung,* July 19, 1999.

Hicklin, M. *War-Damaged Children: Some Aspects of Recovery* (1946).

Hilliard, R. L. *Surviving the Americans: The Continued Struggle of the Jews After Liberation* (New York, 1997).

Hilton, E. E. Schneider. *Displaced Person: A Girl's Life in Russia, Germany, and America* (Baton Rouge, La., 2006).

Hilton, L. J. "Pawns on a Chessboard? Polish DPs and Repatriation from the US Zone of Germany, 1945–1949," in J.-D. Steinert and I. Weber-Newth (eds.), *Beyond Camps* (2005).

Hirschmann, I. A. *The Embers Still Burn* (New York, 1949).

Hitchcock, W. I. *The Bitter Road to Freedom: A New History of the Liberation of Europe* (New York, 2008).

Hoffman, E. *Lost in Translation: A Life in a New Language* (1989; 1998).

Hogan, J. *The Marshall Plan: America, Britain and the Reconstruction of Western Europe, 1947–1952* (Cambridge, England, 1987).

Holian, A. "Displacement and the Post-war Reconstruction of Education: Displaced Persons at the UNRRA University of Munich, 1945–48," *Central European History* 17 (2008), pp. 167–95.

————. "From political prisoners to displaced persons. Nationalism, Anti-communism and Ambivalence in the Formation of a Polish DP Community," in J.-D. Steinert and I. Weber-Newth (eds.), *Beyond Camps* (2006).

Holborn, L. W. *The International Refugee Organization: A Specialized Agency of the United Nations. Its History and Work, 1946–1952* (1956).

Holleufer, H. von. "Seeking New Horizons in Latin America: The Resettlement of 100,000 European Displaced Persons between the Gulf of Mexico and Patagonia (1947–1951)," *Jahrbuch für Geschichte Lateinamerikas* 39 (2002), pp. 126–62.

Homze, E. L. *Foreign Labor in Nazi Germany* (Princeton, N.J., 1967)

Hoopes, T., and D. Brinkley. *FDR and the Creation of the U.N.* (New Haven, Conn., 1997).

Horne, A. *Harold Macmillan,* vol. 1: *1984–1956* (1989).

Horsburgh, P. G., and H. A. Raeburn. "The Health Problem in Berlin (July 1945–January 1946)," *British Medical Journal* 1 (1946), pp. 423–9.

Hrabar, R., et al. *The Fate of Polish Children During the Last War* (Warsaw, 1981).

Hrycyszyn, M. *God Save Me from My Friends: A Ukrainian Memoir* (Cambridge, England, 2006).

Hulme, K. *The Nun's Story* (1956).

————. *Undiscovered Country: The Search for Gurdjieff* (1966; Lexington, Ky., 1997).

————. *The Wild Place* (Boston, 1953).

Humbert, A. *Résistance: Memoirs of Occupied France* (Paris, 1946; 2008).

Huntford, R. *Nansen: The Explorer as Hero* (1997; 2001).

Huxley, J., et al. *When Hostilities Cease* (1943).

Hyman, A. S. *The Undefeated* (Jerusalem, 1993).

Ignatieff, M. *Blood and Belonging: Journeys into the New Nationalism* (1994).

Isajiw, W. W., et al. (eds.). *The Refugee Experience: Ukrainian Displaced Persons After World War II* (Edmonton, 1994).

Iwańska, A. *Polish Intelligentsia in Nazi Concentration Camps and American Exile: A Study of Values in Crisis Situations* (Lewiston, N.Y., 1998).

Jackson, K. *Humphrey Jennings* (2004).

Jacobmeyer, W. *Vom Zwangarbeiter zum heimatlosen Ausländer: Die Displaced Persons in Westdeutschland, 1945–1951* (Göttingen, Germany, 1985).

Janco, A. P. "The Soviet Refugee: Problem of Imposture and Contested Identity in the Displaced Persons' Camps, 1945–1947," in J.-D. Steinert and I. Weber-Newth (eds.), *Beyond Camps* (2008).

Jansen, M., and B. de Jong. "Stalin's Hand in Rotterdam: The Murder of the Ukrainian Nationalist Yevhen Konovalets in May 1938," *Intelligence and National Security* 9 (1994), pp. 676–94.

Jaroszyńska-Kirchmann, A. D. *The Exile Mission: The Polish Political Diaspora and Polish Americans, 1939–1956* (Athens, Ohio, 2004).

Jay, D. *Change and Fortune: A Political Record* (1980).

Johnson, P. *A History of the Jews* (1993).

Judt, T. *Postwar: A History of Europe Since 1945* (2005).

———. *Reappraisals: Reflections on the Forgotten Twentieth Century* (2008).

Kaplan, I. "Marsch aus den Kauferinger Lagern" (The March from the Kaufering Camps), *Fun Letstn Khurbn* 5 (May 1947).

Kay, D., and R. Miles. *Refugees or Migrant Workers? European Volunteer Workers in Britain, 1946–1951* (1992).

Kee, R. *Refugee World* (Oxford, 1961).

Kennedy, D. M. *Freedom from Fear: The American People in Depression and War, 1929–1945* (New York, 1999).

Kershaw, I. *Hitler 1936–1945: Nemesis* (2001).

Kersten, K. *The Establishment of Communist Rule in Poland, 1943–1948* (Berkeley, Calif.: 1991).

Kessner, T. *Fiorello H. La Guardia and the Making of Modern New York* (New York, 1989).

Kindleberger, C. P. *The German Economy, 1945–1947* (Westport, Conn., 1989).

———. *Marshall Plan Days* (Boston, 1987).

Kinnear, M. *Woman of the World: Mary Craig McGeachy and International Cooperation* (Toronto, 2004).

Klausner, A. J. *A Letter to My Children from the Edge of the Holocaust* (San Francisco, 2004).

———. *Weddings: A Complete Guide to all Religious and Interfaith Marriage Services* (Columbus, Ohio, 1986).

Klemmé, M. *The Inside Story of UNRRA: An Experience in Internationalism. A Firsthand Report on the Displaced People of Europe* (New York, 1949).

Knef, H. *The Gift Horse* (New York, 1971).

Kochavi, A. J. *Post-Holocaust Politics: Britain, the United States and Jewish Refugees, 1945–1948* (Chapel Hill, N.C., 2001).

Königsweder, A., and J. Wetzel. *Waiting for Hope: Jewish Displaced Persons in Post–World War II Germany* (Evanston, Ill., 2001).

Korboński, S. *Warsaw in Chains* (1959).

Kossert, A. *Kalte Heimat: Die Geschichte der deutschen Vertriebenen nach 1945* (Munich, 2008).

Kramer, A. *The German Economy, 1945–1951* (Oxford, 1991).

Krockow, C. von. *Die Reise nach Pommern: Bericht aus einem verschweigenen Land* (Stuttgart, 1985).

———. *The Hour of the Women* (1991).

Kulischer, E. M. *The Displacement of Population in Europe* (Montreal, 1943).

Kunz, E. F. *Displaced Persons: Calwell's New Australians* (Canberra, 1980).

Kynaston, D. *Austerity Britain, 1945–1951* (2007).

Laar, M. *The Forgotten War: Armed Resistance Movement in Estonia in 1944–1956* (Tallinn, 2005).

Lagrou, P. *The Legacy of Nazi Occupation: Patriotic Memory and National Recovery in Western Europe, 1945–1965* (Cambridge, England, 2000).

Lampe, J. R. *Yugoslavia as History* (Cambridge, 1996).

Lane, A. B. *I Saw Poland Betrayed* (1948; Boston, 1965).

Lane, A. T. *Victims of Stalin and Hitler: The Exodus of Poles and Balts to Britain* (Basingstoke, 2004).

Laqueur, W. *A History of Zionism: From the French Revolution to the Establishment of the State of Israel* (New York, 2003).

Lauren, P. G. *The Evolution of International Human Rights: Visions Seen* (2nd ed., Philadelphia, 2003).

Lavsky, H. *New Beginnings: Holocaust Survivors in Bergen-Belsen and the British Zone in Germany, 1945–1950* (Detroit, 2002).

Leiby, J. *A History of Social Work and Social Welfare in the United States* (New York, 1978).

Leith-Ross, F. *Money Talks: Fifty Years of International Finance* (1968).

Leivick, H., et al. *Belsen* (Tel Aviv, 1957).

Levi, P. *The Truce* (1965; 1987).

Levin, D. *The Litvaks: A Short History of the Jews in Lithuania* (Jerusalem, 2000).

Levy, I. *Witness to Evil: Bergen-Belsen, 1945* (1995).

Lewis, N. *Naples '44* (1978).

Lewycka, M. *A Short History of Tractors in Ukrainian* (2005).

Lieven, A. *The Baltic Revolution: Estonia, Latvia, Lithuania and the Path to Independence* (1993; New Haven, Conn., 2005).

Littman, S. *Pure Soldiers or Sinister Legion: The Ukrainian 14th Waffen-SS Division* (Montreal, 2003).

London, L. *Whitehall and the Jews, 1933–1948* (Cambridge, England, 2000).

Lotnik, W. *Nine Lives: Ethnic Conflict in the Polish-Ukrainian Borderlands* (1999).

Louis, W. R. *The British Empire in the Middle East, 1945–1951: Arab Nationalism, the United States, and Postwar Imperialism* (Oxford, England, 1984).

Luciuk, L. (ed.). *Heroes of Their Day: The Reminiscences of Bohdan Panchuk* (Toronto, 1983).

———. *Searching for Place: Ukrainian Displaced Persons, Canada, and the Migration of Memory* (Toronto, 2000).

———. "Unintended Consequences in Refugee Resettlement: Postwar Ukrainian Refugee Immigration to Canada," *International Migration Review* 20 (1986), pp. 467–82.

Macardle, D. *Children of Europe: A Study of the Children of Liberated Countries: Their Wartime Experiences, Their Reactions, and Their Needs, with a Note on Germany* (1951).

McClelland, G. *Embers of War: Letters from a Quaker Relief Worker in War-Torn Germany* (1997).

McCullough, D. *Truman* (New York, 1992).

MacDonogh, G. *After the Reich: From the Liberation of Vienna to the Berlin Airlift* (2007).

McDowell, L. *Hard Labour: The Forgotten Voices of Latvian Migrant Volunteer Workers* (2005).

MacInnes, C. *To the Victor the Spoils* (1950; 1986).

Mackenzie, M. D. *Medical Relief in Europe: Questions for Immediate Study* (1942).

Macmillan, H. *The Blast of War, 1939–1945* (1967).

———. *War Diaries: The Mediterranean, 1943–1945* (1984).

McNeill, M. *By the Rivers of Babylon: A Story Based upon Actual Experiences Among the Displaced Persons of Europe* (1950).

Magocsi, P. *A History of Ukraine* (Toronto, 1996).

Mankowitz, Z. W. *Life Between Memory and Hope: The Survivors of the Holocaust in Occupied Germany* (Cambridge, England, 2002).

Marrack, J. "Food for Starving Europe" in J. Huxley et al., *When Hostilities Cease* (1943).

Marrus, M. *The Unwanted: European Refugees from the First World War Through the Cold War* (Oxford, England, 1985).

Martin, J. I. *Refugee Settlers: A Study of Displaced Persons in Australia* (Canberra, 1965).

Matusow, A. J. *Farm Policies and Politics in the Truman Years* (Cambridge, Mass., 1967).

Mazower, M. (ed.). *After the War Was Over: Reconstructing the Family, Nation and State in Greece, 1943–1960* (Princeton, 2000).

———. *Dark Continent: Europe's Twentieth Century* (1998).

———. *Inside Hitler's Greece: The Experience of Occupation, 1941–44* (1993; New Haven, Conn., 2001).

———. *Hitler's Empire: Nazi Rule in Occupied Europe* (2008).

Medlicott, W. N. *The Economic Blockade* (1952).

Meehan, P. *A Strange Enemy People: Germans Under the British, 1945–1950* (2001).

Mekas, J. *I Had Nowhere to Go* (New York, 1991).

Mendelsohn, E. *The Jews of East Central Europe Between the World Wars* (Bloomington, Ind., 1983).

Mikołajczyk, S. *The Pattern of Soviet Domination* (1948).

Milosz, C. *The Captive Mind* (1953; Harmondsworth, England, 1980).

Milton, S., and F. D. Bogin (eds.). *Archives of the Holocaust,* vol. 10, *American Jewish Joint Distribution Committee* (New York, 1995).

Mishell, W. W. *Kaddish for Kovno: Life and Death in a Lithuanian Ghetto, 1941–1945* (Chicago, 1988).

Monnet, J. *Memoirs* (New York, 1978).

Moorehead, A. *Eclipse* (1945).

Moorehead, C. *Dunant's Dream. War, Switzerland and the History of the Red Cross* (1998).

———. *Human Cargo. A Journey Among Refugees* (2005).

Morgan, F. *Peace and War* (1961).

Morris, B. *1948: A History of the First Arab-Israeli War* (New Haven, Conn., 2008).

Mosley, L. *Report from Germany* (1945).

Murphy, C. J. "SOE and Repatriation," *Journal of Contemporary History* 36 (2001), pp. 309–23.

Murphy, H. B. M. "The Assimilation of Refugee Immigrants in Australia," *Population Studies* 5 (1952), pp. 179–206.

———. (ed.). *Flight and Resettlement* (Geneva, 1956).

———. "The Resettlement of Jewish Refugees in Israel, with Special Reference to Those Known as Displaced Persons," *Population Studies* 5 (1952), pp. 153–74.

Murphy, R. *Diplomat Among Warriors* (New York, 1964).

Nachmani, A. *Great Power Discord in Palestine: The Anglo-American Committee of Inquiry into the Problems of European Jewry and Palestine, 1945–1946* (1987).

Nadich, J. *Eisenhower and the Jews* (New York, 1953).

Naimark, M. *Fires of Hatred: Ethnic Cleansing in Twentieth-Century Europe* (Cambridge, Mass., 2001).

————. *The Russians in Germany: A History of the Soviet Zone of Occupation, 1945–1949* (Cambridge, Mass., 1995).

Namias, J. *First Generation: In the Words of Twentieth-Century American Immigrants* (Boston, 1978).

Nardini, J. E. "Survival Factors in American Prisoners of War of the Japanese," *American Journal of Psychiatry,* 109 (1952), pp. 241-8.

National Planning Association. *Relief for Europe* (Washington, D.C., 1942).

————. *UNRRA: Gateway to* Recovery (Washington, D.C., 1944).

Nesaule, A. *A Woman in Amber: Healing the Trauma of War and Exile* (New York, 1995).

Nevins, A. *Herbert H. Lehman and His Era* (New York, 1963).

Nicholas, H. G. (ed.). *Washington Despatches: Weekly Political Reports from the British Embassy* (1981).

Nicholas, L. H. *Cruel World: The Children of Europe in the Nazi Web* (New York, 2005).

Niewyk, D. L. (ed.). *Fresh Wounds: Early Narratives of Holocaust Survival* (Chapel Hill, N.C., 1998).

Niewyck, D., and F. Nicosia. *The Columbia Guide to the Holocaust* (New York, 2000).

Nolte, H.-H. (ed.). *Häftlinge aus der UdSSR in Bergen-Belsen: Dokumentation der Erinnerungen: "Ostarbeiterinnen" und "Ostarbeiter," Kriegsgefangene, Partisanen, Kinder, und zwei Minsker Jüdinnen in einem deutschen KZ* (Frankfurt am Main, 2001).

Novick, P. *The Holocaust in American Life* (Boston, 1999).

Nowakowski, T. *The Camp of All Saints* (New York, 1962).

Oakley, A. "Eugenics, Social Medicine, and the Career of Richard Titmuss in Britain, 1935–1950," *British Journal of Sociology* 42 (1991), pp. 165–94.

O'Connor, F. *A Good Man Is Hard to Find and Other Stories* (1968).

Oldfield, S. *Women Humanitarians: A Biographical Dictionary of British Women Active Between 1900 and 1950* (2001).

Olsen S. (ed.), *Harold Nicolson: Diaries and Letters, 1930–1964* (1984).

Orwell, G. *I Belong to the Left, 1945* (2001).

————. *Smothered Under Journalism, 1946* (2001).

OSE. *Report on the Situation of the Jews in Germany, October–December 1945* (Geneva, 1946).

Overy, R. *The Morbid Age: Britain Between the Wars* (2009).

Padover, S. K. *Psychologist in Germany: The Story of an American Intelligence Officer* (1947).

Papanek, E. "'They are not expendable': The Homeless and Refugee Children in Germany," *Social Service Review* 20 (1946).

Patenaude, B. *The Big Show in Bololand: The American Relief Expedition to Soviet Russia in the Famine of 1921* (Stanford, Calif., 2002).

Patt, A. J. *Finding Home and Homelands: Jewish Youth and Zionism in the Aftermath of the Holocaust* (Detroit, 2009).

Patterson, J. T. *Grand Expectations: The United States, 1945–1974* (New York, 1996).

Patterson, W. P. *Ladies of the Rope: Gurdjieff's Special Left Bank Women's Group* (Fairfax, Calif., 1998).

Paul, K. *Whitewashing Britain: Race and Citizenship in the Postwar Era* (Ithaca, N.Y., 1997).

Pavlowitch, S. K. *The Improbable Survivor: Yugoslavia and Its Problems* (1988).

Peck, A. (ed.). *American Jewish Archives Cincinnati: The Papers of the World Jewish Congress, 1945–1950. The Liberation and the Saving Remnant* (New York, 1990).

————. (ed.). *Among the Survivors: The Landsberg DP Letters of Major Irving A. Heymont* (Cincinnati, 1982).

————. "'Our Eyes Have Seen Eternity': Memory and Self-Identity Among the Sher'erith Hapletah," *Modern Judaism* 17 (1997), pp. 57–74.

Pedersen, S. *Eleanor Rathbone and the Politics of Conscience* (New Haven, 2004).

Pelly, M. E., et al. (eds). *Documents on British Policy Overseas*, series I, vols. 5–6 (1990–1991).

Penrose, E. F. "Negotiating on Refugees and Displaced Persons, 1946," in R. Dennett and J. E. Johnson (eds.), *Negotiating with the Russians* (Boston, 1951).

Perl, G. *I Was a Doctor in Auschwitz* (New York, 1948).

Peters, N. *Milk and Honey—But No Gold: Postwar Migration to Western Australia, 1945–1964* (Crawley, Western Australia, 2001).

Petrovich, M. B. "The View from Yugoslavia," in T. T. Hammond (ed.), *Witnesses to the Origins of the Cold War* (Seattle, 1986).

Pettiss, S. and L. Taylor. *After the Shooting Stopped: The Story of an UNRRA Welfare Worker in Germany, 1945–1947* (Victoria, B.C., 2004).

Pimlott, B. *Hugh Dalton* (1986).

————. (ed.). *The Second World War Diaries of Hugh Dalton* (1986).

Pinson, K. S. "Jewish Life in Liberated Germany—a Study of the Jewish DPs," *Jewish Social Studies,* 9 (1947), pp. 101–26.

Polenberg, R. *One Nation Divisible: Class, Race, and Ethnicity in the United States Since 1938* (Harmondsworth, England, 1980).

"Potiphar." *They Must Not Starve* (1945).

Proudfoot, M. "The Anglo-American Displaced Persons Program for Germany and Austria," *American Journal of Economics and Society* 6 (1946), pp. 33–54.

————. *European Refugees: 1939–52. A Study in Forced Population Movement* (1957).

Purrs, A. "'How Those Brothers in Foreign Lands are Dividing the Fatherland': Latvian National Politics in Displaced Persons Camps after the Second World War," in Gatrell and Baron (eds.), *Warlands.*

Rapaport, I. *Shake Heaven and Earth: Peter Bergson and the Struggle to Rescue the Jews of Europe* (Jerusalem, 1999).

Raphael, C. "The Litvak Connection and Hasidic Chic," *Commentary,* May 1976.

Reich, W. (ed.). *Hidden History of the Kovno Ghetto* (Boston, 1997).

Reid, A. *Borderland: A Journey through the History of Ukraine* (1997).

Reilly, J. *Belsen* (1998).

————. "British policy," in M. Z. Rosensaft (ed.), *Life Reborn* (2001).

Reinisch, J. "Introduction: Relief in the Aftermath of war," *Journal of Contemporary History* 43 (2008), pp. 371–404.

————. "Public Health in Germany Under Soviet and Allied Occupation" (PhD thesis, University of London, 2004).

————. "'We Shall Build Anew a Powerful Nation': UNRRA, Internationalism and National Reconstruction in Poland," *Journal of Contemporary History* 43 (2008), pp. 451–76.

Rendel, G. *The Sword and the Olive: Recollections of Diplomacy and the Foreign Service, 1913–1954* (1957).

Revutsky, V. "Theatre in the Camps," in Isajiw et al (eds.) *The Refugee Experience.*

Richie, A. *Faust's Metropolis: A History of Berlin* (1998).

Rieber, A. J. (ed.). *Forced Migration in Central and Eastern Europe, 1939–1950* (2000).

Robbe-Grillet, A. *Ghosts in the Mirror* (1988).

Roberts, A. *Masters and Commanders* (2009).

Rose, N. *Chaim Weizmann: A Biography* (1986).

———. *"A Senseless, Squalid War": Voices from Palestine 1945–1948* (2009).

Rosensaft, H. *Yesterday: My Story* (Washington, D.C., 2004).

Rosensaft, M. Z. (ed.). *Life Reborn: Jewish Displaced Persons, 1945–1951* (Washington, D.C., 2001).

Royal Institute of International Affairs. *Relief and Reconstruction in Europe: The First Steps. Report of a Chatham House Study Group* (1942).

Rutland, S. D. "Sanctuary for Whom? Jewish Victims and Nazi Perpetrators in Post-war Australian Migrant Camps," in J.-D. Steinert and I. Weber-Newth (eds.), *Beyond Camps* (2006).

Ryan, A. A., Jr. *Quiet Neighbors: Prosecuting Nazi War Criminals in America* (New York, 1984).

Ryder, S. *Child of My Love: An Autobiography* (1997).

Rystad, G. (ed.). *The Uprooted: Forced Migration as an International Problem in the Post-war Era* (Lund, Sweden, 1990).

Sabbagh, K. *Palestine: A Personal History* (2006).

Sachar, H. M. *A History of Israel from the Rise of Zionism to Our Time* (New York, 2007).

Saldukas, L. *Lithuanian Diaspora* (Vilnius, 2002).

Salomon, K. *Refugees in the Cold War: Towards a New International Refugee Regime in the Early Postwar Era* (Lund, Sweden, 1991).

Salter, A. *Memoirs of a Public Servant* (1961).

Sanders, R. *The High Walls of Jerusalem: A History of the Balfour Declaration* (New York, 1984).

Sangster, J. "The Polish Dionnes': Gender, Ethnicity, and Immigrant Workers in Post–Second World War Canada," *Canadian Historical Journal* 88 (2007), pp. 469–500.

Savage, A. *Return to Ukraine* (College Station, Tex., 2000).

Save the Children Fund. *Children in Bondage: A Survey of Child Life in the Occupied Countries of Europe and in Finland* (1942).

Schieder, T. (ed.). *Documents on the Expulsion of the Germans from Eastern-Central-Europe*, 4 vols. (Bonn, 1955–1960).

Schoenberg, H. W. *Germans from the East: A Study of their Migration, Resettlement, and Subsequent Group History Since 1945* (The Hague, 1970).

Schwarz L. *The Redeemers: A Saga of the Years 1945–1952* (New York, 1953).

———. (ed.). *The Root and the Bough* (New York, 1949).

Searle, G. R. "Eugenics and Politics in Britain in the 1930s," *Annals of Science* 35 (1979), pp. 159–69.

Segelman, R. "The Psychology of Jewish Displaced Persons," *Jewish Social Service Quarterly* 23 (1947), pp. 363–5.

Segev, T. *One Palestine Complete* (New York, 2000).

———. *The Seventh Million: The Israelis and the Holocaust* (New York, 1991).

Sereny, G. *Albert Speer: His Battle with Truth* (1995; 1996).

———. *The German Trauma: Experiences and Reflections, 1938–2000* (2000).

Shapira, A. *Land and Power: The Zionist Resort to Force, 1881–1948* (New York, 1992).

Shawcross, W. *The Quality of Mercy: Cambodia, Holocaust, and Modern Conscience* (1994).

Shephard, B. *After Daybreak: The Liberation of Belsen, 1945* (2005).

———. "The Medical Relief Effort at Belsen," *Holocaust Studies* 12 (2006), pp. 31–50.

———. *A War of Nerves: Soldiers and Psychiatrists, 1914–1994* (2000).

Sherman, A. J. *Mandate Days: British Lives in Palestine* (London, 1997).

Sherwood, R. E. *White House Papers of Harry L. Hopkins,* vol. 2 (1949).

Siedlecki, J. N. *Beyond Lost Dreams* (Edinburgh, 1994).

Simpson, C. *Blowback: America's Recruitment of Nazis, and Its Effects on the Cold War* (New York, 1988).

Sington, D. *Belsen Uncovered* (1946).

Sjöberg, T. *The Powers and the Persecuted* (Lund, Sweden, 1991).

Skidelsky, R. *John Maynard Keynes,* vol. 3, *Fighting for Britain* (2001).

Skultans, V. *The Testimony of Lives: Narrative and Memory in Post-Soviet Latvia* (1998).

Smereka, V. *The Girl from Ukraine* (Leeds, England, 2008).

Smith, J. E. (ed.). *The Papers of General Lucius D. Clay* (Bloomington, Ind., 1974).

Smith, M. J. *Dachau: The Harrowing of Hell* (1972; New York, 1995).

Snetsinger, J. *Truman, the Jewish Vote, and the Creation of Israel* (Stanford, Calif., 1974).

Snowden, F. M. *The Conquest of Malaria: Italy, 1900–1962* (New Haven, Conn., 2006).

Snyder, T. *The Reconstruction of Nations: Poland, Ukraine, Lithuania, Belarus, 1569–1999* (New Haven, Conn., 2003).

Somers, E. and R. Kok (eds.). *Jewish Displaced Persons in Camp Bergen-Belsen, 1945–1950* (Amsterdam, 2003).

Speer, A. *Inside the Third Reich* (1970).

Srole, L. "Why the DP's Can't Wait," *Commentary,* January 1947.

Stadulis, E. "The Resettlement of Displaced Persons," *Population Studies* 3 (1953), pp. 207–37.

Stafford, D. *Endgame 1945: Victory, Retribution, Liberation* (2007).

Stargardt, N. *Witnesses of War: Children's Lives under the Nazis* (2005).

Steinert, J.-D. "Food and the Food Crisis in Post-war Germany, 1945–1948: British Policy and the Role of British NGOs," in F. Trentmann and F. Just (eds.), *Food and Conflict in Europe in the Age of the Two World Wars* (Basingstoke, England, 2006).

Steinert, J.-D., and I. Weber-Newth (eds.). *Beyond Camps and Forced Labour: Current International Research on Survivors of Nazi Persecution. Proceedings of the International Conference, London, 29–31 January 2003* (Osnabrück, 2005).

———. *Beyond Camps and Forced Labour: Current International Research on Survivors of Nazi Persecution. Proceedings of the International Conference, London, 11–13 January 2006* (Osnabrück, 2008).

Stewart, N. *The Royal Navy and the Palestine Patrol* (2002).

Stoessinger, J. D. *The Refugee and the World Community* (Minneapolis, 1956).

Stone, I. F. *Underground to Palestine* (1946; 1979).

Subtelny, O. *Ukraine: A History* (Toronto, 1988).

Sudoplatov, P. *Special Tasks* (Boston, 1994).

K. Sword, et al. *The Formation of the Polish Community in Great Britain 1939–1950* (1989).

Tannahill, J. A. *European Volunteer Workers in Britain* (Manchester, 1958).

Taveth, S. *Ben-Gurion and the Holocaust* (New York, 1996).

———. *Ben-Gurion: The Burning Ground, 1886–1948* (Boston, 1987).

Terry, N. "Conflicting Signals: British Intelligence on the 'Final Solution' Through Radio Intercepts and Other Sources, 1941–1942," *Yad Vashem Studies* 32 (2004), pp. 351–96.

Ther, P. "The Integration of Expellees in Germany and Poland After World War II: A Historical Reassessment," *Slavic Review* 55 (1996), pp. 799–805.

Ther, P., and A. Siljak (eds.). *Redrawing Nations: Ethnic Cleansing in East-Central Europe, 1944–1948* (Lanham, Md., 2001).

Thernstrom, S., et al. (eds.). *The Harvard Encyclopedia of American Ethnic Groups* (Cambridge, Mass., 1980).

Thomas, H. *Armed Truce: The Beginnings of the Cold War, 1945–1946* (New York, 1987).

———. *John Strachey* (1973).

Tolstoy, N. *Victims of Yalta* (1977).

Tooze, A. *The Wages of Destruction: The Making and Breaking of the Nazi Economy* (2006).

Topping, A. "The Task of UNRRA: Medical Services in the Liberated Countries," *British Medical Journal* 1 (1945), pp. 816–17.

Toranska, T. *Oni: Stalin's Polish Puppets* (1987).

Tory, A. *Surviving the Holocaust: The Kovno Ghetto Diary* (Cambridge, Mass., 1990).

Trepman, S. "On Being Reborn," in H. Leivick et al., *Belsen* (Tel Aviv, 1957).

Truman, H. S. *Memoirs,* vol. 1, *Years of Trial* (1955).

Ulam, A. B. *Expansion and Coexistence: The History of Soviet Foreign Policy from 1917–1967* (1968).

Urquhart, B. *A Life in Peace and War* (New York, 1991).

Vachon, J. *Poland 1946* (Washington, D.C., 1995).

Vandenberg, A. H., Jr. (ed.). *The Private Papers of Senator Vandenberg* (New York, 1953).

Van Reenan, A. J. *Lithuanian Diaspora: Koenigsberg to Chicago* (Lanham, Md., 1990).

Vernant, J. *The Refugee in the Post-war World* (1953).

Vida, G. *From Doom to Dawn: A Jewish Chaplain's Story of Displaced Persons* (New York, 1967).

Vincent, C. P. *The Politics of Hunger: The Allied Blockade of Germany, 1915–1919* (Athens, Ohio, 1985).

Vinen, R. *The Unfree French: Life under the Occupation* (2006).

Walker, P. Gordon *The Lid Lifts* (1945).

Wasserstein, B. *Britain and the Jews of Europe,* 2nd ed. (Leicester, England, 1999).

Weindling, P. *Epidemics and Genocide in Eastern Europe, 1890–1945* (Oxford, 2000).

Weissman, B. B. *Herbert Hoover and Famine Relief to Soviet Russia, 1921–1923* (Stanford, Calif., 1974).

Wilmington, M. W. *The Middle East Supply Centre* (1972).

Wilmot, P. *A Singular Woman: The Life of Geraldine Aves, 1898–1986* (1992).

Wilson, A. *The Ukrainians: Unexpected Nation* (New Haven, Conn., 2002).

Wilson, F. *Aftermath: France, Germany, Austria, Yugoslavia* (West Drayton, England, 1947).

———. *In the Margins of Chaos: Recollections of Relief Work in and Between Three Wars* (1944).

Wilson, R. *Quaker Relief: An Account of the Relief Work of the Society of Friends, 1940–1948* (1952).

Winder, R. *Bloody Foreigners: The Story of Immigration to Britain* (2005).

Woodroofe, K. *From Charity to Social Work: In England and the United States* (1962).

Woropay, O. *On the Road to the West: Diary of a Ukrainian Refugee* (Wetherby, Yorkshire, England, 1982).

Wyman, D., and R. Medoff. *Race Against Death: Peter Bergson, America and the Holocaust* (New York, 2004).

Wyman, M. *DPs: Europe's Displaced Persons, 1945–1951* (1989; Ithaca, N.Y., 1998).

Yablonka, H. *Survivors of the Holocaust: Israel After the War* (Basingstoke, England, 1999).

Ybarra, M. J. *Washington Gone Crazy: Senator Pat McCarran and the Great American Communist Hunt* (Hanover, N.H., 2004).

Yergin, D. *Shattered Peace: The Origins of the Cold War and the National Security State* (1977; Harmondsworth, England, 1980).

Zahra, T. *Kidnapped Souls: National Indifference and the Battle for Children in the Bohemian Lands* (Ithaca, N.Y., 2008).

———. "Lost Children: Displacement, Family and Nation in Postwar Europe," *Journal of Modern History* 81 (2009), pp. 45–86.

Zangwill, I. *The Melting Pot* (1909).

Zayas, A. M. de. *Nemesis at Potsdam* (1979).

Zertal, I. *From Catastrophe to Power: Holocaust Survivors and the Emergence of Israel* (Berkeley, Calif., 1998).

Ziemke, E. F. *The U.S. Army in the Occupation of Germany* (Washington, D.C., 1975).

Zolberg, A. R. *A Nation by Design: Immigration Policy in the Fashioning of America* (Cambridge, Mass., 2006).

Zubkova, E. *Russia After the War: Hopes, Illusions and Disappointments, 1945–1957* (Armonk, N.Y., 1998).

Acknowledgments

My grateful thanks to Jake Arnold-Forster for the extended loan of his grandfather's papers; to Colonel Rupert Prichard, OBE, for permission to quote from the papers of Sir Frederick Morgan; and to Dr. Yair Grinberg for corresponding with me. It has been a pleasure to get to know Menachem Rosensaft.

My debt to other scholars is substantial. Mark Mazower provided initial encouragement. Jair Kessler and Tony Judt awarded me Visiting Research Fellowships at the Remarque Institute, New York University. The Beinecke Library at Yale University granted me a Donald C. Gallup Fellowship; my thanks especially to Barbara A. Shailor. Jessica Reinisch invited me into the Birkbeck fold and has been a stalwart friend. Brian Bond, Allan Young, and José Brunner gave me the chance to try out my ideas. Matthew Frank, Nick Stargardt, and Alex Clarkson generously shared their research. My old comrades in arms, Raye Farr and Martin Smith, have been patient listeners. I alone am responsible for the final product.

For generous help, I also thank Nick Baron, Yehuda Bauer, Danny Cohen, Marta Dyczok, Peter Gatrell, Josef Grodzinsky, Anna Jaroszyńska-Kirchmann, Zeev Mankowitz, Edith Raim, Gitta Sereny, Hans-Dieter Steinert, Reiner Schulze, Tomas Venclova, Paul Weindling, and Tara Zahra.

I am indebted to the librarians and staff of the United Nations Archives, the Imperial War Museum (especially Rod Suddaby and the Department of Documents), the Wiener Library, the British Library, the National Archives, London, the United States Holocaust Memorial Museum, the Yale University libraries, the London Library, the Bristol University Library, the Columbia University Library, the Bodleian and Rothermere Libraries, Oxford, and New York University.

Tim Cole, Anne Deighton, Prosper Devas, Atina Grossmann, Rhodri and Leonie Hayward, Boyd Hilton, Marylla and Julian Hunt, Tristram Hunt, Diana Jeater, Jair Kessler, Mark Kidel, Cathy Merridale, Matthew Parker, Peter Romijn, Silvia Salvatici, Hew Strachan, Flora Tsilaga, and Jay Winter have provided moral support. My sister, Caroline Moser, and her husband, Peter Sollis, gave me shelter in both London and Washington.

At Bodley Head, Will Sulkin has been wonderfully supportive and Jörg Hensgen a dream editor, combining saintly patience with ruthless excision. Dan Franklin was involved in the initial commission, and Tessa Harvey has been a perceptive reader. At

Knopf, Carol Brown Janeway believed in the project; Elizabeth Lee patiently shepherded it to completion. I am fortunate to have Clare Alexander as my agent and friend.

My wife, Sue, has sustained me through a long writing process. She was required to play many roles and was magnificent in all of them. Our trips to Eastern Europe together have made this book memorable for me.

Index

PHOTOGRAPH CREDITS

German soldiers and refugees in Berlin: Getty Images

DPs in Frankfurt train station: Getty Images

DPs in assembly line: Getty Images

Russians at Mosbach: Getty Images

Returning concentration camp survivors: Getty Images

La Guardia and Lehman: Getty Images

La Guardia at Funk Kaserne: United Nations Archives

Lieutenant General Sir Frederick Morgan: Getty Images

Habets and Hulme in Wildflecken: Beinecke Library, Yale University

Heymont and Ben-Gurion at Landsberg: United States Holocaust
    Memorial Museum

DPs at Weilheim: American Friends Service Committee

Football match at Belsen: Netherlands Institute for War
    Documentation

Jewish survivors of Buchenwald: Getty Images

Baltic Cygnets: Getty Images

Zinaida Supa in New York: U.S. National Archives

A NOTE ON THE TYPE

The text of this book was set in Bembo, a facsimile of a typeface cut by Francesco Griffo for Aldus Manutius, the celebrated Venetian printer, in 1495.

The present-day version of Bembo was introduced by the Monotype Corporation of London in 1929. Sturdy, well-balanced, and finely proportioned, Bembo is a face of rare beauty and great legibility in all of its sizes.

Composed by Creative Graphics, Allentown, Pennsylvania
Printed and bound by Berryville Graphics, Berryville, Virginia
Book design by Robert C. Olsson
Map by Reginald Piggott